BEHIND THE BER

Behind the Berlin Wall

East Germany and the Frontiers of Power

PATRICK MAJOR

OXFORD

UNIVERSITY PRESS

OXFORD

UNIVERSITY PRESS

Great Clarendon Street, Oxford OX2 6DP

Oxford University Press is a department of the University of Oxford.
It furthers the University's objective of excellence in research, scholarship,
and education by publishing worldwide in

Oxford New York

Auckland Cape Town Dar es Salaam Hong Kong Karachi
Kuala Lumpur Madrid Melbourne Mexico City Nairobi
New Delhi Shanghai Taipei Toronto

With offices in

Argentina Austria Brazil Chile Czech Republic France Greece
Guatemala Hungary Italy Japan Poland Portugal Singapore
South Korea Switzerland Thailand Turkey Ukraine Vietnam

Oxford is a registered trade mark of Oxford University Press
in the UK and in certain other countries

Published in the United States
by Oxford University Press Inc., New York

© Patrick Major 2010

British Library Cataloguing in Publication Data

Data available

Library of Congress Cataloging in Publication Data

Major, Patrick.
Behind the Berlin Wall : East Germany and the frontiers of power / Patrick Major.
p. cm.
Includes bibliographical references and index.
ISBN 978–0–19–924328–0
1. Germany (East)—History. 2. Germany (East)—Politics and government. 3. Germany (East)—Social conditions.
4. Power (Social sciences)—Germany (East)—History. 5. Berlin Wall, Berlin, Germany, 1961–1989.
6. Walls—Social aspects—Germany (East)—History. 7. Boundaries—Social aspects—Germany (East)—History.
8. Germany (East)—Boundaries—Germany (West) 9. Germany (West)—Boundaries—Germany (East) 10. Cold
War. I. Title.
DD282.M35 2009
943'.1087—dc22
2009026991

Typeset by Laserwords Private Limited, Chennai, India
Digitally printed and bound
in Great Britain by
CPI Antony Rowe, Chippenham and Eastbourne

ISBN 978–0–19–924328–0 (Hbk.)
ISBN 978–0–19–960510–1 (Pbk.)

To my father, John Major (1936–2009), my first historian

Acknowledgements

My thanks go to the many people who have helped in the archives on this long project, above all Volker Lange of the Bundesarchiv Berlin, whose untimely death saddened me greatly. I wish also to thank the Nuffield Foundation and the University of Warwick's Humanities Research Centre for their financial support, as well as colleagues Colin Jones and Margot Finn for reading the manuscript, and Leo Schmidt for checking one chapter. Various German friends put up with the Wall, and put me up too, including Ralf Haselow and Katrin Rump, Susanne and Johannes Gaebler, Ute Engelhardt, and Katrin and Annika Eickmann. I wish also to thank all those who agreed to interviews, but appear here anonymized. Throughout, my parents, John and Rosemary, have followed the project with interest and been a pillar of support. Above all, I thank my wife Jennifer, who helped me over the final wall.

Contents

List of Illustrations

Abbreviations

AZKW	Amt für Zoll und Kontrolle des Warenverkehrs (Office of Customs and Excise)
BAB	Bundesarchiv Berlin
BAK	Bundesarchiv Koblenz
BArch	Bundesarchiv (Federal Archive)
BDVP	Bezirksbehörde der Deutschen Volkspolizei (Regional Authority of the German People's Police)
BfV	Bundesamt für Verfassungsschutz (Federal Office to Defend the Constitution)
BL	Bezirksleitung (Regional Leadership)
BLHA	Brandenburgisches Landeshauptarchiv (Brandenburg State Main Archive)
BMG	British Military Government
BMfgF	Bundesministerium für gesamtdeutsche Fragen (Federal Ministry of All-German Affairs)
BMfIB	Bundesministerium für innerdeutsche Beziehungen (Federal Ministry of Inner-German Relations)
BPA	Bezirksparteiarchiv (Regional Party Archive)
BPKK	Bezirksparteikontrollkommission (Regional Party Control Commission)
BPO	Betriebsparteiorganisation (Works Party Organization)
BStU	Bundesbeauftragte/r für die Unterlagen des Staatssicherheitsdienstes der ehemaligen DDR
BT	Bezirkstag (Regional Parliament)
BuVo	Bundesvorstand (Federal Executive)
BV	Bezirksverwaltung/Bezirksvorstand (Regional Administration/ Executive)
DBM	Dokumentationszentrum Berliner Mauer

DDR	Deutsche Demokratische Republik (German Democratic Republic)
DVP	Deutsche Volkspolizei (German People's Police)
EZA	Evangelisches Zentralarchiv
FDGB	Freier Deutscher Gewerkschaftsbund (Free German Trade Union Federation)
FDJ	Freie Deutsche Jugend (Free German Youth)
HU	Humboldt-Universität (Humboldt University)
HV	Hauptverwaltung (Main Administration)
HVDVP	Hauptverwaltung der Deutschen Volkspolizei (Main Administration of the German People's Police)
IA	Innere Angelegenheiten (Internal Affairs)
KL	Kreisleitung (District Leadership)
KMS	Karl-Marx-Stadt (now Chemnitz)
KMU	Karl-Marx-University Leipzig
KPKK	Kreisparteikontrollkommission (District Party Control Commission)
LAB	Landesarchiv Berlin (State Archive Berlin)
LAM	Landesarchiv Merseburg
LPO	Leitende Parteiorgane (Leading Party Organs)
MdI	Ministerium des Innern (Ministry of the Interior)
MdJ	Ministerium der Justiz (Ministry of Justice)
MfHV	Ministerium für Handel und Versorgung (Ministry of Trade and Supply)
MfK	Ministerium für Kultur (Ministry of Culture)
MfS	Ministerium für Staatssicherheit (Ministry of State Security)
MLHA	Mecklenburgisches Landeshauptarchiv (Mecklenburg State Main Archive)
MZAP	Militärgeschichtliches Zwischenarchiv Potsdam (Military History Interim Archive Potsdam, now housed at Freiburg)
NF	Nationale Front

NVA	Nationale Volksarmee (National People's Army)
NVR	Nationaler Verteidigungsrat (National Defence Council)
PB	Politbüro
PdVP	Präsidium der Volkspolizei (Presidium of the People's Police)
PI	Parteiinformation (Party Information)
PL	Parteileitung (Party Leadership)
PM	Paß- und Meldewesen (Pass and Registration)
PO	Parteiorgane (Party Organs)
RdB	Rat des Bezirkes (Regional Council)
RdK	Rat des Kreises (District Council)
RdSB	Rat des Stadtbezirkes (Borough Council)
RIAS	Radio in the American Sector
SächsHStA	Sächsisches Hauptstaatsarchiv (Saxon Main State Archive)
SAPMO	Stiftung Archiv der Parteien und Massenorganisationen der DDR (Archive Foundation of Parties and Mass Organizations of the GDR)
SdM	Sekretariat des Ministers (Minister's Secretariat)
SED	Sozialistische Einheitspartei Deutschlands (Socialist Unity Party of Germany)
Sek.	Sekretariat (Secretariat)
SfHF	Staatssekretär für Hoch- und Fachschulwesen (Secretary of State for Higher and Further Education)
SKK	Sowjetische Kontrollkommission (Soviet Control Commission)
SL	Stadtleitung (City Leadership)
SMAD	Sowjetische Militäradministration in Deutschland (Soviet Military Administration in Germany)
SPD	Sozialdemokratische Partei Deutschlands (Social Democratic Party of Germany)
SPK	Staatliche Plankommission (State Planning Commission)
STA	Stadtarchiv (City Archive)

Abbreviations

StAC	Staatsarchiv Chemnitz (State Archive Chemnitz)
StAL	Staatsarchiv Leipzig (State Archive Leipzig)
TH	Technische Hochschule (Technical Highschool)
ThHStAW	Thüringisches Hauptstaatsarchiv Weimar (Thuringian Main State Archive Weimar)
TNA	The National Archives (London, Kew)
TRO	Transformatorenwerk (Transformer Works)
VEB	Volkseigener Betrieb (People's Owned Factory)
ZAIG	Zentrale Auswertungs- und Informationsgruppe (Central Evaluation and Information Group)
ZERV	Zentrale Ermittlungsstelle für Regierungs- und Vereinigungskriminalität (Central Investigation Agency for Governmental and Organized Criminality)
ZK	Zentralkomitee (Central Committee)
ZKG	Zentrale Koordinierungsgruppe (Central Coordination Group)
ZR	Zentralrat (Central Council)
ZS	Zentraler Stab (Central Staff)
ZV	Zentralvorstand (Central Executive)

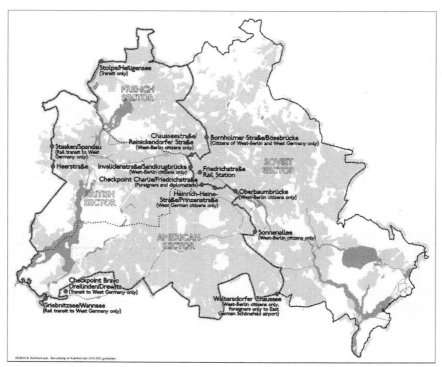

Figure 1. Cold War Berlin.

Source: composed in 2004 by de:Benutzer:Sansculotte. Usage granted under the conditions of the GNU FDL and the CCBYSA 2.0

1

Introduction: The Frontiers of Power

Few historical changes occur literally overnight. Yet, in the early hours of Sunday 13 August 1961 a new landmark appeared on the Cold War's frontline. In the darkness between East and West Berlin, jackhammers tore up roads and pavements, while tramlines and railings were welded into temporary barriers, followed by cinder blocks, barbed wire, and concrete. Its builders, the East German communist party, called it the 'Antifascist Defence Rampart', while the rest of the world knew it as the Berlin Wall, or simply 'the Wall'. Its iconic images still influence our mental picture of East Germany: a fleeing East German policeman frozen in mid-air above a barbed-wire entanglement; a tug-of-war over an elderly woman dangling from an apartment window; US and Soviet tanks point-blank at Checkpoint Charlie. Viewing platforms soon permitted western tourists a glimpse of the sandy no man's land between the front and rear walls, raked clean by day and floodlit at night, known as the 'death-strip'. No trip to West Berlin was complete without a visit to the Haus am Checkpoint Charlie, filled with escape memorabilia and dioramas of the beleaguered demi-city. The Wall was merchandized on postcards and T-shirts; it formed the backdrop to John le Carré and Len Deighton's spy thrillers; legions of graffiti artists spray-painted it; and Johnny Rotten of the Sex Pistols met his nihilistic match in it.[1]

I myself encountered the Wall in the mid-1980s when I lived for a year in West Berlin. Checkpoint Charlie was like a macabre version of the wardrobe in C. S. Lewis's Narnia stories: you began in one world, filled with neon and primary yellows, only to emerge in another, seemingly set in sepia, where the air smelled of brown coal and two-stroke petrol. Part of the Wall's fascination is that it was a primordial, almost fairytale solution to a modern problem, more akin to the Brothers Grimm than the late twentieth century. Of course, humans have always marked boundaries with ditches, fences, and walls, around homesteads, fields, and fortifications. The first recorded walled city was Jericho, 10,000 years ago.[2] Six thousand years later Chinese warlords began immuring whole territories, culminating in the sixteenth-century Great Wall of China.

---

[1] The Sex Pistols, 'Holidays in the Sun', Oct. 1977.
[2] Felipé Fernandez-Armesto, 'This Story Doth a Wall Present', *Index on Censorship (Writing on the Walls)*, 33/3 (2004), 41.

Court scholars championed it as a moral construct to protect civilization from barbarism, and although the Berlin Wall kept transgressors in rather than out, East German propagandists justified it in similarly paternalistic terms as protection against the *Unkultur* beyond.[3] Yet, had the Ming dynasty become a prisoner of its fortification strategy, of an inward-looking Middle Kingdom mentality? We might also ask whether the German Democratic Republic's (GDR) *Betonköpfe* or 'concrete heads', as detractors called them, had likewise succumbed to a bunker syndrome, building ever-more perfect walls, while becoming increasingly detached from reality.

Naturally, one does not have to look as far as China for other precedents. After the annihilation of Varus's legions in the Teutoburg Forest in 9 AD, the Roman Empire withdrew behind the Rhine and Danube, reinforcing natural defences with an artificial perimeter—or *limes*—of roads and forts, fronted by palisades and fencing.[4] Nevertheless, it could not ward off the Vandals and Goths, nor prevent the sacking of Rome 400 years later. As the Roman Empire collapsed into the Holy Roman Empire, so did the resources to sustain such edifices as the *limes*. By the Middle Ages each town had retreated behind its own castellations; gone were the Romans' area defences. Instead, margraves and mounted knights patrolled the imperial margin. Only with mass conscription and industrialization did the brute simplicity of geostrategic wall-building re-emerge, culminating in the Maginot and Siegfried Lines, static defences rendered obsolete by mobile warfare. In the Cold War, however, nuclear deterrence provided a balance of power which froze fronts and stabilized conflict. 'From Stettin in the Baltic to Trieste in the Adriatic', as Winston Churchill famously proclaimed in 1946, 'an iron curtain has descended across the continent'.[5] And even today, a security wall separates Israel from the Palestinian territories.[6]

Policing a border means more than patrolling a strip of land; it involves controlling its hinterland and populace. The frontier is merely the state's outward manifestation. In Plato's ideal state, only loyal citizens would be allowed out, and nobody under forty,[7] while Sparta forbade travel abroad to protect against 'the infection of foreign bad habits'.[8] Labour migration was to be a perennial problem

---

[3] Arthur Waldron, *The Great Wall of China: From History to Myth* (Cambridge: CUP, 1990), 215–26; Julia Lovell, *The Great Wall: China against the World, 1000 BC to 2000 AD* (London: Atlantic, 2006).

[4] C. R. Whittaker, *Frontiers of the Roman Empire: A Social and Economic History* (Baltimore and London: Johns Hopkins University Press, 1994); Derek Williams, *The Reach of Rome: A History of the Roman Imperial Frontier 1st–5th Centuries AD* (London: Constable, 1996).

[5] *New York Times*, 6 Mar. 1946. See also Patrick Wright, *Iron Curtain: From Stage to Cold War* (Oxford: Oxford University Press, 2007), 34–50.

[6] Isabel Kershner, *Barrier: The Seam of the Israeli-Palestinian Conflict* (Houndmills: Palgrave Macmillan, 2006); Ray Dolphin, *The West Bank Wall: Unmaking Palestine* (London: Pluto, 2006).

[7] Plato, *The Laws*, trans. Trevor J. Saunders (Harmondsworth: Penguin, 1970), 500–1.

[8] Alan Dowty, *Closed Borders: The Contemporary Assault on Freedom of Movement* (New Haven and London: Yale University Press, 1987), 9.

for gatekeepers. The dying Roman Empire tried to tackle it by tying peasants to the land by serfdom. Later, in the age of mercantilism and absolutism, as the New World threatened to drain the Old, states further regulated subjects' movements, legislating against the emigration of skilled artisans. By the late eighteenth century passports were obligatory to enter European countries, and by 1914 to leave them too.[9] Yet Enlightenment theorists such as Carl Ferdinand Hommel warned '*against having to make a prison of the state* . . . The very proscription against venturing outside the land renders the inhabitants all the greedier to leave their fatherland and serves only as a warning to foreigners not to settle within it'.[10] Natural patriotism would instead furnish the necessary ties. Even in the age of social Darwinism between nation-states, the intellectual father of *Lebensraum*, the German geographer Friedrich Ratzel, still conceptualized state frontiers as fluid and organic, filtering membranes to keep the body politic 'healthy'.[11]

Few governments had contemplated blocking this interface completely, until the advent of state communism. From 1919 Soviet travel abroad required police permission, and during the 1920s a stringent border regime operated under secret police control.[12] Border violators faced up to three years' imprisonment, or treason charges if heading for capitalist states. In 1932 the USSR even introduced an internal passport system. It was little surprise, therefore, when in 1948 Russia voted against freedom of movement as an automatic human right under the United Nations' convention.[13] Nor was the United States immune from temptations to control citizens' movements, albeit more selectively, for instance in the Internal Security Act of 1950. But it was East Germany that attacked freedom of movement most systematically. The 1963 UN special report on emigration singled out the 'Chinese wall' in Berlin as the worst offender in modern-day history: 'whereas Governments once erected walls to keep foreigners from entering a country, today walls are built—both figuratively and literally—to keep nationals hemmed in'.[14] Indeed, the GDR's 1968 constitution abolished Article 10's previous right of emigration, guaranteeing freedom of travel only 'within the state territory'.[15] The Berlin Wall had become the wall of walls, a *reductio ad absurdam* of the modern state's obsessive desire to regulate its interior.

Yet not all frontiers are visible. Our language is suffused with border metaphors reflecting power structures and no-go areas every bit as real as

---

[9] John Torpey, *The Invention of the Passport: Surveillance, Citizenship and the State* (Cambridge: Cambridge University Press, 1999), 21–121.

[10] Cited in Rolf Henrich, *Der vormundschaftliche Staat: Vom Versagen des real existierenden Sozialismus* (Hamburg: Rowohlt, 1989), 175.

[11] John Prescott, *Boundaries and Frontiers* (London: Croom Helm, 1978), 15–16.

[12] Dowty, *Closed Borders*, 69–70.   [13] Ibid., 112.

[14] José D. Inglés, *Study of Discrimination in Respect of the Right of Everyone to Leave any Country, including his Own, and to Return to his Country* (New York: United Nations, 1963), 4 and 58.

[15] J. K. A. Thomaneck and James Mellis (eds), *Politics, Society and Government in the German Democratic Republic: Basic Documents* (Oxford: Berg, 1989), 50–67.

border checkpoints.[16] This book is also about the invisible frontiers of power staked out behind the literal walls. Sociologist Max Weber was among the first to elaborate a systematic theory of social control, distinguishing between 'power' (*Macht*) and 'rule' (*Herrschaft*). Power signified the imposition of one agency's will, even against that of others, whereas rule involved obedience and thus a degree of legitimacy. His third possibility of 'discipline' reflected simple habituation.[17] All three categories bear on East Germany. Post-GDR social historians adapted Weberian terminology, coining the term 'overruled society' (*durchherrschte Gesellschaft*), rejecting a simple pitting of state against society, with a no-man's land in between, in favour of a vertical co-optation model.[18] Ever since the GDR's foundation in 1949, opinion has been divided over how deep this control went. Was it total? Was at least the intention total? Did East German communism survive by brute force alone, through the Red Army, Stasi, and not least the Wall; or did it manage partial legitimation through a welfare state and an ideology of antifascism-cum-socialism?[19] A key factor in this debate has been the perceived docility of East Germany, particularly vis-à-vis other eastern bloc states. To what extent did this quiescence rest on submission to power or consent to rule?

'Totalitarianists' claim that the party state always presided over an 'over-powered society'. According to Klaus Schroeder: 'The frontiers of power are reached only when the power-wielders no longer encounter obedience among the security forces, police or army to the forcible implementation of their interests'.[20] This does seem a narrow definition, reflecting the political scientist's fixation on the state, and omitting society from the equation. Yet theorists and cultural historians have been equally guilty of fetishizing elite power fantasies, while ignoring their realizability. Reading eighteenth-century prescriptions for a more ordered society—epitomized by the prison, but replicated in factories, schools, barracks, and hospitals—Michel Foucault charted the rise of the modern regulatory state. His pinnacle of rational control was Bentham's imagined Panopticon, that voyeuristic, theatrical penitentiary in which prisoners would learn to surveil themselves. Yet the society-as-prison metaphor is not without relevance to the GDR, as is Foucault's recognition that heavy-handed shows of force could yield to more sophisticated techniques. As he suggested:

[16] For a cultural anthropology of international borders, see Hastings Donnan and Thomas M. Wilson, *Borders: Frontiers of Identity, Nation and State* (Oxford: Berg, 1999), 87 ff.

[17] Max Weber, *Economy and Society: An Outline of Interpretive Sociology* (New York: Bedminster, 1968), i: 212–301, and iii: 941–55. I prefer 'rule' to the more usual 'domination'.

[18] Jürgen Kocka, 'Eine durhcherrschte Gesellschaft', in Hartmut Kaelble *et al.* (eds), *Sozialgeschichte der DDR* (Stuttgart: Klett-Cotta, 1994), 547–53.

[19] For an overview, see Mary Fulbrook, *Anatomy of a Dictatorship: Inside the GDR 1949–1989* (Oxford: Oxford University Press, 1995), 3–13.

[20] 'Vermachtete Gesellschaft': Klaus Schroeder, *Der SED-Staat: Geschichte und Strukturen der DDR* (Munich: Landeszentrale für politische Bildungsarbeit, 1998), 633.

There are two images, then, of discipline. At one extreme, the discipline-blockade, the enclosed institution, established on the edges of society, turned inwards towards negative functions: arresting evil, breaking communications, suspending time. At the other extreme, with panopticism, is the discipline-mechanism: a functional mechanism that must improve the exercise of power by making it lighter, more rapid, more effective, a design of subtle coercion for a society to come.[21]

In the GDR both possibilities existed side by side. The Wall provided a literal 'discipline-blockade', but other 'discipline-mechanisms' were available, both before and after 1961, not least of which was the all-seeing secret police or Stasi, but also citizens' own self-censorship.

Ironically, the Wall did indeed permit the regime to refine its surveillance techniques and achieve a lighter touch within its confines. As Hermann Weber, West Germany's eminent GDR scholar, characterized the period immediately following its building, 'by adaptation to the constraints of a modern industrial society the methods of rule in the GDR altered considerably: they shifted more and more from terror to neutralization and manipulation of the masses'.[22] Within the closed societal laboratory, the regime engaged in ambitious social engineering through positive discrimination towards certain groups and the withering away of others. This socioeconomic leverage involved so-called 'social power', whereby an agency indirectly predisposes citizens through an incentive structure to 'choose' to conform. The key levers of social power were the party, labour, and education. The GDR has consequently been labelled both a 'welfare dictatorship' (*Fürsorgediktatur*), dispensing social security in return for political obedience,[23] and a 'didactic dictatorship' (*Erziehungsdiktatur*), with the party posing as 'guardian' to an immature citizenry.[24] If totalitarian is to mean anything then, it must signify greater sophistication of power, rather than the proverbial secret police knock at the door.[25]

Closely scrutinized, totalitarian control is anything but total, generating resistance by the very attempt to micromanage. Case studies suggest that individuals' self-interest, their so-called *Eigen-Sinn* to borrow Alf Lüdtke's phrase, can create autonomous spaces in defiance of the state, expressed through ritual and even body language.[26] One West German observer famously described

---

[21] Michel Foucault, *Discipline and Punish: The Birth of the Prison* (Harmondsworth: Penguin, 1981), 209.

[22] Hermann Weber, *Geschichte der DDR* (Munich: dtv, 1985), 327.

[23] Konrad H. Jarausch, 'Care and Coercion: The GDR as Welfare Dictatorship', in id. (ed.), *Dictatorship as Experience: Towards a Socio-Cultural History of the GDR* (New York and Oxford: Berghahn, 1999), 47–69.

[24] Henrich, *Der vormundschaftliche Staat*.

[25] Even Cold War broadcasters at the time realized that programmes where 'loud knockings at the door followed by everyone being afraid that the Secret Police have come at last' were counter-productive stereotypes: T. Peters, 'Programme Content of BBC's Soviet Zone German Broadcasts', 3 June 1959, The National Archives (TNA), FO 1110/1240.

[26] Alf Lüdtke, *Eigen-Sinn: Fabrikalltag, Arbeitererfahrungen und Politik vom Kaiserreich bis in den Faschismus* (Hamburg: Ergebnisse, 1993); Thomas Lindenberger (ed.), *Herrschaft und Eigen-Sinn*

the GDR as a 'niche society', where the home acted as a refuge from public conformity, and a safety valve for the regime.[27] The GDR could never completely erase the public–private borderline. In another highly influential anthropology of domination, James Scott argued that throughout history both rulers and ruled have acted out ritualized public contestations of power. Nevertheless, the 'frontier between the public and the hidden transcripts is a zone of constant struggle between dominant and subordinate—not a solid wall'.[28] The subservient become adept at masking their feelings, in words, behaviour, or symbols, while exhibiting contempt for their 'superiors', turning rulers' words against them, and appropriating dominant discourses for their own ends. The subtexts, or 'hidden transcripts', are often far more hostile. As will become evident, many echoes of Scott are to be found in GDR double-speak. Yet, for Lüdtke at least, such self-interest may not always be a conscious act of political opposition. Few everyday actions, even in a state which attempted to politicize most things, defined themselves in terms of the high politics of the 'anti-imperialist struggle', the 'transition to socialism', or the 'antifascist defence rampart'. Home-making, wage-earning and leisure occupied most energies even behind the iron curtain.[29]

    Where does the Wall fit into all of this theorizing? Professional historians have in fact been remarkably coy about it since its fall. It has not been a fashionable subject for research. For self-conscious former West Germans, highlighting it could smack of sanctimonious Cold War recrimination; for East German academics it was often painfully interwoven with their own biographies. Clearly, my choice of topic focuses on the repressive aspects of the East German state and would seem at first sight an object lesson in totalitarianism. The Wall drastically curtailed East Germans' freedom of travel. It also killed hundreds. Even remotely, the Wall affected everybody within the GDR, from the Politbüro, to the regional party leaders, to the rank-and-file functionaries, factory workers, farmers, intellectuals, and teenagers who form the many actors in this story. Yet I wish to avoid the type of military Wall history which recounts, in often mind-boggling detail, its precise physical dimensions,[30] or the journalistic page-turner

in der Diktatur: Studien zur Gesellschaftsgeschichte der DDR (Cologne: Böhlau, 1999). *Eigen-Sinn* suggests the contrariness of an obstreperous child, a form of bloody-mindedness which also betrays the rational self-image of the mentor, in this case the state.

    [27] Günter Gaus, *Wo Deutschland liegt: Eine Ortsbestimmung* (Hamburg: Hoffmann & Campe, 1983), 156–233.

    [28] James C. Scott, *Domination and the Arts of Resistance: Hidden Transcripts* (New Haven and London: Yale University Press, 1990), 14.

    [29] Evemarie Badstübner (ed.), *Befremdlich anders: Leben in der DDR* (Berlin: Dietz, 2000).

    [30] Volker Koop, *'Den Gegner vernichten': Die Grenzsicherung der DDR* (Bonn: Bouvier, 1996); Peter Joachim Lapp, *Gefechtsdienst im Frieden: Das Grenzregime der DDR* (Bonn: Bernard & Graefe, 1999); Alexandra Hildebrandt, *Die Mauer: Zahlen, Daten* (Berlin: Verlag Haus am Checkpoint Charlie, 2001); Hendrik Thoß, *Gesichert in den Untergang: Die Geschichte der DDR-Westgrenze* (Berlin: Karl Dietz, 2004).

which deals with it as a series of sensational escape stories.[31] Such approaches can degenerate into minutiae, like those obsessively recorded by the photographer anti-hero of one Wall novel who:

spent too long on technical views of the barrier, cinder-block walls, layers of concrete slabs, lines of barbed wire on struts, walled-up windows in border houses, guards on three-storey towers, with dogs in the field of fire. He tried for wire nets on roof ridges, sightscreens, shooting stands, because what attracted him about this border was how much more multifaceted and striking things looked when a city was split in two . . .[32]

The author, Uwe Johnson, who himself had fled the GDR, was clearly making a point about the western media's selective vision. But I would suggest that something similar has been happening with historical writing on Germany's division. Twenty years after its demise, we often cannot see the Wall for the bricks.

At the other extreme, however, 'anti-totalitarians' have treated the Wall as a metonym for a reductionist, black-and-white stereotyping of the GDR, and thus a foil for greater historical complexity. One volume on state and society in East Germany punningly titled itself *The Limits of Dictatorship*.[33] According to its editors, however, GDR history was 'more than the history of an untrammelled dictatorship protected by a border of concrete and barbed wire'.[34] There were historical legacies and collective mentalities, as well as the sheer chaos of the early postwar years to consider. The economy also placed severe constraints on party rule. External limitations in the guise of the Soviet Union meant that East German leaders were not masters of their own destiny. Even after August 1961, 'The Wall remained a simultaneous monument to power and impotence'.[35] The influential American historian Charles Maier has also advocated a broader view: 'The Wall at the frontier had made possible all the walls within; the GDR had been a regime of walls, the most effective being those within its citizens' heads'.[36] Even before it fell, GDR dissidents labelled it 'the tip of the iceberg' of a more general 'demarcation syndrome'.[37] More recently still, Thomas Lindenberger

[31] Alan Shadrake, *The Yellow Pimpernels: Escape Stories of the Berlin Wall* (London: Hale, 1974); Anthony Kemp, *Escape from Berlin* (London: Boxtree, 1987); Bodo Müller, *Faszination Freiheit: Die spektakulärsten Fluchtgeschichten* (Berlin: Links, 2000); Christopher Hilton, *The Wall: The People's Story* (Thrupp: Sutton, 2001).

[32] Uwe Johnson, *Zwei Ansichten* (1965; Frankfurt: Suhrkamp, 1992), 140.

[33] Richard Bessel and Ralph Jessen (eds), *Die Grenzen der Diktatur: Staat und Gesellschaft in der DDR* (Göttingen: Vandenhoeck & Ruprecht, 1996). The German 'Grenze' connotes both frontier and limit.

[34] Ibid., 9.   [35] Ibid., 11.

[36] Charles S. Maier, *Dissolution: The Crisis of Communism and the End of East Germany* (Princeton, NJ: Princeton University Press, 1997), 56.

[37] Gruppe Absage an Praxis und Prinzip der Abgrenzung, 'Recht ströme wie Wasser', cited in Hans-Jürgen Fischbeck, 'Das Mauersyndrom: die Rückwirkung des Grenzregimes auf die Bevölkerung der DDR', in Deutscher Bundestag (ed.), *Materialien der Enquete Kommission 'Aufarbeitung von Geschichte und Folgen der SED-Diktatur in Deutschland'* (Baden-Baden: Nomos/Suhrkamp, 1995), v/ii: 1188–211; 1190.

has enjoined social historians to recognize that these frontiers of power did not run neatly between state and society, with a 'free' area beyond the state's ambit. Referring to the 'dictatorship of frontiers', he urged readers not to become fixated on the physical state border: 'In the GDR's interior ran numerous other, invisible borders, which every GDR citizen knew about, regardless of social position. They were by no means unitary, but diffuse and omnipresent, often forming border zones rather than precise demarcation lines'.[38]

All of this is quite true. Yet I would suggest that before turning our backs on the Wall, and becoming lost in a maze of metaphorical walls, we should turn more closely to the real one, with some of the very tools which *Alltagsgeschichte*, or everyday history, has given us.[39] Even concrete has a social history.[40] This involves differentiating between the regime's overt intentionality—that is, its egalitarian social engineering—and the unintended structures of discrimination which the border engendered. It also requires conceptualizing from the bottom up how the GDR's immurement shaped many life stories. As one guest book inscription at an exhibition forty years after its erection pondered: 'The Wall pushed my whole life onto a different track'. In her youth the author had been separated from her boyfriend by the actions of 1961. 'Only 23 years later did I reach the West with an emigration application. I suffered many twists of fate and never did find my friends from back then. How would my life have gone, if . . .??'[41] If?? By bringing ordinary people more firmly back to centre stage, without becoming sentimental or vindictive, and investigating the impact of high politics at the grass roots, we may better understand the human dimensions of the Wall.[42]

Moreover, what even many theoretical accounts implicitly overlook is that, for over a third of its existence, from 1945–61, East Germany remained unwalled. Only from 1961–89 was it the more familiar closed society. One of my aims is to draw attention to this early phase and compare GDR rule before and after the Wall.[43] This was, of course, not the first instance of a historically significant open border. Frederick Jackson Turner, in his renowned 1893 address, argued that American individualism and 'antipathy to control' were consecrated on the wild west frontier. Federal government on the eastern

---

[38] Thomas Lindenberger, 'Diktatur der Grenzen', in id. (ed.), *Herrschaft und Eigen-Sinn*, 32.

[39] Thomas Lindenberger, 'Alltagsgeschichte und ihr möglicher Beitrag zu einer Gesellschafts-geschichte der DDR', in Bessel and Jessen (eds), *Grenzen*, 298–325.

[40] Cor Wagenaar *et al.*, *Ideals in Concrete: Exploring Eastern and Central Europe* (Rotterdam: NAi publishers, 2004).

[41] Marion in 'Buch der Erinnerungen' at Berlin-Wilmersdorf Rathaus, Aug. 2001.

[42] Timothy Garton Ash rightly took to task Cold War politicians' lip service to 'the people' (*die Menschen*), although his own methodological preferences for researching and interviewing elite figures were hardly likely to remedy this. See his *In Europe's Name: Germany and the Divided Continent* (London: Jonathan Cape, 1993).

[43] See also Dierk Hoffmann *et al.* (eds), *Vor dem Mauerbau: Politik und Gesellschaft in der DDR der fünfziger Jahre* (Munich: Oldenbourg, 2003).

seaboard could not impose 'European' values on the pioneer spirit.[44] The East German authorities likewise struggled to assert themselves when their citizens, too, could 'go west'. The open border offered loopholes to dictatorship, and the negotiation of power between gatekeepers and citizenry was not always stacked in the state's favour. Its short-term victories, such as 13 August 1961, stored up the seeds of future problems, as Chapters 7 and 8 will show. The book traces the ebbs and flows of this asymmetric conflict. Many of those East Germans confined within the system undoubtedly perceived themselves at the time as relatively powerless, but it would be condescending to deny individuals any agency in this contest. At a further remove, and with two decades of hindsight, one might see the GDR as one of the first victims of the globalization process which knows no national frontiers. East Germany tried perhaps harder than any modern state to seal itself off from the outside 'first' world of capitalism and democracy. The electronic mass media were nevertheless capable of penetrating the iron curtain in ways which made it increasingly anachronistic and futile.

Economist Albert O. Hirschman was among the first to theorize power in open and closed systems. In his seminal *Exit, Voice and Loyalty*,[45] he argued that any member of an economic, social or political entity faced with an adverse situation has two basic options: either to walk away (exit), or to speak up and complain (voice). 'Voice' could range from 'faint grumbling to violent protest',[46] but was always most effective when collectively articulated, whereas 'exit' was an individual solution, a quiet slipping away. Moreover, the two were diametrically opposed like opposite ends of a see-saw: generally speaking, exit would, according to Hirschman, 'tend to *atrophy the development of the art of voice*'.[47] Nevertheless, both actions encouraged hierarchies to remedy shortcomings, particularly where competition existed. In monopolistic systems, however, 'management'—in this case the communist state—would have less interest in recuperation, especially where a limited outlet existed. We might reasonably ask whether, with the open border, East German communists were indeed happy to see the back of troublemakers. The availability of West Germany as a dumping ground may have encouraged the Stalinist excesses of the 1950s. Equally plausibly, the open frontier before 1961 may have acted as a safety valve for popular discontent and a brake on authoritarianism. This is an important ambiguity and one to which I shall return, although there is no clear answer to this paradox.

Freedom of movement has, nevertheless, generally been seen to increase the room for manoeuvre of those left behind and to encourage reform. Conversely,

[44] Frederick Jackson Turner, 'The Significance of the Frontier in American History', in id., *The Frontier in American History* (New York: Henry Holt, 1920), 1–38.

[45] Albert O. Hirschman, *Exit, Voice and Loyalty: Responses to Decline in Firms, Organizations and States* (Cambridge, MA: Harvard University Press, 1970).

[46] Ibid., 16.   [47] Ibid., 43.

total monopolies with no exit become prisoners of their clients, who have no alternative but voice, forcing the powers-that-be to consider change. As we shall see in Chapter 6, in the 1960s the GDR did attempt to liberalize, but retrenched, leaving it paralysed when Gorbachev initiated *glasnost* and *perestroika* in the 1980s. As Hirschman warned, in totalitarian systems which repress exit and voice simultaneously, long-term deterioration is likely to set in, possibly to the point of no return. By 1989 the GDR did seem beyond help. As one observer put it: 'Those who have locked themselves into the logic of coercion seem, in the end, to be trapped by it'.[48] Importantly, Hirschman also realized that criticism did not preclude loyalty, which has been more systematically pursued by other scholars.[49] To protect the greater good, idealists might blow the whistle, and if complaint had some effect, might delay exit. Even passive citizens have a psychological propensity to rationalize self-sacrifice as time and effort well spent and so become functionally loyal. Thus, like the passenger at the bus stop, the longer the wait invested, the more difficult it is to walk away. Yet, loyalty always implies the possibility of disloyalty. 'The chances for voice to function effectively as a recuperation mechanism are appreciably strengthened if voice is backed up by the *threat of exit*', added Hirschman, 'whether it is made openly or whether the possibility of exit is merely well understood to be an element in the situation by all concerned'.[50] As Chapter 3 will show, moral blackmail was not uncommon before the Wall, but in Chapter 8 the role of 'loyal critics' will also be examined in relation to the collapse of 1989.

 In this way, perhaps, the gulf between totalitarians and *Alltagsgeschichtler* can be bridged; these seemingly antithetical positions are, I would argue, not so far apart as they often imagine. Even totalitarianists would, presumably, have to confirm their theories at the bottom of the pyramid, to see if ordinary citizens did indeed internalize the maxims of the big brother state. Nor do everyday historians necessarily romanticize a grass roots in permanent revolt, but accept that 'little people' could opt into the micro-networks of power, albeit often on their own terms, settling private scores, or drifting as the careerist current took them. Mary Fulbrook has recently described the 'participatory dictatorship' and 'honeycomb state', whose micro-structures burrowed deep into GDR society.[51] What I offer below, therefore, is an interlocking political, social, and cultural history of the impact of the open frontier, followed by border closure, on the East German population at large—an everyday history of high politics, if that is not a

---

[48] Dowty, *Closed Borders*, 229.
[49] Jonathan Grix, *The Role of the Masses in the Collapse of the GDR* (Houndmills: Palgrave, 2000), who talks of 'conditional loyalty'.
[50] Hirschman, *Exit*, 82.
[51] Mary Fulbrook, *The People's State: East German Society from Hitler to Honecker* (New Haven and London: Yale University Press, 2005), 235 ff.

contradiction in terms.[52] It is also a conscious move away from the top-down Cold War histories which have dominated this topic, certainly until recently.[53] But everyday Cold War history does not have to be about inconsequentialities. National division was felt very deeply, as the rupture of emotional ties to family, neighbourhood, and *Heimat*. These issues mattered intensely to contemporaries in the Cold War, and they should matter to historians. Moreover, people power was crucial in bringing down the Wall in 1989 and, as I shall argue, in forcing its erection in 1961.

UNDER EASTERN EYES: POPULAR OPINION IN A CLOSED SOCIETY

> We don't know much about the East Germans really, you know. We get odd bits here and there, but on the whole they're something of a mystery.
>
> John le Carré, *Call for the Dead* (1961)

This more inclusive view of Cold War history necessarily raises its own methodological problems. In 1989 it was easy to read the demonstrators' banners, as was fleetingly possible during the insurrection of 1953, when GDR politics took to the streets. During the long interim, however, East Germans engaged in the venerable practice of *Maul halten* or 'keeping stumm', for fear of being 'put on the black list' as one student put it.[54] What is more, as with the Third Reich, the historian of East Germany is faced with a regime consciously attempting to fabricate and manipulate public opinion. There were none of the conventional outlets of a 'public sphere'—a free press, associational autonomy, or intellectual debate—through which an alternative to the official voice could be heard, at least not until the final months. This is, undoubtedly, a problem, but as Ian Kershaw has shown for Nazi Germany, it is possible to reconstitute some of the 'popular opinion' which persisted beyond the regime's official rhetoric, however impressionistic this might be.[55] It is now almost *de rigueur* to write about 'ordinary Germans' in the Third Reich.[56] Cold War historiography has been generally slow

---

[52] Alf Lüdtke (ed.), *The History of Everyday Life: Reconstructing Historical Experiences and Ways of Life* (Princeton, NJ: Princeton UP, 1995).

[53] See the following chapter for an overview.

[54] SED-ZK (PO), 'Information' Nr. 29, 10 Mar. 1961, SAPMO-BArch, DY30/IV2/5/294, fo. 227.

[55] Ian Kershaw, *Popular Opinion and Political Dissent in the Third Reich: Bavaria 1933–1945* (Oxford: Clarendon, 1983), 4–10.

[56] Daniel J. Goldhagen, *Hitler's Willing Executioners: Ordinary Germans and the Holocaust* (London: Little, Brown & Co., 1996); Robert Gellately, *Backing Hitler: Consent and Coercion in Nazi Germany* (Oxford: Oxford University Press, 2001).

to catch up with history from below, although historians of the interwar Soviet Union have begun to discuss popular opinion under Stalinism, often reaching surprising conclusions on levels of popular support.[57] One of the obvious reasons for this blindspot during East–West hostilities was lack of archival access in the East, for communist and non-communist historians alike. The opening up of the East German archives in 1990, far more extensively than in other former eastern-bloc countries, has transformed the source-base. The vast majority of this material, it must be said, is routinized bumf, and German-speaking histories of the GDR in the 1990s tended to replicate this functionary's eye-view of the system, producing painstaking, but often unimaginative accounts. It took a number of Anglo-American scholars, clearly influenced by advances in the sociocultural study of the Third Reich, to show a concerted interest in popular opinion.[58]

First and foremost for this study, I have used documents from East Germany's communist party, the Socialist Unity Party of Germany (SED); references to 'the party' mean this one. The Central Committee files, as well as police, trade union, and youth movement papers, are housed in the Archive Foundation of the Parties and Mass Organizations of the GDR (SAPMO) in the Bundesarchiv at Berlin-Lichterfelde. One rich quantitative source was Volkspolizei statistics on refugees, which I have collated and present here for the first time, chiefly in Chapter 3. Whereas previous studies have mainly used annual western statistics, the eastern files allow a much finer calibration of the monthly nuances of the exodus. I also ventured into local archives, paying special attention to the industrial areas of Berlin, Saxony, and Saxony-Anhalt, as well as rural districts in Brandenburg and Mecklenburg-Vorpommern. These all contain party and state files at *Bezirk* or regional level, as well as district-level documents down to individual factories. The Ministry of State Security, or Stasi—although I shall also use the formal abbreviation MfS—provided another rich mine of information, at the Federal Commission for the State Security Files (BStU).

On the other side of the iron curtain, West German authorities collected voluminous data on GDR refugees, which were consulted in the Bundesarchiv at Koblenz. In addition, the West German demoscopic agency Infratest, founded in 1947, conducted detailed interviews with East German refugees from the mid-to-late 1950s, not unlike the Harvard Project on Soviet émigrés.[59] Its findings were

---

[57] Robert W. Thurston, *Life and Terror in Stalin's Russia, 1934–1941* (New Haven and London: Yale UP, 1996); Sarah Davies, *Popular Opinion in Stalin's Russia: Terror, Propaganda and Dissent, 1934–1941* (Cambridge: CUP, 1997); Sheila Fitzpatrick, *Everyday Stalinism: Ordinary Life in Extraordinary Times: Soviet Russia in the 1930s* (Oxford and New York: OUP, 1999).

[58] Recent pathbreaking studies have been Mark Allinson, *Politics and Popular Opinion in East Germany, 1945–68* (Manchester: MUP, 2000) and Corey Ross, *Constructing Socialism at the Grass-Roots: The Transformation of East Germany, 1945–65* (Houndmills: Macmillan, 2000). See also Patrick Major and Jonathan Osmond (eds), *The Workers' and Peasants' State: Communism and Society in East Germany under Ulbricht 1945–71* (Manchester: MUP, 2002).

[59] Alex Inkeles and Raymond Bauer, *The Soviet Citizen: Daily Life in a Totalitarian Society* (Cambridge, MA: Harvard University Press, 1961).

then circulated to Federal government agencies, even when they did not make good propaganda and upset Bonn's cold warriors.[60] The American broadcaster RIAS acted as another informal disseminator of opinion, in its radio broadcasts 'From the Zone, for the Zone', preserved at the Deutsches Rundfunkarchiv at Potsdam, along with listeners' letters. Federal Chancellor Konrad Adenauer's papers, as well as British and American assessments from the National Archives at Kew and the microfiched National Security Archive collection,[61] also shed some light on the situation inside East Germany, as do the United States Information Agency's research reports, although the vast bulk cover West Germany.[62] As a westerner myself, who lived in West Berlin for a year in 1985–86, and in East Berlin in the GDR's final months, I make no apologies for focusing exclusively on the eastern experience of the Wall; during its lifetime this was neglected for far too long![63]

The chief communist agency charged with gathering public opinion was the so-called Party Information. It existed at every level of the SED, analogous to the Nazi *Sicherheitsdienst* or SD, which had produced digests of popular opinion in the Third Reich,[64] although it understandably bore a closer family resemblance to Soviet practice.[65] The Party Information reported both on opinion within the party apparatus as well as the population at large, collating information from various sources such as trade unions, coalition parties, and the police. The tenor of reporting follows two main veins: 'fair weather reports' which say what the party leadership wanted to hear, and perhaps betray the reporter's careerism, as well as self-deprecatory 'critiques and autocritiques', indicating where the party could do better. Nevertheless, the leadership was aware of potential distortion, commenting for instance on one local party's submissions: 'A reporting schematic

[60] Bundestag (Ausschuß für gesamtdeutsche Fragen), 11 Nov. 1959, BAK, B 150, 6466, Heft 2.

[61] William Burr and National Security Archive (eds), *The Berlin Crisis 1958–1962: Guide and Index* (2 vols; Washington, DC and Alexandria, VA: National Security Archive and Chadwyck-Healey, 1992).

[62] National Archives and Records Administration (NARA), College Park, MD, RG 306, 1005/1–11.

[63] Initially only West Berliners were studied systematically, giving perhaps the false impression that they were the Wall's main victims: Kurt L. Shell, *Bedrohung und Bewährung. Führung und Bevölkerung in der Berlin-Krise* (Cologne and Opladen: Westdeutscher Verlag, 1965); Richard L. and Anna J. Merritt (eds), *Living with the Wall: West Berlin, 1961–1985* (Durham, NC: Duke University Press, 1985). There was a problem of access to East Germans, of course, which improved with détente. These studies tend to be necessarily impressionistic. See for instance, Jean Edward Smith, *Germany beyond the Wall: People, Politics . . . and Prosperity* (Boston and Toronto: Little, Brown & Co., 1969); Hans Axel Holm, *The Other Germans: Report from an East German Town*, trans. Thomas Teal (New York: Random House, 1970); Anne Armstrong, *Berliners: Both Sides of the Wall* (New Brunswick, NJ: Rutgers University Press, 1973), which still gives considerably more weight to West Berlin.

[64] Heinz Boberach (ed.), *Meldungen aus dem Reich: Die geheimen Lageberichte des Sicherheitsdienstes der SS 1938–1945*, 17 vols. (Herrsching: Pawlak, 1984).

[65] The CPSU's (Communist Party of the Soviet Union) Information Departments, and the NKVD, also produced *svodki* or summaries of the public mood: Davies, *Opinion*, 9–17.

is evident. After good examples (e.g. joy and enthusiasm among the population at the feat of Comrade Gagarin) a few negative examples are given.' But—like a bad student essay—'a problematic, assessment, and conclusion are missing'. Yet, the leadership was equally guilty of suppressing uncomfortable findings. At the party grass roots, with a better claim to have a finger on the popular pulse, this clearly caused frustration. On one East Berlin shop-floor, for instance, SED officials complained that 'we keep giving the party leadership signals and hints. But these never reach the top because they are filtered out in between'.[66] This filtering can occasionally be traced in the files. For instance, in September 1962 the Party Information summarized twenty-nine *vox populi* statements on foreign and economic policy, twenty-three of which were clearly negative, whereas only six were 'positive arguments'.[67] The next day, an edited version was submitted by Horst Dohlus, head of the Party Organs Department, to the Politbüro, containing twenty-one snippets. Seven negatives had been dropped, and one positive, the latter possibly because it was overlong. Yet it was not simply a matter of space. Of the seven excised statements, all could reasonably be adjudged 'extreme', involving fundamental criticisms of socialism or taboos about the Russians or the Wall. Of those criticisms left in, however, some might be read as complaints at the slowness of what were essentially worthy party initiatives, and thus as indirect encouragements.[68]

A final layer of censorship came from Erich Honecker, the GDR's number two in the 1960s, and leader from 1971, who vetted opinion reports before they reached the Politbüro.[69] It has been noted that the quality of GDR reporting declined in the 1970s and 1980s.[70] In the final phases of the regime, Honecker himself was on the receiving end of censorship from Dohlus. It is also clear, nevertheless, that certain information holders were concerned about this self-insulation. A small incident in April 1988 illustrates the point. When the Frankfurt/Oder SED met to discuss internal order, the local Stasi commander, Major-General Engelhardt, called for rapid improvements in production and consumption 'in order to cut the ground from enemy arguments'. (In SED speak the 'enemy' was an amorphous entity which could include both enemies within and without.) As the Party Information defensively glossed, 'the comments are a simplified version and an inadmissible generalization'. Unfortunately, however, they were then printed in the local press and subsequently picked up and broadcast by the western media. The regional party boss was then forced into an

---

[66] SED-ZK (PO), 'Information' Nr. 65, 26 May 1961, SAPMO-BArch, DY30/IV2/5/295, fo. 55.

[67] SED-ZK (PO), 'Argumente zur Politik der Partei', 24 Sept. 1962, SAPMO-BArch, DY30/IV2/5/297, fos. 149–52.

[68] SED-ZK (PO), 'Information an das Politbüro: Zu einigen Problemen der Diskussion in der Bevölkerung', 25 Sept. 1962, SAPMO-BArch, DY30/IV2/5/297, fos. 169–72.

[69] See the various covering notes in SAPMO-BArch, DY 30/IVA2/5/22.

[70] Fulbrook, *Anatomy*, 73.

autocritique, and into disciplining the editor of the offending paper.[71] As well as revealing the regime's paranoia about the western media and the porousness of the GDR's 'closed' public sphere, it also shows that some functionaries, even MfS officers, were prepared to risk their careers to get unwelcome information through. Moreover, at times of crisis, such as 1961 and 1989, citizens were more willing to drop the veneer of conformity and speak their minds.

Problematic, nevertheless, was the unwillingness of reporters to quantify opinions. The official line was usually that the 'overwhelming majority' agreed with government initiatives. If there were exceptions, then such views were held by suitably nebulous 'sections' of the populace. Occasionally one hears second-hand guesstimates relating to specific events, such as the building of the Wall, objecting to official newspaper versions that '100% of the population are for the measures—that's not true'.[72] One shop-floor functionary was told: 'If you want to speak to the colleagues they will throw you out. 90% of people are against these measures anyway'.[73] Similarly, reporters at the DEFA (the GDR's state film company) studios were told that 'The most unpopular thing that could have happened has happened. These measures are rejected by 80% of the population'.[74] In Halle two young women put it at 75 per cent.[75] When a show of hands was requested in one Leipzig factory, seventeen voted against the closure and only eight in favour.[76] These quantifications—the only ones I have found from literally thousands of recorded statements—were, of course, no more objective than the party's version. But they do demonstrate that the 'isolated' cases of dissent conceded by the reporting apparatus may have reflected much more widely held views.

To be fair, there were official attempts to combat biased reporting. In its 1960 guidelines the Party Information was exhorted to 'be true to life and may neither cosmetically enhance the real situation nor paint it distortedly black. It must be based on typical facts, but also signal both positive and negative extremes'.[77] Elaborate procedures were devised for broadening the source-base. The SED had alternative sources that did not contaminate the Party Information pool. From August 1953 the MfS's Central Evaluation and Information Group (ZAIG) collected opinion reports, starting with workers, then including the rest

---

[71] SED-ZK (PO), 'Information . . .', 19 May 1988, SAPMO-BArch, DY30/2181, fos. 82–4.

[72] FDJ-ZR (Org-Instruk), 'Argumente und Meinungen von Jugendlichen . . .', 15 Aug. 1961, SAPMO-BArch, DY 24/3.725.

[73] FDGB-BuVo (Org), 'Klassenfeindliche Tätigkeit . . .', 16 Aug. 1961, SAPMO-BArch, DY30/IV2/6.11/65, fos. 223–30.

[74] SED-ZK (PO), '8. Kurzinformation', 15 Aug. 1961, SAPMO-BArch, DY30/IV2/5/433, fo. 24.

[75] FDJ-ZR (Org-Instruk), 'Auszüge aus den Berichten . . .', 31 Aug. 1961, SAPMO-BArch, DY24/A3.935.

[76] 'Informationsbericht vom 18.8.1961', StAL, BPA SED Leipzig, IV2/12/595.

[77] SED-ZK, 'Richtlinien für die Aufgaben und Arbeitsweise der Parteiinformation . . .', SAPMO-BArch, DY30/JIV2/3/699, fos. 13–22.

of the population.[78] At the outset it employed just four operatives at the centre, and two or three in each region, but by 1989 it numbered 423 workers, sifting information from tens of thousands of the Stasi's 'unofficial collaborators'.[79] Early on, however, the MfS insisted on corroborated evidence and vetted informants for trustworthiness. It would be wrong, therefore, to think the authorities whitewashed everything coming from below. But there were limits to how much the populace was willing to tell the party directly, unless alcohol had removed inhibitions (which it often did).[80] Functionaries noted how citizens would clam up at the approach of a 'bonbon wearer' (a reference to the red enamel party lapel badge). 'The comrades should try taking off their party badges and going outside', one veterinarian told investigators, 'and then they would hear what the population is saying'.[81]

The SED gradually sought more anonymous means of gauging opinion. Initial attempts were not so happy. The so-called 'consciousness analyses' (*Bewußtseins-analysen*) of the 1960s, prepared by regional Ideological Commissions, acted as progress reports along the road to socialism. Like previous assessments, these suffered from a rose-tinted, ideological bias, stressing the GDR's historical mission, antipathy to West Germany, and affinity with the Soviet Union, but they did at least attempt an overview.[82] The most serious break with tradition came with the establishment in 1964 of the Central Committee's Institute for Demoscopy (Institut für Meinungsforschung). Although the results—despite the protestations of one former associate[83]—were heavily skewed towards what respondents thought the powers-that-be wanted to hear, they do highlight differing attitudes between classes and age groups. At its inaugural meeting, its new head, Karl Maron, argued that, faced with a complex, industrialized society, the party needed to know what was alienating GDR citizens.[84] The Institute went to great pains to guarantee anonymity, so that respondents should give 'their own opinion and not that of others'. No help was to be given during filling in. If asked, questionnaires were being conducted simply with 'government

[78] Alf Lüdtke, ' " . . . den Menschen vergessen"?—oder: Das Maß der Sicherheit: Arbeiterver-halten der 1950er Jahre im Blick vom MfS, SED, FDGB und staatlichen Leitungen', in id. and Peter Becker (eds), *Akten, Eingaben, Schaufenster: Die DDR und ihre Texte* (Berlin: Akademie, 1997), 189–91.

[79] Walter Süß, 'Die Stimmungslage der Bevölkerung im Spiegel von MfS-Berichten', in Eberhard Kuhrt (ed.), *Die SED-Herrschaft und ihr Zusammenbruch* (Opladen: Leske & Budrich, 1996), 239.

[80] Dohlus to Honecker, 1 Dec. 1966, SAPMO-BArch, DY30/IVA2/12/140.

[81] SED-PL Humboldt-Universität, 'Information', 16 Aug. 1961, SAPMO-BArch, DY30/IV2/9. 04/495, fos. 59–62.

[82] SED-BL Potsdam (Agit-Prop), 'Konzeption für die Ausarbeitung einer Analyse der Bewußt-seinsentwicklung im Bezirke', 23 Aug. 1967, BLHA, Bez. Pdm. Rep. 530/3188.

[83] Heinz Niemann, *Meinungsforschung in der DDR: Die geheimen Berichte des Instituts für Meinungsforschung an das Politbüro der SED* (Cologne: Bund, 1993); ibid., *Hinterm Zaun: Politische Kultur und Meinungsforschung in der DDR—die geheimen Berichte an das Politbüro der SED* (Berlin: edition ost, 1995).

[84] Maron's notes, 7 July 1964, SAPMO-BArch, DY30/IVA2/9.02/31.

Introduction 17

support'.[85] Indeed, enough uncomfortable information seeped through to have Honecker abandon the experiment in 1976 and close the Institute. In the same year the Stasi's ZAIG stopped reporting on the populace at large.[86] In its later stages, therefore, the leadership lived in a self-imposed popular opinion blackout.

In order to counter resistance to propaganda frequently regarded as 'primitive' and 'too hard',[87] the party also manufactured public opinion, in so-called 'declarations of support' (*Zustimmungserklärungen*). These were usually short, written statements supporting current government initiatives and signed by one or more individuals. Sometimes a rally would issue a collective declaration of support.[88] The pick of these were then published in the press as the *vox populi*, often supplying names and addresses of signatories for added authenticity. Since such material was also recycled in opinion reports, there was a danger of the regime believing its own propaganda. Moreover, many of these declarations were solicited under conditions which could hardly be described as voluntary. Agitation groups were dispatched to residential areas in order to conduct 'discussions' (*Aussprachen*), or in difficult cases, 'confrontations' (*Auseinandersetzungen*). The feelings of many who had been doorstepped in this way were not necessarily welcoming. Occasionally the door was unceremoniously slammed in the face of agitprop officials with muttered references to this sort of thing having happened once before.

The fact that all declarations were written, moreover, meant a considerable degree of premeditation. For instance, comrade dairyman Alfred W. greeted one SED initiative thus:

I agree with every word of the SED Central Committee resolution on the results of the Moscow talks. Straight after reading the communiqué of the Moscow talks I gained a full insight into the certainty of victory of the socialist over the capitalist world system. I, too, am for a life without wars, without the destruction of our autonomous values, for it will bring a bright future for all working people, for which it is worth working and fight-ing.[89]

Evidently, many opted for an easy life by such statements. This often degenerated into a charade, with even the Party Information complaining that 'one noticed from workers' conference speeches, especially from shop-floor comrades, that their contributions had been "drycleaned" by local leaderships. They often stepped up with verbatim manuscripts and came across woodenly'.[90] Other

---

[85] SED-ZK (Institut für Meinungsforschung), 'Merkblatt für Interviewer', n.d., SächsHStA, BPA SED Dresden, IV2/5/131.

[86] Personal communication by Jens Gieseke, BStU.

[87] SED-ZK (Agit), n.d., SAPMO-BArch, DY30/IV2/9.02/6, fos. 55–60.

[88] For a selection of *Zustimmungserklärungen* see LAB, BPA SED Berlin, IV2/12/1276.

[89] SED-ZK (PO), 'Information', 6 Jan. 1961, SAPMO-BArch, DY30/IV2/5/294, fo. 4.

[90] SED-ZK (PO), 'Information ...', 16 May 1962, SAPMO-BArch, DY30/IV2/5/297, fo. 45.

assessments were patently lifted from the current media line. As one district in Saxony complained: 'The available opinions often paraphrase the word on current political events as broadcast on radio or written in the press'.[91] Reading between the lines of some *Zustimmungserklärungen*, however, one can sometimes detect veiled criticism, deliberately taking the party at its word and alluding to abandoned promises. As one stated: 'If we conduct the discussion of the Plan with the same precision as the Soviet cosmonauts carried out their formation flight, we shall achieve the Plan targets and strengthen the socialist camp'.[92] Yet, such superhuman yardsticks could easily become rods for the party's own back.

Even the SED could not ignore the fact that, back down on Earth, there were severe grounds for complaint. Everyday problems such as housing repairs, waiting lists for cars, or applications to travel abroad could become major bones of contention. The regime attempted to head off some of this discontent with a Workers' and Peasants' Inspection, a trouble-shooting ombudsman to monitor the state apparatus. Founded in 1963, it was to expose deficiencies on the shop-floor and in the health, education and retail sectors, 'unrelentingly' and 'with the support of the public, regardless of personal standing'.[93] It achieved a certain respect. The system also permitted a gentle self-mockery, in the satirical magazine *Eulenspiegel* for instance, whose readers could smile at the pompousness of functionaries or the hypocrisy of ideological fellow travellers. Socialist satire stereotyped a number of shortcomings, always safely contained behind inverted commas or folksy euphemisms, so-called 'hot potatoes'. To its credit, *Eulenspiegel* fought against this sanitization, but lost. From 1965 its editors were ordered to make satire 'partisan'.[94] This partly explains the huge vogue for unofficial political jokes in the GDR, which ignored the taboos on criticizing the system as a whole or leadership personalities.[95] One Neubrandenburg mayor, for instance, related how 'A man is walking across the Alexanderplatz with a pound of margarine dangling before him and half a pound of butter behind him and a potty on his head'. Asked to explain the strange attire, he explained 'that butter is a thing of the past, margarine a thing of the future, while those at the top keep shitting on us'.[96] Ouch!

[91] Various KLs, May–Oct. 1960 in StAC, SED-BL KMS, IV2/5/42.

[92] SED-ZK (PO), 'Argumente zur Politik der Partei', 24 Sept. 1962, SAPMO-BArch, DY30/IV2/5/297, fos. 149–52.

[93] Hartmut Mummert, 'Die Arbeiter-und-Bauern-Inspektion in der DDR zwischen Anspruch und Wirklichkeit: Zur Geschichte eines Volkskontrollorgans', *Hefte zur DDR-Geschichte*, 58 (1999), 10.

[94] Eulenspiegel (ed.), *Spötterfunken: Karikaturen aus zehn Jahren deutscher Entwicklung* (East Berlin: Eulenspiegel Verlag, 1959); Sylvia Klötzer, 'Über den Umgang mit heißen Eisen: *Eulenspiegel*(eien)', in Simone Barck *et al.* (eds), *Zwischen 'Mosaik' und 'Einheit': Zeitschriften in der DDR* (Berlin: Ch. Links, 1999), 105–15.

[95] Helga and Klaus-Dieter Schlechte (eds), *Witze bis zur Wende: 40 Jahre politischer Witze in der DDR* (Munich: Ehrenwirth, 1991).

[96] SED-ZK (PO), 'Information . . .', 4 July 1961, SAPMO-BArch, DY30/IV2/5/36, fos. 200–3.

A more systematic index of popular grievances, and one which will be returned to throughout, was petitions (*Eingaben*). Viewers of *Good Bye, Lenin!* (Becker, 2002) may be familiar with the mother firing off these barbed entreaties to the powers-that-be. Rather than seeking 'bourgeois' legal redress, however, citizens in a people's democracy sought social justice from their rulers direct. Yet, unlike some historical precedents, such as collective *cahiers de doléance* in revolutionary France, GDR petitioning was kept solitary.[97] I have drawn chiefly on petitions to President Pieck, and following his death in 1960, to the Council of State, in which housing and travel figured prominently, as well as complaints to the People's Police, or Volkspolizei, which stood in the immediate firing line on travel matters. In February 1961 the Council of State actively encouraged more petitions, promising an end to 'heartless bureaucracy' and faster processing. The numbers duly doubled, from 52,000 to nearly 102,000 annually.[98] Almost every organ of government had its own petitions office, however. Mühlberg estimates an annual total of nearly 1 million petitions, a mixture of entreaties, demands, and complaints.[99] Although local authorities became skilled at deflecting them,[100] it should not be forgotten that many were upheld by the higher authorities. Citizens also became adept at turning the party's rhetoric back on itself in support of claims for resources in short supply. Party leader Ulbricht even claimed that it was 'self-evident that problems are discussed in the population and that many of them can only be solved during the further construction of socialism'—with one notable exception: 'I do not include here petitions to travel to West Germany'.[101] To borrow party jargon, freedom of travel was the system's 'neuralgic point', and as one early oral history argued, 'the inner German border is the crucial key to the history of the GDR'.[102]

For our purposes, petitions represent Hirschman's category of 'voice', and one which was increasingly forced into the arena of unsanctioned dissent.[103] Socially, it is clear that freedom of travel was more salient for members of the educated

[97] Lex Heerma van Voss (ed.), *Petitions in Social History* (Cambridge: Cambridge University Press, 2001), 1–10.

[98] See BAB, DA-5/5999.

[99] Felix Mühlberg, *Bürger, Bitten und Behörden: Geschichte der Eingabe in der DDR* (Berlin: Dietz, 2004), 175.

[100] Jonathan R. Zatlin, 'Ausgaben und Eingaben: Das Petitionsrecht und der Untergang der DDR', *Zeitschrift für Geschichtswissenschaft*, 45 (1997), 906.

[101] 'Ausführungen des Genossen Ulbricht . . . ', n.d., BAB, DA-5/167, fos. 221–4.

[102] Lutz Niethammer *et al.*, *Die volkseigene Erfahrung: Eine Archäologie des Lebens in der Industrieprovinz der DDR* (Berlin: Rowohlt, 1991), 26.

[103] Regionally, some areas were more prone to petition the Council of State than others, and at different times. In 1961 Dresden was most plaintive (0.71 per cent of the populace), closely followed by Leipzig, Karl-Marx-Stadt and Halle at over 0.6 per cent, with East Berliners least likely to petition (0.29 per cent), followed by Potsdam at less than 0.4 per cent. This would support Hirschman's thesis that areas with greatest potential to exit the GDR were least likely to voice complaint. Yet, as the GDR aged and the outlet to the West was closed, this pattern switched. By 1970 Berlin had reached pole position, at 0.66 per cent, followed by Potsdam at 0.41 per cent, a pattern repeated with minor changes ten years later in 1980. BAB, DA-5/5999.

intelligentsia, the *Mittelstand*, and women of all classes, than it was for other groups.[104] Furthermore, the special status of travel petitions is revealed by the fact that from the 1970s the security section of the SED's Central Committee, in conjunction with the MfS, became the arbiter on travel and emigration. Indeed, the vast majority of its surviving files consist of alphabetized special pleading by citizens to travel west. Although, overall, housing petitions predominated over the GDR's lifetime, providing a salutary reminder that most inhabitants wanted to make a go of it, travel touched an especially raw official nerve. The GDR was full of taboos, yet the desire to leave the country was tantamount to a rejection of socialism, and thus 'hostile to the state'. It was also the issue which evoked the greatest sense of abnormality in recollections by former citizens.[105] But first, in order to make sense of East Germany's fragile existence on the eve of the Wall, we must turn to the dual foreign and domestic crises at the Cold War's epicentre: in Berlin.

---

[104] Felix Mühlberg, 'Eingaben als Instrument informeller Konfliktbewältigung', in Badstübner (ed.), *Befremdlich anders*, 237.
[105] See Mary Fulbrook's survey in the final chapter of id. (ed.), *Power and Society in the GDR, 1961–1979: The 'Normalisation of Rule'?* (New York: Berghahn, 2009).

PART I

BEFORE THE WALL

2

East Germany's Dual Crisis: Politics and Economics on the Eve of the Wall

Existing accounts of the second Berlin crisis—starting with Khrushchev's 1958 ultimatum and ending with the building of the Wall in 1961—have treated it primarily as an episode in international relations, the classic superpower confrontation of the European Cold War. We consequently know much about top-level contingency planning and crisis management in Washington[1] and the Kremlin,[2] as well as among the junior partners in Whitehall,[3] the Quai d'Orsay,[4] West Germany and West Berlin.[5] Since the fall of the Wall, the so-called 'New Cold War History' has unearthed mountains of documents

Histo

---

[1] Jack M. Schick, *The Berlin Crisis, 1958–1962* (Philadelphia: University of Pennsylvania Press, 1971); Robert M. Slusser, *The Berlin Crisis of 1961: Soviet-American Relations and the Struggle for Power in the Kremlin, June–November 1961* (Baltimore: Johns Hopkins University Press, 1973); Heribert Gerlach, *Die Berlinpolitik der Kennedy-Administration: Eine Fallstudie zum außenpolitischen Verhalten der Kennedy-Regierung in der Berlinkrise 1961* (Frankfurt: Haag & Herchen, 1977); Honoré M. Catudal, *Kennedy and the Berlin Wall Crisis: A Case Study in US Decision Making* (West Berlin: Berlin-Verlag, 1980); Michael Beschloss, *Kennedy versus Khrushchev: The Crisis Years 1960–63* (London: Faber, 1991); Joachim Arenth, *Der Westen tut nichts! Transatlantische Kooperation während der zweiten Berlin-Krise (1958–1962) im Spiegel neuer amerikanischer Quellen* (Frankfurt: Peter Lang, 1993); John C. Ausland, *Kennedy, Khruschchev and the Berlin–Cuba Crisis, 1961–1964* (Oslo: Scandinavian University Press, 1996); Rolf Steininger, *Der Mauerbau: Die Westmächte und Adenauer in der Berlinkrise 1958–1963* (Munich: Olzog, 2001).
[2] Gerhard Wettig, *Chruschtschows Berlin-Krise 1958 bis 1963: Drohpolitik und Mauerbau* (Munich: Oldenbourg, 2006); Vladislav M. Zubok, 'Khrushchev and the Berlin Crisis (1958–1962)' (Cold War International History Project, Working Paper No. 6, May 1993).
[3] John P. S. Gearson, *Harold Macmillan and the Berlin Wall Crisis, 1958–62: The Limits of Interest and Force* (Basingstoke: Macmillan, 1998); Sabine Lee, 'Perception and Reality: Anglo-German Relations and the Berlin Crisis 1958–1959', *German History*, 13 (1995), 47–69; Victor Mauer, 'Macmillan und die Berlin-Krise 1958/59', *Vierteljahrshefte für Zeitgeschichte*, 44 (1996), 229–56; Ann Tusa, *The Last Division: Berlin and the Wall* (London: Hodder & Stoughton, 1996).
[4] Erin R. Mahan, *Kennedy, de Gaulle and Western Europe* (Houndmills: Palgrave, 2002).
[5] Hanns Jürgen Küsters, 'Konrad Adenauer und Willy Brandt in der Berlin Krise 1958–1963', *Vierteljahrshefte für Zeitgeschichte*, 40 (1992), 483–542; Diethelm Prowe, 'Der Brief Kennedys an Brandt vom 18. August 1961: Eine zentrale Quelle zur Berliner Mauer und der Entstehung der Brandtschen Ostpolitik', *Vierteljahrshefte für Zeitgeschichte*, 33 (1985), 373–83; id., ' "Ich bin ein Berliner": Kennedy, die Mauer und die "verteidigte Insel" West-Berlin im ausgehenden Kalten Krieg im Spiegel amerikanischer Akten', in Landesarchiv Berlin (ed.), *Berlin in Geschichte und Gegenwart* (Berlin: Siedler, 1989), 143–67.

from previously inaccessible archives behind the iron curtain.[6] Nuclear fears, diplomatic recognition for the post-1945 settlement, and Chinese rivalry were undoubtedly all Soviet motives. The focus has remained, nevertheless, on high politics, pursuing convoluted paper trails in search of elusive smoking guns. Yet, remarkably little changed internationally as a result of the crisis: the Kremlin failed to prevent an atomic-capable Bundeswehr; no peace treaties were signed; and it was another decade before there was significant movement between the two Germanys. Nevertheless, following post-revisionist trends within Cold War historiography away from bipolar models of superpower conflict, recent research on the Wall crisis stresses regional players. It has been persuasively argued, by Michael Lemke but above all Hope Harrison, that the GDR leadership was instrumental in escalating the crisis.[7]

Relations between the Soviet and East German comrades had never been easy, ever since the founding of the GDR in October 1949. When the second Berlin crisis began, the East German state was less than a decade old. It was not inconceivable that Moscow would make a German–German deal, sacrificing the SED's partial gains.[8] West Berlin, situated deep within the surrounding GDR, presented both problems and opportunities for the eastern bloc. Given its exposed position, it was an easy pressure point on the West, but it also rendered the GDR geopolitically 'hollow'. While the Kremlin may have seen Berlin as leverage to solve other problems, Berlin *was* the fundamental problem for the SED, which lobbied Khrushchev to stick to what it saw as core demands. This is not the place for a recapitulation of the diplomatic battles being waged, yet I do wish to show that much of the pressure on the GDR leadership was coming from below, from its own populace. Ordinary East Germans were largely sceptical of the leadership's international gambits, and indeed of the ability of Cold War leaders on both sides to resolve their differences. Unless the SED could lend credibility to the latest campaign, international instability would result in a continuation of the domestic legitimacy crisis of the young Workers' and Peasants' State.

Furthermore, I wish to highlight the systemic 'crisis behind the crisis': the domestic economic breakdown inaugurated by Ulbricht's July 1958 pledge to overtake West German consumer goods production by 1961. This was a miniature version of Khrushchev's ambitious 1957 scheme to beat the United

---

[6] See 'Cold War International History Project Bulletin' (Washington, DC, 1992 ff.); also online: http://wilsoncenter.org/index.cfm?topic_id=1409&fuseaction=topics.home.

[7] Michael Lemke, *Die Berlinkrise 1958 bis 1963: Interessen und Handlungsspielräume der SED im Ost-West-Konflikt* (Berlin: Akademie Verlag, 1995); Hope M. Harrison, 'Ulbricht and the Concrete "Rose": New Archival Evidence on the Dynamics of Soviet–East German Relations and the Berlin Crisis, 1958–1961' (Cold War International History Project, Working Paper No. 5, May 1993); id., *Driving the Soviets up the Wall: Soviet-East German Relations, 1953–1961* (Princeton: Princeton UP, 2003). See also Matthias Uhl and Armin Wagner (eds), *Ulbricht, Chruschtschow und die Mauer: Eine Dokumentation* (Munich: Oldenbourg, 2003).

[8] Dirk Spilker, *The East German Leadership and the Division of Germany: Patriotism and Propaganda 1945–53* (Oxford: Oxford University Press, 2006).

States at its own consumer game. The GDR economy had indeed made great strides to overcome wartime destruction and Soviet dismantling, which had removed around 30 per cent of industry, yet manufacturing was still fragile, suffering from dwindling raw materials and manpower.[9] Besides production bottlenecks, there was a crisis of consumption. 1958 witnessed the lifting of rationing, yet distribution proved unequal to increased demand for even basic foodstuffs and clothing. The forced collectivization of agriculture, accelerated in spring 1960, only exacerbated the problem in public eyes. Then came the threat of an embargo of West German exports to the GDR in the autumn, to which the SED responded with its own autarky programme. Such developments would have placed enormous strains on the East German economy at the best of times, but at the height of a self-imposed race with West Germany, they proved disastrous. In conjunction with the diplomatic brinkmanship occurring in the international arena, many thought the GDR was on the verge of collapse, but would not go down without a fight.

I am particularly concerned with the effects of the dual crises on the wider East German public. In most accounts the 'people' are allocated a walk-on—or in this case walk-off—part in the drama. Between 1945 and 1961 approximately one in six East Germans left the country. Those who stayed behind could also cause severe difficulties. In fact, ordinary East Germans were, as will become evident, the root cause of the chronic instability of the young Workers' and Peasants' State. Individually, these departures may have been pinpricks, but together this massive brain-drain forced the GDR into a struggle for survival. Neither the superpowers nor their allies could control the exodus, which will be examined in more detail in Chapter 4. But if any Cold War crisis was simultaneously a 'people's crisis', it must surely have been the Berlin crisis of 1958–61. Even diplomatic historians now accept that public opinion mattered. As John Lewis Gaddis not so recently lamented: 'So what *did* ordinary people during the Cold War really think?'[10] The first half of this chapter is an attempt to do exactly that. The interaction between high and low politics will become evident, in ways which I hope will become more commonplace in the 'new' New Cold War history.

However, diplomatic historians, versed as they are in painstaking reconstructions of policy formulation, should be forewarned that public perceptions of events at the top were hazy and ill-informed—one cannot expect the career diplomat's lapidary prose. There was often a considerable time-lag in responses to events. Only educated elites were likely to keep abreast of media debates. Nevertheless, the East German state forced its citizenry to discuss current diplomatic

[9] Rainer Karlsch, *Allein bezahlt? Die Reparationsleistungen der SBZ/DDR 1945–1953* (Berlin: Links, 1993).

[10] John Lewis Gaddis, 'On Starting All Over Again: A Naïve Approach to the Study of the Cold War', in Odd Arne Westad (ed.), *Reviewing the Cold War: Approaches, Interpretations, Theory* (London: Cass, 2000), 36.

initiatives in countless public gatherings, recorded by the Party Information. Perforce, therefore, the East German public was arguably better informed than its West German counterpart. Many, of course, took a localized view of high politics, asking how it was going to affect them personally. Indeed, the social history of Germany's Cold War has begun to reveal that international ruptures were frequently perceived through the prism of family relations.[11] In long conversations with one old lady in West Berlin in the 1980s, postwar events were recounted to me in terms of which family members had remained 'over there'; which daughter-in-law had married into the Nazi hierarchy and gone west; or which son had joined the East German military and been barred from visiting his mother. National division tore through the social fabric far less neatly than the new lines on the map.

COLD WAR BERLIN: A TALE OF TWO CITIES

The diplomatic falling out of 1958–61 had a long pre-history. Even before war's end, the former German capital had putatively been split into sectors, originally three, but joined in spring 1945 by a fourth French sector.[12] In the meantime, it remained for the Allies to capture the city. Despite Churchill's gung-ho calls for an Anglo-American charge across the north German plain, Eisenhower left it to Moscow. In a battle costing 304,000 casualties, the Red Army finally encircled the city in late April 1945, street-fighting its way to the garrison's surrender on 2 May.[13] An orgy of raping and looting followed, confirming many Germans' prejudices about 'Asiatic barbarism'. Yet, although the Soviets' blood sacrifice fuelled later moral claims to all Berlin, for the moment the Allies honoured their wartime agreements. In July 1945, as American and British troops withdrew from captured Saxony and Thuringia to allow in the Red Army, western Allied contingents entered their sectors of Berlin. The Americans occupied the southwestern city, including large leafy areas of the Grunewald; the British took a central slice reaching from their headquarters near the Olympic Stadium in the west to the Brandenburg Gate in the east; the French received two rather rundown boroughs in the north. Meanwhile, the Soviets controlled eight boroughs in the city's eastern half, including many workers' districts, but also the former government quarter of Mitte, which formed a salient into West Berlin. The seat of Allied military government for all Germany, the Allied Control Council,

---

[11] John Borneman, *Belonging in the Two Berlins: Kin, State, Nation* (Cambridge: Cambridge UP, 1992).

[12] Tony Sharp, *The Wartime Alliance and the Zonal Division of Germany* (Oxford: Clarendon, 1975), 187–99.

[13] Anthony Read and David Fisher, The *Fall of Berlin* (London: Hutchinson, 1992), 468; Alexandra Richie, *Faust's Metropolis: A History of Berlin* (London: HarperCollins, 1998), 547–603; Antony Beevor, *Berlin: The Downfall 1945* (London: Penguin, 2002), 386.

and the city's military administration, the Kommandatura, both resided in the American sector. The Rathaus, on the other hand, lay in the Soviet sector. There were also a number of exclaves, such as the Soviet war memorial in Tiergarten, inside the British sector, and the British-held hamlet of Staaken within the Soviet Zone.

In the early occupation years, however, common problems of survival masked geopolitical fissures. Seventy per cent of Berlin lay devastated after sustained aerial and ground assault.[14] In the summer of 1945 bluebottles still swarmed over the bodies under the rubble; refugee convoys flooded in, awaiting relocation; and a thriving black market arose. Eating became the main preoccupation. Inhabitants bartered watches, cigarettes, and household goods, and women and boys sometimes even offered themselves, for food.[15] The Soviets insisted, however, that the western Allies supply their own sectors by rail, while they themselves used *payoks*, or food parcels, to win over hungry German officials. Like all postwar German cities, rural provisioning trips became vital. Ordinary Berliners from both halves of the city thus hiked to outlying Brandenburg, rucksack on back, oblivious to the ideological boundaries they were crossing.[16]

It was not long, however, before simmering municipal rifts erupted in 1948 into international crisis with the Berlin blockade. In the spring, alarmed at preparations for a separate West German state, Russia had flexed its veto on the Allied Control Council, before Marshal Sokolovsky walked out in March.[17] The Soviets launched parallel spoiling tactics on the transit routes to West Berlin, turning back Allied trains which refused checks, and closing all but the Berlin–Helmstedt line. US military governor Lucius D. Clay responded with a 'Little Airlift' in April–May to bring in supplies for American personnel.[18] But Soviet restrictions continued, for instance against barge traffic, and on 12 June the Berlin–Helmstedt autobahn was ominously closed for indefinite repairs. The introduction of a separate western currency, the deutschmark, proved the final straw for Moscow. Although the new money was intended only for the western zones, when on 23 June the Soviets announced their own ostmarks, to include all Berlin, the western Allies extended the deutschmark to the western sectors.[19] In retaliation Moscow severed all traffic to and from the beleaguered half-city, owing to 'technical difficulties', and electricity from power stations in

---

[14] Richie, *Faust's Metropolis*, 531.

[15] Jennifer V. Evans, 'Bahnhof Boys: Policing Male Prostitution in Post-Nazi Berlin', *Journal of the History of Sexuality*, 12 (2003), 605–36.

[16] Paul Steege, *Black Market, Cold War: Everyday Life in Berlin, 1946–1949* (Cambridge: Cambridge University Press, 2007), 18–63.

[17] Ann and John Tusa, *The Berlin Blockade* (London: Hodder & Stoughton, 1988), 102.

[18] W. Phillips Davison, *The Berlin Blockade: A Study in Cold War Politics* (Princeton, NJ: Princeton University Press, 1958), 74.

[19] Gerhard Keiderling, *'Rosinenbomber über Berlin': Währungsreform, Blockade, Luftbrücke, Teilung* (Berlin: Dietz, 1998), 55–64.

East Berlin was all but cut off. Only when the West abandoned moves towards a separate West German state, or so the Kremlin implied, would normal service be resumed. The US military were initially divided over how to respond. The Pentagon was inclined to abandon West Berlin, but Clay argued that withdrawal would be politically disastrous, mooting an armoured probe along the transit autobahn. The less risky solution, exploiting a loophole in air traffic control regulations, was an airlift.[20] Over the next eleven months all supplies were flown in, from coal to powdered food.[21] Feeding West Berlin became the key to winning the blockade, as the Soviets attempted to lure western residents to register for rations in the eastern sector. Yet, even at the lowest trough, in February 1949, only 100,000, or 5 per cent, of West Berliners complied.[22] This, at least, was the official story. There was, in fact, never a complete blockade. East Berliners brought food parcels to western relatives and the Volkspolizei regularly confiscated contraband from West Berliners on foraging trips. Smugglers would smash eggs on station platforms and pour milk and flour down washbasins, rather than let them fall into 'enemy' hands.[23] It is clear that many West Berlin businesses, starved of raw materials, would have collapsed without a furtive black market across the sector boundary in defiance of the official counter-blockade.[24] Yet by the spring of 1949, as Allied planes shuttled in ever-increasing tonnages, the Soviet Union was seeking a diplomatic way out of a public relations disaster. By April secret negotiations were under way and on 12 May the blockade was lifted.

During the 1950s the city split further apart. Until 1956, the Soviets retained Goebbels' former radio studios in the British sector, forcing the western Allies to set up rival stations such as Radio in the American Sector (RIAS) and Sender Freies Berlin, which, according to eastern propaganda, were poisoning the airwaves, but were still avidly listened to in the East.[25] In a typical Cold War absurdity, the municipal railways were split between the overground S-Bahn, run by the East, and the underground U-Bahn, run by the West. The U-Bahn, with many stations under the Mitte salient, thus offered a relatively unmolested route

---

[20] Jean Edward Smith, *The Defense of Berlin* (Baltimore, MD: Johns Hopkins Press, 1963), 94.

[21] Thomas Parrish, *Berlin in the Balance: The Blockade, the Airlift, the First Major Battle of the Cold War* (Reading, MA: Addison-Wesley, 1998); Michael D. Haydock, *City under Siege: The Berlin Airlift, 1948–1949* (Washington, DC: Brassey's, 1999), 180–8.

[22] Steege, *Black Market* 214–17.

[23] Paul R. Steege, 'Totale Blockade, totale Luftbrücke? Die mythische Erfahrung der ersten Berlinkrise, Juni 1948 bis Mai 1949', in Burghard Ciesla *et al.* (eds), *Sterben für Berlin: Die Berliner Krisen 1948: 1958* (Berlin: Metropol, 2000), 59–77; here 68.

[24] Volker Koop, *Kein Kampf um Berlin: Deutsche Politik zur Zeit der Berlin-Blockade 1948/1949* (Bonn: Bouvier, 1998), 211–46; William Stivers, 'The Incomplete Blockade: Soviet Zone Supply of West Berlin, 1948–49', *Diplomatic History*, 21 (1997), 569–602.

[25] DIVO, 'Radio Listening and TV Viewing in East Germany', Oct. 1959, NARA, RG 306, 1005/11. See also Wolfgang Schivelbusch, *In a Cold Crater: Cultural and Intellectual Life in Berlin, 1945–1948*, trans. Kelly Barry (Berkeley, CA: University of California Press, 1998), 107–26.

out under the sector boundary. The Friedrichstraße interchange in particular was a warren of tunnels, impossible for the East German customs to control fully. GDR cinema depicted an 'underground' overrun by western gangsters and Mata Haris, seducing weak-willed passengers into betraying socialism.[26] Likewise, S-Bahn stations in West Berlin were off-limits to Allied personnel and West Berlin police, treated as East Berlin enclaves, as was West Berlin's main railway station, the Bahnhof Zoo.[27] The Zoo also attracted 'speculators', exploiting the twin currencies. Quickly, an unofficial exchange rate of 1 deutschmark to 5 ostmarks emerged, abused by western bargain-hunters after cheap haircuts or knock-down Zeiss cameras. The West Berlin chamber of commerce even ran an advertising campaign against the fictitious Herr Schimpf and Frau Schande—Mr Blame and Mrs Shame—who endangered jobs at home by taking their custom to 'the other side'.[28] East Berlin also attempted deterrence, demanding pass permits and identity cards in shops, although many West Berliners continued, as the Volkspolizei disapprovingly noted, 'to shop and visit hostelries, friends and relatives'.[29] And although in October 1957 East Germany changed its own currency, it was only months before the black economy reasserted itself.[30]

On 17 June 1953 Berlin once again attracted world attention when demonstrations by building workers in the eastern sector's Stalinallee escalated into GDR-wide strikes and insurrections. Sparked by mismanaged work quotas and ration cards, during a period of Moscow-inspired liberalization following Stalin's death in March, numerous grievances were aired, from violent anti-communism to pro-democracy demands. Demonstrators marched on the government quarter, opened prisons and set fire to some party offices, as crowds milled to and fro across the still open sector boundaries. Only the reluctant appearance of Soviet tanks in the late afternoon restored order. Despite party damage limitation exercises and conspiracy theories blaming the CIA, simmering discontent persisted, although the spontaneous nature of the explosion had also revealed the difficulties of concerted action against the SED regime.[31] Nonetheless, 17 June became *the* skeleton in the closet for most party apparatchiks, and critics liked to remind them of it.[32] The crisis of 1958–61 was naturally very different, a wasting

[handwritten margin note: legitimacy]

[26] *Zugverkehr unregelmäßig* (Freund, 1951).

[27] Burghard Ciesla, ' "Über alle Sektorengrenzen hinweg . . .": Die deutsche Reichsbahn und die Berlinkrisen (1945–1958)', in id. *et al.* (eds), *Sterben für Berlin?*, 133–51.

[28] Katherine Pence, 'Herr Schimpf und Frau Schande: Grenzgänger des Konsums im geteilten Berlin und die Politik des Kalten Krieges', in Ciesla *et al.* (eds), *Sterben für Berlin?*, 185–202.

[29] HVDVP (PM), '1. Halbjahresbericht . . .', 23 July 1957, BAB, DO-1/11/918, fos. 3–20.

[30] Gerhard Keiderling and Percy Stulz, *Berlin 1945–1968: Zur Geschichte der Hauptstadt der DDR und der selbständigen politischen Einheit Westberlin* (East Berlin: Dietz, 1970), 389–90.

[31] Ilko-Sascha Kowalczuk *et al.* (eds), *Der Tag X: 17. Juni 1953: Die 'Innere Staatsgründung' der DDR als Ergebnis der Krise 1952/54* (Berlin: Links, 1995).

[32] Gareth Pritchard, *The Making of the GDR, 1945–53* (Manchester: Manchester University Press, 2000), 211–17.

sickness rather than a violent convulsion, but it is clear that local SED officials, on shop-floors and in the streets, were being pushed onto the defensive. Policing the frontiers of power at the grass roots, while the powers-that-be appeared to be bungling diplomacy and the economy, became an increasingly uncomfortable experience.

The divided city also proved a spies' paradise. On the Teufelsberg, or 'Devil's Mount' of piled-up bomb rubble, the Americans built a signals intelligence centre. More daringly, in 1955, the CIA and MI6 launched Operation Gold, to tunnel 500 yards under the sector boundary to tap Russian cable-traffic. Unknown to western intelligence, however, mole George Blake had already betrayed the operation to the KGB, who waited before 'accidentally' stumbling on the tunnel and exposing it to the world press.[33] Nor were the eastern secret services averse from snatching targets off West Berlin streets.[34] In 1954 even the head of West Germany's counter-intelligence, Otto John, was allegedly drugged and abducted to East Berlin, where he publicly denounced West German rearmament. For their part, the eastern authorities also complained of West Berlin as a forward base for espionage into the communist hinterland.[35] Allied military missions roved the GDR, scouting, according to the MfS, for 'tactical bases in the event of the hostile powers' planned counter-revolutionary and warlike operations'. The Stasi counted 40 American intelligence operations in West Berlin spreading black propaganda in the East or debriefing agents, prior to another alleged 'X Day' à la 1953.[36]

By the late 1950s, therefore, West Berlin presented several problems to the eastern authorities, unable to drive out the western garrison in 1948–49. Although the Red Army outnumbered it by twenty-five to one, a military solution was a nuclear non-starter. The airlift had also demonstrated the inviolability of the air corridors to the West, through which hundreds of thousands of escaping East Germans continued to flee with impunity. West Berlin had been the poorer sibling in the late 1940s, awash with unemployment and refugees, but now the SED claimed that the 'Frontstadt'—the front city in mocking allusion to wartime Nazi propaganda—was provoking the peace-loving East with its 'shopwindow politics'.[37] The opulent Kaufhaus des Westens offered the best in consumer luxury, but then most ordinary shops in the western

---

[33] David Stafford, *Spies beneath Berlin* (London: Murray, 2002); David E. Murphy *et al.*, *Battleground Berlin: CIA vs. KGB in the Cold War* (New Haven: Yale University Press, 1997), 208–37.

[34] Arthur L. Smith, *Kidnap City: Cold War Berlin* (Westport, CT: Greenwood, 2002).

[35] Paul Maddrell, *Spying for Science: Western Intelligence in Divided Germany 1945–1961* (Oxford: Oxford University Press, 2006).

[36] MfS, 'Materialien zu Fragen der Einmischung der USA . . .', n.d. [May 1960], BStU-ZA, MfS-SdM 290, fos. 20–88.

[37] 'Das wahre Gesicht der Frontstadt Berlin', *Tatsachen und Argumente*, 25 (East Berlin, n.d.); Allgemeiner Deutscher Nachrichtendienst (ed.), *Tatsachen über Westberlin: Subversion, Wirtschaftskrieg, Revanchismus gegen die sozialistischen Staaten* (East Berlin: Kongreß, 1962).

sectors provided cheaper and better-quality goods. Even Dresdeners came to buy the ingredients for their traditional Christmas *stollen*.[38] Cross-border cinemas offered forbidden Hollywood fruit to eastern moviegoers. The eastern authorities resorted to painting the West as a 'swamp' of black marketeers, spies, and, as one East German magazine suggested—photographing the bright lights of the Kurfürstendamm through a pair of nylon-sheathed legs—loose women.[39] The Stasi's 1959 exhibition, 'No Chance for NATO Agents', greeted visitors with a giant western spider spinning its web across the city. Exhibits warned of the man 'who only wanted to sell mushrooms, but returned a spy', or the CIA nightclub owner who recruited innocent young girls from the East German sticks into becoming scantily clad go-go dancers.[40] A sign of the East's weakness was the resort to such moral arguments to create an invisible *cordon sanitaire*, a zone of transgression from which good citizens should, but often would not, hold back. Policing the Cold War frontline in the name of peaceful coexistence felt like fighting a losing battle.

DIPLOMATIC DEADLOCK: THE SECOND BERLIN CRISIS

It was therefore a shock, but not a total surprise when, in November 1958, Nikita Khrushchev served notice on the three western powers to evacuate West Berlin within six months. The Kremlin leader had always considered the western city a 'festering sore' on the GDR, but also the 'testicles of the West'. 'Every time I want to make the West scream', he remarked, 'I squeeze on Berlin.'[41] At times during the prolonged crisis the world seemed to teeter on the brink of war. Historians have suggested various motives, ranging from quirks of personality and Soviet domestic pressures,[42] to attempts to impress Chinese and western observers, to hopes of removing nuclear weapons from West Germany.[43] While hard evidence from the Kremlin's inner sanctum is only just emerging,[44] it now seems that traditional, top-down bipolar models of Cold War dynamics, painting Khrushchev as the driving force, are misleading. Some of the reasons lay closer to home, made in the GDR. Hope Harrison has even provocatively suggested that a weak GDR effectively blackmailed Moscow into

---

[38] Interview with Mr and Mrs Sch. and Mr and Mrs L., Dresden-Weißig, 22 Aug. 1996.

[39] *Neue Berliner Illustrierte*, 44 (1959).

[40] BStU-ZA, ZAIG 10353, fo. 149 and ZAIG 10366, fo. 179.

[41] Nikita Khrushchev, *Khrushchev Remembers: The Last Testament*, ed. and trans. Strobe Talbott (Boston: Little, Brown, 1974), 501.

[42] James G. Richter, *Khrushchev's Double Bind: International Pressures and Domestic Coalition Politics* (Baltimore: Johns Hopkins University Press, 1994).

[43] Marc Trachtenberg, *A Constructed Peace: The Making of the European Settlement, 1945–1963* (Princeton, NJ: Princeton University Press, 1999), 251–6.

[44] Aleksandr Fursenko and Timothy Naftali, *Khrushchev's Cold War: The Inside Story of an American Adversary* (New York: Norton, 2006).

propping it up, becoming the East German tail that 'boldly wagged the [Soviet] dog'.[45]

Up to 1958 Soviet diplomacy had followed a twin track of addressing the Berlin problem only in the wider context of the German question. This included forcing recognition of contested postwar borders, not only the Oder–Neisse frontier between Poland and East Germany, but all new eastern-bloc frontiers. It also sought to neutralize the Federal Republic and detach it from NATO. One means to this end would be a peace treaty between the former anti-Hitler coalition on the one hand, and the two German states on the other, as a prelude to unification on a neutralist model. Adding eastern Europe's states into the equation would help to overcome the Soviet Union's isolation in the face of the three western powers, since West Germany's size threatened to swamp the GDR in any settlement. According to eastern logic, this intra-German inferiority could be further offset by insistence on government-to-government talks, hammered out between equally weighted delegations. The stock western response throughout the 1950s was to call for free elections before negotiations, thus hoping to undermine the communists' position at the ballot-box before they reached the negotiating table.

The other, perhaps more realistic eastern goal was gradual, de facto recognition by the West of the GDR. Ever since East Germany's foundation, the Federal Republic had refused to recognize what it regarded as an illegitimate Stalinist creature. Bonn claimed the sole right to represent the German nation. Even internal Federal correspondence referred to the GDR as the 'Soviet Zone' (later this was commuted to placing 'GDR' inside inverted commas). Unlike international frontiers, West German atlases showed the inner German border as a dotted line. In 1955 Bonn enshrined non-recognition in the so-called Hallstein Doctrine, which refused diplomatic relations with any state which itself recognized East Germany.[46] Among the states denying the GDR were, of course, the American, British, and French occupation forces in Berlin. In practical terms this meant that Allied troops would not deal with East German officials. If military personnel were stopped by the Volkspolizei in transit, they would sit tight until a Soviet officer intervened. After one incident when the Stasi had caught American officers spying near Karl-Marx-Stadt, it was forced to hand them over to the Soviets, who promptly released them. According to an irate Ulbricht: 'The members of the western military missions are laughing at our State Security officials—they despise and insult them.'[47] When entering East Berlin, the western Allies refused to show ID to East German border

---

[45] Harrison, *Driving*, 139.

[46] William Glenn Gray, *Germany's Cold War: The Global Campaign to Isolate East Germany, 1949–1969* (Chapel Hill, NC: North Carolina University Press, 2003), 49.

[47] Ulbricht to Khrushchev, n.d. [1959], SAPMO-BArch, DY30/J IV2/202/127. This flouting of GDR authority is wholly borne out by British recollections: Tony Geraghty, *Brixmis: The Untold Exploits of Britain's Most Daring Cold War Spy Mission* (London: HarperCollins, 1996).

police, still treating the eastern sector as under quadripartite Allied jurisdiction. The East Germans, on the other hand, regarded East Berlin as the GDR's capital. Like it or not, the Berlin and German questions were intimately linked.[48]

Part of communist strategy was, moreover, to tie the fate of the GDR to the wider interests of the eastern bloc. East Germany was being built up as a showcase for socialism; a defeat there, it was suggested, would be the thin end of the wedge against communism elsewhere. With the growing rift between Moscow and Beijing, Khrushchev was also keen to impress Mao Zedong that he was not 'soft'.[49] Up to 1958 the Soviet leader had indeed acted the reasonable statesman, the author of peaceful coexistence. The East Germans, on the other hand, tended towards a 'maximalist' policy on West Berlin, hoping for direct control.[50] Khrushchev, too, appears to have overestimated the ease with which he could pressurize the West, but when brinkmanship threatened actual war, the Kremlin leader usually rediscovered an eleventh-hour pragmatism which pulled him back.[51]

What did the average East German make of all this? The connections between foreign and domestic policy were closer in the GDR than in most states. Ever since the early occupation the Soviets had realized that championing national reunification might be one way to overcome popular anticommunism. SED-Soviet behind-the-scenes discussions betrayed concern about the propaganda impact of foreign policy initiatives, among both East and West Germans.[52] Bonn could not be allowed to seize the initiative in the German question. In the early 1950s the East certainly claimed to be making most of the national running. Since the abandonment of reunification in favour of 'peaceful coexistence' in 1955, however, the communists felt more vulnerable, especially when the Adenauer government paid its own lip service to reunification efforts after 1958. As long as the German question remained open, uncommitted East Germans might harbour hopes that the socioeconomic clock could be turned back. The SED's Party Information labelled this the 'it-could-turn-out-different' attitude, a form of domestic Hallstein doctrine ascribed to wide sections of the rural population, the *Mittelstand* and intelligentsia.

Pre-emptively, therefore, the party would follow each diplomatic initiative with a barrage of media coverage, and its agitators engaged the population in 'discussions', at the workplace or on the doorstep, often based on readings of the current diplomatic notes. Invariably, a party spokesperson was on hand to give the official view. The archives are full of foreign policy opinion reports. For

---

[48] Lemke, *Berlinkrise*, 98.

[49] Vladimir Zubok and Constantine Pleshakov, *Inside the Kremlin's Cold War: From Stalin to Khrushchev* (Cambridge, MA: Harvard University Press, 1996), 199.

[50] Lemke, *Berlinkrise*, 109.   [51] Wettig, *Chruschtschows Berlin-Krise*, 37–9.

[52] For instance, the SED wished to have the Khrushchev Ultimatum in time for its elections: Harrison, *Driving*, 108.

example, in May 1959, during the Geneva summit, SED agitators painstakingly recorded 120,574 house meetings; 26,515 public fora; 65,118 'differentiated' one-to-one talks; as well as 2,580 rallies across the GDR. A total of 8 million signatures had been collected.[53] East Germans nevertheless had other sources of information than SED agitprop. Many tuned in to western radio broadcasts and, increasingly, television. The West's call for free elections is thus echoed frequently, categorized by the party as 'enemy discussions' or 'RIAS arguments'. Indeed, it became all too easy for the SED to write off any adverse comment as an imported conspiracy. Moreover, although the East's foreign policy gambits were designed to stabilize the domestic situation by reinforcing the GDR's sense of permanence, through diplomatic recognition from outside, the high-risk means employed only succeeded in panicking the populace, forcing the authorities to consider ever more drastic solutions.

After flying a kite in a speech earlier in the month, on 27 November 1958 Khrushchev sent his ultimatum to the three western Allied powers, in typically strident language. He blamed the breakdown of the anti-Hitler coalition on their alleged flouting of the Potsdam Agreement and nuclear rearmament of West Germany. Berlin acted as 'a smouldering match held against a powder-barrel'. Berating the western powers for their 'sabre-rattling', he blamed them for stalling discussions on a German peace treaty. The West German government, which 'systematically fans the "cold war"', came under fire for neither accepting a second German state, nor a German confederation. The four-power status of Berlin, Khrushchev argued, had de facto been superseded, since the western powers were abusing the western sectors as a 'State within a State', a 'springboard for increased espionage, diversionist, and other subversive activity' against the GDR, and a source of 'indirect aggression' against the Soviet Union. The USSR no longer considered itself bound by wartime partition agreements. More alarmingly for the West, Khrushchev mooted 'handing over to the German Democratic Republic . . . functions which were temporarily performed by Soviet organs', for instance territorial 'sovereignty on land, water, and in the air', which meant, of course, control over access to West Berlin. The note's central proposal was for ending the western Allied occupation of West Berlin and its 'normalization' as a demilitarized 'Free City', analogous to neutral Austria. It also alluded to direct negotiations between the East and West German governments, signifying recognition of a sovereign GDR and, by extension, of all postwar international borders. Yet, by hinting that 'the most correct and natural solution' would be simply to incorporate West Berlin, 'separated from the German Democratic Republic as a result of foreign occupation', into the GDR, from which this was a concessionary step back, the binding nature of the offer remained open to doubt. Moreover, by setting a six-month deadline,

---

[53] SED-ZK (Agit-Prop/Org), 'Informationsbericht . . .', 22 June 1959, SAPMO-BArch, DY30/IV2/5/290, fos. 319–30.

Khrushchev was underlining that this was an ultimatum, which, if not accepted, left 'no subject for talks between the former Occupying Powers on the Berlin question'.[54]

Public responses across the GDR recorded the usual high numbers of declarations of support, but often tied to hopes for reunification.[55] The Party Information admitted 'a great deal of confusion'. Many assumed the West would not comply, wanting to know the East's response. In East Berlin, for instance, the question was raised 'almost everywhere' of 'what happens if the western powers do not accept the proposals within six months?' Would there be a second blockade?[56] According to western pollsters, East Germans were more insistent on a western hard line than even West Berliners.[57] The partisanship hoped for by the SED was often undermined by arguments about even-handedness. The Americans could not be expected to yield more than the Soviets: 'This is repeatedly described as "unfair", "unjust" or "unreasonable".'[58] There was speculation, particularly in areas liberated by the Americans in 1945, that as a quid pro quo some GDR territory would be exchanged with the West, such as Thuringia or Saxony.[59] There were revisionist hopes regarding the Oder–Neisse frontier in the east, many harboured by former expellees from the eastern territories (approximately one in five of GDR citizens). One farmer near Görlitz explained how 'the implementation of this note will contribute to the further consolidation of the GDR, not a pleasant prospect for him since he sees his entry into the collective farm drawing ever nearer.'[60] More sophisticated arguments citing international law suggested that the ultimatum itself violated Potsdam. DEFA film studio workers, for example, cited Allied Control Council agreements granting West Berlin to the western occupiers: 'The Soviet Union is not entitled to break the agreement unilaterally.'[61] Most assumed that West Berliners would have no interest in the proposals. Why should they wish to sacrifice their higher standard of living? There was also doubt in many quarters that East Germany could sustain the additional burden of West Berlin. In Dresden for instance, there were fears that Soviet subsidies to West Berlin would lead to

[54] Foreign Office (ed.), *Selected Documents on Germany and the Question of Berlin, 1944–1961* (London, 1961), 318–33.

[55] Unless otherwise stated: SED-ZK (Org), 'Berichte über die Stimmung zur Note der Sowjetunion . . .', 28–9 Nov. 1958, SAPMO-BArch, DY30/IV2/5/288, fos. 177–210.

[56] SED-BL Berlin (Org/Kader), 'Dritte Einschätzung . . .', 30 Nov. 1958, LAB, BPA SED Berlin, IV2/5/699.

[57] DIVO, 'East Zone Opinions towards Current Issues', 1959, NARA, RG 306, 1005/11, 14.

[58] SED-BL Berlin (Org/Kader), 'Fünfte Einschätzung . . .', 3 Dec. 1958, LAB, BPA SED Berlin, IV2/5/699.

[59] Allinson, *Politics*, 120.

[60] SED-KL Görlitz (Org/Kader), unnamed, undated report, SächsHStA, BPA SED Dresden, IV2/5/127, fos. 106–07.

[61] SED-ZK (Org), '5. Bericht . . .', 29 Nov. 1958, SAPMO-BArch, DY30/IV2/5/288, fos. 197–210.

shortages in the provinces.[62] Sporadic voices demanded a plebiscite on a Free
City, while others wanted this in East Berlin too (which clearly was *not* the
communists' intention!).[63] Others wondered whether a third German territory
would only complicate reunification. Analogies were occasionally made with the
pre-1939 Polish corridor: 'A Free City is not an appropriate solution. Danzig
was a permanent bone of contention and war was waged because of it.'[64] What
currency would it use?[65] Others quizzed arrangements for transit and air travel,
clearly aware of the implications for those wishing to use West Berlin to leave
the GDR. These were therefore not just rhetorical questions. Many hoped that
renewed negotiations would undo some of the constraints on their daily lives
imposed by the Cold War; and by reopening the German question with such
fanfare, the communists had raised many more hopes than they could possibly
satisfy.

The western Allies' response was mixed.[66] US Secretary of State Dulles played
with the idea of recognizing the East Germans as 'agents' of the Soviet Union,
in order to make dealing with them more palatable. There were Pentagon plans
to send a military probe along the transit route, to be followed up by divisional
forces should resistance be encountered. Dulles even told Adenauer that the
United States was prepared to fight a nuclear war for Berlin, which seems to
have alarmed rather than reassured the Federal Chancellor.[67] The British were
more conciliatory. A four-power foreign ministers' conference might be one way
to soften the six-month ultimatum. Prime Minister Macmillan even travelled
to Moscow, against the wishes of Adenauer and the Americans, but returned
empty-handed.[68] In the meantime the Soviets brought the issue of a peace
treaty, alluded to in the ultimatum, to the fore. On 10 January 1959 the USSR
issued another note,[69] decrying the fact that, fourteen years after the war, there
was still no peace treaty with Germany. A settlement, it was argued, would
be a first step towards a rapprochement between the two German states, to be
signed by the FRG and the GDR, and possibly even a confederation of the
two, on behalf of 'Germany'. The Allied and associated powers to sign on behalf
of the victors naturally included every eastern-bloc state. In a long, aggressive
preamble the blame was laid squarely on the western Allies for disingenuously

---

[62] SED-BL Dresden (Org/Kader), '4. Kurzbericht . . . ', 2 Dec. 1958, SächsHStA, BPA SED
Dresden, IV2/5/127, fos. 10–12.
    [63] SED-BL Berlin (Org/Kader), 'Erste Einschätzung . . . ', 27 Nov. 1958, LAB, BPA SED Berlin,
IV2/5/699.
    [64] SED-BL Berlin (Org/Kader), 'Vierte Einschätzung . . . ', 27 Nov. 1958, LAB, BPA SED
Berlin, IV2/5/699.
    [65] SED-BL Berlin (Org/Kader), 'Erste Einschätzung . . . ', 27 Nov. 1958, LAB, BPA SED Berlin,
IV2/5/699.
    [66] Steininger, *Mauerbau*, 41–58.
    [67] John Lewis Gaddis, *We Now Know: Rethinking Cold War History* (Oxford, 1997), 141.
    [68] Gearson, *Harold Macmillan*, 56–78.
    [69] Foreign Office (ed.), *Selected Documents*, 351–69.

prolonging wartime occupation rights in the service of the Cold War, as a concealed 'NATO strong-point situated in the centre of the German Democratic Republic'. A draft peace treaty was appended, which envisaged both German states withdrawing from NATO and the Warsaw Pact, but maintaining a defence force (minus nuclear weapons, missiles, bombers, or submarines) and various safeguards against a revival of militarism and Nazism. The eastern territories were to be formally renounced. Privately, according to Khrushchev, the spectre of a peace treaty was to act as a 'Damocles' sword' over the western powers, to pressure them into recognizing the GDR.[70]

The response among ordinary East Germans to this new initiative was mixed, too. 'Negative discussions' focused on the recognition of Germany's current borders. There were frequent references to Potsdam's stipulation that the Oder–Neisse frontier was provisional, pending a peace treaty. Expellees, or 'resettlers' as they were called in the GDR, would sometimes greet the draft in principle, but not the renunciation clauses: 'Why doesn't the East hand back the eastern territories? After all, the western powers had to give back the Saar.'[71] Agitators in Erfurt found themselves confronted by resettlers accusing them of having 'no national pride'. In Merseburg, a communist heartland, party functionaries were 'almost helpless' against these arguments. More alarmingly, party comrades were occasionally heard making revisionist arguments themselves, citing some unlikely sources: 'Lenin already said that annexationist peace treaties harbour the seeds of a new war. The drawing of the Oder–Neisse frontier is such an annexation.' One farmer comrade faced party proceedings for baldly stating: 'Silesia is our home. We are attached to it, and if necessary, I would be capable of taking up arms to return to it.'[72] These were, of course, extreme cases. There are also many examples of refugees consciously declaring their support by renouncing their former *Heimat*, or, like the resettlers of Dippoldiswalde, who simply asked how they would be compensated. Yet, these contrary opinions give a sense of the perceived fluidity of the German question even a decade and a half after the war. The disarmament clauses of the draft were also hotly debated, especially among youths: 'Can one talk about a sovereign German state if, as it says in the treaty, Germany may not produce U-boats, bombers etc. If Germany is attacked, what will it defend itself with?'[73] As elsewhere, a key reservation was how the West would react. On past form, it was expected to demur. In Cottbus, for example, growing scepticism was reported, especially among the intelligentsia, the *Mittelstand* and farmers—in other

[70] Hope Harrison, 'The Berlin Crisis and the Khrushchev–Ulbricht Summits in Moscow, 9 and 18 June 1959', *Cold War International History Project Bulletin*, 11 (1998), 213.

[71] Following a referendum in 1955, the French-administered Saarland had acceded to the FRG.

[72] SED-ZK (Org), 'Informationsbericht', 13 Jan. 1959, SAPMO-BArch, DY30/IV2/5/289, fos. 21–32, and following reports, fos. 33–56.

[73] SED-ZK (Org), '2. Bericht . . . ', 12 Jan. 1959, SAPMO-BArch, DY30/IV2/5/289, fo. 17.

words, precisely those groups targeted by 'national' propaganda. As throughout the crisis, 'third way' arguments cropped up regularly: 'Each side should take a step back and they will come to an agreement.' At the same time many voices reflected the powerlessness ordinary citizens felt when following these high-level discussions. Resignation thus became a key undertone in the early months of the crisis.

Khrushchev let the six-month deadline pass, but did secure a summit in Geneva in May 1959, this time with German delegations in attendance.[74] There was still deadlock. Despite perceived initial successes in seizing the national initiative, the SED began to despond about public interest, noting foreign policy fatigue. East Germans had already witnessed the abortive Stalin notes of 1952, as well as the previous Geneva summit of 1955. Apathy expressed itself in views such as 'In Geneva there will be no agreement, the western powers do what they like, there have already been a lot of conferences where nothing happened, this won't be any different.' There were also widespread reports of a wait-and-see attitude among farmers baulking at collectivization. The intelligentsia and the urban *Mittelstand* were the other key 'wavering' or pessimistic groups.[75] Again, when talks resumed in July observers noted that: 'Besides the generally optimistic mood, some of the population are losing interest in the conference.' Bonn's 'spoiling propaganda' was having its effect.[76] This evidence is echoed in the BBC's East German listeners' letters: 'No one believes in a summit conference or reunification' or 'Our faith even in some easing of our position has gone.'[77] Responses to Khrushchev's visit to the United States in September 1959 only reflected popular impatience: 'The two statesmen should have negotiated from the outset and saved the wasted time in Geneva.'[78] This disaffection was reinforced a year later when, after the USSR's shooting down of an American U-2 spy plane, the Paris summit of May 1960 collapsed almost before it had begun. Many respondents could understand Soviet anger, but thought Khrushchev should nevertheless have negotiated. 'Among many colleagues, especially women,' it was reported in Berlin, 'disappointment, and in some cases consternation, prevails at the fact that the summit conference, on which one had "pinned all hopes", will not take place. The view is cropping up repeatedly that it will probably now come to war.'[79] One new farmer near Leipzig, four of whose children

---

[74] Harrison, 'Berlin Crisis', 204–17.

[75] SED-ZK (Agit-Prop/Org), 'Informationsbericht . . .', 22 June 1959, SAPMO-BArch, DY30/IV2/5/290, fos. 319–30.

[76] SED-ZK (Org), 'Informationsbericht', 21 July 1959, SAPMO-BArch, DY30/IV2/5/291, fo. 56.

[77] BBC (German Audience Research), 'Report on Mail Received . . .', 16 Nov. 1959, TNA, FO 1110/1240.

[78] NF-BA Leipzig, 'Informationsbericht Nr. 13/59', 15 Sept. 1959, StAL, BT and RdB Leipzig, 4102, fos. 15–19.

[79] SED-BL Berlin (Org/Kader), 'Stellungnahmen und Maßnahmen . . .', 17 May 1960, SAPMO-BArch, DY30/IV2/5/984, fos. 294–312.

had moved to West Germany, explained how 'cat-and-dog' high politics was often measured by everyday yardsticks: 'Everyone expected a lot of the summit conference. We thought it would finally bring back German unity so that we might see our children again. Everyone in the village was very disappointed at the summit's collapse.'[80] The view from below thus typically linked the political to the personal.

As the crisis deepened, Soviet and East German agendas diverged. For Khrushchev, Berlin remained a lever to solve several problems at once, using the threat of GDR sovereignty to force a back-down over nuclear weapons in the FRG, or to force wider negotiations over a peace treaty. Whether he entertained serious hopes of acquiring control of West Berlin remains doubtful. The East Germans, for their part, had taken the Soviet leader at his word, assuming that the six-month deadline was real. In February 1959, for instance, Ulbricht submitted detailed proposals to Moscow about how the GDR might take over air traffic control.[81] But there were already misgivings among GDR officials that the Kremlin was not fully committed, fuelled in March 1959 when Khrushchev relaxed the deadline. A year later he was telling the GDR leader to be patient for a peace treaty: 'We are realists and we will never pursue a gambling policy. . . . We had better wait, and the matter will get more mature.'[82] Despite later promises of a separate peace treaty in 1961, the GDR leader remained sceptical and began to seek ways to hold Moscow to its promises. The East Germans engaged in various unilateral ploys to up the ante. Since 1955 they had designated East Berlin as their capital, whereas the West treated it as a quadripartite entity, providing much fertile ground for conflict. In early September 1960, for five days, East German police introduced passport controls for West Germans entering East Berlin in retaliation for what they called the 'revanchist rally' being held by expellee groups in the western sectors. The western commandants immediately protested. Later that month Soviet diplomats became alarmed after an altercation between US Ambassador Dowling and East German Vopos (Volkspolizei) at the Brandenburg Gate who had demanded his credentials.[83] Normally, the diplomatic flag was enough to be waved through. The East Germans had clearly acted on their own initiative and upset the Soviets. Ulbricht stuck to his guns, however, insisting that states which did not recognize the GDR must identify themselves, and even suggested changing signs at the sector boundary to read 'You are entering the Capital of the GDR'.[84]

[80] 'Meinungen zur Gipfelkonferenz', 23 May 1960, SAPMO-BArch, DY30/IV2/5/916, fos. 382–3.

[81] 'Probleme im Zusammenhang mit der Übergabe der Rechte der sowjetischen Vertreter betreffend Westberlin und die Regierung der Deutschen Demokratischen Republik', 4 Feb. 1959, SAPMO-BArch, DY30/JIV2/202/127.

[82] Schick, *Crisis*, 121–2.

[83] MfAA to Ulbricht, 23 Sept. 1960, SAPMO-BArch, DY30/JIV2/202/127.

[84] Ulbricht to Khrushchev, 18 Oct. 1960, SAPMO-BArch, DY30/JIV2/202/127.

In late November 1960 the East Germans and Soviets held a crisis management meeting in Moscow. Ulbricht prophesied that 'the conflicts in Berlin will increase'. Khrushchev listened, but believed the 'western powers will not start a war over the peace treaty'.[85] Three diplomatic scenarios were agreed: the best case was western agreement to a four-power peace treaty with the two Germanys and West Berlin as a Free City; a compromise solution would be an eighteen-month to two-year interim agreement on West Berlin while treaty negotiations continued; the worst-case scenario would be western refusal and a separate eastern-bloc peace treaty with the GDR.[86] In the event, none of these materialized. But in January 1961 Ulbricht kept up the pressure, reminding his Soviet ally to exploit the West Germans' preoccupation with Bundestag elections in the autumn and the inexperience of the new American President Kennedy. The GDR wished to see the Allied Kommandatura, espionage agencies, military missions, and radio stations all dissolved, and troop contingents reduced prior to removing them altogether.[87] A GDR delegation even pointedly visited Beijing in the same month without informing Moscow, at a time when the Sino-Soviet split was deepening. Nonetheless, in March Kennedy made it clear that concessions agreed by the Eisenhower administration at Geneva were now off, although he did agree to a face-to-face meeting with Khrushchev. The Vienna summit in June 1961 is generally agreed to have been a diplomatic disaster. Both world leaders had been primed to expect flexibility; instead, they met with intransigence. Khrushchev reiterated that Moscow would 'never, under any conditions, accept US rights in West Berlin after a peace treaty had been signed'.[88] In an accompanying aide-memoire, despite some concessions, the Kremlin leader maintained that 'all questions of communications by land, water, or air through the German Democratic Republic will be settled only by appropriate agreements with the German Democratic Republic.' To lend urgency, a renewed six-month deadline was added.[89] It appeared that the Kremlin's patience with its own ultimatory politics had run out.

Ulbricht reinforced this message at a highly publicized press conference on 15 June, where he also uttered the notorious phrase 'Nobody has the intention of building a wall.'[90] Whether this was a verbal slip or calculated, it had the effect of increasing the refugee flow into West Berlin. The term 'wall' also began to crop up in popular opinion reports. For instance, according to one rumour: 'After the signing of a peace treaty with the GDR a wall will be erected around the GDR

---

[85] 'Aktenvermerk über die Unterredung des Genossen Walter Ulbricht mit Genossen N.S. Chruschtschow', n.d. [30 Nov. 1960], SAPMO-BArch, DY30/JIV2/202/30.

[86] Harrison, 'Concrete "Rose" ', 28.

[87] Ulbricht to Khrushchev, 18 Jan. 1961, SAPMO-BArch, DY30/JIV2/202/129.

[88] Foreign Relations of the United States, 1961–1963, xiv: *Berlin Crisis, 1961–1962*, ed. Charles S. Sampson (Washington, DC: USGPO, 1993), 87–94: 95.

[89] Foreign Office (ed.), *Selected Documents on Germany*, 443–7. This was eventually dropped in October, much to the annoyance of the East Germans.

[90] *Neues Deutschland*, 17 June 1961, 5.

and we won't see our relatives any more.'[91] Others were less clear, believing that a visa regime would be introduced for West Berlin, like the one operating for West Germany. Many simply did not know what to think. A separate peace treaty in itself seemed rather pointless. What was clear was that this would have implications for the balance of power within the GDR. There were, among farmers in Saxony for instance, claims that 'after the signing of a peace treaty the "thumb screws" will be tightened. They say that there is only one way out, as long as West Berlin is open. When West Berlin is closed the collective farmers will have their backs to the wall regarding communal working.'[92]

The unravelling international crisis also increased fears of the outbreak of war among East German citizens. A rather aggressive television address by the Kremlin leader did little to calm nerves; nor did Kennedy's 'three essentials' of 25 July, stating the US's willingness to go to war to defend West Berlin. 'With the offensive exposition of our policy', admitted one SED apparatchik rather drily, 'negative arguments crop up in ever larger volume, indicating that the assessment of the Moscow Declaration did not succeed in achieving clarity on the basic questions of our policy among wide segments of the population.'[93] Memories of the outbreak of the Second World War were also still fresh, as one female part-time worker explained: 'I haven't read all the things in the newspapers about the peace treaty. I just don't have enough time. But one thing is clear to me as a woman and mother, there must not be a war. It would be terrible if my children were to experience what my generation had to live through.'[94] To a limited extent the SED could exploit these fears and pose as the guarantor of peace. The 'militarists' and 'revanchists' were allegedly all on the other side. It was evident from conversations with the populace, however, that the East was being increasingly blamed for the escalation. In Schwerin one farmer argued that 'there is no danger of war from West Germany', while others complained that 'we [the East] tend to overdo it'.[95] Indeed, all too often the West was implicitly being encouraged to stand firm and not repeat the mistakes of appeasement twenty years before.

For others, the type of war being threatened encouraged resignation. Once Sputnik was launched in October 1957, it was clear that nowhere was safe from intercontinental nuclear attack. Khrushchev liked to remind western diplomats of the atomic kilotonnage required to incinerate their respective homelands, adding that 'we may die but the rockets will fly automatically'.[96] From 1958–59 the Soviets began secretly deploying intermediate-range nuclear missiles in the

---

[91] FDGB-BuVo (Org), 'Zusammenfassung . . . ', 4 Aug. 1961, SAPMO-BArch, DY34/22677.
[92] SED-BL KMS (PI), 'Informationsbericht . . . ', 1 July 1961, StAC, SED-BL KMS, IV2/5/21, fos. 146–53.
[93] SED-ZK (PO), 'Kurzinformation', 17 June 1961, SAPMO-BArch, IV2/5/295, fo. 130.
[94] FDGB-BuVo (Org), '4. Information', 21 June 1961, SAPMO-BArch, DY34/22677.
[95] SED-BL Schwerin (PO), 'Informationsbericht', 12 July 1961, MLHA Schwerin, BPA SED Schwerin, IV2/5/644, fos. 1–11.
[96] Foreign Relations of the United States, 1958–1960, viii: *Berlin Crisis, 1958–1959*, ed. Charles S. Sampson (Washington, DC: USGPO, 1993), 941–3: 942.

GDR, although the West suspected and they were subsequently withdrawn.[97] The SED, for its part, believed that the prospect of a nuclearized West German Bundeswehr would provoke public support.[98] In early 1958 the GDR had started its own shelter-building programme. Yet critics in the street differentiated between official peace propaganda and the new air-raid protection measures: 'Moreover, many believe there can be no effective protection whatsoever in an atomic war.'[99] Promises of reductions in conventional Soviet forces were weighed against Moscow's continued nuclear stockpiles.[100] Fears of an actual outbreak of hostilities seem to have reached their peak immediately before and after the building of the Wall. In mid-June 1961 the view that 'there will be war' was reported in all strata, even among SED members.[101] There were numerous fears in Karl-Marx-Stadt, for example, that 'it is coming to the crunch and then there will be war', since the Americans would not freely renounce West Berlin.[102] Potsdamers asked what would happen 'if the western powers force a passage to Berlin with tanks'.[103] Later in August the Soviets resumed nuclear testing, further undermining the East's peace-loving credentials. The SED and the Kremlin, therefore, came to be viewed as part of the problem, not the solution. Large swathes of GDR popular opinion, powerless to influence superpower high politics in any meaningful way, developed a form of hostage syndrome. Keen not to antagonize those brandishing the weapons, they remained reassuring in public; but in private few felt that the cause of either superpower was worth dying for, and as conditions deteriorated many believed the only safe place was as far away from Berlin as possible.

OVERTAKING WITHOUT CATCHING UP: THE GDR'S ECONOMIC MISSION IMPOSSIBLE

The diplomatic impasse was reinforced by a near economic breakdown within the GDR, in a second crisis whose seeds had been sown months before the international crisis. At the SED's Fifth Party Convention in July 1958 Ulbricht

---

[97] Matthias Uhl and Vladimir I. Ivkin, ' "Operation Atom": The Soviet Union's Stationing of Nuclear Missiles in the German Democratic Republic, 1959', *Cold War International History Project Bulletin*, 12/13 (2001), 299–304.

[98] Harrison, *Driving*, 126–29.

[99] SED-ZK (Org), 'Informationsbericht Nr. 3/58', 23 Jan. 1958, SAPMO-BArch, DY30/IV2/5/287, fos. 32–9.

[100] SED-ZK (Org), '3. Bericht . . .', 19 Jan. 1960, SAPMO-BArch, DY30/IV2/5/292, fos. 24–27.

[101] SED-ZK (PO), 'Kurzinformation', 17 June 1961, SAPMO-BArch, IV2/5/295, fo. 130.

[102] SED-BL KMS (PI), 'Erste Stellungnahmen . . .', 19 June 1961, StAC, SED-BL KMS, IV2/5/21, fos. 130–8.

[103] SED-BL Potsdam (Volksbildung/Kultur), 'Information . . .', 17 July 1961, BLHA, Bez. Pdm. Rep. 530/IV2/5/899.

had outlined the new Economic Main Task, to catch up with, and overtake, per capita consumer goods production in West Germany by 1961.[104] A miniature version of Khrushchev's challenge to overtake the United States, this was a fantastically bold claim, since, despite a small downturn in 1958, the Federal economy was still enjoying exceptionally high growth. (East German statisticians may secretly have been hoping for a slow-down of capitalism to allow them to 'overtake without accelerating'.[105]) Beforehand, Ulbricht had explained to Moscow how he intended to demonstrate the 'superiority of the socialist social order' and to make the GDR 'an attractive example for the working class and all West Germany's working people as well as the other capitalist countries of Europe.' This would reverse the poles of the German–German economic magnet, which had already drawn 1.9 million East Germans westwards. Currently, he conceded that the GDR was 'far behind' West Germany's industrial and consumer production, 'which is viewed by the population as the yardstick for living standards'. A shopping list of items showed FRG superiority in cars, refrigerators, and televisions, as well as fruit and coffee. Whereas West Germany commanded the Ruhr's heavy industry and had benefited from Marshall Aid, the GDR was not self-sufficient in raw materials, devoid of hard coal and iron ore. Moreover, as Ulbricht was well aware, Soviet dismantling had decimated East German industry, which had relied on its heavy engineering to the detriment of infrastructural renewal in the energy and chemicals sectors. He was therefore asking the socialist bloc for substantial subsidies, amounting to 2 billion rubles over 1959–62, as well as 300 million rubles of hard currency. Iron ore, rolled steel, copper, and aluminium, as well as consumer goods, would all have to be imported for the crash programme.[106]

Initially, the Economic Main Task provided a psychological boost and growth rates in industrial production rose significantly: 10.9 per cent in 1958 and 13.1 per cent in 1959.[107] This optimism carried on well into 1960. Yet the long-term investment in chemicals and metallurgy, plus the new priority on consumer goods, starved vital sectors such as engineering. The immediate shop-floor response among engineers and workers was local scepticism and practical reminders about shortages of raw materials.[108] In the crucial chemicals industry in Halle there were 'frequent hard confrontations with pessimistic views among economic functionaries'.[109] The local party had resorted to naming and shaming

[104] Walter Ulbricht, *Der Kampf um den Frieden* (Dietz: East Berlin, 1958), 44–5.

[105] Dietrich Staritz, *Geschichte der DDR*, 2nd edn (Frankfurt: Suhrkamp, 1996), 176–7.

[106] SED-ZK to CPSU-CC, 3 May 1958 (draft), SAPMO-BArch, DY30/JIV2/202/28.

[107] André Steiner, 'Vom Überholen eingeholt: Zur Wirtschaftskrise 1960/61 in der DDR', in Burghard Ciesla *et al.* (eds.), *Sterben für Berlin? Die Berliner Krisen 1948–1958* (Berlin: Metropol, 2000), 249.

[108] SED-ZK (Org), 'Informationsbericht', 8 Aug. 1958, SAPMO-BArch, DY30/IV2/5/288, fos. 70–71.

[109] SED-ZK (Org), 'Zu einigen Fragen . . . im Bezirk Halle', 25 Aug. 1958, SAPMO-BArch, DY30/IV2/5/288, fo. 110.

doubters in its factory broadsheet. Elsewhere, workers complained that they would have to shoulder the burden of modernization, as in 1953. The Main Task became an increasing hostage to fortune throughout the crisis, since it promised such tangible improvement. Economics students at Leipzig, in a view echoed throughout the GDR, believed that the party had 'bitten off more than it could chew'.[110] When one doctor sat listening to a comrade extolling the virtues of the Task, he asked if he also 'believed in Father Christmas'.[111]

To its credit, the party recognized that part of the solution was to raise productivity, not just production, among workers. On paper, the fact that East German workers were paid a piece rate and not an hourly wage, seemed to favour high output. Yet the system of quotas—'norms' in GDR parlance—had been set so low that workers were regularly overfulfilling them and earning handsome bonuses. When the party had tried to tackle the problem in 1953, by resetting quotas 10 per cent higher, this had become a major factor in the outbreak of the 17 June uprising. Thereafter, the SED preferred not to grasp the quota nettle.[112] At the Leuna works, for example, an 'unspoken moratorium' existed between shop-floor and management, who were 'both fixated on fulfilling the plan at any price',[113] which in practice meant quantity over quality. If frustrated economics functionaries attempted to revise norms unilaterally, this could lead to rumblings. When the director of one engineering works announced over the tannoy that norms exceeding 150 per cent would no longer be paid, workers immediately threatened to strike.[114] Although strikes were banned in the GDR, there were wildcat stoppages every year. Admittedly, these were highly localized, fleeting, and economistic, with an average participation of ten (frequently members of the same work brigade). Very often strikers were punishing the bureaucratic apparatus for reneging on wage increases or premiums. In 1960 the unions counted 166 such stoppages, as well as 72 cases of sabotage and 44 of arson, concentrated in the building, metal, and textile industries, with high incidences in Dresden and Halle.[115] Local union officials, afraid of criticism, often tried to defuse the situation without alerting the 'state organs', failing which the MfS would be called in. Less spectacular, but more prevalent perhaps, was *Arbeitsbummelei*, or 'sciving', including absenteeism, alcoholism, and shoddy work. This was, of course, a venerable tradition, but not expected in a worker

[110] SED-PL KMU, 'Informationsbericht', 15 Apr. 1961, SAPMO-BArch, DY30/IV2/9.04/558, fos. 60–6.

[111] 'Analyse über die Republikflucht im Städtischen Hufelandkrankenhaus und im Städtischen Krankenhaus in Berlin-Buch', n.d. [1959], SAPMO-BArch, DY30/IV2/19/53.

[112] Jeffrey Kopstein, *The Politics of Economic Decline in East Germany, 1945–1989* (Chapel Hill, NC: University of North Carolina Press, 1997), 35–40.

[113] SED-ZK (PO), 'Information' Nr. 39, 27 Mar. 1961, SAPMO-BArch, IV2/5/294, fos. 326–27.

[114] SED-ZK (PO), 'Information' Nr. 56, 4 May 1961, SAPMO-BArch, IV2/5/295, fos. 6–18.

[115] SED-ZK (Gewerkschaften/Sozial), 'Arbeitsniederlegungen und Konflikte im Jahre 1960', 9 Feb. 1961, SAPMO-BArch, IV2/6.11/9, fos. 6–10.

state. Union officials had watched sickness rates rise steadily since 1953, so that by 1960 6 per cent of the workforce was off at any one time. The East German head cold reportedly lasted fifteen days, four days above the European average.[116] Institutionalized drinking was rife. At a building-site in Stralsund, for example, the SED work brigadier discovered his entire brigade drinking in its portacabin in the morning. When he remonstrated, they became violent, forcing him to seek shelter in a lorry cab.[117] Naturally, the SED regarded such behaviour as objectively counter-revolutionary, but was forced to tolerate it since much indiscipline was caused by production downtime generated within the system.[118]

The way out of the productivity dilemma was seen to lie in quality not quantity. Planners realized that the GDR was facing a labour shrinkage, not only from migration west, but due to an ageing population and women's growing tendency towards part-time work. Technology and rationalization became the watchwords. Wars were waged on wastage levels with model practice named after 'innovators', such as the Mitrofanov Method, which involved workers disassembling their machinery, as well as the Christoph, Wehner, and Seifert methods. But, despite a limited sense of empowerment, by the late 1950s, East German workers were beginning to experience 'method fatigue'. Each new scheme was greeted with a mixture of frustration and condescension. Economics apparatchiks also preferred to play safe and go for quantity over quality, remaining suspicious of procedures which threatened to halt production altogether. Before the 1960s the East German economy was simply not in a position to automate large sections of its industry.[119]

As a stop-gap, the SED relied on politicizing workers. Shop-floor evidence reveals an unreceptive audience. Participation in the 1958 Socialist Competition, which played off factories and work brigades against each other, captured only 59.3 per cent of workers, but was far lower in Berlin and its environs as well as in the engineering and building industries.[120] More long-term were the Socialist Work Brigades, encouraged to accept higher quotas and help out less activistic workmates, but by November 1959 only 21.1 per cent of industrial workers belonged to these elite bodies.[121] As a dispirited shop-steward at a large Berlin works recognized, his workers were materialists: 'They are for the GDR in the sense that they don't want any bosses, fascists and militarists back. Not all are

---

[116] 'Bericht über die Entwicklung des Krankenzustandes . . .', n.d. [1962], SAPMO-BArch, DY30/IV2/6.11/53, fos. 407–20.

[117] SED-ZK (PO to Sicherheit), 29 Oct. 1960, SAPMO-BArch, DY30/IV1/12/112, fos. 257–58.

[118] Andrew I. Port, *Conflict and Stability in the German Democratic Republic* (Cambridge: Cambridge University Press, 2007), 164–94.

[119] Steiner, 'Vom Überholen eingeholt', 248.

[120] SED-ZK (Gewerkschaften), 'Ergänzung . . .', 9 June 1958, SAPMO-BArch, DY30/IV2/6.11/52, fos. 64–72.

[121] 'Übersicht über sozialistische Brigaden und Gemeinschaften nach Bezirken, Stand 14.11. 1959', SAPMO-BArch, DY30/IV2/6.11/52, fo. 148.

consciously for the Workers' and Peasants' State. Their attitude to the GDR is always connected to questions and answers about their personal life, for which they have high aspirations'.[122] At Zeiss in Jena, East Germany's flagship optics works, workers acknowledged their sociocultural opportunities in the GDR, 'but overall the standard of living in West Germany is described as better'.[123] The only short-term reward that the system could offer was higher wages which it could ill afford. Thus, local works hoarded workers, seeking to retain them with perks and higher pay. From 1958 to 1961 alone, average wages went up a staggering 18.4 per cent, far ahead of projected productivity increases.[124]

The GDR was also chronically short of raw materials. Bottlenecks existed, for instance, in sheet steel, to be stamped into housings for industrial switchboxes and domestic refrigerators, or rolled into refinery pipelines and tubes for vacuum cleaners. The chassis of the Trabant car was notoriously improvised from a superior form of laminated cardboard for lack of tensile steel. While production lines waited for supplies, workforces stood idle, sweeping up or playing cards. Where was the GDR to find its raw materials? Could the East wean it off western dependencies? In 1959 the GDR's State Planning Commissioner was in Moscow negotiating for subsidies, but came away with only half of what was needed, concluding, less than a year into the Economic Main Task, that it was just 'not realizable'.[125] By the summer of 1960 the GDR's shortages were reaching crisis proportions, but a letter from Ulbricht requesting more steel and credit was rejected by Moscow in September.[126] The GDR continued to outsource specialized steels or chemicals in the West, but for these hard currency was needed. This placed the GDR in a three-way, economic catch 22: in order to generate hard currency it needed to export manufactured goods; to produce manufactured goods it had to import raw materials; and to import raw materials it required hard currency. It soon became apparent that the GDR was slipping irretrievably behind in the race to catch up with the FRG: in 1960 the already strong West German economy grew by 11.6 per cent; East Germany's by only 8.2 per cent.[127]

Despite political division, trade between the two Germanys continued. Indeed, the GDR could not have survived without West German imports. The whole Energy Programme and parts of the Chemicals Programme, which involved a second giant complex at Leuna, were dependent on the import of pipelines from the FRG under the Interzonal Trade Agreement. Every year the GDR spent

[122] SED-GO VEB TRO, 'Einschätzung', 1 July 1958, LAB, BPA SED Berlin, IV7/23/19.
[123] SED-BPO Carl Zeiß Jena, 'Bericht . . .', 24 Aug. 1955, SAPMO-BArch, DY30/IV2/5/843, fos. 85–99.
[124] Staatliche Zentralverwaltung für Statistik, n.d., SAPMO-BArch, DY30/IV2/6.08/46, fo. 185.
[125] Leuschner, 'Ergebnis der Beratungen über die ökonomischen Fragen', 17 June 1959, SAPMO-BArch, DY30/JIV2/202/29.
[126] Pervukhin to Ulbricht, 13 Sept. 1960, SAPMO-BArch, DY30/JIV2/202/29.
[127] Steiner, 'Auf dem Weg zur Mauer?', 110 n. 36.

a billion deutschmarks on West German imports, and 600–700 million on other capitalist markets. The main engineering dependencies were in maritime diesel engines; turbine housings; and essential equipment for cement factories, steel mills, and refineries, including roller bearings, armatures, compressors, high-voltage cables, switches, and gauges. In the chemicals industry dyestuffs, photochemicals, and pharmaceuticals were also heavily imported from the FRG.[128] Already, however, the West was delaying delivering coal and steel from the Ruhr. Worse was to follow. On 30 September 1960, in retaliation for the GDR's introduction of a visa regime for West Germans entering East Berlin—and here again we see the nexus between the international and internal crises—the Federal government announced an end to the trade agreement as of 31 December. This caused considerable panic. The State Planning Commission predicted 'difficult situations' in the year ahead, and that 4–500 engineering, textile, building, and chemicals works might come to a standstill and 'perhaps even some branches of industry would have to go on to short time'.[129] But Ulbricht immediately spotted the possibilities of turning the bleak situation to the GDR's advantage. In October he warned Khrushchev of the dangers of a trade embargo, reminding him that the economic crisis was exacerbated by the 'current international situation' which was hampering trade with the capitalist exterior. A planned steel mill at Eisenhüttenstadt would not be online until 1970. The Plan was consequently extremely 'tight'. Furthermore,

[w]e literally recycle every hard mark we have to spend on imports several times over. We cut back and redeploy. But it all naturally has a limit. If the cloth is not sufficient, one can cut it at whichever corner one will, here and there one can add a patch, but overall the cloth remains too small and no needle and scissors will make it fit.[130]

The flight of skilled workers was also undermining 'a decisive foundation of our production'. By the year's end the GDR would be 575 million rubles in debt. In an earlier draft, warnings had been direr still. Lack of economic support would 'naturally entail great, very great political ramifications. Please allow us to reiterate strongly that the economic development of the GDR—in practice its very existence—depends upon us being able to import . . . the necessary raw materials'.[131]

At a crucial meeting on 30 November 1960 in Moscow, the Soviet and East German leaderships tried to work out a coping strategy. Despite all Ulbricht's previous entreaties, Khrushchev feigned ignorance of the GDR's dependency on West Germany: 'Only Adenauer's cancellation rubbed our noses in the fact.' The Soviet leader estimated a fifty–fifty chance that the FRG would implement

[128] Büro Apel to Wirtschaftskommission (Abt.-Ltr.), 17 May 1961, SAPMO-BArch, DY30/IV2/ 2.029/115, fos. 102–126.
[129] Steiner, 'Auf dem Weg zur Mauer?', 99.
[130] Ulbricht to Khrushchev, 19 Oct. 1960, SAPMO-BArch, DY30/J IV2/202/29.
[131] Ulbricht to Khrushchev (draft), n.d. [Oct. 1960], SAPMO-BArch, DY30/JIV2/202/29.

an embargo, but doubted whether the other western European states would follow suit. If necessary, the GDR could apply pressure on the FRG through Berlin to reinstate the agreement, since 'the GDR had the longer lever'. (The East Germans had indeed suggested making the continued servicing of the access routes to West Berlin contingent upon continued trade ties.[132]) In any event, it was agreed to devise a maximal and minimal autarky programme: the former in case of an embargo; the latter to sort out the GDR's long-term raw material supply.[133] What followed was the so-called 'undisruptability' campaign (*Störfreimachung*). Engineers and planners had to review their supply needs with a view to minimizing and even eliminating FRG imports. In December the government called on all engineers for 'extreme parsimoniousness with all material'.[134] Each factory was required to draw up a contingency plan. At the same time the GDR started switching from pre-war German industrial norms, which regulated everything from the size of screws to the quality of paint, to Soviet-style norms, further complicating research and development. Some engineers appear to have embraced the task, but others remained to be convinced. The mood by summer 1961 was one of frustration and resignation. At a discussion with research scientists in July, party officials were bombarded with complaints. One professor from Halle-Wittenberg University believed the GDR was going 'downhill'; his colleague described confidence in party policy as in 'ruins'. Professor H. of VEB Vakutronik noted sarcastically that the difference between capitalism and socialism was that 'the capitalist economy works, while in the socialist economy general chaos reigns'. Press reports on economic progress were dismissed as 'eyewash'. Especially alarming for the SED was the fact that the party's inability to manage the economy was affecting scientists' 'assessment of our political fundamentals': SED jargon for the future of socialism.[135]

At the eleventh hour, on 29 December 1960, the East Germans managed to negotiate a reinstatement of the trade agreement, thus averting an embargo. Yet the economic apparatus pushed ahead with *Störfreimachung*, clearly hoping to achieve a major restructuring of the economy and integration into the Soviet plan. In the meantime Moscow's advice was to buy up steel and finished goods in the West, regardless of the debt run up, in order to relieve the USSR. Mikoyan reassured his counterpart Leuschner that in the current year the Soviet Union would help the GDR: 'But in future this would not be possible.'[136] The Soviets were clearly becoming increasingly resentful at having to bail out the former

[132] Steiner, 'Auf dem Weg zur Mauer?', 105.
[133] 'Aktenvermerk über die Unterredung . . .', n.d. [30 Nov. 1960], SAPMO-BArch, DY30/JIV2/202/30.
[134] Ministerrat, 'Stellungnahme', 5 Dec. 1960, SAPMO-BArch, DY30/JIV2/2/735, fos. 34–7.
[135] Arbeitsgruppe Forschung & technische Entwicklung, 'Zu einigen Problemen . . .', 13 July 1961, SAPMO-BArch, DY30/IV2/2.029/199, fos. 65–79.
[136] Leuschner to Ulbricht, 27 Jan. 1961, SAPMO-BArch, DY30/JIV2/202/30.

enemy. Already in November 1960 Khrushchev had made it clear that he was not prepared to subsidize the GDR with Soviet gold reserves.[137] One important rationale for the Wall when it came, therefore, was to scale back Moscow's economic aid to what was becoming an economic black hole.

The GDR's economic problems were not only on the production side.[138] In 1958 the government had lifted rationing, largely for political reasons, since the 'adversary' was using ration cards for anti-socialist propaganda.[139] The Fifth Party Convention also made great play of consumer goods. Yet, despite the relatively high prices of de-rationed goods, the system could not cope with increased demand, including, it must be said, many West Berliners buying on the cheap.[140] Already by early 1959 the leadership recognized that there had been a serious miscalculation of food supply, especially of meat and dairy products.[141] Coffee, cocoa, tropical fruits, but also textiles and shoes, had to be purchased in hard currency on the world market. In June, in one of many begging letters, Ulbricht asked Moscow for 1.15 billion rubles' worth of imports in these areas, over half on credit.[142] This was only partially forthcoming, since the USSR was facing its own agricultural failures, so much so that within a year of the Main Economic Task being announced, GDR functionaries were admitting privately that the great leap forward was unfeasible. Although the GDR might catch up on bicycles and some dairy products, it was still lagging on cars, washing-machines, and refrigerators, and was hopelessly behind on luxury items.[143] The distribution apparatus was sluggish, and many products were rotting in warehouses awaiting packaging.

The Fifth Party Convention had also announced the final stage of the collectivization of the countryside, started in 1952 on a voluntary basis, and then stepped up in 1958. In the spring of 1960 the heat was turned up, when 265,000 farmers were cajoled into joining in short order.[144] Factory workers and megaphone-toting party functionaries descended on villages to elicit signatures to join the state Agricultural Production Collectives (LPGs). Reluctant farmers were branded anti-socialists or militarists. 'In the morning the brigade comes to recruit for the LPG', complained one woman in Magdeburg, 'and if it is unsuccessful, then the police come in the afternoon.'[145] In several cases recalcitrant farmers barricaded themselves in their farms, and in a few even committed suicide rather

[137] Harrison, 'Concrete "Rose" ', appendix A.

[138] Mark Landsman, *Dictatorship and Demand: The Politics of Consumerism in East Germany* (Boston, MA: Harvard University Press, 2005), 173 ff.

[139] Ulbricht to Khrushchev, 12 May 1958, SAPMO-BArch, DY30/JIV2/202/39.

[140] Pence, *Rations to Fashions*, ch. 9.

[141] Leuschner to Ulbricht, 3 Mar. 1959, SAPMO-BArch, DY30/JIV2/202/29.

[142] Ulbricht to CPSU, June 1959, SAPMO-BArch, DY30/JIV2/202/29. See also Harrison, 'Berlin Crisis', 211.

[143] Leuschner, 'Ergebnis der Beratungen über die ökonomischen Fragen', 17 June 1959, SAPMO-BArch, DY30/JIV2/202/29.

[144] Staritz, *Geschichte der DDR*, 190.

[145] SED-ZK (LPO), 'Bericht über die politische Lage . . . ', 17 Mar. 1960, SAPMO-BArch, DY30/IV2/5/292, fos. 122–9.

than join. The northern regions were collectivized first, perhaps because there were fewer traditional smallholdings at stake, although it is clear that many 'new farmers', beneficiaries of 1945's land reform, also feared returning to the status of estate workers. Soon after the announcement of full collectivization on 14 April 1960, farmers were complaining about being tricked by broken promises. A significant minority of LPG members unilaterally resigned from collectives. A year after collectivization 17,000 'individual farmers' were still counted—tiny compared with the half million new collective farmers—but still a thorn in the authorities' side.[146] 'Fire brigades' of party officials roved the countryside for recantations. Farmers' wait-and-see attitude also manifested itself in the fact that, rather than removing the marker stones around plots, some merely buried them in situ. In terms of output, there were problems with animal husbandry, with high death rates among livestock. A total of 1.25 million pigs died in 1960, and over 210,000 cattle and almost 115,000 sheep.[147] A drought in 1959 had depleted cattle feed dangerously, but the party files are also filled with reports of sabotage. In 1960, 862 rural fires were reported, 206 of which were considered arson.

Whatever the causes, rapid collectivization was widely held responsible for the poor supply of foodstuffs in the early 1960s. The party became particularly sensitive to this issue since the Federal media were reporting famine in the GDR, even offering food aid. Despite the lifting of rationing, under-the-counter 'customer lists' continued.[148] Meat, including sausages, was being sold out of hours. It was common practice for female factory workers to knock off early to beat the queues and track down the last bread or vegetables in the shops. One party investigator went to find out for himself how bad the situation in Brandenburg was. The local comrade's wife complained that not even potatoes were available in the nearby greengrocer's, requiring extensive traipses around town and separate queuing for each and every item. The two men then set off on a potato hunt, securing their booty only after a 45-minute wait.[149] It is important to note that this was not just part of the GDR's chronic problem with an underperforming economy. Things became tangibly worse in the early 1960s. In Potsdam doubts were 'greater than a few months ago and are currently growing'.[150] The MfS also reported a 'very negative mood' among the populace: 'The shortages lead for example in Glienicke to views that the current conditions are far worse than during rationing and that under these circumstances the

---

[146] MfS-Kollegium, 1 Mar. 1961, BStU-ZA, MfS-SdM 1557, fo. 55.   [147] Ibid., fo. 69.
[148] Burghard Ciesla and Patrice Poutrus, 'Food Supply in a Planned Economy: SED Nutrition Policy between Crisis Response and Popular Needs', in Jarausch, *Dictatorship as Experience*, 143–62: 149.
[149] SED-BL Potsdam (Kühne), Aktennotiz, 7 Aug. 1961, BLHA, Bez. Pdm. Rep. 530/IV2/5/899.
[150] SED-BL Potsdam (Org-Kader), 'Bericht über die politische Lage', 10 Nov. 1960, BLHA, Bez. Pdm. Rep. 530/1620.

building of socialism is a doubtful matter.'[151] No longer were citizens comparing the situation with the disaster years 1945–48, happy to see any improvement. There were pointed questions about, why, fifteen years after the war, the GDR was still not able to feed itself.

Yet not just food was the problem. Finding small items, such as towels, cutlery, and bath-plugs, became the bane of many East Germans' lives. At Zeiss in Jena workers were indignant at the long queues for shoes which always formed when new stock arrived, asking 'how long this is supposed to go on for'.[152] In February 1960 the State Planning Commission even launched a 'Thousand Little Things' campaign to improve the provision of services and household goods.[153] Another chronic problem was the housing shortage. In November 1960 12 per cent of the Leuna workforce were looking for somewhere to live, almost double the figure of five years before.[154] In Jena accommodation seekers had risen from 8.1 per cent in 1947, to 8.4 per cent in 1953, to 9.9 per cent in 1960. At the Zeiss works 567 employees were homeless.[155] Local housing offices were deluged with plaintive letters about overcrowded accommodation and leaking roofs. Among the petitions to the state president, housing regularly figured as the number one popular grouse, constituting around 40 per cent.[156] The party even organized 'repair brigades' to try to rectify defects in new apartments. As the MfS acknowledged, 'examples of this sort could be cited *ad infinitum*'.[157]

Despite the relative improvements compared with the hunger years 1945–48, the yardstick for East Germans always remained the 'golden West' in the here and now. 'The presence in Berlin of an open and essentially uncontrolled border between the socialist and capitalist worlds', complained Soviet ambassador Pervukhin in 1959, 'unwittingly prompts the population to make a comparison between both parts of the city, which, unfortunately, does not always turn out in favour of Democratic [East] Berlin.'[158] In one Leipzig office conversations

revolve exclusively around the satisfaction of personal needs. For instance on the supply of televisions, refrigerators, cars etc., and on the price differences of consumer goods

[151] MfS-BV Potsdam, 'Einschätzung der Lage im Grenzgebiet am Ring um Westberlin', 13 May 1960, BStU-ZA, Allg. S 204/62, viii, fos. 105–9.

[152] SED-BPO Carl Zeiß Jena, 'Informationsbericht', 19 Oct. 1960, SAPMO-BArch, DY30/IV2/5/843, fos. 155–61.

[153] Tausend kleine Dinge: Reparaturen und Dienstleistungen (1960), SAPMO-BArch, DY30/IV2/6.08/10, fos. 1–17.

[154] SED-KL Leuna to SED-BL Halle, 23 Nov. 1960, LAM, BPA SED Halle, IV2/5/663, fos. 118–21.

[155] 'Bericht über die Lage im Wohnraum in Jena', 23 Sept. 1960, SAPMO-BArch, DY30/IV2/5/843, fos. 162–7.

[156] Taken from BA, DA-5/5999.

[157] MfS-ZAIG, 'Bericht über die Entwicklung der Republikflucht im Zeitraum Oktober-Dezember 1960 . . . ', 3 Feb. 1961, BStU-ZA, ZAIG 412, fo. 14.

[158] Harrison, *Driving*, 99.

compared with the western zone, such as nylon stockings and the fact that personal freedom is restricted because the GDR did not have enough holiday resorts.[159]

By mid-1961 the SED leadership was acknowledging that it was in an economic crisis. Even Ulbricht conceded before the Politbüro that 'the general figures that our production is growing by so-and-so much are no more use to us. Nobody believes them anyway.'[160] The Economics Commission also reported widespread 'disbelief in the superiority of the planned economy and disbelief in the figures'.[161] The solution found was a typically East German one: simply no longer to publish statistics and to go into a collective act of denial.

GRASS-ROOTS CRISES

In conclusion, how did the dual diplomatic and economic crises affect the frontiers of power? The regime had clearly been hoping to strengthen its position by seizing the initiative over the Berlin question and the economic race with West Germany. Indeed, international and internal consolidation were intimately connected in party thinking. The SED spoke of the 'unity of politics and economics': ideological clarity in the head about the long-term victory of socialism over capitalism would create the self-sacrifice necessary to raise output and overcome the GDR's structural deficiencies. If East Germans could be convinced that the world balance was tipping in favour of communism, they might also be persuaded to come to terms with changes closer to home. Yet ordinary citizens tended to invert such logic. With such huge outlays on space exploration, for instance, why was socialism unable to solve the basic food supply? Frustrated shoppers joked that 'There'll be butter again soon. Gagarin is already on his way to the Milky Way.' Puns played on the word *kürze*, meaning both a short time and a short amount. Hence, '*In kürze gibts alles!*' (roughly, 'we have an abundance of nothing'). The image of catching up with the West had been a hostage to fortune from the start, as when one wit, referring to the growing defections to the FRG, commented: 'Oh really, we're supposed to be overtaking West Germany—but we're not even all there yet.'[162] Another suggested a new emblem for the GDR: instead of hammer, dividers, and wheat sheaves, he proposed a 'hippopotamus with the water lapping around its neck, but still holding its mouth wide open'.[163]

---

[159] RdB Leipzig (Inneres), 'Bericht über den Stand der Bevölkerungsbewegung . . .', 19 May 1960, StAL, BT/RdB Leipzig, 1629, fos. 139–42.

[160] 'Protokoll der Beratung im Politbüro vom 6. Juni 1961 zu Fragen der Versorgung', SAPMO-BArch, DY30/J IV2/2/766, fo. 185.

[161] SED-PB (Wirtschaftskomm.), 16 June 1961, SAPMO-BArch, DY30/IV2/2.101/24.

[162] SED-ZK (PO), 'Information' Nr. 65, 26 May 1961, SAPMO-BArch, DY30/IV2/5/295, fos. 53–61.

[163] FDGB-BuVo (Org.), 14 Aug. 1961, SAPMO-BArch, DY30/IV2/6.11/65, fos. 206–07.

It proved difficult for agitators to engage the public in discussions of international affairs when there were so many unresolved bread-and-butter issues closer to home. As one passer-by bluntly put it: 'Stuff the peace treaty—first sort out the butter supply.'[164] Two disillusioned agitprop functionaries in Weimar warned: 'As long as we have to queue for tomatoes and no potatoes are to be had, we'll never enthuse people.'[165] In the sleepy corner of Suhl in the south-western GDR there were no significant discussions of the Vienna summit between Kennedy and Khrushchev in June 1961: 'They are drowned in the lively debates about supply questions.'[166] There was a pronounced primacy of economics over politics in the immediate concerns of the population. It was always possible to sign a declaration on the Berlin question or the peace treaty without much thought, but the poor state of the economy was an everyday reality which united vast swathes of the populace. As one observer at the TRO works in Berlin commented: 'For about the last eighteen months conversations with colleagues show that confidence in state, government and party is not consolidating but crumbling away more and more—especially since the contradiction between promises about the Economic Main Task and the actual situation has grown so great.'[167] Citizens drew increasingly political inferences. Overhasty collectivization was one of the common explanations for the food crisis, even when the real reasons were more complex and mundane.[168] Taboos were broken, for instance when Brandenburg housewives commented: 'Is it back to that: guns instead of butter!',[169] or 'That's the way Hitler began; first the butter, then the meat, then war.'[170] Rumours even spread that the chronic shortage of washing-powder was because its phosphorus ingredient was being used for munitions.[171] The party was under attack over many of its core values.

Rank-and-file SED members were reportedly going onto the defensive, being 'driven into a corner' or 'wavering'. In one local unit comrades were 'weak-kneed'.[172] Queues became dangerous places for the SED faithful, with some functionaries removing party insignia before joining them. In Berlin a 'not

[164] 'Bericht über die Stimmung in der Partei und der Bevölkerung in Jena-Stadt . . .', 21 June 1961, SAPMO-BArch, DY30/IV2/9.04/545, fos. 17–21.

[165] SED-ZK (PO), 'Information' Nr. 81, 10 July 1961, SAPMO-BArch, DY30/IV2/5/295, fo. 157.

[166] SED-ZK (PO), 'Schwerpunkte . . .', 13 June 1961, SAPMO-BArch, DY30/IV2/9.02/50, fos. 3–7.

[167] 'Stimmungsbericht . . .', 1 June 1961, LAB, BPA SED Berlin, IV7/23/20.

[168] SED-ZK (LPO), 'Information über die Lage in der Versorgung . . .', 4 Nov. 1960, SAPMO-BArch, DY30/IV2/12/112, fos. 267–70.

[169] SED-ZK (PO), 'Information' Nr. 30, 10 Mar. 1961, SAPMO-BArch, DY30/IV2/5/294, fos. 236–49.

[170] SED-ZK (PO), 'Information' Nr. 70, 12 June 1961, SAPMO-BArch, DY30/IV2/5/295, fo. 96.

[171] SED-BL Schwerin (PO), 'Kurzer Bericht . . .', 1 Dec. 1961, MLHA Schwerin, BPA SED Schwerin, IV2/5/644, fos. 315–18.

[172] SED-BPL VEB Entwicklungsbau Pirna, 'Informationsbericht', 3 July 1961, SächsHStA, BPA SED Dresden, IV2/6/42, fos. 71–73. See also Allinson, *Politics*, 121–2, for Thuringia.

inconsiderable portion of the members and candidates avoid confrontations, both in the members' meetings and in public, by not joining in discussions'.[173] In Potsdam the party reported 'signs of capitulation' among some functionaries.[174] At one trade union meeting a member dared to say: 'We shouldn't speak so much of the front between the GDR and West Germany, since this front runs through the middle of the GDR. It exists between the government and the population, and 95 per cent are against the government.' Strong words indeed, but as the reporter observed: 'In many cases the responsible economic functionaries remain silent during such provocations.'[175] It was also noted that some comrades were beginning to chime in with the chorus of discontent. At the Zeiss works one communist, in the party since 1920, claimed the 'party was making mistake after mistake and we have to bail them out down here. The Central Committee should issue an autocritique.' Others believed that 'they'll get a shock at the top when the whole shop falls apart'.[176] In Oranienburg the deputy mayor and local party boss even faced disciplinary proceedings for claiming that the situation was as bad as 1953, accused of 'politically caving in to enemy pressure'.[177]

Despite the torrents of ink spilt over the second Berlin crisis, it in fact achieved very little: the western Allies did not withdraw; there was no peace treaty; the GDR was only half-heartedly recognized ten years later. Likewise, the economy did not immediately revive and attempts to modernize it were effectively abandoned in 1971. Yet, although the international frontiers did not shift, and East Germany lagged further behind the West German economic miracle, the dual crises had a destabilizing effect on the domestic population. For ordinary citizens, the border was not simply a matter of international law, but part of their daily lives: how they got to work; how they visited family; how they spent their leisure time. Many were revisionist towards the eastern territories. It became evident, moreover, that there was a distinct primacy of domestic politics over international politics. What popular opinion also reveals about political communication in the GDR is that individuals were prepared to send critical signals up the apparatus, but the latter showed little responsiveness. Unlike the study of foreign policy and public opinion in a democracy, where an elected leadership is bound to pay some attention to the electorate, frustrated voices in the GDR found themselves being displaced into other channels of less sanctioned

[173] SED-ZK (PO), 'Einige wichtige Probleme im Bezirk Berlin' [Vorlage to SED-PB], 19 July 1961, SAPMO-BArch, DY30/IV2/5/13, fos. 142–63.
[174] SED-BL Potsdam (Org-Kader), 'Bericht über die politische Lage', 10 Nov. 1960, BLHA, Bez. Pdm. Rep. 530/1620.
[175] SED-ZK (PO), 'Kurzinformation . . .', 27 July 1961, SAPMO-BArch, DY30/IV2/5/13, fos. 183–7.
[176] 'Bericht über die Stimmung in der Partei und der Bevölkerung in Jena-Stadt . . .', 21 June 1961, SAPMO-BArch, DY30/IV2/9.04/545, fos. 17–21.
[177] SED-ZK (LPO), 'Informationsbericht', 2 July 1960, SAPMO-BArch, DY30/IV2/5/293, fos. 14–31.

dissent. One of these was Hirschman's act of exit. The following chapter will examine more closely the everyday power struggles over the open border. Only then can one appreciate how the diplomatic and economic crises were symptoms of a broader 'people's crisis', which neither the superpowers nor their allies could control.

3

Crossing the Line: *Republikflucht* between Defection and Migration

Between 1945 and the building of the Wall in 1961 3.5 million, or one in six, East Germans crossed the iron curtain to the West[1]—proportionally thirty times as many as fled the Third Reich.[2] Whereas West Germany's population swelled from 47.3 to 56.2 millions from 1948 to 1961, the GDR, despite a birth surplus, dwindled from 19.1 to 17.1 millions. The act even had an official name: *Republikflucht* or 'flight from the Republic', with connotations of *Fahnenflucht*, or military desertion from the flag. Absconders were crossing a frontline and leaving fellow fighters for socialism in the lurch. As one police commander put it, even for non-communists, '*Republikflucht* is betrayal of the Workers' and Peasants' State, betrayal of the GDR's working people'.[3] As part of an elaborate conspiracy theory, western militarists were allegedly recruiting cannon fodder and industrialists hiring cheap labour to destabilize the rival German state: '*Republikflucht* is systematically organized by agencies in Bonn and is considered an essential means in their waging of the "Cold War" . . . with an eye to weakening the German Democratic Republic by the systematic removal of certain occupational groups.'[4] It was estimated that the economic cost by 1961 was 120 billion marks.[5] Towards the end of the crisis it was even suggested that Adenauer was manipulating the refugees as Hitler had stoked up the Sudeten crisis in 1938, as a pretext for invasion.

[1] The West German authorities registered 2,557,697 asylum-seekers; the Volkspolizei counted a total of 2,458,671 illegal and 311,700 legal departures (the latter mainly elderly people and dependants). On top of this, an estimated 876,200 Soviet Zonal refugees left between 1945 and 1949, whereas a half million 'returnees' and immigrants entered from West Germany by 1961. Federal sources were taken from BAK, B136/821 & 2718–22; Volkspolizei figures from BAB, DO-1/8/298(2)-302(1).

[2] Approximately 300,000 Jews and 30,000 political persecutees: Werner Röder, 'Die Emigration aus dem nationalsozialistischen Deutschland', in Klaus J. Bade (ed.), *Deutsche im Ausland: Fremde in Deutschland: Migration in Geschichte und Gegenwart* (Munich: Beck, 1993), 348–51.

[3] 'Disposition', 13 Nov. 1958, BAB, DO-1/34/27105.

[4] SED-PB, 'Bericht der Kommission zu Fragen der Republikflucht', 25 May 1956, SAPMO-BArch, DY30/JIV2/2/483, fos. 25–34.

[5] Henrik Bispinck, ' "Republikflucht": Flucht und Ausreise als Problem für die DDR-Führung', in Dierk Hoffmann *et al.* (eds), *Vor dem Mauerbau: Politik und Gesellschaft in der DDR* (Munich: Oldenbourg, 2003), 285.

This was a charge vigorously contested by West German leaders, whose radio broadcasts urged East Germans to hold out in the 'Zone', pending reunification.[6] Yet for the West, too, the exodus was a form of political defection. The FRG thus spoke of *Republikflüchtlinge* rather than *Republikflüchtige*.[7] However, whereas the East stressed pull factors, the West discerned mainly push factors, generated by intolerable living conditions and totalitarian repression. This reading had obvious propaganda uses, especially in contrasting the alienating experience of communism with the more 'natural' order in the Federal Republic.[8] Given the absence of free GDR elections, western politicians delighted in paraphrasing Lenin that leavers were 'voting with their feet'. 'The Free World Greets You', proclaimed banners at reception centres, while the western media sensationalized escapes from the clutches of communism. Arrivees, sitting anxiously before screening panels, also had a vested interest in claiming political persecution, which entitled them to housing benefits and financial compensation. In any case, as part of the FRG's diplomatic Cold War, all East Germans were entitled to Federal citizenship. Away from the public spotlight, however, western administrators soon realized that a form of economic migration was occurring. Recent research has also presented this revisionist conclusion, to which I shall return below.[9] However, in order to convince Federal taxpayers and shame the SED, Bonn did not speak of 'migrants' in the 1950s, but 'refugees'. Likewise, GDR officials who denied the primacy of politics were accused of ideological laxity.

SITUATIONAL FACTORS

Nevertheless, before tackling politics and economics, let us add another category, namely situation, to explain why one person absconded while another remained. Situation was partly an external given, where personal circumstance collided with high politics. It was a matter of historical accident on which side of the iron curtain individuals happened to be in 1945. Many leavers were seeking to reunite

[6] Bundesministerium für innerdeutsche Beziehungen (ed.), *Der Bau der Mauer durch Berlin: Die Flucht aus der Sowjetzone und die Sperrmaßnahmen des kommunistischen Regimes vom 13. August 1961 in Berlin* (Bonn: BMfiB, 1986), 27–30.

[7] Damian van Melis and Henrik Bispinck (eds), *'Republikflucht': Flucht und Abwanderung aus der SBZ/DDR* (Munich: Oldenbourg, 2006), 15. *Flüchtling* means refugee; *Flüchtiger* suggests a criminal on the run.

[8] For a selection of contemporary publicity material: Harald von Koenigswald, *Menschen von drüben* (Bonn: BMfgF, 1958); id., *Sie suchen Zuflucht* (Esslingen: Bechtle, 1960); id., *Bauern auf der Flucht* (Bonn: BMfgF, 1960); BMfgF (ed.), *Jeder Fünfte* (Bonn, n.d.); Erika von Hornstein, *Die deutsche Not* (Cologne: Kiepenheuer & Witsch, 1960).

[9] Helge Heidemeyer, *Flucht und Zuwanderung aus der SBZ/DDR 1945/1949–1961* (Düsseldorf: Droste, 1994); Volker Ackermann, *Der 'echte' Flüchtling: Deutsche Vertriebene und Flüchtlinge aus der DDR 1945–1961* (Osnabrück: Universitätsverlag Rasch, 1995).

families, not as an ideological statement, but to normalize daily life. In the early postwar years, and beyond, there was considerable natural internal migration between the two recovering Germanys. Yet amid the arbitrariness of national partition a pattern emerged: expellees from beyond the Oder–Neisse and youths proved more volatile; family, locale, or old age tied others down. As one witness who discarded thoughts of leaving recorded:

> The roots to my home were too strong for me to cut. And besides: why should I leave my familiar landscape and its inhabitants only because others laid claim to it? Who entitled the self-appointed representative of the dictatorship of the proletariat to define my *Heimat* as its property and subjugate the people within it?[10]

In fact, future research will probably reveal as much about the reasons for staying as for leaving.[11]

Wartime evacuees had tended to retreat eastwards, away from Allied bombing. Often they had a long wait for rehousing in their home towns, especially in heavily targeted conurbations. One Hamburg woman living in Schwerin did not receive such permission until 1961.[12] Then came the protracted *Völkerwanderung* westwards from the former eastern territories. Approximately 4 million refugees entered the Soviet Zone, or 23 per cent of the population by 1950. Initially, newcomers wished to make a go of it and the proportion of fleeing expellees was well below average. Yet locals tended to treat 'resettlers' as second-class citizens.[13] The real trigger to move on, however, came in 1952 with Bonn's Equalization of Burdens Law, compensating expellees. From 1950 to 1961 1.2 billion deutschmarks were disbursed to former GDR expellees, with significant sums coming on stream in 1953.[14] The corresponding jump in flights by this group was thus hardly coincidental. Expellee districts—mainly in the north—were abnormally prone to *Republikflucht*, sometimes reaching three times the national average. As Frankfurt/Oder reported on recently repatriated Germans from Poland: 'they are using the GDR as a spring-board to get to West Germany.'[15] In other areas of Brandenburg 'easterners' were staying just a few months before moving on; the belief was widespread 'that for a *Republikflucht* one must photograph one's property and bring documents on ownership—such as extracts from the land register—in order to demonstrate ownership in West

---

[10] Johannes Richter in Carl-Christoph Schweitzer *et al.* (eds), *Lebensläufe: hüben und drüben* (Opladen: Leske & Budrich, 1993), 321.

[11] Jan Palmowski, *Inventing a Socialist Nation: Heimat and the Politics of Everyday Life in the GDR, 1945–90* (Cambridge: Cambridge University Press, 2009).

[12] MfS-ZAIG, 'Bericht über die Entwicklung der Republikflucht im Zeitraum 1.4.61–13.8.61 . . .', 3 Oct. 1961, BStU-ZA, ZAIG 412, fo. 72.

[13] Alexander von Plato and Wolfgang Meinicke, *Alte Heimat—neue Zeit: Flüchtlinge, Umgesiedelte, Vertriebene in der Sowjetischen Besatzungszone und in der DDR* (Berlin: Verlags-Anstalt Union, 1991), 56–65.

[14] BAK, B136/2719, fo. 181; B136/2720, fo. 25.

[15] HVDVP, 'Republikfluchten . . .', 2 Nov. 1957, BAB, DO-1/11/964, fos. 193–201.

Germany.'[16] There was even some solidarity among expellee communities. On 13 February 1960 five farming families, originally from Latvia, then transplanted to the Ukraine by Nazi resettlement before enjoying the land reform in 1945, fled en masse from the commune of Niemberg in Halle.[17] This was their third move in twenty years—just some of the wandering souls of the early GDR.

Among East Germans themselves rootedness varied by region, as Figure 2 clearly demonstrates. Initially there was greater uniformity, with border regions slightly more susceptible. Later on, southern *Bezirke* proved more immune to *Republikflucht*. It is possible that in areas such as Saxony, less pronounced wartime upheaval promoted greater social cohesion. With the notable exception of Dresden, the southern cities had been spared heavy bombing and ground-fighting. Whereas Magdeburg, Frankfurt, and Prenzlau in the north had been devastated, Leipzig and Karl-Marx-Stadt were only moderately damaged, and Thuringia almost unscathed. Saxony was an industrialized region and remained so, attracting an internal migration. In the north, on the other hand, there had been much greater dislocation of social networks under the land reform, ending centuries of Junker patronage.[18] Here a long-established 'flight from the land' continued, as young country-dwellers sought work in the towns. In the rural areas of the south, on the other hand, smallholding, including workers' cottage gardens, provided a stronger incentive to stay. Moreover, Cottbus and Dresden contained the homelands of the slavic Sorb minorities in the Ober- and Niederlausitz and witnessed consistently low losses.

Although Germany was divided, it was still criss-crossed by family ties. The war had scattered populations, entailing convoluted comings-and-goings only visible at the micro-level. Eduard K., for instance, returned as a PoW from Russia to his native Dortmund in West Germany, where he married a former East German with six children. In January 1956 they moved to the GDR, where K.'s step-son had supposedly inherited land. But then K. returned to Dortmund, seeking an apartment, while wife and children stayed in West Berlin. Apparently unsuccessful, the family returned to the GDR once again, only to be deported when K. refused to work on a collective.[19] Beneath the polarizing high politics of the Cold War there were many such complex realities on the ground. The family was often all that could be salvaged from the National Socialist disaster, but parental authority seemed to be under renewed SED attack. When the state threatened to disrupt kinship ties, the natural reaction of many family heads was to protect the primary group. As one artisan explained: 'I believe that family ties between parents and children, and relationships of various orders, where one part

---

[16] MdI (IA), 'Analyse der Republikfluchten im Sektor Landwirtschaft', n.d. [1959], SAPMO-BArch, IV2/13/622.

[17] MdI, 'Informationsbericht . . . ', n.d., BAB, DO-11/34/21718.

[18] Christian Nieske, *Republikflucht und Wirtschaftswunder: Mecklenburger berichten über ihre Erlebnisse 1945 bis 1961* (Schwerin: Helms Thomas Verlag, 2002).

[19] Leiter des Notaufnahmeverfahrens in Uelzen, 6 Aug. 1957, BAK, B 150/4083a.

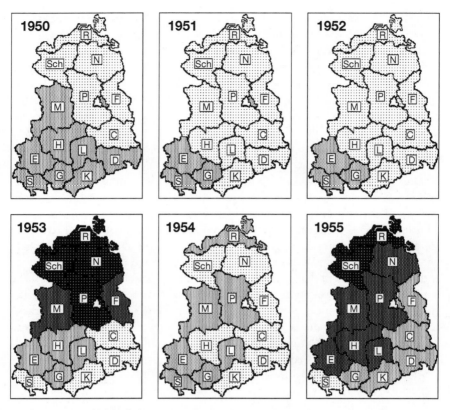

Figure 2a. *Republikflucht* by area, 1950–61 (as percentage of regional populace).
Source: DVP figures. See Note 1. C, Cottbus; D, Dresden; E, Erfurt; F, Frankfurt; G, Gera; H, Halle; K, Karl-Marx-Stadt; L, Leipzig; M, Magdeburg; N, Neubrandenburg; P, Potsdam; R, Rostock; S, Suhl; Sch, Schwerin. East Berlin is between Potsdam and Frankfurt. The figures for 1961 have been averaged over the pre-Wall months, not the entire year.

lives in West Germany and the other in the GDR, cannot simply be forbidden by legal directives.'[20] The importance of family is also revealed in letters, for instance from one Berlin doctor:

I have no more next of kin, neither parents nor brothers and sisters nor other relatives. Separation from a person very close to me, living in West Germany, with whom I would like to share my life, is a great burden. Moreover, my and my parents' friends, whom I regard as kin, live in West Germany. The considerable difficulties in receiving an interzonal pass, since my visit was not to 'family', which I had to endure last year too, make these personal issues intolerable in the long term.[21]

20 Konsumgenossenschaft Köthen, 3 June 1961, BAB, DO-1/34/27105.
21 Dr Hildegard Sch. to Dr Sch., 29 Apr. 1959, SAPMO-BArch, DY30/IV2/19/56.

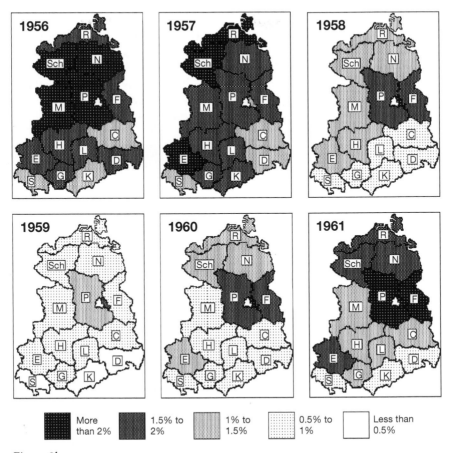

Figure 2b.

It was thus not uncommon, well into the 1950s, to see East–West family reunions take place: 17 per cent of asylum cases from 1953 to 1961 occurred for this purpose alone.[22] Fifty-three per cent of all refugees arrived as families, with especially heavy concentrations in 1953, 1956, 1958, and 1960, in other words, at times of greatest socioeconomic uncertainty. One frequent reason cited by parents leaving was to <u>secure their children's futures.</u> Travelling as a group nevertheless aroused particular suspicion, so that relatives disguised their togetherness, sometimes sitting in separate railway compartments or taking alternative routes, some via Berlin, others across the Demarcation Line.[23] Relatives in the West were also crucial in overcoming inhibitions about starting over. Frequently, western municipal authorities refused residence permits without evidence of outside support. Otherwise, refugees faced months or even years inside

[22] Heidemeyer, *Flucht*, 47.   [23] Herrlitz interview, 9 Sept. 1996.

a transit camp, awaiting placement.[24] Of course, as more people fled west, this generated an extended kinship network of its own. As the Volkspolizei noted, 'family ties to West Germany caused by *Republikflucht* have risen year on year'.[25] Thirty per cent of Leuna workers in 1961 were estimated to have western friends and relations, who were suspected of inciting them to leave.[26] Since dependants left behind in the GDR were in turn discriminated against, by being barred from education or refused travel permits, the state was actually increasing the likelihood of their departure too: *Republikflucht* became a chain reaction.

Yet these were not the mass expellee treks of 1945, where whole communities had been uprooted. About half of *Republikfluchten* occurred as isolated acts. (Indeed, some flights 'for family reasons' were using the border as a surrogate for divorce.) Individuals had different tolerances, and situational factors therefore require psychological as well as sociological explanation, based on the particular power relationships in a person's immediate environment. The youth of those leaving is also striking, when compared with the national average (see Figure 3). Although 18- to 24-year-olds constituted a small proportion of the overall population, they were massively overrepresented among *Republikflüchtige*, especially young men.[27] Some of the reasons were universal: youths had fewer responsibilities and were more employable; others were specific to postwar Germany. Absent war-dead fathers and working mothers undermined the parental authority which might have tethered some youngsters. In a survey of 558 young refugees in the mid-1950s, 40 per cent had lost one or both parents, in most cases the father.[28] There was also a natural youthful rebelliousness. Many older observers took an indulgent view of 'tearaways', bored by socialist reality where, according to youths from Fürstenwalde, 'there is only work, otherwise there is nothing on offer and nothing happening'.[29] Even youngsters being groomed for the apparat could bridle at the prospects ahead. Helmut S. wrote to his SED parents from the West in 1961 of his disillusionment with the party. In the army, too, he had experienced a 'lack of enthusiasm, incompetence, petty-mindedness, pessimism, take-it-or-leave-it attitudes, meetings and conferences—and no visible development'. At his journalism school in Leipzig 'came the borderlines again':

[24] Günter Köhler, *Notaufnahme* (Berlin: Stapp, 1991).
[25] HVDVP, 'Vorlage für die Mitglieder des Kollegiums . . .', 1 June 1961, BAB, DO-1/11/967, fos. 93–122.
[26] SED-KL Leuna (KPKK), 'Analyse . . .', 10 July 1961, LAM, BPA SED Halle, IV/412/235, fos. 118–25.
[27] Peter Skyba, *Vom Hoffnungsträger zum Sicherheitsrisiko: Jugend in der DDR und Jugendpolitik der SED 1949–1961* (Cologne: Böhlau, 2000), 331–57.
[28] Infratest (ed.), *Jugendliche Flüchtlinge aus der SBZ: Die menschlich-soziale, geistige und materiell-berufliche Eingliederung jugendlicher Sowjetzonen-Flüchtlinge* (Munich, May 1957), 35.
[29] SED-ZK (Arbeitsgruppe Jugendfragen), 'Republikflucht von Jugendlichen . . .', 10 Nov. 1960, SAPMO-BArch, IV2/16/230.

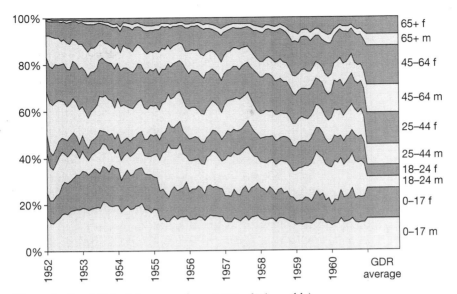

Figure 3. *Republikflucht* by age and sex, 1952–60 (monthly).
Source: BMfFV figures. See Note 1. GDR average from *Statistisches Jahrbuch der DDR*.

I won't have my hand held like a child any longer. How is a young person here supposed to mature into a personality . . .? I believe in the collective, in commonality . . . but one cannot arbitrarily mould any given group of people into a collective. . . . I am not entering the bourgeois world to make it easy on myself. . . . I am leaving precisely because it is too comfortable here. . . . In future I shall be Me and not my dossier.[30]

Yet situational explanations did not appeal to the SED for several reasons. For one, there was little that could be done about them. Moreover, the party habitually denied agency to ordinary citizens, casting them as dupes of capitalist conspiracies. The younger generation, for instance, was being 'blinded' by the facade of western 'shop-window politics'.[31] Girls, in particular, were caricatured as vulnerable to consumerism and sexploitation. Local parties were constantly berated as 'politically blind' for believing in the 'fairytale' of *Republikflucht* for 'family reasons'.[32] The real causes were, according to the leadership, to be found in western radio propaganda, recruitment agencies, and defeatist rumours. Nevertheless, the repeated nature of such chidings suggests that everyday factors and personal self-determination were only too real.

[30] Helmut S. to his parents, n.d. [1961], SAPMO-BArch, DY30/JIV2/202/65, fos. 141–52.
[31] 'Illegale Abwanderungen Jugendlicher', n.d., BAB, DO-1/34/21723.
[32] 'Material für die Besprechung . . .', SAPMO-BArch, DY30/IV2/13/395.

POLITICAL FACTORS

This is not to deny political motivations. The monthly figures in Figure 4 show considerable peaks and troughs, in both East and West German statistics. First, there were annual rhythms. Flights always rose in summer and at Easter, as holidays offered pretexts for otherwise incriminating luggage. Seasonal work was another cyclical factor. But some years were obviously far worse than others. The first half of 1953 was very costly. A lull followed until 1955–57, which saw sustained losses, followed by the quietest period of all in 1959, with matters deteriorating in 1960 and becoming critical again in 1961. It is tempting to see the bigger swings as responses to the changing political climate in the GDR and to read off *Republikflucht* like traces on a sociopolitical seismograph. This is certainly how Federal observers interpreted shifts, annotating charts of the exodus with references to political campaigns and diplomatic initiatives, some of which are replicated in Figure 4.[33]

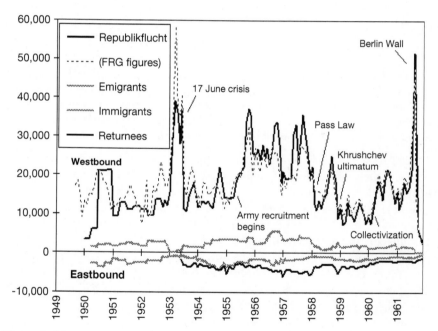

Figure 4. Movements across the open border, 1949–61 (monthly).
Source: DVP and BMfFV figures. See Note 1. DVP figures were quarterly until October 1952 (averaged here). Immigrants and returnees were not listed separately until June 1953.

[33] See for instance BMfiB (ed.), *Bau der Mauer*, final pull-out sheet. See also Johannes Kurt Klein, 'Ursachen und Motive der Abwanderung aus der Sowjetzone Deutschlands', *Aus Politik und Zeitgeschichte*, B 26/55 (15 June 1955), 361–83.

One political calibration is the number of so-called C-certificates issued by the Federal authorities to asylum-seekers, given only to those who had left under ideological duress. After the turbulent year of 1953, in the second half of which 25.3 per cent of refugees were considered political, these dropped in the mid-1950s, reaching a low of 7.4 per cent in 1957, but then rising again in 1958 to 15.2 per cent and achieving a new high of 21.1 per cent in 1960.[34] A roller-coaster pattern of 'politicals' emerged, high at each end of the pre-Wall period and dipping in the middle. Certainly, in the early years of the 'antifascist-democratic upheaval' of 1945–48, the refugee flow included many party-political opponents leaving the Soviet Zone. It has even been suggested that the SED was not unhappy to see the backs of potential troublemakers. In the first wave were former National Socialists, fearful of reprisals and denazification. Yet, soon the Cold War added new enemies. Already in 1945–46 several prominent SPD (Social Democratic Party of Germany) leaders opposed to the SED merger, such as Hermann Brill and Gustav Dahrendorf, had fled west. Also among Christian Democrats and Liberals there were departures by zonal politicians such as Hermes and Kaiser, as well as local defections, in Thuringia for instance, where a whole swathe of 'bourgeois' leaders left.[35] There were, moreover, various 'natural' class enemies, such as Junker landowners and factory bosses, who were encouraged to leave.[36] By contrast, SED members proved demonstrably more loyal to the Workers' and Peasants' State. In the traumatic year of 1953 the party registered 7,370 card-carrying defections or 0.6 per cent of its membership, against 1.6 per cent among the adult population.[37] During the 1950s the annual figure hovered around 8,000, but by 1960 was only 4,470, or 0.3 per cent (against 1.2 per cent nationally), indicating an increasingly stable core. For party careerists, western contacts were frowned upon and few would have deluded themselves about employment prospects in an increasingly anti-communist Federal Republic.

Among non-party members of any hue, *Republikflucht* generally rose during periods of heightened class struggle, such as that ushered in by the 'construction of socialism' in July 1952 and ended by the abortive insurrection of 17 June 1953. It is quite clear that emigration was part, and not a displacement, of this popular discontent, contrary to Hirschman's seesaw model. Most flights occurred *before* the uprising, not after.[38] The Volkspolizei recognized that, indeed, as ideological pressure intensified, '*Republikflucht* has risen substantially

---

[34] Heidemeyer, *Flucht*, 47.   [35] Allinson, *Politics*, 28–9.

[36] van Melis, *'Republikflucht'*, 20–1.

[37] Of these, around one-third were former Social Democrats, a tenth former Communists, and the rest 'newcomers': Renate Wanstrat, *Strukturanalyse der politisch nicht anerkannten Flüchtlinge in West-Berlin* (West Berlin: Verwaltungsdruckerei, 1953), i, 14.

[38] See also Corey Ross, 'Before the Wall: East Germans, Communist Authority, and the Mass Exodus to the West', *Historical Journal*, 45 (2002), 471–4.

and become a focus of police activity.'[39] Internally, the authorities admitted that their own insensitive policies, 'lacking any finesse', were alienating leavers.[40] This included criminalization of certain sectors. Thus, while in 1949 only 341 people had absconded to avoid prosecution, in 1953 it was 13,060.[41] This was compounded by interzonal travel restrictions in the early spring. The western authorities reported an ensuing panic, 'a mass-induced fear of not being able to get away in time before obstacles were placed in the way of flight'.[42] Conversely, when the New Course, promising reforms, was announced a week before the uprising, flights dropped by 80 per cent, a trend reinforced by the closure of the border for three weeks in the wake of 17 June. Yet, once reopened, departures resumed as suspects and parolees fled.[43]

The most prominent group of 1953, however, was farmers (see Figure 6). The SED had recently introduced the Agricultural Production Collective, or LPG, but still on a voluntary basis, yet already 'kulak' farmers were being prosecuted for undershooting grain quotas. According to the Volkspolizei, the number of *Großbauern* leaving in February 1953 was ten times that of the previous September. Yet significant numbers of smallholding 'new farmers', beneficiaries of the 1945 land reform, were also heading west.[44] The *Mittelstand* felt next in line. Artisans, businessmen, and factory owners left in massive numbers in 1953, following the introduction of Manual Production Collectives. Significantly, neither farmers nor the *Mittelstand* were natural candidates for flight. Farmers were tied to the land, and the commercial sector to its businesses.[45] Members of the 'old' *Mittelstand* of artisans and shopkeepers knew there was little call for them in the West, so it was all the more remarkable when these groups departed. When they did, there were sometimes symbolic burnings of bridges, such as the smashing of glasshouses by market gardeners.[46]

Overall, 1953 witnessed massive losses across the board and was a truly exceptional year. At other times, many political defections occurred not so much from principled anti-communism, as in avoidance of specific obligations. A classic case was informing for the Stasi.[47] If individuals had fallen foul of the system

[39] 'Analyse über die Motive der Republikflucht', 1953, BAB, DO-1/11/962, fos. 67–80.

[40] 'Bericht über die Entwicklung der Republikflucht im März 1953', 24 Apr. 1953, SAPMO-BArch, DY30/IV2/13/394.

[41] 'Abwanderung aus der DDR . . . 1950–1953', BAB, DO-1/11/962, fos. 159–60.

[42] Senator für Sozialwesen, 'Die Flüchtlingssituation am 15. Mai 1953', 18 May 1953, LAB, B Rep. 008–02/241.

[43] 'Kurzbericht . . . Republikflucht nach dem 17. Juni 1953', 26 Oct. 1953, SAPMO-BArch, DY30/IV2/13/394. For instance, of the 600 parolees in Karl-Marx-Stadt after the 'fascist excesses', only forty-two remained in the GDR by the end of 1954: 'Bericht über die illegalen Abwanderungen . . . 1954', SAPMO-BArch, DY30/IV2/13/396.

[44] Maron to SKK, 2 Aug. 1952, BAB, DO-1/11/961, fos. 114–20.

[45] Antonia Maria Humm, *Auf dem Weg zum sozialistischen Dorf? Zum Wandel der dörflichen Lebenswelt in der DDR von 1952 bis 1969* (Göttingen: Vandenhoeck & Ruprecht, 1999), 48–9.

[46] MdI (IA), 'Informationsbericht Nr. 3 . . .', 24 Mar. 1960, SAPMO-BArch, IV2/13/368.

[47] See refugee statements 1, 4, 9, 11, 12, 13 in BMfIB (ed.), *Bau der Mauer*, 43–82.

in even a minor way, MfS officers could entrap them into observing colleagues. Anonymous telephone calls and feelings of being watched were common reasons given for pre-emptively leaving. Another example is the recruitment of young men into the armed forces in the mid-1950s. Ever since the Garrisoned Volkspolizei (KVP) had been set up in 1948, there had been discipline problems. In 1952 2,900 Vopos fled, and in 1953 4,731, yet by the late 1950s numbers were down to the low hundreds. The leakage became more general, however, with the expansion of the police into a standing army in 1955–56. Rather than introduce a conscription law, the SED relied on coercive voluntarism. In spring 1955 pressure mounted, and as Figure 3 shows, the proportion of young men aged 18 to 24 soared—a perfect example of the regime politicizing the populace from above by moving the goalposts of social obligation, as even the authorities recognized:

Whereas until KVP recruitment it was almost exclusively persons blinded by trash literature, propaganda and relatives, and sometimes openly negative attitudes towards our Workers' and Peasants' State, now it is a circle sometimes described as industrious and disciplined. In many cases they are members of the Free German Youth and even young members of our party.[48]

Whether these were out-and-out critics of the regime is doubtful. Even West German officials understood that many deserters were leaving for general reasons, for 'a better life'. The decision was not one between East and West, since most youngsters had little basis for comparison, but was a bid for 'self-determination'. Even this was a minority motive, with a quarter of all deserters simply seeking to evade the tedium of political indoctrination and another fifth fearing recriminations for minor infractions.[49] Such liberty was therefore largely negatively conceived—freedom from state meddling rather than for the exercise of abstract civil rights.[50]

In 1958, however, more general political factors re-emerged, for instance in a wave of anti-clericalism. Ulbricht issued his socialist 'ten commandments' and schools sidelined religious instruction. The state also pressured citizens into leaving the church, with 158,736 Protestants quitting in that year alone.[51] When the Federal Lutheran church agreed to minister to the new Bundeswehr, the SED immediately accused all pastors of being in league with the 'other side'. And as noted above, the Berlin crisis, but also the economic race with the FRG, made 1958 a highly political year. The MfS commented in its annual report that: 'A far stronger tendency, and obviously still growing, is for politico-ideological confusion and insufficient socialist consciousness to be determining

---

[48] Untitled, 1955, BAB, DO-1/11/963, fos. 70–99.

[49] H. von zur Mühlen, 'Die Volkspolizei-Deserteure im Notaufnahmeverfahren von 1952 bis 1954', 18 Mar. 1955, BAK, B150/5941/1.

[50] Infratest (ed.), *Jugendliche Flüchtlinge*, 45 and 47.

[51] Robert F. Goeckel, *The Lutheran Church and the East German State: Political Conflict and Change under Ulbricht and Honecker* (Ithaca: Cornell University Press, 1990), 21.

causes of *Republikflucht*, while "personal or material reasons" only serve as an external pretext or trigger.'[52] The group which merited closest Stasi attention as 'especially grave' was the intelligentsia, not just intellectuals, but all those with a university education. In 1958 these even defied the general downward trend (see Figure 5). Whereas previously, fleeing doctors had mainly blamed 'aggravation at incorrect treatment', 'now more and more messages and letters left behind openly cite political rejection of our system and policies'.[53] Among these, one doctor complained about

the incessant hammering home of political theses in words and writing, films and books and even work conferences. It is the constraint of genuine free intellectual activity by scientists and university lecturers, the diversion from our proper tasks, so important for the public, who basically need some occasional leisure, playful flights of fancy and sometimes contemplative concentration. It is the lack of a feeling of freedom, replaced by a caged sensation. . . . It is the deep dreariness which overshadows life in almost all intellectual professions in the GDR.[54]

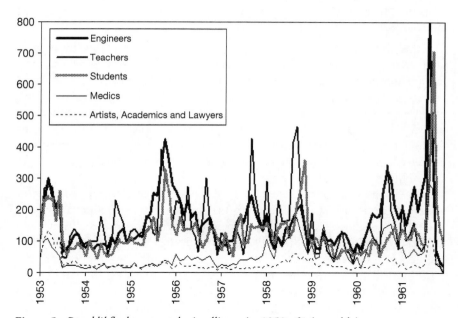

Figure 5. *Republikflucht* among the intelligentsia, 1953–61 (monthly).
Source: DVP figures. See Note 1.

[52] MfS, 'Bericht über die Entwicklung der Republikflucht im Jahre 1958', 20 Mar. 1959, BStU-ZA, ZAIG 186, fos. 1–21.
[53] 'Entwurf einer Information über die Lage im Gesundheitswesen . . .', 23 Apr. 1959, SAPMO-BArch, DY30/IV2/19/53.
[54] Dr H.A. to Dr Sch., 29 June 1958, SAPMO-BArch, DY30/IV2/19/55.

Another commented on the atmosphere of uncertainty which gave him palpitations every time he left his surgery, wondering whether he had said too much to a patient:

Any genuine political or ideological conversation conceals the danger of personal jeopardy, since, even if one can trust the interlocutor, one does not know what a third party encountered by the speakers will make of the subject. But the fact that people demand an opinion of us, and then only a particular one when it is needed, and then try to force us to say something which is not our opinion at all, is so humiliating that I simply cannot bear it any longer.[55]

Dr B. and his wife, who had given up a private practice in 1953 to take up a public post, counted themselves as disillusioned sympathizers:

Impressed by the lessons of the past we were positively inclined to many of the progressive 'achievements'. From our surgery we thoroughly welcomed equal rights for women, the enormous support of the health service by the state, discrimination against racial hatred, efforts to preserve peace, the condemnation of war as a means to solve national conflicts and much more, and tried to do our bit to realize these projects. On top of this we endeavoured to understand the fundamentals of this development by studying Marxist theory. Yet we foundered on one core question: *class warfare!*[56]

Indeed, Infratest studies conducted among refugees arriving in the FRG showed that 85 per cent of the intelligentsia viewed their flight as political. However, certain professions felt more exposed to political sanctions than others. Artists and medics were rated lowest, with teachers and academics next, and economists, engineers, and administrators feeling most vulnerable.[57] The 1958 crisis nevertheless reveals that even groups who had tried to keep their heads down earlier were fleeing in greater numbers. As Figure 5 shows, the highest rises were among academics, medics, and teachers.

Academics stood out in particular.[58] In 1958 the SED had launched a campaign against 'petit-bourgeois' elements on campuses, extending Marxist–Leninist studies to even science courses and introducing military training. From April the number of faculty members defecting began to rise dramatically.[59] SED attempts to inculcate a partisan view of socialist scholarship were widely rejected in favour of 'universal knowledge'. Academics still regarded themselves as a professional estate bound by its own rules. Thus, accepting a chair in the West was defended

---

[55] Dr Josef H. to Chefarzt Dr Karl V., 9 Dec. 1958, StAL, BT, RdB Leipzig, 1629, fos. 33–5.

[56] Ernst and Irmgard B., 1 Jan. 1959, SAPMO-BArch, DY30/IV2/19/56.

[57] Infratest (ed.), *Die Intelligenzschicht in der Sowjetzone Deutschlands*, vol. 2: *Analyse der Fluchtgründe* (Munich, 1959), Schaubilder 1 and 5.

[58] See also Ilko-Sascha Kowalczuk, *Geist im Dienste der Macht: Hochschulpolitik in der SBZ/DDR 1945 bis 1961* (Berlin: Links, 2003), 515–25; and John Connelly, 'Zur "Republikflucht" von DDR-Wissenschaftlern in den fünfziger Jahren', *Zeitschrift für Geschichtswissenschaft*, 4 (1994), 331–52.

[59] SfHF, 'Quartalsanalyse der Republikfluchten (IV. Quartal 1959)', n.d., SAPMO-BArch, DY30/IV2/9.04/669, fos. 157–62.

as a normal career move, although recipients were liable to be stripped of their titles by their home universities.[60] There were also plenty of push factors. Dr O., who had taken a job at a hydrobiological institute in Denmark, explained that low salary, but also low academic prestige, had been alienating factors. Now, he had a well-equipped laboratory with his own assistant: 'Everything which could only be acquired (or not, as the case may be) with great difficulty, long telephone calls, applications to the rectorate or to Professor K. in person, is routine here.'[61] At Jena, the rector himself, Professor H., fled in August 1958, on the eve of the university's four-hundredth anniversary.[62] Other prominent intellectuals included Ernst Bloch, Professor of Philosophy at Leipzig. After being attacked by the SED as a 'seducer of youth', he stopped lecturing in 1957, and in 1961 opted for the FRG, explaining:

In the first years of my work at the university I enjoyed unrestricted freedom of speech, writing, and teaching. In recent years the situation has increasingly changed. I was driven into isolation, had no opportunity to teach, contact with students was broken, my best pupils were persecuted, punished, the possibility of publicistic activities was forbidden, I could not get published in any journal, and the Aufbau-Verlag in Berlin did not fulfil its contractual obligations regarding my works. So began a tendency to bury me in silence.[63]

The universities of Berlin, Leipzig, and Halle were most badly depleted, with the faculty of medicine accounting for half of all academic losses, followed by science and technology. The humanities, by contrast, were generally less susceptible, reflecting higher ideological conformity and poorer re-employment prospects. Students were also leaving in droves, and whereas previously many had waited until after finals, more first and second years began to leave,[64] including the 21-year-old Rudi Dutschke, future leader of the West German student movement, who fled on his scooter just days before the Wall.[65]

More teachers began to go, too. In April 1958 polytechnics had been announced as part of the further socialization of education, including the switch from half-day to all-day schooling and the sidelining of religious instruction, which offended many practising Christian educationalists. Yet there was general disquiet about politicizing the classroom.[66] In 1958 nearly 11 per cent of

---

[60] BMfiB (ed.), *Bau der Mauer*, 115.

[61] Jürgen O. to Helmuth, 3 Aug. 1961, SAPMO-BArch, DY30/IV2/9.05/143, fos. 272–74.

[62] Foreign Office (Information Research Dept.), 'The Refugee Flow Westwards', May 1960, TNA, FO 975/137.

[63] Cited in Weber, *Geschichte*, 284.

[64] SED-PL (Humboldt-Uni), 'Republikfluchten 1959', 29 Feb. 1960, SAPMO-BArch, DY30/IV2/9.04/669, fos. 144–7. See also Waldemar Krönig and Klaus-Dieter Müller, *Anpassung-Widerstand-Verfolgung: Hochschule und Studenten in der DDR 1945–1961* (Cologne: Verlag Wissenschaft und Politik, 1994), 394–428.

[65] Ulrich Chaussy, *Die drei Leben des Rudi Dutschke: Eine Biographie* (Berlin: Links, 1993), 30.

[66] Joachim S. Hohmann, ' "Wenn Sie dies lesen, bin ich schon auf dem Weg in den Westen": "Republikflüchtige" DDR-Lehrer in den Jahren 1949–1961', *Zeitschrift für Geschichtswissenschaft*,

leavers were heads or deputy heads, and sixth-form teachers were more likely to abscond than junior school colleagues. Stress-related disorders, such as stomach ulcers, were rising. More alarming for the state was the fact that many younger, GDR-trained cadres were going, and not just Nazi-vintage teachers as the SED liked to believe. In 1958 31.5 per cent were under thirty, reaching 36.8 per cent by 1960.[67] At the same time the FRG relaxed regulations that eastern staff must sit catch-up exams. The authorities also became alarmed at the example disappearing teachers were setting pupils. Over 3,000 sixth-formers fled in 1958, compared with fewer than 250 in 1957. The university quota system meant that many were being rejected and recommended instead for a 'practical year' on the production line. Intelligentsia parents were apparently particularly upset at the discrimination their offspring faced in favour of workers' children.[68]

Doctors became *the* professional group most likely to depart, upset by plans for the wind-down of private practices, and fearing salary cuts once the Berlin crisis was resolved.[69] There were also grumblings that 'comrade doctors' were being promoted over non-party colleagues, or had sewn up lucrative army contracts. Since doctors were relatively privileged, the authorities could discern few pecuniary reasons, but noted instead 'that a hostile basic attitude to the GDR was masked by a decent existence and high material income'.[70] Doctors also relished their travel privileges, which allowed them to attend medical congresses in West Germany. There they could observe the advantages of professional status—doctors' wives were still greeted as 'Frau Doktor'—as well as the benefits of a doctor–patient ratio half the GDR's. In 1958 it was noted with alarm that more physicians were fleeing than graduating, one in ten of them specialists. The country was becoming critically short of GPs, ear, nose, and throat specialists, ophthalmologists, neurologists, and paediatricians. When the X-ray specialist in Suhl fled, the entire populace had to travel to neighbouring Erfurt for radiology.[71] By 1959 there were only two eye specialists in Frankfurt/Oder, and four paediatricians in Neubrandenburg.[72] Karl-Marx-Stadters were 'indignant' that their new outpatients clinic was closed for lack

45 (1997), 317. See also id., *Lehrerflucht aus SBZ und DDR 1945–1961: Dokumente zur Geschichte und Soziologie sozialistischer Bildung und Erziehung* (Frankfurt: Peter Lang, 2000).

[67] 'Überblick der Entwicklung der Republikfluchten der Lehrer und Pionierleiter . . .', n.d., SAPMO-BArch, DY30/IV2/9.05/143, fos. 36–38; SED-ZK (Volksbildung), 'Analyse . . .', 9 Mar. 1961, SAPMO-BArch, DY30/IV2/9.05/143, fos. 250–70.

[68] SfHF, 'Analyse der Republikfluchten II. Quartal 1960', 8 Aug. 1960, SAPMO-BArch, DY30/IV2/9.04/669, fo. 232.

[69] Anna Sabine Ernst, *'Die beste Prophylaxe ist der Sozialismus': Ärzte und medizinische Hochschullehrer in der SBZ/DDR 1945–1961* (Münster: Waxmann, 1997), 54–72.

[70] RdB Leipzig (Gesundheits- & Sozialwesen), 'Analyse zur Republikflucht der Ärzte', 14 Jan. 1959, StAL, BT/RdB Leipzig, 1629, fos. 24–7.

[71] SED-ZK (Gewerkschaften, Sozial- & Gesundheitswesen), 'Die Lage unter der medizinischen Intelligenz', 21 June 1958, SAPMO-BArch, DY30/IV2/19/53.

[72] 'Entwurf . . .', 23 Apr. 1959, SAPMO-BArch, DY30/IV2/19/53.

of personnel.[73] Even in the GDR's elite teaching hospital, the Berlin Charité, losses were becoming critical. From 1955 to 1960 it lost 140 doctors (almost a quarter of its complement) and 245 other medical staff, including a number of professors.[74] Since each *Republikflucht* increased the burden among remaining colleagues, they too became more likely to flee. The only recourse was to bring in medics from neighbouring eastern bloc countries. As well as doctors, support staff were leaving, drawn by the opening of a new clinic in West Berlin's Steglitz. East Berlin nurses, it was reported, 'want to be dressed as in the West and glorify everything smuggled in from West Berlin. Many frequent West Berlin bars, have fiancés and friends and shop there.' The fact that patients and nurses were having to purchase equipment such as catheters across the border, or that surgical steel made in the GDR rusted, was also having 'grave ideological consequences'.[75]

The final social group to be noticeably dislocated by a political campaign was farmers (see Figure 6), who had been relatively immobile since 1953. The prospect of collectivization had been looming over the countryside since 1952, but in 1960 it became a reality. Farmers who could not face work in an LPG began to flee.[76] Rural *Republikfluchten* shot up in March 1960, peaking in April and May. Arrivees in the West complained of the psychological terror used to intimidate recalcitrant farmers into collectivizing. Brandenburg was a particular hotspot, reflecting the high number of resettlers there. As well as farmers and their dependants, the whole agrarian infrastructure of tractor drivers, vets, and agronomists was leaving. Rumours abounded that all arrivals in the FRG would receive a tenant farm and 5,000 deutschmarks, as well as an automatic C-certificate. Many apparently already had long-standing links with West German communities, particularly religious believers who received parcels from parish sponsors.[77] The breaking of ties to the land also had an unsettling effect on the rest of the population, and was often far more visible, as farms were left derelict for passers-by to see.

As well as domestic politics, the high politics of the Berlin crisis could influence whether to go or stay. Negotiations could, on the one hand, retard *Republikflucht*, but when these broke down, uncertainty ensued. This, at least, was the Stasi's conclusion, which ascribed the lowest recorded level of December 1958 to hopes pinned to 'the Soviet Berlin proposals'.[78] Likewise, the head

[73] SED-ZK (Gesundheitspolitik), 'Bericht über den Einsatz . . . im Bezirk Karl-Marx-Stadt', 27 Oct. 1960, SAPMO-BArch, DY30/IV2/9.04/669, fos. 270–76.
[74] MdI (IA) to Maron, 1 Feb. 1961, BAB, DO-1/34/21719.
[75] 'Analyse . . .über die Republikflucht im Städtischen Hufelandkrankenhaus und im Städtischen Krankenhaus in Berlin-Buch', n.d. [1959], SAPMO-BArch, DY30/IV2/19/53.
[76] Arnd Bauerkämper, *Ländliche Gesellschaft in der kommunistischen Diktatur: Zwangsmodernisierung und Tradition in Brandenburg 1945–1963* (Cologne: Böhlau, 2002), 456.
[77] MdI (IA), 'Analyse der Republikfluchten in der Landwirtschaft', 12 May 1960, SAPMO-BArch, IV2/13/622.
[78] MfS, 'Bericht über die Entwicklung der Republikflucht im Jahre 1958', 20 Mar. 1959, BStU-ZA, ZAIG 186, fos. 1–21.

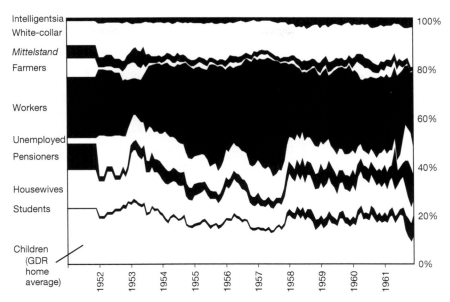

Figure 6. *Republikflucht* by social group, 1952–61 (monthly percentages).
Source: DVP. See Note 1.

of West Berlin's Marienfelde reception camp reported early in the crisis, from conversations with refugees, that: 'In general the situation is not taken too seriously. . . . They even expect a possible alleviation of the situation from the forthcoming negotiations. The threats by the Soviet Union and the Soviet occupation regime are often described as a bluff.' Trust in the steadfastness—or indifference—of the West, seems to have encouraged a wait-and-see attitude.[79] It also seems plausible that 1954's Berlin Council of Foreign Ministers and 1955's Geneva summit had had a similar pacifying effect, and that during the Geneva conference in 1959 farmers were openly deferring decisions to leave pending the outcome. However, high-political bickering militated against these tendencies. As the six-month deadline for the first Khrushchev ultimatum approached, the intelligentsia apparently panicked.[80] The number of doctors leaving in April 1959 tripled over the previous month, and teachers more than doubled, amid rumours that: 'On 26 May 1959 the hatches will be battened down, the last opportunity to jump is then closed; it's time to pack your bags.'[81] By June, however, with the Geneva summit under way, levels normalized. Conversely,

[79] Leiter des Notaufnahmeverfahrens in Berlin, 'Ursachen der Abschwächung des Flüchtlings-stroms', 6 Feb. 1959, BAK, B 106/24843.
[80] 'Jahresanalyse . . . 1959', n.d., BAB, DO-1/11/966, fos. 90–105.
[81] 'Entwurf . . .', 23 Apr. 1959, SAPMO-BArch, DY30/IV2/19/53.

when the Paris summit collapsed a year later, in May 1960, over the U-2 incident, flights rose. Academics were reported to 'be disappointed at the failure of the summit' and fearful of the rescinding of travel to the West.[82] As the Volkspolizei summarized: 'whenever the adversary plays up the West Berlin question, a rise in *Republikfluchten* was ascertained'.[83] The temporary closure of East Berlin to West Germans in September 1960 increased edginess. Engineers expected an 'intensification of the situation leading to a blocking of the sector boundary. There is talk of a certain stampede panic.'[84] Indeed, in the months before the actual building of the Wall, there were constant rumours circulating in the GDR that the borders would be closed one way or another, and, as evidenced in the previous chapter, the stalled diplomatic offensive of 1958–61 only fuelled such suspicions.

There is thus much to be said for a 'repoliticization' of *Republikflucht* from 1958 to 1961 as a result of more aggressive social and foreign policies. However, these factors, even at their peak, probably still only accounted for a minority, largely confined to the intelligentsia. Between 1953 and 1961, it should be remembered, only 14.2 per cent of refugees were deemed even by the Federal authorities to have left the GDR under political duress.[85] Nevertheless, it became a truism for some observers (usually West German) to assume that the go-getters left, while only the no-hopers remained: 'the daft residue' ('der doofe Rest' as a colloquial 'DDR' abbreviation had it). This assumes a great deal. Many who chose to stay did so out of political principle and were prepared to cause trouble. Christians felt a calling to remain.[86] Marxist dissidents also had a mission to reform what they saw as a travesty of true socialism. And as we shall see in a later chapter, East Germans were by no means the passive dupes some West Germans would like to have believed, but were masters of passive resistance and low-level dissent.

ECONOMIC FACTORS

Nor does politics explain the overall bulge in departures from 1955–57. By the mid-1950s, would-be SED reformers were beginning to doubt party conspiracy theories.[87] 'One should no longer speak of *Republikflucht*, since the majority

---

[82] SfHF, 'Analyse der Republikfluchten II. Quartal 1960', 8 Aug. 1960, SAPMO-BArch, DY30/IV2/9.04/669, fos. 223–40.

[83] 'Stand und Entwicklung der Bevölkerungsbewegung im Jahre 1960', 13 Feb. 1961, BAB, DO-1/11/967, fos. 37–60.

[84] Magistrat von Groß-Berlin (IA), 'Bericht - III. Quartal 1960', 22 Oct. 1960, BAB, DO-1/34/530/2.

[85] Heidemeyer, *Flucht*, 47 and 55.

[86] Karl-Heinz Ducke in Schweitzer *et al.* (eds), *Lebensläufe*, 91–9.

[87] Peter Grieder, *The East German Leadership, 1946–1973: Conflict and Crisis* (Manchester: Manchester University Press, 1999), 118.

of cases were not *Republikflucht* but emigration', noted a policy discussion in November 1956. 'The majority of those leaving the German Democratic Republic are doing so not because they disagree with our order, but above all for economic and other reasons. They are not fleeing but emigrating.'[88] Recent research on western policies has tended to confirm the migratory aspects of the exodus.[89] A disproportionate number of refugees were of working age. Already in the late nineteenth century there had been a labour migration from the less developed East to the more industrialized West. Figure 3 suggests elements of the classic migration curve, as proportionally more breadwinning males departed in the first half of the 1950s. Although the criminalization of *Republikflucht* forced many to take their immediate families with them, explaining the high numbers of housewives and children in the early 1950s, the tail of older people, especially women, grew perceptibly in the latter half of the decade.[90]

With such a strong neighbouring economy in the Federal Republic there were obviously strong pull factors at work. By the mid-1950s the FRG had overcome its unemployment problems and needed skilled labour. In 1955, according to one West German civil servant, the 'tangibly growing labour shortage' required coordination between the refugee administration and the Ministry of Labour.[91] Unlike the earlier influx of expellees into the western zones, billeted in rural areas such as Bavaria, Lower Saxony, and Schleswig-Holstein, until the manufacturing centres revived, the lion's share of GDR refugees were placed straight into industrial *Länder* such as North Rhine-Westphalia (37 per cent), Baden-Württemberg (18 per cent) and West Berlin (9 per cent).[92] A seasonal job market also developed, for instance in the building industry, as casual labour migrated to West Germany in the summer, only to return in October, helping to explain the fluctuations of refugees and returnees in Figure 4.[93]

Much head-hunting was market-driven and privately sponsored, rather than the government conspiracy the SED claimed. Some western firms wrote directly, or via representatives, to skilled workers with job offers.[94] Among the professions, specialist congresses for doctors, technicians, or engineers, and even the GDR's

---

[88] SED-ZK (Leitende Staatsorgane), 'Niederschrift . . . zu den Fragen der Republikflucht am 23.11.1956', 4 Dec. 1956, SAPMO-BArch, DY30/IV2/13/397.

[89] Heidemeyer, *Flucht*, 35–6 and 57; this was even recognized at the time in some quarters: Dietrich Storbeck, 'Flucht oder Wanderung?', *Soziale Welt*, 14 (1963), 153–71.

[90] For an integrated approach to postwar demographic shifts see Siegfried Bethlehem, *Heimatvertreibung, DDR-Flucht, Gastarbeiterzuwanderung: Wanderungsströme und Wanderungspolitik in der Bundesrepublik Deutschland* (Stuttgart: Klett-Cotta, 1982), 81–106 on the GDR.

[91] 'Teilniederschrift über die Dienstbesprechung . . .', 24 May 1955, BAK, B 150/4080a. See also Bethlehem, *Heimatvertreibung*, 86.

[92] *Statistisches Jahrbuch für die Bundesrepublik Deutschland: 1962* (Stuttgart: Kohlhammer, 1962), 68.

[93] Seifert, 'Republikfluchten', 16 Sept. 1957, BAB, DO-1/11/964, fo. 161.

[94] For a selection see: BStU-ZA, ZAIG 10353–4.

own Leipzig trade fairs, provided a meeting-place for employers and potential employees. Moreover, despite national division, company loyalties had not been completely ruptured. There is indeed evidence that, as entrepreneurs relocated westwards, they encouraged former workers in the East to follow, for instance at the Zeiss optics works in Jena and its western spin-off, Zeiss Opton in Baden-Württemberg.[95] The former IG Farben was also scattered between the Leuna chemicals plant and Agfa-Wolfen film factory in the East, and Bayer, Hoechst, and BASF in the West. Western personnel departments allegedly kept card indexes on workers, sending food parcels for long service to former eastern employees. In the district of Forst in Cottbus, textile workers jokingly called the new western plant at Iserloh 'Little Forst',[96] and at one friendly football match between two sister works, three eastern players even 'transferred' themselves, permanently, at half-time.[97]

Nevertheless, the Volkspolizei soon began to distinguish between such 'active recruitment', and passive recruitment generated by the Federal boom, media, and tourism, as well as 'the whole way of life in West Germany'.[98] Anyone with access to the western press could read the jobs columns, and word-of-mouth, letters from former workmates and radio ensured that East German workers had a clear picture of the labour market. The Leipzig police intercepted letters from departed workers which 'depict West German conditions and their personal experience in the rosiest of colours and incite them to *Republikflucht*'. It was here that young East Germans were gaining 'notions of the "golden West", of an unbridled, easy life'.[99] Regina V., for instance, a technical drawer, itemized to her friend the new coat, dress, leather shoes, bedclothes, and towels she had bought with her first wage packet.[100] Former workmates swaggered in front of ex-colleagues in their new chrome-plated cars. One doctor was visited by the wife of a former colleague, 'dripping in gold from head to toe' and rhapsodizing about conditions in the West.[101] Indeed, one of the SED's stock conspiracy theories was to blame the moral corruption of menfolk on their consumerist wives. Among the bourgeoisie, in particular, it was claimed that parents-in-law were pressuring sons-in-law to provide their daughters with modern comforts such as foreign holidays, cars, and a lavish social life.[102]

[95] 'Bericht einer Brigade der Kreisleitung der SED Jena-Stadt . . .', 17 Nov. 1957, SAPMO-BArch, DY30/IV2/5/843, fos. 4–11.
[96] Untitled, 1955, BA, DO-1/11/963, fos. 70–99.
[97] 'Beispiele über Republikfluchten . . .', BAB, DO-1/11/962, fos. 161–2.
[98] HVDVP, 'Analyse', 1956, BAB, DO-1/11/963, fos. 225–9.
[99] 'Staatsanwaltschaft', n.d. [May 1961], StAL, BT/RdB Leipzig, 3930, fos. 10–12.
[100] Seifert, 'Republikfluchten', 10 Oct. 1955, BAB, DO-1/1/963, fo. 50.
[101] 'Argumente zur Begründung der R-Flucht im Ges.-Wesen', 18 Apr. 1959, SAPMO-BArch, DY30/IV2/19/56.
[102] SfHF, 'Analyse der Republikflucht', 8 Aug. 1959, SAPMO-BArch, DY30/IV2/9.04/669, fos. 94–107.

There were, nonetheless, important push factors in the East German economy too.[103] Workers at dismantled factories—nearly a third suffered this fate—did not always find work when production resumed and so headed west instead.[104] The Economic Main Task exposed further underlying weaknesses in the command economy, unable to keep up with a generous wage system, which raised many workers' hopes through ambitious training schemes, only to dash them on the production line. Many leavers regarded themselves as skilled workers being paid unskilled rates. Among engineering workers leaving in 1959–60, well over half were described as unskilled and nearly half of Halle's leavers,[105] despite the fact that over two-thirds of male workers in the GDR were categorized as skilled.[106] In particular, younger workers finishing apprenticeships found themselves employed below expectations.[107] In Neubrandenburg youths even had their workbooks stamped with the words 'Only to be employed in agriculture or the Volkspolizei'. A trained mechanic in Berlin complained in his letter of resignation of 'continuous down-time, in which I joined in almost every unskilled worker's job, from store worker, potato carrier, driver's mate, mail-order worker, coalman, furniture haulier, transport worker to navvy'.[108] Since workers were paid a piece rate, idle production lines meant thinner wage packets. At one dockyard in Rostock several hundred workers were on stand-by, caused by raw material shortages, poor management, and a labour surplus: 'Repeatedly the workers express such views as: if we don't achieve continuous production soon, we're going west.'[109]

The key economic group, for the SED, was the so-called 'technical intelligentsia'.[110] Engineers were in greatest demand in the West, but under enormous pressure in the East to fulfil the plan and deluged in paperwork. British observers noted that ever

more refugees who had held positions of some responsibility [had] decided to come out because their jobs had become impossible to perform as a result of defections further

---

[103] This is somewhat underplayed in Jörg Roesler, 'Rübermachen': Politische Zwänge, ökonomisches Kalkül und verwandschaftliche Bindungen als häufigste Motive der deutsch-deutschen Wanderungen zwischen 1953 und 1961, *Hefte zur DDR Geschichte*, 85 (2004).

[104] Seifert, 'Republikfluchten', 18 Sept. 1957, BAB, DO-1/11/964, fo. 162.

[105] SPK (Kader), 'Bericht über die Republikabgänge . . . im Bereich des Maschinenbaus', 30 July 1960, SAPMO-BArch, IV2/2.029/114, fos. 92–105; SED-BL Halle (Sicherheit), 'Einschätzung des Standes der Republikfluchten . . .', 26 Aug. 1960, LAM, BPA SED Halle, IV/2/4/992, fos. 50–61.

[106] 'Übersicht über die Anzahl der Produktionsarbeiter . . .', n.d., SAPMO-BArch, DY30/IV2/6.08/46, fos. 220–2.

[107] 'Analyse über Republikfluchten . . .', n.d. [1956], BAB, DO-1/34/21723.

[108] 'Stand und Entwicklung der Bevölkerungsbewegung im Jahre 1960', 13 Feb. 1961, BAB, DO-1/11/967, fos. 37–60.

[109] 'Jahresbericht zur Bevölkerungsbewegung über die D-Linie', BAB, DO-1/34/21723.

[110] Raymond G. Stokes, *Constructing Socialism: Technology and Change in East Germany, 1945–1990* (Baltimore: Johns Hopkins University Press, 2000), 45–6.

down the line. The effect of the refugee flow on the economy is relative to the magnitude of the tasks which the economy is set.[111]

By 1959 it was mainly younger engineers, employed in research and planning offices, who felt most constrained. Furthermore, the technocratic career ladder was tied to SED membership, which also alarmed the pre-1945 'old intelligentsia'. When staff saw colleagues under MfS investigation for shortcomings, flight often seemed the easiest way out. Construction engineers in the capital were thus suffering from 'fear of responsibility' because of 'overhasty deadlines'.[112] One disappearing engineer refused to be made accountable for what he saw as a catalogue of planning errors.[113] At another office several engineers felt 'constantly threatened'. Following the arrest of their former technical director, two other section heads had fled in sympathy.[114] Dr Gerhard R., technical chief of the Institute of Semiconductors in Frankfurt/Oder for eight years, wrote to his former boss: 'I have had to realize that the non-party scientist is only supported in his work as long as he is absolutely needed'; skilled personnel were being steadily replaced by party men. After the MfS had attempted to pump him for information on colleagues, he became aware of 'an extensive system of all-round control, surveillance and informing on the leading staff in the institute'.[115] Indeed, in the GDR context it makes little sense neatly to disaggregate politics and economics.

In the chemicals industry the story was little different. GDR delegates were being barred from attendance at western conferences for fear of exposing East Germany's technological backwardness. Again there were complaints about the mass of paperwork in the planned economy. Reporters typically highlighted cases of recruitment by West German firms. Many senior chemists, taking their research teams with them, were apparently hoping to receive pensions from the estate of IG Farben.[116] Nor could these losses be made good by the return of 'specialists' deported to the Soviet Union in 1946. Of fifty-five returning chemical experts, twenty-six immediately fled west. In 1960 *Republikflucht* by the intelligentsia assumed disastrous proportions at the GDR's elite chemicals plants. Leuna lost twenty-two, compared with eleven the previous year; Buna seventeen versus six; and the Wolfen film and paints factories nineteen and seventeen, versus four and one respectively. Moreover, a new, younger pattern emerged. West German plants were apparently sending congratulatory telegrams

[111] Ledwidge to Duff, 27 July 1961, TNA, FO 371/160503/CG1018/22.
[112] Zentralkommission f. Staatl. Kontrolle, 'Republikflucht von Ingenieuren und Angestellten . . .', 14 Oct. 1955, SAPMO-BArch, DY30/IV2/13/396.
[113] Willi W. to Herr L., 18 Feb. 1953, SAPMO-BArch, DY30/IV2/13/394.
[114] MdI (IA), 'Vermerk zur Fragen der Bevölkerungsbewegung im PKB-Kohle Berlin . . .', 10 July 1959, BA, DO-1/34/21721.
[115] Gerhard R. to Prof. F., 5 Nov. 1960, DY30/JIV2/202/68.
[116] 'Bericht über die Republikabgänge aus der chemischen Industrie', 23 Apr. 1959, SAPMO-BArch, DY30/IV2/9.04/669, fos. 72–87.

to students receiving distinctions in exams.[117] Half of 1960's leavers were under thirty and thus products of the GDR's education system, but complaining of having 'no real future in the plant'.[118] The MfS confirmed that 'various older members of the intelligentsia cling to their posts without being competent to fill them'.[119]

The result of the domestic crisis was that by 1960, in crucial areas of the economy, engineers and skilled workers were leaving in irreplaceable numbers. In Berlin the Television Works in Köpenick lost twenty-one engineers and seventy-five skilled workers; the Radio Works eleven and sixty-four; TRO two and sixty-two respectively.[120] As a whole, the chemicals industry lost 2,211 workers, and engineering 8,402, including 2,406 in electronics, as well as 1,723 from heavy industry and 3,328 from construction.[121] The exodus was also having knock-on effects for those remaining. Fleeing shopkeepers left behind dissatisfied customers. Individual factories took to self-provisioning. The State Planning Commission began to warn of serious problems ahead. The labour pool was threatening to shrink by almost 10 per cent over the course of the current Seven-Year Plan, as reserves dried up.[122] By May 1961, even Ulbricht admitted that the failures of the Economic Main Task were causing more flights, which, in a vicious cycle, were forcing the leadership to scale back planning targets.[123] What had started as an attempt by economic means to create East Germany's own pull factor was only accelerating the brain-drain.

TRIGGER FACTORS

Situational predispositions, political convictions, and economic difficulties formed a complex cocktail of motives, but which often still required a catalyst. Without the benefit of hindsight, it was difficult for the would-be leaver to discern a clear point of no return amidst what were often creeping developments. Nor should one forget the strong pressures to stay: family loyalties, educational

---

[117] MdI (IA), 'Analyse über die Republikfluchten aus der chemischen Industrie', n.d. [June 1959], BAB, DO-1/34/21721.

[118] SED-BL Halle (BPKK), 'Analyse über die Rep. Flucht', Feb. 1961, LAM, BPA SED Halle, IV2/4/995, fos. 36–48.

[119] MfS-ZAIG, 'Bericht über die Entwicklung der Republikflucht 1960 . . .', 28 Oct. 1960, BStU-ZA, ZAIG 247, fo. 102.

[120] PdVP Berlin (K), 'Republikfluchten', 21 Jan. 1961, LAB (STA), Rep. 26.1/Nr. 481, fos. 1–5.

[121] 'Stand und Entwicklung der Bevölkerungsbewegung im Jahre 1960', 13 Feb. 1961, BAB, DO-1/11/967, fos. 37–60.

[122] Jörg Roesler, 'Ende der Arbeitskräfteknappheit in der DDR? Erwartete und unerwartete Wirkungen der Grenzschließung auf wirtschaftlichem Gebiet' in Daniel Küchenmeister (ed.), *Der Mauerbau: Krisenverlauf—Weichenstellung—Resultate* (Berlin: Berliner Debatte, 2001), 74–87.

[123] Steiner, 'Vom Überholen eingeholt', 260.

opportunities, job responsibilities, and roots to home and hearth.[124] The decision to go could be an agonizing one, as one doctor explained:

You know my practice, you know how attached I am to my patients, to my magnificent apartment and my colleagues. I am sitting here in the same mood as yesterday on Christmas Eve, as I went with my wife through all the rooms, through everything we had built up from nothing, since as Silesians we had lost everything. I am sitting here at a friend's without any immediate prospect of a post or apartment, and know that I will have a significantly more difficult time in the near future. . . . And despite this, yesterday I left behind everything I had previously treasured in the GDR, since it had finally become clear to me that staying in the GDR was jeopardizing my freedom.[125]

So how did individuals take the plunge? Many *Republikfluchten* were well prepared and executed with almost military precision. Given Stasi surveillance and the penalties attached, departure had to be discreet, prepared in secret before slipping quietly away. The state often remained in the dark about motives. As one shop-floor comrade lamented, 'one can do little to prevent *R-Fluchten* because if it is mentioned, everybody keeps quiet'.[126] From 1952 to 1960 47 per cent of refugees arrived alone. There were frequent letters of apology to remaining relatives. Soon after absconding, Günter K. sought forgiveness from his wife Regina for concealing his impending departure. As a trusted party security functionary in Leipzig, he had said nothing to his parents either.[127] Dr Z. had decided a year in advance that he was leaving, and drove every Sunday to West Berlin—a total of 126 times!—where family possessions were sent to Nuremberg in 465 separate parcels.[128] During the 1953 crisis the West Berlin authorities had also noticed that the numbers of 'spontaneous' flights were far fewer than calculated departures, indicating unhappiness brewing over a long period. 'These prepare the flight often not only days but weeks before departure and it requires only a last slight impetus in order to go.'[129]

Sometimes the desire to leave remained latent, slowly kindled by the 'policy of pinpricks' by small-time state officials, as one doctor put it,[130] or by another as 'an accumulation of small everyday unpleasantnesses'.[131] It often took only a trivial incident to trigger the final decision. Some bore the hallmarks of a hasty departure, with reading glasses left behind or valuables left standing. One SED policy-maker diagnosed *Republikflucht* as 'above all a psycho-political problem.

---

[124] Thomas Scholze and Falk Blask, *Halt! Grenzgebiet! Leben im Schatten der Mauer* (Berlin: BasisDruck, 1992), 56.

[125] R.U. to Chefarzt, n.d., SAPMO-BArch, DY30/IV2/19/56.

[126] SED-ZK (PO), 'Information' Nr. 53, 26 Apr. 1961, SAPMO-BArch, DY30/IV2/5/294, fos. 495 and 496.

[127] Günter K. to Regina K., 30 Aug. 1960, SAPMO-BArch, DY30/IV2/12/112, fo. 215.

[128] VPKA Leipzig (PM), 'Analyse . . . Juli 1961', 2 Aug. 1961, StAL, BDVP 24.1/494, fo. 96.

[129] Senator für Sozialwesen, 'Die Flüchtlingssituation Mitte Juni 1953', n.d., LAB, B Rep. 008–02/241.

[130] SED-ZK (Gesundheitspolitik) to Hager, 8 Sept. 1960, SAPMO-BArch, DY30/IV2/19/55.

[131] Stellv. Kreisarzt Saalfeld to Wetzel, 12 Sept. 1960, BAB, DO-1/34/21721.

Some of our population have no sense of political security, but instead a feeling of political pressure and insecurity, when an essentially inconsequential cause triggers a *Republikflucht*.'[132] This was also recognized at local level: 'Aggravation at the many petty things which constrain daily work, and are not changed despite constant hints, becomes the straw which breaks the camel's back. A short circuit reaction leads to *Republikflucht*.'[133] Here is a case in point, where one blown fuse blew another:

The physicist Günther Sch., employed at the Institute of Semiconductor Technology in Teltow, bought a refrigerator which needed repairing a short time later, and he vented his irritation to a workmate. The colleague informed the party secretary about comrade Sch.'s allegedly negative attitude. Without checking the circumstances or talking to the physicist, the party secretary held a discussion with other colleagues about the incident. Sch., who heard of it, felt threatened and discriminated against compared with other colleagues, and committed *Republikflucht*.[134]

Observers in the West also knew about the 'short circuit reaction'. They believed that most East Germans had learnt to accommodate themselves to the regime, some more superficially than others. Sixty-nine per cent of the intelligentsia interviewed by Infratest were deemed to be conforming; 19 per cent superficially; but only 10 per cent could be said to be actively opposing.[135] Nevertheless, considerable emotional energy and self-denigration was invested in kow-towing to superiors, particularly when expertise was sacrificed to political correctness. As the Czech dissident Václav Havel also noted when dealing with incompetent superiors, 'nothing remains forgotten. All the fear one has endured, the dissimulation one has been forced into, all the painful and degrading buffoonery, and, worst of all, perhaps, the feeling of displayed cowardice—all this settles and accumulates somewhere on the bottom of our social consciousness, quietly fermenting.'[136] Beneath the veneer of conformist behaviour, attitudes could still be critical. As one departing professor wrote:

No letter in my whole life has been as hard as this one. For more than ten years I have been trying to save face, to remain honest to myself but still to give the state its due. I cannot do so any longer. I had to be hypocritical and deceive those who trusted me.[137]

The longer this process had gone on, the more individuals had to lose in breaking out. An element of guilt prevented much further introspection.

---

[132] 'Hauptgründe für die Republikflucht', SAPMO-BArch, DY30/IV2/13/397.

[133] SED-ZK (Gesundheitspolitik), 'Bericht über den Einsatz . . .', 27 Oct. 1960, SAPMO-BArch, DY30/IV2/9.04/669, fos. 270–6.

[134] 'Beispiel Ursachen RF I. Quartal 1961', BAB, DO-1/11/967, fos. 78–83.

[135] Infratest (ed.), *Die Intelligenzschicht in der Sowjetzone Deutschlands, Bd. II: Analyse der Fluchtgründe* (Munich, October 1959).

[136] Václav Havel, *Living in Truth* (London: Faber, 1987), 31.

[137] K. to Dekan of Fak. f. Technologie, TH Dresden, 28 July 1960, SAPMO-BArch, DY30/IV2/9.04/668, fo. 85.

Flights occurred when the discrepancy between outward behaviour and under-lying attitudes became too great. Trigger factors were divided by Infratest into political, work-related, and home-related. For instance, among the intelligentsia 50 per cent of ruptures were adjudged political; 28 per cent career-related; and 20 per cent family-related and 'apolitical'.[138] A strong majority found the deci-sion to leave difficult, mainly because of their jobs, but also for ethical and family reasons, with 30 per cent fearing their future in the West and 19 per cent still feeling attached to their *Heimat*. Fewer than a quarter found the break easy.[139] Over half claimed to have made no serious preparations for flight; a third had seriously contemplated leaving; and a further 14 per cent had actually made concrete preparations. Almost half the sample ascribed the final decision to some change in their circumstances, with only a quarter acting on their own volition.

In the final analysis it is difficult to disentangle politics, from economics, from situation, as one British observer visiting a refugee camp in West Germany in early August 1961 discovered, while interviewing a group of articulate technicians. The dreariness of the regime, fears for their children's future, lack of consumer commodities, and the general absence of individual liberty were all cited as long-term causes. 'I had the impression strongly, however, . . . that although the actual decision to flee was often prompted by some change in individual material circumstances, hatred of the political manifestations of Communism was at least as strong a factor as living conditions.'[140] Perhaps. What does seem clear is that the push factors inside the GDR were getting worse in the late 1950s and early 1960s, and that for the intelligentsia political factors were re-emerging which had lain dormant since 1953. As even Ulbricht candidly admitted in January 1961: 'In my assessment 60 per cent of *Republikfluchten* can be ascribed to deficiencies in our own work.'[141]

DISAPPEARING ACTS: BLACKMAILING THE SYSTEM

Like most dictatorships, the GDR secretly wished to be loved. 'We need everybody' ran one favourite slogan. This was certainly the official line after 1952, not only for prestige but for economic reasons. Consequently, for those who remained in East Germany the open border offered negotiating possibilities. As observed in the introduction, Hirschman suggested that when individuals can exit a situation, their bargaining power with authority is significantly strengthened. In the wording of petitions Mühlberg has likewise identified a rhetoric of threat, where leaving the country was the most extreme variant.[142]

---

[138] Infratest (ed.), *Intelligenzschicht*, ii, 8.   [139] Ibid., 52.
[140] Welbore Ker minute, n.d. [Aug. 1961], TNA, FO 371/160503/CG1018/26.
[141] Ulbricht at SED-PB, 4 Jan. 1961, SAPMO-BArch, DY30/I IV2/2/744, fos. 12–114.
[142] Mühlberg, *Bürger, Bitten und Behörden*, 233–6.

Ross, too, has highlighted the uses of the open border in dealing citizens a 'trump card' versus the state.[143] Most of these pre-Wall negotiations appear to have been self-interested, however, rather than to recuperate the system as a whole, which is an important distinction to make with the situation before 1989. The regime itself had chosen a system of divide and rule, privileging certain groups over others, and the population responded in kind. The stakes in the everyday frontiers of power were often low, but all the more vigorously contested. Loyalty was conditional, and citizens were quite prepared to explore how far they could exact local patronage in return for their continued willingness to stay in the GDR.

The intelligentsia, in particular, recognized its scarcity value and was prepared to make loaded demands, for salary increases, housing, or research materials.[144] At the Wolfen paint plant in December 1960, for instance, sixty-three pay rise applications were pending, where white-collar workers were dropping heavy hints that 'in Leverkusen [home of Bayer], or other large factories in West Germany, more money would be paid for the same job'.[145] There were also complaints about accommodation, with engineers refusing to join housing associations with three- to four-year waiting lists or to accept poky apartments. Some doctors

assume . . . that they are 'scarcity goods' in the GDR and can 'reap the consequences' at any time, making demands for unjustifiable western trips and unnecessary congress visits, sixth-form and university places for intellectually mediocre and politically negative children, demands for the approval of private practice for purely commercial reasons instead of state work, demands for payment over the going rate for contracts above the quota, etc.[146]

There were even cases of absentee citizens writing from West Germany with wish-lists to secure their return. Dr U. cited his good surgical statistics: 'My minimum requirement would be what I had in Apolda', with a salary of 3,000 marks (he claimed he could earn fivefold in the FRG) and support for his post-doctoral research, but preferably his own district hospital, adding: 'Anyway, the matter is not urgent. I am not on the street or starving.'[147] It was also possible for academics to play see-saw politics after being offered jobs in the West. Dr P. of Leipzig left in July 1959. A specialist in oriental law, he was head-hunted by Munich and offered a chair. Three Leipzig professors then wrote to the Secretary for Higher Education, requesting that P. be given his

---

[143] Corey Ross, *Constructing*, 143–60; id., 'Before the Wall: East Germans, Communist Authority, and the Mass Exodus to the West', *Historical Journal*, 45 (2002), 459–80: 478.

[144] See also Ross, 'Before the Wall', 471–8.

[145] SPK (Chemie), 'Auszug aus dem Situationsbericht des VEB Farbenfabrik Wolfen vom 6.12.1960', SAPMO-BArch, DY30/IV2/6.03/62, fos. 258–9.

[146] 'Beispiele für Ursachen der Republikflucht nach Berichten und Briefen', n.d. [1959], SAPMO-BArch, DY30/IV2/19/56.

[147] Dr Dr Kurt U. to Prof. Dr S., May 1959, SAPMO-BArch, DY30/IV2/19/56.

own institute and chair, unsuccessfully as it transpired.[148] As well as pure self-interest, however, there were nascent signs of professional lobbying, more worrying to the regime. One group of doctors thus demanded a form of co-determination in policy-making and legislation, and a break with Health Ministry nepotism.[149]

This bargaining was not limited to social elites. According to the Interior Ministry it was spreading to workers too: 'There is a widespread popular belief that one first has to commit RF to obtain an apartment or a better-paid position. Likewise, returning persons are supposedly treated much more generously than citizens who support the construction of our Republic.'[150] One professional comedian even mocked the situation on stage: 'If it is a flat you quest, then wander over to the West. Upon your re-embarkment, your reward is an apartment.'[151] Petitions desks bore the brunt of this popular resentment. Herr P. wrote indignantly to President Pieck:

This is a fine thing: these returnees are just laughing at us oldsters. They bunk, we work, they come back because the streets are not paved with gold on the other side, but then move happy as Larry into waiting apartments. We have the privilege of keeping working while suffering the housing shortage.[152]

Willy M. complained that 'while doctors (who stay over there with their cars) and businessmen are issued interzonal passes, I, with my honest and positive willingness to help in the reconstruction, am refused one. How can one honestly believe in justice and right?'[153] Loyal citizens 'drew comparisons with their own situation' and stressed 'their skilled work and positive attitude to the Workers' and Peasants' State'.[154] Workers in particular felt discriminated against, pointing to their 'achievements on the production line and sometimes in the National Reconstruction Programme'.[155] The very egalitarian basis of socialism was being questioned. Young men also realized that with a criminal record for *Republikflucht* they could render themselves unfit for military service in the GDR.[156] What is more, the level of threat appears to have been linked to the state's perceived willingness to make concessions. Especially once the New Course was launched in 1953, which softened the rapid construction of socialism announced the year before, 'petitioners are trying to assert their housing wishes by "threatening"

---

[148] SED-ZK (Wissenschaften), 'Mitteilung an die Abteilungsleitung', 31 July 1959, SAPMO-BArch, DY30/IV2/9.04/668, fos. 94–6.

[149] MfS-ZAIG, '2. Bericht', 8 Jan. 1959, BStU-ZA, ZAIG 166, fo. 8.

[150] 'Vorschläge für die Beratung der Kommission des ZK am 28.2.1957', 28 Feb. 1957, BAB, DO-1/34/21723.

[151] 3rd quarter 1956 *Eingaben* report, SAPMO-BArch, DY30/IV2/5/252.

[152] June 1953 *Eingaben* report, SAPMO-BArch, DY30/IV2/5/251, fo. 118.

[153] 3rd quarter 1958 *Eingaben* report, SAPMO-BArch, DY30/IV2/5/253.

[154] 4th quarter 1959 *Eingaben* report, SAPMO-BArch, DY30/IV2/5/253.

[155] 2nd quarter 1960 *Eingaben* report, SAPMO-BArch, DY30/IV2/5/253, fos. 71–149.

[156] 'Beispiel Ursachen RF I. Quartal 1961', BAB, DO-1/11/967, fos. 78–83.

to go to West Germany should their request be refused'.[157] By 1956, the year of destalinization, there was an epidemic of such threats. Thus, while travel petitions abated because of the liberalization of interzonal traffic (see below), this merely opened another door of complaint on the housing front. Local authorities were instructed to call petitioners' bluff, and although many threats turned out to be empty, officials had to invest a huge amount of time and effort in personal interviews.

In response, the regime developed a repertoire of concessionary policies. It would be wrong, therefore, to see the SED as totally inflexible. Already in June 1953, under Soviet pressure,[158] it was admitted in the famous Politbüro resolution introducing the New Course that 'serious mistakes' had been made, leading to 'numerous persons leaving the Republic'. Returnees were to have confiscated property, jobs, and ration cards restored, and farmers in particular were to have their holdings returned or receive compensation.[159] At the same time—and the importance of this cannot be overemphasized—legal travel to the West was massively expanded, as Figure 7 attests in the following chapter. Further reforms came in 1956 with destalinization. Doctors were to be exempt from some public chores, and to receive the top ration card, additional Intourist holidays to the Soviet Union, and loyalty bonuses.[160] Teachers were also concili- ated with higher salaries and more sixth-form provision for their offspring, while summer camp duty—many an educator's annual horror—was abolished.[161] Yet, given the state's limited resources, concessions had to be rationed, often to the intelligentsia. In September 1958 the SED sought to placate doctors, promising more research and publication opportunities, access to West German congresses and more university places for privileged children. Private practices and pharmacies were to continue. Even holidays and pensions were to be handled by a special doctors' commission.[162] When the mass exodus resumed in 1960, moreover, a high-level trouble-shooting team of Mielke as Minister of State Security and Honecker as SED security chief, as well as the Interior Minister and the SED's ideological chief, Kurt Hager, was tasked with drawing up a containment policy.[163] Hager appealed to material needs. Party and state were to curb their own sectarian behaviour, ministries to investigate 'how the intelli- gentsia can be unburdened of superfluous reports, statistics and investigations',

---

[157] Apr. 1954 *Eingaben* report, SAPMO-BArch, DY30/IV2/5/251, fo. 472.

[158] Bispinck, 'Republikflucht', 291.

[159] SED-PB communiqué, 9 June 1953, in SED-ZK (ed.), *Dokumente der Sozialistischen Einheitspartei Deutschlands*, iv, 428–31.

[160] Gew. f. Gesundheitswesen-ZV to FDGB-BuVo, 17 July 1956, SAPMO-BArch, DY30/IV2/ 19/54.

[161] Gew. Unterricht & Erziehung-ZV, 'Beschluss des Politbüros über Maßnahmen gegen die Republikflucht', 20 July 1956, SAPMO-BArch, DY30/IV2/9.05/142, fos. 14–21.

[162] 'Zu Fragen des Gesundheitswesens und der medizinischen Intelligenz', in SED-ZK (ed.), *Dokumente der Sozialistischen Einheitspartei Deutschlands* (East Berlin, 1961), vii, 348–52.

[163] SED-ZK (Sek), 5 Oct. 1960, SAPMO-BArch, DY30/J IV2/3/706, fo. 2.

and the State Planning Commission to provide more housing. Yet more trips were to be organized to the socialist bloc and local councils to supply more fashion goods.[164] But even at this late stage, in November 1960, it is clear that the party leadership was thinking in public policy terms, rather than physical walls.

The response of those targeted was sceptical acceptance. Improvements were viewed as a tactical 'withdrawal by the party'.[165] Conversely, it was expected that if the Berlin crisis were resolved 'to the GDR's satisfaction, the previous position of doctors will be revised and all privileges dropped'.[166] One dentist was contemptuous of the carrot-and-stick approach of the visiting law enforcement officers who inspected his apartment:

Since all the objects whose absence might arouse suspicion of *Republikflucht* were in the flat, the men contented themselves with promising my wife heaven and earth if I do not 'flee the Republic'. I just needed to express a wish regarding a practice or a new apartment and it would be fulfilled.[167]

Unmoved, he fled. In prominent cases the state resorted to outright bribery to retain experts. In late 1960 Professor D., paediatrics director at the Berlin Charité, was offered a chair at Gießen in West Germany. Fearful of western publicity, the Secretary of Higher Education, the rector of the Humboldt University, President of the Academy of Sciences, and Minister of Health, all held personal talks with D. to dissuade him. The Stasi was called in to ascertain his weaknesses, suggesting a top-of-the-range Volga car, 'since the comrades of the MfS indicated that the D. family, especially his wife, was open to material gain'. A large villa was also dangled, but after much agonizing, D. finally fled, leaving his apartment with all his furniture and clothes, 'in great haste'.[168] Occasionally colleagues would even be sent to retrieve departed doctors, offering immunity from prosecution and help with accommodation, on condition that they brought their family back with them.[169]

The reaction of other citizens to these privileges was one of envy, and contempt for the SED. Workers in particular felt aggrieved at the double standards of the Workers' and Peasants' State. A system of what amounted to selective bribery revealed the materialistic calculations behind a regime which was becoming a travesty of socialist idealism. Some party members also found

[164] Hager, 'Entwurf einer Vorlage an das Politbüro beim Zentralkomitee der SED', 1 Nov. 1960, SAPMO-BArch, DY30/IV2/9.05/143, fos. 198–220.

[165] MfS-ZAIG, '2. Bericht', 8 Jan. 1959, BStU-ZA, ZAIG 166, fo. 1.

[166] 'Analyse über die Republikfluchten der medizinischen Intelligenz im Jahre 1959', 12 Mar. 1960, SAPMO-BArch, DY30/IV2/9.04/669, fos. 148–54.

[167] H.K. to Gew. Gesundheitswesen, 16 Nov. 1959, SAPMO-BArch, DY30/IV2/19/56.

[168] 'Information über die Republikflucht von Prof. Dr. D., Direktor der Univ. Kinderklinik der Charité - Berlin', 5 Jan. 1960, SAPMO-BArch, DY30/IV2/19/56.

[169] 'Zurückgewinnung von republikflüchtigen Ärzten . . .', 20 Oct. 1958, SAPMO-BArch, DY30/IV2/19/55.

the barefacedness of the concessionary policies hard to swallow. According to one comrade at the Humboldt University's medical faculty: 'Intelligentsia policy basically means greasing people's palms.' At the same meeting there was criticism of the hypocrisy whereby a professor could move to West Berlin with Central Committee permission, while nurses were forbidden even to shop there.[170] Police in East Berlin even joked that they needed new equipment for dealing with intelligentsia crimes: a bouquet of flowers and a red carpet.[171] This ability to blackmail the system evidently stressed local functionaries and may have tempted some to wash their hands of fractious citizens, to put a stop to 'pussy footing' and 'sentimentality' in the words of one.[172] The party leadership, for its part, criticized local hardliners. After no less a person than Walter Ulbricht had publicly hinted that the GDR was well rid of its kulak farmers, the *Republikflucht* Commission warned against creating the impression 'that we attach no importance to their staying here. We are fighting for every inhabitant of our Republic.'[173] But the party was not always on message. As even the MfS recognized, functionaries' 'heartless, bureaucratic, administrative and sometimes sectarian behaviour' could be counter-productive.[174] 'We should simply let all the indifferent go to West Germany', said staff at the Karl Marx University in Leipzig, 'this is a healthy cleansing process and they are not to be halted anyway.'[175] One schools inspector did not lament the loss of teacher Z., 'who in no way belongs in our socialist school. There is surely not one colleague at the B. upper school who regrets this case.'[176] A cadre functionary at the EKB chemicals works also discerned a silver lining to some departures: 'We can only be glad that Dr H. has bunked. He would only have made more trouble for us.'[177] Local housing offices viewed *Republikflucht* as a solution to housing shortages, much to the chagrin of the Central Committee, which complained that 'various state institutions are working against one another'.[178] State agencies, especially

[170] SfHF, 'Information für Gen. K. Hager', 3 Sept. 1960, SAPMO-BArch, DY30/IV2/9.04/669, fos. 241–53.
[171] SED-ZK (Sicherheitsfragen), 'Bericht über die Kampf- und Einsatzbereitschaft der Kräfte des Präsidiums der Deutschen Volkspolizei in Berlin', 24 July 1961, SAPMO-BArch, DY30/JIV2/202/65, fos. 108–26.
[172] SED-ZK (Org), 'Einschätzung der Bezirksparteiaktivtagungen zur Auswertung des 33. Plenums', 13 Nov. 1957, SAPMO-BArch, DY30/IV2/5/286, fos. 218–32.
[173] SED-ZK (Staatliche Verwaltung), 'Massnahmen der Abteilung . . .', 24 Mar. 1953, SAPMO-BArch, DY30/IV2/13/394.
[174] MfS-ZAIG, 'Bericht über die Entwicklung der Republikflucht im Zeitraum Oktober-Dezember 1960 . . .', 3 Feb. 1961, BStU-ZA, ZAIG 412, fo. 9.
[175] SED-PL KMU, 'Informationsbericht', 9 Aug. 1961, SAPMO-BArch, DY30/IV2/9.04/558, fos. 148–50.
[176] SED-ZK (Volksbildung), 'Analyse des Standes der Republikfluchten im Jahre 1960', 9 Mar. 1961, SAPMO-BArch, DY30/IV2/9.05/143, fos. 262.
[177] 'Bericht über die Republikabgänge aus der chemischen Industrie', 23 Apr. 1959, SAPMO-BArch, DY30/IV2/9.04/669, fos. 72–87.
[178] 'Jahresbericht über die Durchführung der Maßnahmen zur Bekämpfung der Republikflucht', 21 Jan. 1955, SAPMO-BArch, DY30/IV2/13/396.

grass-roots functionaries, usually tried to scapegoat the police, which in turn complained how 'party, state and economic functionaries at regional and local level are in many cases putting in a good word for persons whose journey has justifiably been rejected by the Volkspolizei', resulting in the 'disorientation' of visa staff.[179] Countless examples could be given of local authorities ducking the issue.[180]

Republikflucht thus hovered in an uncomfortable space between taboo and open secret. Rather than encouraging an egalitarian society, the open border led to an endless round of negotiations of power at the local level, in which there always seemed to be an exception to every rule. The 1950s are often described as the 'ideological' decade, as opposed to the more pragmatic mature regime, but material incentive was already being used as a party tool. Leavers realized their market value in this economy of favours, since the departure of others was creating much room at the top. They were in a win–win situation, since the possibilities of employment in the FRG were high, but so too was the need for experts in the GDR, just as had been the case in the early Soviet Union. For those threatening a disappearing act, it may well have been only that: an act. Nevertheless, it was a threat enacted by enough of the population—the equivalent of one or two apartments on every staircase, two or three colleagues in every work brigade, up to five children in every classroom—that it carried weight. It was a nettle the regime was reluctant to grasp. At the apex of the pyramid of power SED leaders could claim a far-sighted and indulgent magnanimity, but at the grass roots there was a greater temptation to see the open border as a short-term solution to local difficulties. Strategists realized that the only long-term solution was to address the push factors at home, but these were largely conceived as economic (the Main Economic Task), rather than political. In the short term the authorities tended to think in terms of controls and closures. It is to the state's counter-measures, a tightrope walk between repression and liberalization, that we now must turn.

[179] HVDVP, 'Vorlage für die Mitglieder des Kollegiums . . .', 1 June 1961, BAB, DO-1/11/967, fos. 93–122.
[180] See also Ross, 'Before the Wall', 462–6.

4

Holding the Line: Policing the Open Border

The German–German border had always been more than just a line on the Cold War map. It marked the potential flashpoint between two military superpowers, as well as the interface between competing socioeconomic systems. For millions of ordinary Germans, however, it was a hurdle to be negotiated every day—on the way to work, family, or private pursuits. In its early years, it proved remarkably porous. It was, of course, really two borders: one the sector boundary in Berlin, sometimes only a white stripe in the road, or a sign informing potential trespassers that 'You are leaving the American Sector', or just as frequently an invisible line along housefronts or tramlines. The other was the 'mainland' inner-German border between the British and American Zones on the one hand, and the Soviet on the other. This so-called Demarcation Line reached from the Baltic in the north, along the river Elbe, down through the Harz Mountains, before turning east along the Czech frontier. The often difficult terrain made this frontier permeable, too, especially to those with local knowledge.[1] In toto, the double frontier ran for close on a thousand miles, presenting a considerable policing challenge to the young East German state. The early Volkspolizei was constrained not only by deficient training and equipment, but was constantly having to look over its shoulder to the Soviet big brother, for fear of triggering a diplomatic, or worse, a military incident. Nevertheless, the compulsion to control the border became symptomatic of East Germany's quest for recognition by the outside world.

Notwithstanding Allied Control Council proposals in December 1945 to open up zonal boundaries to travel and commerce, in July 1946 they were temporarily closed.[2] From October German travellers required thirty-day interzonal passes, until their abolition in 1953, when the GDR replaced them with visas. Furthermore, in December 1946 a lightly armed German Border Police began supporting Soviet patrols, each unit covering an average 10-kilometre sector of the Demarcation Line or 'green frontier'.[3] By 1948 some 10,000 officers were

---

[1] Edith Sheffer, 'On Edge: Building the Border in East and West Germany', *Central European History*, 40 (2007), 307–39.
[2] Smith, *Defense of Berlin*, 98.
[3] Dietmar Schultke, *'Keiner kommt durch': Die Geschichte der innerdeutschen Grenze 1945–1990* (Berlin: Aufbau Taschenbuch Verlag, 1999), 20.

on duty, playing cat and mouse with bootleggers trafficking in machine-tools, alcohol, cigarettes, textiles, and soap.[4] It was also not unknown for Soviet troops to pursue illegal border-crossers into the Allied zones, frequently firing after and occasionally killing them, or even for unwitting German farmers to graze their cattle across the ill-defined border.[5] In April 1948, moreover, the Volkspolizei's 'Berlin Ring' detachment was formed, guarding seventy-one road and seventeen rail and canal checkpoints along the 300-kilometre border around Greater Berlin. During the blockade alone, it claimed to have apprehended 214 spies, 22,418 criminals, 668 racketeers, and 2,115 smugglers.[6] Yet this was probably a drop in the ocean compared with those who eluded them.

In June 1950 the Soviets eventually devolved checkpoint duty onto the GDR Border Police (Allied personnel and foreigners were still dealt with by Russians), followed the next year by an East German customs and excise, the AZKW. Yet little had changed upon the founding of the GDR. When, for instance, a sports club in the border town of Eisfeld was denied passes to nearby Coburg in Bavaria, members simply crossed illegally.[7] At this stage approximately 40,000 East Germans and 10,000 West Germans transgressed the Demarcation Line monthly. Nor should it be forgotten that there was considerable legitimate East–West travel, mainly by rail. Between spring 1950 and spring 1961 13.1 million visits to West Germany were formally approved by the Volkspolizei, with 8.4 million in the opposite direction, despite official attempts to curb regional authorities' 'over-generosity' in issuing visas.[8] When socialist celebrities such as playwright Bertolt Brecht were fast-tracked, however, this could cause resentment elsewhere. Western travel was becoming a coveted but unevenly distributed commodity.[9]

A quantum leap in border consolidation occurred in May 1952, following the foundering of the famous Stalin Notes and West Germany's subsequent military integration into the western bloc. Now Stalin instructed that the Demarcation Line 'be seen as a frontier and not as a simple border but a dangerous one'.[10] Accordingly, on 26 May a 5-kilometre Exclusion Zone was created, requiring a permit, including a 500-metre 'protection strip' and a 10-metre 'control strip' at the border itself, razed of vegetation and ploughed over to expose tell-tale

[4] Alois Buckler, *Grenzgänger: Erlebnisse aus den Jahren 1947–1961 an der innerdeutschen Grenze* (Leipzig: Thomas, 1991); Frank Grube and Gerhard Richter, *Die Schwarzmarktzeit: Deutschland zwischen 1945 und 1948* (Hamburg: Hoffmann & Campe, 1979), 101–4.

[5] See Public Safety (Land Niedersachsen), 'British-Russian Zonal Border Incidents', Mar. 1948–Mar. 1949, TNA, FO 1050/596.

[6] Ritter and Lapp, *Grenze*, 18.

[7] 'Quartalsbericht der Abt. Verwaltungspolizei d. Landesbehörde d. Volkspolizei Thüringen für die Monate Januar, Februar, März 1950', BAB, DO-1/8/41381.

[8] Seifert to SKK, 20 Sept. 1950, DO-1/11/936, fos. 66–9; Reinwardt to Innenministerien der 5 Länder, 20 Aug. 1951, DO-1/11/937, fo. 68.

[9] Brecht and Weigel to Fischer, 12 Dec. 1950, DO-1/11/936, fos. 89–90.

[10] Stalin, 7 Apr. 1952, in *Cold War International History Project Bulletin*, 4 (Fall 1994), 48.

footprints. Even Baltic holidaymakers required a permit. At the same time German–German road and rail links were drastically reduced to five and six respectively, and 200 of the 277 routes connecting West Berlin with the eastern city and its GDR hinterland were severed, as well as all direct telephone lines. A total of 35,000 border police, with new uniforms and military ranks, were authorized to fire on 'border violators', as indeed they had been since 1947. A night-time curfew was introduced in the Exclusion Zone and the Border Police started recruiting Auxiliary Volunteers in local villages to act as eyes and ears, soon numbering some 5,000.[11] The Stasi also played an increasing role. In Operation Vermin in June 1952, the MfS supervised the deportation from the Exclusion Zone of over 11,000 inhabitants deemed a danger to public order, despite some local armed resistance.[12] A further 10,000 *Republikfluchten* from border areas had occurred by the end of the year, and, indeed, the whole national pattern of *Republikflucht* altered (see Figure 8). Whereas in 1950 just over 30 per cent fled via Berlin, by 1953 this had tripled to almost 90 per cent, before stabilizing at around 50 per cent in the mid-1950s. Crucially, too, there was a drastic, tenfold reduction in the interzonal passes issued, limited only to emergencies such as close bereavement. Accordingly, by the end of 1952 police complaints had quadrupled.[13] For the first time, the border was becoming a high-profile source of discontent in the GDR.

Nor should the Federal Republic's gatekeeping function be left out of the equation. Indeed, early on it rejected more refugees than it accepted from the GDR. From 1949 to 1951 145,789 were granted asylum, while 247,536 were rejected, and 109,000 were simply turned around on the spot.[14] Although a large proportion of rejects in West Berlin refused to leave and continued to live a shadowy existence, the municipal authorities were extremely reluctant to issue residence permits for fear of overcrowding the island half-city.[15] Western authorities often means-tested arrivees before issuing permits, presenting another bureaucratic barrier to migration. Bonn's politicians broadcast to inhabitants of the 'Zone' to hang on, and wait for reunification. Thus, in January 1950 the Federal Minister of Expellees publicly implored East Germans 'please not to come here without dire need'.[16] In November 1960 the Synod of the Evangelical Church called on clergy, doctors, and teachers to remember their duty to God to stand by their parishioners, patients, and pupils.[17] Only in the final days of the

---

[11] Bundesministerium für innerdeutsche Beziehungen (ed.), *Die Sperrmaßnahmen der DDR vom Mai 1952* (Bonn: BMidB, 1987), 7–32.

[12] Inge Bennewitz and Rainer Potratz, *Zwangsaussiedlungen an der innerdeutschen Grenze: Analysen und Dokumente* (Berlin: Links, 1994), 13–99; Udo Gentzen and Karin Wulf, 'Niemand wußte, wohin wir gebracht werden . . . ': *Zwangsumgesiedelte von 1952 und 1961 berichten über ihr Schicksal* (Hagenow: Boizenburg, 1993).

[13] 'Abteilung PM 1', BAB, DO-1/11/913, fo. 162.   [14] LAB, B Rep. 008–02/241.

[15] Wanstrat, *Strukturanalyse*.   [16] Cited in Ackermann, *Flüchtling*, 97.

[17] 'Wort der Synode der Evangelischen Kirche der Union an die Gemeinden zum Bleiben in der DDR', Nov. 1960, EZA, 104/595. See also Eberhard Schmidt *et al.* (eds), *Gehen oder*

crisis did West Berlin's mayor, Willy Brandt, question the logic of telling GDR citizens 'to stay put. This was a question which every individual must decide for himself.'[18] Yet this counsel was still kept behind closed doors.

Paradoxically, the GDR authorities did not pay much initial heed to the exodus. Certainly, in October 1947 the Volkspolizei's K-5 section, forerunner of the Stasi, had been tasked with monitoring movements to the West, but with limited success.[19] Only in mid-1951 did the Volkspolizei list *Republikflucht* as a '*Schwerpunkt*'.[20] A sharp rise in flights in 1952–53 prompted a rethink, however, and the founding of a Politbüro *Republikflucht* Commission in September 1952. In mirror image of western conspiracy theories, it rather fancifully proposed the 'systematic recruitment of scientists, doctors, specialists, artists and skilled workers from West Germany with a view to taking up work in the GDR'.[21] Members of GDR delegations were to have quiet words with West German colleagues to invite them east. Yet as Figure 4 shows, the numbers moving from West to East remained modest, despite raised hopes in 1959, when immigrants momentarily outweighed emigrants in some areas.[22] By the time of the Wall, while every sixth citizen had left the GDR, in the FRG it was only every eighty-sixth. Of the latter, well over half were returning *Republikflüchtige*. A total of 36.8 per cent came from the industrial centres of North Rhine-Westphalia, and 10.9 per cent from Baden-Württemberg.[23] Many were homesick youngsters, unable to integrate in the FRG. Those without relatives in the West found it particularly difficult to settle, feeling isolated or like second-class citizens.[24] There is also anecdotal evidence that Protestant East Germans experienced alienation in the Catholic south.[25] Among the early eastward immigrants from the FRG, it was estimated that about half involved postwar family reunions, or were spouses of returnees; around a third were job-seekers; and 10 per cent cited political reasons, such as draft-dodging, although communists were encouraged to stand

bleiben: Flucht und Übersiedlung von Pfarrern im geteilten Deutschland (Leipzig: Evangelische Verlagsanstalt, 2002).

   [18] 'Record of a Meeting between the Commandants and the Governing Mayor held in the office of the British Commandant on July 21, 1961', n.d., TNA, FO 371/160507/CG10112/17.

   [19] Van Melis, *'Republikflucht'*, 22–3.

   [20] HVDVP (PM), 'Bericht über das III. Quartal 1951', 20 Oct. 1951, BAB, DO-1/11/912, fos. 46–68.

   [21] SED-PB, 6 Jan. 1953, Anlage 7: 'Richtlinien über Maßnahmen gegen die Republikflucht und zur Werbung von Fachkräften in Westdeutschland', 7 Jan. 1953, SAPMO-BArch, DY30/J IV2/2/256, fos. 30–40.

   [22] MdI (IA), 'Presseauswertung der Bevölkerungsbewegung in die DDR', 23 Oct. 1959, SAPMO-BArch, DY30/IV2/9.02/131, fos. 14–20.

   [23] HVDVP, 'Vorlage für die Mitglieder des Kollegiums . . .', 1 June 1961, BAB, DO-1/11/967, fos. 93–122.

   [24] Schröter, Gerhard, *Jugendliche Flüchtlinge aus der Sowjetzone* (Munich: infratest, 1958), 68–70. See also Frank Hoffmann, *Junge Zuwanderer in Westdeutschland: Struktur, Aufnahme und Integration junger Flüchtlinge aus der SBZ und der DDR in Westdeutschland (1945–1961)* (Frankfurt am Main: Peter Lang, 1999).

   [25] Interview with Mr and Mrs L., 22 Aug. 1996.

and fight in the West.[26] Among the inbound economic migrants, however, the annual numbers of intelligentsia, *the* official target group, continued to drop throughout the 1950s, from a little under a thousand to a few hundred annually. Even given the FRG's early high unemployment and the closure of many Ruhr pits in 1958, as well as the rationalization of agriculture, the hoped-for influx of skilled labour did not materialize.[27]

A very high proportion of first-time arrivals left the GDR again, disappointed at what they found, and returnees were also prone to recommit *Republikflucht*.[28] By 1961 only about one-third of arrivees and returnees were still in the country.[29] Part of the problem was chronic suspicion by local officials. The Volkspolizei kept newcomers under surveillance and the welcome afforded was often brusque. About one in seven were deported straight back to the West as 'asocial elements', including former *Republikflüchtige*. As was reported of one reception centre: 'The overall condition of the Eisenach resettler camp is reminiscent of prisoner-of-war camps (apart from rations and barbed wire) familiar from the fascist era, including old military beds and cupboards, beds with straw sacks.'[30] In other reception hostels there were regular punch-ups and 'mutinies against the house rules'.[31] Even for those who made it beyond the camps there were integration difficulties. Factory workers were monitored and kept apart from one another. Of the 1,199 returnees and arrivees at the Buna plant between 1955 and 1959, for instance, two-thirds were gone again by 1960.[32] For those who had not grown up in the GDR, it could be a culture shock. One fiancée from Cologne who moved to Erfurt was 'deeply shaken by the poor food supply' and long queues, quickly persuading her husband-to-be to come back with her to the West.[33] West–East migration was largely a failure.

One other group which profited daily from the open border were the so-called *Grenzgänger*, or border-crossers. Three-quarters were East and West Berliners who lived in one half of the city, but worked in the other, while another

[26] HVDVP (Hauptabt. K), 'Zuwanderung von Personen aus Westdeutschland und Westberlin in das Gebiet der DDR für das Jahr 1951 sowie für das I. und II. Quartal 1952', 22 Sept. 1952, SAPMO-BArch, DY30/J IV2/202/68.
[27] 'Bericht über die Bevölkerungsbewegung für das Jahr 1959 (bis November)', 17 Dec. 1959, SAPMO-BArch, IV2/16/230.
[28] Andrea Schmelz, *Migration und Politik im geteilten Deutschland während des Kalten Krieges: Die West-Ost-Migration in die DDR in den 1950er und 1960er Jahren* (Opladen: Leske & Budrich, 2002), 303–11.
[29] 'Thesen zur Analyse über Rückkehrer und Zuziehende aus Westdeutschland und Westberlin', BAB, DO-1/11/967, fos. 26–33.
[30] 'Bericht über die illegalen Abwanderungen . . . im Jahre 1954', SAPMO-BArch, DY30/IV2/13/396.
[31] HVDVP (PM), '1. Halbjahresbericht . . .', 23 July 1957, BAB, DO-1/11/918, fos. 3–20.
[32] SED-BL Halle (BPKK), 'Beantwortung einiger Fragen zur Halbjahres-Analyse 1959', 28 Mar. 1960, LAM, BPA SED Halle, IV/2/4/992, fos. 16–36.
[33] SfHF, 'Quartalsanalyse der Republikfluchten (I. Quartal 1960)', n.d., SAPMO-BArch, DY30/IV2/9.04/669, fos. 187–96.

quarter commuted from the Brandenburg hinterland, up to 4 hours daily.[34] In the early Cold War there had been more west–east commuters than vice-versa, especially at times of high unemployment such as the blockade. Thus, in 1949 approximately 100,000 West Berliners and 50,000 East Berliners engaged in *Grenzgängerei*.[35] In the long term, however, as the western city gradually recovered, the lure of the deutschmark prevailed. The numbers of west–east commuters shrank during the 1950s to around 11,000, servicing a number of hospitals and theatres in East Berlin, but half of whom were actually employed in the GDR's West Berlin railway exclaves.[36] Although movement in the opposite direction initially also dwindled, to around 30,000, it began to grow again in the mid-fifties, reaching just over 63,000 by the time the Wall went up.[37] Some had worked in larger factories such as Siemens and AEG since before the First World War, or were managers living in leafy GDR suburbs such as Klein-Machnow. Proportionally more smaller enterprises and workshops came to rely on eastern labour, however, joined by some 10,000 moonlighters, many of them women working part-time, such as shop-assistants, putting-out seamstresses, and the so-called 'scrubbing-brush brigade' of cleaners. Building workers jobbed in West Berlin in the summer, and returned east in the winter. There was a shift in 1960, however, as the GDR economy deteriorated and ever more industrial *Grenzgänger*—the GDR's proletarian elite—headed west, growing by about 800 a month between July 1960 and June 1961.[38]

Grenzgänger could provoke a copycat chain reaction. For instance, in the state-owned department store on the Alexanderplatz in the heart of East Berlin, two sales assistants had left in 1960, but visited ex-colleagues in the food hall to regale them, in the disapproving words of one reporter, with 'everything they could buy with the extortionate rate-of-exchange'. Younger colleagues were visibly impressed, but supervisors feared confronting staff for fear of seeing more leave.[39] There was in fact a general fluctuation occurring on the Berlin job market. In July 1961 the Ministry of Electrical Industries even adopted an emergency plan to reduce job-shifting at the major electro-works and the state went so far as to introduce labour exchanges. On the eve of the Wall, the GDR economy was getting into serious difficulties, when East Berlin was short of approximately 9,000 workers and individual factories such as the Television Electronics Works, the Köpenick and Adlershof cable works, and the Berlin Lightbulb Works were

---

[34] 'Einpendler nach Berlin (West)', n.d. [1958], LAB, Rep. 4/Acc. 1650/Nr. 24/1.

[35] Jörn Schütrumpf, 'Zu einigen Aspekten des Grenzgängerproblems im Berliner Raum von 1948/49 bis 1961', *Jahrbuch für Geschichte*, 31 (1984), 337.

[36] For an oral history: Erika M. Hoerning, *Zwischen den Fronten: Berliner Grenzgänger und Grenzhändler 1948–1961* (Cologne: Böhlau, 1992).

[37] Klein to Lemmer, 2 Aug. 1961 in Verein Berliner Mauer (ed.), *Die Berliner Mauer* (Dresden: Michel Sandstein Verlag, n.d.), 94–5.

[38] Schütrumpf, 'Zu einigen Aspekten', 345.

[39] HO-Warenhaus am Alex (Kader), 'Republikfluchten . . .', 10 May 1961, SAPMO-BArch, DY30/IV2/6.10/68, fos. 47–52.

all far behind plan. At the Transformer Works, too, the cadre section noted that if until recently accessions and departures had cancelled each other out, now the pool was shrinking: 'If a foreman or section head in 1959 could watch a colleague's departure with equanimity, because a replacement could be found elsewhere, that is no longer possible today.'[40]

The incentives to work in West Berlin were simply too great. Its Senate had established a Wage Equalization Exchange in 1949, whereby easterners working in the West received 25–40 per cent of wages in hard currency. They could thus buy cars, televisions, and refrigerators in deutschmarks, while paying subsidized rents, gas, and electricity in ostmarks. With a soft–hard rate of exchange of five to one, *Grenzgänger* could thus lead a relatively opulent existence. The GDR's *Eulenspiegel* magazine caricatured one larger than life *Grenzgänger* sitting bricklaying in the western sector and receiving cash in hand from a rotund western businessman, while toasting his giant feet through the window of his home in the East.[41] Not all of this was party propaganda. There is evidence that the general public resented such privileges and welcomed punitive measures when they came. There was even a note of criticism that the regime had waited too long to get a grip: 'It is often said that it was high time and we are reproached for not having done something much earlier. They are talking about years, not days or weeks.'[42] A few authoritarians even demanded that *Grenzgänger* be deported or made to wear a 'G' on their clothing.[43] The more tolerant preferred to differentiate between older commuters—in 1961 60 per cent were over 45—many of whom had built up pension rights started under Weimar, and younger opportunists.[44] Yet, besides withholding a considerable labour resource, worth a billion marks annually, border-crossers posed a political problem, importing western ideology into their locale: '*Grenzgänger* hardly join in social life and try to move about the residential quarter as inconspicuously as possible.' They often had their own *Stammtisch* at local pubs. Some, however, 'act as labour recruiters and even try to incite our workers'. One former quality controller at East Berlin's Borsig locomotive works, now at its sister plant in Tegel, was even apparently encouraging wage demands.[45]

Another group considered infected with westernism—so-called 'ideological *Grenzgänger*'—was youth. Annually, the authorities would seize hundreds of thousands of 'trash and smut' publications from adolescents, smuggled chiefly

[40] 'Analyse über die Fluktuation im VEB TRO "Karl Liebknecht" ', n.d. [1961], LAB (STA), Rep. 411/Nr. 1511.

[41] *Eulenspiegel*, 7: 46 (Nov. 1960), 1.

[42] 'Berichterstattung der Operativgruppe vom 3. August 1961', LAB, BPA SED Berlin, IV2/12/1278.

[43] SED-BL Berlin (Org-Kader), 'Kurzinformation', 9 Aug. 1961, LAB, BPA SED Berlin, IV2/3/633.

[44] SED-ZK (Sicherheit), 23 July 1961, SAPMO-BArch, DY30/J IV2/202/65, fos. 85–92.

[45] MdI, 'Einschätzung des Grenzgängerproblems im demokratischen Berlin und in den Randgebieten', 10 Jan. 1961, SAPMO-BArch, DY30/IV2/13/366, fos. 85–9.

from West Berlin.[46] Among one haul representing 'American unculture', thirty comics were analysed. A total of 523 crimes were ascertained in twenty-four varieties, including poisoning and sexual murder, resulting in 255 deaths, and, as the indignant reporter added, 'The overwhelming majority of these crimes were committed by a positively-portrayed hero.'[47] Youngsters were also attracted by the possibilities of buying fashion items and records in the West. As one recalled:

At the beginning of the fifties, when I was 16, I was always going to West Berlin with my friends. Four or five times a week, if not every day. We crossed at Schilling Bridge via the so-called open checkpoint. Then we went to the cinema for 25 west pfennigs. They showed films with John Wayne and Gary Cooper which were really something for us. And we would buy chewing gum and stick it under our seats. . . . we thought it was a knockout . . .[48]

At Potsdamer Platz, as well as north in Wedding and south in Kreuzberg, there were indeed several subsidized 'border cinemas' in West Berlin catering to an eastern clientele with a mixture of newsreels and superannuated B-movies. By 1960 an impressive 27 per cent of patrons of West Berlin cinemas were East Germans,[49] including an estimated 90 per cent of East Berlin youngsters. East German girls idolized West German film stars, as random locker checks revealed.[50] One appalled SED observer reported how 'the cinemas in the vicinity of Schlesisches Tor show special performances with almost solely American-produced films, dominated by shoot-outs, murders and other acts of violence, and last but not least, eroticism.'[51] In response, East Berlin cinemas felt under pressure to liven up their repertoire, and those near the sector boundary were indeed permitted to show 'lighter' films than elsewhere.[52] Yet, even in the hinterland, cinemas consciously advertised their 'westernness'.[53]

Radio was another loophole. Younger listeners were particularly enthralled by Radio Luxembourg and RIAS, sending in copious fan mail. With the arrival of Bill Haley and Elvis Presley, the authorities began to identify rockers, or

---

[46] Korn to Mielke, 20 Jan. 1962, BStU-ZA, MfS-SdM 1007, fo. 323.

[47] Magistrat von Groß-Berlin (Volksbildung), 'Teilbericht über Probleme der Jugendgefährdung', 19 Dec. 1960, SAPMO-BArch, DY30/IV2/16/230.

[48] Horst H., born in 1936 in Rebecca Menzel *Jeans in der DDR: Vom tieferen Sinn einer Freizeithose* (Berlin: Links, 2004), 12.

[49] BMG Berlin to Foreign Office, 17 Sept. 1961, TNA, FO 371/160508/CG10112/25.

[50] Magistrat von Groß-Berlin (Volksbildung), 'Teilbericht über Probleme der Jugendgefährdung', 19 Dec. 1960, SAPMO-BArch, DY30/IV2/16/230.

[51] Berliner Zahlungsverkehr (Geldumlauf), 'Analyse des Besuches von Westberliner Kinos durch Bewohner unseres Wirtschaftsgebietes', 16 Apr. 1956, SAPMO-BArch, DY30, IV/2/2.026/75, fos. 45–52.

[52] 'Vorschläge zur Verbesserung der Filmarbeit in Berlin', 1 Feb. 1956, SAPMO-BArch, DY30, IV/2/2.026/75, fos. 2–10.

[53] Ross, *Constructing Socialism*, 139.

Halbstarke, as the new enemy, huddled around their transistor radios on street corners. This was a contagion which spread easily, even to 'positive youths'.[54] The number of gangs with western role models, and in Berlin often actual members and leaders, rose alarmingly, reaching 250 in 1959 across the GDR. They ranged from loose organizations to tightly knit groups with logos, membership fees, and names such as 'Outpost of the Free World', 'Texas Gang', 'Jeans Gang', 'Leather Jacket Crew', as well as various rock'n'roll and Presley appreciation societies. The generation gap between the party and its youth soon showed. Baffled policemen phonetically transcribed English names: '*Blutjings*' for blue jeans and '*Tinetschel*' for teenager. Taunting the communist youth organization, the FDJ (Free German Youth), as well as the Volkspolizei, was a popular pastime, even culminating in mass assaults on police stations.[55] Leipzig and its Clara-Zetkin-Park became the centre of the alternative scene. After the local press had attacked the dress sense of *Halbstarke*, dubbing them 'scarecrows', youths held an 'enlightenment march' through the suburbs in 1959.[56] Feuding gangs even merged, seeking showdowns with Volkspolizei auxiliaries, suitably dubbed 'sheriffs'.[57] Nor were these groups totally apolitical. Some called for the disbanding of the army and border police.[58] Yet, however hard the authorities tried, alternating between carrot and stick, co-opting parents and barbers, and confiscating apparel, they were never able to stamp out the phenomenon. As will become evident below, this was to remain the case even after the building of the Wall, when the electronic media became doubly important as hidden portals to the West.

The *Republikflucht* Commission also encouraged horror stories about the fate of refugees in a heartless West, including French Foreign Legion press gangs and 'young girls forced into prostitution'.[59] The MfS faked mailshots from remorseful refugees, warning of a West Germany plagued by poverty, degradation, and suicide, where engineers worked as porters and doctors as usherettes. One unfortunate supposedly made ends meet as a 'nude model for a female cubist painter' (clearly the Stasi's idea of the ultimate class enemy). According to another returning 'mother': 'When my little one asked me why I could not buy her the chocolate on sale in the shop-window . . . the tears welled up in my eyes, although I am not one for sentimentality.' The East, on the other

[54] 'Der Kampf gegen Jugendkriminalität und Rowdytum im Bezirk Leipzig', n.d. [Schriftenreihe der DVP], StAL, BDVP 24/113, fos. 107–34.
[55] SED-ZK (Org-Instruk), 'Einschätzung der gegenwärtigen Bandentätigkeit . . . ', 4 Dec. 1959, SAPMO-BArch, DY30/IV2/16/230.
[56] BDVP Leipzig (Kripo), 'Bericht über die Entwicklung des Rowdytums und dessen Bekämpfung', 21 Jan. 1960, StAL, BDVP 24/113, fos. 145–53.
[57] The English word was used: StAL, BDVP 24/113, fos. 135–40.
[58] BDVP Leipzig, 'Niederschrift über die Beratung über Fragen der Jugendkriminalität und des Rowdytums in der Stadt Leipzig am 29. Oktober 1958', 30 Oct. 1958, StAL, BDVP 24/113, fos. 86–9.
[59] SED-ZK (Staatliche Verwaltung), 'Vorschläge für Maßnahmen gegen die Republikflucht und zur Werbung von Fachkräften in Westdeutschland', 22 Sept. 1952, SAPMO-BArch, DY30/IV2/13/393.

hand, offered 'secure, orderly conditions'.[60] Although the propaganda may have been clumsy, the idea behind it was not so ill-conceived. When asked what they found best about the GDR, refugees would regularly mention the welfare system, or if youths, the scholarships, sports facilities, and outdoors activities on offer.[61] Posters showed masked figures stealing away in the night, clutching bags labelled 'education' and 'stipend'. Others depicted footprints heading west, ending as skeletal feet in the Federal wilderness.[62] Brochures appeared with titles such as 'We Came from the Golden West' and 'Home Again',[63] while pulp novels such as *Twilight*, *Temptation* and *Dangerous Love* dramatized the decisions involved.[64]

East German cinema, too, was enlisted to fight ideological border-crossing. *Alarm at the Circus* (Klein, 1954) tells the 'true-life story' of two West Berlin boys, press-ganged into stealing horses from an East Berlin circus. West Berlin is a den of iniquity, populated by spivs in brothel-creepers and leering American GIs. Behind a faked SED sign announcing 'We Are Rebuilding', the gang symbolically dismantle a wall at the sector boundary to prepare their getaway. The young protagonists' growing fondness for the animals, however, and admiration for the GDR's educational opportunities, allow the Volkspolizei to foil the plot. The film ends with the boys being feted in the circus, encircled by friends rather than exploiters. This was a theme repeated in *Sheriff Teddy* (Carow, 1957), about a young West Berlin tearaway, Kalle, the diminutive leader of a West Berlin gang of would-be cowboys, led astray by comics and B-movies. When his family moves to the eastern sector, Kalle is socialized into more acceptable norms, but not without several runs-in with his teachers. Propagandists liked to play on the audience's emotions. *Berlin Romance* (Klein, 1956), a kitchen sink drama in divided Berlin, depicts Uschi from East Berlin and Hans from West Berlin in their attempts to resolve their love, in spite of everyday obstacles, eventually by marriage. And *Life Begins* (Carow, 1959), based on the true story of Karin N., portrays the dilemma of a doctor's daughter who follows her father west, but soon sees beyond the glittering lights, and on her own initiative returns east to her friends and socialism.[65] The most memorable of these morality tales, however, was East Germany's answer to Hollywood's teen movies, *Berlin—Ecke Schönhauser* (Klein, 1957).[66] This semi-documentary 'social study' follows a gang

[60] For a selection see: BStU-ZA, ZAIG 10354, fos. 91–103.

[61] Gerhard Schröter, *Jugendliche Flüchtlinge aus der Sowjetzone* (Munich: infratest, 1958), 35.

[62] 'Von Deutschland nach Deutschland: Flucht und Ausreise aus der SBZ/DDR 1945 bis 1989' (exhibition held at the Erinnerungsstätte Notaufnahmelager Marienfelde, Sept.–Oct. 2000).

[63] SED-ZK (Agit), 'Materialien zur Bekämpfung der Republikflucht', 5 Jan. 1957, SAPMO-BArch, DY30/IV2/9.02/6, fos. 12–15.

[64] Käthe Muskewitz and Bruno Stubert, *Zwielicht* (Berlin: Das Neue Berlin, 1955); Werner Reinowski, *Die Versuchung* (Halle: Mitteldeutscher Verlag, 1956); Georg Redmann, *Gefährliche Liebe* (Berlin: Das Neue Berlin, 1960).

[65] On the real Karin N. see SAPMO-BArch, DY30/IV2/9.05/143, fos. 325–67.

[66] Joshua Feinstein, *The Triumph of the Ordinary: Depictions of Daily Life in the East German Cinema, 1949–1989* (Chapel Hill, NC: University of North Carolina Press, 2002), 45–77.

from the street corners of East Berlin to the clutches of a West Berlin reception camp, complete with interrogators and hooligan guards. Scriptwriter Wolfgang Kohlhaase went to great lengths to 'understand' teens who 'just don't know where to let off steam'.[67] Like *Rebel without a Cause*, broken families are to blame for their alienation, while the state offers a surrogate family. In the final scene, the police sergeant is forgiving but vigilant: 'Think about how all of this could happen. I am responsible, you are responsible. If we aren't there, our enemies will be.'

Intermittently, naming and shaming of defectors in positions of responsibility was encouraged in order to stoke up moral outrage. When writer and academic Alfred Kantorowicz fled in 1957, a hate campaign ensued against 'the renegade', *pour encourager les autres*.[68] In the case of one consultant doctor from Dresden, the press accused him of 'basely betraying and leaving our Republic in the lurch'. Instead of being true to his Hippocratic Oath, Dr S. had gone to the half of Germany 'where atomic death is being prepared'.[69] In other cases public meetings issued condemnations in the press. Open letters were also signed by remaining doctors to colleagues to live up to their 'moral and ethical duty' and not to burden colleagues with more work.[70] In other cases the SED drew attention to the high cost of training some of the disappeared, at the expense of the 'worker's shilling'. But public gatherings often ended in collective shoulder-shrugging. Dealing with *Republikflucht* became another routinized chore for the state and party apparatus. The Volkspolizei produced painstaking monthly and annual statistics, copies of which were sent off to the Soviet embassy.[71] Cadre departments, such as the Erfurt SED's security section, listed losses in minute detail, by abode, age, party membership, and social background. There were, however, no practical suggestions for how to stop the flow.[72] The party appears to have preferred to discuss the problem behind closed doors, as part of its self-confessed 'mystery-mongering'.[73]

1953: OPENING GAMBLE

Despite all of its moralizing, the party realized that it also needed a preventative solution. The June 1953 uprising, which as we have seen was preceded by massive

---

[67] Poiger, Uta G., *Jazz, Rock and Rebels: Cold War Politics and American Culture in a Divided Germany* (Berkeley, CA: University of California Press, 2000), 124.

[68] Josie McLellan, *Antifascism and Memory in East Germany: Remembering the International Brigades 1945–1989* (Oxford: OUP, 2004), 196.

[69] 'Das Vertrauen mißbraucht', *Sächsische Zeitung*, 23 Apr. 1958.

[70] Open letters, Sept. 1960, SAPMO-BArch, DY30/IV2/19/56.

[71] See for instance the covering notes in BAB, DO-1/8/318/2. Other copies went to Sorgenicht (ZK), Szinda (MfS), Hegen and Seifert (MdI). These files, which carried a '*Vertrauliche Verschlußsache*' designation, were only declassified internally in November 1988, at a time when the SED was re-examining its travel policy. See also Zubok and Pleshakov, *Inside*, 248–9.

[72] SED-BL Erfurt (Sicherheitsfragen), 'Bericht über die illegalen Abwanderungen . . .', 12 Aug. 1961, ThHStAW, SED-BL Erfurt, IV2/3/387.

[73] 'Analyse der illegalen Abwanderungen im 1. Halbjahr 1957', BAB, DO-1/34/21723.

Republikflucht, gave serious pause for thought. The Politbüro even reversed earlier policies of confiscating leavers' property and relocating their remaining relatives within the GDR.[74] Among the climb-downs, travel was drastically liberalized, as evidenced in Figure 7. The Interior Minister successfully requested more latitude in dealing with travel applications.[75] Accordingly, in November the interzonal pass was dropped in favour of the so-called PM 12a visa, and West German visitors' residence permits could be obtained by relatives in the GDR, rather than by lengthy correspondence. The Volkspolizei's Pass and Registration section thus entered a 'liberal' phase, justified by reference to the New Course and the growing numbers of returnees.[76] In the wake of destalinization in 1956 the SED again enacted conscious reforms to staunch losses. The party needed to be more self-critical of MfS surveillance techniques and overzealous customs officials: 'Every *Republikflucht* is inevitably a criticism of the work of the state apparatus and so a criticism of our work too.'[77] In June the Politbüro duly ordered a catalogue of measures: more travel visas, even for state employees; the Ministry of Transport was to encourage greater tourism to the GDR; intelligentsia children were to receive more university places; and the attorney general was to ensure 'democratic legality', including an amnesty for petty offenders who had absconded.[78]

The gamble had costs, of course. By 1957 there were 2.8 million east–west visits—compared with fewer than 51,000 in 1952!—and 1.4 million in the other direction. The number of refusals was relatively low: in 1957 only 6.4 per cent.[79] Despite the fact that would-be travellers could expect to wait for 2–4 hours in the mid-1950s, in rooms festooned with agitprop, the opening up of travel seemed to be having the desired effect on the public mood. In 1957, the Interior Ministry noted with some satisfaction that the recent measures had 'contributed substantially to the calming of the situation of the population'.[80] On GDR national holidays East Germans took the opportunity to go shopping in the West, and those close to the border would sometimes go every weekend. Since Christmas 1956 the Federal Republic was supplying 10 deutschmarks and travel assistance. Even comrades and state functionaries were reported to be accepting these, claiming that they were 'breaking' the FRG 'from within'.[81]

Inevitably, however, it was recognized by the police that many citizens were abusing freedom of travel to commit *Republikflucht*. From 1954 to 1957 half of all defections were carried out 'legally', by PM 12a travel visa (see Figure 7,

---

[74] Van Melis, '*Republikflucht*', 41.

[75] Maron to Stoph, 31 July 1953, DO-1/11/939, fos. 76–7.

[76] HVDVP (PM), 'Bericht über Maßnahmen zur Normalisierung der Beziehungen zwischen der DDR und Westdeutschland', 14 June 1955, DO-1/11/941, fos. 64–6.

[77] 'Hauptgründe für die Republikflucht', SAPMO-BArch, DY30/IV2/13/397.

[78] In BA, DO-1/34/21723.

[79] HVDVP, 'Interzonenverkehr', n.d. [1957], BAB, DO-1/11/964, fo. 117; HVDVP, 'Vorlage für die Mitglieder des Kollegiums . . .', 1 June 1961, BAB, DO-1/11/967, fos. 93–122.

[80] HVDVP (PM), 'Vermerk', 13 Mar. 1957, BAB, DO-1/11/964, fos. 93–8.

[81] HVDVP (PM), '1. Halbjahresbericht . . .', 23 July 1957, BAB, DO-1/11/918, fos. 3–20.

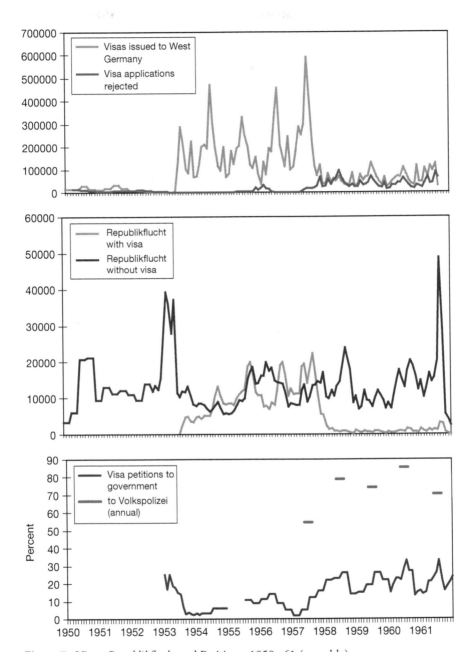

Figure 7. Visas, *Republikflucht* and Petitions, 1950–61 (monthly).

Source: DVP. See Note 1, Chapter 3; petitions to State President until Pieck's death in September 1960; thereafter to Council of State.

central panel). Many a postcard was sent from the safety of a West German post office, informing superiors that the colleague in question would 'not be returning from holiday'. The authorities inferred that friends and relations in the West were to blame. The Volkspolizei noted that mainly women and children chose the 'safe' option, as well as citizens in the southern provinces, while menfolk were more likely to take the Berlin route. During 1957, therefore, the authorities considered ways of reversing some of the concessions of the previous four years, conscious that they were walking a tightrope. The Soviets and East Germans began meeting monthly to discuss the exodus.[82] A central registry of high-risk persons was mooted. Local police and employers were to vet applicants' risk of defection, and workplace personnel offices to discourage travel. From September state employees were no longer permitted to go to the 'capitalist exterior', except in exceptional circumstances. The following month constraints were applied more widely to the general public. Those at risk of fleeing or who had departed relatives, as well as 'speculators', were to be turned down.[83] The party leadership began to emit a harder line. Before the Central Committee, Hanna Wolf, director of the Karl Marx Party Highschool, attacked the question of 'the hard and the soft course, the hard and the soft comrades'. She left listeners in no doubt which side she was on: 'when a comrade hears that someone has committed *Republikflucht*, the first reflex must be . . . "that is a swine!", and I can deal with the "psychology" later'.[84] Most tellingly, in a reversal of visa liberalization, only 612,686 persons received travel permission in 1958—less than a quarter of the previous year. Almost as many applications were rejected as accepted. This had the desired gate-keeping effect, since 'legal' *Republikfluchten* by visa fell by over 90 per cent compared with 1957, and departures overall sank.[85]

At the same time the regime further criminalized departure from the GDR. Already the state was empowered to seize defectors' property, but this was rather like closing the gate after the horse had bolted. Paradoxically, the law punished aiding and abetting of *Republikflucht*, but not the act itself. In 1955, for instance, 408 people were thus prosecuted, including one exemplary eight-year sentence for allegedly luring young girls to a bordello for American officers.[86] Although fines and imprisonment were available for illegally crossing the Demarcation Line, they did not apply to those entering West Berlin. Anybody with an identity card could enter the western sectors relatively unmolested. In December 1957, however, the existing Pass Law, which punished unauthorized travel abroad with up to three years' imprisonment, was extended to include the territory of the

---

[82] Harrison, *Driving*, 100.

[83] HVDVP (PM), 'Ausgabe von Personalbescheingungen (PM 12 a)', 11 Dec. 1957, BAB, DO-1/11/947, fos. 104–5.

[84] 33rd SED-ZK, 16–19 Oct. 1957, in BMfVFK (ed.), *Der Bau der Mauer*, 91.

[85] HVDVP (PM), 'Reiseverkehr', 26 Aug. 1958, BAB, DO-1/11/948, fos. 67–9.

[86] 'Bericht über die Republikfluchten aus der Deutschen Demokratischen Republik für die Zeit vom 1.1.1954 bis 31.12.1955', n.d., BAB, DO-1/11/963, fos. 100–29.

FRG and West Berlin. Even preparations for departure were prosecutable.[87] Crossing the sector boundary without a visa thus became far more risky, while the Demarcation Line itself was further fortified with new fences, ditches, and alarms.

Both of these actions—visa restrictions and Pass Law—gave the authorities an often neglected weapon in policing the outflow, and qualify claims that the drop in flights in 1958–59 represented, according to one prominent GDR scholar, 'signs of social consolidation'.[88] This unwittingly echoes official wishful thinking at the time that the dip was ascribable to the Seven-Year Plan and 'intensified political agitation on the perspectives for the whole population in socialism'.[89] The regime even raised its hopes that it had turned the corner of *Republikflucht*. As aggravated citizens queued at police stations, however, only to be fobbed off with excuses about security, or polio epidemics in West Germany, tempers frayed. A staple grouse in letters to the BBC, for example, was the difficulty of obtaining travel permits.[90] Opinion reports on the Pass Law revealed a 'multitude of confused and hostile arguments'. Tractor drivers north of Berlin claimed that all that was now needed to complete the 'prison' was a wooden fence: 'Probably they want to seal us off hermetically now, that is, ring down the iron curtain for fear of western influences.'[91] Aggrieved citizens held the party's own patriotic rhetoric against it, asking how blocking family ties would help the national question.[92] The state had no right. In Neubrandenburg, 'the existence of two opposing states is not acknowledged in the question of travel—instead people proceed from the basis of one Germany'.[93] Others believed that the Pass Law was one of the chief causes of the continuing exodus. According to Dr F. of Bischofswerda:

It had become intolerable for me to be dependent in the long term on the good will or caprices of the police authorities as to whether, how often and when I could visit my closest family inside Germany. I consider it the most primitive right of my personal freedom to choose my domicile where I like.[94]

[87] Karl Wilhelm Fricke, *Politik und Justiz in der DDR: Zur Geschichte der politischen Verfolgung 1945–1968: Bericht und Dokumentation*, 2nd edn. (Cologne: Verlag Wissenschaft und Politik, 1990), 417–19.

[88] Staritz, *Geschichte der DDR*, 169.

[89] HVDVP (PM), 'Analyse der Bevölkerungsbewegung für das Jahr 1959', 1 Feb. 1960, BAB, DO-1/11/919, fos. 24–39.

[90] BBC (German Audience Research), 'Report on Mail in German from Listeners in the Soviet Zone and Other Countries, October 16–31 1959', 31 Oct. 1959, TNA, FO 1110/1240.

[91] SED-ZK (Org), 'Informationsbericht Nr. 1/58', 9 Jan. 1958, SAPMO-BArch, DY30/IV2/5/287, fos. 1–13.

[92] SED-ZK (Org), 'Informationsbericht Nr. 2/58', 15 Jan. 1958, SAPMO-BArch, DY30/IV2/5/287, fos. 14–31.

[93] BDVP Neubrandenburg (Politabteilung), 'Einschätzung', 28 June 1961, BAB, DO-1/11/951, fos. 90–4.

[94] SED-ZK (Gesundheitspolitik), 'Information für Genossen Hager . . . ', 2 June 1960, SAPMO-BArch, DY30/IV2/19/56.

One defector who had gone to join his wife-to-be claimed: 'Had it been possible to visit my family at regular intervals, I would have had no reason to leave the GDR.'[95] The MfS also noted that most of those turned down still 'try by threatening a complaint or *Republikflucht* to force a permit'.[96] It seemed that the SED had taken a step too far into the private sphere, breaking an unwritten pact. From the figures themselves (see Figure 6), the intelligentsia in particular appear to have reacted badly to the new dispensation, viewing it as a breach of trust, whereas groups such as workers were more susceptible to obstacles placed in their way.

There is other evidence that the drop in *Republikflucht* concealed many simmering discontents. Applications for formal emigration jumped in 1958, but were stonewalled by the Interior Ministry.[97] The number of actual emigrations allowed thus dropped by two-thirds (see Figure 4). Petitions to the state and police regarding travel consequently soared. Whereas in the first quarter of 1957 petitions to President Pieck on travel had almost died out at 2 per cent (compared with 22 per cent in spring 1953), these were back at 22 per cent in spring 1958.[98] The President's petitions desk reported a 'lack of understanding', with many pensioners writing in, 'often in an aggressive and demanding form'. Inge R. of Dresden warned that 'by compulsory measures you only aggravate people, not win them'.[99] The Volkspolizei bore the brunt of public irritation, however. Petitions to its Pass and Registry section had made up only a quarter of all police complaints in the first quarter of 1957, but by the final quarter constituted over two-thirds. In 1958 this rose to 79 per cent, and in 1960 to a staggering 85 per cent. The volume of complaints also exploded, quadrupling in the same period.[100] The content of the petitions is also revealing. Pieck's office commented that 'in a considerable proportion . . . correspondents ignore the fact that we currently have two independent states in Germany'. Lore F. wrote: 'One can refuse passes abroad but not to West Germany which still belongs to us.' Or Gudrun S.: 'I was at the interzonal pass office in Erfurt yesterday. The aggravation among the population at not being issued passes is unimaginable.'[101] According to a third, 'the filled-out application form was crumpled up by the Volkspolizei officer before my mother's eyes and thrown in the wastepaper basket'.[102] Travel was clearly an issue which could rouse the passions almost more than any other.

[95] HVDVP (Leiter), 'Republikfluchten', 8 Jan. 1958, BAB, DO-1/11/965, fos. 7–13.
[96] MfS-ZAIG, 'Bericht über die Entwicklung der Republikflucht im Zeitraum vom 1.4.61–13.8.61 . . . ', 3 Oct. 1961, BStU-ZA, ZAIG 412, fo. 64.
[97] MdI (IA), 'Jahresanalyse . . . 1958', 3 Feb. 1959, SAPMO-BArch, DY30/IV2/13/400.
[98] SAPMO-BArch, DY30/IV2/5/252–53.
[99] Präsident der DDR (Staatssekretär) to SED-ZK (PO), 28 Oct. 1957, SAPMO-BArch, DY30/IV2/5/252, fos. 279–327.
[100] BAB, DO-1/11/49–50.
[101] Präsident der DDR (Staatssekretär) to SED-ZK (PO), 29 Oct. 1958, SAPMO-BArch, DY30/IV2/5/253, fos. 1–70.
[102] Ibid., report for 2nd quarter of 1960, SAPMO-BArch, DY30/IV2/5/253, fos. 71–149.

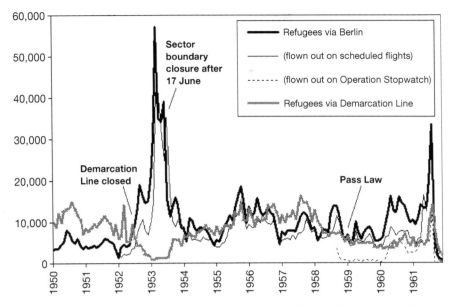

Figure 8. *Republikflucht* via Berlin and the Demarcation Line, 1950–61 (monthly).
Source: BMfFV figures. See Note 1, Chapter 3.

Moreover, the new clamp-down had the effect of funnelling more and more of the exodus towards Berlin. As Figure 2 shows, whereas in 1957 *Republikflucht* had been evenly spread across the GDR, in 1958, as well as dipping overall, it became localized around Berlin. Defection became increasingly a crime of opportunity, favouring those with local connections. Figure 8 shows the Berlin factor in more detail. In fact, numbers taking this route may have been even higher in the later stages of the crisis—as many as 85–95 per cent—as refugees arriving in West Berlin flew out and then registered in West Germany.[103] Absconders bluffed their way to the capital, carrying ostensible presents for family celebrations, onward tickets to holiday destinations on the Baltic, or chits claiming official business. To avoid S-Bahn checks, some boarded the interzonal train with just a platform ticket, happy to risk the penalty fare.[104]

In the final stages of the open-border crisis, desperate efforts were made to seal off Berlin from its hinterland, a tall order, since East Berlin was the capital of the GDR and hub of its transport network. Earlier proposals for the diversion of long-distance trains around Berlin, and lengthy border controls of

[103] Acland to Zulueta, 30 June 1961, TNA, FO 371/160656/CG1821/5; 'Stand und Entwicklung der Bevölkerungsbewegung im Jahre 1960', 20 Jan. 1961, BAB, DO-1/34/21723.
[104] 'Verhinderung von Republikfluchten', 10 Aug. 1961, BAB, DO-1/11/967, fo. 145.

S- and U-Bahn traffic, had been rejected.[105] Even in 1960 the Volkspolizei was limited to monitoring Berlin-bound vehicles 'under the pretext of technical checks'.[106] 'Train escort squads' with wanted lists decanted suspected absconders into special holding compartments. Besides its local constables and Auxiliary Volunteers, the police co-opted mayors, employers, banks, and post-offices. Parcels were confiscated in their tens of thousands. The MfS recruited informers among taxi ranks and railway ticket offices. Anybody selling off valuables such as cars was automatically investigated and the Stasi took to interviewing would-be leavers as a psychological deterrent.[107] Thus, between May 1960, when the new stringency began, and the building of the Wall, over 50,000 suspects were detained by the authorities. For every one held, however, six managed to evade the police cordon. As the MfS concluded, 'a comprehensive sealing-off of West Berlin is not possible and therefore the combating of *Republikflucht* cannot be left to the security organs of the GDR alone'.[108]

The authorities also tried to grasp the *Grenzgänger* nettle. SED campaigns to isolate them had initially been patchy, relying on suasion and naming and shaming. Berlin's Transformer Works implored employees not to succumb to the 'egotistical wolf's morality'.[109] Persistent offenders were sometimes deprived of their flats or fined. In other cases children were barred from higher education. In mid-1958 measures were stepped up when the Volkspolizei searched apartments for western consumer goods. But this simply prompted many to flee once and for all, with numbers going up fivefold in the late summer.[110] In spring 1961 the SED contemplated more swingeing deterrents, such as charging for rent, gas, and electricity in hard currency,[111] but thought better of forcing commuters to exchange hard currency one to one, leaving only 'pocket money'.[112] In July a decree made ownership of cars, televisions, refrigerators, and washing-machines dependent on a certificate of permanent employment in the GDR.[113] Then, on 5 August, apparently ignorant that this measure would soon be redundant, the city council announced that commuters would be forcibly registered between 9

[105] MfS (Chef der Transportpolizei), 'Vorschläge . . .', 17 Feb. 1956, SAPMO-BArch, DY30/IV2/13/397.
[106] HVDVP (Kripo), 'Thesen . . .', 7 July 1960, BA, DO-1/34/21721.
[107] MfS-ZAIG, 'Bericht über die Entwicklung der Republikflucht 1960 . . .', 28 Oct. 1960, BStU-ZA, ZAIG 247, fos. 70–114.
[108] MfS-ZAIG, 'Bericht über die Entwicklung der Republikflucht im Zeitraum Oktober-Dezember 1960 . . .', 3 Feb. 1961, BStU-ZA, ZAIG 412, fo. 4.
[109] 'Zum Grenzgängerproblem', 27 June 1961, LAB (STA), Rep. 411/Nr. 402.
[110] Senator für Arbeit & Sozialwesen, 'Jahresbericht 1958 . . .', LAB, Rep. 4/Acc. 2140/Nr. 192.
[111] 'Vorschläge zur weitgehenden Eindämmung der Grenzgänger-Bewegung . . .', 24 Mar. 1961, SAPMO-BArch, JIV2/202/65, fos. 36–39.
[112] 'Maßnahmen zur weitgehenden Eindämmung der Grenzgänger-Bewegung . . .', 6 June 1961, SAPMO-BArch, JIV2/202/65, fos. 66–72.
[113] Schütrumpf, 'Zu einigen Aspekten', 349.

and 19 August,[114] provoking a final counter-productive wave of 8–9,000 flights in the final weeks before the Wall.[115]

In the last days of the crisis the party reached for ever-more fantastical conspiracy theories to explain the losses. The MfS, in Operation Checkmate, orchestrated show trials against 'recruiters'.[116] Cross-examinations were scripted to incriminate the West Berlin Senate, complete with Stasi camera directions for televised confessions and sentences.[117] On 2 August 1961 five people were duly convicted. The main defendant, accused of luring away over 100 members of the intelligentsia, received fifteen years' penal servitude.[118] At the same time 'Committees against Human Trafficking' were formed across the GDR, taking it upon themselves to impound passports, as well as condemning recruitment in the most lurid manner: 'With carrot and stick, in the manner of the slave trade, many West Berlin spy organizations and Senate offices are trying to recruit people from our Republic', announced one works' tannoy, but 'behind the glittering facade lurks naked, raw and ruthless violence'.[119] *Neues Deutschland* carried heart-rending stories of child snatching, claiming that 'no means are too low for the modern slave traders in Bonn and West Berlin to force people from our state into their clutches'.[120] Yet, all too often, loaded terms such as 'people trafficking' and 'head-hunting' rebounded on the SED as diversionary 'sledgehammer' propaganda.[121]

The exodus assumed crisis proportions in the summer of 1961. The backlog of refugees in West Berlin threatened to overwhelm the Allies' resources, as billets ran out and Tempelhof's air capacity reached breaking point. The mood among the GDR populace was one of exasperation and confusion. Some local parties felt obliged to produce 'missing' leaders in order to quell speculation that rats were leaving a sinking ship.[122] West German observers described 'disaffection, passivity, and susceptibility to "western propaganda" ', although no danger of strikes.[123] It was not like 1953. Instead, a muted *Torschlußpanik*, a stampede panic, spread fears that the borders were about to close, including the idea of a 'special exclusion area' around Greater Berlin. Matters were not helped by Ulbricht's unsolicited reassurance at a press conference on 15 June that 'No-one has any intention

[114] Magistrat von Groß-Berlin (Wirtschaftsrat), '2. Situationsbericht zur Durchführung der Registrierung', 9 Aug. 1961, LAB (STA), Rep. 124/Nr. 216.

[115] Schütrumpf, 'Zu einigen Aspekten', 351–2.

[116] MfS, 'Aktion "SCHACH" ', 19 July 1961, BStU-ZA, ZAIG 10366, fos. 102–14.

[117] MfS (Agit) minutes of SED-ZK, 25 July 1961, BStU-ZA, ZAIG 10366, fos. 13–14.

[118] Mehls, *13. August*, 27–8.   [119] Untitled, undated, LAB (STA), Rep. 411/Nr. 402.

[120] *Neues Deutschland*, 11 Aug. 1961, 1.

[121] SED-PL KMU, 'Bericht', 11 Aug. 1961, SAPMO-BArch, DY30/IV2/9.04/558, fos. 151–6.

[122] SED-BL Erfurt (Org-Kader), 'Informationsbericht Nr. 23/61', 14 Aug. 1961, ThHStAW, SED-BL Erfurt, IV2/3/387.

[123] 'Politische Entwicklung in der Sowjetzone Deutschlands', 4 Aug. 1961, TNA, FO 371/ 160656/CG1821/10.

of erecting a wall.'[124] And despite subsequent claims that the Allies had known since 1958 of an Operation Chinese Wall to seal off Berlin,[125] West German intelligence reported to Adenauer that, although 'the island of West Berlin has now become a matter of life or death for the Communist regime', further travel restrictions would be 'intolerable to the whole population'.[126] On 12 August the British, too, were putting a brave face on the crisis: 'The Russians are probably more impressed by the dangers of disturbances if the escape route is completely cut than by the current damage to the D.D.R.'[127] Instead, British Military Government seemed set for more of the same. A day later, everything changed. 13 August 1961 was to go down as the darkest day of Germany's Cold War.

SHUTTING THE GATE: THE DECISION TO BUILD THE WALL

The final decision-making for total border closure occurred only days before the Wall went up. It had to, in order to avoid a mass stampede for the exit. Yet historians will search in vain for explicit references to an impending border closure; even behind closed doors leaders talked in euphemistic code, of the need to 'implement the peace treaty', rather than the erection of a wall. Insiders knew, of course, that a peace treaty would have given the East Germans a free hand to close the border, and was thus not simply of academic interest, but Moscow insisted on the indirect approach. With hindsight, it seems that the SED had contemplated border closure for some time, but had been consistently vetoed by the Russians. As early as February 1952 East Berlin had suggested to the Soviet Control Commission isolating West Berlin from its hinterland, but had been overruled by Moscow in March 1953.[128] Following the 17 June insurrection the sector boundary had indeed been sealed for three weeks, but then reopened. And although the East Berlin Police Presidium maintained a contingency 'Anton Plan' for complete closure of the sector boundary, in the mid-1950s it contented itself with gradually throttling cross-border traffic and trade.[129] Meanwhile, the Demarcation Line between the two Germanys was tightened. In 1955 East German border police took over guard duty from the

---

[124] *Neues Deutschland*, 17 June 1961, 5.   [125] Catudal, *Kennedy*, 226–7.

[126] BfV, 'Sowjetzonale Maßnahmen zur Eindämmung der sogenannten "Republikflucht" ', 20 July 1961, BAK, B136/3925.

[127] BMG Berlin to Foreign Office, 12 Aug. 1961, TNA, FO 371/160656/CG1821/8.

[128] Stefan Creuzberger, 'Abschirmungspolitik gegenüber dem westlichen Deutschland im Jahre 1952', in Gerhard Wettig (ed.), *Die sowjetische Deutschland-Politik in der Ära Adenauer* (Bonn: Bouvier, 1997), 12–36: 23.

[129] Armin Wagner, *Walter Ulbricht und die geheime Sicherheitspolitik der SED: Der Nationale Verteidigungsrat der DDR und seine Vorgeschichte (1953 bis 1971)* (Berlin: Links, 2002), 434.

Russians and by 1959 barbed wire covered 1,000 kilometres of the 1,400-kilometre intra-German frontier. Wooden posts were replaced with concrete, and 500 observation towers erected, surrounded by bunkers and alarms.[130] Propagandists cultivated an image of order at the 'border between two worlds', defending socialism against revanchist capitalism.[131] Nevertheless, even as late as November 1960, East Berlin and the Kremlin talked only of 'security measures', of stepped-up internal controls, such as patrols of access roads—but no physical edifice.[132] The sensitivity of quadripartite Berlin, in which even the tiniest procedural move could flare into nuclear war, meant that Moscow was always likely to suppress unilateral moves by its junior ally.

Yet since this crucial meeting also signalled the Kremlin's resistance to subsidizing the GDR indefinitely, the East Germans began to look for alternatives. As we have seen, in January 1961 the SED Politbüro launched a high-level troubleshooting group including Honecker and Mielke to combat the refugee flow. Despite subsequent claims that in March 1961 Ulbricht approached the Warsaw Pact with various options, including a blockade or a quarantined Greater Berlin,[133] there is no direct evidence of this from the record. Ulbricht pleaded for aid in stabilizing the East German economy which was subject to 'systematic recruitment' of skilled workers by Bonn: 'West Berlin represents a great hole in the middle of our Republic costing us more than a billion marks a year.' Yet the East German leader stressed the gradualism of the planned expulsion of the western powers: 'We have no abrupt change of all circumstances in mind, but a transitional stage.'[134] The overall tone was to emphasize economic and diplomatic initiatives, playing up the dangers of West German revisionism east of the Oder-Neisse for the benefit of the eastern bloc audience. Nevertheless, from March 1961 the border police were supposedly hoarding barbed wire and concrete posts, to cover all eventualities.[135] Moreover, from May the East German and Soviet armies began secret planning for a military escalation of the crisis, should it be necessary, and a third of the GDR's riot police were transferred to Berlin in June.[136]

In these months there is no doubt where the pressure to act was coming from: the GDR. On the eve of Khrushchev's important international engagements, Ulbricht regularly lobbied for action. It was clear to the Stasi that a second

---

[130] Schultke, *"Keiner kommt durch"*, 45.

[131] *Reporter an der Grenze* (East Berlin: Verlag Ministerium des Innern, 1960).

[132] Steiner, 'Auf dem Weg?', 108.

[133] Norman Gelb, *Berlin Wall* (London: Michael Joseph, 1986), 65.

[134] SAPMO-BArch, DY30/J IV2/202/251.

[135] Hauptmann Ganßauge in *Es geschah im August* (Karsten and Hertle, 2001), ARD TV documentary, 13 Aug. 2001.

[136] Matthias Uhl, ' "Westberlin stellt also ein großes Loch inmitten unserer Republik dar": Die militärischen und politischen Planungen Moskaus und Ost-Berlins zum Mauerbau', in Dierk Hoffmann *et al.* (eds), *Vor dem Mauerbau: Politik und Gesellschaft in der DDR der fünfziger Jahre* (Munich: Oldenbourg, 2003), 314–18.

blockade would be a non-starter, since West Berlin was too well provisioned.[137] Yet, although the MfS had warned that the West suspected something might be in the offing for August or September, on 19 May 1961 GDR leaders formally asked the Soviets to close the sector border at all costs. Ambassador Pervukhin reported the SED's impatience: 'Our friends would like to establish now such a control on the sectoral border between democratic and West Berlin which would allow them to, as they say, close "the door to the West".'[138] The failure of the Vienna summit between Kennedy and Khrushchev in early June undoubtedly strengthened Ulbricht's hand, but still the Kremlin hesitated. On 4 July Pervukhin relayed SED plans for border controls following a peace treaty, but advised that a full-scale closure would be difficult, both technically and politically. The first line of attack should be on overland and air corridors between West Berlin and the FRG. Nevertheless, contingency measures were laid for 'introducing a state border regime on the sectoral border'.[139] While holidaying in the Crimea, Khrushchev weighed up his options. Meanwhile Honecker, as SED security chief, and Verner, as Berlin party boss, were in Moscow for talks with the CPSU's Germany spokesman, Karpin. It was clear to them that the Soviets 'still do not know how all these issues are to be solved practically, because they still do not have a definite picture of individual problems'.[140] Berlin was told, nevertheless, to prepare itself well for the forthcoming Warsaw Pact gathering of international party leaders, where politico-economic as well as military questions would be on the agenda, regarding 'especially West Berlin'. At this late stage, however, the SED Politbüro's working group was still focusing on 'legal methods of conducting the battle against the flight wave'.[141] Thus, less than a month before the Wall went up, schemes were being devised which were soon to be redundant. An emergency Central Committee meeting on 28 July, for instance, discussed how trains might be diverted around East Berlin and youths forbidden from travelling west. And as we have seen, local Committees for the Protection of GDR Citizens and Prevention of Slave Trading were to be established, and *Grenzgänger* compulsorily registered, thus generating a last counter-productive wave of *Republikflucht* in early August.[142]

It is unclear what finally prompted Khrushchev to give a green light. Perhaps he wished to 'wall in' Ulbricht and prevent him from encroaching on West Berlin?[143] The Wall was a consolation prize—what Khrushchev later called 'the maximum of what was possible'—but also a means of controlling the

---

[137] MfS, 'Sonderbericht über weitere Vorbereitungen für eine Luftbrücke nach Westberlin', 13 May 1961, BStU-ZA, MfS-SdM 1898, fos. 209–12.

[138] Harrison, *Driving*, 170.   [139] Harrison, *Driving*, 185.

[140] 'Besondere Informationen an Genossen Walter Ulbricht', 15 July 1961, SAPMO-BArch, DY30/JIV2/202/130.

[141] SED-PB, 18 July 1961, SAPMO-BArch, DY30/J IV2/2/777.

[142] SED-PB, 28 July 1961, SAPMO-BArch, DY30/J IV2/2/780.

[143] Harrison, 'Concrete "Rose" ', 55.

East Germans.[144] The Kremlin was quick to nip in the bud the GDR leader's more far-fetched suggestions, such as blockading West Berlin's air corridors with barrage balloons.[145] Zubok and Pleshakov highlight growing Soviet resentment at supplying the bottomless pit of the GDR economy. In November 1960 Gosplan head Kosygin had complained at the levels of foodstuffs demanded from a USSR which was experiencing severe difficulties itself. Khrushchev allegedly exploded at Ulbricht's request for Soviet guest workers, adding: 'We won the war. Our workers will not clean your toilets.'[146] Poland, too, was baulking at coal deliveries.[147] Internal SED statistics show that, apart from Bulgaria, Comecon was only providing about 20 per cent of what East Berlin thought had been agreed, with particular disappointment at Poland, Rumania, and Czechoslovakia.[148] From these eastern allies' point of view, making the GDR a showcase of socialism was turning into a costly albatross around their necks.

Our sketchy knowledge of the final moments is based mainly on memoir literature which places Soviet assent sometime in July. It is possible that Kennedy's 'three essentials' speech on 25 July, at which he dug his heels in over West Berlin but implicitly washed his hands of East Berlin, removed the Kremlin leader's last inhibitions. The following day he instructed Ulbricht that 'we have to use the tension in international relations now to circle Berlin in an iron ring'.[149] A few days later Senator Fulbright explicitly conceded the GDR's right to close its border. The Stasi assiduously gathered evidence of American non-interventionism, for instance Senator Hubert Humphrey's claim to Willy Brandt that 'if the "rights of the military" were not infringed, he saw no reason for military intervention', as well as Kennedy's reported claim that: 'We Americans cannot jump into a world war for the sake of this city.'[150] Certainly, events moved very quickly after this juncture, but only because the SED had already done much of the groundwork. Khrushchev, poring over a bad map of Berlin, discussed border control with Pervukhin, who was to consult with Ulbricht. When he did so, he was surprised at how well-developed the East German leader's thoughts were.[151] Towards the end of July, heeding a National Defence Council directive of May, the SED's Security Department produced a detailed plan of 'pioneer measures' required to seal off West Berlin, as well as readiness reports on the Border Police and Volkspolizei. Although 54

[144] Khrushchev on 26 Feb. 1962, in Douglas Selvage, 'The End of the Berlin Crisis, 1961–62', *Cold War International History Project Bulletin*, 11 (1998), 225.

[145] Uhl, 'Westberlin', 318.   [146] Zubok and Pleshakov, *Inside*, 249.

[147] Douglas Selvage, 'The End of the Berlin Crisis, 1961–62', *Cold War International History Project Bulletin*, 11 (1998), 218–29: 219.

[148] SED-ZK (Politbüro), 12 Sept. 1961 (appendix 1), SAPMO-BArch, DY30/J IV2/2/790, fos. 14–23.

[149] Fursenko and Naftali, *Khrushchev's Cold War*, 377.

[150] MfS, 'Sonderbericht Nr. 9–61', 7 Aug. 1961, BStU-ZA, MfS-SdM 1898, fo. 191.

[151] Julij A. Kwizinskij, *Vor dem Sturm: Erinnerungen eines Diplomaten* (Berlin: Siedler, 1993), 179.

kilometres of border were already fenced off, another 92 kilometres remained
to be sealed, requiring an estimated 485 tonnes of barbed wire and 27,000
man-hours. Notwithstanding a ready supply of concrete posts available from the
prison factories at Bautzen and Torgau, the GDR's barbed-wire stockpiles, held
mainly at the Demarcation Line, would only accomplish just over a third of the
task.[152] (The shortfall was made up by imports from Poland and Czechoslovakia,
not West Germany as is sometimes claimed.[153]) At the same time contingency
plans envisaged cutting S- and U-Bahn traffic between East and West Berlin,
except at Friedrichstraße and Potsdamer Platz.[154] Meanwhile, the GDR's Interior
Ministry began covert action under its armed forces commander, Willi Seifert,
a former Buchenwald inmate with first-hand experience of high security, and
one of the key behind-the-scenes figures in the ensuing events. On 31 July the
Border Police were ordered to start top-secret preparations for the 'reinforced
technical expansion' of the border around West Berlin. The next day lorry-loads
of construction materials began to wend their secret way from the Demarcation
Line to the Berlin Ring, using every conspiratorial precaution to keep even drivers
in the dark.[155]

Nevertheless, such a momentous decision required Warsaw Pact blessing.
Surrounded by eastern bloc communist leaders, on 3 August Khrushchev
outlined three options: a separate peace treaty, which might entail western
sanctions; border closure; or to do nothing, which would require ongoing
Comecon subsidies to East Germany.[156] Although the Kremlin may well have
favoured the latter, the gathered eastern Europeans had no desire to become
permanent blood donors to the GDR. Ulbricht played on their fears of West
German revanchism. The build-up of the Bundeswehr allegedly represented
'the well-known "Drang nach Osten" whereby German imperialism since time
immemorial has launched its aggression against the peoples of eastern and
south-eastern Europe'.[157] The open border had caused the GDR considerable
economic damage, requiring 'the removal of the espionage centres in West
Berlin and *complete control of traffic*'.[158] This would entail East German checks
on transit and air traffic between West Berlin and West Germany as well as
special passes for East German citizens to cross the state frontier, which, in the

[152] SED-ZK (Sicherheit) to Ulbricht, 24 July 1961, SAPMO-BArch, DY30/JIV2/202/65, fos. 82–126.

[153] MdI (Versorgungsdienste), 'Auskunftsbericht Nr. 17', 29 Aug. 1961, BAB, DO-1/11/1077, fos. 83–84.

[154] 'Massnahmen zur Sicherstellung der Kontrolle des Verkehrs . . . ', n.d., SAPMO-BArch, DY30/JIV2/202/130.

[155] NVA (Inst. f. Deutsche Militärgeschichte), 'Die Nationale Volksarmee in der Aktion vom 13. August 1961', 20 Feb. 1964, BA-MZAP, Strausberg, AZN 32588, 35.

[156] Bernd Bonwetsch and Alexei Filitow, 'Chruschtschow und der Mauerbau: Die Gipfelkonferenz der Warschauer-Pakt-Staaten vom 3.-5. August 1961', *Vierteljahrshefte für Zeitgeschichte*, 48 (2000), 155–98: 167–8.

[157] Ulbricht speech, 3 Aug. 1961, SAPMO-BArch, DY30/J IV2/201/1216, fo. 8.

[158] Ibid., fo. 26. Emphasis in original.

unexpurgated version of the speech, 'will be sealed off'.[159] Ulbricht thought it improbable, nonetheless—despite 'sabre-rattling'—that the western powers would resort to military measures, although 'it would be wrong to close one's eyes to the fact that, with the resolution of the decisive questions standing before us, military complications are also possible'.[160] More likely was an economic embargo, a factor which allowed Ulbricht to remind his audience that some partners were not sticking to their agreed deliveries of bottleneck goods. Polish leader Władysław Gomułka then obliged by calling for the border to be shut.[161] Eastern bloc representatives were excluded, however, from detailed discussions of military aspects of the operation, which were dealt with behind closed doors between the CPSU and SED.[162] In Ulbricht's almost indecipherable handwritten notes of his meeting with Khrushchev, we read: 'What is the way out? . . . Close the border': '13 August—midnight'.[163]

Meanwhile, the SED had been put on 'highest battle-readiness', braced for an economic embargo. With June 1953 obviously in mind, the party was to secure all factories and public places and personal weapons were broken out.[164] On Ulbricht's return from Moscow planning went into overdrive. On Monday, 7 August, the SED's Politbüro confirmed the date for the coming Saturday night/Sunday morning, when fewest East Germans would be going to work. On Wednesday Honecker, charged with running the operation, closeted himself with Transport Minister Kramer in the Police Presidium and drafted a ground plan. At midnight on the appointed day Honecker would gather seven other leaders at his headquarters, including the ministers of the Interior, Security, and Transport. Then at 1 a.m. Interior Ministry forces, the Berlin and Potsdam Task Forces, and the Kampfgruppen militia were to be alerted. From 4 a.m. agitators were to appear at all railway stations. Finally, the MfS was to screen the border population for 'enemy elements'.[165] The Stasi was, nevertheless, initiated into the secret only very late, on 11 August,[166] drawing up plans under its operation 'Rose' to monitor communications and transport, guarding against 'the counter-revolutionary forces of 1953 in the GDR and 1956 in Hungary and Poland'.[167]

[159] Bonwetsch and Filitow, 'Chruschtschow', 169.

[160] Ulbricht speech, 3 Aug. 1961, SAPMO-BArch, DY30/J IV2/201/1216, fo. 50.

[161] Bonwetsch and Filitow, 'Chruschtschow', 174.

[162] 'Vorschläge zur Durchführung der Beratungen', 31 July 1961, SAPMO-BArch, DY30/J IV2/202/130.

[163] '3. August', SAPMO-BArch, DY30/3682, fos. 148–51. Interestingly, even at this stage the notes only mentioned 'closing external border ring—exit of GDR citizens only by special pass'.

[164] 'Direktive zur Schaffung einer hohen Kampfbereitschaft der Partei . . . ', 4 Aug. 1961, SAPMO-BArch, DY30/IV2/5/36, fos. 41–52.

[165] 'Plan der Maßnahmen (geschrieben 9.8.61 v. EK f. EH)', BA-MZAP, VA-01/39575.

[166] MfS, 'Protokoll über die Dienstbesprechung am 11.08.1961', 18 Aug. 1961, BStU-ZA, MfS-SdM 1557, fos. 231–7.

[167] MfS-BV Frankfurt/Oder, 'Einsatzplan', 12–13.8.1961, Dokumentationszentrum Berliner Mauer.

In the event, the operation proceeded smoothly. At 4 p.m. on 12 August Ulbricht signed responsibility over to Honecker. The bloc party leaders were then invited to the First Secretary's summer residence at Döllnsee, deep in the East German hinterland, 'just in case', as he explained to the Soviet ambassador.[168] After dinner Ulbricht let them into the secret, holding an impromptu session of the Council of Ministers, which duly rubber-stamped the measures. At 8 p.m. Army General Hoffmann opened his sealed orders, and at 9 p.m. the Volkspolizei was alerted. The Border Police was ordered to undertake 'intensified border security' at the 'State Border West', preventing transgression in both directions. Heavy border units were to form a flying reserve and reconnoitre the 'adversary'.[169] By 3.10 a.m. the units involved had completed their encirclement of West Berlin and by 6.30 a.m. the last checkpoint had been closed.[170]

The forces involved were divided into three echelons. In the first were Border and Riot Police, unrolling the barbed wire, backed by human cordons of Volkspolizei and Kampfgruppen factory militia, who kept an eye on the frontline comrades. Indeed, in the first fortnight, thirty-six Border and seventy Riot police, many of them raw recruits, deserted; some volunteers were clearly reporting for border duty specifically to abscond.[171] Among the regular Volkspolizei discipline was better, with only three desertions in the first fortnight, most famous of which was Conrad Schumann's leap over the barbed wire, caught for posterity by a western photographer.[172] However, 111 Vopos were dismissed during the crisis for defeatism and spreading enemy arguments.[173] The Kampfgruppen, although amateurs who in fact took a long time to mobilize, were usually SED members and viewed as loyal. In the crucial Berlin-Mitte sector only two defected.[174] They were also seen as the potentially most trigger-happy—so much so that they were not issued with live ammunition. Instead a constant stream of bouquets of flowers and hot soup was ferried out to these political representatives of the working class, who, in their peaked caps and baggy fatigues, became the official symbols of the action.[175]

[168] Kwizinskij, *Sturm*, 184.

[169] DGP-Kommando, 'Befehl Nr. 002/61', 12 Aug. 1961, in Werner Filmer and Heribert Schwan, *Opfer der Mauer: Die geheimen Protokolle des Todes* (Munich: Bertelsmann, 1991), 328–30.

[170] BEL Berlin to Ulbricht, 13 Aug. 1961 (7.00 a.m.), LAB (STA), Rep. 303/26.1/Nr. 227, fos. 4–7.

[171] 'Fahnenfluchten neueingestellter Angehöriger des Kommando-Grenze . . .', 30 Nov. 1961, SAPMO-BArch, DY30/IV2/12/47, fos. 288–94.

[172] SED-ZK (Sicherheit), 'Bericht über die Fahnenfluchten in den bewaffneten Kräften der DDR in der Zeit vom 01.07.–31.08.1961 . . . ', 15 Sept. 1961, SAPMO-BArch, DY30/IV2/12/47, fos. 247–55.

[173] HVDVP (Pol. Verw.), 'Zwischenbilanz . . .', 2 Oct. 1961, BAB, DO-1/11/321, fos. 116–27.

[174] VPI Berlin-Mitte (Polit-Abt.), 'Bericht . . .', 1 Sept. 1961, LAB, BPA SED Berlin, IV2/12/1414.

[175] April Eisman, 'Picturing the Berlin Wall in 1960s East Germany', paper at 'Berlin, Divided City' conference, Austin, Texas, 28–29 Mar. 2008.

In the second echelon were regular soldiers of the National People's Army (NVA) providing a demonstrative presence. In the event of western Allied intervention the Soviet Red Army was on standby as a third tier, but was never called upon.[176] Like most of those involved, the divisional and regimental NVA commanders only learned of the operation during the evening of 12 August. Three days before, Minister of National Defence Hoffmann had been given the task of drawing up a blind order of march. The next day two motorized rifle divisions were sent on routine manoeuvres away from Berlin, and then, on the evening of 12 August, in radio silence, took up position 1,000 metres from the border, one in the city and one in the countryside along the Western Ring. According to the minister's orders, however, 'The use of firearms is categorically forbidden and will occur only at my command. Ammunition in the tanks is to be sealed. . . . Only guards and patrols are to receive live ammunition.'[177] Accordingly, guns and artillery were pointed away from West Berlin so as not to provoke the West, thus belying the official rationale for the operation.

'The adversary was unable to discover our plan', Ulbricht later boasted. 'All orders were worked out, everything had been passed in Moscow, everything sat in the safe. Still they suspected nothing.'[178] Kennedy was out cruising off Martha's Vineyard; Macmillan was grouse shooting in Scotland; Brandt was on the election trail. But even if they had known more, the West would not have intervened. Kennedy had candidly admitted shortly before the final dénouement that Washington could not have prevented a border closure: 'I can hold the Alliance together to defend West Berlin but I cannot act to keep East Berlin open.'[179] When he saw his prophecy come true, he told aides: 'It's not a very nice solution, but a wall is a hell of a lot better than a war.'[180] Nevertheless, Honecker kept to a provisional 'Stage I' of the operation during the first week, ready to back down if necessary. In the first hours barbed-wire entanglements were simply trailed across open spaces, and railings, lamp-posts, and other fixtures improvised as barriers. In some areas tram lines were prised up, cut and welded into tank traps. Then in the following days posts were erected to support a wire-mesh fence, concrete blocks emplaced and sections of wall built at key points such as Potsdamer Platz. Yet, only four days into operations, it was clear to the SED 'that the West will not undertake anything special'.[181] Accordingly, on 21 August the GDR went over to Stage II of a 'regular border control', involving a heavy-duty, 2-metre-high wall of concrete breeze blocks, commandeered from the GDR's building programme, topped with concrete lintels and barbed wire, as well as a second tier of obstacles. Under armed guard, builders in their white overalls began

---

[176] Uhl, 'Westberlin', 320–6 and 328–9.   [177] Schultke, *"Keiner kommt durch"*, 53.
[178] 'Rede des Genossen Walter Ulbricht im Politbüro am 22.8.1961', 22 Aug. 1961, SAPMO-BArch, DY 24/3.727.
[179] Gaddis, *We Now Know*, 148.   [180] Gaddis, *We Now Know*, 149.
[181] Honecker, 'Schlußfolgerungen', n.d. [notes for Zentralstab session of 17 Aug. 1961], BA-MZAP, VA-01/39577, fos. 132–5.

to brick up housefronts.[182] Five of the remaining twelve crossing-points were also closed and West Berliners no longer allowed into East Berlin. New guard towers and searchlights were erected.[183] Security officials paced out the sector boundary for loopholes. Alerted by a dislodged manhole cover, the Stasi even descended into the sewers, welding up the final escape routes with underwater grilles, and congratulating itself that MfS officers, 'despite their desk duties, have remained true workers.'[184] The Berlin Wall had arrived.

[182] 'Bericht der Kommission des Stadtbezirks Mitte . . . ', 24 Aug. 1961, LAB (STA), Rep. 124/213.
[183] RdSB Friedrichshain, 'Vorschlag zur erweiterten Sicherung der Grenze . . . ', 19 Aug. 1961, LAB (STA), Rep. 124/213.
[184] Generalmajor Beater, 'Bericht für das Kollegium des MfS', Dec. 1961, BStU-ZA, MfS-SdM 1558, fo. 96.

PART II

BEHIND THE WALL

5

Walled in: 13 August 1961

The first East Germans to witness the new landmark in the early hours of 13 August were either late-night revellers or early risers. 'You've picked a very inconvenient time for it,'[1] complained the head of Berlin Transport, called away from a party. Outside Rita's Dance Palace, close to Bernauer Straße, fifteen irate youths ran amok. Elsewhere, transport personnel, attempting their usual short-cut across West Berlin to Treptow, threatened to strike, but retraced their steps. A group of musicians encountering the same difficulty became abusive,[2] as did one bus conductor who had to be physically restrained after shouting 'We live in a prison anyway.'[3] A tram conductress in Köpenick tearfully rued the lack of national solidarity.[4] This eclectic mix of views was typical of the fragmented responses to the overnight changes; unlike 17 June 1953, the populace was on the back foot and it took days if not weeks for the new power-political landscape to sink in. Realizing that bus and railway stations would be focal points, the party flooded them with agitprop cadres, armed with leaflets and ready-made arguments. At Friedrichstraße, the main rail interchange, passengers heading for West Berlin dispersed peacefully, their mood described as 'variable'. A large number, when prompted, publicly welcomed the action, adding that it should have come sooner. Others kept quiet.[5] During the morning, crowds milled about, trying to take in the situation from the advertising pillars now plastered with the government decree. Many were in shock, 'dazed' as one youth put it.[6] Recollections, too, betray the sense of stunned disbelief:

In the train the mood was low. No-one spoke. The nearer we came to Berlin the worse it got. There were constant checks in the train to see if anyone was travelling who had

[1] SED-ZK (PO), 'Kurzinformation', 13 Aug. 1961, SAPMO-BArch, DY30/IV2/5/433. fo. 1.

[2] PdVP Berlin (Polit-Abt.), 'Informationsbericht Nr. 1', 13 Aug. 1961, LAB (STA), Rep. 303/26.1/230, fo. 1. See also Corey Ross, 'East Germans and the Berlin Wall: Popular Opinion and Social Change before and after the Border Closure of August 1961', *Journal of Contemporary History*, 39 (2004), 25–43; 32 ff.

[3] SED-BL Berlin (Org-Kader), 'Information . . .', 13 Aug. 1961 (7.50 a.m.), LAB, BPA SED Berlin, IV2/12/1278.

[4] PdVP Berlin (Polit-Abt.), 'Stimmungsbericht vom 13.8.61, 09.00 Uhr', 13 Aug. 1961, LAB (STA), Rep. 303/26.1/230, fo. 4.

[5] BEL Berlin to Ulbricht, 13 Aug. 1961 (7.00 a.m.), LAB (STA), Rep. 303/26.1/227, fos. 4–7.

[6] SED-KL Neustrelitz (Org-Kader), 'Informationsbericht 8.00 Uhr', 14 Aug. 1961, MLHA Schwerin, BPA SED Neubrandenburg, IV2/11/976.

no business in Berlin. When we arrived, East Berlin was dead. It was as if a bell-jar had been placed over it and all the air sucked out. The same oppressiveness which hung over us, hung over all Berlin. There was no trace of big city life, of hustle and bustle. Like when a storm moves across the city. Or when the sky lowers and people ask if hail is on the way.[7]

Nor did many realize how permanent the new dispensation was. They had already witnessed the sector boundary's closure and reopening in 1953, as well as temporary closures in 1957 and the brief exclusion of West Germans in September 1960. Thus, initially, bystanders asked when the measures would be lifted. 'It is nothing to get het up about', explained one *Grenzgänger*. 'In a few days the measures are bound to be relaxed, so you may as well stay at home for a few days.'[8] Many requests betrayed the expectation that people could still go about their business, including 'visits to the sick, family dos, visits to the cemetery and trips to allotments to pick fruit and feed rabbits etc.'[9] Individuals still believed that an exception would be made for them. Defensive SED agitators in fact encouraged citizens to believe the measures would be rescinded once a peace treaty had been signed. Accordingly, during the first week tens of thousands of easterners applied in good faith for passes to West Berlin, to no avail.[10] Some clung to the hope of a diplomatic solution. After the end of the year, however, when a peace treaty had not materialized, the finality of the situation was evident even to 'optimists'.[11]

Keen to play down the situation, the Party Information described 13 August in Berlin, without irony, as 'a normal Sunday afternoon'.[12] Similar claims were made in the provinces.[13] Outside the capital there was certainly some equanimity, but only very rarely did officials try to quantify sentiment. In communist bastions such as Halle the SED claimed that proportionally more older citizens supported the action, but youngsters tended towards neutralism or hostility.[14] The intelligentsia and *Mittelstand* were apparently also more inscrutable. However, this silence, which marks 13 August off from the explosion

---

[7] Karin Schöpau in Anke Gebert (ed.), *Im Schatten der Mauer: Erinnerungen, Geschichten und Bilder vom Mauerbau bis zum Mauerfall* (Berne: Scherz, 1999), 207–13; 207.

[8] FDJ-ZR (Org-Instruk), 'Argumente . . .', 13 Aug. 1961, SAPMO-BArch, DY24/A 3.975.

[9] SED-BL Berlin (Org-Kader), 'Information . . .', 13 Aug. 1961 (10 a.m.), LAB, BPA SED Berlin, IV2/12/1278.

[10] BEL Berlin to Ulbricht, 13 Aug. 1961 (11.00 p.m.), LAB (STA), Rep. 303/26.1/227, fos. 25–28.

[11] SED-ZK (PO), 'Bericht über die Führungstätigkeit der BL Berlin . . .', 8 Feb. 1962, SAPMO-BArch, DY30/IV2/5/296, ff. 74–84.

[12] SED-ZK (PO), 'Kurzinformation Nr. 5', 13 Aug. 1961, SAPMO-BArch, DY30/IV2/5/433, fo. 12.

[13] BDVP-BEL KMS, '1. Bericht . . .', 13 Aug. 1961, StAC, SED-BL KMS, IV2/12/5, fos. 1–2; SED-SL Dresden (PI), 'Kurzbericht Nr. 5', 13 Aug. 1961, SächsHStA, BPA SED Dresden, IV2/5/134, fos. 108–09.

[14] SED-SBL Halle-Süd, 'Kurzinformation', 15 Aug. 1961, LAM, BPA SED Halle, IV/2/4/992, fos. 59–63.

of 17 June 1953, cannot always be interpreted as simple indifference. Much tight-lipped behaviour suggests conscious restraint, such as one farmer's ditty: 'Drink your fill and stuff your gut—if it's politics, keep your gob shut.'[15] Those who did speak out were liable to arrest, as the files abundantly attest. Yet, during moments of crisis some citizens dropped their guard and one does not have to scratch very deep to discover widespread feelings of resentment and betrayal. 'While youths spoken to individually in factories and at home generally react positively', noted one reporter, 'when they can act anonymously, they try to provoke.'[16] Although early Stasi assessments bullishly stressed the fragmented but manageable nature of protests, weaker in the provinces 'while they display a somewhat greater, but in no sense overwhelming scope in democratic Berlin,'[17] the MfS conceded that the measures dominated conversation for days.[18] Letter intercepts painted a gloomier picture: 'They claim that an unimaginable mood is abroad among the population in the Zone. People are beat, have no proper desire to work anymore and are all very embittered.'[19]

There were, of course, some who genuinely welcomed the measures. It would be historically dishonest to deny that there were not. What can probably never be answered satisfactorily is exactly how many. At the time, however, even the Party Information was sceptical of blithe claims that the mood was 'happy'.[20] Many declarations of support were couched in official terminology, parroting the party daily, *Neues Deutschland*.[21] Yet, even where there was political sympathy, there were severe reservations about the means employed. Government overreaction was a frequent accusation. Moderates suggested that the solution was to raise living standards, not walls.[22] Some were put off by thuggish press language, 'especially the crude terminology used against Brandt and Adenauer', described as 'demagoguery'.[23] Leipzig's main daily had 'sunk to the level of the [West German tabloid] *Bildzeitung*',

[15] 'Sauf Dich voll und fress Dich dick: doch halt Dein Maul von Politik.' SED-BL Potsdam, 13 Aug. 1961, BLHA, Bez. Pdm. Rep. 530/IV2/5/1021.

[16] SED-SL Leipzig, 'Bericht über den weiteren Verlauf der Aussprachetätigkeit . . .', 13 Aug. 1961, StAL, BPA SED Leipzig, IV2/12/595.

[17] MfS-ZAIG, 'Bericht über die Reaktion der Bevölkerung . . .', 15 Aug. 1961, BStU-ZA, ZAIG 526, fo. 2.

[18] MfS-Verwaltung Groß-Berlin (Informationsgruppe), 'Lagebericht Nr. 3', 18 Aug. 1961, LAB, BPA SED Berlin, IV2/12/1278.

[19] MfS-BV Frankfurt/Oder (Abt. M), 'Stimmungen der Bevölkerung der DDR . . .', 17 Aug. 1961, DBM, 'Berlin, 13. August 1961'.

[20] SED-BL Berlin (Kultur), 'Einschätzung der Stimmung unter der Intelligenz', 1 Sept. 1961, LAB, BPA SED Berlin, IV2/9.02/1002.

[21] SED-BL Berlin (Kultur), 'Erste Einschätzung der Stimmung unter den Kollegen des Märkischen und der staatlichen Museen . . .', 2 Sept. 1961, LAB, BPA SED Berlin, IV2/9.02/1002.

[22] 'Einschätzung der politischen Situation im Bereich der Deutschen Akademie der Wissenschaften zu Berlin', 8 Sept. 1961, SAPMO-BArch, DY30/IV2/9.04/272, fos. 384–86.

[23] SED-ZK (Agitation), 'Argumente der Intelligenz, Stichtag 20.9.61', SAPMO-BArch, DY30/IV2/9.02/6, fos. 48–54.

according to one educated group.[24] Karl-Eduard von Schnitzler's notorious 'Schwarzer Kanal' television programme was likewise criticized as 'too offensive, too ice-cold and calculating'.[25] There were even a number of satirical songs on the airwaves, in which the state came across as gloating. Evidently, many tuned in to western radio and television too, necessitating the banning of transistor radios in some workplaces.[26] Although the eastern media did not broadcast pictures of events, citizens were frequently overheard describing pavements being ripped up and barbed wire being deployed.[27] Calls for free elections also echoed western broadcasts. Even in Dresden, colloquially known as the 'Valley of Blissful Ignorance' because of its poor international radio reception, 'very many know exactly when, how and what has been going on in Berlin'.[28]

Where 'positive' opinions were recorded, many appear to have been rationalizations of self-interest rather than principled support for socialism. As the Party Information recognized, 'direct support is always linked with pleasure or even *Schadenfreude* regarding the *Grenzgänger*'.[29] According to one Brandenburg tractorist, there would be no more 'swaggering' by travellers to the West.[30] There was also relief on some shop-floors that the acute labour shortage might be eased. Although such views were welcomed by the party apparatus, they did not demonstrate the desired level of class or geopolitical consciousness.[31] Once ordinary citizens realized that they too were affected, the mood changed. In Berlin, for instance, anti-*Grenzgänger* sentiment declined markedly after the first 36 hours.[32] Arguments against speculators certainly persisted somewhat longer outside Berlin, reflecting deep-seated provincial resentment that Berliners had benefited disproportionately from their proximity to West Berlin. But many declarations of support included a veiled criticism of the state for having tolerated the situation for so long. Others were prepared to defend older commuters who had worked for up to forty years in West Berlin, and who would now lose their pensions.[33]

[24] SED-PL KMU, 'Informationsbericht', 23 Aug. 1961, SAPMO-BArch, DY30/IV2/9.04/558, fos. 189–94.
[25] Wyschofsky, 'Forum mit leitenden Angehörigen der Intelligenz des VEB Filmfabrik Wolfen', 16 Sept. 1961, SAPMO-BArch, DY30/IV2/6.03/62, fos. 356–8.
[26] FDGB-BuVo (Org), 'Klassenfeindliche Tätigkeit ...', 15 Aug. 1961, SAPMO-BArch, DY30/IV2/6.11/65, fos. 212–20.
[27] BEL KMS, '3. Bericht', 13 Aug. 1961, StAC, SED-BL KMS, IV2/12/5, fos. 6–9.
[28] FDJ-BL Dresden to FDJ-ZR, 15 Aug. 1961, SächsHStA, BPA SED Dresden, IV2/5/135, fos. 111–15.
[29] SED-BL Berlin (Org-Kader), 'Information zu den Schutzmaßnahmen', 13 Aug. 1961 (5.45 p.m.), LAB, BPA SED Berlin, IV2/3/633.
[30] SED-BL Potsdam (PI), 13 Aug. 1961, BLHA, Bez. Pdm. Rep. 530/IV2/5/1021.
[31] MfS-Verwaltung Groß-Berlin (Informationsgruppe), 'Lagebericht Nr. 2', 17 Aug. 1961, LAB, BPA SED Berlin, IV2/12/1278.
[32] SED-BL Berlin (Org-Kader), 'Information zu den Schutzmaßnahmen', 14 Aug. 1961, LAB, BPA SED Berlin, IV2/12/1278.
[33] SED-BPO Farbenfabrik Wolfen, 'Kurzinformation', 16 Aug. 1961, LAM, BPA SED Halle, IV425/115, fos. 199–200.

There were, conversely, accusations of hypocrisy at the continued encouragement of West Berliners to work at hospitals and theatres in the East.

This was where the official logic, that the border had been closed to protect East Germans from West German aggression, began to break down. The official defensive rationale was soon exposed when westerners continued to enter East Berlin. At the Natural History Museum in Berlin-Mitte staff thus asked: 'Why are the Kampfgruppen standing with their guns pointing east and their backs to the Brandenburg Gate. "Are the guns", they ask, "pointing at our own population"?'[34] In Potsdam, too, complaints circulated that 'the armed forces are not there to secure our border against Berlin, but because of our own population'.[35] Indeed, even the SED reporting apparatus could not conceal the fact that the majority of the populace (rightly) believed that the border had been closed simply to stop *Republikflucht*. In fact, for those who dared, the direct comparison with fascist incarceration was drawn, mirroring claims in the western media. As one transport worker in Görlitz commented: 'Barbed wire on the streets and it looks like the concentration camps in the old days.'[36] 'The barbed wire just needs electricity and the concentration camp will be complete,' added another.[37] Given the SED's own antifascist rhetoric, anticommunists always drew such parallels with particular relish. Indeed, the technical mastermind behind much of the wall-building, Willi Seifert, had experienced Buchenwald camp first-hand from the inside. Counter-arguments—such as one local party's line that 'this barbed wire is fending off inhumanity because the barbs are directed against militarism'—rang correspondingly hollow.[38]

As the thirteenth wore on, comment became more hostile, or in SED-speak, 'in sections of the population there is a certain volatility of views and opinions'.[39] Propagandists in Berlin noted the relatively few open declarations of support. Instead, there were 'a whole number of negative statements', including 'deepening of national division by us', 'infringement of freedom', 'no democracy', and 'fear of war'.[40] By mid-morning, these were becoming more frequent, sometimes aimed at government and party. Youths mocked the new barbed-wire entanglements,

[34] SED-ZK (Wissenschaften), 'Information über die Stimmung an unseren wissenschaftlichen Einrichtungen . . .', 16 Aug. 1961, SAPMO-BArch, DY30/IV2/5/433, fos. 75–80.

[35] SED-BL Potsdam (Org/Kader), 'Information über die Lage', 15 Aug. 1961, BLHA, Bez. Pdm. Rep. 530/IV2/5/1021.

[36] SED-KL Görlitz, telephone report, 7.30 p.m., 14 Aug. 1961, SächsHStA, BPA SED Dresden, IV2/5/135, fos. 12–14.

[37] FDGB-BuVo (Org), 'Erste zusammenfassende Information . . .', 19 Aug. 1961, SAPMO-BArch, DY34/22677.

[38] SED-KL Nauen, 'Kampf für den Frieden ist oberstes Gebot der Menschlichkeit!' (leaflet), BLHA, Bez. Pdm. Rep. 530/IV2/5/1025, fo. 165.

[39] NVR-ZS, 'Protokoll der Lagebesprechung am 16. August 1961' (8–9.30 p.m.), BA-MZAP, VA-01/39573, fos. 26–32.

[40] SED-BL Berlin (Org-Kader), 'Information zu den Schutzmaßnahmen', 13 Aug. 1961 (10 a.m.), LAB, BPA SED Berlin, IV2/12/1278.

shouting: 'Socialism triumphant, marching inexorably onwards!'[41] Meanwhile, the party kept the 'neuralgic points' under close observation,[42] while police patrols filmed street scenes.[43] Nevertheless, during the afternoon there were several gatherings behind the sector boundary by curious but aggressive East Berliners, mainly youths, with encouraging crowds on the other side. At half a dozen crossing-points groups of several hundred loitered, and in some cases tried to break through to the western sectors.[44] In Mitte and Treptow, when hundreds of youths attempted to remove barbed wire, police forced them back into the hinterland, in one case at bayonet point.[45] Then, at around 5 p.m., around 5,000 people gathered either side of the Brandenburg Gate, with some West Berliners even carrying banners into the East before being dispersed by water cannon.[46] Over the following days, however, it was West Berlin youths, caricatured as hooligans in the GDR media, who caused the Volkspolizei most headaches. In a series of running battles along the sector boundary, stones and tear-gas canisters were exchanged, and border installations vandalized, until the West Berlin police intervened to keep onlookers back. American troops also played 'chicken', driving up to the border at speed, but stopping short only feet from East Berlin.[47] The mood was understandably extremely tense.

In general, however, young East Germans were the most vociferous critics of the measures, displaying a more developed sense of 'personal freedom' than the older generation. Thus, in Potsdam: 'While, as a rule, our agitators encountered or could generate understanding among the majority of older citizens'—an ambiguous phrase in itself—'this was not the case with a large number of youths.'[48] Accordingly, the GDR media geared much propaganda to middle-aged fears of disorder, playing up disturbances by 'rowdies'. Assorted youths, some on motorbikes, loitered for long periods during 13 August at Glienicke Bridge between Potsdam and West Berlin, and in Hennigsdorf youths jeered at passing army units.[49] One biker gang, including a woman to the authorities' disgust, was arrested for 'reconnoitering' the border and threatening to 'knock off

[41] SED-BL Berlin (Org-Kader), 'Information zu den Schutzmaßnahmen', 13 Aug. 1961 (10.45 a.m.), LAB, BPA SED Berlin, IV2/12/1278.

[42] SED-BL Berlin, notes for *Aktiv-Tagung* on 13 Aug. 1961, LAB (STA), Rep. 124/212.

[43] PdVP Berlin (Instrukteurgruppe VPI Lichtenberg), 'Bericht', 13 Aug. 1961, LAB (STA), Rep. 303/26.1/230, fos. 17–19.

[44] SED-ZK (PO), '2. Kurzinformation', 13 Aug. 1961, SAPMO-BArch, DY30/IV2/5/433, fo. 4.

[45] Stab des MdI (Information), 'Informationsbericht für die Berichtszeit bis 23.00 Uhr', 13 Aug. 1961, BAB, DO-1/11/321, fos. 18–19.

[46] HVDVP (Operativstab), 'Zwischenbericht . . .', 14 Aug. 1961, BAB, DO-1/11/1129, fo. 140.

[47] MfS-ZAIG, 'Bericht', 23 Aug. 1961, BStU-ZA, ZAIG 526, fos. 40–1.

[48] SED-BL Potsdam to Honecker, 13 Aug. 1961, BLHA, Bez. Pdm. Rep. 530/IV2/5/1032.

[49] DGP-5. Grenzbrigade (Aufklärung), 'Informationsbericht . . .', 13 Aug. 1961, BLHA, Bez. Pdm. Rep. 530/IV2/5/1021.

the Volkspolizei'.[50] At one cafe youths in leather jackets 'provoked', complaining: 'It stinks here. We can't go to the cinema, it's so boring.'[51] Similar voices were heard across the whole of the GDR, not just in the environs of Berlin. In Halle, for instance, youngsters mourned the loss of western fashion items such as jeans.[52] Once the physical niche of West Berlin was blocked, many youngsters appeared to go into a collective sulk and, in the party jargon, to 'stand on the sidelines' of social development.

Away from the immediate frontline, older East Germans tended to construct more sophisticated political objections. Some drew attention to breaches of international law, such as the Potsdam Agreement or the United Nations charter.[53] Hopes of a response from the international community allegedly encouraged 'wavering' attitudes, as observers waited for political action or economic sanctions from the West.[54] When the Americans sent a token military convoy to West Berlin on 20 August, GDR security forces went to great lengths to keep citizens away from the transit autobahn. Nevertheless, in some nearby villages rumours circulated that the 'liberators' were coming amid surreptitious waving, and a motorcycle gang tagged along at one point.[55] There was also alarm at US Vice President Johnson's concurrent visit, in case he tried to enter the eastern sector.[56] When Adenauer toured West Berlin on 22 August, around a hundred East Berliners waved across the wire at Bernauer Straße, and one woman who had shouted 'freedom' was duly arrested, to boos from a neighbouring house.[57] Yet, as in 1953, anti-appeasers were to be disappointed, and apart from gestures of solidarity, the West did little to unsettle the East. After 13 August 1961 help from outside was a forlorn hope.

Another repeated popular criticism was that the East was deepening the division of Germany. Until 1955, when it embraced co-existence, the SED had always portrayed itself as the champion of national unity. Even the campaign for a separate peace treaty had been conducted as a rearguard action from this position. East Germans thus felt aggrieved when the final nail in the coffin of national unity was driven home by their own government. Berliners felt doubly

---

[50] 'Anlage 2a & 2b zum Informationsbericht v. 23.8.61, 3.00 Uhr', LAB (STA), Rep. 303/26.1/230, fos. 173–5.
[51] SED-BL Berlin (Org-Kader), 'Information . . .', 13 Aug. 1961 (8.15 p.m.), LAB, BPA SED Berlin, IV2/3/633.
[52] SED-SL Halle (Org-Kader), 'Kurzinformation', 13 Aug. 1961, LAM, BPA SED Halle, IV2/55/1145, fos. 193–4.
[53] Loose doc., MLHA Schwerin, BPA SED Neubrandenburg, IV2/11/976.
[54] 'Zusammenfassung der Berichte der Einsatzleitungen der Bezirke', n.d. [15 Aug. 1961], BA-MZAP, VA-01/39577, fos. 223–29.
[55] 'Einschätzung der Lage im Bezirk Potsdam am 20.08.1961', 20 Aug. 1961, BA-MZAP, VA-01/39577, fos. 142–7.
[56] NVR-ZS, 'Protokoll der 11. Lagebesprechung am 20. August' (9–11.30 a.m.), BA-MZAP, VA-01/39573, fos. 72–81.
[57] MfS-ZAIG, 'Bericht', 22 Aug. 1961, BStU-ZA, ZAIG 526, fo. 35.

riven.[58] Nor was national consciousness the preserve of the *Mittelstand*, as the Party Information liked to believe. 'We are all Germans. Be good Germans and see reunification not from a class point-of-view', workers told one unionist who concluded, with some surprise, that 'in the working class, even in the German Democratic Republic, there are still—and 13 August and discussions in the following days showed that—really strong nationalist views and opinions, which the adversary is now latching onto.'[59] Despite all attempts to inculcate a cold civil war 'other', many ordinary East Germans appear to have clung to older notions of the nation, a community of need under attack from global outside interests.

More immediate, however, was the 'war psychosis' which had characterized the Berlin crisis from the start. But this was now an emergency with no way out, generating paralysis and 'lassitude at the workplace and at home. Often it is pointed out that there is no point in achieving anything, since there will soon be war'.[60] The presence of the National People's Army, the NVA, in the heart of the capital was viewed with alarm, and seen by some as a prelude to hostilities, belying the SED's defensist line. Occasional mutterings were heard that 'with tanks one cannot be for peace'[61] or, as armoured cars rolled down the Stalinallee, the manager of one music shop ironically accompanied them on the piano with 'Deutschland, Deutschland über alles'.[62] In the surrounding countryside guests cut short holidays, alarmed at nearby troop movements. Women were allegedly particularly susceptible, and in some of Berlin's predominantly female electronics workforces there were reports of crying fits.[63] Older people, for whom memories of the last war were still fresh, were also especially pessimistic: 'Now there is an acute danger of war, since in 1914 and 1939 it started just like this.'[64] It also seems clear that most regarded the East as escalating the situation and did not believe in officially propagated western militarism. In Zschopau in the south, housewives claimed 'that the borders are being closed by us and so we are the ones who are pushing towards war'.[65] At the paediatrics section of the Charité, the presence of tanks and militia was 'proof that we were being aggressive and the danger came from us. If the GDR wanted peace then it could not act with

---

[58] SED-ZK (PO), '2. Kurzinformation', 13 Aug. 1961, SAPMO-BArch, DY30/IV2/5/433, fo. 5.

[59] 10th FDGB-BuVo, 25 Aug. 1961, SAPMO-BArch, DY30/IV2/611/39, fos. 265–6.

[60] Untitled report for Hermann Matern, n.d. [Aug. 1961], BA-MZAP, VA-01/39577, fos. 157–64.

[61] SED-BL Berlin (Org-Kader), 'Information . . .', 13 Aug. 1961 (10 a.m.), LAB, BPA SED Berlin, IV2/12/1278.

[62] SED-BL Berlin (Org-Kader), 'Information . . .', 16 Aug. 1961 (3 a.m.), LAB, BPA SED Berlin, IV2/12/1278.

[63] FDGB-BV Groß-Berlin (Sek.), 'Information', 14 Aug. 1961, SAPMO-BArch, DY34/22232.

[64] BEL KMS, '2. Bericht', 13 Aug. 1961, StAC, SED-BL KMS, IV2/12/5, fos. 3–5.

[65] BEL KMS, '4. Bericht', 13 Aug. 1961, StAC, SED-BL KMS, IV2/12/5, fos. 10–13.

tanks and bayonets' which, according to the speaker, 'went against Lenin whose first maxim had been peace'.[66]

As in previous 'hot' wars, one knee-jerk response was a wave of panic buying.[67] On Monday, 14 August, hoarders were mainly after food. One woman purchasing 20 pounds of salt explained that it was 'good protection against radio-active rays'.[68] The press actively mocked such incidents: 'Do these people really believe that they can survive an atomic war with 10 lbs. of coffee and 50 packets of pepper?'[69] This irrational buying was then exacerbated by widespread rumours of a currency reform, so that shoppers started 'investing' in expensive consumer items such as jewellery. In one Dresden store a customer thus paid 8,000 marks for a music centre, well above the average worker's annual wage. Canny shop managers even took the opportunity to shift otherwise unsaleable stock. Although the wave began to subside in mid-week, the following Saturday crowds re-assaulted the shops, leading the Ministry of Trade and Supply to buy in chocolate, coffee, cigarettes, and liquor to preserve normality. Washing-powder was also imported into Berlin, as shop assistants painted anti-hoarding slogans on shop-fronts, or forcibly emptied overfilled baskets at the checkout. Some 'serial shoppers' were even arrested.[70] But the so-called war psychosis also served the SED's purposes. As part of a hostage syndrome, some citizens colluded in keeping the situation calm, for fear of the state sparking off a war which would take everybody down with it. Others were concerned not to throw away the gains of the postwar reconstruction, so painstakingly built up over the previous sixteen years.

The sudden amputation of the two halves of Berlin sliced through innumerable personal bonds and family ties. One interviewee with parents-in-law in Bavaria described the immediate emotion as one of sadness, an intangible homesickness: 'now it's all over'.[71] Many family members were visiting friends or relatives in West Berlin when it happened. One boy had been faced with the agonizing decision whether to stay with his aunt in the West, or return to his parents in the East.[72] The regime was ruthless in applying travel restrictions. Any GDR citizen caught behind the Wall, even spouses of West Germans, had to stay put. In many cases, however, it was precisely in the private sphere that many East Germans felt that the state had gone too far, breaching the unwritten social contract of the 1950s, whereby citizens conformed in public, but were left to

---

66 SED-ZK (Wissenschaften), 'Informationsbericht über die Stimmung an der Humboldt-Universität . . .', 16 Aug. 1961, SAPMO-BArch, DY30/IV2/5/433, fos. 69–74.
67 MfHV, 'Übersicht über die Entwicklung im Handel nach dem 13.8.1961', n.d., SAPMO-BArch, DY30/IV2/6.10/115, fos. 150–60.
68 BMG Berlin to Foreign Office, 20 Nov. 1961, TNA, FO 371/160504/CG1018/56.
69 MfHV, 'Bericht', 18 Aug. 1961, SAPMO-BArch, DY30/IV2/6.10/115, fos. 135–43.
70 Zentrale Kommission für Staatliche Kontrolle, 'Information Nr. 5', 16 Aug. 1961, BA-MZAP, VA-01/39577, fos. 61–81.
71 Herr Sch. interview, Dresden-Weißig, 22 Aug. 1996.
72 Joachim H. interview, 2 Feb. 1996.

their own devices at home. Even for those without western relatives, West Berlin had been a regular shopping destination. Party comrades, too, found it difficult to accept the new constraints. Generally, it was reported that 'the measures of 13 August are politically understood and acknowledged in principle; people are finding difficulties, however, in coming to terms with the personal sacrifices entailed (travel to the West, conferences abroad).'[73] Some of those quizzed added their own qualifications to messages of support. Frau K. of Pirna agreed 'that the measures are right, only from a family point of view it was a personal hardship for her, since she had all her relatives in West Berlin'.[74] In Potsdam it was those in the border districts to West Berlin who felt most aggrieved, cut off from relations.[75] Yet, even in remote Zittau, factory workers refused to sign declarations of support, 'since everybody has the right to visit their relatives in West Germany'.[76] Elsewhere, those with western kin refused to join in political discussions. The intelligentsia were singled out as particularly insistent on this issue. Letter intercepts also revealed the emotionality of the event, including one from Fürstenberg to West Berlin: 'when we heard the terrible news on Sunday everything was clear to us. The tears shed would fill a lake and still not have stopped flowing. The fun has gone out of everything.'[77]

Once Stage II of the border closure commenced in the second week, and especially once West Berliners were barred from the eastern sector ten days after the action, the personal factor became even more acute. 'The main discussion point is that henceforth families are completely torn asunder', reported the Berlin SED. 'More than previously there is talk that we have perpetrated an irreversible division.'[78] At some plants, such as the Television Works, agitators despaired of ever being able to justify the latest twist: 'They cannot cope with arguments where many young girls work who spent most of their spare time in West Berlin.'[79] Likewise, police at checkpoints confronted by West Berliners carrying funeral wreaths found it difficult to turn them away, vainly telephoning headquarters for discretionary permits.[80] Women were identified as particularly prone to venting their private anger in the public sphere. At one meeting a Quedlinburgerin, who was swiftly arrested, railed against the barbed wire: 'I am

---

[73] Wyschofsky, 'Forum mit leitenden Angehörigen der Intelligenz des VEB Filmfabrik Wolfen', 16 Sept. 1961, SAPMO-BArch, DY30/IV2/6.03/62, fos. 356–8.

[74] SED-KL Pirna, telephone report, 1.05 p.m., 13 Aug. 1961, SächsHStA, BPA SED Dresden, IV2/5/134, fos. 13–15.

[75] SED-BL Potsdam to Honecker, 15 Aug. 1961, BLHA, Bez. Pdm. Rep. 530/IV2/5/1032.

[76] SED-KL Zittau, 'Informationsbericht, 11.00 Uhr', 15 Aug. 1961, SächsHStA, BPA SED Dresden, IV2/5/135, fos. 125–7.

[77] MfS-BV Frankfurt/Oder (M), 'Stimmungen der Bevölkerung der DDR . . .', 17 Aug. 1961, DBM, 'Berlin, 13. August 1961'.

[78] SED-BL Berlin (Org-Kader), 'Information zu den Schutzmaßnahmen', 23 Aug. 1961 (2.30 p.m.), LAB, BPA SED Berlin, IV2/12/1278.

[79] SED-BL Berlin (Org-Kader), 'Berichterstattung der Operativgruppe vom 25.8.1961', LAB, BPA SED Berlin, IV2/12/1278.

[80] MfS-ZAIG, 'Bericht', 23 Aug. 1961, BStU-ZA, ZAIG 526, fo. 47.

a German woman and that is why my heart bleeds at such inhumanity. Only monsters can do such a thing.'[81] Another wrote to the Evangelical Church, in the mistaken belief that it was acting on behalf of separated families: 'I, too, belong to the hardest-hit, since for months I have been living separated from my husband. I hardly need to underline to you that this state of affairs is almost unbearable.' The writer went on to describe how another woman, separated from husband and children, had recently hanged herself.[82] The western media also focused on the human interest stories, filming bridal couples standing on chairs to wave over the Wall at parents-in-law or conversations between East Berliners in upper-floor windows and relatives down below. Waving and shouting across the Wall were forbidden, however, as 'contact with the enemy', and were soon blocked by wooden sight-screens, rendering the closure seemingly absolute.

CAPTIVE AUDIENCES: REBUILDING STATE AUTHORITY BEHIND THE WALL

The SED leadership was clearly concerned that its grass-roots members should take advantage of the new momentum. It paid close attention to the response times on 13 August for what was an unpopular task.[83] As noted above, the SED felt on the defensive on the eve of the Wall. The Party Information now betrayed its high hopes with reports of increased local activity. Members' meetings were supposedly being held 'in a critical and militant atmosphere', and in districts such as Karl-Marx-Stadt 'especially older comrades' were making a show, 'displaying their fighting experience from before 1933 and during fascism'.[84] Yet although 13 August was an efficient operation, it was not quite as rosy as such reports suggest. In Berlin activist meetings were held early in the morning of 13 August, and generally the party managed participation levels of 85 per cent compared with 30–50 per cent earlier in the summer. At the Kabelwerk Oberspree and other electronics factories some comrades stayed at their posts for 36 hours. Yet six weeks after the action the Berlin SED had won only 1,226 new applicants, a figure with which it was immensely disappointed, also recording 'tendencies to yield and capitulationist behaviour'.[85] In Potsdam the SED criticized a number of comrades for 'out-and-out sciving' on the big day, such as the mayor of Markendorf who simply locked himself in his flat.[86]

---

[81] 'Protokoll über das Seminar mit den Büromitgliedern der Kreisleitungen am 3. Okt. 1961', LAM, BPA SED Halle, IV/2/2/45.

[82] Anonymous letter to EKD, 15 Mar. 1962, EZA, 104/596.

[83] SED-KL Bischofswerda, telephone report, 8.45 a.m., 14 Aug. 1961, SächsHStA, BPA SED Dresden, IV2/5/134, fos. 129–31.

[84] SED-ZK (PO), 'Information . . .', 18 Aug. 1961, BA-MZAP, VA-01/39577, fos. 118–24.

[85] Untitled, undated document: LAB, BPA SED Berlin, IV2/12/1278.

[86] SED-BL Potsdam to SED-ZK, 13 Aug. 1961, BLHA, Bez. Pdm. Rep. 530/IV2/5/1030.

The local party took to task 'unstable and wavering' comrades who were sent on refresher courses, delegated to the militia or the army, or in some cases even expelled.[87] At traditional weak spots, such as the Humboldt University, 'several comrades are afraid that we are acting too sharply and unconvincingly'.[88] Even in a bastion such as Halle, party disciplinary proceedings rose from 743 in the first half of 1961 to 1,219 in the second, with many intelligentsia comrades punished for attempting 'to force an autocritique on the party leadership'.[89] In Leipzig 207 comrades were admonished for 'waverings', absenteeism on 13 August, 'conciliationism' and 'liberalism'.[90] One recalcitrant female comrade in Görlitz sarcastically wished she had 'fallen into the slave-traders' hands. The party did not help me to get a trip west, and so I don't have any time for the party.'[91]

The FDGB trade union was generally even more prone to 'going native' than the party. On 13 August several union leaders apparently applied for leave or stayed at home.[92] Although most full-time functionaries remained firm under pressure, part-time officials were less steadfast. In 20 enterprises in Berlin-Prenzlauer Berg, especially semi-state and locally organized plants, the FDGB noted that even shop-floor chairmen disowned the measures.[93] IG Printing and Paper came in for particular criticism for 'opportunism', as well as local health sector shop stewards.[94] Among the unions' voluntary workers the mood was even more despondent. One liaison officer at the Warnow shipyard complained that 'the government itself has made a mockery of the trust of the population and can no longer use the excuse—when difficulties arise—that spies are to blame'. Another simply told the government to 'kiss my . . .'.[95] In one branch meeting in Prenzlauer Berg only two members actually stood by the measures, while others muttered that Sunday the thirteenth had revealed 'a lot of little Ulbrichts among us'.[96] All of this would suggest that many party members shared a widespread resentment that 13 August had infringed their own private sphere or threatened to undermine the *modus vivendi* with local clienteles.

[87] SED-BL Potsdam to Honecker, 19 Aug. 1961, BLHA, Bez. Pdm. Rep. 530/IV2/5/1032.

[88] SED-PL HU, 'Bericht über das Anlaufen des Studienjahres 1961/62', 11 Sept. 1961, SAPMO-BArch, DY30/IV2/9.04/495, fos. 69–77.

[89] SED-BL Halle (BPKK), 'Analyse . . .', 22 Jan. 1962, LAM, BPA SED Halle, IV/2/4/993, fos. 55–79.

[90] See lists of SED-BPKK Leipzig in StAL, BPA SED, IV2/4/356.

[91] SED-KL Görlitz, telephone report, 3.00 p.m., 14 Aug. 1961, SächsHStA, IV2/5/135, fos. 10–11.

[92] SED-ZK (PO), 'Einige Probleme der Gewerkschaftsarbeit . . .', 15 Sept. 1961, SAPMO-BArch, DY30/IV2/5/295, fo. 226.

[93] SED-ZK (Gewerkschaften & Sozialpolitik) to Ulbricht, 21 Aug. 1961, SAPMO-BArch, DY30/IV2/611/39, fo. 111.

[94] Herbert Warnke at 10th FDGB-BuVo, 24 Aug. 1961, *Tribüne*, 200 (supplement), 29 Aug. 1961, 6.

[95] FDGB-BuVo (Org), 'Informationsbericht Nr. 6', 16 Aug. 1961, SAPMO-BArch, DY 34/22677.

[96] FDGB-BV Groß-Berlin (Sek.), 'Information', 29 Aug. 1961, SAPMO-BArch, DY 34/22232.

Another response by embattled functionaries was to take it out on their erstwhile tormentors. A significant amount of physical, if still ritualized, violence was meted out in the immediate wake of the Wall, in which indignant workers supposedly dispensed natural justice, according to the widespread motto 'Those who won't hear it, must feel it.' In Eilenburg comrade E., who had hurt his hand beating up detainees, boasted to the local doctor about how he had got his injury. 'Dentists', he warned, 'would be getting a lot of work in the near future.'[97] Yet this was not simply local activism run amok. The press cynically sanctioned violence. 'Step right up if you want to dance', announced one newspaper, describing how a man 'pirouetted from fist to fist, and when he was able to walk again, was given a secure car-ride'.[98] Paul Fröhlich, Leipzig party boss, told local police not to tolerate drunken insults anymore: 'Lay them out so that they never want to drink again. (Laughter.) I think we understand each other, comrades.'[99] The FDJ, too, was enjoined to set up 'orderly groups' to patrol areas otherwise dominated by gangs of rowdies: 'There is no discussion with provocateurs. They will be first thrashed and then handed over to the state organs.'[100] When the party leadership distanced itself from this use of brute force a few weeks later, clearly alarmed at the counter-productive propaganda it was making as local cadres ran riot, it typically forgot its own role.[101] One can only describe these methods as neo-fascist, reminiscent of SA violence after the Nazi *Machtergreifung*, and a number of comrades had the courage to say so at the time, refusing to join in.[102]

The legal apparatus was also cranked up. 'Incitement' or 'state slander' might mean as little as insulting a policeman, or breaking the Pass Law, but in the wake of the Wall prosecutions soared. In Berlin police patrolled bars frequented by *Grenzgänger*, refusing to turn a deaf ear.[103] Collective farmer Kurt F. from Seelow was arrested for shouting while drunk: 'You bloody dogs, now we are all right in the bag, you bloody Communist gang.' Likewise, railwayman Franz L. from Strausberg 'provocatively demanded a ticket to Charlottenburg' in West Berlin, adding that 'there was no freedom in the GDR'.[104] Yet, even the authorities recognized that insults, vandalism, and rumour-mongering were

---

[97] SED-ZK (PO), 'Information über Vorgänge im Kreis Eilenburg', n.d. [Jan. 1962], SAPMO-BArch, DY30/IV2/5/296, fos. 46–50.

[98] Weber, *Geschichte der DDR*, 330–1.

[99] 'Referat des Genossen Paul Fröhlich vor den ABV am 17.8.1961', StAL, BPA SED, IV2/6/454, fo. 165.

[100] FDJ-ZR to FDJ-BLs, 13 Aug. 1961, SAPMO-BArch, DY24/3.934.

[101] SED-ZK (PO), 'Einige Probleme der Massenarbeit . . .', 21 Sept. 1961, SAPMO-BArch, DY30/IV2/5/37, fos. 37–49; 'Protokoll über das Seminar mit den Büromitgliedern der Kreisleitungen am 3. Okt. 1961', LAM, BPA SED Halle, IV2/2/45.

[102] SED-PL KMU, 'Informationsbericht', 26 Aug. 1961, SAPMO-BArch, DY30/IV2/9.04/558, fos. 195–8.

[103] PdVP Berlin (Operativgruppe), 'Zwischenbericht', 21 Aug. 1961, LAB, BPA SED Berlin, IV2/12/1275–1.

[104] Schrauer to MdJ, 16 Aug. 1961, SAPMO-BArch, DY30/IV2/13/423.

simply letting off steam: 'organized and concerted enemy activity could not be ascertained in investigations hitherto'.[105] Nevertheless, the Volkspolizei detained a relatively large number. By early September 6,041 people had been brought in for questioning nationwide, including 3,108 arrests, over half from Berlin and Potsdam. About one in twelve, especially where *Republikflucht* was involved, were handed over to the MfS.[106] These figures compare with high arrest levels after 17 June 1953, but included a political component. The Ministry of Justice required judges to consider the 'social danger' represented by offenders. Courts were encouraged to impose heavier, faster sentences than normal in order to achieve a 'general preventive effect'.[107] 'Fast-track courts' were organized, in which the accused agreed to confess. In Potsdam three such trials were held on 15 August, including some of the strikers mentioned below, where courts were directed to convene even at night.[108] Between 16 and 17 August the first 'accelerated proceedings' were held in Berlin, five against attempted escapers and two for state slander. Verdicts were to reflect the ideological causes of criminal acts, usually as a consequence of western influence, as well as the 'political implications of the measures to protect our borders'.[109] By the end of the first week, there had been thirty-seven such hearings in East Berlin, 133 in Potsdam and eighteen in Frankfurt/Oder, with eighty-six people sentenced to less than six months, and 104 to longer sentences.[110] On 24 August the courts were given an additional weapon against 'asocial and workshy elements' in the 'Movement Restriction Decree', which even allowed internment in a work education camp, itself an innovation made possible by the Wall.[111] In the first month sixty-one people received custodial sentences and 105 movement bans, with Potsdam and Leipzig making particularly heavy use of the new powers.[112] According to Ministry of Justice guidelines, proceedings were to be an 'expression of the will of the popular masses' and trials were to be heavily publicized in the press.[113]

The implications were not lost on key ulterior targets, such as the intelligentsia. As already noted, the middle classes had already predicted that if the border

[105] PdVP/BEL Berlin to Ulbricht, 5 Sept. 1961, LAB (STA), Rep. 303/26.1/227, fo. 184.

[106] HVDVP (Operativstab), 'Operativer Bericht in Erfüllung der Beschlüsse des Ministerrates der DDR', 4 Sept. 1961 (4 a.m.), BAB, DO-1/11/1130, fo. 209.

[107] MdJ, 'Vertrauliche Anleitung zur Rechtsprechung . . .', 7 Sept. 1961, SAPMO-BArch, DY30/IV2/13/423.

[108] MdJ (Hauptabt. II), 'Bericht über die Instruktion bei der Justizverwaltungsstelle Potsdam am 15. August 1961', SAPMO-BArch, DY30/IV2/13/423.

[109] Oehmke, '4. Bericht, 16.8.1961 6,30 Uhr bis 17.8.1961 7,30 Uhr', 17 Aug. 1961, SAPMO-BArch, DY30/IV2/13/423.

[110] HVDVP (Operativstab), 'Operativer Bericht', 21 Aug. 1961 (4 p.m.), BAB, DO-1/11/1130, fo. 86.

[111] Falco Werkentin, *Politische Strafjustiz in der Ära Ulbricht* (Berlin: Links, 1995), 264–70; Fricke, *Politik und Justiz*, 431–61.

[112] MdJ (Hauptabt. II), 'Bericht über die Durchsetzung der Verordnung über Aufenthalts-beschränkung', 22 Sept. 1961, SAPMO-BArch, DY30/IV2/13/423.

[113] MdJ, 'Anleitung Nr. 2/61 zur Verordnung über Aufenthaltsbeschränkung vom 24.8.1961', n.d., SAPMO-BArch, DY30/IV2/13/423.

were closed, 'a "new course", a harder course will come'.[114] At Leipzig University, Professor Müller-Hegemann, who had previously ridiculed 'slave-trading' propaganda, was singled out to deliver the autocritique on 14 August: 'You will all have heard of such cases where medics said: "I demand this and that!" or "my son who is studying in West Berlin should be allowed to visit here, or I'm leaving!" ', he told listeners. 'Since yesterday the situation has altered fundamentally. Now we face the task of re-educating these somewhat pampered fellow citizens.'[115] Similar confrontations occurred at the Academy of Sciences in Berlin and Halle University,[116] and in industry the unions reported 'stronger than previous *sectarian tendencies*' towards white-collar workers.[117] At the Leuna plant, for example, workers claimed 'that now we can finally speak plainly ['deutsch reden'] with the intelligentsia'.[118] In the state apparatus, too, there was a desire to take off the kid gloves. A policeman told one senior doctor at the visa desk that 'now the "Intelligenzlerei" was over'.[119] At the Charité hospital, *the* previous *Republikflucht* hotspot, the professor of forensic medicine welcomed the fact that research would no longer be disrupted by fleeing colleagues. A professor of ophthalmology, presumably a Wehrmacht veteran, now wanted to 'run the clinic like a good field dressing station'.[120] Junior doctors, conversely, went into a collective sulk, shunning party colleagues. Previously oppositional Humboldt professors simply kept stumm.[121] Yet the whispered fears of blocked careers and intellectual isolationism did not merge into anything approaching collective protest. Nor did the great clamp-down materialize. In October Kurt Hager, the SED's cultural spokesman, went to great lengths to reassure his audience that 'leftist exaggerations and excesses' were not on the agenda, although access to western know-how would be 'regulated'.[122] Indeed, western publications were almost immediately confined to the so-called 'poison cabinet' of libraries and research institutes, replacing previous travel privileges with a virtual system of knowledge access.[123]

[114] Untitled report for Hermann Matern, n.d. [Aug. 1961], BA-MZAP, VA-01/39577, fos. 157–64.

[115] 'Stenografisches Protokoll einer Aussprache mit Genossen der Intelligenz am 14.8.1961', StAL, BPA SED, IV2/3/286, fos. 167–257.

[116] 'Einschätzung der politischen Situation im Bereich der Deutschen Akademie der Wissenschaften zu Berlin', 8 Sept. 1961, SAPMO-BArch, DY30/IV2/9.04/272, fos. 384–6.

[117] FDGB-BuVo (Org), 'Informationsbericht Nr. 7/61', 16 Aug. 1961, SAPMO-BArch, DY34/22677.

[118] SED-KL Leuna, 'Meinungen zu den Massnahmen vom 13.8.61', 29 Aug. 1961, LAM, BPA SED Halle, IV412/279, fos. 12–13.

[119] SED-PL KMU, 'Informationsbericht', 8 Sept. 1961, SAPMO-BArch, DY30/IV2/9.04/558, fos. 218–23.

[120] SED-BL Berlin (Agit-Prop), 'Die Lage an der Medizinischen Fakultät . . .', 17 Aug. 1961, LAB, BPA SED Berlin, IV2/12/1278.

[121] SED-ZK (Wissenschaften), 'Information an Abteilungsleitung über die Professorenaussprache . . .', 16 Aug. 1961, SAPMO-BArch, DY30/IV2/9.04/496, fos. 332–4.

[122] Speech to Kulturbund, 1 Oct. 1961 in Richter (ed.), *Mauer*, 145–55: 154.

[123] SED-PB, 22 Aug. 1961, SAPMO-BArch, DY30/JIV2/2/787.

Workers, despite their ideologically protected status, were another target group. The regime had clearly not ruled out another insurrection like 1953, and the files are dotted with outbursts or graffitied insults keeping the memory alive.[124] During an innocent power cut in Berlin on 16 August, for instance, four women in a butcher's thought this was the signal: 'Hey, it looks like this is it, now's the strike!'[125] Yet, the expectation was that someone else would do the striking. When power resumed, it was back to normal. The SED had been shrewd in picking a Sunday for the operation, taking the wind out of sails by Monday morning. Unlike 1953, in 1961 the government drove events, while the populace struggled to keep up. As one youth in Königs-Wusterhausen said in mock admiration: 'You've definitely prepared yourselves better than on 17th June '53, eh?'[126] Although there were no strikes on the previous scale, it is worth recording those which did occur. Often they were local trials of strength, where shop-floor representatives had to be prodded into taking a hard line from above by the national union, the FDGB. Overall, stoppages in the third quarter of 1961 were down by nearly half on 1960, and those linked to 13 August tended to take place in and around Berlin.[127]

In 1953 Berlin construction workers had been at the forefront of protest and so were under closest scrutiny. Now their mood was described as 'very reticent'.[128] Only one youth brigade at the Hotel Moskau building site on the Stalinallee actually refused work, cold-shouldering its foreman, but was carefully chaperoned by the party flying squad.[129] The tactic of concentrating party forces at trouble spots proved effective. At VEB Bauhof in Berlin-Friedrichshain, for example, a meeting of 120 building workers was going rather stormily: 'There were interjections (from a *Grenzgänger* it transpired) which culminated in claims that the cruelty came from here and not the other side, heckles such as "the barbed wire was put up here and not by the West" and many other arguments.'[130] Only after a telephone call to the district leadership for reinforcements, did the meeting calm down. At VEB Luckenwalder Beschläge, an armature factory in Brandenburg, ten workers in the mould shop conducted a stoppage on 14 August. Six could be persuaded to desist, but four continued, arguing that 'they would not resume work until the tanks and street barriers had been

[124] BEL KMS, '5. Bericht', 13 Aug. 1961, StAC, SED-BL KMS, IV2/12/5, fos. 14–17.
[125] BEL Berlin to Ulbricht, 16 Aug. 1961 (3.00 a.m., 8.00 p.m., 9.00 p.m., 12.00 a.m.), LAB (STA), Rep. 303/26.1/227, fos. 59–70.
[126] FDJ-ZR (Org-Instruk), 'Argumente und Meinungen von Jugendlichen . . .', 13 Aug. 1961, SAPMO-BArch, DY24/A3.975.
[127] FDGB-BuVo (Org), 'Analyse der klassenfeindlichen Tätigkeit im III. Quartal 1961 . . .', 2 Oct. 1961, SAPMO-BArch, DY30/IV2/6.11/65, fos. 293–300.
[128] SED-ZK (PO), '7. Kurzinformation', 14 Aug. 1961, SAPMO-BArch, DY30/IV2/5/433, fo. 21.
[129] SED-BL Berlin (Org-Kader), 'Information . . .', 14 Aug. 1961, LAB, BPA SED Berlin, IV2/12/1278.
[130] RdSB Friedrichshain (Bauamt), 'Politische Einschätzung . . .', 23 Aug. 1961, LAB, BPA SED Berlin, IV4/01/241.

removed'.[131] The works manager, desperate for his superiors not to find out, initially tried to reason with the strikers, asking them to go home after they started drinking. In the afternoon, behind his back, union representatives then called in the Stasi, who interrogated the 'provocateurs', including the ringleader who was also a party comrade, before arresting three of them and putting them before an emergency court. At VEB Holzindustrie Hennigsdorf during the same morning, after 'violent discussions against the measures' in the carpentry shop, thirteen workers downed tools. Local FDGB leaders immediately appeared and conducted the 'confrontation'. Work was then resumed, but in the afternoon forty workers stopped work, demanding 'that the measures be reversed and free elections carried out'. Furthermore: 'We were not consulted before the implementation of the measures, although we are always told "plan together, rule together". The labour code is incomplete because it contains no right to strike. The tanks, troops and concrete posts must go.' The stand-off was only broken when nearby steelworkers loyal to the regime were posted in the factory, after which four ringleaders were arrested and expedited behind bars.[132]

Elsewhere on the fourteenth actions were limited to labour indiscipline short of clearly identifiable stoppages. A plan by four workers at the Concrete Works at Berlin-Köpenick to issue a dawn resolution criticizing the measures was foiled after a tip-off.[133] At the Elisabeth-Hütte in Brandenburg five colleagues failed to turn up for work, although Monday morning absenteeism was not uncommon. At VEB Gablona in Jüterbog, in the tool section, there was effectively no work between 6.30 a.m. and 7.45 a.m., during which the border closure was discussed: 'Only when leading cadres were deployed was work resumed.'[134] At a building site in Peitz eighteen young colleagues dawdled until noon, in protest at no longer being able to shop in West Berlin. At several other building sites in the Potsdam region there were 'negative discussions' and drinking, for instance at VEB Montagebau at Potsdam, where work was only begun at 9.30 a.m. At VEB Ausbau Potsdam, in Luckenwalde, there was no work all day. A tractor station brigade in nearby Milow 'sat in the pub and drank'.[135] In a few other incidents the impetus for symbolic stoppages appeared to come from the West. The Federal unions had called for 15 minutes' silence in West Berlin at 2 p.m. on 14 August and 2 minutes throughout West Germany at 11 a.m. the following day. In East

[131] SED-ZK (PO), 'Arbeitsniederlegung . . .', n.d. [14 Aug. 1961], BA-MZAP, VA-01/39577, fos. 148–9.
[132] SED-KL Hennigsdorf, 'Bericht über die provokatorischen Vorkommnisse im VEB Holzindustrie Hennigsdorf', 14 Aug. 1961 (6 p.m.), BLHA, Bez. Pdm. Rep. 530/IV2/5/1021.
[133] BEL Berlin to Ulbricht, 14 Aug. 1961 (6.00 a.m.), LAB (STA), Rep. 303/26.1/227, fos. 33–8.
[134] SED-BL Potsdam (Org-Kader), 14 Aug. 1961 (1.00 p.m.), BLHA, Bez. Pdm. Rep. 530/IV2/5/1021.
[135] SED-BL Potsdam (PI), 'Zu einigen Erscheinungen auf den Baustellen', 14 Aug. 1961, BLHA, Bez. Pdm. Rep. 530/IV2/5/1021.

Berlin factory officials noticed several 'coincidental' breaks by workers.[136] The largest plant affected, if only briefly, was the Carl Zeiß optics works in Jena. After a stilted official debate on the fourteenth, the next day discussions were overheard about the planned West German sympathy stoppage. Then, at the appointed time, comrade U.—to the horror of the local SED—downed tools in his section. The FDGB immediately sent in its local leaders, but could not move colleagues to distance themselves from U., who was expelled from the party on the spot.[137] On the same day in the central Berlin post office, approximately 100 women workers held a 2-minute silence at 11 a.m.: 'Colleagues who wanted to work or spoke were told to be silent.'[138]

There were probably many more small-scale acts of defiance which did not reach official ears, but nothing which endangered production. Inside the major factories SED and FDGB certainly maintained the upper hand and the vast majority of East German workers dutifully clocked on. The Berlin unions' mood by Monday evening was one of relief, having expected 'a harder discussion and more open rejection', especially from former SPD members: 'many of the waverers are quite impressed by our assertive attitude and are saying "they" are obviously stronger than we thought'.[139] Honecker, supervising operations, also reviewed the situation with obvious satisfaction, but called for maintained vigilance: 'No carelessness must creep in.' The armed forces were to remain on high alert, with 'constant observation and dispersal of groups forming at the border and in the rear'.[140] In the industrial provinces, too, the party reported that it had been 'on the offensive', not allowing the adversary to 'get a purchase'.[141]

In response, workers resorted to passive resistance. Industrial sabotage rose in the third quarter of 1961: taps were left running; objects dropped into machinery; fires started; windows smashed; death threats posted; and graffiti scrawled. Individual workplaces organized go-slows.[142] A classic technique was to stonewall functionaries. At one Saxon works: 'The colleagues explained that they had no opinion of their own, despite the fact that before and after these meetings there was lively discussion. Upon the approach of the district SED comrade these conversations immediately stopped.'[143] LEW Hennigsdorf

[136] SED-BL Berlin (Org-Kader), 'Information . . .', 16 Aug. 1961 (3 a.m.), LAB, BPA SED Berlin, IV2/12/1278.

[137] SED-BPO Carl Zeiß Jena, 'Informationsbericht', 15 Aug. 1961, SAPMO-BArch, DY30/IV2/5/844, fos. 153–5.

[138] FDGB-BuVo (Org), 'Klassenfeindliche Tätigkeit . . .', 16 Aug. 1961, SAPMO-BArch, DY30/IV2/6.11/65, fos. 223–30.

[139] FDGB-BV Groß-Berlin (Sek.), 'Information', 14 Aug. 1961, SAPMO-BArch, DY34/22232.

[140] NVR-ZS, 'Protokoll der Lagebesprechung vom 14. August 1961' (8–10.15 p.m.), BA-MZAP, VA-01/39573, fos. 1–5.

[141] SED-BL Potsdam to Honecker, 14 Aug. 1961, BLHA, Bez. Pdm. Rep. 530/IV2/5/1032.

[142] 'Grundorganisationen, die durch ernste Erscheinungen zu Schwerpunkten der politischen Arbeit werden müssen', 26 Aug. 1961, LAB, BPA SED Berlin, IV2/3/633.

[143] BEL KMS, '11. Bericht', 15 Aug. 1961, StAC, SED-BL KMS, IV2/12/5, fos. 37–39.

was characterized by 'steadily deepening *silence* among the workers'.[144] In the ensuing weeks this uncomfortable atmosphere continued: 'Some comrades are no longer greeted by non-party members. If a group of colleagues are chatting at the workbench and a comrade joins them wanting to chip in, the colleagues silently go about their work.'[145] At the Brandenburg steel and rolling mill, too, reporters could almost cut the silence and at the Funkwerk in Köpenick it was described as 'icy'.[146] But occasionally, discussions could become more irate, for instance among former Social Democratic railwaymen in Neustrelitz, where, apart from the union representative, 'no-one present defended our Workers' and Peasants' State. Some stood in the background and observed the excited arguments and said nothing at all.'[147] Undercover western reporters also suggested that local functionaries beat a retreat from overt confrontations.[148] This pattern of passive resistance was already well-established in the 1950s, reminiscent of 'pre-modern' forms of informal protest which tested rather than breached the limits of control. But importantly, this behaviour continued behind the Wall, which, as we shall see below, did not cure shop-floor problems overnight.

A case in point is the treatment of the party's public enemy and scapegoat number one, the *Grenzgänger*, those Cold War commuters between the two Berlins. Far-sightedly, the SED recognized their potential to improve GDR work discipline. The Council of Ministers decreed that they be re-employed in their old workplaces, but dispersal for security reasons frequently undermined this gesture.[149] There was undoubtedly some hostility among former workmates to the reappearance of former absentees. Employees at the Signal Works in Treptow only grudgingly readmitted one colleague, arguing that he had 'left the brigade in the lurch'.[150] Some newcomers attempted to overcome antagonism by throwing parties and handing round western cigarettes. Economic functionaries were sceptical, however, that this frostiness was all due to loyalty to the Workers' and Peasants' State, 'but really for fear that some good skilled workers might

---

[144] FDGB-BuVo (Org), 'Klassenfeindliche Tätigkeit . . .', 16 Aug. 1961, SAPMO-BArch, DY30/IV2/6.11/65, fos. 223–30.

[145] SED-BL Potsdam to SED-ZK, 'Informationsbericht BPO LEW "Hans Beimler" ', 5 Sept. 1961, BLHA, Bez. Pdm. Rep. 530/IV2/5/1032.

[146] SED-ZK (Org-Kader), 14 Aug. 1961, SAPMO-BArch, DY30/J IV2/202/65, fos. 131–2 and fos. 133–5.

[147] FDGB-BV Neubrandenburg, 14 Aug. 1961, MLHA Schwerin, BPA SED Neubrandenburg, IV2/11/976.

[148] Kanitz, 'Conditions in East Berlin since the Imposition of Restrictions', 17 Aug. 1961, TNA, FO 371/160503/CG1018/31.

[149] Ministerrat, 'Anordnung über die Eingliederung von Rückkehrern und Zuziehenden sowie ehemaliger Grenzgänger in den Arbeitsprozeß', 14 Aug. 1961, SAPMO-BArch, DY30/JIV2/2/784, fo. 11.

[150] SED-ZK (PO), 'Information' Nr. 6, 14 Jan. 1961, SAPMO-BArch, DY30/IV2/5/294, fo. 56.

ruin their norms'.[151] At the Signalwerk *Grenzgänger* were warned 'not to work so fast and to take more breaks in order not to squeeze the norm',[152] a story repeated elsewhere.[153] At VEB Berlin Brake Works initially well-disciplined commuters were soon joining in boozing sessions and at VEB '7th October' the six newcomers quickly fell into absenteeism.[154] Intensive, but nonetheless chaotic, efforts were made to register *Grenzgänger*. On 24 August the GDR introduced labour exchanges, previously derided as instruments of capitalism, to curb the endemic job changing in the GDR and funnel workers into nationalized industry. As British observers noted, 'An ordinance of this nature could not have been introduced as long as the Berlin escape route was open.'[155] Former sixth-formers studying in West Berlin were to be given work placements, and while science undergraduates were to be allowed to continue their studies, with a fast track for medical students, humanities undergraduates 'are without exception to be sent onto the production line'.[156] Yet, in placement interviews *Grenzgänger* were generally reported to be 'making demands such as top wages, normal shift, no to certain factories, no heavy work'.[157] It was also noticed that former border-crossers were bypassing registration points and negotiating with employers direct, often in the private sector. The authorities had estimated as many as 70,000 *Grenzgänger*, yet by the end of September only 33,000 had registered. Many female part-time workers chose not to work, while many young men found themselves in the armed forces. Even priority works in the electrical sector remained below target. All told, only 18,000 were allocated work in the state sector.[158] Besides the conscious evasion of a more politicized workplace, it would seem that the labour market was not in a position to absorb all *Grenzgänger* properly, and even skilled workers were forced into unskilled jobs.[159]

Beyond this specific group, the state had hoped to use the Wall to attack general labour indiscipline. Before workers at the Berlin Sports Hall, Ulbricht announced that 'now, after 13 August, a great upturn is underway'.[160] Local

[151] SED-BL Berlin (Org-Kader), 'Information . . .', 15 Aug. 1961 (5.30 p.m.), LAB, BPA SED Berlin, IV2/12/1278.

[152] FDGB-BV Groß-Berlin (Sek.), 'Information' 24 Aug. 1961, SAPMO-BArch, DY34/22232.

[153] PdVP Berlin (K), 'Ordnung und Sicherheit in den Schwerpunktbetrieben . . .', 10 Nov. 1961, LAB (STA), Rep. 26.1/481, fos. 143–72.

[154] PdVP/BEL Berlin to Ulbricht, 5 Sept. 1961, LAB (STA), Rep. 303/26.1/227, fo. 184.

[155] BMG Berlin (External Dept.) to Chancery, Bonn, 6 Sept. 1961, TNA, FO 371/160661/CG2181/7.

[156] SED-PB, 22 Aug. 1961 (Appendix 5), SAPMO-BArch, DY30/JIV2/2/787, fos. 19–23.

[157] SED-BL Berlin (Org-Kader), 'Information . . .', 14 Aug. 1961 (4 p.m.), LAB, BPA SED Berlin, IV2/3/633.

[158] SPK (Arbeitskräfte), 'Analyse über die Durchführung des Arbeitskräfteplanes in der Zeit von Januar bis September 1961', 14 Oct. 1961, SAPMO-BArch, DY30/IV2/6.08/46, fos. 99–108.

[159] Magistrat von Groß-Berlin/Wirtschaftsrat, '18. Situationsbericht . . .', 28 Aug. 1961, LAB (STA), Rep. 124/216.

[160] FDGB-BuVo, *Unser Aktionsprogramm für den Friedensvertrag* (East Berlin, Nov. 1961), 13–17.

functionaries pledged 'order at the border and order on the shop-floor!'[161] 'Self-obligations' duly emerged, as brigades promised to produce a few more units there, or finish the Plan so many days ahead of schedule.[162] This was a heavily formalized ritual, yet the Politbüro wanted a more systematic campaign, the so-called Production Drive.[163] 'Spontaneously' demanded by workers at VEB Elektrokohle of Berlin-Lichtenberg, it addressed issues such as short-time, quality work, economizing, and 'undisruptability', under the motto 'produce more in the same time for the same money'. The economic apparatus was also hoping to close the wages productivity scissor and throttle 'consumer ideology' among workers. The 'new morality' involved an 'honesty towards oneself as well as society'. Socialist patriotism would strengthen the economy and improve the negotiating position of the GDR for a peace treaty.[164] This was the nearest the party had dared come to grasping the 'hot potato' of work-sciving since 1953. The shop-floor response was predictably negative. The Production Drive was a pretext for tightening norms and freezing wages. Workers felt singled out at the expense of managers and the intelligentsia. 'Start at the top, with the men in coats', suggested one Halle worker.[165] Some pleaded, perhaps disingenuously, that there were no more ergonomic reserves left in their work routine. Others complained that they were simply being asked to offset the labour being poured into building the Wall.[166] Factories resorted to management by decree, extracting unpaid overtime to catch up on Plan deficits. Economic functionaries failed to put quality over quantity. The Production Drive sank into the usual routine of 'number-fiddling and top-down activism'.[167] For workers at Bergmann-Borsig it was meaningless while raw materials were missing.[168] Managements were fearful of pressing too hard, lest workers shift jobs.[169] Leuna still noticed workers clocking off early and rising sickness rates.[170] At Zeiß the party was gripped by

[161] FDGB-KV Dessau, 'Wie hat die Kreisgewerkschaftsorganisation Dessau . . . die besten Erfahrungen im Produktionsaufgebot verallgemeinert', 20 Jan. 1962, SAPMO-BArch, DY30/IV2/6.11/54, fos. 4–19.

[162] For a selection of these highly artificial *Zustimmungserklärungen*, many semi-printed, see LAB (STA), Rep. 303/26.1/227, fos. 187–255.

[163] SED-ZK (Politbüro), 29 Aug. 1961, SAPMO-BArch, DY30/JIV2/2/788. See also Ross, 'East Germans', 36–7.

[164] FDGB-BuVo, 'Seminarplan', 11 Sept. 1961, SAPMO-BArch, DY30/IV2/6.11/53, fos. 31–7.

[165] SED-SBL Halle-Süd, 'Informationsbericht', 12 Oct. 1961, LAM, BPA SED Halle, IV/2/4/992, fos. 113–29.

[166] Generalmajor Beater, 'Bericht für das Kollegium des MfS', Dec. 1961, BStU-ZA, MfS-SdM 1558, fo. 76.

[167] FDGB-BuVo (Org), '1. Information . . .', 19 Sept. 1961, SAPMO-BArch, DY34/22677.

[168] SED-ZK (PO), 'Bericht zu einigen Problemen in der Arbeit der Berliner Parteiorganisation', 29 Nov. 1961, SAPMO-BArch, DY30/IV2/5/37, fos. 77–82.

[169] SED-ZK (Gewerkschaften & Sozialpolitik), 'Zentralvorstand IG Metall', 24 Oct. 1961, SAPMO-BArch, DY30/IV2/6.11/53, fos. 456–60.

[170] VEB Leuna-Werk (Arbeitsdirektion), 'Aufgaben der Arbeitsnormung im Jahre 1962', 30 Jan. 1962, SAPMO-BArch, DY34/22377.

'depression'.[171] The notion that 13 August had brought about a fundamental change in workers' mentality was thus far from the truth. Whereas in 1961 there had been 135 labour stoppages, in 1962 there were 144.[172] The unions never published final figures on participation in the Production Drive, which quietly died a death in 1962.

The Ministry of Agriculture hoped that 13 August would have a similar consolidating effect on the overhasty collectivization of 1960. Resignations from LPG collectives had indeed been 'almost completely withdrawn', but there were signs of the state's continued weak foothold in the countryside. The harvest was slow coming in, despite an emergency decree. Former Nazi *Bauernführer* and 'kulaks' still exerted influence from behind the scenes, often from the local pub. On the less stringent Type I collectives many farmers performed their 8-hour day for the state, but farmed for themselves on the side. Reactionary views persisted that 'it might turn out different' and the capitalist smallholding would return.[173] Yet it was far easier for the authorities to isolate opponents on the land. In many cases co-opted fellow workers and apparatchiks would literally surround a miscreant in a miniature show trial. Using the decree of 24 August, the Potsdam Volkspolizei and MfS launched five such operations against 'enemy activity' and *Arbeitsbummelei*, distributing leaflets at 'backward' collectives. By the month's end twenty-five people had been sent for work re-education.[174] Thus, one cooperative worker, 'known for drunkenness, poor work discipline and an attempt to leave the Republic illegally', was put before over 100 dairyworkers who 'demanded the immediate detention of dairyman M. in a work camp'.[175] Likewise, the Erfurt authorities started making examples of 'workshy elements'.[176] In the Karl-Marx-Stadt region, too, 'several incorrigibles were put behind lock and key', and one farmer even deported to West Germany.[177] Local agronomists, police, and workers from 'sponsor' factories concentrated their forces on collectives which had still not merged their plots of land. In Saxony 'serious distortions' in party policy occurred as previously frustrated officials took it upon themselves to push the

171 SED-BPO Carl Zeiß Jena, 'Informationsbericht', 19 Oct. 1961, SAPMO-BArch, DY30/IV2/5/844, fos. 203–7.

172 FDGB-Bundesvorstand, 'Analyse über Arbeitskonflikte, die zu Arbeitsniederlegungen führten, und über klassenfeindliche Tätigkeit im Jahre 1961', 1 Feb. 1962; FDGB-Bundesvorstand, 'Entwicklung der Arbeitsniederlegungen im Jahre 1962', n.d., SAPMO-BArch, DY30/IV2/6.11/66, fos. 27–36 and fos. 257–69.

173 Ministerium für Landwirtschaft, 'Einschätzung der Entwicklung der LPG nach dem 13.8.1961', 2 Sept. 1961, SAPMO-BArch, DY30/IV2/7/376, fos. 49–62.

174 BDVP Potsdam (Abt. K), 'Zur Lage in der Landwirtschaft', 29 Aug. 1961, BLHA, Bez. Pdm. Rep. 530/IV2/5/1023, fos. 185–94.

175 RdK Pritzwalk to RdB Potsdam, 30 Aug. 1961, BLHA, Bez. Pdm. Rep. 401/3796, fo. 82.

176 'Einschätzung der massenpolitischen Arbeit nach dem 13.8.1961 im Kreis Erfurt-Land', 4 Sept. 1961, ThHStAW, SED-BL Erfurt, B IV2/7/20.

177 SED-BL KMS (Landwirtschaft), 'Bericht für Genossen Rolf Weihs', 22 Aug. 1961, StAC, SED-BL KMS, IV2/7/9, fos. 152–57.

collectivization process further ahead, issuing LPGs with deadlines to merge into super-LPGs.[178] Other, more local reports promised much, but cited little evidence of an overnight change in the countryside. The Potsdam MfS claimed that the border closure had ushered in a 'transformation process in the political thinking of the collective farmers'. Nevertheless, the examples cited showed that farmers continued to plough their own furrow, and that local agricultural officials were unwilling to risk a trial of strength.[179] Around Karl-Marx-Stadt, too, the last region to collectivize fully, there was still little enthusiasm for joint working of the land, and indeed signs of 'passive resistance'.[180] The Ministry still had to combat 'corner-cutting, disorder, fodder wastage, high animal losses' only with 'tellings-off, general statements and administrative measures without unmasking the hostile forces . . . and raising the authority of the state'.[181]

Another target group was young men to be recruited into the armed forces. Before the Wall recruiters had relied on heavy-handed persuasion to perform 'honorific service', but there was no GDR conscription. The result was a chronic shortfall in induction quotas, for instance, by nearly half in Halle in February 1961.[182] One reason was factories hoarding manpower.[183] Yet, with the border closed young men could no longer evade the mustering committees. Nevertheless, the state still tried to preserve the fiction of voluntarism. On 17 August the FDJ issued a 'Call to Arms'. 'Every proper man with his heart in the right place' was encouraged to join up: 'Peace must be armed!'[184] Some youths clearly objected to this manufactured consensus, pointing out that 'if the borders were reopened, thousands of youths would immediately run away'.[185] Repeatedly addressees refused, calling for a law or preferring to show solidarity at the workplace (army pay was poor in comparison). And not a few thought the GDR had lost the moral high ground to a West Germany where national service was already compulsory.[186]

[178] SED-ZK (PO), 'Mitteilung über die Arbeit des Genossen H. . . .', 26 Sept. 1961, SAPMO-BArch, DY30/IV2/5/37, fos. 33–5.

[179] MfS-BV/BDVP Potsdam, 'Die Lage in der Landwirtschaft im Bezirk Potsdam', 1 Dec. 1961, SAPMO-BArch, DY30/IV2/7/401, fos. 184–223.

[180] SED-BL KMS, 'Bericht', 17 Sept. 1961, StAC, SED-BL KMS, IV2/5/22, fos. 43–57.

[181] Ministerium für Landwirtschaft, 'Einschätzung der Entwicklung der Lage auf dem Lande in Vorbereitung der Wahlen zum 17. Sept. 1961', 17 Sept. 1961, SAPMO-BArch, DY30/IV2/7/376, fos. 65–83.

[182] NVA-Bezirkskommando Halle, 'Kurze Einschätzung der Lage für die SED-Bezirksleitung', 24 Feb. 1961, LAM, BPA SED Halle, IV2/4/991, fos. 25–28.

[183] Corey Ross, ' "Protecting the accomplishments of socialism": The (re)militarisation of life in the GDR', in Patrick Major and Jonathan Osmond (eds), *Workers' and Peasants' State* (Manchester: MUP, 2002), 78–93: 84.

[184] *Neues Deutschland*, 18 Aug. 1961, 5.

[185] SED-KL Leuna, 'Meinungen zu den Massnahmen vom 13.8.61', 29 Aug. 1961, LAM, BPA SED Halle, IV/412/279, fos. 12–13.

[186] FDJ-ZR (Org-Instruk), 'Meinungen und Argumente . . .', 20 Aug. 1961, SAPMO-BArch, DY24/3.725.

Volunteering was not a success, despite encouragements to the 'many girls who shamed boys who wavered and hesitated'.[187] At Wolgast near Rostock only twenty-nine of fifty youths summonsed appeared: no-one was prepared to sign up, and after refusing to listen to Ulbricht's speech, all 'demonstratively left the room'.[188] Likewise, at a sewing-machine factory near Karl-Marx-Stadt, the meeting collapsed when only one of the 166 invitees turned up. At the miners' hospital at Erlabrunn, at a special muster before the Minister of Justice herself, thirty-six youths appeared but none signed.[189] These were very dispiriting results for a Free German Youth still encompassing less than half the youth population. For non-affiliated youth, universities, schools, and factories became the pressure points. Students were a tough nut to crack, however, evincing pacifism, Christian conscience, and repugnance at supposed 'cadavre obedience'.[190] Recalcitrant undergraduates at the Humboldt University only acceded after 'a very hard confrontation'.[191] Refuseniks at Leipzig were ex-matriculated. On some shop-floors factory ordinances were issued, delegating young workmates to the NVA, photographing the role models and publicizing them over the tannoy.[192] But when this occurred at a clothing works in Reichenbach, 110 of the 120 workers stopped work.[193] By 28 August there were 41,616 signatures altogether, lowest in Berlin, but clearly not enough to man an army.[194] The next day the Politbüro bit the bullet of legislation for a compulsory military draft, but to be kept secret until after the upcoming elections.[195] Within three days of these, on 20 September, the Defence Law appeared. Another pacifist wave occurred, including symbolic protests, such as the wearing of black by one school class in Anklam, which led to mass expulsions and the firing of staff.[196] But some youths now realized the inevitability of conscription, attempting to take last-minute advantage of the perks of volunteering, such as choice of armed service. Finally, in January 1962 conscription was introduced. There were a number of calls for conscientious objection,[197] but the vast majority of young East German men reported for duty

---

[187] FDJ-ZR (Sek), 'Einschätzung der ersten Ergebnisse bei der Führung des Aufgebots . . .', 21 Aug. 1961, SAPMO-BArch, DY24/3.725.

[188] HVDVP (Operativstab), 'Operativer Bericht . . .', 20 Aug. 1961 (4 a.m.), BAB, DO-1/11/1130, fo. 62.

[189] BEL KMS, '27. Bericht', 19 Aug. 1961, StAC, SED-BL KMS, IV2/12/5, fo. 110.

[190] SED-PL KMU, 'Einschätzung der politischen Arbeit unter den Studenten', 23 Sept. 1961, SAPMO-BArch, DY30/IV2/9.04/558, fos. 243–68.

[191] SED-PL HU, 'Bericht über das Anlaufen des Studienjahres 1961/62', 11 Sept. 1961, SAPMO-BArch, DY30/IV2/9.04/495, fos. 69–77.

[192] SED-BL Leipzig (Org-Kader), '12. Bericht . . .', 24 Aug. 1961, StAL, BPA SED Leipzig, IV2/12/594.

[193] 'Arbeitsniederlegung im VEB Vogtl. Bekleidungswerk Reichenbach, Werk III', n.d. [Sept. 1961], StAC, SED-BL KMS, IV2/5/22, fos. 16–17.

[194] 'Statistik über Kampfauftragserfüllung', 28 Aug 1961, SAPMO-BArch, DY24/3.935.

[195] SED-PB, 29 Aug. 1961, SAPMO-BArch, DY30/JIV2/2/788.

[196] SED-ZK (Volksbildung), 'Information', 26 Sept. 1961, SAPMO-BArch, DY30/IV2/9.05/27, fos. 29–31.

[197] Neugebauer to Hager, 14 Feb. 1962, SAPMO-BArch, DY30/IV2/9.05/27, fos. 111–13.

and enrolment went smoothly.[198] Yet, the fact that the SED had been forced to introduce conscription over its preferred didactic means of 'volunteering', represented a defeat behind the Wall.

By September the regime deemed the immediate crisis to be over. The *Kampfgruppen* had returned to work on 25 August.[199] There had been no major strikes. The harvest was in. The government had grasped the nettle of conscription for the armed forces. Although the party had apprehensions that the imminent elections could turn into a protest vote, when it came to polling on 17 September, 98.4 per cent ritually affirmed the single list, but with a noticeably lower turnout in Berlin and among young voters.[200] Arrests for anti-state behaviour ran on into October, but by then it was the West Berlin police who were spending more time dealing with unruly protestors in the West. The international aftershocks rumbled on until the end of October, with the famous armoured stand-off at Checkpoint Charlie, but domestically the SED had weathered the Wall crisis.

PERFECTING THE 'ANTIFASCIST DEFENCE RAMPART'

> The Wall was supposed to protect for hundreds of years to come; painstaking construction, utilizing the building know-how of all known epochs and peoples, and a permanent sense of personal responsibility on the part of the builders, were absolute job specifications.
>
> Franz Kafka, 'Building the Great Wall of China'

The term 'Wall' remained taboo in the GDR for most of its twenty-eight-year lifetime. Only in 1989 did Honecker use the word publicly. During the crisis various euphemisms were rigidly applied, including the 'measures' of the Council of Ministers, or 'border securification'. In late 1961, however, the Politbüro's Horst Sindermann coined the future designation 'Antifascist Defence Rampart' (*antifaschistischer Schutzwall*).[201] Doggedly, the GDR adhered to its conspiracy theory of a West bent on destroying it from without, seeking to elide the Third Reich and Federal Republic as revanchist, militarist aggressors. It also attempted to normalize the border by claiming, in the words of the Council of Ministers, that such levels of control were 'usual at the borders of any sovereign state'.[202] In its early days, when still improvised and incomplete, there were nevertheless still

---

[198] Wansierski to Honecker, 5 Apr. 1962, SAPMO-BArch, DY30/IV2/12/57, fos. 71–2.

[199] BEL Berlin to Ulbricht, 26 Aug. 1961, LAB (STA), Rep. 303/26.1/227, fos. 135–40.

[200] SED-ZK (PO), 'Abschlußbericht über die Vorbereitung und Durchführung der Wahlen . . . am 17.9.1961', 13 Oct. 1961, SAPMO-BArch, DY30/IV2/5/295, fos. 270–84.

[201] Horst Dieter Schlosser, *Die deutsche Sprache in der DDR zwischen Stalinismus und Demokratie* (Cologne: Verlag Wissenschaft und Politik, 1990), 216. The German *Wall* is a false friend to the English wall.

[202] *Neues Deutschland*, 13 Aug. 1961, 1.

ways through for the intrepid. By 20 September 1961 the authorities had counted
284 escapes, having foiled another 257, mostly by young people. Favourite routes
were out of windows overlooking the border, either abseiling or leaping onto
the waiting blankets of the West Berlin fire brigade; swimming across rivers and
canals, or diving off moving boats or trains; dodging between the gravestones
of the cemeteries which lined the northern perimeter; or simply by cutting the
barbed wire on top of the makeshift wall and climbing over while a guard's back
was turned.[203]

The Wall presented the ultimate challenge, and its tales of escape fed images
of an uncowed East German spirit in the western media and at exhibitions at the
Haus am Checkpoint Charlie.[204] Each new attempt had to be more ingenious
than the last, ramming the Wall with locomotives, diggers, and armoured buses,
or on pulley systems, home-made planes, and hot-air balloons. Among the first
and most spectacular was the hijacking on 18 August of the *Binz* ferry, along
with 150 passengers, by twelve members of the Protestant Junge Gemeinde
who forced it across the Baltic only to be intercepted by NVA *Schnellboote* just
before the Swedish coast.[205] Increasingly, however, outside help was needed from
so-called 'escape helpers', initially idealistic student volunteers or recently fled
East Germans wishing to rescue loved ones, but in what became an ever-more
commercial venture. False passports could be smuggled into East Berlin. Or
West Berliners attempted to cut through from the West, releasing friends and
relatives waiting on the other side. After a tip-off in December 1961, a firefight
ensued in one such incident at Staaken, in which a West Berlin student died
in no-man's land.[206] Tunnels were also built from the West by escape helpers
through the sandy soil below Bernauer Straße. All told, thirty-nine tunnels have
been counted (including nine from the East) through which 250–300 people
fled, almost all before 1965.[207] One of the first and most macabre started
in a cemetery in Pankow where over twenty escapees disguised as mourners
'descended' into the underworld. Perhaps the most indefatigable tunneller was
Harry Seidel, a former GDR racing cyclist, who had himself escaped in August
1961, and who turned his prodigious feats of endurance to rescuing his wife and
child later that year. His athleticism allowed him to vault the Wall, climb house

[203] 'Grenzdurchbrüche', n.d., LAB (STA), Rep. 303/26.1/239, fos. 157–64.

[204] Rainer Hildebrandt, *Es geschah an der Mauer/It Happened at the Wall. Eine Bilddokumentation
des Sperrgürtels um Berlin (West), seine Entwicklung vom '13. August' 1961 bis heute mit den
wichtigsten Geschehnissen*, 8th edn (Berlin: Arbeitsgemeinschaft 13. August, 1978); Anthony Kemp,
Escape from Berlin (London: Boxtree, 1987); Bodo Müller, *Faszination Freiheit: Die spektakulärsten
Fluchtgeschichten* (Berlin: Links, 2000); Ellen Sesta, *Der Tunnel in die Freiheit: Berlin, Bernauer
Straße* (Berlin: Ullstein, 2001).

[205] Werkentin, *Politische Strafjustiz*, 258.

[206] MfS-ZAIG, 'Einzelinformation über Grenzprovokationen', 10 Dec. 1961, BStU-ZA, ZAIG
525.

[207] Marion Detjen, *Ein Loch in der Mauer: Die Geschichte der Fluchthilfe im geteilten Deutschland*
(Munich: Siedler, 2005), 95–163 and 442–5.

facades, and at one point to jump two floors from Stasi detention. In March 1962 Seidel was nearly caught, dragging a mortally wounded comrade back from a shoot-out at a tunnel entrance, before finally being arrested while trying to extract others in November 1962. In the most notorious tunnel incident, in October 1964, however, fifty-seven people crawled through a passageway dug from a cellar in the West to an outside lavatory in East Berlin. After another betrayal, shooting broke out, leaving one border guard dead. Thereafter, the MfS used infiltration, counter-tunnelling, and listening equipment to foil further subterranean attempts. As the urban route became more dangerous, the determined turned to the Demarcation Line, where 40 per cent of escapes proved successful in 1961–62, including desertions by border guards. Escapers devised ever more ingenious ways of arming themselves, testing minefields or diving underwater across rivers. In February 1962, for instance, twelve would-be escapees were caught with home-made snow camouflage and a smoke screen, as well as sulphuric acid for throwing at guards.[208]

In the absence of early foolproof barriers, especially in Berlin where the border was more easily approachable, guards were encouraged to shoot. 'Arrest by firearm', as the jargon put it, was *the* most controversial aspect of the frontier regime.[209] Already, according to a SMAD (Soviet Military Administration in Germany) directive of August 1947, border police, after calls and warning shots, were permitted to fire on border-crossers at the Demarcation Line.[210] This was repeated in an MfS directive of May 1952, as well as in detailed Border Police regulations in 1958, which formed the core of all later orders. After Willy Brandt's plea in August 1961 for Germans not to fire on Germans, Ulbricht was keen to stifle such 'pacifist behaviour': 'Some say Germans cannot shoot at Germans. If they are impudent, we shall fire on Germans representing imperialism. Whoever provokes will be shot.'[211] Honecker echoed this: 'Firearms are to be used against traitors and border violators. . . . A field of vision and fire is to be created in the Exclusion Zone.'[212] This was subsequently translated into Defence Ministry Order No. 76/61, requiring border guards to use their firearms 'to arrest persons who do not heed the directives of the border sentry by not stopping at the call of 'Halt—stand still—border sentry' or after the discharge of a warning shot, but who obviously are trying to violate the state frontier of the GDR and no other means of arrest exist.'[213] This particular version lasted formally until February 1964, but *de facto* until 1972, when

[208] NVA-Kommando Grenztruppen (Grenzsicherung), 'Bericht über die Ergebnisse der Grenzsicherung im Jahre 1962', 21 Jan. 1963, BA-MZAP, GT 1186, fos. 194–225.

[209] Uwe Gerig, *Morde an der Mauer* (Böblingen: Tykve, 1989).

[210] Schultke, *"Keiner kommt durch"*, 177.

[211] 'Rede des Genossen Walter Ulbricht im Politbüro am 22.8.1961', 22 Aug. 1961, SAPMO-BArch, DY 24/ 3.727.

[212] 'Protokoll über die Lagebesprechung des zentralen Stabes am 20.09.1961, von 08.30 Uhr bis 09.30 Uhr', 20 Sept. 1961, BA-MZAP, VA-01/39573, fos. 92–8.

[213] Koop, *'Den Gegner vernichten'*, 499–500.

regulations were relaxed and sentries allowed discretionary use of firearms, although, as Honecker reiterated in May 1974, 'As always, ruthless use of firearms must be made upon border breakthrough attempts, and comrades who have successfully utilized their firearms are to be commended.'[214] Since 1967, the order of the day, repeated every watch, demanded that 'border violators are to be arrested or annihilated'.[215] The only restrictions were a categorical ban on firing into West Berlin, for fear of international incidents, augmented by Honecker's policy in the 1980s of suspending shooting during diplomatic visits. Only in April 1989 was shoot-to-stop lifted, except in self-defence, then completely abolished on 21 December 1989 by the new Minister of Defence.[216]

The first fatal shooting after the Wall occurred at 4.15 p.m. on 24 August when Günter Litfin, a 24-year-old former *Grenzgänger*, leaped into the river Spree within sight of the Reichstag, despite a warning.[217] Shot in the head by a burst of automatic fire, Litfin's body was later dredged up before the western media. At his funeral 800 mainly older people gathered, while 'progressive' citizens tried in vain to quash neighbourhood rumours that the dead man had been an innocent victim.[218] Meanwhile, the party press smeared him as a homosexual.[219] Five days later, on 29 August, the 27-year-old Roland Hoff tried to swim the Teltow Canal, ignoring a warning shot:

> At that point Officer X gave the order for aimed fire. Officer X fired 18 shots from his sub-machinegun in short bursts; Soldiers P. and L. a total of 9 shots from their carbines. A militiaman arriving on the scene also discharged one aimed shot. . . . Rounds were not observed impacting on the western side. After the aimed fire the person immediately sank into the canal and did not resurface. A briefcase bobbed up which was recovered about 20 m downstream by a Kampfgruppe comrade.[220]

Attempts could even develop into regular firefights between eastern and western police. At 8.10 p.m. on 4 October 1961 two border guards in the city centre engaged in a roof-top chase with Bernd Lünser, which was to end in his death:

> After cries for help, the civilian was promised support by West Berlin police. When they realized our guards were in pursuit, reinforcements from the Riot Police arrived and the West Berlin police opened fire on our guards with pistols, approx. 10 rounds. Sgt. P. was wounded by a shot through the upper thigh. In their struggle Sgt. P. and the escapee

---

214 Peter Przybylski, *Tatort Politbüro: Die Akte Honecker* (Berlin: Rowohlt, 1991), 185–6.
215 Ritter and Lapp, *Grenze*, 66.   216 Ritter and Lapp, *Grenze*, 44.
217 BEL Berlin to Ulbricht, 25 Aug. 1961, LAB (STA), Rep. 303/26.1/227, fos. 130a–4.
218 BEL Berlin to Ulbricht, 1 Sept. 1961, LAB (STA), Rep. 303/26.1/227, fo. 170. See also Jürgen Litfin, *Tod durch fremde Hand: Das erste Maueropfer in Berlin und die Geschichte einer Familie* (Husum: Verlag der Nation, 2006).
219 *Neues Deutschland*, 2 Sept. 1961, cited in Frederick Taylor, *The Berlin Wall: 13 August 1961 to 9 November 1989* (London: Bloomsbury, 2006), 262.
220 Filmer and Schwan (eds.), *Opfer der Mauer*, 83–4.

slid and were both left hanging in the guttering. As a result of two warning shots . . . the escapee extricated himself from Sgt. P. and ran back across the roofs . . . By this point the West Berlin fire-brigade was in position with a jumping blanket, trying to orientate the civilian. At the moment the escapee was aligning himself with the jumping blanket, Sub-Lt. H. fired 3 aimed shots from his 'M' pistol, of which the 3rd shot was probably a hit and the escapee fell from the roof of the five-storey house in a horizontal position with arms outstretched.[221]

The most notorious incident of all occurred on 17 August 1962, however, when the 18-year-old Peter Fechter was shot near Checkpoint Charlie. Hit in the back and abdomen while scaling the Wall, he lay for an hour in no-man's land, slowly bleeding to death, while border guards took cover, apparently fearful of being shot at themselves. All of this was captured by western cameras and the photograph of Fechter's lifeless body being carried away became an icon of West German anticommunism.[222] Soviet vehicles were subsequently stoned by West Berliners as they passed through the checkpoint, and among eastern onlookers the Stasi reported 'extremely negative discussions'.[223]

The regime was understandably keen to suppress news of such incidents, and East German trigger-happiness even led to calls for restraint from Soviet superiors.[224] MfS disinformation campaigns denied any killings at the Wall. The wounded were held in isolation wards, and only close relatives of the dead were informed, sometimes with misleading death certificates, but never permitted to view the body, which was often pre-emptively cremated.[225] By far the bloodiest years were the 1960s. A further 1,000 were seriously injured and 72,000 imprisoned for attempting to escape.[226] A definitive death toll at the inner German border will probably never be reached, given the legal and forensic difficulties of identifying perpetrators and victims. Does a woman missing, presumed drowned in the Baltic count the same as a man shot dead at the Wall? The official West German agency at Salzgitter, set up in November 1961, reported 274 killings, including 114 at the Wall,[227] while the central police investigation agency in West Berlin (ZERV) pursued 421 and 122 cases respectively.[228] Since these were judicial bodies investigating premeditated killings, deaths by misadventure were not included. The 'Arbeitsgemeinschaft 13.

[221] Ibid., 86–7.
[222] Pertti Ahonen, *Death at the Berlin Wall* (Oxford: Oxford University Press, 2011).
[223] MfS-ZAIG, 'Bericht', 17 Aug. 1962, BStU-ZA, ZAIG 10725, fos. 371–3.
[224] Harrison, *Driving*, 212.
[225] Polly Feversham and Leo Schmidt, *Die Berliner Mauer heute: Denkmalwert und Umgang* (Berlin: Verlag Bauwesen, 1999), 117.
[226] Bernd Eisenfeld, 'Flucht und Ausreise—Macht und Ohnmacht', in Eberhard Kuhrt (ed.), *Opposition in der DDR von den 70er Jahren bis zum Zusammenbruch der SED-Herrschaft* (Opladen: Leske and Budrich, 1999), 383.
[227] Heiner Sauer and Hans-Otto Plumeyer (eds), *Der Salzgitter Report: Die Zentrale Erfassungsstelle berichtet über Verbrechen im SED-Staat*, 2nd edn (Frankfurt: Ullstein, 1993), 255–317.
[228] ZERV, *Jahresbericht 2000* (Berlin: Polizeipräsident, 2001), 8.

August' at the Haus am Checkpoint Charlie, continuing its posthumous war on the GDR, has insisted on higher but speculative totals, including accidents and East German deaths at the iron curtain in other eastern bloc countries. From 372 cases announced in 1992, its running total rose to 1,135 in 2005, bolstered at various times by up to 30 per cent of hearsay claims or unidentifiable remains.[229] This 'holistic' accounting has now discarded the latter, but added new categories, such as spies abducted to Moscow and executed, and speaks no longer of victims of the border regime, but of 'Germany's division'.[230] Most recently Hans-Hermann Hertle of the Zentrum für Zeithistorische Forschung and Gerhard Sälter of the Dokumentationszentrum Berliner Mauer have embarked on a project to document the Wall's dead qualitatively as well as quantitatively.[231] The provisional total for Berlin is ninety-nine GDR refugees killed while attempting to escape, and twenty-seven from East and West caught up in firefights or killed accidentally.[232]

There were, of course, also eight border guards who died at the Wall, which the regime exploited to the full. On 23 May 1962, when a teenager swimming a canal came under fire, West Berlin police retaliated, a ricochet killing sentry Peter Göring. The photograph of his startled corpse appeared under the headline 'Murder Attack . . . Anger Fills Our Land'.[233] The following month, sentry Reinhold Huhn was shot dead during a stop-and-search by an escape helper.[234] Like Göring, he received a state funeral, lying in an open coffin for parties of young pioneers to pay their respects. As *Neues Deutschland* emotively reported: 'the flags with funeral garlands were dipped, tears ran down the pain-filled faces, pioneers raised their hands in an honour salute'.[235] Huhn's barracks bed was symbolically kept made up and his grave tended in a rather macabre death cult. But few realized at the time that, of the two dozen officially commemorated border guards, half had been shot by their own side, such as Egon Schultz, caught in crossfire, although the autopsy findings on the fatal Kalashnikov bullet were suppressed.[236] GDR propagandists were disappointed, moreover, that the public was not always ready to accept such martyrs. When Thuringians were quizzed

[229] Arbeitsgemeinschaft 13. August (ed.), '121. Pressekonferenz: Bilanz der Todesopfer des DDR-Grenzregimes', 11 Aug. 1999.

[230] Hans-Hermann Hertle and Gerhard Sälter, 'Die Todesopfer an Mauer und Grenze: Probleme einer Bilanz des DDR-Grenzregimes', *Deutschland Archiv*, 39 (2006), 667–76: 673.

[231] Interim results are available at www.chronik-der-mauer.de.

[232] Hans-Hermann Hertle, *Die Berliner Mauer: Monument des Kalten Krieges* (Berlin: Links, 2008), 104.

[233] *Neues Deutschland*, 25 May 1962, 1.

[234] MdI (Kommando Bereitschaftspolizei), 'Auswertung besonderer Vorkommnisse in den Grenzbrigaden (B)', 22 June 1962, BA-MZAP, VA-07/8448, fos. 256–63. See also Peter Kirschey, *Der Tod des Gefreiten Reinhold Huhn* (Berlin: Spotless, 1999).

[235] *Neues Deutschland*, 22 June 1962, 1.

[236] Dokumentationszentrum Berliner Mauer, 'Tunnel 57/Egon Schultz': see in particular the autopsy report.

on Göring's death, one youth asked 'why are you making so much of it? People dying everyday are not even mentioned.' Others argued that, 'We built the Wall in the first place, which had to lead to provocations. Aren't our soldiers who shoot at border violators just as much murderers?'[237]

The only long-term solution to such negative publicity was to deter escapes by making the frontier near impregnable. On 14 September 1961 Soviet Marshal Koniev directed the NVA to undertake 'the heavy-duty and technical expansion of the border', including 'wire fencing, minefields, signals, observation towers and controls and patrols'.[238] In October concrete chicanes were emplaced at crossing-points after a number of 'severe border breakthroughs' by vehicles and locomotives, and over the winter building continued apace. Then, in June 1963 a 10-metre control strip was introduced in Berlin itself and even graveyards were cleared of occupants. Buildings and allotments abutting the sector boundary were razed, although the ground-floor facades of the Bernauer Straße remained as an eery reminder until the late 1970s.[239] U- and S-Bahn entrances were sealed up, while unseen guards peered from platform pillboxes at the western trains which continued to trundle through the 'ghost stations' under East Berlin.[240] Loopholes on the 'green line' were also closed. Rather than a wall, the inner-German border was guarded by three lines of wire-mesh fencing, including a 100-metre defoliated fire zone.[241] Rivers and canals received underwater grilles, guarded above by boats, which also patrolled coastal waters. A cost-effective means of closing off open country was mines, 1.3 million of which covered about 20 per cent of the border.[242] Most notorious of all were the SM-70 'self-firing devices', boobytraps strung along the frontline fence before being dismantled in 1983–84. As tests revealed, their eighty steel splinters could penetrate an inch of wood and were deadly far beyond the 'optimal' 10 metres.[243] Last but not least, dog-runs were placed in no-man's land, or on frozen rivers, so that by 1989 3,000 Alsatians helped to guard the frontier. The Border Troops also practised defence in depth, using local contacts, police, and Stasi to intercept would-be escapees. The Volkspolizei's Auxiliary Volunteers, usually reservists or ex-policemen, patrolled their district for a few hours a week, on the look-out for strangers. Whereas in 1962 71.5 per cent of detainees had been caught directly at

---

[237] SED-KL Heiligenstadt, 'Einschätzung . . .', 6 June 1962, ThHStAW, SED-BL Erfurt, IV2/9.01/13.

[238] Ritter and Lapp, *Grenze*, 30.   [239] Feversham and Schmidt, *Berliner Mauer*, 175.

[240] Heinz Knobloch, *Geisterbahnhöfe: Westlinien unter Ostberlin*, 3rd edn (Berlin: Links, 1994); Udo Dittfurth, *August 1961: S-Bahn und Mauerbau: Die Berliner S-Bahn im Jahr 1961* (Berlin: GVE, 2006), 26–71.

[241] MdI, 'Befehl Nr. ?/61: Gewährleistung der Sicherheit im Sperrgebiet an der Westgrenze der Deutschen Demokratischen Republik', n.d. [Sept. 1961], SAPMO-BArch, DY30/JIV2/3/763, fos. 29–44.

[242] Ritter and Lapp, *Grenze*, 107; Schultke, *"Keiner kommt durch"*, 64.

[243] Schultke, *"Keiner kommt durch"*, 82.

the frontier, by 1988 it was only 31 per cent of the 2,312 arrestees, demonstrating the successes of policing the hinterland.[244]

As in 1952, security also involved borderzone deportations. In Berlin about 4,000 people were removed, as plain-clothes militia guarded apartment windows while police read out eviction orders.[245] In Bernauer Straße, where the house-fronts marked the border, 149 families were targeted, described as ex-fascists, criminals, former *Grenzgänger*, or simply as 'known to be hostile in the past'. Although there was little physical resistance, there were last-minute breakouts. Marianne S. abseiled down a washing-line, abandoning 1,600 marks in her rush; but when the 77-year-old Frieda Schulze climbed out onto the window-ledge, a tussle ensued between militiamen trying to drag her back in and West Berliners pulling her out, resolved only when West Berlin police tear-gassed the apartment.[246] The next day 80-year-old Olga Segler was less fortunate, dying from injuries sustained in her fall. After this experience the municipal authorities went over to blanket evictions and demolitions. At the Demarcation Line, too, residents were expelled in Operation Consolidation.[247] Originally over 10,000, or 2.7% of the border population, had been earmarked, including nearly 1,000 former Nazi functionaries and over 1,000 'reactionaries', as well as over 750 returnees and immigrants, sixty-four 'workshy and asocial' elements and eight priests.[248] In the event, a modified evacuation occurred between 20 and 25 September 1961, and by 4 October 3,200 suspect persons had been deported by the Volkspolizei, after limited passive resistance.[249]

Since the Border Troops had become such a huge undertaking—over 38,000 men by 1961—they were transferred in September 1961 from the police to the army as the 'Kommando Grenze'. National service swelled this to 52,000 by 1963, recruited only from those without western relatives. Duties consisted of patrolling, usually in random twosomes, laying ambushes, or manning watchtowers, and night patrols had to take a 4-hour 'service nap' in the early evening. Guards were also categorized according to reliability in so-called 'blood groups', with only class-conscious 'A-graders' permitted to patrol alone up to the wire. 'B-graders' could only operate alongside a category-A comrade, and D-graders remained behind the border installations under A-category supervision.[250] Needless to say, the MfS saturated the border regiments with informants. Nevertheless, from 1961 to 1989 well over 2,000 guards deserted. From the outset there had been

[244] Schultke, *"Keiner kommt durch"*, 108–9. Two-thirds were seized by the Volkspolizei and Transport Police, a quarter by the Border Troops and a mere 4 per cent by the MfS.
[245] Scholze and Blask, *Halt! Grenzgebiet!*, 104–06.
[246] SED-KL Berlin-Mitte to SED-BL Berlin, 25 Sept. 1961, LAB, BPA SED Berlin, IV4/04/235.
[247] Bennewitz and Potratz, *Zwangsaussiedlungen*, 100–69.
[248] HVDVP (Leiter), '2. Bericht ... Ausweisung von Personen aus dem Grenzgebiet ...', 20 Sept. 1961, BAB, DO-1/11/779, fos. 180–4.
[249] HVDVP (Leiter), '4. Bericht ... Ausweisung von Personen aus dem Grenzgebiet ...', 4 Oct. 1961, BAB, DO-1/11/779, fos. 193–6.
[250] Schultke, *"Keiner kommt durch"*, 101.

concern at western attempts to influence them, both in personal conversations *propaganda* across no-man's land, 'luring' them with cigarettes or sending recently deserted comrades to fraternize, as well as poster hoardings and a set of mobile loudspeaker vans, the 'Studio on the Wire'.[251] The GDR deployed its own counter-batteries in a decibel war which neither side won, as well as erecting sight-screens to shield sentries from visual contact. Border Troops were also subjected to heavy doses of political indoctrination.[252] Songs celebrated the defence of socialism, reviving Spanish Civil War slogans:

> They shall not pass, comrades, that's a promise!
> We shan't let the misguided out of our land,
> Nor let the seducers in to us.
> We prevent the abuse of stupidity.
> That's a promise, comrades, they shall not pass!
> Neither the incendiaries into our reborn land,
> Nor those here led astray into the siren swamp.
> We protect the suicidal from their own deeds.
> That's a promise, comrades, they shall not pass!
> We shall dig out the burrowers,
> Stand fast against the onslaughts.
> Against the brown-black flood the rampart will hold.
> We swear: They shall not pass, comrades, that's a promise![253]

Like most GDR institutions, the Border Troops fetishized statistics, registering 'provocations' in lovingly rendered graphics, including every western tourist who approached the Wall. Frontier culture also included heavy doses of kitsch. Chunky bronze maquettes of idealized border sentries, permanently vigilant, adorned many a guardroom sideboard.

How many guards lived up to this image is hard to say. Listening to foreign radio was forbidden, but random checks on transistor radios revealed that this rule was regularly flouted. Stasi investigations concluded that, although most officers were enrolling for 'political–ideological' reasons, many NCOs were after material advantages, such as pay and housing, a place at university, or promotion. Semi-secret interviews with guards revealed uncertainty but a desire to justify their actions as 'normal' by international standards.[254] Most guards were prepared to carry out their duties conscientiously, although there were still 'conflicts' over willingness to shoot.[255] A significant number of sentries shot wide,

[251] NVA (Stadtkommandantur Berlin), 'Probleme der verstärkten klassenmäßigen Erziehung . . .', 31 Oct. 1963, LAB, BPA SED Berlin, IV2/12/1275–2.
[252] Dirk-Arne Walckhoff, *Der 13. August 1961 in der Traditionsarbeit der Grenztruppen der DDR* (Hamburg: Lit-Verlag, 1996).
[253] Koop, *'Den Gegner vernichten'*, 162.
[254] Privatarchiv Buyens, Mappe '1 Berlin', 788–92. See also Gisela Karau, *Grenzerprotokolle: Gespräche mit ehemaligen DDR-Offizieren* (Frankfurt: dipa, 1992).
[255] Schultke, *"Keiner kommt durch"*, 120.

especially in the later years. The routine of patrolling the border and manning the watch-towers was excruciatingly boring for most. The Border Troops lived an isolated, spartan existence, with rare leave and strict discipline. Drinking could be heavy, and every year the MfS had to investigate dozens of suicide attempts. Occasionally flashes of humanity would leak across the wire, in the form of returned greetings or smiles, but when in the presence of an officer, guards turned their backs or retreated behind binoculars and cameras.

From 1965 a new generation of prefabricated Wall was introduced in Berlin. Would-be escapers had first to negotiate a concrete 'hinterland wall', followed a few yards later by the border signal fence, alarmed with sensors. Then came a sandy 'protection strip', 50- to 70-metres wide, punctuated by guard-towers and floodlights, and capped by an anti-vehicle ditch and 'control strip', raked smooth every day to capture tell-tale footprints. Finally, there was the 'forward blocking element', the ultimate obstacle, made of concrete slabs slung horizontally between steel or concrete posts and topped with an anti-grip pipe. Painted white to silhouette would-be escapers, it contrasted with the grey rectangles along the rear wall. Finally, in 1975, emerging from behind the previous wall like a snake shedding its skin, came the 'Border Wall 75', beloved of graffiti artists for its smooth finish. Razor wire replaced barbed wire to the rear; improved, all-weather guard-towers were erected, connected to command centres; and the new frontline wall was constructed of free-standing L-shaped, prefabricated concrete sections, 3.6 metres high, originally designed for agricultural outhouses. At their testing ground at Neu-Zittau the Border Troops went to great lengths to beat the new installation, deploying athletes, crowbars, lorries, and explosive charges, all to no avail.[256] And this increasing refinement of the border achieved the desired effect. Whereas in 1962 5,761 'barrier breakers' were recorded, by the 1970s this had dwindled to under a thousand per year, reaching an all-time low of 160 in 1985.[257]

In its later years the Wall was remodelled somewhat in the light of détente. The SED was keen to achieve a 'neater' effect to soothe western eyes. Thus, in 1984, in return for a billion deutschmark credit from Bavaria's Franz Josef Strauß, slightly lower, less forbidding sections were introduced at Checkpoint Charlie, where most foreign tourists entered the GDR. Shrubberies to mask searchlights were laid between the Brandenburg Gate's pillars, which never had the 'death-strip' of other sections. The Reichstag's hinterland wall was also cladded to give the impression of stonework in keeping with the surrounding nineteenth-century architecture. At the same time it was decided to remove the fragmentation devices. A delicate mine clearance operation began in 1983, including landmines, which were fully removed by 1985.[258] From then on border units relied on a signal fence, short-circuited when scaled. Beyond that was a

---

[256] Feversham and Schmidt, *Berliner Mauer*, 35.
[257] Ritter and Lapp, *Grenze*, 167.   [258] Koop, *Gegner*, 315–20.

3-metre-high fence, too finely meshed for fingers to gain a purchase, and topped by razor wire.[259] High tech was another solution. By 1989 70 kilometres of fence were protected by halogen lights, designed to blind trespassers. Projected plans for a 'millennium wall' even included microwave, radio, and vibration sensors, as well as pyro-electric alarms and laser barriers.[260] Thankfully, these remained figments of the GDR's security mania.

In its immediate shadow, the border became a grim, everyday reality for a section of the populace. Within 500 metres of the Wall and 5 kilometres of the German–German border, special restrictions regulated comings and goings in the Exclusion Zone.[261] It was an isolating experience, even for the trustees permitted to live on the Cold War's frontline. In 1964 186 residents of Kremmener Straße, signed a petition asking for West Berlin relatives to be able to visit them in the Zone. The signatures even contained SED members, and complained of being second-class citizens, of 'living in a ghetto' and suffering from 'barbed wire fever'.[262] One pastor painted a yet more dismal picture of families in his Brandenburg parish, which had had strong links with West Berlin:

Especially older parishioners are suffering from the division. Their children have married into the neighbouring parishes; they often only know their grandchildren from pictures. Many have passed on without seeing their relatives again. Often the local pastor stands with neighbours and friends *alone* by the coffin; the relatives stand by the wire, for they hear the bells and the distance is not great. The number of those taking their own lives is shattering. If the mood has calmed somewhat, the order at the so-called 'border' has etched itself deep into minds and lives.

As the pastor continued, the expulsion of inhabitants to increase security in the Exclusion Zone was particularly unsettling:

I experienced many things in the war, but this is scarcely describable in words. Fear sits on those affected like a storm warning, the fear that one day or one night they too will have to vacate their houses and apartments. It is no exaggeration when I say that people can find no peace.[263]

Besides Berlin, the 'mainland' border covered about 200,000 of the population.[264] Certain places, such as Mödlareuth between Bavaria and Thuringia, were physically bisected by the border, with a wall running down the village centre. Life there was subject to numerous restrictions. No returnees or immigrants were allowed to live there, or rowdies or 'asocial elements' or those with criminal

---

[259] Ritter and Lapp, *Grenze*, 107–10. [260] Schultke, *"Keiner kommt durch"*, 95–6.
[261] Scholze and Blask, *Halt! Grenzgebiet!*.
[262] SED-ZK (Parteiorgane), 'Bericht', 2 Nov. 1964, SAPMO-BArch, DY30/IVA2/5/23.
[263] Evangelisches Pfarramt Schönefeld & Groß Ziethen, 'Gemeindebericht', 1 July 1963, EZA, 104/942.
[264] Andreas Hartmann, *Grenzgeschichten: Berichte aus dem deutschen Niemandsland* (Frankfurt: S. Fischer, 1990); Torsten Neuborg (ed.), *Mitten in Deutschland: Menschen an der Grenze: Gespräche und Fotos vor und nach dem 9. November 1989* (Frankfurt and Leipzig: Insel, 1991).

convictions. Visitors required special permits. One set of guidelines to visiting tourists reminded them that, 'You are in a position of trust to spend your vacation in a resort directly at the state border to the FRG, and we expect that you justify this trust at all times during your visit.' Although visitors were encouraged to go rambling, they had better not stray too close to the Exclusion Zone.[265] GDR maps of the border regions went over to marking the West simply as blank *terra incognita*: here, the world as socialism knew it, ended.[266]

[265] Ritter and Lapp, *Grenze*, 100–01.
[266] Daphne Berdahl, *Where the World Ended: Re-Unification and Identity in the German Borderland* (Berkeley, CA: University of California Press, 1999), 146–52.

6

In the Shadow of the Wall: Coming to Terms with Communism

For the SED, following 13 August, it was business as normal in the enclosed GDR. Now, without outside disturbance, the state could go about the steady building of socialism. The economy would flourish and living standards rise. The Wall had also allegedly saved the peace. Defensively, the press insisted that East German soldiers were 'good Germans': 'The howls of the NATO "lads without a fatherland" will not provoke them.'[1] *Neues Deutschland* mocked the West's helplessness, printing facsimiles of western headlines, including the famous *Bild* tabloid headline 'The West is doing NOTHING!'[2] Revanchist dreams of marching back under the Brandenburg Gate were now scuppered forever. Cartoons depicted the West German policy of strength as a clapped-out car disintegrating against a GDR border post, while Adenauer and Brandt bickered.[3] As the Wall's first anniversary approached, the GDR press cited non-aligned comment, in India, Denmark, and Mexico, on the need for closure, under headlines such as 'GDR Defence Rampart Serves World Peace' or 'Defence Rampart Brought Security'.[4] Karl Gass's post-Wall documentary, *Behold This City*, attacked a militaristic West Berlin and fixed the GDR's iconic image of 13 August: American tanks pulled up short at Checkpoint Charlie, seemingly by a lone Vopo.[5] Later TV documentaries reiterated the peace-loving rationale of the Wall, intercutting newspaper headlines from 1939 and 1961 to suggest parallels between the Sudeten and Berlin crises, between Hitler and Adenauer. The stakes were high: 'To be or not to be, peace or war.'[6]

Yet, beneath the foreign policy rhetoric, the SED paternalistically appealed to 'German' virtues of orderliness: 'Now children will be protected from

---

[1] *Neues Deutschland*, 15 Aug. 1961, 1.

[2] Ibid., 17 Aug. 1961, 1.   [3] Ibid., 18 Aug. 1961, 5.

[4] Ibid., 2 Aug. 1961, 1; ibid., 7 Aug. 1962. In similar vein: Anita Dasbach Mallinckrodt, *Propaganda hinter der Mauer: Die Propaganda der Sowjetunion und der DDR als Werkzeug der Außenpolitik im Jahre 1961* (Stuttgart: Kohlhammer, 1971), 117–26. See also Kara S. Fulcher, 'Walling in and Walling Out: The Politics and Propaganda of the Second Berlin Crisis, 1958–1962' (PhD thesis, Princeton, 1997).

[5] *Schaut auf diese Stadt* (Gass, 1962).

[6] 'Drei Jahre danach: Der 13. August 1961 aus heutiger Sicht' (DFF, 1964).

child-snatchers; families from people-trafficking blackmailers; factories from
head-hunters. Humans will be protected from monsters, order from the disorderly, the hard-working from workshy speculators, our citizens' peace and
security from the cold warriors.'[7] This was a continuation of the moral *cordon sanitaire*, contrasting a 'clean' GDR with the decadent morass of West
Berlin. The domestic function of the Wall was also evident from internal
communist correspondence. Writing to Khrushchev a month after the Wall,
Ulbricht identified a 'turn-around' in popular thinking, enabling a 'fundamental discussion of the long-term future': 'Many people talked of the fact
that they could no longer regularly travel to their aunt or uncle, but in reality they meant that the western position is now shattered and there is no
other way but to orientate oneself to the Workers'-and-Peasants' State and
the socialist camp.' Those hoping for a quadripartite reunification or 'concessions from both sides' were now forced to 'think things through'.[8] Thus,
as well as a physical function, the Wall served a psychological purpose, to
force neutralists off the sidelines. The Party Information prepared a long
assessment of the short-term effects of the 'measures' which reached similar
conclusions:

Among large sections of the population the standing of the Workers' and Peasants' State
and our Party has grown. The consistent and smooth implementation of the measures,
which the class enemy was powerless to resist, brought out more clearly for many citizens
the true balance of power and the superiority of the socialist camp. Among all strata of
the population it has become clearer that nothing will change in the GDR's social order.[9]

Doubtless, this view contained much wishful thinking by the East German
leadership, which still placed its greatest faith in the working class and greatest
mistrust in the middle classes. Yet inevitably, the building of the Wall must
be seen as a turning-point in the East German public's coming to terms with
communism.[10] The German word *Anpassung*—accommodation—describes the
process of adapting to force of circumstance, of making the best of a bad
job. The population had, of course, little choice, short of the type of internal emigration familiar from the Third Reich. British observers, too, noted
that citizens were 'acutely conscious that the situation within the DDR has
changed radically'. As one former doctor explained to embassy officials, since
resistance would be futile the population would now have to adapt: 'He compared it with the period 1933–34 in Germany when people realized that the

  [7] *Neues Deutschland*, 14 Aug. 1961, 1.
  [8] Ulbricht to Khrushchev, 15 Sept. 1961, SAPMO-BArch, DY30/JIV2/202/130.
  [9] SED-ZK (PO), 'Information über den politisch-ideologischen Zustand der Arbeiterklasse
und der einzelnen Bevölkerungsschichten vor und nach dem 13.8.1961 . . .', 22 Sept 1961,
SAPMO-BArch, DY30/IV2/5/295, fos. 235–57.
  [10] Anke Gebert (ed.), *Im Schatten der Mauer: Erinnerungen, Geschichten und Bilder vom Mauerbau
bis zum Mauerfall* (Berne: Scherz, 1999).

National Socialist Party had come to stay and they then jumped on the party bandwagon.'[11] Another man put it more succinctly: 'if you can't beat them, join them'.[12]

Grass-roots GDR officialdom was also keen to document the new deference. 'State authority has grown', reported the backwater of Schmalkalden. 'After 13 August numerous citizens—especially from the middle classes and intelligentsia—no longer make their wishes and representations to the state organs as demands and conditions, but deliver them politely and objectively.'[13] The Volkspolizei noted a gratifying rise in positive suggestions from the population, who had quickly abandoned complaints about travel.[14] Petitions, too, 'currently have the feel of begging letters'.[15] Much of this was undoubtedly lipservice, since East Germans were masters of double-speak. A more difficult question, since the change happened overnight but lasted a generation, is whether, over the long term, they came to accept the Wall. For those directly in its shadow, the answer is probably no, at least not in the medium term. In Berlin-Lichtenberg four years after its erection, it was still the attitudinal yardstick.[16] In Potsdam's border areas in 1966 even the SED conceded that few locals cooperated with the security forces.[17] In Berlin, although hostile discussions were on the wane, 'this has less to do with conviction about its necessity than with habituation'.[18] From my own experience, too, regularly visiting a family within two minutes' walk of the Wall in the mid-1980s, it is true that one could temporarily blot out what lurked around the corner. When directly confronted, however, the Wall never lost its shocking character.[19] As one British journalist recorded: 'I saw an East German drunk one night near to Checkpoint Charlie. Crossing the road with a stagger, he suddenly saw the Wall looming ahead. He knelt down, prayed and crossed himself: then held up his hands in surrender.'[20]

Psychologically, however, many felt that the wrong people had been penalized: precisely those who had stayed and remained loyal to the GDR. Dr S. at Buna

---

[11] BMG Berlin (External Dept.) to Chancery, Bonn, 18 Sept. 1961, PRO, FO371/160503/CG1018/37.

[12] Dieter Hildebrandt, *Die Mauer ist keine Grenze: Menschen in Ostberlin* (Düsseldorf: Diederichs, 1964), 20.

[13] SED-Sek., 'Information der Abteilung Agitation des ZK über die Lage und Stimmung im Kreis Schmalkalden', 27 Sept. 1961, SAPMO-BArch, DY30/JIV2/3/766, fos. 35–50.

[14] HVDVP (Sek.), 'Quartalsanalyse . . . III. Quartal 1961', n.d. [1961], BAB, DO-1/11/50, fos. 198–221.

[15] Untitled material in BAB, DA-5/167, fos. 130–9.

[16] SED-KL Lichtenberg (Org/Kader), 'Einschätzung der Bewußtseinsentwicklung . . . ', 23 Sept. 1965, LAB, BPA SED Berlin, IVA4/03/88.

[17] SED-BL Potsdam (Agit-Prop), 'Bericht vor dem Sekretariat des ZK . . . ', 19 Oct. 1966, BLHA, Bez. Pdm. Rep. 530/3187.

[18] Draft for a Bewußtseinsanalyse, Jan. 1967, LAB, BPA SED Berlin, IVA2/9.01/490.

[19] Interview with Mr and Mrs Sch. and Mr and Mrs L., Dresden-Weißig, 22 Aug. 1996.

[20] Bernard Newman, *Behind the Berlin Wall* (London: Hale, 1964), 162.

'considered the measures a vote of no confidence in his person'.[21] A Dresdener complained that 'we are now being punished because we did our job loyally and dutifully and stayed here'.[22] Perhaps this reaction was best captured by novelist Uwe Johnson whose heroine D. suffers a prolonged anxiety attack: 'Locked into this state she felt double-crossed, duped, deceived; the feeling was like an insult one cannot return; it constricted her throat, almost imperceptibly impeding her breathing, wanting out.'[23] The SED had effectively placed itself *in loco parentis*, and now became the object of a simmering resentment over this permanent grounding. And as we shall see below, it was often those holding positions of responsibility within the system, such as members of the armed forces, who were kept most firmly away from the West, creating antagonisms among even regime carriers.

For psychoanalyst Hans-Joachim Maaz the Wall was merely the outer manifestation of a 'blocked' authoritarian society, of 'walled-in, bounded-in life', crippling its members' personalities.[24] The GDR populace, trained from an early age to obey and not to overstep the mark, exhibited signs of alienation. The pressures of hierarchy and taboo were supposedly displaced into internal Freudian repression, leading to character deformation aimed at 'fitting in, control, order, discipline, exertion and performance'.[25] Obviously, one cannot put an entire nation on the psychohistorian's couch, but there is some evidence that incarceration had psychosomatic effects. In the 1970s the defecting director of an East Berlin psychiatric hospital claimed to have diagnosed 'Wall sickness'. Taking secret notes, he believed that the initial shock of 13 August had led to 'creeping physical disorders'. Separation from loved ones was causing curious symptoms: one hysterical woman could not open her mouth; another, with few relatives in the East, experienced 'pent-up' emotions; others complained of depression leading to insomnia and paranoia. Alcoholism, violent tendencies and claustrophobia were diagnosed. As Frau M., a 46-year-old housewife in the Exclusion Zone, put it: 'everything cramped up inside me'.[26] For those already susceptible, national division and Cold War paranoia could distort their whole perception of reality, such as the young man caught distributing leaflets on 'secret television', allegedly broadcast by the West German military–industrial complex, sending 'small black threads floating through the air, especially when the Centre is watching you read or write'.[27] It also seems likely that in areas

[21] SED-KL Buna to SED-BL Halle, 14 Aug. 1961, LAM, BPA SED Halle, IV2/55/1145, fos. 129–31.
[22] FDGB-BV Dresden (Org), '2. Situationsbericht', 16 Aug. 1961, SächsHStA, BPA SED Dresden, IV2/5/136, fos. 18–21.
[23] Uwe Johnson, *Zwei Ansichten* (1965; Frankfurt: Suhrkamp, 1992), 47. Author's translation.
[24] Hans-Joachim Maaz, *Der Gefühlsstau: Ein Psychogramm der DDR* (Berlin: Argon, 1990), 15.
[25] Maaz, *Gefühlsstau*, 69.
[26] Dietfried Müller-Hegemann, *Die Berliner Mauer-Krankheit: Zur Soziogenese psychischer Störungen* (Herford: Nicolaische Verlagsbuchhandlung, 1973), passim.
[27] Wansierski to Mielke, 3 Nov. 1971, SAPMO-BArch, DY30/IVA2/12/140.

close to Berlin the suicide rate went up perceptibly, as well as doubling among young people, although there was not the epidemic suspected by the western media.[28]

Nevertheless, living in a permanent state of resentment is difficult for most human beings. Besides, writing off the post-1961 GDR as a glorified prison,[29] or as 'Stasiland',[30] risks condescension towards its non-communist citizens, reminiscent of Cold War narratives of helpless easterners waiting to be rescued by the West. Consciously or unconsciously, many East Germans carved out a normality for themselves in the Wall's shadow, living 'within socialism'. Even vociferous critics of the GDR, such as historian Hermann Weber, recognized that the population had to 'come to an arrangement' with the regime and 'make the best of their situation', simply because they had no other choice.[31] As Mary Fulbrook has also recently suggested: 'Within the undesired but unchallengeable confines of a walled-in state, it was in most people's interests to be able to lead as comfortable, enjoyable and healthy lives as possible.'[32] This is not an apologia for the Wall, but a recognition that even under dictatorship individuals have agency. Lives may indirectly be shaped by Foucault's 'discipline-blockade', but cannot be consciously led in this knowledge day in, day out. Coping strategies were developed. Rita Kuczynski, for example, fled into obsessive piano practice during the first days, but then, after two suicide attempts, engaged in a form of inner emigration, separating her private from her public persona.[33] Another tactic, echoing Scott's weapons of the weak, was humour. East Germans developed a large repertoire of political jokes, including many oblique jibes over travel. The following could be heard regularly:

One evening St. Peter was sitting inside the gates of Heaven. He heard a knock, went outside, and found Ulbricht there. 'Well, you've got a nerve!' said St. Peter. 'A Communist leader, an atheist—for years you have persecuted Christians: and now, just because you are dead, you want to come into Heaven. No fear! Downstairs with you! Go to hell!' Three evenings later St. Peter heard another knock on the gates, went out, and was surprised to find the Devil himself. The Devil was claiming political asylum.[34]

These witticisms included a high degree of self-deprecation, yet this willingness to see the irony of the situation did something to defuse East Germans' anger, and reflected a growing identity as long-suffering easterners, but where the barbs were constantly pointed at the regime.

[28] Udo Grashoff, *'In einem Anfall von Depression . . . ': Selbsttötungen in der DDR* (Berlin: Links, 2006), 218–27.
[29] Taylor, *Berlin Wall*, 186–201.
[30] Anna Funder, *Stasiland: Stories from behind the Berlin Wall* (London: Granta, 2003).
[31] Weber, *DDR*, 98.   [32] Fulbrook, *People's State*, 18.
[33] Rita Kuczynski, *Mauerblume: Ein Leben auf der Grenze* (Munich: Claassen, 1999), 70.
[34] Newman, *Behind the Berlin Wall*, 76.

Others have compared the numbing process to that of an amputee, as Berliners developed a 'phantom pain' and symptoms of 'hospitalism'.[35] One of the rather obvious healing factors was geographic distance from the Wall. Saxons were assigned border duty because they supposedly did not have the same personal ties as Berliners. Away from the direct centre of operations, out of sight could become out of mind. When the local party interviewed residents on Leuna's housing estates, several hours south-west of Berlin, responses were relatively conformist, praising the end of economic exploitation and espionage. Only those who had relatives actively complained. One teacher talked of the closure being 'quite disruptive', since he had relatives on the other side, but qualified himself that it was all for the sake of peace. A housewife explained matter-of-factly that 'every bastard who bust up with his wife scarpered'. Only a few responded along the lines that it was politically correct, if inhumane.[36] Thus it is clear that distance did not mean indifference, but even East Berliners grew apart from West Berlin. As one woman recalled, 'the high-rise buildings towering on the other side appeared completely unreal as if on another planet'.[37] By architectural sleight of hand, town planners also built a screen of buildings along the Leipzigerstraße, to shield downtown East Berlin from the city lights and political message boards of the West.[38]

Another part of the answer is generational. For those old enough to remember a united Germany (anyone over twenty-five), or Germany before dictatorship (anyone over forty), the building of the Wall had a marked effect; we have already seen that national sentiments were still strong during 1961. It is more difficult to assess the 'middle' generation. There were certainly opportunities for young adults who had remained in the GDR after the great 1950s brain-drain. The expansion of university education began to tell in the 1960s, creating some system loyalty among socialist careerists. Yet it was precisely the eighteen to thirty group who had had most contact with the West. Less conflicted was the successor generation. Dorothee Wierling's collective biography of the cohort born in 1949 covers perhaps the youngest group aware of a before and after the Wall; they were eleven or twelve when it went up. Yet these interviews reveal an adolescent generation susceptible to SED propaganda who recall confusion and panic, but were very hazy about the political implications of border closure at the time.[39] Then there were the nearly 6 million East

---

[35] *Markierung des Mauerverlaufs: Hearing am 14. Juni 1995: Dokumentation* (Berlin: Senatsver-waltung für Bau- und Wohnungswesen, 1995), 11.

[36] July 1963 survey in LAM, BPA SED Halle, IVA2/9.01/29.

[37] Feversham and Schmidt, *Berliner Mauer*, 121.

[38] Alan Balfour, *Berlin: The Politics of Order 1737–1989* (New York: Rizzoli, 1990), 204.

[39] Dorothee Wierling, *Geboren im Jahr Eins: Der Jahrgang 1949 in der DDR: Versuch einer Kollektivbiographie* (Berlin: Links, 2002), 180–4. See also Thomas Davey, *Generation Divided: German Children and the Berlin Wall* (Durham, NC: Duke University Press, 1994).

Germans born after the Wall who knew only the closed society.[40] For them, the 'West' was a second-hand notion, something talked about by older relatives or watched on TV. Yet, the career opportunities which perhaps pacified the middle generation contained the seeds of destruction for the generation of 1949. Lutz Niethammer was among the first to point out that without the open border guaranteeing rapid advancement to those prepared to stay in socialism and fill the empty seats, upward mobility turned into social stagnation, as functional elites clung to their positions.[41] By the 1970s the GDR was turning into a system which could not reproduce itself. As Ralph Jessen has also argued: 'It was blocked from without by the Wall, and blocked from within by a frozen, rigid social structure. . . . [T]he Wall became a real hurdle to upward movement within society.'[42] As we shall see, the sorts of ambitious young people who had left in the 1950s began to seek ways out three decades later.

From the mid-1960s 'the West' also became more morally ambivalent for many eastern observers. The Adenauer government appeared authoritarian and secretive following the *Spiegel* affair of 1962, and in 1965 a series of war crimes trials in the Federal Republic revealed that there was indeed much unfinished denazification to be done. The shooting of Benno Ohnesorg, a bystander at a demonstration in West Berlin in June 1967, incensed the student New Left there, and created an embattled minority for East Germans to sympathize with. Ohnesorg's funeral cortège was granted a guard of honour through the GDR. Despite the surface similarities, however, the western students' often unreflective loyalty to Marx and Lenin put off East German dissidents, who had little time for utopian socialism.[43] Crucially, as will be seen in the final chapter, the Americans' adventurist foreign policy in Vietnam was used to relativize the faults of the Wall. But this could cut both ways. As one discussant pointed out: 'We don't have to get excited if women and children in Vietnam are being murdered. We are murdering our own children at the border.'[44] Yet the point remained that the West could be morally culpable too. There was not the same blind faith by the 1980s as in the 1950s, once economic recession had become a demonstrable downside of capitalism.

---

[40] Michael Simmons, *The Unloved Country: A Portrait of East Germany Today* (London: Abacus, 1989), 119.

[41] Niethammer *et al.*, *Volkseigene Erfahrung*, 44–5.

[42] Ralph Jessen, 'Mobility and Blockage during the 1970s', in Jarausch (ed.), *Dictatorship*, 341–60; 346. See also Heike Solga, *Auf dem Weg in eine klassenlose Gesellschaft? Klassenlage und Mobilität zwischen Generationen in der DDR* (Berlin: Akademie, 1995); Johannes Huinink *et al.*, *Kollektiv und Eigensinn: Lebensverläufe in der DDR und danach* (Berlin: Akademie, 1995).

[43] Michael Geyer in Carl-Christoph Schweitzer *et al.* (eds), *Lebensläufe—hüben und drüben* (Opladen: Leske & Budrich, 1993), 139–40.

[44] SED-ZK (PO), '3. Information über die Stimmung der Bevölkerung zum Briefwechsel der SED und SPD', 1 Apr. 1966, SAPMO-BArch, DY30/IVA2/5/22.

The generation behind the Wall also witnessed a gradual growing apart from their West German cousins at the family level. Hardest hit were East Berliners, cut off from West Berliners ten days after the Wall rose. Even telephone lines were cut. As Christmas 1962 approached, for instance, complaints mounted at the inhumanity of this familial apartheid.[45] The regime relented in 1963, however, and for the next three Christmases West Berliners were permitted across at the festive season, albeit under close Stasi surveillance.[46] Inevitably, there were calls for reciprocal visits in the other direction,[47] or for individual family members to be allowed out while relatives stood surety for them.[48] Yet the party liked to report cases where East Berlin's poor relations complained of being patronized by their western visitors. Some described them as 'hard currency speculators, on the make, who just boast and spoil the festive peace'.[49] Instead, East German citizens, with a new sense of national pride, would show their in-laws the 'achievements of socialism'. As the fondness of absence wore off, westerners apparently 'just want to play the benevolent uncle and then eat us out of house and home'.[50] These were just the earliest manifestations of what would become palpable East–West family tensions, a ritual of perceived condescension by '*Besserwessis*' towards less fortunate '*Ossis*', and it is understandable that those on the receiving end would be driven to defend aspects of 'their' world. (Northern Britons or Americans from the southern states might have shared some of these emotions towards their own national 'other halves'.) By 1988 84 per cent of West Germans were reported as having no contacts with the GDR whatsoever.[51]

Feeling condescended to by the 'golden West' created a negatively defined identity, which may have been magnified in people's memories by post-unification resentments after 1990. Far more difficult for the SED was the inculcation of a positive identification with the GDR, although this was not for want of trying. In March 1962 the GDR's National Front launched its National Document, which conceded 'that the German nation today is split into two states which oppose each other on German territory', but wished to convince East Germans that they lived in the better half.[52] The rationale behind this was class based, that the working population embodied the GDR nation and the Federal Republic was in the hands of a clique of capitalists and revanchists. This view repeatedly met with

[handwritten in margin: End is better / rationale]

[45] SED-KL Berlin-Mitte, 'Feindtätigkeit im Kreisgebiet', 12 Dec. 1962, LAB, BPA SED Berlin, IV4/04/233.
[46] Gerhard Kunze, *Grenzerfahrungen: Kontakte und Verhandlungen zwischen dem Land Berlin und der DDR 1949–1989* (Berlin: Akademie, 1999), 48–216.
[47] SED-ZK (PO), 'Information', 19 Dec. 1963, SAPMO-BArch, DY30/IVA2/5/22.
[48] NF-Nationalrat, 'Information Nr. 11', 23 Mar. 1965, SAPMO-BArch, DY30/IVA 2/9.02/75.
[49] SED-BL Berlin (Wirtschaft), 'Stimmungen und Meinungen zur Passierscheinfrage aus den Z-Betrieben der Berliner Industrie', 25 Feb. 1964, LAB, BPA SED Berlin, IVA2/6/387.
[50] SED-ZK (PO), 'Information über die Durchführung des Passierscheinabkommens', 3 Nov. 1964, SAPMO-BArch, DY30/IVA2/5/22.
[51] Garton Ash, *In Europe's Name*, 148.   [52] Ulbricht cited in Weber, *DDR*, 98.

incomprehension. The intelligentsia, youth, and former *Grenzgänger* were in the forefront of hostile arguments. In the capital, 'one keeps sensing the search for a third way. There are widespread arguments that we are placing socialism above the interests of the nation.'[53] In the party's so-called 'consciousness analyses' conducted during the 1960s a stock question remained attitudes to national division, as the party sought reassurance about its separate identity. However, in Dresden in 1963, for instance, the intelligentsia continued to fail to grasp the class nature of the national question, which was constantly being clouded by the measures of August 1961. Youths were beset with 'pessimism, moaning (*Nörgelei*) and a lack of understanding for the SED's peace and economic policies'.[54] Four years later in Berlin it was reported that national division was taken for granted or 'the "4 great powers" are made responsible. Likewise the ideology persists of the "little man" who cannot influence "big politics".'[55] The newly founded Institute for Demoscopy reached the further conclusion that over a quarter of respondents thought both German governments should make concessions, with this figure reaching over two-fifths in the *Mittelstand*.[56] Neutralism and a third way were definitely not party policy, but were widely held views at the grass roots. Nor could the party convince its key citizens that the FRG belonged in their *Feindbild* or enemy stereotype: only just over a third of men of military age said they would fire on Bundeswehr troops if called to, with another 23 per cent saying 'no' and an unusually high 40 per cent hiding behind 'don't knows'.[57]

Other alarming trends emerged, moreover, during the West German SPD's tentative moves towards *Ostpolitik* launched in the mid-1960s.[58] The intellectual father of 'change through rapprochement', Egon Bahr, advocated 'loosening up of the frontiers and the Wall' by acknowledging the SED's security fears directly.[59] When the SPD called the SED's bluff over organizing speaker exchanges in 1966, the East German population, including local party members, showed

[53] SED-ZK (PO), 'Information über die Rechenschaftslegung und Neuwahl in den Parteigruppen und Grundorganisationen', 21 Mar. 1962, SAPMO-BArch, DY30/IV2/5/296, ff. 186–203.

[54] 'Einschätzung der politischen Stimmung unter der Arbeiterklasse, den Genossenschaftsbauern, der Intelligenz und aller Schichten der Bevölkerung unseres Bezirkes', 29 July 1963, SächsHStA, BPA SED Dresden, IVA2/9.01/395.

[55] In LAB, BPA SED Berlin, IVA2/9.01/490.

[56] SED-ZK (Inst. f. Meinungsforschung), 'Bericht über eine Umfrage zu einigen Problemen der nationalen Politik in beiden deutschen Staaten', 22 July 1965, SAPMO-BArch, DY30/IVA2/9.02/31. Also printed in Heinz Niemann, *Meinungsforschung in der DDR: Die geheimen Berichte des Instituts für Meinungsforschung an das Politbüro der SED* (Cologne: Bund, 1993), 78–108.

[57] Institut für Meinungsforschung, 'Bericht über eine Umfrage zu einigen Problemen der nationalen Sicherheit', 27 Jan. 1968, SAPMO-BArch, DY30/IVA2/9.02/32.

[58] Heinrich Potthoff, *Im Schatten der Mauer: Deutschlandpolitik 1961 bis 1990* (Berlin: Propyläen, 1999).

[59] 1963 Tutzing speech cited in Garton Ash, *In Europe's Name*, 176–7. See also Peter Bender, *Neue Ostpolitik: Vom Mauerbau zum Moskauer Vertrag* (Munich: dtv, 1986).

considerable sympathy for Bahr's position.[60] In all strata, according to opinion reports, 'so-called small steps' and 'human alleviation' were seen as the correct way ahead, and there was much criticism of SED intransigence.[61] One citizen argued that 'if one builds a garden fence around a house, one has a gate and lets visitors in and out'. Others complained that 'the Wall costs a lot of money' or that the GDR should join the UN, since freedom of movement was a human right.[62] 'There are two souls in my body', admitted one trade unionist. 'One wants to explain our policy to my colleagues openly; the other says I cannot avoid agreeing with the SPD about the Wall, travel, and orders to shoot.'[63] Corrective discussions unintentionally provoked arguments against border security, especially in Berlin, or revealed popular scepticism over Bonn's alleged militarism.[64] Disconcerted, in June 1966 the SED dropped continued dialogue under a pretext.[65]

Yet the logic of détente persisted, especially when it served the Soviet Union's purposes in the late 1960s. Other SPD successes, such as the new Federal Chancellor Willy Brandt's visit to Erfurt in March 1970, where he was cheered by East German crowds, caused further consternation in Berlin. In Ulbricht's twilight months, and then consistently under Honecker's leadership, the GDR finally abandoned national unification rhetoric and pursued instead a policy of 'delimitation' (*Abgrenzung*). In 1973 the new SED leader thus explained that despite cultural and linguistic affinities, the two German states were marked by 'different, indeed contradictory social structures'.[66] The SED started replacing the word 'German' with 'GDR' at every turn. The 1974 constitution dropped its 1968 predecessor's claims that the GDR was a 'socialist state of the German nation'. Instead, ideologues such as Hager argued that there had always been two competing German nations throughout Germany's history, a bourgeois and a proletarian which had roots in the Peasants' Revolt and the 1848 Revolutions. Nevertheless, while delimitation was developed as the politically correct line for the GDR, its economy became increasingly enmeshed in that of the Federal Republic, so that the idea that the GDR was an autonomous state was a fiction by 1989.

[60] SED-ZK (PO), '1. Information über die Stimmung der Bevölkerung zum Briefwechsel SED/SPD', 28 Mar. 1966, SAPMO-BArch, DY30/IVA2/5/22.

[61] SED-ZK (PO), 'Information . . . zum Meinungsaustausch zwischen der SED und SPD', 3 June 1966, SAPMO-BArch, DY30/IVA 2/5/22.

[62] SED-ZK (PO), '2. Information . . . ', 30 Mar. 1966, SAPMO-BArch, DY30/IVA2/5/22.

[63] SED-ZK (PO), '3. Information . . . ', 1 Apr. 1966, SAPMO-BArch, DY30/IVA2/5/22.

[64] SED-BL Berlin (PO), 'Information . . . ', 26 May 1966, LAB, BPA SED Berlin, IVA2/5.01/330.

[65] A. James McAdams, *Germany Divided: From the Wall to Reunification* (Princeton, NJ: Princeton University Press, 1993), 74. For the continued rapprochement in the 1980s see Rolf Reißig, *Dialog durch die Mauer: Die umstrittene Annäherung von SED und SPD vor der Wende* (Frankfurt: Campus, 2002).

[66] Bundesministerium für innerdeutsche Beziehungen (ed.), *DDR-Handbuch*, 3rd edn (Cologne: Verlag Wissenschaft und Politik, 1985), vol. i: 1.

'TO BE A ROCK AND NOT TO ROLL'? LIBERALIZATION BEHIND THE WALL

The greatest lesson which the party learned from building the Wall was that, '[t]hough the population had to make its peace with the GDR, the SED had also to find a modus vivendi with all those who remained in the country'.[67] Whereas before the Wall the state could partially wash its hands of its fractious citizenry, it was now learning that a captive audience had a price. If the open border had acted as a safety valve, now any tensions within the country would have to be resolved or faced down. Flexibility might work better. Relatively soon, the party reined in sectarian tendencies to throw the party's weight around and bully the populace with the 'politics of the fist'. Undoubtedly, the second wave of destalinization, launched by Khrushchev in October 1961, played its part. In November Ulbricht disabused those hoping 'to take educational work lightly because today we have no open border, or to replace it with administrative measures' as 'sorely mistaken'.[68] In December the MfS also counselled against maintaining the high levels of custodial sentences introduced in the wake of 13 August.[69] GDR justice became less heavy-handed from 1962/63, witnessing the mass release in summer 1962 of almost half of all prisoners.[70] Although these moves took some time to gather momentum, the period 1963–65 can be seen as one of relative openness, the equivalent of Khrushchev's 'thaw' in the Soviet Union. Yet just as the Kremlin leader did not survive his final reforms, there was a definite limit to how far East German liberalization behind the Wall was prepared to go.

The economy is a case in point. One of the internal myths of 13 August was that the measures had solved the GDR's economic problems overnight, once westerners could no longer plunder the East. In the short term it is difficult to find the economic miracle the SED claimed. Instead, in the run-up to the first Christmas behind the Wall: 'Repeatedly the argument is cropping up: "It's getting worse and worse since the borders have been closed, and that's supposed to be the victory of socialism." '[71] At the Buna chemical plant food was still the main topic of conversation in November 1961, with gripes that 'since 13.8.1961 there has been a continual worsening'.[72] A printer at the party newspaper complained that: 'All day I run around looking for a cooking pot.

---

[67] Allinson, *Politics*, 130.   [68] Cited in Staritz, *Geschichte der DDR*, 203.

[69] Armin Mitter, *Brennpunkt 13. August 1961: Von der inneren Krise zum Mauerbau* (Berlin: Presse- und Informationsamt des Landes Berlin, 2001), 72.

[70] Werkentin, *Politische Justiz*, 271–80 and 407; Fricke, *Politik und Justiz*, 461.

[71] SED-ZK (PO), 'Information' Nr. 97, 4 Dec. 1961, SAPMO-BArch, DY30/IV2/5/295, f. 348.

[72] SED-KL Buna, 'Bericht zum Produktionsaufgebot', 15 Nov. 1961, LAM, BPA SED Halle, IV405/207, fos. 104–8.

Before 13.8. you said the West Berliners were buying everything up. But now there is even less and it is getting worse day by day.'[73] This was not just a problem of perception. Precisely a year after the Wall went up, the Ministry of Trade and Supply admitted that: 'Over the last months the supply of important basic foodstuffs has continually gone down compared with previous years.' Fish, meat, eggs and dairy products were in such short supply that queuing had begun again and 'goods are sold out within a few hours'. In some areas meat and butter were beneath levels during rationing, and since June the ministry had been cutting meat with water and fishmeal. Cheese was only available on prescription.[74] On the same day the graffito appeared at Leuna: 'Communists, give us more to eat, or have you forgotten the 17th of June?'[75] In fact the authorities were using the new latitude permitted by the Wall to raise prices in order to absorb the wage overhang which had developed with the open border.[76] Not until 1963 did the GDR turn the food supply corner, although there were still queues and empty shelves, and customers were disgruntled at creeping price rises,[77] and only on the second anniversary of the Wall could the SED talk of basic satisfaction among the population.[78] Among those without 'connections' the general standard of living may not have stabilized until 1967.[79]

Consequently, it is against this persistent economic malaise that one should judge the party's adoption in 1963 of the so-called New Economic System of Planning and Leadership (NÖS), as much an act of necessity as of calculated liberalization.[80] Centralized planning was partially delegated to individual enterprises, but also to whole branches of industry, and the system was to be incentivized with limited profits to act as 'economic levers'. This was, moreover, a turn away from Comecon integration which the autarky campaign had advocated; NÖS demanded an opening to western technologies in order to improve productivity, requiring higher exports there, and as the reforms progressed, increasingly enlisted the 'scientific-technological revolution'. Finally, it envisaged a fundamental rise in workers' productivity, the stumbling block of all previous reforms. As André Steiner summarizes: 'At bottom the reformers were attempting

[73] SED-ZK (PO), 'Information über die Rechenschaftslegung und Neuwahl in den Parteigruppen und Grundorganisationen', 21 Mar. 1962, SAPMO-BArch, DY30/IV2/5/296, fo. 190.
[74] SED-ZK (Handel, Versorgung & Außenahndel), 'Information über die Lage in der Versorgung bei den wichtigsten Nahrungsgütern', 14 Aug. 1962, SAPMO-BArch, DY30/IV2/6.10/17, fos. 200–10.
[75] SED-ZK (PO to Sicherheitsfragen), 14 Aug. 1962, SAPMO-BArch, DY30/IV2/12/114, fos. 70–1.
[76] André Steiner, 'Eine wirtschaftliche Bilanz der Mauer', in Hertle *et al.* (eds), *Mauerbau*, 195.
[77] SED-ZK (PO), 'Zu einigen Problemen des Handels und der Versorgung', 14 May 1963, SAPMO-BArch, DY30/IVA2/5/24.
[78] SED-ZK (PO), 'Information', 7 Aug. 1963, SAPMO-BArch, DY30/IVA2/5/22.
[79] Peter Hübner, *Konsens, Konflikt und Kompromiß: Soziale Arbeiterinteressen und Sozialpolitik in der SBZ/DDR 1945–1970* (Berlin: Akademie, 1995), 169.
[80] Monika Kaiser, *Machtwechsel von Ulbricht zu Honecker: Funktionsmechanismen der SED-Diktatur in Konfliktsituationen 1962 bis 1972* (Berlin: Akademie, 1997), 57–64.

to simulate market economy mechanisms without introducing the basics of a market economy.'[81]

Workers were as sceptical as ever, viewing NÖS as a smokescreen for wage and bonus squeezes; the intelligentsia were resistant to schemes for productivity-related pay. The SED predicted problems with apparatchiks, too, who thought 'that it is "nothing new" and merely study those passages of the document which "apply to them" or wait for orders "from above" '.[82] A year later it was reported that 'old habits of mechanically adding a few per cent to the previous year's results, without proceeding from the economically optimal Plan, are not overcome'.[83] There was also considerable resistance to constant demands to improve productivity. The emphasis on technology often only highlighted lack of investment. At one Leipzig ironworks workers were in a state of dejection at the end of 1965: 'The know-it-alls should try coming to Mölkau and maintaining iron at 1500 degrees with furnace technology from 1918.' Elsewhere there were complaints that workers were still bearing the brunt of modernization. 'Our high-grade machines go for export and nothing remains for us. We have to work with antiquated machines. We talk of the technological revolution, but get no new plant and the raw materials allocations etc. are cut.'[84] Such problems were raising fundamental doubts about the planned economy. Again and again, complaints were levelled that not enough raw materials were reaching shop-floors, nullifying any sophisticated planning. At the Oberspree Transformer Works in 1965 'most work regulations are based on the AEG technology of circa 1936'.[85] Research and development was constantly being placed on the back burner. Two years later the works could not even keep up with previous years' production, leading to 'resignation'.[86] Ulbricht reported some progress to Moscow, but 'in comparison with other socialist countries the GDR's workers have a relatively high standard of living. Yet the working class compare—as do other working strata of the GDR—their material situation *not* with the workers in Poland, the Soviet Union, in Bulgaria and other socialist countries, but above all with the material situation of workers in West Germany.'[87]

Hardliners in the Politbüro, including Honecker and Günter Mittag, began to voice their disquiet at the reforms. The new Brezhnev leadership in Moscow

[81] André Steiner, *Von Plan zu Plan: Eine Wirtschaftsgeschichte der DDR* (Munich: DVA, 2004), 131.
[82] SED-ZK (PO), 'Information', 9 Aug. 1963, SAPMO-BArch, DY30/IVA2/5/24.
[83] SED-ZK (PO), 'Information', 18 July 1964, SAPMO-BArch, DY30/IVA2/5/24.
[84] SED-ZK (PO), 'Information über politisch-ideologische Probleme bei der Planvorbereitung 1966 und der Erfüllung des Planes 1965', 15 Dec. 1965, SAPMO-BArch, DY30/IVA2/5/25. Emphasis in original.
[85] SED-BL Berlin (Büro f. Ind. & Bauwesen), 'Zu Problemen des VEB Transformatorenwerk', 2 Mar. 1964, LAB, BPA SED Berlin, IVA2/6/390.
[86] SED-BL Berlin, 'Einschätzung der Lage im VEB TRO . . .', 1 June 1967, LAB, BPA SED Berlin, IVA2/6/390.
[87] Ulbricht to CPSU, 6 Sept. 1965, SAPMO-BArch, NY4182/1206, fos. 107–33.

appears to have lent them discreet support. The pressure became so much for Erich Apel, head of the State Planning Commission, that he committed suicide in December 1965.[88] At the same time NÖS was duly watered down, and other aspects were abandoned in 1967, followed by renewed retrenchments after the suppression of the Prague spring in 1968 (an example to the conservatives of where economic liberalization could lead). The GDR suffered consumer goods shortages in 1970 and inflation, and soon after Ulbricht's removal in May 1971, the SED resolved to reintroduce central planning.[89] Thereafter, Honecker concentrated on guaranteeing the basic standard of living in the so-called 'unity of economic and social policy'. This involved massive subsidies for everyday items, public transport, and housing, but at the expense of infrastructural investment. The GDR was effectively living on tick, increasingly from the West. And far from 'solving' East Germans' consumer needs, the satisfaction of basic needs simply created more sophisticated aspirations which could only be met by imports.

At the same time, commentators have pointed to the cultural liberalization which could occur in the shadow of the Wall. Particularly in the years 1963–65 there was a wave of cinematic and literary experimentation. Films such as *Das Kaninchen bin ich* (I am the rabbit) and *Denk bloß nicht, ich heule* (Just don't think I'm crying) were not afraid to show the growing pains of socialism. The regime also consciously curried favour with the younger generation, permitting greater personal freedom. It had not forgotten that this was the group which had felt hardest hit by the Wall.[90] In the weeks following 13 August the FDJ had lost some 300,000 or 9 per cent of its membership, with higher rates in Berlin and Potsdam.[91] In September 1963, however, the party leadership issued a communiqué recognizing the problems of the younger generation and announcing an end to 'spoon-feeding, finger-pointing and managerialism'.[92] Ironically, this compensatory 'opening inwards' as Dorothee Wierling has called it, would hardly have been possible without the external closure.[93] The new policy was undoubtedly popular, since it offered a social compact of non-interference in private leisure in return for efficient work under NÖS. It is evident, too, that young people had a very clear notion of where the frontier of their personal privacy began and where the state's domain ended. The popular cultural revolution of the 1960s, and Beatlemania in particular, tested the cultural frontiers of power behind the Wall. What follows is a case study of a failed experiment in cultural

[88] Kaiser, *Machtwechsel*, 105–32.   [89] Grieder, *East German Leadership*, 165–70.

[90] Marc-Dietrich Ohse, *Jugend nach dem Mauerbau: Anpassung, Protest und Eigensinn* (Berlin: Links, 2003).

[91] Dorle Zilch, *Millionen unter der blauen Fahne* (Rostock: Verlag Jugend und Geschichte, 1994), 53.

[92] McDougall, *Youth Politics*, 153–63; 157.

[93] Dorothee Wierling, 'Die Jugend als innerer Feind: Konflikte in der Erziehungsdiktatur der sechziger Jahre', in Hartmut Kaelble *et al.* (eds), *Sozialgeschichte der DDR* (Stuttgart: Klett Cotta, 1994), 408.

relaxation demonstrating that this was 'liberalization within limits'.[94] Moreover, when the authorities burned their fingers on popular music, it was used as a pretext to dismantle other reforms in December 1965.

As was hinted at in Chapter 3, the corrupting influence of rock'n'roll in the 1950s had already alarmed the GDR's moral guardians. It was perceived as more dangerous than jazz, which was containable to an arty intellectual milieu.[95] Nevertheless, there had been echoes of Nazi campaigns against jazz as degenerate music, including the same discourse on 'German' melody versus 'primitive' rhythm.[96] However, by the 1960s the media limited themselves to mocking beatniks and existentialists in their goatee beards and polo-neck sweaters. It was also clear that several members of the SED Central Committee's cultural section were secret jazz fans themselves. Rock'n'roll was more threatening because it appealed to a mass audience, above all working-class youth, encouraging them to dance in public, as well as breaking down some of the gender norms so prized in the short-back-and-sides culture of the GDR. As Wierling has pointed out, it was appealing to the SED's own supposed clientele.[97] The fact that boys were sporting quiffs and paying excessive attention to their appearance was seen as effeminate; the supposedly lewd dancing of girls and their overt sexuality was also making some censors hot under the collar.[98] Official descriptions of rock'n'roll stressed its dehumanizing and narcoticizing aspects. Bassists were depicted as 'glassy-eyed', with twitching bodies and insistent beats. In the FDJ's *Junge Welt* Elvis sang 'like a crow with whooping cough . . . with a wild hip-swinging à la Marilyn Monroe'.[99] After Bill Haley's tour of West Germany in October 1958, the GDR went over to labelling him a 'rock'n'roll gangster'. These generational battles obviously took place in western societies too, but without the GDR's overt politicization. Caricatures of teenagers involved in the 17 June 1953 uprising depicted them in jeans and Texas shirts, lobbing bricks at the forces of law and order. Rock'n'roll was allegedly turning its audience into a fifth column for NATO, the musical accompaniment to the increasing social anomie of western capitalism.

What was especially alarming was the fact that these influences continued to invade the closed GDR. In 1961 the SED's culture section issued a document, 'NATO Politics and Dance Music', according to which 'western hits of this ilk are

[94] Mark Fenemore, 'The limits of repression and reform: youth policy in the early 1960s', in Major and Osmond (eds), *Workers' and Peasants' State*, 171–89; 177.

[95] Toby Thacker, 'The fifth column: Dance music in the early German Democratic Republic', in Major and Osmond (eds), *Workers' and Peasants' State*, 227–43.

[96] 'Zu einigen Fragen der Tanzmusik im Rundfunk', n.d. [1957], SAPMO-BArch, DY30/IV2/9.06/293, fos. 10–26.

[97] Wierling, 'Jugend als innerer Feind', pp. 409–10.

[98] Uta G. Poiger, *Jazz, Rock and Rebels: Cold War Politics and American Culture in a Divided Germany* (Berkeley, CA: University of California Press, 2000), 175–82.

[99] Cited in Michael Rauhut, *Beat in der Grauzone: DDR-Rock 1964 bis 1972—Politik und Alltag* (Berlin: BasisDruck, 1993), 31.

penetrating over the airwaves. The use of reactionary western films in the GDR is impossible, incoming trash and smut literature is confiscated, as happens with illegally imported records with damaging hit music.' Yet, all that the authorities could place in the way of radio listening was 'a steady campaign of persuasion'.[100] The post-Wall GDR was thus never a truly hermetically sealed society. Moreover, the surrounding eastern bloc was far more tolerant of beat, forcing the party to police all fronts.[101] Since radio, like television, could not be jammed, the GDR had to learn to live with popular music. Tape-recorders could record warbly versions of western hits. Yet, it was not simply an ideological problem, but one of economics. Radio stations were required to pay royalties in hard currency for western numbers. In the late 1950s, for instance, 87 per cent of state coffee bars' royalties, and 77 per cent from private cafés, went west.[102] Moreover, the GDR record industry could not produce vinyl in sufficient quantity or quality to satisfy eastern demand.[103] Enviously, agitprop functionaries realized that pop was creating the mass audience to which they aspired. Subconscious capitalist messages were filtering through, requiring that 'we must "package" the content of our new texts at least as mass-consciously'.[104] If they could capture that audience by channelling the dance craze into socialist directions, they could perhaps win the propaganda battle. The proffered solution was a healthy, GDR-style *Tanzmusik*, offering better musicianship and a humanist message. Socialist versions of the Twist were developed, such as the 'Lipsi'. Hardliners, however, were always suspicious of populism at the expense of ideological purity and organizational control of the youth movement, of agendas to 'soften up' certain areas, as the Radio Committee put it.[105] Between these two poles the debate continued. Purists, echoing the Frankfurt School's criticisms of the manipulative tendencies of the culture industry, insisted that Tin Pan Alley was simply a branch of monopoly capitalism. Reformers countered that this was the music of an oppressed American racial minority, or downplayed it as harmless fun.

In 1963–64, however, reformers in the Politbüro's Youth Commission under Kurt Turba won ground, with backing from Ulbricht. One of the key catalysts for change was the British music scene of the early 1960s. The SED's culture section detected a happy medium between the 'crass musical decadence' of American

---

[100] SED-ZK (Kultur), 'NATO-Politik und Tanzmusik', n.d. [1961], SAPMO-BArch, DY30/IVA2/9.06/159.

[101] Timothy Ryback, *Rock around the Bloc: A History of Rock Music in Eastern Europe and the Soviet Union* (New York: Oxford University Press, 1990), 50–65.

[102] Weber, *Geschichte der DDR*, 314.

[103] 'Stand und Entwicklung der Schallplattenproduktion der DDR', n.d., SAPMO-BArch, DY30/IV2/9.06/253, fos. 76–90.

[104] Radio DDR, 'Zur Situation der Tanzmusik in der DDR', 8 Aug. 1960, SAPMO-BArch, DY30/IV2/9.06/293, fos. 33–38.

[105] 'Bericht über die Beratung von Musikfragen im Komitee des Rundfunks am 22.1.1957', n.d., SAPMO-BArch, DY30/IV/2/9.06/293, fos. 27–31. See also McDougall, *Youth Politics*, 166, who places much of the blame with Honecker and the FDJ national leadership.

rock'n'roll and the 'lacrimose sentimental crooning' of West Germany.[106] There were many early Shadows imitators, since instrumentals had no problem lyrics, but it was the breakthrough of the Beatles which caused a major rethink. Lennon and McCartney were providing the missing melodies. In contrast, the Rolling Stones were denigrated as morally degenerate and became synonymous with 'bad' beat music.[107] In parallel, the GDR authorities doggedly promoted a home-grown dance music scene, with properly trained vocalists and musicians who could read sheet music, yet the verdict of the public was almost universally negative, ranging 'from pitiful contempt to coarse insults'. Youths simply brought their tape-recorders into youth clubs and played medleys of radio hits. According to one expert, the eastern public was apparently absorbing western dance music 'like a dry sponge water': 'Every attempt to prevent it was met by increased pressure from the public who closed ranks, wanting their toy all the more . . . , finding it absurd when the charade was repeated every two years.'[108]

By 1964 the Beatles were being popularized in the GDR's own media, hitting magazine covers, with a compilation album appearing on the Amiga label the following year. In 1964 at an International Hits Festival, touring Czech Beatlesesque bands were received with wild approval, while the GDR's rather tame Christel Schulze was whistled down.[109] Home-grown talent was consistently mocked unless it copied western styles. In Berlin there were perhaps 100 beat bands by October 1965, made up mainly of young workers, students, and even some army recruits. The British influence was unmistakeable. Groups had to have the authentic ring of the Beatles or the Rolling Stones, hence the 'Butlers', 'Bottles', 'Brittels', 'Five Stones', 'Musik Stones', or just 'Beatmen' and 'Guitarmen'. Others paid lipservice to socialism, calling themselves the 'Sputniks' or 'Luniks' after the Soviet space programme. Most notorious for the authorities was the 'Diana-Show-Band', which drew large audiences, some of which ended in brawls. Although FDJ members' attitudes to beat were hardly any different from non-affiliated youths,[110] the party, through its youth movement, still attempted to ride the popular wave. At the FDJ's Germany Rally Games of 1964 a new radio station, DT-64, was founded, to appeal to a younger audience.[111] Soon, however, DT-64 disc jockeys were transgressing the state's own 60:40 rule, playing more than their quota of western titles. The Central Committee's cultural section secretly monitored transmissions, noting

[106] SED-ZK (Kultur), 'Zur Vorlage über die heitere Muse, insbesondere Tanzmusik', 14 May 1965, SAPMO-BArch, DY30/IVA2/9.06/159.

[107] SED-ZK (Kultur), 'Gutachten zur Beat-Musik' (for Honecker), 13 Dec. 1965, SAPMO-BArch, DY30/IVA2/9.06/159.

[108] Natschinski to Bentzien, 23 Mar. 1964, SAPMO-BArch, DY30/IVA2/9.06/159.

[109] Tauche, 'Information über den Einfluß und die Entwicklung der Beatel-Gruppen', 22 July 1964, StAL, BPA SED Leipzig, IVA2/9.02/365.

[110] SED-BL Berlin (Jugendkomm.), 'Einige Angaben über die Beatgruppen in der Hauptstadt', 5 Oct. 1965, LAB, BPA SED Berlin, IV/A-2/16/659.

[111] McDougall, *Youth Politics*, 166–7.

with displeasure the number of English-language 'boys', 'girls', 'darlings', and 'parties' passing the announcers' lips.[112]

The internal debate reached a minor crescendo in spring 1965 when *Neues Deutschland* published an article praising dance music as above politics, to the protests of the Central House of Culture.[113] Yet, when the interested parties met in Leipzig, including the GDR's star band, The Butlers, only the Central House and the local council were prepared to defend the official line that beat musicians were workshy and hooligan elements. Tellingly, the local FDJ interjected that 'youth wants to hear this music. That's why we have to promote the guitar groups in order to win over young people for FDJ work.'[114] Subsequently, in the summer a musicians' talent competition was held across the GDR, to culminate in a final in Berlin, with the FDJ hoping 'to use the guitar competition to strike a note for our socialist *joie de vivre*'.[115] Unfortunately for the organizers, events degenerated into scenes of chaos and the competition was prematurely broken off in October. The degree to which the party had lost control of the 'movement' was betrayed in internal discussions. Even Kurt Turba, Ulbricht's reforming young turk, was at a loss, citing Honecker, that: 'Either we let the beat wave roll or put ourselves at its crest and place our stamp on the movement.'[116]

Ominous developments had occurred in September, when the real Rolling Stones played the Waldbühne in West Berlin. After an insultingly short set the audience trashed the arena, leading to a press outcry in the West. With schadenfreude *Neues Deutschland* carried a facsimile of *Bild-Zeitung*'s front page. In October 1965 the authorities then effectively banned most of the beat groups—including fifty-four out of fifty-eight groups in the Leipzig area, which had become the GDR's Merseyside—claiming that they were infringing the 60:40 rule, indulging in 'excesses' on stage, using English band names, sciving work, and dropping out.[117] The old press stereotypes re-emerged, deriding beat bands as animalistic and asocial: 'Their long, straggly hair, which they wear as an external mark of their mentality, is blinkering them so much that they cannot see how abnormal, unhealthy and inhumane their behaviour has become. . . . Heads are for thinking, not platforms for unaesthetic haircuts. Here culture rules, not unculture.'[118] Copies of the article were demonstratively hung up in schools. Agitprop was even carried onto the dance floors, with youths

[112] Czerny, 'Einschätzung DT 64', 26 Aug. 1965, SAPMO-BArch, DY30/IVA2/9.06/159.

[113] SED-ZK (Kultur), 'Abschließende Bemerkung zur Auseinandersetzung über den Artikel 'Butlers Boogie' im "Neuen Deutschland" vom 4.4.1965', 6 Dec. 1965, SAPMO-BArch, DY30/IVA2/9.06/159.

[114] 'Kurzbericht über die Besprechung bei der Bezirksleitung der FDJ in Leipzig am 13. Mai 1965, 14.00 Uhr', 13 Nov. 1965, SAPMO-BArch, DY30/IVA2/9.06/159.

[115] FDJ-ZR, 'Standpunkt des Zentralrates der FDJ zur Arbeit mit den Gitarrengruppen', n.d. [20 Apr. 1965], SAPMO-BArch, DY30/IVA2/9.06/159.

[116] SED-BL Berlin (Jugendkomm.), 'Information über eine Aussprache beim Genossen Kurt Turba am 5.10.1965', 6 Oct. 1965, LAB, BPA SED Berlin, IVA2/16/659.

[117] Untitled, StAL, BDVP 24.1/236, fo. 135.   [118] *LVZ*, 20 Oct. 1965, 6.

button-holed between numbers.[119] For their part, teenagers objected to being labelled dirty or workshy, pointing out the SED and FDJ's hypocrisy in banning what they had until recently sponsored.[120] Then, on 31 October 1965 2,500 young people, including 500–800 beat fans, confronted by a large number of *FDJ'ler* and security personnel, went onto the streets of Leipzig to protest at the ban. Without banners or slogans, they were dispersed by the police and 357 were loaded onto waiting lorries, forcibly shorn of their moptops, and transported to nearby open-cast mines for one to three weeks' forced labour, in what was an orchestrated 'overreaction' by the state.[121] Several 'ringleaders' were even put on trial. Nevertheless, in the following days and nights, slogans appeared on walls and pavements with messages such as 'Only the Beatles for us'.[122]

In fact, the whole liberalization experiment had shown that those listening to western music were by no means a dangerous fifth column, but simply bored youngsters. More often than not they went out of their way to disavow the 'scruffs' (*Gammler*) attacked by the authorities. Youths instead pleaded for 'private freedoms'. In confrontations, band members were at pains to work out a modus vivendi, but were prepared to argue their corner. One of The Guitarmen of Leipzig thus objected to recent newspaper articles claiming that he had paraded in tiger skins half-naked, explaining that the offending article was made of material from the state retail store and that the band had only been barefoot.[123] Berlin youths rejected demands to cut their hair.[124] Nor could the state have it all its own way with the bands who survived the ban. When the Berlin Sputniks played in Karl-Marx-Stadt in November 1965, they immediately departed from the agreed script, to the great annoyance of the local FDJ. When confronted in the interval, the lead singer complained that: 'Before the Germany Rally the Central Council [of the FDJ] and DT-64 practically dragged us out of the cellar. They implored us on bended knee, we were popularized and praised with all means, just so that we could say that in the GDR we have our beat groups, but now it's all different.'[125]

The final nail in the beat coffin came in December 1965 with the eleventh Plenum of the SED, sometimes dubbed the '*Kahlschlag*' or 'firebreak' conference. As well as 'yeah, yeah, yeah music', Honecker inveighed against experimental cinema and literature. In the run-up culture functionaries were told that artistic

[119] Beier to Lauter, 26 Oct. 1965, StAL, BPA SED Leipzig, IVA2/9.02/365.

[120] SED-BL Leipzig (PO), 'Information', 27 Oct. 1965, StAL, BPA SED Leipzig, IVA2/16/464, fos. 102–07.

[121] McDougall, *Youth Politics*, 191.

[122] SED-BL Leipzig (PO), 'Information', 20 Nov. 1965, StAL, BPA SED Leipzig, IVA2/16/464, fos. 148–58.

[123] RdB Leipzig (Schulen), 'Information', 18 Nov. 1965, StAL, BPA SED Leipzig, IVA2/16/464, fos. 121–22.

[124] SED-BL Berlin (PO), 'Information', 11 Nov. 1965, LAB, BPA SED Berlin, IVA2/5.01/336.

[125] 'Information der FDJ-Bezirksleitung Karl-Marx-Stadt', 30 Nov. 1965, SAPMO-BArch, DY30/IVA2/9.06/159.

freedom was 'working objectively towards the enemy, to target the intelligentsia and youth through a policy of liberalization and the spread of immorality and so soften up the GDR from within'.[126] Ideological chief Kurt Hager diagnosed a cultural divide between those who had experienced fascism and the post-fascist generation. The latter appeared more susceptible to the 'sex propaganda' from the West. The SED, on the other hand, fought to defend decency and morals.[127] At the 11th Plenum, meeting from 15 to 18 December 1965, reforms were reversed. Ulbricht announced the 'second stage' of NÖS, which signalled a partial return to centralization and a command economy. Erich Honecker delivered a speech on the ideological and cultural tasks ahead, criticizing 'damaging tendencies' in film, television, theatre, and literature, which through the 'representation of alleged mistakes spread scepticism and immorality'. The poet and songwriter Wolf Biermann, writer Stefan Heym, and dissident chemist Robert Havemann were singled out. Honecker, reiterating the SED's obsession with purity, demanded a 'clean canvas' for a 'clean state'.[128]

The liberalization experiment had been very short-lived. Indeed, has this intra-mural reform been exaggerated at the expense of the basic power structures within the post-1961 GDR?[129] There was certainly some jockeying for position behind the scenes in the SED leadership, and Ulbricht's newly discovered modernization was partially checked by Honecker and associates before he was finally ousted in 1971. Over time, however, the authorities realized that rock music could not simply be banned by decree. Young East Germans continued to listen to Radio Luxembourg, or to watch 'Beat-Club' on West German television. School comrades would write to West Berlin radio stations with pseudonyms and requests, and although occasionally docked marks when discovered, continued undaunted.[130] One indicator of this losing battle was official attitudes to jeans. In the late 1950s the Leipzig Volkspolizei could still seriously consider arresting wearers of 'rivet-pants', as they were disparagingly referred to.[131] By 1968 this taboo was quietly dropped.[132] As the western counter-culture turned against the war in Vietnam, it also began to share common ground with East German anti-imperialism and thus became more acceptable. By the later 1960s, therefore,

---

[126] 'Konzeption für die Beratung mit den Sekretären und Abteilungsleitern für Kultur der Bezirksleitungen am 6.12.1965', SAPMO-BArch, DY30/IVA2/5/57.

[127] 'Protokoll über ein Seminar der Ideologischen Kommission . . . auf dem Gebiet der Kultur, am 7. Dezember 1965', n.d., SAPMO-BArch, DY30/IVA2/9.01/21.

[128] Günter Agde (ed.), *Kahlschlag: Das 11. Plenum des ZK der SED 1965: Studien und Dokumente* (2nd edn Berlin: Aufbau, 2000), 238–51.

[129] Thomas Lindenberger, 'Diktatur der Grenze(n): Die eingemauerte Gesellschaft und ihre Feinde', in Hertle *et al.*, *Mauerbau*, 203–13.

[130] Interview with 'Henja', a sixth-former at Bischofswerda in the late 1960s, 30 Mar. 2001.

[131] BDVP Leipzig, 'Niederschrift über die Beratung über Fragen der Jugendkriminalität und des Rowdytums in der Stadt Leipzig am 29. Oktober 1958', 30 Oct. 1958, StAL, BDVP 24/113, fos. 86–9.

[132] Rebecca Menzel, *Jeans in der DDR: Vom tieferen Sinn einer Freizeithose* (Berlin: Links, 2004), 90–2.

many music restrictions were lifted. In 1971 the new SED leadership—ironically Honecker had been 1965's leading anti-reformer!—preferred to judge youths by their 'socialist behaviour and achievements for our state', rather than by their dress sense. There was also a growing satisfaction that GDR songwriters were beginning to find their own style, a form of ballad-rock.[133] 'Under concrete circumstances, and since the ether cannot be hermetically sealed off, the task is to consider the real situation and the needs of young people'; Western music was to be used selectively, but 'flexibly,' sifting out the brutal in favour of the humane.[134] By the 1970s bands such as the Puhdys were allowed to play in DEFA's greatest ever screen success, *The Legend of Paul and Paula*, in which alternative lifestyles were on display (still to the horror of the older generation of letter-writers). Indeed 'Ost-Rock' became one of the GDR's greatest exports, with the Puhdys touring West Germany and the USA in the 1980s. By then the wearing of denim and long hair was almost de rigueur among the young adult population, years after it had gone out of fashion in the West. The party leadership was at pains to supply jeans en masse, even importing a stonewash facility, aware that GDR fashions were out of step with international trends.[135]

Yet, popular music never quite lost its dangerous edge.[136] In 1975 the band Renft, the successor to The Butlers, was banned for the 'Rock Ballad of Little Otto', which alluded to a failed *Republikflucht*. Two years later, two of its members were deported from Stasi incarceration to the FRG.[137] Pop also became the vehicle for privately sponsored détente by such figures as the West German rock singer Udo Lindenberg, who, besides a leather biker's jacket personally donated to 'Honey' Honecker, offered to add his voice against re-armament, but at the price of touring the GDR.[138] It was the lure of western hard currency which persuaded the SED to relent and allow a limited number of western 'progressive' artists to play in the GDR, since the regime could market the broadcast rights to the western networks. Each of these events was laden with a frisson of unpredictability. Lindenberg was only allowed to play to a handpicked audience and the full-scale tour never materialized; the Cologne band BAP were refused entry visas at the last minute; and when Bruce Springsteen played the Berlin Cyclodrome in 1988, it was a slightly surreal experience for me to be surrounded by tens of thousands of East Germans singing along to 'Born in the USA', despite its ostensibly self-critical lyric. Nor did Lindenberg and

---

[133] SED-ZK (Kultur), 'Zu einigen politisch-ideologischen Problemen unserer gegenwärtigen Situation auf dem Gebiete der Tanzmusik', 4 May 1971, SAPMO-BArch, DY30/IVA2/9.06/159.

[134] SED-ZK (Kultur) to Hager, 14 Dec. 1971, SAPMO-BArch, DY30/IVA2/9.06/159.

[135] 'Information über die gemeinsame Beratung zur Entwicklung, Produktion und dem Verkauf von Erzeugnissen der Jugendmode am 19. März 1985', SAPMO-BArch, DY30/IV2/2.039/267, fos. 1–11.

[136] Antonia Grunenberg, *Aufbruch der inneren Mauer: Politik und Kultur in der DDR 1971–1990* (Bremen: Temmen, 1990).

[137] Klaus Renft, *Zwischen Liebe und Zorn: Die Autobiografie* (Berlin: Schwarzkopf, 2001).

[138] Rauhut, *Schalmei und Lederjacke*, 67–127.

his Panikorchester allow Honecker to forget the Wall. In the 1983 video to his 'Express Train to Pankow', the singer bats a tennis ball into the 'death strip', turning to the camera in mock alarm. However well meaning, Lindenberg effectively destroyed Honecker's street credibility.

Other western artists had criticized the border. David Bowie's highly emotional 'Heroes', recorded in West Berlin, stated that 'the shame was on the other side'. When Bowie and Genesis played an open-air concert in West Berlin near the Wall in 1987, several thousand East Berliners congregated on the other side. As security forces attempted to disperse them, there were shouts of 'The Wall must go' and 'We want freedom!'[139] Punk also challenged the authorities, as certain groups attempted to opt out, seeking their own private spaces within a heavily circumscribed system.[140] Yet, these were groups immune to the limited consumerism of Honecker's social policy, practising instead a rejectionist asceticism. More important was when mainstream groups such as City dared to challenge the system from within. Their 1987 number 'Wall to Wall' ('Wand an Wand') was overtly about two potential lovers, neighbours separated by a partition wall, but included the lines: 'Despite only twenty centimetres, we will never touch. If we want to meet, we have to leave the house. When you laugh, it drifts across as if from another land. Wall to wall.'[141] The metaphor was not lost on the censor, which banned public transmission. Whether these groups, along with the bearded environmentalists and the sandal-wearing Protestant nonconformists, constituted an emerging civil society will be returned to later. Yet one group which *has* been viewed as a substitute public sphere was artists and writers. Did they provide the missing voice in the GDR? Did they oppose the Wall or retreat into inner emigration?

WRITING ON THE WALL: GDR INTELLECTUALS FROM INNER TO OUTER EMIGRATION

The wall is there. It is like nature. If you lived beside the sea, you'd accept the sea the way we accept the wall. . . . It is as if the wall has been there for a thousand years.

Thomas Brasch, exiled East German writer, 1981[142]

---

[139] Miriam Jokiniemi, 'From "Mauer-Blues" to "Der Tag, an dem die Mauer fiel"': The Berlin Wall in Contemporary Songs and Ballads', in Ernst Schürer *et al.* (eds), *The Berlin Wall: Representations and Perspectives* (New York: Peter Lang, 1996), 228–49; 237.

[140] Roland Galenza and Heinz Havemeister (eds), *Wir wollen immer artig sein . . . : Punk, New Wave, HipHop, Independent-Szene in der DDR 1980–1990* (Berlin: Schwarzkopf, 1999).

[141] City, 'Wand and Wand', *Casablanca* (Amiga, 1987).

[142] Cited in Anthony Bailey, *Along the Edge of the Forest: An Iron Curtain Journey* (London: Faber, 1983), 139.

GDR writers have had a mixed press since 1989. Revelations about the Stasi involvement of leading lights such as Christa Wolf and Sascha Anderson have suggested complicity with the system, the one public the other clandestine. Relatively speaking, members of the Writers' Association did indeed enjoy a privileged existence, which militated against dissidence.[143] The right to travel could be dangled as a carrot before potential malcontents, such as the fictional pseudo-intellectual W. in Hilbig's *'I'*, whose Stasi case officers manipulate his desire to see the West: 'To stay or not to stay, that was the question.'[144] As will become evident below, a significant number of the Prenzlauer Berg set, including Anderson, were spirited out of the country, sometimes by mutual consent. Literature could, on the other hand, provide a coded medium for veiled criticism. By its very nature, the Wall conjured up taboo, 'the fairy tale mechanism and psychology of the forbidden door or the forbidden box that should not be opened'.[145] The border offered an almost irresistible set of metaphors which the Ministry of Culture had to censor or let pass. Rather absurdly even Sartre's *Le mur* had to be translated as *Die Wand* in order to avoid the more correct *Die Mauer*.[146]

Initially, however, the Wall was a political issue which could not be ducked, not least because East German authors were publicly challenged to speak out. The first intellectual assault came not from the East, but the West. On 14 August 1961 Günter Grass, the FRG's self-appointed critical conscience, wrote to Anna Seghers, chair of the GDR Writers' Association, drawing parallels between the incarceration under way and the concentration camp victims in her wartime antifascist novel, *The Seventh Cross*. If they were prepared to attack authoritarianism and former Nazis in the West, why did East German colleagues not speak out? Unanswered, two days later Grass and Wolfdietrich Schnurre sent an open letter to all GDR writers, declaring that 'barbed wire, machine-pistols and tanks are not the means to make conditions in the GDR bearable for your state's citizens. Only a state no longer sure of its citizens' support tries to save itself in this way.' They added: 'there is no "inner emigration", even between 1933 and 1945 there was none. Whoever remains silent is guilty.'[147] Stephan Hermlin responded on behalf of the Writers' Association, repeating the usual externalization logic that it was an action directed against the same neo-Nazi tendencies Grass decried, drawing emotive parallels with Hitler's *Machtergreifung*, which could have been stopped 'if, back then, red tanks had stood at the Brandenburg

---

[143] Jeannette Madarász, *Conflict and Compromise in East Germany, 1971–1989: A Precarious Stability* (Houndmills: Palgrave, 2003), 177–8.

[144] Wolfgang Hilbig, *'Ich'* (Frankfurt: Fischer, 1993), 154.

[145] Koepke, 'The Invisible Wall', in Schürer *et al.* (eds), *Berlin Wall*, 74.

[146] *Wand* connotes an internal wall; *Mauer* is the more correct translation. My thanks to Siegfried Lokatis for this information.

[147] In Hans Werner Richter, (ed.), *Die Mauer oder der 13. August* (Reinbek bei Hamburg: Rowohlt Taschenbuch, 1961), 62–6.

Gate'.[148] Behind the scenes, the Central Committee's cultural section noted the 'old confusions'.[149] In public, however, the state's artistic elite maintained ranks.[150] At the DEFA film studios, too, there was uncomfortable conformity, although the director Slatan Dudow and the character actor Erwin Geschonnek were reprimanded for their absenteeism on 13 August.[151]

For very different reasons, a number of other intellectuals, by no means all regime supporters, condoned the measures, including chemist Robert Havemann, who later became the focus of intellectual opposition in the GDR.[152] For these 'true' socialists, now was a chance to begin afresh and for the state to end its hypocritical policy of selective privileges. The playwright Heiner Müller came out in favour, too, accounting the Wall 'right and necessary' for a 'critical and realistic' fresh start.[153] Such 'leftist illusions' were nevertheless soon dispelled by the regime's subsequent behaviour. The poet Heinz Kahlau also remembered: 'My friends and I believed that now that we had closed the shop . . . we could talk turkey. There was a period, perhaps two or three years, of hope among many that we would get real socialism.'[154] Rolf Henrich, another later dissident, shared this false dawn, only to have it dispelled once and for all by the crushing of the Prague Spring in 1968, aided and abetted by the GDR.[155] Unabashed criticism came only from the *enfant terrible* of the GDR, the bawdy singer–songwriter Wolf Biermann, who variously anthropomorphized Berlin as a woman ('I cannot leave you any longer, In the West stands the Wall, In the East wait my friends'[156]), or as the stinking arsehole of a divided Germany, over which he imagined himself serenely floating. Meanwhile the ghosts of his comrades-in-arms, such as the French poet Villon, performed antics atop the Wall, playing tunes on the barbed wire while the guards provided a macabre accompaniment of machine-gun fire.[157] Yet, Biermann still believed he was criticizing the SED rather than the GDR, singing 'I live in the better half and have twice the pain', doubly frustrated at the squandering of true socialism. When the son of his friend Havemann, Florian, escaped west, Biermann was ambivalent about such egoism: 'The GDR in the long run, Needs neither Wall nor prison. We shall see to that! Then the people will flee to us in droves . . . In spite of everything, I shall sing here and stay.'[158]

[148] In ibid., 66–8.

[149] Wagner to Ulbricht, 5 Oct. 1961, in Matthias Braun, *Drama um eine Komödie: Das Ensemble von SED und Staatssicherheit, FDJ und Ministerium für Kultur gegen Heiner Müllers 'Die Umsiedlerin oder Das Leben auf dem Lande' im Oktober 1961* (Berlin: Links, 1995), 132.

[150] Stiftung Archiv der Akademie der Künste (ed.), *Zwischen Diskussion und Disziplin: Dokumente zur Geschichte der Akademie der Künste (Ost)* (Berlin: Henschel, 1997), 192–9.

[151] Feinstein, *Triumph of the Ordinary*, 123.   [152] Maier, *Dissolution*, 30.

[153] Matthias Braun, *Drama um eine Komödie* (Berlin: Links, 1995), 18.   [154] Ibid., 18 n. 42.

[155] On Sabine Christiansen talk show, ARD, 12 Aug. 2001.

[156] 'Berlin, Du deutsche, deutsche Frau', on *VEBiermann* (Zweitausendeins, 1998).

[157] 'Ballade auf den Dichter François Villon' and 'Deutschland—ein Wintermärchen', on *Chausseestraße 131* (Wagenbach, 1969).

[158] 'Es senkt das deutsche Dunkel' and 'Enfant perdu', on *Warte nicht auf beßre Zeiten* (CBS, 1973).

As tempers died down several retrospective East German novels did appear, revealing more complexity than the histrionics of August 1961. A new realism was preached behind the Wall, following the 'Bitterfeld path' of 1959 towards grittier, socialist realist *Bildungsromane* in which flawed heroes choose socialism over capitalism. The first such book 'artistically to marshal the "raw material" of reality', as an approving censor put it,[159] was Brigitte Reimann's 1961 *Arrival in the Everyday (Ankunft im Alltag)*, soon followed by her 1963 *The Siblings*, which describes a sister's attempts to prevent her brother from committing *Republikflucht* in the spring of 1961.[160] Typical was the depiction of national division as private drama. Elisabeth, a painter from a bourgeois family, who has already witnessed one former lover fleeing west, herself considers flight after sexual discrimination at her factory, but decides to stand her ground. It is her arch-rival who retreats, in a curious reversal of the border image, to a house in the country 'with a high, silver-bronze fence and a ferocious alsatian which slopes along the bars and guards the private garden of Eden'.[161] Her brother Uli, who is contemplating defection, is immature, uncommitted, and overfond of Anglicisms—a beatnik and 'pseudo-rebel'.[162] Elisabeth's failure to get through to him, again using loaded imagery, is 'like standing before an insuperable wall, before a gate shot with seven bolts'.[163] Elisabeth becomes a socialist of the heart, and the parental home a symbol of the wider *Heimat*, reassuring and safe. Indeed, for Reimann, referring to the 'old ballad in which a father cuts the table-cloth between himself and his son', national division runs deepest in the private sphere: 'The unholy border cut the white, damask sheen of the table-cloth—the invisible swing-barrier which went right through the middle of our family.'[164] Generation gaps, fostered by suspicion of those who had witnessed (and supported) Nazism, help to reinforce the political symbolism of the border. At the story's climax, after a verbal montage of Nazi racial imagery and capitalist advertising slogans, the sister berates her brother: 'You haven't even understood that your stepping over the border is a step back into the past, that you are not swapping Germany for Germany.'[165] In a typical GDR syllogism, the West equals the past, and the past is bad, so the West is bad. Under this barrage, Uli capitulates, unpacks his belongings and stays.

Most famous of these works was Christa Wolf's *Divided Heavens*, also of 1963, which deals with a couple on the eve of the Wall, one of whom, Manfred, commits *Republikflucht*, while his fiancée Rita briefly follows him, only to return.[166] Significantly, the Wall itself hardly features; instead, as the story's title hints, the divisions are between value systems. The cynical Manfred comes from a depoliticized bourgeois background; Rita, the village innocent, matures to accept

---

159 Eva Strittmatter, reader's report, 19 Apr. 1961, BAB, DR-1/5061a, fo. 372.
160 Brigitte Reimann, *Die Geschwister* (Berlin: Aufbau-Verlag, 1963).   161 Ibid., 211.
162 Ibid., 245.   163 Ibid., 120.   164 Ibid., 78.   165 Ibid., 250.
166 Christa Wolf, *Der geteilte Himmel* (Halle: Mitteldeutscher Verlag, 1963).

socialist responsibility.[167] The factory where she is gaining work-experience, and whose director commits *Republikflucht* in the spring of 1960, becomes a metaphor for GDR society, divided into those prepared to roll up their sleeves and those exhibiting '*schadenfreude* that the ship on which they were sailing was sinking on the open sea'.[168] Although Wolf privileges private concerns, the high politics of the Berlin crisis always hover menacingly, like the anonymous forces of nature or nuclear conflagration, as a brewing storm or 'a malevolently glowing sunball' sending its 'fiery breath over the land'.[169] Yet, Wolf did not allow her heroine to sink into despondency, nor the story completely into the socialist realist rut, although one lector thought it too 'didactic'.[170] Gagarin's manned orbit provides a mythical counter to these dark forces, as his capsule races like a 'scalpel across every meridian, slitting open the earth's crust down to its boiling, red-hot core'.[171] (In the film version, too, history seems to stand still at this point, as the actors become frozen on celluloid, while the Cold War rages above.[172]) Although, throughout, the sky appears to look on impassively at the tragedy unfolding below, as Rita reminds Manfred on their parting, 'the heavens are the very first to divide'.[173] Since the couple has already grown apart before 13 August, the Wall merely seals an existing state, providing relief rather than anguish. Unlike Reimann, where familial belonging overcomes potential division, personal ties are not enough for Wolf. The story pleased the cultural functionaries, too, because:

Even if this short novel's focus is more on the representation of the two lovers' inner life than on rendering their environment, it is still clear that love is not independent of the big questions of our age.... On the contrary, the very relationship between Rita and Manfred reflects ... the contradictions between the Old and New ... Christa Wolf shows this frontier through the heart of Germany very clearly. She draws the ideological border through the very love between Rita and Manfred.[174]

The novel was complex in its narrative structure and by no means glossed over the human costs of this decision—at one point Rita attempts suicide—but in the prologue and epilogue Wolf implicitly defended the decision of August 1961 for permitting a reversion to normality: 'So we returned to our daily work

---

[167] Anna Kuhn, *Christa Wolf's Utopian Vision: From Marxism to Feminism* (Cambridge: Cambridge University Press, 1988), 48.

[168] Ibid., 80.   [169] Ibid., 111.

[170] Mitteldeutscher Verlag to MfK on Christa Wolf's *Der geteilte Himmel*, 23 Nov. 1962, BAB, DR-1/2087a, fos. 386–7. The publisher was most concerned with the depiction of Manfred, fearing a one-sided depiction of the intelligentsia.

[171] Ibid., 228. Wolf also inserts quotes verbatim from Gagarin's memoirs.

[172] *Der geteilte Himmel* (Wolf, 1964).   [173] Ibid., 298.

[174] MfK (HV Verlage & Buchhandel), 'Stellungnahme zu Christa Wolfs Erzählung "Der geteilte Himmel"', 29 Sept. 1963, BAB, DR-1/2087a, fos. 388–94. It is clear that some of the 'Bitterfeld school' did not like the book, reacting sensitively to Wolf's attacks on small-minded functionaries in the story, accusing her of 'not depicting one "normal" comrade' in an editorial discussion. Manfred's character also had to be toned down to avoid alienating the intelligentsia.

which we had interrupted for an instant.' Rita is now an integrated member of the socialist community. The final message is of security: 'Yet she is not afraid. That offsets everything: the fact that we grow accustomed to sleeping soundly. That we live to the full as if there were a superabundance of this strange stuff life. As if it could never end.'[175]

The former deputy head of the State Planning Commission, Fritz Selbmann, also tried his hand at novel writing, with *The Sons of the Wolves* (1967), reconstructing the effects of the border closure on an electrical works in Berlin-Köpenick. The anti-hero is the works director, Heinz Lorenzen, a Social Democrat of bourgeois origin, who makes his career in the GDR. Despite the party's best efforts, however, Lorenzen is progressively corrupted by the open border and visits to West Berlin into betraying the Plan. The dangers of 13 August 1961 come from the 'other side', from the same rent-a-mobs who had allegedly instigated 17 June 1953. The border becomes a warlike 'front', the dividing line between the 'new' world in the East and the 'old' world in the West. In the former the factory militias stand 'calm and disciplined'; on the other side they are 'screaming and cursing demonstrators'.[176] The positive figures in the novel all feel reassurance on 13 August. The westernized Domino gang, on the other hand, 'wanderers between two worlds', feel trapped now that 'the border was shut and the garden of poisoned delights was closed and walled up'.[177] The gang's last desperate bid to flee across the Wall is foiled by the Volkspolizei in the novel's climax. Nevertheless, Selbmann offers redemption. Initially negative figures such as Graaff, the former *Grenzgänger*, knuckle down; he becomes a work brigade leader. Lorenzen himself is a lost cause, however, too morally 'eaten-away' to be reformed—a son of the pre-socialist wolf ethos—justifying his ultimate arrest by the Stasi. Captain Bethke, while pocketing the pistol with which Lorenzen was about to shoot himself, gives him the by now familiar line that this is for his own good: 'Do you know, laddy, the first time I saved you was from the black [SS] bandits in the camp. The second time, I saved you on 16 June '53 from the West Berlin thugs. And now, now I have to save you a third time, this time from yourself.'[178] This was the GDR's tough love.

For this early generation of writers 13 August meant defending party paternalism, but it was difficult to combine the moral choice for socialism from below, which the socialist realist plot required, with the fact that the state had imposed this choice unilaterally from above. But it was an enduring format.[179] The best later example was probably Jürgen Höpfner's *Switching Points*, a rite

---

[175] Ibid., 317

[176] Fritz Selbmann, *Die Söhne der Wölfe* (Halle: Mitteldeutscher Verlag, 1967), 52. See also Birgit Frech, *Die Berliner Mauer in der Literatur: Eine Untersuchung ausgewählter Prosawerke seit 1961* (Pfungstadt: Edition Ergon, 1992), 82–94.

[177] Ibid., 557.   [178] Ibid., 577–8.

[179] Alessandra Jaforte, *Die Mauer in der literarischen Prosa der DDR* (Frankfurt: Peter Lang, 1991); Dieter Sevin, *Textstrategien in DDR-Prosawerken zwischen Bau und Durchbruch der Berliner*

of passage novel of teenagers set on the eve of the Wall, whose tone was far more ambivalent.[180] What many of these works also have in common is an implicit gendering of the East–West moral divide: in almost all cases the East is feminized and the West masculinized. Even GDR authors writing from exile, such as Uwe Johnson, who had fled in 1959, adopted this stereotype in his 1965 *Two Views*.[181] The male photographer B., obsessed with sports cars, represents the superficial materialism of the West; the female nurse D. embodies the more caring but brooding nature of the East. Their fleeting love affair is thus doomed to fail even before the Wall physically separates them. Indeed, when B. helps D. to escape, nothing changes and they remain separated. The very structure of the novel, a series of alternating portraits with almost no dialogue between the two main characters, reinforces this apartness.

It should be noted that these 'quality' writers were already borrowing from a repertoire well established in the GDR's more trashy world of thrillers and romances, which had a much higher readership than the works traditionally studied by Germanists. Just as Anglo-American readers probably derived most of their notions about the Wall from the works of thriller writers such as John le Carré and Len Deighton,[182] East Germans had their own equivalents. Yet, whereas the British, post-Bondian spy story toned down the Cold War to the grey realities of the Wall, eastern popular authors did precisely the opposite. J.C. Schwarz picked the doctor–nurse romance, where bosoms heaved with alarming regularity, to mock the bourgeois world of medics and their come-uppance on 13 August. The convertee in this narrative is Dr Rimkeit, whose brother succumbs to *Republikflucht*, but who learns to resist temptation himself. Here, the West is caricatured as venal and populated by agents looking like 'Hollywood divas'—all the East can offer in reply is girlish fringes and freckles.[183] Such glamorization—the 'superficial "shining lights" of the capitalist way of life', as one lector commented rather derisively,[184] or 'western standard = world standard', according to another[185]—of course risked making the West more attractive still. And just as Ian Fleming's James Bond, who only encountered the Berlin Wall in his final mission,[186] was arguably more tourist than spy, East German thriller writers provided a vicarious taste of the forbidden Non-Socialist Exterior. Harry Thürk specialized in South-East Asia. Wolfgang Schreyer set

Mauer (Heidelberg: Winter, 1994); Ursula Jakobsen, *Berührungen: Deutsche Schriftsteller vor und nach der Mauer* (Rottenburg: Mauer Verlag, 2005).

[180] Jürgen Höpfner, *Gleisverwerfung* (Halle and Leipzig: Mitteldeutscher Verlag, 1982).

[181] Uwe Johnson, *Zwei Ansichten* (1965; Frankfurt: Suhrkamp, 1992).

[182] See Patrick Major, 'Coming in from the Cold: The GDR in the British Spy Thriller', in Arnd Bauerkämper (ed.), *Britain and the GDR: Relations and Perceptions in a Divided World* (Philo: Vienna, 2002), 339–52.

[183] J.C. Schwarz, *Das gespaltene Herz* (East Berlin: Tribüne, 1962).

[184] Ursula Mießner, 'Lektorat', 4 Feb. 1962, BAB, DR-1/5073, fos. 303–6; 305.

[185] Martin Freitag, 'Einschätzung', 5 Feb. 1962, BAB, DR-1/5073, fos. 307–8.

[186] Ian Fleming, 'The Living Daylights', in *Octopussy* (London: Jonathan Cape, 1966).

most of his spy stories in the Caribbean, paying lavish attention to the creature comforts and in-flight entertainment of his protagonists: 'In the first-class dining room it was even quieter, almost like an expensive restaurant. A uniformed girl served the first course. The gap between the seating was wider, the upholstery plusher; there were white table-cloths and smart overhead ambient lighting.'[187] Despite the Ministry of Culture's concerns about Schreyer's 'petit-bourgeois' tendencies,[188] such 'airport literature' served an important escapist function in a country where the real terminals flew to so few destinations.

A series of retrospective films by DEFA also dealt with recent events. Some could be surprisingly direct. *Chin Hook* opens with the former *Grenzgängerin* Carolin waking to the news of the 'measures' and rushing to the wire, where she flirts with militiaman Georg, played by star Manfred Krug, in the hope of finding a way through. Yet the film's message is about coming to terms with the new situation. Georg sets about persuading her, quirkily and undogmatically, to make the best of it: 'There are some things you can't grasp in ten minutes. . . . You're a victim? It's caught you out, so to speak. Why actually? We both live in the eastern sector. We both eat our bread here.' Gradually, Carolin comes to see the 'positive' side of socialism, becoming a shop-assistant and donning the housewife's apron (yes, the GDR was always post-feminist), but in a state where jazz, if somewhat martial, fills the soundtrack, and reconstruction and prosperity beckon. Yet her happiness, still conceived in terms of marital bliss, is jeopardized when her past as a call-girl in West Berlin threatens to catch up with her in the shape of a former pimp, the dapper but unscrupulous Bubi, now also trapped in the East. Ultimately, it is Georg who must learn to compromise, remaining immune to Bubi's blackmail attempts and showing him the 'worker's fist' while holding Carolin in with his socialist love.[189] Another film which ended with a fight, and may have been a surrogate action film of the type now out of bounds behind the Wall, was *The Skinhead Gang*, also set in the days of August 1961, as a group of westernized bikers terrorize a Baltic seaside resort. Earning their name by shaving their heads to resemble Yul Brynner—who ironically was on concurrent GDR release in *The Magnificent Seven*—this film purported to be based on a true-life incident. But with nowhere left to flee, it is only a matter of time before the local law enforcement, a detective with an almost Dr Doolittlean way with his Alsatian dog, finally tracks them down and restores law and order.[190] One notorious film, *Sunday Trippers*, even applied comedy to 13 August, as a group of bourgeois find that this particular Sunday has put an end to their

---

[187] Wolfgang Schreyer, *Tempel des Satans* (East Berlin: Verlag des MfNV, 1960), 156.

[188] Helga Hielscher, 'Verlagsgutachten' for *Preludio 11*, 28 May 1964, BAB, DR-1/5071, fos. 100–4.

[189] *Der Kinnhaken* (Thiel, 1962).

[190] *Die Glatzkopfbande* (Groschopp, 1963). For the real back story see Mark Fenemore, *Sex, Thugs and Rock 'n' Roll: Teenage Rebels in Cold-War East Germany* (New York: Berghahn, 2008), 219–30.

escapism. As scriptwriter Wolfgang Kohlhaase recalled: 'We thought we could do something to contribute to the lightening-up of . . . the public mood. That was a mistake.'[191]

The didactic tone and personification of moral stances in these films was typical. In *Julia Lives* a young border guard falls in love with two women, Penny, the daughter of a bourgeois professor, and Li, the hardworking nurse. Leaving the pregnant Li, he sets about rehabilitating the bourgeoise.[192] . . . *And Your Love Too*, set before and after the Wall, likewise romanticizes the East–West conflict. Two brothers, the politically correct Ulli (in shirt and tie), played by another DEFA star, Armin Mueller-Stahl, and the renegade Klaus (in leather jacket), are both in love with Eva. Initially she opts for Klaus and his trips to West Berlin. The whole film is narrated in a series of flashbacks, which act as a subtle mechanism to historicize and 'contain' recent events, leading towards Eva's decision for honest living and recognition that 'somewhere there must be a limit'. Nevertheless, the film's ending was ambiguous and open: 'And so we both realized that that wasn't the end of it. Nothing is at an end.' Moreover, in the climactic scene where Klaus attempts but fails to cross the Wall, the border guards fire in the air, while it is the West Berlin police who return aimed fire. Cinematically, too, the film was daring in showing documentary footage of the building of the Wall, blended into experimental *cinéma-vérité* street scenes from the period, lending the film a neo-realist aesthetic.[193] The Ministry of Culture had particular misgivings, however, that the Wall was depicted too much as a 'prison wall' and that Klaus's labour education camp resembled a Nazi concentration camp.[194] Other realist transgressions, such as Belgian filmmaker Frans Buyens' 1965 documentary *Deutschland, Terminus Ost*, filmed in the GDR and capturing interviews with slightly startled East Berliners, and even border guards against the background of the actual Wall, were pulled from public screening soon after completion.[195] Others which chose a surrealist route, such as Konrad Petzold and Egon Günther's *The Suit* (1961), an adaptation of Andersen's emperor's new clothes fairytale, was banned because it was set in a walled city.[196]

And then there were a number of spy films proper. In *For Eyes Only*, the GDR's answer to *The Spy Who Came in from the Cold*, scripted by the prolific Harry Thürk, the Stasi agent operating in the West on the eve of the Wall is a clean-cut family father, whose cover story is that he has committed *Republikflucht*. Even DEFA could not resist a classic infiltration scene, but this time from East to West, through the nocturnal border installations, with the tension provided this time

---

[191] Cited in Feinstein, *Triumph*, 126, on *Sonntagsfahrer* (Klein, 1963).
[192] *Julia lebt* (Vogel, 1963).
[193] . . . *und deine Liebe auch* (Vogel, 1962). Allan, 'Projections of History', in Andrew Plowman *et al.* (eds), *Divided, But Not Disconnected: German Experiences of the Cold War* (Oxford: Berghahn, forthcoming).
[194] Allan, 'Projections of History'.   [195] Personal communication of Thomas Heimann.
[196] Feinstein, *Triumph*, 130, on *Das Kleid*.

by western guards. His mission as a mole in the CIA, whose operatives' penchant for wearing sunglasses indoors is clearly affecting their counter-intelligence capabilities, is to steal the West's secret invasion plans for the East. In another twist, the Stasi man has to break back into East Germany, charging down a checkpoint with a safe stowed in the back of his family hatchback, under cover of some decidedly low-tech smoke bombs (the screen MfS evidently did not run to a 'Q' section). The final scene is a classic GDR wish fulfilment fantasy, showing the supposed renegade revealing himself to his son as a loyal defender of the Workers' and Peasants' State.[197] Armin Mueller-Stahl reprised this storyline ten years later as the intelligence gatherer Werner Bredebusch, alias Achim Detjen, in the highly popular TV series *The Invisible Cross-Hair*. Detjen is another mole infiltrated into the Federal Republic in search of the 'black protocol' to document Bonn's revanchism. Here the undercover police wear leather coats and black fedoras in mirror image of western clichés of the Stasi, both borrowing from a common Gestapo stereotype. The same surrogate, titillatory tourism occurs as with Schreyer, as one visit to a Bonn nightclub reveals:

The current owner from America has applied a liberal dose of wild west romance. A touch of saloon from the cowboy film, a touch of speakeasy from the prohibition years and a touch of sultry sex from the store of Hollywood's dream factory, the whole vigorously shaken and stirred—that is the 'Golden Nugget'. Here no-one bats an eyelid when the striptease girls appear in cowboy costume and drop their gunbelts last of all.[198]

Bredebusch's undercover life in the Federal Republic is a constant voyage of temptation through the world of capitalism, with tension generated by the audience's fear that he might succumb. Yet, viewers were surely invited to share the voyeuristic pleasures of the West along the way.

Mueller-Stahl made one more espionage-related film in 1977, *Escape*, a film warning against the dangers of West German escape helpers, in which the doctor–hero contemplating *Republikflucht* struggles in vain to extricate himself from their machinations, ending up abandoned and dying on a lonely country road.[199] The film backfired, however, since Mueller-Stahl himself was soon to leave the country in the wake of the affair which was to shake and polarize the GDR's artistic community. The authorities had always had the option of deporting troublemakers. On 16 November 1976 they used it against the most high-profile dissident voice in the country: Wolf Biermann. The angry young singer–songwriter of the early 1960s, already banned from public performance

---

[197] *For Eyes Only: streng geheim* (Veiczi, 1963).

[198] Otto Bonhoff and Herbert Schauer, *Das unsichtbare Visier*, i: *Kennwort 'Vergißmeinnicht'* (East Berlin: Militärverlag, 1975), 268.

[199] *Die Flucht* (Gräf, 1977). See the agonised discussion of how to tackle this 'hot potato' in BA-FA, DR-1/419, MfK (HV Film), 'Stenographische Abnahme vom Band des Auswertungsgespräches über den Film "Die Flucht" vom 13.11.1978'. Director Gräf had even filmed illegally in the Exclusion Zone. The film's licence was revoked in 1985. See MfK (HV Film), Protokoll Nr. 339/85, 24 Oct. 1985 in same file.

Criticism

since 1965, was on tour in Cologne in West Germany when his citizenship was revoked in absentia, effectively deporting him. Such a step had already been considered in 1974, but resisted in the interests of the GDR's international prestige. To the SED's surprise, however, thirteen of the GDR's leading writers, including Christa Wolf and Stefan Hermlin, as well as sculptor Fritz Cremer, publicly criticized the action, asking the Politbüro to reconsider, in a statement leaked to the West.[200] Despite a series of confrontations, none of the signatories would recant. Yet the party managed to defuse the situation, refraining from a public showdown. Even if they formed a tentative 'counter-elite', these renowned personalities were still protected, and had never previously challenged the system per se. Non-personalities were more likely to face punishment. Jürgen Fuchs, a minor poet who had signed the petition, was arrested and interrogated for nine months, before being deported to the West.[201] In the wider sphere, local parties and artists' groups were forced to engage in the venerable practice of disavowal. The long-term result of the Biermann Affair was, nonetheless, to discredit even further the Writers' Association—Hermlin and Fühmann effectively withdrew from its activities—and to persuade younger authors to maintain their distance, or to enter the more bohemian scene of Prenzlauer Berg.[202]

Following the affair, several other artists and critical intellectuals decided to leave. Biermann's ex-wife, Eva-Maria Hagen, a DEFA screen star, and her daughter, Nina, soon to become a punk icon in the West, were among the first. Author Thomas Brasch followed with his wife, the actress Katharina Thalbach.[203] Between 1976 and 1989 the Writers' Association lost thirty of its members in this manner,[204] and all told a hundred of the GDR's leading literati and artists emigrated, including Reiner Kunze, Sarah Kirsch, Klaus Schlesinger, and Hans Joachim Schädlich. Others, including Günter Kunert, Erich Loest, Jurek Becker, and Monika Maron, lived in the West as GDR citizens on permanent visas.[205] In June 1977 jazz singer and screen actor Manfred Krug, arguably the most popular figure in the GDR and another Biermann signatory, emigrated after complaining that his career was being blocked. As in many of these cases, his send-off by friends, at which twenty-five bottles of vodka and sixty bottles of sekt were consumed, resembled a wake, veering between revelry and tears.[206] He was

---

[200] Roland Berbig *et al.* (eds), *In Sachen Biermann: Protokolle, Berichte und Briefe zu den Folgen einer Ausbürgerung* (Berlin: Links, 1994).

[201] Jürgen Fuchs, *Gedächtnisprotokolle* (Reinbek bei Hamburg: rororo, 1978).

[202] Paul Kaiser and Claudia Petzold, *Boheme und Diktatur in der DDR: Gruppen, Konflikte, Quartiere 1970–1989* (Berlin: Fannei & Walz, 1997).

[203] Stefan Wolle, *Die heile Welt der Diktatur: Alltag und Herrschaft in der DDR 1971–1989* (Berlin: Links, 1998). Katharina Thalbach might be more familiar to some cinéastes as the mother in *Sonnenallee*.

[204] Madarász, *Conflict*, 165.

[205] Andrea Jäger, *Schriftsteller aus der DDR: Ausbürgerungen und Übersiedlungen von 1961 bis 1989* (Frankfurt: Verlag Peter Lang, 1995).

[206] Manfred Krug, *Abgehauen* (Düsseldorf: Econ, 1996), 255–65.

soon followed by Mueller-Stahl. From the authorities' point of view, keeping such talents pent up within the GDR was in danger of generating too many critical voices within. If authors really wanted to, manuscripts could be smuggled to the West and published in the FRG. Yet, comparisons must inevitably be drawn with neighbouring countries such as Poland with its Adam Michnik or Czechoslovakia with its Václav Havel. They went on to become key intellectual leaders of the revolution in 1989. In the GDR such voices had become a rather distant echo from outside.

A compromise solution for the state was to allow critical views to be published in the West, while authors remained in the GDR. In the case of Stefan Heym, the Ministry of Culture allowed trips to West Berlin, as long as he avoided 'unhelpful polemics and speechifying', and undertook not to read from his novel on the 1953 uprising, *Fünf Tage im Juni*.[207] The Stasi could play games of carrot and stick with aspiring authors, promising publication in the GDR for good behaviour, or outlets in the West. Sascha Anderson thus published with the left-wing Rotbuch Verlag in West Berlin, including the cryptic:

> go over the border
> on the other side
> stands a man and says:
> go over the border
> on the other side
> stands a man and says:
> go over the border
> on the other side
> stands a man and says:[208]

Or Stasi case officers could promise to open the secret door. In 1986 Anderson finally made it to West Berlin, only for it to be revealed after the fall of the Wall that all along he had been informing on his fellow Prenzlauer Berg writers, and had continued to do so from exile.[209] In this case, the MfS had played the wall game and won.

In consequence, it is difficult to see the East German artistic elite as either a clear-cut cheerleader for the system or as the counter public sphere which has been discerned elsewhere. Perhaps Anderson expressed this form of inner emigration best: 'neither for, nor against, but outside'.[210] It is true that Czechoslovakia and Poland kept their intellectuals; for them there was no other western half in which they could have practised their métier. The GDR authorities could siphon off troublemakers to the West, but as the Biermann case had shown, this could come

---

[207] MfK (HV Verlage & Buchhandel, Haid) memorandum, 11 Feb. 1965, SAPMO-BArch, DY30/IVA2/9.04/489.

[208] Sascha Anderson, *Jeder Satellit hat einen Killersatelliten* (West Berlin: Rotbuch, 1982), 25.

[209] Joachim Walter, *Sicherungsbereich Literatur: Schriftsteller und Staatssicherheit in der Deutschen Demokratischen Republik* (Berlin: Propyläen, 2001), 639–42.

[210] Gareth Dale, *Popular Protest in East Germany, 1945–1989* (London: Routledge, 2005), 96.

at massive political cost. It was also possible for these leavers to recycle their ideas and contacts back into the East, for instance via the lively gallery scene in West Berlin, or even via exhibitions held in the Federal Republic's Permanent Mission in East Berlin. From 1986 GDR 'delimitationists' were further hampered by the cultural cooperation agreement signed with the West. As in the case of the economy and popular music, the West began to penetrate the GDR *volens nolens*. And even if it was possible for the Stasi to infiltrate the Prenzlauer Berg scene, it could not prevent it from happening altogether.[211] Thus, the state's attempts to control artistic output by controlling the means of (re)production became redundant as artists began to engage in samizdat publishing, organizing their own galleries and happenings with themselves as an audience.[212] Yet this was at best a semi-public sphere, and one which always required the oxygen of western publicity. And since writers and artists formed such a privileged group within GDR society, ultimately they cannot be regarded as typical East Germans, but as we shall see in the next chapter, their treatment did filter down to other, more ordinary citizens and influenced their attempts to break out of the walled society.

LOOPHOLES

The Wall was never a truly hermetic barrier. Like a one-way valve, it operated in one direction, yet western influences continued to seep into the GDR from the outside. The regime was to discover a whole series of potential sources of leakage. The Leipzig Trade Fair, for instance, projected the GDR's quest for 'world standard' (*Weltniveau*), but it also attracted many visitors from the West. From the 1960s, it could also be a venue for East and West Germans to meet each other clandestinely.[213] Prague fulfilled a similar function on more neutral territory, the host of many a beery football friendly between East and West German teams. During détente, westerners continued to make inroads into the GDR in growing numbers, often literally on the transit autobahnen. Fleetingly, East Germans could drive side by side (or more likely behind) West German Mercedes and BMWs, sharing the same service stations, before turning off at the last exit before the border.[214] Nevertheless, closure was not just a

211 Paul Kaiser and Claudia Petzold, *Boheme und Diktatur in der DDR: Gruppen, Konflikte, Quartiere 1970–1989* (Berlin: Fannei & Walz, 1997).

212 Ilko-Sascha Kowalczuk (ed.), *Freiheit und Öffentlichkeit: Politischer Samisdat in der DDR 1985 bis 1989* (Berlin: Robert Havemann Gesellschaft, 2002).

213 Katherine Pence, ' "A World in Miniature": The Leipzig Trade Fairs in the 1950s and East German Consumer Citizenship', in David F. Crew (ed.), *Consuming Germany in the Cold War* (Berg: Oxford, 2003), 21–50; 40.

214 Friedrich Christian Delius and Peter Joachim Lapp, *Transit Westberlin: Erlebnisse im Zwischenraum* (Berlin: Links, 1999).

question of concrete and chicanes. In the electronic age, radio and television could transcend the Wall in an instant. This may not yet have been the age of the internet, but some of the first signs of globalization, of the creation of a virtual media landscape, were already beginning to make their mark on the closed society.

Even what would appear at first sight to have been the easiest gate to police, the post, proved highly problematic. Although printed matter sent to private individuals was regularly impounded, for the determined it was still possible to acquire forbidden texts, such as the science fiction authors Angela and Karlheinz Steinmüller, who smuggled Orwell's *Nineteen Eighty-Four* in from Hungary, 'stuffed between pullovers and paprika salami'.[215] More generally, East Germans continued to receive a taste of the West in the form of 'care packets' from western friends and relations, often sponsored by Federal government agencies as state–private networks to overcome national division.[216] Initially western packages had contained staples such as flour or vegetables to combat the perceived hunger crisis in the 'Zone'. But gradually senders were advised by western charities to send little luxuries, which also made good advertising for the economic miracle in the West. Many East Germans remembered with nostalgia the smell of unwrapping shortage goods such as real coffee or chocolate. As one recipient wrote in her thank-you note: 'By the way, with Pid deodorant I make a good impression on everyone—the fragrance of the big wide world! Then I have the little *4711* bottle of eau de cologne in my handbag and everyone sniffs: "Aha, the West!" '[217] The building of the Wall witnessed a surge in parcel sending, prompting a defensive posture by GDR propaganda against these Trojan 'gifts of love'.[218] The post-box became a new internal border for the GDR customs and Stasi to police.[219] Between January and August 1962 51,000 packages were impounded.[220] However, the MfS's Section 12 was not above simply lifting some of the choicer items. Yet while officials could X-ray for suspect items, reading matter became a particular headache—it had to be read!—so that backlogs of unread material accumulated at post-offices. Meanwhile, the GDR's official media were discreetly permitted to subscribe to western lifestyle magazines to keep abreast of fashions, including the Paris shows, allowing readers 'to dream

Western influence

[215] Angela and Karlheinz Steinmüller, *Andymon: Eine Weltraum-Utopie* (Berlin: Shayol, 2004), 292.

[216] Christian Härtel and Petra Kabus (eds), *Das Westpaket: Geschenksendung, keine Handelsware* (Berlin: Links, 2000).

[217] Ina Dietzsch, 'Geschenkpakete—ein fundamentles Mißverständnis: Zur Bedeutung des Paketaustausches in persönlichen Briefwechseln', in Härtel and Kabus (eds), *Westpaket*, 105–17; 112.

[218] Petra Kabus, 'Liebesgaben für die Zone: Paketkampagnen und Kalter Krieg', in Härtel and Kabus (eds), *Westpaket*, 121–31; 129.

[219] Generalmajor Beater, 'Bericht für das Kollegium des MfS', Dec. 1961, BStU-ZA, MfS-SdM 1558, fo. 93.

[220] Verner to Honecker, 8 Oct. 1962, SAPMO-BArch, DY30/IV2/12/114, fos. 92–4.

their way out of their little world', although they had to walk a constant tightrope between meeting needs and unleashing unfulfillable desires.[221]

Eventually the GDR saw the wisdom of channelling some of this small-scale consumer demand into its own coffers, setting up its Genex mail-order business for western benefactors (its catalogues were banned from the GDR for fear of alerting the home population to the level of export goods involved). Delicatessens and luxury goods were introduced in specialist GDR outlets such as 'Delikat' and 'Exquisit', but these often raised the hackles of those who could not afford them.[222] This proved even worse with the introduction of Intershop duty free outlets, founded in February 1962 and aimed initially at western travellers, which accepted only foreign hard currency. With the *Ostpolitik* treaties of 1971–72, numbers of western visitors began to rise dramatically, so that by the late 1970s 6.4 million West Germans and Berliners were arriving annually, bringing in hard currency in the form of gifts, tips, and bribes.[223] The regime connived in the venality of its citizenry, however, by amending the law in 1974 to allow East Germans to hold convertible currency. The West German deutschmark became the GDR's covert second currency, of which the state was keen to relieve its citizens in return for 'Forum cheques' redeemable at—where else?—Intershop. This only exposed the GDR's hypocrisy in such matters. I still recall the rage I felt, not just for being relieved by a border policeman of a pack of blank video cassettes destined for an East German host, which he duly receipted as illegal contraband, but for his parting shot that I could, of course, buy the very same cassettes at Intershop. Petitions reveal that many East Germans felt the same way: 'These Intershops remain reserved for people who receive hard currency as gifts. That is really a very unfair thing in a socialist state! You can be ever such a good worker or GDR citizen, but without "western connections" you won't be able to buy these things.'[224] Others saw Intershops benefiting only western tourists and undermining the state's egalitarian claims.[225] By the regime's final days the newly founded GDR's Freethinkers' association was accusing the party of generating 'consumer avarice', a grubby mockery of the high ideals of socialism.[226] These were just a few examples of 1960s GDR political correctness being eroded by 1980s economic imperatives, and at the same time gently fanning the consumerist desires of the population.

---

[221] Torben Müller, 'Vom Westen lernen, heißt improvisieren lernen: *Guter Rat*—eine sozialistische Verbraucherzeitschrift', in Simone Barck *et al.* (eds), *Zwischen "Mosaik" und "Einheit": Zeitschriften in der DDR* (Berlin: Links, 1999), 69–76; Evemarie Badstübner, 'Auf 80 Seiten um die Welt: *Das Magazin* zwischen 1954 und 1970', in ibid., 189–201; 199.

[222] SED-BL Berlin (PO), 'Information', 26 May 1966, LAB, BPA SED Berlin, IVA2/5.01/330.

[223] Katrin Böske, ' "Selbstverständlich kein standiger Begleiter des Sozialismus": Der Intershop', in Härtel and Kabus (eds), *Westpaket*, 213–29; 217.

[224] Ibid., 223.

[225] SED-BL Karl-Marx-Stadt to SED-ZK, 20 Nov. 1978, SAPMO-BArch, IVB2/5/1001.

[226] Verband der Freidenker der DDR, 'Information', 6 Oct. 1989, SAPMO-BArch, DY30/IV2/2.039/317, fos. 9–11.

Policing the airwaves was a different matter altogether. The GDR was always fighting a losing battle over radio listening.[227] It saw itself confronted by a battery of hostile broadcasters:

What RIAS cannot manage with its heavy-handed yokel-baiting, Radio Luxembourg is supposed to achieve with schmaltzy hit parades and idiotic write-ins. If that does not work, the BBC is ready with its 'objective', refined news programmes, and failing that, then Sender Freies Berlin or West Germany's Black Channel jump into the breach. The right thing for every taste.[228]

There was relatively little the party could do, however, apart from keep an eye on people's dials during house-calls or pledge school classes not to copy the cartoon character 'Zacharias of RIAS', whose donkey's ears always pricked themselves to 'listen in' to western stations.[229] As should already be clear, young listeners regularly flouted such injunctions in the case of beat. Transistor technology made the portable *Kofferradio* next to uncontrollable. Television, however, was still on the cusp of mass ownership in 1961. (There were just over 1 million television viewers nationwide.[230]) This may have encouraged one of the more bizarre GDR prophylactic campaigns, when the party became a latter-day King Canute in 'Operation Blitz against NATO Broadcasters' in September 1961. The FDJ, entrusted with the action, claimed that although physical east–west border-jumping was over, 'many citizens still have their antennae pointed to the West. They are still ideological *Grenzgänger*.'[231] The oxhead-shaped aerials required to receive western channels were readily visible from the ground, making owners easy targets. Groups of FDJ thus descended on local communities, demanding that licence holders either dismantle antennae, or in extreme cases party officials even climbed up onto roofs and sawed off offending aerials.

What Operation Blitz revealed was that there were limits beyond which the party could not go.[232] Public reactions were almost universally hostile to 'an invasion of personal freedom'.[233] The methods used were particularly odious. In Stalinstadt FDJ orderlies 'chanted the names of known listeners to NATO

---

[227] Infratest (ed.), *Empfangsmöglichkeit und Nutzung westdeutscher und westlicher Auslands-Sender in der SBZ: Ergebnisse einer Umfrage bei Ostzonenflüchtlingen* (September/October 1955).

[228] FDJ-ZR (Agit-Prop), 'Materialien über die Rolle der NATO-Kriegssender und des schwarzen Kanals', 1 Sept. 1961, SAPMO-BArch, DY24/A3.935.

[229] The GDR adopted Nazi terminology: *hören* was not enough, but *abhören*.

[230] *Neues Deutschland*, 10 Apr. 1961, 3; Infratest (ed.), *Fernsehempfang in der SBZ: Empfangsmöglichkeiten, Zuschauerverhalten, Beurteilung* (May 1961).

[231] FDJ-ZR (Agit-Prop), 'Materialien über die Rolle der NATO-Kriegssender und des schwarzen Kanals', 1 Sept. 1961, SAPMO-BArch, DY24/A3.935.

[232] SED-KL Torgau, '17. Informationsbericht', 22 Aug. 1961, StAL, BPA SED Leipzig, IV2/12/598.

[233] FDJ-ZR (Org-Instruk/Agit-Prop), 'Zusammenstellung der Argumente der Aktion "Blitz kontra NATO-Sender"', 8 Sept. 1961, SAPMO-BArch, DY24/A3.935.

programmes and stuck posters on their doors'.[234] In some cases donkey's ears were pinned on entrances to stigmatize recalcitrants, causing some to complain of Nazi-style intimidation.[235] Even party comrades in Karl-Marx-Stadt had objected to having their leisure activities dictated.[236] In Erfurt some threatened to resign over the issue.[237] The rest of the population soon picked up on this. One local was insistent: 'Only when the big party comrades in the village remove their aerials will I do the same.' Instead of such enforced 'voluntarism', citizens demanded legislation. Others defended their right to be informed of both sides' arguments, which the party attacked as 'objectivism'. There were also the usual accusations of SED hypocrisy, since the GDR produced sets with western reception, and its own western broadcaster, Freiheitssender 904, aimed at Bundeswehr troops, regularly blared out popular music. The FDJ reported that Blitz was proving counter-productive: 'through a ban we are encouraging a spirit of opposition. Pupils will then only tune in to western broadcasters secretly and all the more fervently.'[238] By the mid-1960s viewers craved more sport and feature films, and associated western schedules with modernity. Importantly, too, taboos about western forbidden fruit began to break. Among artisans in Magdeburg, for instance, 'in a small circle, at the workplace, in the brigade, in the pub, but especially on the train they talk about what they have watched without embarrassment'.[239]

Discussions with the post-office revealed that there was no effective means of jamming TV transmissions. Local authorities tried to encourage 'group viewing', but closet viewers were soon erecting receivers inside attics or behind net curtains. A black market in home-made western antennae sprang up, and by the mid-1960s the party was listening to fatalistic assessments from its grass roots that 'western television is admittedly politically damaging, but so widespread that nothing serious can be done about it'. Sixty to 90 per cent of the population were estimated to be watching western programmes. The SED reporter was philosophical: 'We live in a technological age where the mass media work in both directions. This brings advantages as well as disadvantages, which we simply have to put up with.'[240] It was known that some comrades, even, were postponing meetings so as not to miss episodes of western police

---

[234] FDJ-ZR (Org-Instruk/Agit-Prop), 'Pressematerial', Sept. 1961, SAPMO-BArch, DY24/A3.935.

[235] SED-ZK (Agitation), n.d., SAPMO-BArch, DY30/IV2/9.02/6, fos. 55–60.

[236] BEL KMS, '38. Bericht', 27 Aug. 1961, StAC, SED-BL KMS, IV2/12/5, fos. 193–9.

[237] SED-ZK (PO), 'Bericht über die Auswertung des Standes der Parteiwahlen . . .', 19 Mar. 1962, SAPMO-BArch, DY30/IV2/5/296, fos. 168–69.

[238] 'Information über die politischen Auseinandersetzungen mit Lehrern, Eltern und Schülern gegen den Empfang von Westsendern', 4 Oct. 1961, SAPMO-BArch, DY30/IV2/9.05/27, fos. 26–7.

[239] SED-ZK (Agit), 'Zum Einfluß des Westfernsehens', 21 July 1966, SAPMO-BArch, DY30/IVA2/9.02/31.

[240] SED-ZK (PO), 'Information über den Einfluß feindlicher Rundfunk- und Fernsehsender . . .', 15 July 1966, SAPMO-BArch, DY30/IVA2/5/23.

dramas. Technical programmes and advertising were other favourites: 'Very often prices or the state of equipment in factories are compared with our own. Not infrequently discussions end in comments that "this and that could be cheaper over here" or "if only we had such machines in our works".'[241] This inevitably led to doubts about the GDR's historical mission to catch up with the West; or viewers recognized products made in the GDR but marketed under capitalist brands, thus fuelling widespread resentments that they were becoming part of a global putting-out system.

By 1971 approximately 85 per cent of the GDR populace owned a television set. Western viewing became a nightly habit. Some of the programming schedules of western stations were specifically geared to fit in with eastern routines, since shift patterns meant most East Germans turned in by 10 p.m. In May 1975 the SED's Central Committee even announced that no more measures would be taken against reception of western broadcasts. Admittedly, the information technology revolution had not yet taken full root, even in the West, let alone the East. Yet with the advent of computers, mobile phones and faxes, satellite television and video recorders, the days of the GDR's ability to seal itself off were surely numbered. And although the Internet was only in its infancy when the Wall finally fell, it is hard to imagine how the GDR could have resisted the relentless march of techno-globalization, especially when it was struggling to develop its own microchip technology. Even though the border troops were experimenting with electronic devices to make the Wall more impassable, there was a limit to what a physical solution could achieve. Moreover, the SED was to discover that it would become ever more difficult to close all the doors in the Wall from East to West. By the 1980s the GDR had developed a form of 'West' syndrome, an inferiority complex whereby everything western was assumed to be better.[242] The glimpses of the Non-Socialist Exterior afforded by the gaps in the Wall were to stoke up the desire to travel. And rather than satisfying the basic material needs of the population so that they could then attend to their spiritual transformation into socialist human beings, the economic reforms of the 1960s and 1970s merely created consumerist aspirations which could not be met in the shadow of the Wall.

241 Ibid.
242 Hans-Hermann Hertle and Stefan Wolle, *Damals in der DDR: Der Alltag im Arbeiter- und Bauernstaat* (Munich: Bertelsmann, 2004), 331–9.

7

Wanderlust: Travel, Emigration and the Movement

Before the law stands a gatekeeper. To this gatekeeper comes a man from the country and requests admission to the law. But the gatekeeper says that he cannot grant him admission now. . . . 'If it tempts you so, try to enter in defiance of my veto. But mark you: I am mighty. And I am only the lowliest gatekeeper. Yet from room to room stand other gatekeepers, one mightier than the next.'

Franz Kafka, 'Vor dem Gesetz' (1919)

In Kafka's parable the man from the country wastes his whole life waiting for justice, trying to bribe even the fleas on the gatekeeper's collar and agonizing whether to bluff his way through a gateway which turns out to be made only for him. All walls have gates, even the 'Antifascist Defence Rampart', and the regime consciously exploited its position as gatekeeper, but ultimately less effectively than Kafka's guard. Yet East Germans were not gullible yokels; they became seasoned complainants.[1] A western observer in the mid-1970s, during the GDR's 'golden years', thought that travel 'is probably the single most important grievance which young East Germans have'.[2] This chapter will examine the day-to-day impact of *Ostpolitik* on East Germans' elusive freedom of movement, especially in the 1970s and 1980s. Did the desire to travel, and the willingness to protest against the absence of this basic human right, constitute a valid part of the East German citizens' campaign which helped to bring down the regime in 1989? This momentous year will be case studied in the next chapter, but as Charles Maier has suggested, the desire for freedom to travel was far more widespread than for abstract intellectual freedoms.[3] Here again, we must distinguish between the desire to come and go, and permanent emigration. Unlike previous studies,

---

[1] Jochen Staadt, 'Eingaben: Die institutionalisierte Meckerkultur in der DDR: Goldbrokat, Kaffee-Mix, Büttenreden, Ausreiseanträge und andere Schwierigkeiten mit den Untertanen' (Berlin: Forschungsverbund SED-Staat paper, 1996).

[2] Jonathan Steele, *Socialism with a German Face: The State that Came in from the Cold* (London: Cape, 1977), 212.

[3] Maier, *Dissolution*, 125. For other anecdotal evidence see Jürgen Kleindienst (ed.), *Mauer-Passagen: Grenzgänge, Fluchten und Reisen 1961–89* (Berlin: Zeitgut, 2004).

my analysis pays equal attention to the former, and seeks its answers in longer-term developments, decades and not just months before the fall of the Wall. Furthermore, there were potentially fatal tensions between the proponents of 'exit' and 'voice'. When dissident activists were asked in 1989 what their chief stumbling block was, they pointed accusingly at emigration.[4] Was this justified? Those intent on leaving the system undoubtedly had to develop some activist skills to attract media attention to their cause, and could become temporary allies of the political opposition in the 1980s. Yet was this merely a means to an end? Were they interested in reforming the system as such, and when they had achieved their goal of the West, would they keep up the pressure from outside?

By the 1980s the SED may have felt like the sorcerer's apprentice, overwhelmed by a rising tide of would-be travellers, but in the immediate wake of the Wall it still felt in control. Besides a few tens of thousands of family reunions in the early 1960s, involving mainly children and older people, in November 1964 it ventured to permit GDR pensioners to visit the West. From then on at least 1 million OAP trips occurred annually, reaching an average 1.5 million in the 1980s. (However, those with relatives in the armed forces or security services were excluded.) From 1972 OAPs could even travel several times a year for up to thirty days.[5] In GDR vernacular, these superannuated citizens had reached their 'coming of travel age' (*Reisemündigkeit*).[6] It was often surmised in the West that the GDR cynically wanted to unburden itself of its senior citizens' welfare. A small number did not return, but most did. Some even complained of being patronized by western relatives. One woman's 'sister would not walk down the street with her because of her tatty clothing'; a couple from Leipzig returned early, worried about becoming a burden: 'Shopping became a trauma for me because of the high prices.'[7] Others enjoyed the experience, commenting on westerners' openness and high standard of living. By the 1970s the divergences were even more apparent. The majority were impressed by West German cities, goods, and services. Nevertheless, socially and emotionally there was a widespread consensus that 'we wouldn't want to live there in the long term'. The hectic lifestyle, materialism, egocentricity, and interpersonal coldness had been off-putting. Regular visitors cited increasing differences of opinion with hosts, especially at alleged West German condescension. In the

[4] Garton Ash, *In Europe's Name*, 196.

[5] Hartmut Zimmermann (ed.), *DDR-Handbuch*, 3rd edn (Cologne: Verlag Wissenschaft und Politik, 1985), vol. 1, 635.

[6] Hans-Jürgen Fischbeck in Zusammenarbeit mit Ludwig Mehlhorn und Stephan Bickhardt, 'Das Mauersyndrom—die Rückwirkung des Grenzregimes auf die Bevölkerung der DDR', in Deutscher Bundestag (ed.), *Materialien der Enquete Kommission 'Aufarbeitung von Geschichte und Folgen der SED-Diktatur in Deutschland'* (Baden-Baden: Nomos/Suhrkamp, 1995), vol. V/2, 1196.

[7] Nationale Front (NF, Nationalrat), 'Meinungen, Fragen und Argumente von DDR-Bürgern im Rentenalter die nach Westdeutschland und Westberlin reisen', 27 Nov. 1964, SAPMO-BArch, DY30/IV A 2/9.02/75.

East, on the other hand, social security and low criminality were ranked highly, as might be expected among pensioners, but, as one put it: 'In the GDR I feel comfortable, it's our *Heimat*. Here there's calm and security.'[8] Now, one might object that this was exactly what the SED wanted to hear, but institutionalization affected not only senior citizens. When the 40-year-old Rita Kuczynski was allowed over in 1985, she panicked when exiting a checkpoint 'behind which, over time, I had made myself at home'.[9] Moreover, these selective concessions evidenced a tangible drop in travel petitions (see Figure 10), many of which had been penned by the elderly although the younger generation continued to feel excluded.[10]

The only younger people who could travel in the 1960s were the so-called *Reisekader* or 'travel cadres', on official business. Government ministers, works directors, and theatre intendants had to write to the Interior Ministry on behalf of employees even for the most mundane of trips west, which amounted to a few thousand annually.[11] Nevertheless, the GDR's desire to achieve 'world standards' militated against total isolationism. Cultural ambassadors such as author Dieter Noll might grace book launches and film premieres in West Germany.[12] Inevitably, some beneficiaries abused these highly coveted trips abroad to defect. Delegation members would occasionally slip their minders and abscond, often in 'third-party' countries.[13] Consequently, the Interior Ministry vetted every applicant, and rejected those deemed untrustworthy.[14] At the 1972 Munich Olympics, for instance, the GDR authorities turned down 18,000 of the 20,000 tickets offered by the West German Olympic association.[15] Yet only very rarely were private trips granted, in cases involving serious illness and where the workplace was prepared to bear the 'political responsibility'.[16]

The remaining population had to content itself with organized holidays within the GDR, to the Baltic resorts or the Harz and Erzgebirge mountains. But even these were heavily bureaucratized and backlogged. For foreign travel, as Figure 9 reveals, in the 1960s only limited places were available in the eastern

[8] SED-ZK (Parteiorgane/Agitation), 'Information über Diskussionen, Argumente und Meinungen von Rentnern, die seit dem 1.1.1970 zu Besuchen in Westdeutschland und Westberlin weilten', 14 Sept. 1970, SAPMO-BArch, IV A2/902/22.

[9] Kuczynski, *Mauerblume*, 219.

[10] 'Beispiele über Nichtbeantwortung bzw. ungenügende Beantwortung von Fragen und Kritiken der Bevölkerung', n.d. [1965], SAPMO-BArch, DY 30/IV A 2/9.02/75.

[11] For a selection, see BAB, DO-1/8/51010 and BAB, DO-1/8/41623.

[12] *Junge Welt*, 27 Sept. 1966.   [13] See some of the reports in BAB, DO-1/8/41386.

[14] Maron to Ministerium für Außenhandel und Innerdeutschen Handel, 6 Dec. 1961, BAB, DO-1/11/951, fos. 173–4.

[15] Daniel Wilton, 'Regime versus People? Public Opinion and the Development of Sport and Popular Music in the GDR, 1961–1989' (PhD thesis, University College London, 2004), 96–7.

[16] Hauptverwaltung Deutsche Volkspolizei (PM), 'Einschätzung des Reiseverkehrs. . .', 7 Nov. 1961, BAB, DO-1/11/951, fos. 138–46.

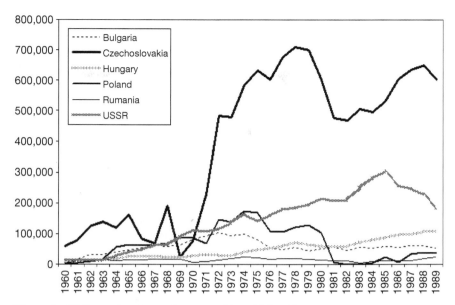

Figure 9. GDR tourist trips to the eastern bloc, 1960–89.
Source: Deutsches Reisebüro statistics from *Statistisches Jahrbuch der DDR*, 1960–89.

bloc.[17] Czechoslovakia remained by far the GDR's most frequented destination, although Poland, Bulgaria, and the Soviet Union catered for growing demand in the 1970s. Freedom of travel had been significantly increased in 1972 with the introduction of visa-free travel to most eastern neighbours. Indeed, hitchhiking around the more liberal East became part of the GDR 'hippy trail'.[18] However, in response to the upheavals in Poland, in October 1980 visa-free travel there was suspended, just as the shutters had come down on Czechoslovakia after 1968, and again in the 1980s. From a peak in 1985, when Gorbachev had come to power, the Soviet Union also became more restricted. Thus, compared with the 1970s, for many holidaymakers the 1980s must have seemed a regressive decade, including Herr P., who had been waiting since 1957 for a chance to revisit the Alps, and since 1972 to see the Caucasus: 'I have walked the neighbouring countries, I have travelled their rivers by boat — now the possibilities are exhausted. Patience has its limits . . . I am close to death and feel perfectly entitled to demand something.'[19]

There was probably another reason why the regime was reluctant to open up completely to the East. The eastern bloc became the outlet of choice for

[17] SED-KL Borna to SED-BL Leipzig, 10 Feb. 1965, StAL, BPA SED Leipzig, IV A2/16/461.
[18] Tilo Köhler, 'Einmal Varna und zurück: Tramp nach Osten', in Michael Rauhut and Thomas Kochan (eds), *Bye Bye Lübben City: Bluesfreaks, Tramps und Hippies in der DDR* (Berlin: Schwarzkopf, 2004), 296–304.
[19] Helmut P., 20 Aug. 1987, SAPMO-BArch, DY 30/1028, fos. 14–17.

post-Wall *Republikfluchten.* 'Holidaymakers' would fly out on forged passports, sometimes aided by West German escape helpers, or stow away on long-distance trucks travelling between Scandinavia and southern Europe, forcing the MfS to send operative units to Prague and Budapest, on the look-out for would-be leavers. In Bulgaria, for instance, every summer a small detachment of Stasi observers worked the beaches of the Black Sea resorts, trying to prevent escapes to Turkey. Although not quite as brutal as the 'Antifascist Defence Rampart', the Czech–Hungarian iron curtain was also heavily patrolled, and allied border troops routinely returned failed escapers for interrogation and prosecution. Only Poland resisted to any extent, as did Yugoslavia, which allowed asylum seekers to proceed to their destination of choice. All told, 14,737 would-be escapers were repatriated from 1963–88.[20]

The removal of Ulbricht in 1971 coincided with a number of international agreements creating further breaches in the Wall, this time to the West. Preceded by Brandt's *Ostpolitik* treaties with the Soviet Union and Poland, in September 1971 the Four-Power Agreement was signed between the former Allies to alleviate transit through the GDR. In December the two German states then signed their first treaty, the Transit Agreement, which regulated traffic between the FRG and West Berlin, followed in May 1972 by a Traffic Treaty on the passage of persons and goods through permanent crossing-points. In December came the Basic Treaty, in which the two states professed good neighbourliness and the inviolability of the intra-German border. 'Permanent representatives' were to be exchanged in lieu of ambassadors. Telephone lines were reconnected between East and West Berlin. Federal citizens, previously allowed only one annual visit, were now permitted multiple trips, and could visit friends as well as relatives. A crucial change occurred on the other side of the Wall, too, in 1972: GDR citizens other than pensioners were to be allowed to visit parents and children in the FRG 'on urgent family matters', or what I shall call compassionate leave, including births, christenings, confirmations, communions, weddings, jubilee birthdays, serious illness, and death. Throughout the 1970s 40–50,000 such annual trips west raised enormous hopes: from 1972 travel petitions began to rise again after consistently sinking over the previous decade.[21] What such leave of absence also achieved by the stroke of a pen was to turn East Germany into a two-tier society: those with 'grade-one' western relatives, as GDR bureaucrats called immediate family, and those without, who now regarded themselves as 'hostages' for the lucky few.[22]

---

[20] Monika Tantzscher, 'Die verlängerte Mauer: Die Zusammenarbeit der Sicherheitsdienste bei der Verhinderung von "Republikflucht" über andere Ostblockstaaten', in Heiner Timmermann (ed.), *Die DDR: Erinnerung an einen untergegangenen Staat* (Berlin: Duncker & Humblot, 1999), 91–122.

[21] Staatsrat, 1972 *Eingaben* report, BAB, DA-5/9026.

[22] NF (Nationalrat), 'Zweiter Bericht über Meinungsäußerungen, Argumente und Fragen zum Vierseitigen Abkommen über Westberlin', 15 Sept. 1971, SAPMO-BArch, DY30/IVA2/9.02/75.

COMPASSIONATE LEAVERS

The German fate: queuing in front of a counter.
The German ideal: sitting behind that counter.

Kurt Tucholsky (1930)[23]

The SED Central Committee's Security Section files are filled with hundreds of thousands of applications for compassionate leave, many laboriously handwritten, and the various gatekeepers' verdicts. Applicants first of all needed permission from their employer's cadre department. Those seeking exemptions were subject to MfS screening, to verify their 'positive or at least loyal attitude to the GDR' and 'ideal, material and family ties'.[24] If they got this far, they would be notified that their matter was being dealt with by the Pass and Registration section at the local police station. It seems, however, that the police could be more restrictive than the leadership, often blocking applications.[25] These cases were then informed that for 'security reasons' they could not travel, leaving them perplexed as to how they could possibly be jeopardizing the GDR.[26] Behind the scenes, the MfS vetted applicants whose relatives had already committed *Republikflucht*, or who were born in the West, or, like comrade Bruno A., were 'single, all dependants and relatives live in the FRG. Local security organs therefore refuse a trip.'[27] Rejectees included a divorcee whose 'son illegally left the GDR',[28] a woman whose mother had fled, leading to her husband's dismissal from the Volkspolizei, or another deemed to be closer to her son in West Germany than to the one in the GDR.[29] Since a sixth of the population had committed *Republickflucht* before the Wall, leaving behind an even longer string of 'grade-one' relatives, this was a sizeable minority. Perhaps as many as every second GDR family had western relations of some degree on other.[30]

Yet local officials soon began applying a whole range of social rather than political or security hurdles, which reflected the GDR's peculiarly petit bourgeois morality. Decision-makers regularly passed value-judgements on applicants, often culled from the constable on the beat, the *Abschnittsbevollmächtigter*,

---

[23] *Die Weltbühne*, 27 May 1930, 799.
[24] Bernd Eisenfeld, 'Flucht und Ausreise—Macht und Ohnmacht', in Eberhard Kuhrt (ed.), *Opposition in der DDR von den 70er Jahren bis zum Zusammenbruch der SED-Herrschaft* (Opladen: Leske & Budrich, 1999), 384.
[25] Else B. to SED-ZK, 19 June 1974, SAPMO-BArch, DY30/IVB2/12/88, fos. 344–5.
[26] Elfriede A. to SED-ZK, 28 Oct. 1977, SAPMO-BArch, DY30/IVB2/12/85, fos. 297–7.
[27] Ministerium des Innern (MdI) (PA), 11 May 1976, SAPMO-BArch, DY30/IVB2/12/85, fo. 21.
[28] MdI (PA), 17 Jan. 1974, SAPMO-BArch, DY30/IVB2/12/85, fo. 9.
[29] MdI (PA), 5 May 1976, SAPMO-BArch, DY30/IVB2/12/85, fo. 85.
[30] Karl F. Schumann, 'Flucht und Ausreise aus der DDR insbesondere im Jahrzehnt ihres Untergangs', in Deutscher Bundestag (ed.), *Materialien der Enquete Kommission*, vol. V/2, 2372.

or from conversations with colleagues. It was important to evidence so-called 'societal ties', sometimes a euphemism for 'hostages', but also for the candidate's proficiency as a 'socialist personality'. Roswitha A. failed the respectability test because 'she is twice divorced and has no ties to the GDR';[31] another for having too many affairs with married men;[32] a third for not having an 'orderly family', since of her eleven children, eight were in care.[33] 'Rowdyism' and alcoholism were further negatives.[34] How much of this was based on hearsay is hard to tell, but at least one comrade applicant was turned down based on 'indications from the population in her place of residence'—in other words neighbours.[35]

Applicants in the state apparatus faced additional obstacles, having to convince first their local parties, then the regional leadership, before going to the Central Committee for arbitration.[36] Those entrusted with secret information were generally automatically excluded. Some applicants listed their service in the armed forces, clearly hoping to demonstrate loyalty, only to have this cited as the reason for rejection.[37] Teachers, too, were refused on principle. Thus, one educationalist in Grimmen was told by the SED 'that he had to be a role-model in overcoming family hardships arising from the political demarcation from West German imperialism'.[38] One comrade with a daughter and son-in-law in the East German customs was also routinely rejected by the district police.[39] Or else local party collectives pleaded on behalf of members, as in the case of the deputy editor of *Freie Welt*, whose SED praised her 'politico-ideological principle, her high sense of responsibility and her exemplary editorial and societal work', adding that she had gained the GDR's order of merit and the German–Soviet Friendship Society's badge of honour (in gold).[40] Consequently, it was often those most ostensibly loyal to the state, but expecting some form of reward, who were excluded. This was to have important effects in the final years of the GDR in eroding the loyalties of 'regime-carriers'.

[31] MdI (PA), 28 May 1974, SAPMO-BArch, DY30/IVB2/12/85, fo. 138.
[32] MdI (PA), 14 Aug. 1980, SAPMO-BArch, DY30/IVB2/12/85, fo. 149.
[33] MdI (PA), 10 Sept. 1973, SAPMO-BArch, DY30/IVB2/12/85, fo. 292.
[34] MdI (PA), 10 June 1978, SAPMO-BArch, DY30/IVB2/12/88, fo. 29; MdI (PA), 12 Mar. 1975, SAPMO-BArch, DY30/IVB2/12/88, fo. 289.
[35] SED-KL Oscherleben to SED-ZK (Sicherheit), 13 June 1973, SAPMO-BArch, DY30/IVB2/12/88, fo. 369.
[36] See, for instance, VEB Kombinat Tiefbau Berlin on Gustel B., 26 July 1972, SAPMO-BArch, DY30/IVB2/12/88, fos. 362–3, and fos. 364–5.
[37] Peter B. to SED-ZK, 11 Sept. 1974, SAPMO-BArch, DY30/IVB2/12/88, fos. 250–3.
[38] SED-KL Grimmen to SED-ZK (Sicherheit), 12 Mar. 1974, SAPMO-BArch, DY30/IVB2/12/85, fos. 32–3.
[39] Zollverwaltung der DDR (Kader) to SED-ZK (Sicherheit), 27 Aug. 1975, SAPMO-BArch, DY30/IVB2/12/85, fos. 74–5.
[40] Berliner Verlag to Modrow, 26 Oct. 1972, SAPMO-BArch, DY30/IVB2/12/85, fos. 239–40. In this case even the ZK's Agitation section was to intercede with the security section.

From the outside, this bureaucratic edifice was as inscrutable as Kafka's existential house of justice. In the interests of state security, applicants were not told why they had been turned down. A game of 'second-guessing' ensued. One tactic was to find someone in authority higher up the hierarchy, leapfrogging gatekeepers. One woman explained: 'Since I am no longer prepared in future to expose myself cap-in-hand (*als Bittsteller*) to the dubious legality of decisions and recommendations of the organs of the Ministry of the Interior', she was turning to the party.[41] Comrades regularly used their 'connections' to speed up decisions. Those in the public eye were usually treated with far more decorum than the general public. The classical singer Theo Adam was thus granted repeated visits to the Bayreuth festival, and the rock band The Puhdys was issued a long-stay visa to West Germany in 1985, with spouses, at the behest of the SED's cultural chief, Kurt Hager.[42] The über-gatekeeper was, of course, Erich Honecker, who enjoyed being arbiter. Indeed, in the final years would-be travellers increasingly chose to go straight to the top, from 1,400 in 1983 to almost 5,000 in 1988,[43] half of which amazingly enough succeeded.[44] Yet perhaps this was not so surprising. Honecker's own high-profile visit to the Federal Republic in 1987, not as a pensioner but as head of state, had set something of a precedent.[45]

One way of short-circuiting procedures or reversing decisions was to file a parallel petition or *Eingabe*. The general tone of these had changed significantly upon the building of the Wall. Now letter-writers acknowledged the state. For instance, according to the Council of State in 1963: 'As a rule it is emphasized that they are good-willed and have proven by their activity at work and in social life that they are loyal to the Republic. Very often they point to special achievements and awards.'[46] Petitions included 'an increasing number of vouchsafes such as leaving behind family members, confirmations of good family and financial circumstances, as well as material and monetary guarantees.'[47] Later, Honecker's petitions office noted the same deference: 'personal achievements, such as one's own home, car etc. as well as a secure future in the GDR are cited as evidence that they would never leave the GDR'.[48] Petitioners became skilled at special pleading, especially in cases of death or serious illness, mimicking party-speak or citing Central Committee resolutions.[49] Frequently, they would invoke antifascist

[41] Bibiana T.-G., 3 Nov. 1988, SAPMO-BArch, DY30/1003, fos. 24–5.
[42] See SAPMO-BArch, DY30/1028, fos. 149–96.
[43] Figures in SAPMO-BArch, DY30/2589.
[44] 'Information über eingegangene Eingaben im 2. Halbjahr 1986', 5 Feb. 1987, SAPMO-BArch, DY30/2590, fo. 66.
[45] See Staatsrat, 1987 *Eingaben* report, BAB, DA-5/11423.
[46] Staatsrat, 1963 Eingaben report, BAB, DA-5/5977.
[47] Kanzlei des Staatsrates, 1 Sept. 1964–31 Aug. 1965, BAB, DA-5/5978.
[48] 'Information über eingegangene Eingaben im 2. Halbjahr 1987', 10 Feb. 1988, SAPMO-BArch, DY30/2590, fo. 95.
[49] Staatsrat, 1973 *Eingaben* report, BAB, DA-5/11380.

services rendered and public duties to the Workers' and Peasants' State, such as Helga T., who had 'performed literally every voluntary job going'[50] or another who had helped to build this state, as a 'rubble child'.[51]

Gradually, however, petitions became an arena to let off steam in the face of state intransigence, suggesting that they were becoming blocked as a channel of political communication. One can trace this sometimes in the increasingly aggressive tone of follow-up petitions. One couple wrote to the Central Committee twenty times in two years, gradually moving from complaints at the local authority's foot-dragging to more sweeping critiques of 'real existing socialism'.[52] Moreover, from Figure 10 we see that the absolute number of petitions on travel and emigration to the Council of State rose, particularly in the 1980s. In 1987–88, they even topped housing as the GDR's standard bugbear, reaching nearly 44,000, an unheard-of proportion of 38.6 per cent. How do we explain this qualitative and quantitative shift? One answer lies in the increasing internationalization of the problem. The Basic Treaty of 1972 was in the public domain, and although petitions officers pooh-poohed many complaints as inspired by the western media, rejections 'caused ever more forceful, sometimes very aggressive and agitated demands for granting applications'.[53] The GDR's accession to the UN in September 1973, which held freedom of travel to be a human right, delivered a new set of arguments.[54] The GDR's 1974 constitution in fact included the clause: 'Everyone is free to leave every country, including his or her own.' That year a West German lobby, the Society of Human Rights, intervened on behalf of would-be travellers for the first time. Some petitioners even asked to be relieved of their GDR citizenship, while citing the UN.[55] Further ammunition was provided by the Helsinki Conference on Security and Cooperation in Europe (CSCE) in 1975. The GDR signed up to 'basket 3', to facilitate family reunions and 'travel for personal and professional reasons'. Among subsequent travel petitions every fourth letter cited Helsinki, whereby 'citizens deduced more far-reaching rights for themselves or treated the formulations as the force of law'. Furthermore, 'it was variously stated that the signature of Comrade Honecker in the final declaration could not be a mere cipher and therefore their travel or emigration application had to be permitted'.[56] People started demanding that relatives once and twice removed be included.[57] The Federal Republic acted as a surrogate public sphere, with petitioners threatening to contact its Permanent Mission in East Berlin or

---

50 Helga T., 25 May 1983, SAPMO-BArch, DY30/1003, fo. 52.
51 Eveline T., 1 June 1987, SAPMO-BArch, DY30/1003, fos. 167–8.
52 Erika and Rudolf M., SAPMO-BArch, DY30/1054, fos. 203–42.
53 Staatsrat, 1st quarter 1973 *Eingaben* report, BAB, DA-5/9026.
54 Staatsrat, 1973 *Eingaben* report, BAB, DA-5/11380.
55 Staatsrat, 1974 *Eingaben* report, BAB, DA-5/11381.
56 Lehmann to Semler, 29 Aug. 1975, BAB, DA-5/9013.
57 Staatsrat, 1975 *Eingaben* report, BAB, DA-5/11382.

'other international organizations'.[58] The GDR's long quest for international recognition had thus brought some unwelcome side-effects. The catch-22 for petitioners, however, unknown to them, was that every petition invoking human rights automatically landed in the wastepaper basket. They would be forced to seek other avenues of unsanctioned dissent outside official channels.

The Federal Republic continued to keep up the humanitarian pressure by attaching political strings to its humanitarian aid in the 1980s. This was fully what the architects of the Social Democrats' 1960s *Ostpolitik* had intended, but their legacy was continued under the Christian Democrats who took office in 1982. Thus pensioners and children visiting East Germany were exempted from sharp increases in compulsory hard currency exchange and tripwire mines were dismantled at the inner-German border. Bavarian Minister President Franz Josef Strauß then negotiated two separate 1-billion-mark loans in 1983 and 1984 which may have prolonged the GDR's creditworthiness, but which also made explicit the cash for reform nexus. This was a period when East Germany was entering a balance of payments crisis, in constant need of hard currency and thus vulnerable to economic leverage from the West, somewhat to the alarm of the Soviet 'friends'. The GDR was also coming under pressure to live up to its international CSCE human rights obligations, with further rounds of negotiations in Madrid in 1983 and later in Vienna in 1988. The mixed signals from the Soviet leadership, on the one hand for flexibility and reform, as well as toughness in the face of Reaganite rearmament, placed the GDR in a dilemma.

Nonetheless, in February 1982, a first extension of the compassionate leave ordinances was wrung out of the GDR, in which the criteria were publicly set out in the GDR's *Gesetzblatt*. The number of birthdays was extended; it was also possible for grandparents and half-siblings to travel ('grade-two relatives' in GDR bureaucratese).[59] At the same time, the possibilities were extended for youths to travel outside the eastern bloc, with the exception of military cadres. There was a corresponding doubling of those applying and travelling. However, the liberalization of short-term travel 'for humanitarian reasons' of December 1985 had a still greater impact. According to GDR statistics, whereas 139,012 non-pensioners had travelled west in 1985, in 1986 it was 525,265, and 1,097,399 the following year.[60] The gatekeepers were evidently taken aback by the enormity of demand.[61] Criteria were duly loosened towards those previously convicted, or 'secret-bearers', but still the authorities insisted on a 'basic loyal attitude to the social conditions of the GDR' and that the GDR be 'represented with dignity'.[62] Family ties were still also mandatory. Yet relatives were now defined to include uncles, aunts, nephews, nieces, cousins, step-parents, and

---

[58] Staatsrat, 1st half 1975 *Eingaben* report, BAB, DA-5/9026.
[59] *Gesetzblatt der DDR*, 17 Mar. 1982, 181.
[60] Figures in SAPMO-BArch, DY30/IV2/2.039/306 and 307.
[61] MdI, 'Einschätzung', 30 Jan. 1987, BAB, DO-1/8/41626.
[62] 'Erfordernisse. . .', SAPMO-BArch, DY30/IV2/2.039/306, fo. 5.

-children. Nevertheless, those without western relatives were still excluded, as were married couples, families, men under twenty-six, or those wishing to visit recently emigrated persons. The two-tier society persisted.

Despite the secrecy of this new government ordinance, applicants soon detected the new latitude available to visa officers, and were determined to test it. Increasingly, demands were made for explicit justifications of rejections. The Interior Ministry noticed, moreover, that citizens were enquiring who had no western relatives (over 100,000 in 1986), and rejectees frequently interpreted the decision as a personal slight which altered their relationship to the state. This tendency deepened, so that by 1988, rather than documenting loyal obedience, as the petitioners of the 1960s and 1970s had done, citizens were 'making their future societal behaviour conditional on acceptance', threatening otherwise to boycott workplace initiatives and social activities, to resign from honorific positions, hand back distinctions, refuse to vote, or renounce their citizenship.[63] As reports in Dresden and Schwerin revealed, 'some citizens during interviews and petitions are making demands. They consider their applications not as exceptions to the legal regulations, but as their right.'[64] Some indeed sought legal redress. Furthermore, every fourth applicant rejected in 1987 or deemed ineligible filed a petition (5,885 to Honecker, 11,886 to the Council of State, as well as 35,199 to the Interior Ministry and 17,579 to the regional police authorities, and 29,606 to individual police stations).[65] In these, too, applicants cited parallel cases, or threatened to escalate to an emigration application.[66] So grew the rudimentary beginnings, if not of a civil society, then at least of a civic consciousness, a culture of complaint in the closed society.

At this stage, in early 1987, the regime still thought that the gambit was paying off. Although 50–60 per cent of all *Republikfluchten* in the 1980s occurred during compassionate leave, including over 3,000 in 1987 and 5,000 in 1988, this was still only a tiny percentage of all travellers (0.23 per cent in 1987). Of those remaining in the West, it was the intelligentsia who interested the party most, including a high proportion of university-educated and skilled citizens, 'who are increasingly using links back into the GDR', to encourage relatives to follow them or to make petitions.[67] What is more, when party members failed to return, this could create particularly bad publicity,[68] as when Ingrid Stoph, daughter of the Minister President, had defected. Nevertheless, Wolfgang Herger, head of the SED's Security section, was convinced that the original

---

[63] 'Einschätzung über Reisen. . .', 20 July 1988, SAPMO-BArch, DY30/IV2/2.039/306, fos. 213–23.

[64] 'Bericht über die Untersuchungen durch die Abteilung für Sicherheitsfragen. . .', SAPMO-BArch, DY30/IV2/2.039/306, fo. 81.

[65] MdI (PM), 'Einschätzung', 1 Feb. 1988, BAB, DO-1/8/41628.

[66] 'Information über Bestrebungen von Bürgern der DDR, die DDR zu verlassen', n.d. [1986], SAPMO-BArch, DY30/IV2/2.039/306, fo. 45.

[67] 'Erfordernisse', n.d., SAPMO-BArch, DY30/IV2/2.039/306, fo. 11.

[68] MdI, 'Einschätzung', 20 July 1988, BAB, DO-1/8/54472.

decision to liberalize had been vindicated: '500,000 "sensible" citizens have contributed to implementing our peace policy.'[69] By October 1987, however, the Interior Ministry was less sure, following conversations between Honecker, MfS chief Erich Mielke, and Egon Krenz as Politbüro Security secretary, to devise a thorough cost–benefit analysis 'in which all positive and negative sides are set down'.[70] This was no doubt prompted by ongoing CSCE negotiations, when the SED had been asked by the Soviets in July 1987 to supply details and justifications of their travel policies while talks were under way in Vienna, after which the GDR was expected to deliver new concessions in 1988. It was philosophically reasoned that liberalization had solved some conflicts, but created others.[71]

Meanwhile, the logic of liberalization proceeded. Travel on compassionate leave witnessed further reforms in March 1988, when in that month alone 145,053 travel applications were processed, despite restrictions on married couples and skilled workers.[72] Indeed, the slight overall slow-down in compassionate travel in 1988, revealed in Figure 10, partly explains the growing aggression.

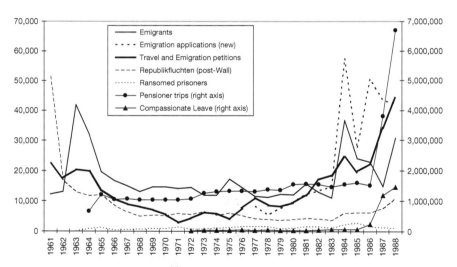

Figure 10. Travel and emigration from East to West Germany, 1961–88.
Source: Eisenfeld, 'Flucht und Ausreise', 397–9; Plück, 'Innerdeutsche Beziehungen', 2024–5; travel and migration petitions, BAB, DA-5/5977, 5978, 9025–27, 11378–87, 11419–25.

[69] 'Vermerk über die Beratung. . . am 22.01.1987. . . ', 23 Jan. 1987, BAB, DO-1/8/41626.
[70] MdI (PM), Vermerk, 16 Oct. 1987, BAB, DO-1/8/41628.
[71] See BAB, DO-1/8/41630.
[72] Hans-Hermann Hertle, *Der Fall der Mauer: Die unbeabsichtigte Selbstauflösung des SED-Staates*, 2nd edn (Opladen: Westdeutscher Verlag, 1999), 79. See also 'Information über eingegangene Eingaben im 2. Halbjahr 1988', 1 Feb. 1989, SAPMO-BArch, DY30/2590, fo. 116.

Moreover, for two years the sheer volume of applications had begun to over-whelm the system, despite the use of computers and electric typewriters. Queues at the Dresden police pass sections had risen since 1986 from one to 2–3 hours. Case officers at the visa desks were apparently being worked 'to the physical and psychological limit'.[73] By 1987 the sickness rate of the mainly female staff in Pass and Registration was over 40 per cent. In 1988 those at the counter-face reported:

The interviews with citizens make clear that trips to the Non-Socialist Exterior are increasingly considered a matter of course and upon non-acceptance of an application for lacking criteria there are stubborn and increasingly aggressive demands for its processing. Above all, by referring to publications in the FRG mass media a 'right' to travel is inferred.

Applicants were supposedly even dredging up long-lost relatives in the West simply to test the system. Yet, the police lamented, official arguments 'are crushed by the citizens' various counter-arguments'. Some wanted to know how social engagement was to be expected without the incentive of travel. One complained that 'Erich Honecker travelled to the FRG with a full sack in order to shine; now after his return he is turning off the tap again'. Another woman threatened a sit-down strike before the Central Committee building. Some visitors were even beginning to tear up their useless passports outside police stations. Long-standing Vopos in Magdeburg commented that 'such circumstances have never been known before'. Moreover:

The colleagues working on travel are increasingly being confronted by citizens with queries on applications and rejections outside of working hours. In public, at home, while shopping, going to the doctor's or hairdresser's, unwholesome scenes are enacted, and the comrades can only defend themselves against these citizens with difficulty.[74]

The travel experiment had threatened to get out of control in 1988, but in November the authorities further liberalized, prompted by the recently concluded Vienna CSCE treaty, printed in *Neues Deutschland*, which promised the right to leave and return to one's home country unhindered.[75] By no longer requiring employer appraisals, and introducing a complaints procedure in January 1989, police and Interior Ministry officials evidently hoped to relieve some pressure. At the same time the Travel Decree shifted the goal posts closer together for 'grade-two relatives', excluding uncles and aunts, nephews and nieces, grandparents, and married couples from travelling together.[76] The result was 'a clear increase in aggressive, demanding, libellous and sometimes impertinent behaviour as well as a sinking threshold of threats and implementation of

[73] 'Bericht über die Untersuchungen durch die Abteilung für Sicherheitsfragen. . . ', SAPMO-BArch, DY30/IV2/2.039/306, fo. 84.

[74] MdI, 'Information', 14 Apr. 1988, SAPMO-BArch, DY30/IV2/2.039/306, fos. 197–211.

[75] *Neues Deutschland*, 14 Dec. 1988, 6.

[76] Walter Süß, *Staatssicherheit am Ende: Warum es den Mächtigen nicht gelang, 1989 eine Revolution zu verhindern* (Berlin: Links, 1999), 145–6.

provocative-demonstrative actions and criminal acts'.[77] Vastly more persons were applying without having western relatives at all. The selective nature of the reform led to complaints

that the decree is only of interest to citizens who have relatives in the Non-Socialist Exterior and who derive their 'advantage' from it. In this connection some declare that the population is thus being divided into two classes and the section without the opportunity to travel is having to generate the necessary hard currency travel money for the other half.[78]

In spring 1989 queues of up to seventy were already waiting outside visa offices in Berlin, Leipzig, and Dresden before they opened each morning. In the first nine months of that momentous year, 1,625,387 compassionate leave applications were made, twenty times the annual average when the process had begun in the early 1970s, of which just over a quarter were deemed ineligible or rejected outright.[79] Aggrieved rejectees accused local officials of 'subjectively' interpreting regulations to deny them their rights. As citizens in Frankfurt/Oder complained: 'they feel disenfranchised and treated like children and expected something different from the CSCE process'. A doctor in Dresden was shown out after claiming that 'we are being sorted out like half-, quarter- and eighth-Jews'. Some threatened not to vote in the forthcoming local elections. There was also a rising tendency to go through the complaints procedure. Some even offered small bribes.[80] The Security section even backtracked in March, allowing 'outlaws' as well as in-laws to count as relatives, thus sending the numbers up again.[81] In May, at the time of controversial local elections, visa desks were under orders to minimize rejections, which indeed fell to 1.9 per cent (compared with 41 per cent in January).[82] The stop–start nature of this gatekeeping had in fact done more to undermine regime credibility, and as we shall see in the next chapter, by May 1989 leavers had a potential alternative way out.

Liberalization was also threatening to undercut all of the party's efforts at *Abgrenzung* and vilification of West Germany. No longer was experience of the West reliant on the hearsay of the over-sixties, although the numbers of pensioners skyrocketed in 1987–88 too. By 1989 approximately 3.5 million East Germans held a passport, and, as Figure 10 shows, over a million trips by younger persons were being granted. Although some returnees, suffering from what the party described as 'egotistical and petit-bourgeois consumer mentality', raved about the West, just as many had found capitalism an unnerving and

---

[77] MdI, 'Information', 17 July 1989, SAPMO-BArch, DY30/IV2/2.039/309, fo. 59.
[78] SED-ZK (Sicherheit), 'Information und Schlußfolgerungen', 28 Feb. 1989, SAPMO-BArch, DY30/IV2/2.039/307, fos. 51–67.
[79] SAPMO-BArch, DY30/IV2/2.039/306–7.
[80] See the regional BDVP reports to the MdI in BAB, DO-1/8/41627.
[81] Süß, *Staatssicherheit*, 147.   [82] Eisenfeld, 'Flucht und Ausreise', 396.

not all possible

expensive experience. Some took the same negative view of western 'hectic and stress' as pensioners, recognizing that western affluence was not always evenly distributed.[83] This mixed reaction is borne out by subsequent testimony, and so was not just SED wishful thinking.[84] Nevertheless, to the consternation of the party:

The majority of travellers appreciate the social security in the GDR, but many have illusions about the real situation in the FRG and in West Berlin. They allow themselves to be blinded by the external facade of the FRG and Berlin. In this regard they evaluate their trip upon return in terms of leisure activities, living and working conditions, failing to recognize the shortcomings of the capitalist system, such as social insecurity, unemployment, future uncertainty, ruthlessness and social coldness.[85]

It was also noted that returnees were often reticent to talk. When pressed, however, 'many show that they are impressed by the apparently functioning consumer society'. They were overwhelmed by the goods on offer, but also the clean towns compared with the 'socialist environment'.[86] It was evident, therefore, that the privileged few in the two-tier society—by now as many as a quarter of the population if we include pensioners—were capable of infecting the excluded majority with a tantalizing view of the West. The secretive nature of the compassionate leave procedures had merely generated suspicion, and as was shown time and again, had tended to displace legal applicants into the petitions procedure, from which it was a small but significant step to an emigration application.

THE EMIGRATION SEEKERS

—the old fool has joined the queue
Of all those screaming down the heavens:
The citizens with an 'application'—oh, how many
Tens of thousands! All want to go west.

Wolf Biermann, 'Legende vom sozialistischen Gang' (1976)

Travel was one thing; permanent emigration quite another. Yet, the two were intimately linked. As we have seen, the threat to submit an emigration application was a means to 'supercharge' a compassionate leave petition. But whoever really did apply to emigrate became ineligible to travel, thus increasing the recourse to fundamentalism. The state's thinking was ostensibly rational: whoever had

---

[83] BDVP Suhl, 'Informationsbericht', 2 June 1986, BAB, DO-1/8/51052.
[84] Sabine Krätzschmar and Thomas Spanier, *Ankunft im gelobten Land: Das erste Mal im Westen* (Berlin: Links, 2004).
[85] 'Information', n.d. [1987], SAPMO-BArch, DY30/IV2/2.039/306, fo. 276.
[86] Dickel to Krenz, 16 Jan. 1989, SAPMO-BArch, DY30/IV2/2.039/309, fos. 7–14.

demonstrated the will to leave the country permanently would surely use a trip west to commit *Republikflucht*. Nevertheless, it was a mechanism ratcheted to go in only one direction.[87] Growing governmental resistance was also a reflection of the changing social demographic of emigrants. Initially, it was a means of dumping unwanted citizens. The post-Wall purge of 1963–64 involved many children, and subsequent police statistics recorded what proportion were beyond working age or were invalids. As late as 1974, for instance, of the 11,760 adults emigrating, 8,318 were in these 'unproductive' categories.[88] For fifteen years, until the 1980s, the numbers hovered at a little over 10,000 per annum, and appeared to be a system stabilizer.

By the 1970s, however, rumours had spread that people in their prime, such as those wanting to marry across the Wall, could lodge an application to leave permanently.[89] The Interior Ministry's initial tactic was neither to confirm nor deny, and hope that the problem would go away by itself. It was a Kafkaesque achievement in its own right to discover even where to submit an application, and applicants often waited months or even years before receiving any acknowledgement. Moreover, those who took this dramatic step were stigmatizing themselves severely and required extreme tenacity. As Gareth Dale has observed, this form of exit was no longer private, but heavily politicized.[90] There was no going back, literally, once one had left the GDR in this way. The state would confiscate remaining property such as houses and cars. If applicants persisted, initially 'soft' pressure would be applied at house meetings.[91] This was coupled with promises of new jobs or apartments for those willing to retract applications. But as will be seen, the Stasi became a key player in this carrot-and-stick process of trying to win back potential leavers. Applicants' ID cards were confiscated, thus reducing freedom of movement even within the GDR; others were denied visas for the eastern bloc.[92] Emigration seeker status also led to problems at work. In isolated cases applicants would resign jobs, leading to arrest, since it was illegal to refuse work in the GDR.[93] Emigration seekers were thus effectively ostracized and rendered socially dead, requiring a form of withdrawal or inner emigration, bordering on asceticism.[94]

[87] MdI (PA) to SED-ZK (Sicherheit), 10 July 1980, SAPMO-BArch, DY 30/IV B2/12/95, fo. 95.
[88] See SAPMO-BArch, DY30/IVB2/12/17, fo. 65.
[89] Hans-Hermann Hertle and Stefan Wolle, *Damals in der DDR: Der Alltag im Arbeiter- und Bauernstaat* (Munich: Bertelsmann, 2004), 359.
[90] Gareth Dale, *Popular Protest in East Germany, 1945–1989* (London: Routledge, 2005), 88.
[91] Martha B. to SED-ZK, 2 Aug. 1973, SAPMO-BArch, DY30/IVB2/12/182, fos. 195–6.
[92] Familie L. to SED-ZK, 29 July 1979, SAPMO-BArch, DY30/IVB2/12/186, fos. 134–5.
[93] Regine and Martin B. to SED-ZK, 7 Sept. 1976, SAPMO-BArch, DY30/IVB2/12/182, fos. 186.
[94] Hans-Hermann Lochen and Christian Meyer (eds), *Die geheimen Anweisungen zur Diskriminierung Ausreisewilliger: Dokumente der Stasi und des Ministeriums des Innern* (Cologne: Bundesanzeiger, 1992).

In the absence of a transparent procedure, would-be emigrants inevitably resorted to the venerable practice of petitioning. Nevertheless, emigration petitions bore a different character from travel petitions. Their authors were no longer trying to impress the state with their loyalty and evinced a generally more aggressive tone. As with compassionate leave petitions, automatic rejection awaited those who transgressed the hidden eligibility guidelines or referred explicitly to the UN or Helsinki. Many applications sought refuge from the political in the personal. Wary emigration seekers refused to be drawn into political discussions with Internal Affairs staff: 'We emphasize again that this state has no right to keep hold of us as law-abiding citizens. There is no legal basis for this. Our matter is a purely private one, borne by humanitarian intentions and is to be viewed as part of a family reunion.'[95] Another family claimed that the reasons were 'purely private and personal. We are suffering under the spiritual and spatial lack of freedom which is leading to psychological tensions within our family. We—that is, my wife and I—are individualists and cannot identify with this state any longer.'[96] A high proportion of women applicants were seeking to join husbands who had left on previous trips, and surveys conducted with arrivees in the Federal Republic confirmed family reunion as a cardinal factor.[97] The files are filled with countless other 'apolitical', personal cases (without wishing to suggest that the family crises were anything but genuine, or that the state's control of one's personal life is anything but political).[98]

Another set of justifications concerned the poor state of the economy. Here one was on relatively safe ground since the SED's 'unity of economics and politics' programme had implicitly conceded rising living standards as a citizen's right. Moreover, it was easier for the party to suspect leavers of base materialism than high principle. One couple, for example, criticized the lack of tourist destinations, fresh fruit and the fact that 'we have been running around Leipzig for two months in search of coffee filters'. A whole catalogue of living and working conditions was appended.[99] 'I know from western television that you can earn a lot more there and live better than in the GDR', explained a 26-year-old waiter. A 40-year-old construction worker was fed up with traipsing around the shops for goods and was outraged at the prices charged in Delikat shops: 'for chocolate we pay tenfold the amount of the original producer'. And a 25-year-old transport worker was disarmingly honest about his interest since teenagerhood in 'the western way of life': not so much democracy as 'the luxury and creature comforts there.

---

[95] Erika and Rudolf M., 2 May 1983, SAPMO-BArch, DY30/1054, fo. 203.

[96] 1983 application in Eisenfeld, 'Flucht und Ausreise', 409.

[97] Karl F. Schumann, *Private Wege der Wiedervereinigung: Die deutsche Ost-West-Migration vor der Wende* (Weinheim: Studienverlag, 1996), 69–71.

[98] A careful study of the Schwerin applicants' reasons concluded that 'family' was the chief factor up to November 1988. See Jonathan Grix, *The Role of the Masses in the Collapse of the GDR* (Houndmills: Palgrave, 2000), 75.

[99] Udo and Gisela M., 25 Feb. 1985, SAPMO-BArch, DY30/1054, fos. 259–61.

Power of TV

If you have the money, you can afford anything you want.'[100] Many of these aspirations were doubtless fuelled by watching western television advertising, but the numbers citing economic motives steadily rose during the 1980s.[101]

Others chose a slightly riskier avenue, because it was political, of holding the party to its own promises, citing SED documents to this effect.[102] There were complaints at the unfairness and hypocrisy of the whole emigration procedure: 'Unfortunately I am not as grand as Wolf Biermann, Manfred Krug or Armin Mueller-Stahl, whom you can sideline and then deport sometime, when they stop shouting "hurrah" for you.'[103] Again we encounter the perceived inegalitarianism of a system which claimed to be eradicating class barriers. Political jokes attacked the never-never GDR: 'A man from Dresden took his courage in his hands and went to the police station: "I want to leave the country." The police officer asks him: "Where do you want to go then, young man?" "To the GDR," he answers. "But you are already here." The officer is astonished. "No, no", the young man doesn't give up. "At long last, I want to move to the GDR which is described in the newspapers." '[104] Others took a more direct line, criticizing head-on human rights infringements. One group in Jena explained why they wanted to be released from GDR citizenship:

We intend to leave the GDR legally, since we are no longer prepared to renounce the achievements of world civilization, be they the right to express a political opinion, to influence state policy, or the chance to consume goods cultural, ideal or material, for the sake of an ideology and the state behind it, in which intention and reality are drifting apart.[105]

One also suspects that emigration became a front for solving other domestic impasses, and was not always about emigration at all. Despite the high penalties attached, ulterior threats appear to have been more common than with compassionate leave petitions. The Council of State's petitions desk thus noted the old, pre-Wall pattern of linking calls for housing with 'threats—sometimes massive—to leave the GDR illegally'. For example, Herbert J. from Halle warned that: 'If we don't have a new flat by the 15th of August you can get our emigration ready or else we will send pictures abroad showing how GDR citizens live. We're living like animals, not human beings.'[106] A Dresden family cited the

---

[100] 'Aussagen von DDR-Bürgern, die versuchten, illegal die DDR zu verlassen', SAPMO-BArch, DY30/IV2/2.039/308, fos. 51–9.

[101] Hilmer in Deutscher Bundestag (ed.), *Materialien der Enquete Kommission*, vol. vii/1, 325.

[102] Familie M., 30 June 1986, SAPMO-BArch, DY30/1054, fo. 5; Rollo M, 20 Apr. 1986, ibid., fo. 261.

[103] Roland A. to Staatskanzlei Berlin, 18 Apr. 1980, SAPMO-BArch, DY30/IVB2/12/182, fos. 54–5. These were all prominent GDR artists—Biermann had been deported in 1976, while Krug and Mueller-Stahl were allowed to leave the following year.

[104] Cited in Madarász, *Conflict*, 143.

[105] Jena citizens to Volkskammer, 12 July 1983, exhibit in Museum Haus am Checkpoint Charlie, 2001.

[106] Lehmann to Eichler, 3 Jan. 1975, BAB, DA-5/9013.

mould growing on their furniture.[107] Others attacked falling living standards. In such cases the authorities usually tried to remedy the immediate cause of the aggravation, in the interests of achieving a retraction. Such applications could, it has to be said, range from the sublime to the ridiculous and petitions officers must occasionally have wondered if pranks were being played. One woman's reason to leave the country was her inability to get central heating fitted. An agonizing four-page appendix itemized every failed step along the way, forcing no less an authority than the Central Committee to order the regional party to find a plumber, all at the height of the GDR's terminal crisis.[108] Since the state measured its success by the number of 'desisters', applicants enjoyed a certain negative bargaining power. A psychological game of cat and mouse ensued, where applications would be retracted in return for concessions, failing which they would be reinstated.[109] Another high-risk tactic was to file an application as an extreme negotiating position from which to climb down towards a more modest goal, such as a travel visa.[110] Ultimately, the state lost the battle for recantation: after 1985 the proportion of 'desisters' to new applicants shrank year on year. Calling the state's bluff in this way could backfire too, with some embattled tactical emigration seekers finding themselves genuinely wanting out. Moreover, since there was no guarantee of success, hindsight should not blind us to what was an unnerving and isolating experience which left behind much bitterness.[111]

The demographic profile of emigrationists changed radically in the 1980s. In a case study of Schwerin, Jonathan Grix found that over half (51.4 per cent) from 1985–89 were skilled manual workers, with over a fifth in the service sector, and 8.9 per cent in the intelligentsia, and 7.1 per cent managers. Only 2.6 per cent were unemployed. The average age was just under thirty-five.[112] He also discovered the same over-qualification of leavers as had occurred before 1961. By the final fatal weeks before the Wall came down, 46.3 per cent of leavers were aged 18–29, rising to 55.9 per cent in the three months after its fall.[113] Infratest discovered that 60 per cent were male, although many families were also involved, representing a cross-section of East German society, and not just the intellectual Prenzlauer Berg set.[114] We can also discern a geographic

---

[107] Hans-Dieter and Marlene M., 25 May 1982, SAPMO-BArch, DY30/1054, fos. 46–7.

[108] Elke M., 26 Sept. 1989, SAPMO-BArch, DY30/1054, fos. 75–86.

[109] Peter and Marion M., 16 Oct. 1982, SAPMO-BArch, DY30/1054, fos. 192–3.

[110] Peter F. to MdI, 3 June 1982, BAB, DO-1/8/51061.

[111] Stiftung Gedenkstätte Berlin-Hohenschönhausen (ed.), *Die vergessenen Opfer der Mauer: Flucht und Inhaftierung in Deutschland 1961–1989* (Berlin: KOMAG, n.d.); Tina, Österreich, *Ich war RF: Ein Bericht* (Berlin: Verlag Haus am Checkpoint Charlie, 1988); Christel Michael, *Ein Alptraum oder der Weg in die Freiheit*, 2nd edn (Frankfurt: R.G. Fischer Verlag, 1994).

[112] Grix, *Role of the Masses*, 77.

[113] Dieter Voigt *et al.*, 'Die innerdeutsche Wanderung und der Vereinigungsprozeß: Soziodemographische Struktur und Einstellungen von Flüchtlingen/Übersiedlern aus der DDR vor und nach der Grenzöffnung', *Deutschland Archiv*, 23 (1990), 734.

[114] Hilmer in Deutscher Bundestag (ed.), *Materialien der Enquete Kommission*, VII/2, 324.

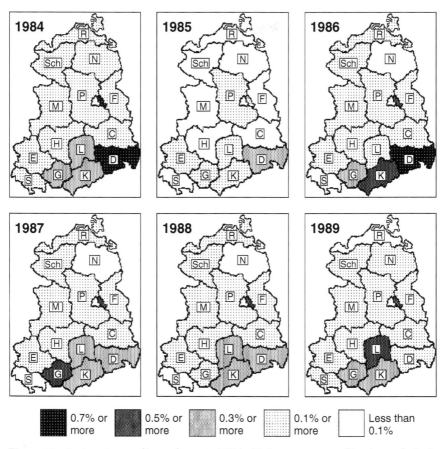

Figure 11. Emigration applicants by area, 1984–89 (as percentage of local population).
Source: SAPMO-BArch, DY30/IV2/2.039, fo. 79.

concentration of applications in the south of the GDR (Figure 11), reflecting collapsing inner-city infrastructures and worse environmental conditions, as well as the relative absence of the electronic window on the West. It was from these areas, too, that there was the greatest internal migration within the GDR.[115]

As with *Republikflucht* before the Wall, it was to be expected that the state would defend itself against emigrationism. Behind the Interior Ministry's front-of-house activities, the Stasi became the key player. To pre-empt the growing problem that emigration would pose once the GDR had signed Helsinki, in 1975 the MfS formed a special Central Coordination Group (ZKG) to combat flight and emigration, with regional offices and a complement growing

---

[115] Steven Pfaff, *Exit-Voice Dynamics and the Collapse of East Germany: The Crisis of Leninism and the Revolution of 1989* (Durham: Duke University Press, 2006), 42.

from 100 to 350 over its twenty-four-year career.[116] In the 1980s the ZKG launched more proactive, so-called 'political-operative' deportations of emigrationist troublemakers, intractables bent upon 'stubbornly achieving their emigration', as well as potential suicides.[117] Some were ground down until they went 'voluntarily', 'incorrigibles' such as Pastor Bartmuß, a former SED member turned minister, who had protested against the demolition of Leipzig's university church in 1968, and had been active in the peace movement since 1981.[118] Or Rudolf Bahro, an ex-SED member turned dissident, who had published *The Alternative* in the West in 1977, and who was jailed and then allowed to emigrate in 1979. Yet, the Stasi had to recognize that political-operative deportation created only 'momentary peace', since cross-border contacts from outside soon stirred up renewed agitation.[119]

In addition, as with almost all aspects of GDR rule, political decisions were corrupted by economic necessities. From 1963 secret negotiations had been initiated by the Federal Republic to buy out political prisoners.[120] The price per head varied with education and length of sentence, but was set at 40,000 deutschmarks in the early 1970s before being raised to 95,847 deutschmarks in 1977. In total the FRG paid out around 3.5 billion deutschmarks in this ransom trade for 34,000 prisoners, although it was soon agreed to make payments in kind via the mediation of the Protestant church. These included coffee, butter, bananas, but later crude oil and raw materials, which the SED's Commercial Coordination usually immediately resold for hard currency. The Soviets, who had their own problems with would-be Jewish emigrants and refuseniks, ominously warned that this trade was beginning to get 'out of control',[121] prompting Honecker to assume personal responsibility: 'permission to leave the GDR is given only with my signature'.[122] West German politicians, on the other hand, began to worry that by ransoming: 'We are removing so-called oppositional elements and normalizing the coercive Communist state. . . . We are sterilizing resistance to the Communists.'[123] Yet the Bonn official in charge of day-to-day policy believed that *Freikauf* 'gnawed away at the foundations' of the GDR, since the word got around that, for the very persistent, a term in prison could be the route out of the country.[124]

---

[116] Wolfgang Mayer, *Flucht und Ausreise: Botschaftsbesetzungen als Form des Widerstands gegen die politische Verfolgung in der DDR* (Berlin: Tykve, 2002), 251–60.

[117] Eisenfeld, 'Flucht und Ausreise', 406.

[118] Ehrhart Neubert, *Geschichte der Opposition in der DDR 1949–1989* (Berlin: Links, 1997), 340.

[119] Eisenfeld, 'Flucht und Ausreise', 387.

[120] Ludwig A. Rehlinger, *Freikauf: Die Geschäfte der DDR mit politisch Verfolgten 1963–1989* (Berlin: Ullstein, 1991), 9 ff.

[121] Hertle, *Fall der Mauer*, 44.

[122] Cited in Timothy Garton Ash, *In Europe's Name: Germany and the Divided Continent* (London: Jonathan Cape, 1993), 145.

[123] Erich Mende quoted in 1984 in Alan Dowty, *Closed Borders: The Contemporary Assault on Freedom of Movement* (New Haven: Yale University Press, 1987), 126.

[124] Rehlinger, *Freikauf*, 54.

In 1977 the ZKG went onto the offensive to reduce the number of first-time emigration applications. The SED reminded state officials that GDR law did not envisage the right to emigrate to non-socialist countries. Only humanitarian cases, as well as older people and those in need of care should be first in line.[125] This approach advocated more carrot and less stick, with the alleviation of grievances such as housing in order to achieve retractions. But it achieved very limited success; within two years the trend of applications was up again, not down. From 1982, therefore, there was a reversion to hard-line pressure at the grass roots, after it was discovered that workplace cadres were passing the confrontational buck. It was also recognized that the non-employment policy towards some emigrationists was only compounding the situation. The Madrid CSCE conference added new fuel to demands. Publicly, in a September 1983 decree, GDR officialdom had to accept the right to emigrate under the rubric of 'family reunions and marriage', but expected that applicants had relatives already in the West or a foreign fiancé.[126] A number of internal criteria nevertheless showed how confused policy was: case officers were to fast-track either pensioners or those with a 'negative-hostile attitude to the GDR'.[127] Yet rewarding bad behaviour only encouraged moderates to up the ante.

The year 1984 was to prove a momentous one for emigration policy. Tactics changed radically in the spring, when 21,000 alleged 'enemies, criminal elements and incorrigibles' were released in one swoop, adding up to almost 37,000 over the whole year. As Figure 10 reveals, this was by far the largest GDR exit for two decades. It was partly a decision forced on the SED by the conditions attached to two Federal billion-mark credits, after which a 'central directive' from Honecker widened the scope for application.[128] Yet, the regime was clearly hoping to lance the boil of emigration once and for all. It had the opposite effect. Although details remained secret, the number of new applications quadrupled to over 57,000. Local officials in fact exploited the regulations to relieve local pressure, thus undermining the hardliners' zero-tolerance approach. The ZKG, on the other hand, feared that mass releases would only encourage incipient embassy occupations, and other actions such as a blockade of the transit routes. The opening of the sluice gates was therefore quickly followed by a police crack-down, including arrests, obstructionism, and a media campaign to denigrate the act of leaving, launched by a newspaper article on 6 March 1985 entitled '20,000 Former Citizens Want to Come Back'.[129] Even the churches were cynically harnessed to this 'broad social front', arguing that loving one's neighbour obligated individuals to stay.[130]

---

[125] SED-ZK (Sek.), 16 Feb. 1977, in Hertle, *Fall der Mauer*, 82.

[126] Hertle, *Fall der Mauer*, 82.

[127] See MdI, 'Zusammenfassende Darstellung', July 1987, BAB, DO-1/8/41630.

[128] Hertle, *Fall der Mauer*, 78.   [129] Eisenfeld, 'Flucht und Ausreise', 391.

[130] Neubert, *Opposition*, 529.

In 1985 13,000 political-operative deportations followed, but by 1986–87 the authorities registered increased activism among groups in Arnstadt, Schwerin, and Jena. Yet the MfS was unwilling to repeat a mass deportation à la 1984, recognizing 'a causal link between large-scale emigrations and the sudden rise in first-time applications'.[131] The Interior Ministry talked of 'stubborn' individuals 'who cannot be won back and represent an immediate danger for state security',[132] and of a 'pull effect' from previously emigrated persons, fetching their relatives after them.[133] Thus, police fought to keep every citizen. Work 'mentors' were to dissuade leavers, meeting fortnightly with ZKG representatives to discuss the best ways of achieving retractions.[134] Gatekeeping had come to resemble an invasive form of social work. Emigration seekers were 'increasingly stubborn, demanding and sometimes aggressive', forming groups of up to sixty. Collective applications appeared. Some were resigning from jobs; others demoralizing the remaining work collective.[135] The authorities were desperate to achieve a 'trend change', aware that the problem was threatening to undermine national security. Instead, however, in 1988 at Honecker's bidding the authorities panicked and reverted to mass deportations and arrests. Between 30 November 1988 and 30 September 1989 86,150 of 160,785 applications for permanent emigration were granted,[136] for 'security considerations' to 'reduce the pressure on the state organs and to avoid foreign policy damage for the GDR'.[137] The MfS had to open 2,000 new investigations, including anybody spotted carrying a placard. Yet, the results were worse than 1984. Complaints reached 70,000, including 30,000 to Honecker himself. Silent marches took place in public. Fines and even confiscations of cars followed. Emigrationist groups sought contact with churches and joined in 'peace prayers'. In Dresden, for instance, on 24 April 1988, forty to fifty emigrationists congregated before the Kreuzkirche and fifteen conducted a sit-down protest.[138] A total of 2,000 MfS investigations were launched against 'provocational-demonstrational actions in public'. Moreover, 273 persons occupied embassies in 1988 and 800 in the first three months of 1989, leading to aggravation among 'legal' emigrationists. Why were embassy-occupiers getting preferential treatment? The Volkspolizei complained of 'supra-regional intensive communication':

Increasingly there are cases of association, group-formation and public appearances of applicants to force permanent exit. Signs of this include so-called silent demonstrations,

[131] Mayer, *Flucht*, 269.
[132] Dickel to Krenz, 1 June 1989, SAPMO-BArch, DY30/IV2/2.039/309, fo. 33.
[133] SED-ZK (Sicherheit), 'Information und Schlußfolgerungen', 28 Feb. 1989, SAPMO-BArch, DY30/IV2/2.039/307, fos. 51–67.
[134] Jan. 1986 directive in Eisenfeld, 'Flucht und Ausreise', 414–15.
[135] SED-ZK (Sicherheit), 'Information über die Vorbeugung und Zurückdrängung von Übersiedlungsersuchen nach der BRD und nach Berlin (West)', 7 Mar. 1988, SAPMO-BArch, DY30/IV2/2.039/308, fo. 70.
[136] Maier, *Dissolution*, 128.   [137] Hertle, *Fall der Mauer*, 139–40.
[138] MdI, 'Information vom 25.04.1988', SAPMO-BArch, DY30/IV2/2.039/308, fos. 118–19.

demonstration walks, events in churches but also before public buildings, various gatherings, joint demonstrative talks with the responsible state organs etc.[139]

Police workers were at a loss: 'The limit of self-esteem is reached when colleagues from the permit desks have to visit the "embassy-occupiers" at home in the evening in order to "quiz them on their emigration wishes" '.[140] Foreign policy issues seemed to be undermining local power structures. Officials from the state apparatus began to resign, leading the Interior Ministry in June 1989 to comment that 'control of the situation regarding the roll-back of applicants for emigration can hardly be guaranteed any more'; the 'possibilities are exhausted'.[141]

FELLOW TRAVELLERS OR OUTRIDERS OF THE MOVEMENT?

Many of these activities sound like a foretaste of 1989, a miniature dress rehearsal for non-violent revolution. Indeed, if we go back through the 1980s, emigrationists were exhibiting classic signs of organized civil disobedience. The secrecy of the whole procedure, and the state's decision in 1977 to bury its head in the sand on petitions, had only resulted in displacing resentment into public spaces. This was anathema to the SED, whose mantra was 'no publicity'. Initially, blocked applicants turned to foreign agencies. As an early example, in January 1976 65 applicants, including fifteen families, had contacted West German TV and in August a doctor from the southern town of Riesa submitted a petition on human rights, joined by twenty-six families and twelve individuals, which was forwarded to the UN and western newspapers.[142] Between 1978 and 1982 several hundred people wrote each year to the UN. Others turned to the FRG's Permanent Mission—6,000 in 1982. If this did not work, then there were threats of more publicity-seeking within the GDR, which threatened to contaminate fellow citizens. However, the authorities decided to prosecute only cases which tried blackmail, or insulted officials, or went public in some way, or demonstrated 'asocial behaviour' by refusing work or neglecting their children's education.[143] (Clearly, some of the state's counter-measures were designed to provoke this behaviour; in one case a foiled escapee had her children taken into care for six years, and after deportation had to protest for four of these at Checkpoint

[139] 'Information', SAPMO-BArch, DY30/IV2/2.039/306, fo. 278.
[140] SED-BPO Magistrat von Berlin, 'Information', 19 Jan. 1989, SAPMO-BArch, DY30/IV2/2.039/307, fo. 25.
[141] MdI, 'Information', 17 July 1989, SAPMO-BArch, DY30/IV2/2.039/309, fo. 67.
[142] Karl Wilhelm Fricke, *Politik und Justiz in der DDR: Zur Geschichte der politischen Verfolgung 1945–1968: Bericht und Dokumentation*, 2nd edn (Cologne: Verlag Wissenschaft und Politik, 1990), 406–7.
[143] Eisenfeld, 'Flucht und Ausreise', 386.

Charlie to secure their release.[144]) The most extreme option was occupation of a foreign embassy. Already five years before the mass embassy sit-ins of 1989, six emigrationists in the US embassy and twenty-five in the Federal embassy in Prague had succeeded in forcing their exit, amid huge press interest.[145]

The sheer numbers involved (well over 300,000 successful and pending applicants throughout the 1980s) meant that a certain solidarity emerged, although it would be premature to call it a movement. Applicants obviously consulted each other. It would seem that some tactics such as vigils were copied from the GDR's incipient peace movement. Local churches became more prominent in offering counselling and facilities for would-be leavers, although their official brief was still to try to reintegrate emigrationists.[146] In Dresden and Jena, around 1983, 'White Circles' were formed, gathering in central squares dressed in white shirts and blouses and silently demonstrating for emigration in linked circles.[147] 'Symbol carriers' also hung white ribbons from car aerials or stuck 'A' for *Ausreiser* on windows and balconies. Following the Jena initiative an East Berlin 'Emigration Community' was founded. In February 1987 300 Dresdeners chanted 'Erich, give us the key!'; in Jena 100 emigration seekers organized a 'walk'; and in Leipzig 300 youths picketed the Leipzig spring fair. And on the day the Vienna chapter of the CSCE was signed in January 1989 fifty-three pro-democracy activists were arrested in Leipzig, mainly emigrationists.[148] As well as joining in prayer meetings, emigrationists started forming 'CSCE working groups'. In the first half of 1989 the Interior Ministry received thirty-three applications to form such associations, such as 'Pro Humanitas' with members from Schwerin, Rostock, Halle, Leipzig, and Berlin.[149]

Crucially, the emigration movement also began to link up with the nascent civil rights movement at the Umweltbibliothek in Berlin, where a working group on 'State Civil Rights of the GDR' was formed in September 1987, which planned collecting signatures on behalf of emigration seekers. In December it issued a first declaration that the GDR was not even respecting its own laws, but was pushing emigration seekers into an 'extra-legal space'. The signatories demanded mechanisms to transform their human rights into civil rights, by a process of law, citing various clauses of the GDR constitution.[150] Yet there were already latent tensions between civil rights activists determined to create a

---

[144] Ines Veith, *Die Frau vom Checkpoint Charlie: Der verzweifelte Kampf einer Mutter um ihre Töchter* (Munich: Knaur, 2006).

[145] Mayer, *Flucht und Ausreise*, 307–36.

[146] Werner Hilse, 'Die Flucht- und Ausreiseproblematik als innenpolitischer Konfliktstoff in der DDR und innerhalb der DDR-Opposition', 391–2.

[147] Eisenfeld, 'Flucht und Ausreise', 388.

[148] Armin Mitter and Stefan Wolle (eds), *'Ich liebe euch doch alle!': Befehle und Lageberichte des MfS Januar–November 1989* (Berlin: BasisDruck, 1990), 11–16.

[149] MdI, 'Information', 17 July 1989, SAPMO-BArch, DY30/IV2/2.039/309, fo. 60.

[150] Declaration of 10 Dec. 1987, in Schwabe and Eckert (eds), *Von Deutschland Ost*, 75–7.

non-communist GDR, but still a GDR, and those using these weapons to turn their back on it. Although emigration seekers cooperated with local opposition members in Jena, or with civil rights activists such as Wolfgang Templin, elsewhere they were viewed with suspicion.[151] As the Stasi summarized: 'In the majority of the so-called church grass-roots groups there continue to be reservations towards applicants for permanent emigration and their efforts to abuse political underground activities for their egotistical goals.'[152]

The first sign of serious internal rifts came in early 1988, ironically when the two movements tried to concert their actions for the first time. On 9 January emigration seekers from eight regions thus met, and decided to join a demonstration to shadow the state's official commemorations of the assassinations of Luxemburg and Liebknecht, on 17 January. On the day itself, however, most were intercepted by the MfS and arrested or deported, including a high proportion of emigration seekers.[153] But included were dissident leaders such as folk singer Stephan Krawczyk and his wife, Freya Klier, who had no intention of leaving, leading to subsequent accusations by other oppositionists that the FRG had unwittingly colluded in stifling protest voices.[154] To make matters worse, those such as Vera Wollenberger who refused to go were imprisoned. Nevertheless, the Berlin deportations encouraged more extreme actions by like-minded emigrationists in the provinces.[155] In the wake of the incident, Krenz reported to Honecker that the mood of applicants was 'extremely aggressive' and that more demonstrations were planned for 1 May. Slogans included 'We won't shake hands with this state; we shall fight for permission to emigrate; any means are just' and 'after the events of 17 January 1988 in Berlin we know how to force our emigration'.[156] Accordingly, on a pre-arranged day in February, 1,344 applicants appeared at local council offices demanding their right to leave. The previous liberalizations of emigration had not led to a reduction. 'On the contrary', as the SED's Security section observed, 'they have repercussions on other citizens and are leading to new applications'.[157]

The organizers of the demonstration at the Umweltbibliothek nevertheless accused the emigrants of 'dividing our movement, usurping and destroying

[151] Neubert, *Opposition*, 530–1.

[152] 1 June 1989 report in Mitter and Wolle (eds), *'Ich liebe euch'*, 46–71; 62. Of course, the secret police themselves had an interest in fragmenting these groups, and no doubt their informal associates planted within the opposition were encouraging these divisions.

[153] Overall sixty-six were arrested, while thirty-seven were released 'after a stern talking-to': Walter Süß, 'Die Stimmungslage der Bevölkerung im Spiegel von MfS-Berichten', in Eberhard Kuhrt (ed.), *Die SED-Herrschaft und ihr Zusammenbruch* (Opladen: Leske & Budrich, 1996), 241–2.

[154] Garton Ash, *In Europe's Name*, 196.   [155] Grix, *Role of the Masses*, 80–1.

[156] SED-ZK (Sicherheit), 'Information über die Vorbeugung und Zurückdrängung von Übersiedlungsersuchen nach der BRD und nach Berlin (West)', 7 Mar. 1988, SAPMO-BArch, DY30/IV2/2.039/308, fos. 70–1.

[157] SED-ZK (Sicherheit), 'Information', 14 Apr. 1988, SAPMO-BArch, DY30/IV2/2.039/308, fo. 104.

the peace movement's structures'.[158] This line has found its way into the historiography of the protest movements and one might be forgiven for thinking that the old battles between exit and voice continue, especially since many of those involved at the time have been the first to write their own histories.[159] (Ultimately, the debate revolves around whether one believes the GDR was ever reformable or simply doomed. It is further clouded by accusations that differences between the two groupings were consciously exploited by the Stasi for its own ends.) One compendious study of GDR opposition only assigned a few brief pages to emigrationists.[160] Others have denied that leaving can be considered oppositional behaviour at all, expressing instead egotistical motives.[161] For some, *Ausreiser* (emigrants) were instead *Ausreißer* (tearaways), kicking over the traces but not exhibiting ethical behaviour. Garton Ash has been more charitable, arguing that the two tendencies 'were not merely complementary' but 'opposite answers to the same challenge': 'Although would-be emigrants often became oppositionists while they remained, and would-be oppositionists very often ended up as emigrants, it was only in the autumn of 1989 that the two movements really came together as one.'[162]

Hirschman, of course, would argue that exit was a priori a form of contrarian action. And as his revision of his theory in the 1990s conceded, exit and voice could function in tandem. Other recent historians have also suggested that in purely functional terms the emigrationists should be considered a legitimate part of the forces which ushered in the GDR's final crisis in 1989. Christian Joppke has even suggested that emigrationists were the only real opposition, since they wished to end SED dictatorship, once and for all, whereas the reform movement clung to the hope that a truly socialist GDR could be saved.[163] This is perhaps an exaggerated position, but reflects the general shift towards a re-evaluation of emigrationism. Church representatives administering pastoral care to would-be leavers later reported to the Bundestag's parliamentary enquiry that their charges had been rather badly done-by by the dissident movement, who owed them more than they would care to admit.[164] Bernd Eisenfeld, himself an *Ausreiser*, has championed emigrationists' 'rehabilitation' within the movement by showing how seriously the Stasi took the problem. Up to 1989, emigrationists were

[158] Wolfgang Rüddenklau, *Störenfried: DDR-Opposition 1986–1989* (Berlin: BasisDruck, 1992), 235–6.
[159] Christof Geisel, *Auf der Suche nach einem dritten Weg: Das politische Selbstverständnis der DDR-Opposition in den 80er Jahren* (Berlin: Links, 2005), 129–39.
[160] Neubert, *Opposition*.
[161] Johannes Raschka, 'Die Ausreisebewegung—eine Form von Widerstand gegen das SED-Regime[?]', in Ulrich Baumann and Helmut Kury (eds), *Politisch motivierte Verfolgung: Opfer von SED-Unrecht* (Freiburg: iuscrim, 1998), 257–74.
[162] Garton Ash, *In Europe's Name*, 202.
[163] Christian Joppke, *East German Dissidents and the Revolution of 1989: Social Movement in a Leninist Regime* (Houndmills: Palgrave, 1994), 205.
[164] Hilse, 'Flucht- und Ausreisebewegung', 394.

simply treated by the MfS as the 'human rights' faction of the various subversive groups within the GDR.[165] Individual case histories of 'incorrigibles' such as Roland Jahn demonstrate, moreover, that not every emigrant who went willingly or unwillingly was prepared to keep quiet in the West. Jahn became a tireless campaigner for the rights of others to leave, even setting up his own radio station for fellow leavers, and it would be churlish to deny him a place alongside other, better-known activists. Balanced against this, however, is the undeniable fact that such cases were the exception rather than the norm. Leavers tended not to hold the ladder at the top for those still trying to get a foot on the bottom rung, and contacts between former emigration seekers tended to evaporate quickly in exile.

I would suggest, however, that we cannot always neatly divide oppositionists from emigrationists. Often, these were the same people at different stages of their falling out with the GDR. In some cases, such as Jahn's, dissidents were forced into becoming émigrés. In 1983 Jahn, who had publicly supported Solidarity's reform moves in Poland, was forced to make an emigration application, which he then retracted, only to be forcibly deported in handcuffs.[166] It thus makes little sense to say that Jahn 'betrayed' the movement. It is naturally understandable that those left behind suffered enormous pangs of self-doubt when fellow fighters abandoned the cause. As one dissident recalled after her best friend had announced that she was making an application: 'That was a slap in the face for me. . . . You didn't want to be the last one. You didn't want to have to shut up shop.'[167] It required an enormous sense of purpose and endurance to continue the reform struggle while familiar faces disappeared. Yet other emigrants had also done their stint in the opposition. Likewise, the protracted nature of emigration procedures meant that emigrationists could spend years in this limbo and became dissidents by default. Since they were often beyond caring what happened to them after prolonged stigmatization, they were also prepared to undertake higher-risk tactics and could 'spearhead' broader initiatives. As the next chapter on the crisis year of 1989 will also make clear, based on studies which have attempted to plot exit against voice to explain the regional specificities of the great change, it would require both strands of non-conformist behaviour to create the tipping-point which would cause the regime to crack. Each on its own was not enough.

The same degree of even limited opposition cannot perhaps be said of the 'compassionate leavers', at least at the time of their applications to leave the GDR. Their only way forward, short of committing *Republikflucht*, was to play the system. Yet the experience of visiting the West usually raised material hopes

---

[165] MfS-ZAIG report, 1 June 1989 in Mitter and Wolle (eds), '*Ich liebe euch*', 46–72; 62–3.
[166] Schwabe and Eckert (eds), *Von Deutschland Ost*, 110–11.
[167] Annabelle Lutz, *Dissidenten und Bürgerbewegung: Ein Vergleich zwischen DDR und Tschechoslowakei* (Frankfurt: Campus, 1999), 133–4.

among returnees and raised the bar of expectations. <u>The relative economic decline of the GDR in the 1980s became all the starker when travellers could make direct comparisons</u>. Furthermore, those who decided to emigrate once and for all must surely have had their hopes raised by the liberalization of compassionate leave. It is no coincidence that travel and emigration grew by the same leaps and bounds in the 1980s. As will become clearer in the following chapter, by 1989 there was a <u>tangible sense of growing privation</u>, not enough to topple a dictatorship, but enough to create a general sympathy among 'bystanders' for those who were prepared to risk their life and liberty during the demonstrations. We must be able to explain why these swelled so considerably in the final weeks before the fall of the Wall. Yet, the very process of <u>applying and petitioning for travel, and doubly so for emigrationists, was a politicizing experience</u>, as *Wanderlust* turned into *Wanderfrust* or travel frustration. East Germans became <u>aware of their human rights</u> in a way which had not been possible in the 1950s. As the files of the Interior Ministry and its legal section show, the GDR came under increasing pressure in the 1980s, through its involvement in <u>international agencies such as the UN, to show that it was reforming itself</u>.[168] The <u>western electronic media</u> ensured that East Germans were aware of these changes, despite all attempts by the authorities to suppress this news. As we have seen, by 1988 the sheer volume of people making use of what few rights had been conceded, threatened to <u>overload the system</u>. Tucholsky's dictum about the ideal position of the bureaucrat–gatekeeper, ensconced behind her counter, was turned on its head: desk duty became a nightmare. Significant numbers of regime carriers were performing their own acts of private exit from the apparatus by the final months. This should give heart to any human rights organization that it is possible to apply serious pressure on an authoritarian regime from the outside.

divided society

This chapter has also demonstrated that, just as Intershops created a divided society which resented the privileging of the few who could bring a taste of the West to themselves, so travel west created a two-tier society which contributed greatly to undermining the SED's egalitarian claims. Travel had become one of the most prized assets in the GDR's economy of favours, but it was a rationed item. Despite the SED's averrals that it was creating a homogeneous, classless society,[169] in the 1980s it was showing signs of fragmentation.[170] The very arbitrariness of eligibility, having 'grade-one or -two' relatives, made a mockery of this egalitarian claim. The issue of travel, like no other, showed that the SED's ideological project had come unstuck. Whereas with housing or other domestic problems, there was a <u>rational hope that personal conformity</u> could

---

[168] See for instance MdI attempts to grapple with accusations of human rights abuses: BAB, DO-1/11330–36.

[169] Sigrid Meuschel, *Legitimation und Parteiherrschaft: Zum Paradox von Stabilität und Revolution in der DDR 1945–1989* (Frankfurt am Main: Suhrkamp, 1992), 306–16.

[170] Madarász, *Conflict*, 186–95.

influence the outcome, the existence or not of western relatives created a society of haves and have-nots. Indeed, it was those most loyal to the regime who tended to be excluded from these privileges. This may partly explain the volatility of the middle-ranking SED members in the crucial months ahead, who could be forgiven for seeing themselves as hostages to socialism.

PART III

BEYOND THE WALL

8

The Fall of the Wall: 9 November 1989

Something there is that doesn't love a wall,
That wants it down.

Robert Frost, 'Mending Wall' (1915)

1989 was to witness the collapse of communism across eastern Europe. Scenes of revellers from East and West Berlin dancing atop the Berlin Wall have remained lodged in memories as the moment the Cold War ended. The 'fall of the Wall' became a metaphor for the end of an era, although it was not until August 1991 that the Soviet Union imploded, taking with it the architect of reform, Mikhail Gorbachev. Nevertheless, the fall of the Wall was a symptom as well as a cause of other changes. Radical challenges to orthodox communism had already been under way for years in Poland and Hungary, where, in the latter instance, citizens had been granted freedom of travel in 1988. The GDR, on the other hand, had always been viewed as the most loyal eastern bloc regime. The Wall's collapse therefore signalled to neighbouring regimes that anything was possible. The contagion of November 1989 soon spread to Czechoslovakia, Bulgaria, and Romania, as regime after regime toppled in the face of popular protest.

The events of 1989 were certainly complex, a concatenation of disparate factors which 'gelled' at a critical juncture to form a terminal crisis.[1] Debates have revolved around the extent to which the East German regime imploded from above, or whether it was effectively challenged from below, or abandoned by its Soviet big brother.[2] Clearly, the fact that not only the GDR, but every eastern European communist state succumbed within months of each other, indicates that they were all facing similar, structural problems. With hindsight it is clear that they were all getting into deep economic difficulties. It was these failings which prompted the new Soviet leader in 1985, Gorbachev, to opt out of the arms race and attempt to reform communism. Again, the Soviet Union's hands-off policy was something which affected every satellite state. The uniqueness of the

---

[1] Detlef Pollack, 'Der Zusammenbruch der DDR als Verkettung getrennter Handlungslinien', in Konrad Jarausch and Martin Sabrow (eds), *Weg in den Untergang: Der innere Zerfall der DDR* (Göttingen: Vandenhoeck & Ruprecht, 1999), 41–81.

[2] Corey Ross, *The East German Dictatorship: Problems and Perspectives in the Interpretation of the GDR* (London: Arnold, 2002), 127.

GDR's situation, however, was its western aspect. The border to the West was to be crucial in determining the course of the demonstrations within the country, but also undermined the efforts of the non-communist opposition once the SED monopoly had been broken.

Honecker

THE CRISIS OF COMMUNISM

When Honecker had come to power in 1971, he had rested his authority on a welfarist 'unity of social and economic policy', promising 3 million new apartments by 1990.[3] Basic services and goods were heavily state subsidized. Bread cost a nominal sum; public transport just 20 pfennigs, the same as in 1945. Yet, to cover these subventions, by 1989 the GDR had run up a western hard-currency debt of 49 billion marks. Debt service amounted to 60 per cent of annual export earnings.[4] By 1980, the GDR would have faced a balance of payments crisis, had western banks decided to foreclose. Increasingly, the GDR was taking goods on credit, only to re-sell them abroad for hard currency to service debts. Many goods originally destined for the home market were also finding their way abroad, much to the ire of ordinary East Germans. Honecker ignored the State Planning Commission's warnings.[5] Raising prices was always ruled out for political reasons. When *Neues Deutschland* broached the issue in February 1989, for instance, 200 readers' letters of complaint reaffirmed the party's belief in the sacred cow of a low cost of living.[6] Instead of fiscal reform, the Ministry of Foreign Trade's Commercial Coordination section (KoKo), under the shadowy Alexander Schalck-Golodkowski, engaged in currency speculation. Only in 1983 was the pressure somewhat relieved, again from the West, by the first of two billion deutschmark credits from Federal Finance Minister, Franz Josef Strauß. In return, the Wall was made porous (see above) and the GDR agreed not to 'overreact' to intermediate nuclear missiles stationed in the FRG. The East Germans also extracted further loans as maintenance subsidies for the East–West transit routes running through the GDR. Thus, in May 1988 Schalck justified to his western interlocutors a requested raise of these costs from 525 to 890 million deutschmark by the increasing volume of travellers to the West requiring hard currency.[7] The political cost of these subventions was, however, more western leverage over human rights issues.

The GDR also faced an energy crisis. Sheltered from the oil crises of the 1970s by Comecon imports, by 1982 East Germany faced shrinking deliveries of Soviet oil and Polish coal. A massive switchover to lignite, or brown coal, resulted. Yet the state's lignite reserves, the source of the briquettes which heated East

---

[3] Steiner, *Plan*, 165–78.   [4] Maier, *Dissolution*, 59–60.   [5] Steiner, *Plan*, 193.
[6] 'Analyse der Leserbriefe zum Artikel . . . ', SAPMO-BArch, DY30/IV2/2.039/268, fos. 57–70.
[7] Hertle, *Fall der Mauer*, 53–4 and 79–80.

Germany's ubiquitous tile stoves, were themselves running low. There was also a hidden environmental crisis looming as a result of the noxious emissions and river pollution created by heavy industry. Particularly near the chemical centres of Halle and Leipzig's open-cast mines, the air was thick with particles and sulphur dioxide. After world oil prices halved in 1986, a new crisis erupted when the USSR refused to increase pre-paid crude oil exports to the GDR. Since the GDR relied on re-exported refined oil for about 30 per cent of its hard currency, this was a double blow. Despite an austerity programme, Honecker still refused to make inroads into the consumer sector. The economy's infrastructure also began to creak ominously, much of it dating back to the First World War.

There were few ways out. The Planning Commission championed high tech, gambling on the GDR becoming a major player in the computer-assisted manufacture of machine-tools. Not only might this generate hard currency from western exports, it would dominate the eastern-bloc market. By 1988, however, micro-electronics had swallowed 14 billion marks in investment and another 14 billion in research and development.[8] Moreover, by 1989 the GDR could manage only 90,000 256-kilobyte chips, lagging far behind *Weltniveau* in quantity, quality, and price.[9] Capital investment also came at the expense of the welfare programme, including ostentatious building projects surrounding the 750th anniversary of Berlin. By 1987–88 the Politbüro and Council of Ministers were becoming deadlocked over whether to grasp the nettle of austerity measures, which would, of course, necessitate price rises and make the malaise public. In April 1988 planning chief Gerhard Schürer even went over the Politbüro to warn Honecker: 'Our Republic is going bust.'[10] Western exports would have to increase more than threefold to cover the rising debt. The leadership declined to take up the challenge, however, accusing the planners of deviating from the party's long-term political strategy.

What was an open economic secret, however, was the failing consumer sector. Relatively high wages and savings meant pent-up purchasing power. High-end goods such as hi-fis, video-recorders, and sports equipment were in great demand, but short supply, or were vastly overpriced relative to western products. Yet by 1987 the MfS reported that shortages of even basic food products, such as pasta and packet soups, were encouraging 'openly expressed doubts about the objectivity and credibility of the balance sheets and economic results periodically published by the mass media of the GDR'.[11] Rumours spread of price rises, especially for shoes, reaching 'provocational' proportions in some districts.[12] In late 1988, the mood was no better.[13] By summer 1989 citizens were becoming

[8] Steiner, 'Zwischen Konsumversprechen', 171.   [9] Maier, *Dissolution*, 75.
[10] Hertle, *Fall der Mauer*, 69.
[11] Krenz to Honecker, 9 Nov. 1987, SAPMO-BArch, DY30/IV2/2.039/268, fos. 5–8.
[12] 'Information des Zentralvorstandes HNG', 11 Apr. 1988, SAPMO-BArch, DY30/IV2/2.039/268, fos. 25–7.
[13] Süß, 'Stimmungslage', 242.

Table 1:   Petitions to the Council of
State, January– 10 October 1989 (excerpts)

Housing allocation	25,890	31%
Building repairs	6,105	7%
Telephone connections	4,070	5%
Trade and retail	5,374	7%
(cars	2,865	4%
(car spares	1,393	2%
Environmental problems	621	1%
Travel	10,902	13%
Emigration	6,390	8%
Total	82,707	

Source: SAPMO-BArch, DY30/IV2/2.039/347, fo. 8

'increasingly critical' of the central and regional economic apparatus, 'demanding changes'. Collective petitions were also emerging. The state's forthcoming fortieth anniversary celebrations became a negative yardstick of failure, including even direct criticisms of socialism itself or its gerontocratic leadership. Visitors to West Germany and West Berlin were passing disparaging comments on the GDR compared with consumer capitalism. 'Goods which years ago belonged to the normal supply are now available only via "good connections", in Delikat shops or by swapping so-called shortage goods', forcing long tramps around the shops. Trade functionaries exhibited 'signs of tiredness' and resignation. Cars were a particular sore point: 'waiting lists for a new purchase of up to 18 years are described as completely unacceptable'.[14] An overview of the everyday economic grievances in the final months of SED control is reflected in the petitions to the Council of State, given in Table 1, which go some way to explaining why the hitherto quiescent GDR population at large provided an audience for the reformers.

Yet, it required some catalyst to change grumbling into an appetite for radical change. The Gorbachev factor has rightly been seen as crucial in the power equation across the eastern bloc, but especially in the GDR, where the bulk of the USSR's European forces were stationed. In 1953 it was Russian tanks which had restored order after the rioting, while the SED Politbüro cowered in the Soviet headquarters; in 1961, it was the Soviet 'third echelon' which had provided the cover for the East Germans to build their wall. When Honecker had replaced Ulbricht in 1971, it had been with the express support of Brezhnev, and Moscow and East Berlin's interests appeared to be in concert.[15] Nevertheless, the ageing Kremlin leader had become increasingly suspicious of the GDR's overtures

[14] Mielke to Krenz, 12 June 1989, SAPMO-BArch, DY30/IV2/2.039/268, fos. 71–83. See also SED-ZK (PO), 'Information über Diskussionen unter der Bevölkerung zu Versorgungsfragen', 28 July 1989, SAPMO-BArch, DY30/IV2/2.039/268, fos. 91–8.
[15] Grieder, *East German Leadership*, 183–7.

Brezhnev Suspicious

towards the FRG under the auspices of *Ostpolitik* and the modernization of its economy. Nor were his successors much more supportive. Various decisions, such as the dismantling of fragmentation devices along the border fence in 1983, or Honecker's visit to Bonn in 1987, were not taken with prior consultation with Moscow, much to the Kremlin's irritation.[16]

Mikhail Gorbachev's leadership of the CPSU, beginning in March 1985, signalled fundamental changes to the special relationship. For his common 'European house', Gorbachev was keen to foster relations with West Germany, even at the GDR's expense, despite all protestations to the contrary. The Soviet General Secretary made Delphic allusions to 'history' solving the German question. Moreover, the Kremlin leader had realized that the arms race could not continue. As protection for his domestic reforms, he was seeking to decrease defence spending, signing agreements in 1987 to reduce intermediate nuclear forces. The GDR's National People's Army was also drawn into planned conventional force cuts. The so-called 'Brezhnev doctrine', giving the Soviet Union the right to intervene in eastern bloc states to preserve socialism, most vividly demonstrated in the crushing of the Prague Spring in August 1968, but tacitly shelved during the Polish crisis of 1980–81, was formally renounced in favour of the 'Sinatra doctrine'.[17] From now on, each socialist state could do it 'its way'. In November 1986 Gorbachev told fellow communist leaders that they must rely on their own legitimacy rather than Soviet intervention,[18] and in July 1988 added: 'Every party is responsible for its own affairs. . . . No attempts can be tolerated not to respect one another or to interfere in the internal affairs of others.'[19] The SED delegation was literally speechless. Moreover, Soviet foreign policy advisers began to think the unthinkable, such as Vyacheslav Dashichev, who publicly spoke of the Berlin Wall as a 'relic of the Cold War',[20] although in January 1989, Honecker notoriously reiterated his faith that the Wall would still stand in '50 or 100 years time'.[21]

Yet, it was domestic reforms—the openness policy of *glasnost* and the restructuring of *perestroika*—which caused equal alarm among the SED leadership. Drafting his speech for the fraternal CPSU Plenary of January 1987, Krenz, Honecker's designated 'crown prince', consciously omitted Gorbachevian phrases, fearing 'misinterpretation of real internal processes in the Soviet Union, but also in the GDR, if they are schematically applied to the conditions in our land'. Since *perestroika* pertained only to developing socialism, the GDR, as a 'developed socialist society', saw itself as exempt. Krenz casuistically rejected the

---

[16] Taylor, *Berlin Wall*, 392–3.

[17] Jeffrey Gedmin, *The Hidden Hand: Gorbachev and the Collapse of East Germany* (Washington, DC: AEI Press, 1992), 19.

[18] Wilfried Loth, 'Die Sowjetunion und das Ende der DDR', in Jarausch and Sabrow (eds.), *Weg*, 124.

[19] Hertle, *Fall der Mauer*, 264.   [20] Gedmin, *Hidden Hand*, 50.

[21] Taylor, *Berlin Wall*, 400.

notion of 'new thinking' for implying a 'community of *guilt* for the explosive international situation'. It was instead chiefly applicable to the imperialist West. Since the party penetrated all levels of society, so it was reasoned, there was an acceptable degree of openness already. In summary, the SED would stick to the 'unity of economic and social policy'.[22] In April the SED's ideological secretary, Kurt Hager, was more dismissive still, making his notorious understatement in an interview with a West German magazine that: 'Just because your neighbour repapers his flat, would you feel obliged to put up new wallpaper in yours too?'[23] In 1988 the GDR even began to distance itself from the USSR. Jokes circulated that a second wall would have to be built, this time to the East. One Politbüro member later complained that 'before we were dealing with a head-on, frontal assault from Germans, but now it is coming every which way from the rear'.[24] In talks with the Soviet leadership Honecker confided his misgivings about the transformation under way in the Soviet Union, which would take time to digest in the GDR.[25] In April articles appeared in *Neues Deutschland* criticizing the attacks on Stalinism in the Soviet Union, and in November the Soviet news digest, *Sputnik*, with the theme 'Stalin and the War', was banned in the GDR. It had unforgivably suggested that the Weimar KPD had been partly responsible for the rise of Hitler.

There was much speculation at the time about whether a German Gorbachev was secretly waiting in the wings of the SED. In February 1989 Schürer had confided to Krenz that he was prepared to act as stalking horse against the SED leader, although the latter was not yet prepared to betray his mentor.[26] For the time being, the SED politbureaucracy kept its collective head down and waited for a 'biological solution'. Besides the later Politbüro challengers to Honecker who eventually toppled him, including Krenz and Schabowski, there were regional leaders such as Hans Modrow in Dresden and Kurt Meyer, Jochen Pommert, and Roland Wetzel in Leipzig. Another group of more intellectually motivated critics included Michael Brie, Rainer Land, Dieter Segert, and Bernd Okun, who wished to see a programmatic renewal. Rolf Henrich, a renegade functionary, also caused a stir with his publication in the FRG in 1989 of *The Guardian State*, attacking bureaucracy and advocating limited free enterprise. Less visible was the former head of overseas intelligence, Markus Wolf, who had broken with the MfS in 1987 and was quietly supporting Moscow-style reform communism.[27] In January 1989 he reportedly warned Honecker: 'If things go on like this, there will be an explosion.'[28] Common to all of these groups, however, was an enduring belief that only the SED was in a position to reform the GDR.

---

[22] 'Januarplenum 1987', SAPMO-BArch, DY30/IV2/2.039/282, fos. 1–82.
[23] Kurt Hager, *Erinnerungen* (Leipzig: Faber, 1996), 385.
[24] Harry Tisch at SED-PB, 29 Aug. 1989 in Stephan (ed.), *'Vorwärts immer'*, 102.
[25] Küchenmeister (ed.), *Honecker-Gorbatschow*, 186–7.   [26] Maier, *Dissolution*, 123.
[27] Markus Wolf, *Spionagechef im geheimen Krieg: Erinnerungen* (Munich: List, 1997), 423–55.
[28] Gedmin, *Hidden Hand*, 84.

Among the intermediate party hierarchy, however, there was clearly disorientation. Thus, when Party Information chief Horst Dohlus convened the regional second secretaries in July 1988, he found them using grass-roots opinion to make indirect criticisms of the regime. It was the classic means/ends dilemma of the GDR:

In the discussion it was emphasized that the working people show high recognition of the successful development of the GDR, its good balance, the growing international esteem of our Republic, as well as its active contribution to the worldwide peace struggle. At the same time this positive development is not infrequently contrasted with shortcomings in the leadership and organization of the factories, supply, especially of spare parts, in the service sector and other local politics problems.[29]

Dohlus reported that party veterans, members of the intelligentsia and young people were especially receptive to new ideas from the East, such as strategic arms reductions.[30] No reform suggestions were relayed to Honecker of applying *perestroika* to the GDR, however. Instead, the Party Information dutifully reported that such solutions were deemed 'neither necessary nor acceptable'. The GDR should be permitted to go its own way and leave Gorbachev to 'control the spirits he had summoned up'.[31] From the perspective of the GDR's political middle management, this made sense. Many had been in-post for decades and had become conservatives by default.

There was also confusion at the mixed signals coming from the Soviet press. 'Who can find their way here?', lamented one Erfurt cadre secretary.[32] When *Sputnik* was banned in November 1988, however, there were unheard of reactions among the party rank and file. The deputy culture minister, Klaus Höpcke, had already criticized the decision.[33] The SED branch at the DEFA film studio issued a declaration registering 'indignation', berating the party for going on the ideological defensive. The ban was 'not acceptable' and would only foster the western media. Discussions revealed a 'devastating' sense of cynicism and of feeling 'gagged'. As one member complained: 'I have been in the party a long time and cannot remember a time when I was so helpless and clueless . . . I am constantly walking onto the non-affiliated members' sword.'[34] Others used

[29] Dohlus to Honecker, 4 July 1988, SAPMO-BArch, DY30/2181, fos. 91–6. Underlining by Honecker.
[30] SED-ZK (PO), 'Information über das Echo unter der Bevölkerung der DDR auf die Vorschläge der UdSSR zur Verminderung der militärischen Konfrontation', 14 July 1988, SAPMO-BArch, DY30/IV2/2.039/330, fos. 38–41.
[31] SED-ZK (PO), 'Information über Meinungen von Bürgern der DDR zum Verlauf und den Ergebnissen der XIX. Parteikonferenz der KPdSU', 5 July 1988, SAPMO-BArch, DY30/IV2/2.039/282, fos. 151–4.
[32] SED-ZK (PO), 'Information über Stimmen und Meinungen in der letzten Zeit im "Neuen Deutschland" veröffentlichten Artikeln aus der sowjetischen Presse', 12 Apr. 1988, SAPMO-BArch, DY30/2181, fos. 53–61.
[33] Gedmin, *Hidden Hand*, 80.
[34] Dohlus to Honecker, 25 Nov. 1988, SAPMO-BArch, DY30/2181, fos. 109–17.

Gorbachev to critique circumstances closer to home, such as the singer Arno Schmidt, on stage in Potsdam in February 1989:

Yes, I am stupid enough to believe that what I read in the paper about New Thinking and Openness is honest. Yes, I am gullible enough to think it possible that a society can purify itself from within and regain its moral health. Yes, I am superficial enough to think *glasnost* is not just something fed to us by the western media, but a rallying cry to make us more courageous, honest and committed. Yes, I am naive enough to hope that honest admission of mistakes and omissions can only make us stronger, in every regard. Yes, I am utopian enough to believe in bottom-up change.[35]

With these 'waverings' in mind, the party announced in the summer a review of the party membership, in an attempt to weed out unsound comrades.[36] As I have argued in Chapter 2, rank-and-file SED members were GDR citizens with a foot in both camps, in state and society. Their behaviour in the gentle revolution of 1989 would be crucial. Would they stick with the party hierarchy, which seemed in no mood for change, or would they join forces with reformers or even groups outside the party? Throughout the 1980s party reformers and civil rights campaigners had inhabited parallel, but 'alien worlds', as one oral history has put it.[37] The invisible boundaries between orthodoxy and 'state enmity' were difficult to transgress for those brought up within the system. For the party, besides organized rallies and indoctrination classes, there were signs of an alternative public sphere, in the FDJ singing movement or in unpublished, 'desk-drawer' manuscripts. Artists and intellectuals proved useful border-crossers between the two communities, including Christa Wolf, Stefan Heym, and Christoph Hein. At the top, however, the SED politbureaucracy lived in seclusion at its compound in Wandlitz. The reformers were even too timid to take advantage of Honecker's gall-bladder operation in August, hamstrung by the need to avoid damaging publicity in the run-up to the country's fortieth anniversary celebrations. On the day itself, the Kremlin leader refrained from direct criticism, but made it clear to the Politbüro by his body language that the time had come for change.[38]

By the spring of 1989, however, SED leaders were looking anxiously over their shoulders at developments elsewhere in the eastern bloc. In March the newly elected Soviet Congress of People's Deputies included reformers calling for a multi-party system and a mixed economy. The Baltic parliaments voted for autonomy and nationalist revolts broke out in the Caucasus and Central Asia. Moreover, in June an electoral pact in Poland led to a humiliating defeat

---

[35] SED-ZK (Abt. PO), 'Information', 21 Feb. 1989, SAPMO-BArch, DY30/2182, fos. 55–6.

[36] Gedmin, *Hidden Hand*, 81.

[37] Rainer Land and Ralf Possekel, *Fremde Welten: Die gegensätzliche Deutung der DDR durch SED-Reformer und Bürgerbewegung in den 80er Jahren* (Berlin: Links, 1998).

[38] Günter Schabowski, *Das Politbüro: Ende eines Mythos: Eine Befragung* (Berlin: Rowohlt, 1990), 74–5.

for General Jaruzelski's communists. In July elections in Hungary brought a victory for opposition candidates, after the symbolic reburial of Imre Nagy, the leader of the failed uprising of 1956. By August Poland had a Solidarity prime minister, Tadeusz Mazowiecki![39] At the same time, student demonstrators for democracy in China were brutally crushed in Tiananmen Square in Beijing. There was therefore plenty of evidence for hardliners in the East German system of the perils of reform. Yet, one should in no sense view the outcome of 1989 as Gorbachev's intention. He had set out to reform communism, not to destroy it. Even up to February 1990 the Soviet leader would attempt to block reunification with West Germany, warning the western allies against interference. It would require something else beyond a faltering revolution from above; instead, it would take a movement from below to make the 'refolution' of 1989.[40]

HIERBLEIBER: THE GROWTH OF THE CITIZENS' MOVEMENT

What began to emerge in the 1980s was a form of civil consciousness in the GDR, primitive and often improvised, but nevertheless growing. Whereas previously grievances had been articulated individually, increasingly groups of citizens came together to protest in what the Stasi called 'combinations' (*Zusammenschlüsse*), wishing to improve the GDR rather than just leave it. These came to be known as the *Hierbleiber* or 'Here-Stayers', in contradistinction to the emigrationists described above. This growth of a nascent civil society alarmed authorities used to keeping citizens in a clientelistic dependency on the state. Moreover, it was far less easy to gain a purchase on idealists of either socialist or Christian extraction, who espoused a peculiarly Marxist–Lutheran brand of self-denial. From 1988 GDR dissidents were increasingly emulating their counterparts in neighbouring eastern bloc states. East Germany was in fact by no means a pacemaker of change, but more often lagged behind, copying outside initiatives, such as the round-table talks in Poland between the government and Solidarity. Moreover, East German oppositionists themselves found it difficult to envisage a reform process without the state. This ran counter to eastern European definitions of civil society as a form of social organization outwith the state.[41] Václav Havel's advice to contrarians was to renounce evasion strategies and confront the lie of state socialism, and instead 'live in truth'.[42]

[39] Gale Stokes, *The Walls Came Tumbling Down: The Collapse of Communism in Eastern Europe* (New York and Oxford: Oxford University Press, 1993), 129–30.

[40] Timothy Garton Ash, *We the People: The Revolution of '89 witnessed in Warsaw, Budapest, Berlin and Prague* (London: Granta, 1990), 19.

[41] Karsten Timmer, *Vom Aufbruch zum Umbruch: Die Bürgerbewegung in der DDR 1989* (Göttingen: Vandenhoeck & Ruprecht, 2000), 63–78.

[42] Havel, *Living in Truth*.

Even prominent later dissident leaders in the GDR started off by trying sanctioned dissent, such as the petition. On 3 April 1986, for instance, twenty-one people, headed by Bärbel Bohley and Monika Haeger, hand-delivered a collective petition to the SED Central Committee. It was targeted at an internal party audience, to be discussed at the forthcoming SED convention: 'Intensified official contacts at party and government level with the outside do not, however, mean world openness. This pseudo-opening is often linked with increased inward pressure.' The petitioners complained that there was not even a party public sphere, while the general population's existence was dominated by other questions. Environmental pollution was not being addressed. Echoing Havel's criticisms, a 'silent consumer contract' was allegedly there to 'keep the population quiet and politically gagged'. Bohley and Haeger criticized the GDR's 'trivial culture and substitute art': 'Classical kitsch and neo-kitsch are both blocking critical consciousness and providing a safety-valve.' Despite claims to be peace-loving, East German society was becoming increasingly militarized. Faced with state sanctions people either 'lose the courage to engage in societal processes. They flee into the private sphere. They leave the GDR, or they identify so strongly with the problems in our land that they accept criminalization or arrest.' The letter closed with a call for a 'constructive dialogue'.[43] At this stage, therefore, leaving the GDR was simply subsumed into the range of dissident options available and reform was not envisaged without the party.

Several other factors broadened the constituency of concerned citizens. From the late 1970s the stationing of intermediate nuclear forces in Europe had led to an unauthorized 'Swords into Ploughshares' anti-nuclear movement. The Chernobyl nuclear reactor disaster of 1986 was a further impetus, as were Soviet firing ranges, littering the landscape with munitions. Projects such as the silicon works at Dresden-Gittersee, necessary for the microelectronics programme, caused local concern. Groups such as the Church Environment Group in Schmalkalden sought to 'codetermine our socialist state and critically collaborate. We regard the state agencies as our partner, with whom we are seeking a dialogue.' Among the basic necessities of life were clean air, food, and water, according to Brecht's dictum: 'Take care that, upon leaving the world, you were not only good, but leave a better world behind.'[44] Such intercessions stressed long-term community interests, representing Hirschman's category of loyalty. Yet the local SED was often at a loss how to handle them, wishing both to co-opt and coerce. In one case two new voices, never in trouble before, had a 'frank' discussion with the Rostock party, after sending an open letter protesting at the Tiananmen Square massacre, at which Chinese student reformers had

---

[43] In SAPMO-BArch, DY30/IV2/2.039/312, fos. 3–18.
[44] SED-ZK (PO), 'Information der Bezirksleitung Suhl über ein besonderes Vorkommnis', 23 Mar. 1989, SAPMO-BArch, DY30/IV2/2.039/330, fos. 1–4.

been brutally repressed in June 1989. They argued 'very emotionally'; 'both are critical, verging on oppositional.' Yet they demanded the right to be consulted in central decision-making, flattering the party 'that today one can say anything in the GDR without being persecuted'. At the same time they were critical of popular inertia, as well as those applying for permanent emigration. The local party's instinct was to recruit them as non-affiliated speakers at local meetings.[45] However, it was to be the top party leadership's reluctance to engage in genuine, two-way dialogue which was to push such disaffected, but essentially collaborative citizens from sanctioned to unsanctioned dissent, from petition to protest.

Protest

But where could a young oppositional movement find the free space to evade being nipped in the bud by the secret police? The churches, especially the Protestant churches, have attracted attention as both sanctuaries for dissent as well as conduits of state control.[46] Ever since the church–state agreement of 1978, the church hierarchy chose conformity, while local activists advocated confrontation. By the late 1980s these tensions were palpable. When I visited a church in Jena in January 1989, its pinboard was festooned with notices about political, environmental, and gay rights activities unheard of in a British parish church. Such grass-roots activism began to filter upwards, in the 'Church from Below' movement. Thus, in summer 1988 church synods in Halle and Rostock issued twenty-point theses echoing *perestroika*.[47] The regime responded by banning several church publications. At the Saxon synod in July 1989 when the regional bishop, Hempel, distanced himself from the activists, there was a polarization between 'positive' bishops (in the SED's eyes) and 'negative' clerics. As party observers noted, however, nearly half the audience was under thirty and evidently sympathized with the troublemakers. Parallel to the official event, an 'Alternative Synod' was held in another Leipzig church, although heavily screened by the security forces.[48] Nevertheless, Detlev Pollack reminds us that such initiatives were borne by only a tiny minority of the populace.[49] The church was also split in its attitude to emigrationism. Like the party, the church leadership argued that 'the GDR needs everyone'. Opting out of society or leaving the GDR were not compatible with Christian conscience. Yet, as we know, some local church leaders took it upon themselves to offer support and guidance to emigration seekers. Some, including later key reformers such as Pastor Rainer Eppelmann, tried to mediate between the two views

Politicise?

[45] Sylvia K. and Rainer B.: SED-ZK (Abt. Sicherheit) to Krenz, 20 Sept. 1989, SAPMO-BArch, DY30/IV2/2.039/312, fos. 135–7.

[46] John P. Burgess, *The East German Church and the End of Communism* (New York: Oxford University Press, 1997), 19–41.

[47] Gedmin, *Hidden Hand*, 70.

[48] SED-ZK (PO), 'Bericht der Bezirksleitung Leipzig . . .', 10 July 1989, SAPMO-BArch, DY30/IV2/2.039/330, fos. 23–8.

[49] Pollack, 'Zusammenbruch', 43.

by formalizing the GDR's faltering steps towards travel reform, calling 'for a friendship society GDR-FRG' to include long-term exchanges and institutional contacts.[50]

More obviously political disaffection flared up around the communal elections of 7 May 1989. The GDR's single-list 'elections' had always achieved incredible, almost unanimous results, in which non-voting was tantamount to anti-state subversion. Now, dissidents tried to catch the state breaking its own rules. Activists organized a concerted boycott, while unofficial tellers checked polling stations and counts. The security organs became particularly alarmed at developments in the capital, but also in Saxony, Potsdam, and Cottbus; or in Leipzig, where four people tried to stage a march to hand over a 'provisional ballot box', but were intercepted by Volkspolizei and MfS.[51] Although voting was down across the population, a 'positive' result of 98.5 per cent was still recorded, thus proving vote rigging in boycotters' eyes. Small numbers of perhaps 200 civil rights activists subsequently protested on the seventh of each month, despite MfS swoops. Others took the state to law for alleged improprieties, filing petitions with the State Attorney, and there was a generally growing GDR litigiousness, ranging from complaints about housing and repairs, to car waiting-lists, to environmental pollution, blocking of applications to visit the capitalist exterior and religious conscience.[52]

complaint

On the eve of the hot autumn of 1989, the SED's Security section summarized the national security threat. One hundred and sixty groupings had been counted, including 150 church grass-roots initiatives, involving 2,500 people. (In other words, the numbers appeared eminently manageable.) These were allegedly forcing the hands of the church hierarchy, or exploiting foreign media to act as dialogue partners for a pluralistic 'counter-public sphere', as well as to 'test state tolerance' by silent demonstrations and non-violent resistance, pressing for human rights changes. 'The behaviour of these forces ranges from politically indifferent, unstable, wavering, to hostile attitudes against socialism in the GDR.' Regarding the May elections, the Security section conceded five times as many non-voters as in 1986; straight 'no' votes were up 18.8 per cent (southern and eastern regions stood out), 'unleashing occasional uncertainties or questions among other citizens, and even party members, regarding the correctness of the election procedure'. Among the emigration movement, protesters were invoking German–German dialogue, as well as events in other socialist countries. Yet, in a typical bout of East German conspiracy theory, the party feared not only organized oppositionists, but non-conformists and even awkward teenagers. Thus, skinheads, punks, heavy metal fans, and goths all counted as 'anti-state',

[50] Bickhardt and Eppelmann, 'Für eine Freundschaftsgesellschaft DDR-BRD', 8 Sept. 1987, SAPMO-BArch, DY30/IV2/2.039/312, fos. 28–30.
[51] SED-ZK (PO), 'Information', 8 May 1989, SAPMO-BArch, DY30/2182, fos. 83–4.
[52] Süß, 'Stimmungslage', 243–5.

as well as the couch potatoes who watched western TV.[53] Nevertheless, a more formal opposition was only to emerge in September 1989 in the wake of a crisis brought on by the perforation of the iron curtain, which was to revive the spectre of mass *Republikflucht* to haunt and ultimately undo the SED.

THE BREACHING OF THE IRON CURTAIN

On 2 May 1989 the Hungarian authorities began to dismantle sections of their iron curtain. The following month Budapest acceded to the Geneva Convention, which forbade the previous practice of returning refugees to their country of origin. As the summer vacation approached there was mounting GDR trepidation, despite reassurances from the Hungarian secret police. The population, too, spread rumours of an impending crack-down on trips to Hungary.[54] For the moment, however, the Austro-Hungarian frontier remained guarded and border-crossers few. Hundreds of those thwarted then sought refuge in the FRG's embassies in Budapest and Prague, as well as the Permanent Mission in East Berlin, leading to their successive closures under the weight of numbers.[55] Events accelerated nevertheless on 19 August, when Hungarian opposition groups organized a 'pan-European picnic' in conjunction with the Euro MP Otto von Habsburg and the reform communist Imre Pozsgay. At the border at Sopron a symbolic border opening including walkabout was staged, publicized even among waiting GDR refugees in Budapest. The Hungarian interior and border authorities then turned a blind eye while over 600 East Germans walked west through an unlocked gate.[56] Two hundred and forty more were able to sneak across three days later, but Hungarian guards and militia were still officially trying to prevent crossings, shooting one refugee dead on 21 August. Budapest was nevertheless tiring of doing the East Germans' dirty work. On 24 August embassy occupiers were flown out with Red Cross papers. The next day Minister President Németh and Foreign Secretary Horn flew secretly to Bonn, announcing that they would permit GDR citizens across the border, in return for which Chancellor Kohl promised an additional credit of 500 million deutschmarks. On 28 August Horn warned the GDR ambassador that Hungary 'cannot be transformed into a giant camp'.[57] By then there were up to 150,000 East Germans in Hungary. The SED Politbüro discussed the exodus for the first time the next day, but remained bullish, blaming the FRG for spreading *Torschlußpanik*.[58] Tellingly,

[53] SED-ZK (Sicherheit), 'Vorlage für das Politbüro', Aug. 1989, SAPMO-BArch, DY30/IV2/2.039/309, fos. 97–119.
[54] Mielke to Krenz, 12 June 1989, SAPMO-BArch, DY30/IV2/2.039/268, fo. 83; Mittig to Krenz, 15 July 1989, SAPMO-BArch, DY30/IV2/2.039/309, fos. 38–45.
[55] Mayer, *Flucht und Ausreise*, 331–5, 356–7 and 362–5.
[56] Timmer, *Aufbruch*, 100.   [57] Hertle, *Fall der Mauer*, 103.
[58] Günter Mittag at SED-PB, 29 Aug. 1989 in Stephan, *'Vorwärts immer'*, 96–107; 105.

the apparatus reverted to terms such as 'slave-trading', last used on the eve of the Wall, spreading reports of holidaymakers being ambushed by lurking western tabloid journalists and 'people-traffickers'.[59] After deadlocked GDR–Hungarian talks, Budapest effectively opened the border on 11 September, resulting in 18,000 crossing in three days.[60] The reactions of those emerging on the other side were ecstatic: 'I have dreamed of flight since I was a child', explained one teacher. 'But I never thought it would come like this.'[61] By 20 September 1989, the GDR had lost 1,653 health workers, including 530 doctors and 145 dentists.[62] By 7 October it was 29,300 all told.[63]

Among the remaining population, the leak in the iron curtain only heated up the travel and emigration movements discussed above to boiling point. Some rejectees for compassionate leave threatened to file an emigration application on the spot, or provocatively requested a visa for Hungary.[64] Citizens were indignant that law-breakers were jumping the queue: 'justice and the law are being turned on their head'. It was also suggested that 'If we had more generous travel opportunities, so many people would not leave the state', or 'The state is driving people to steps they don't want to take.' Applicants refused to leave police premises; Vopos in Schwerin were accused of 'concrete mentality' and 'to blame that so many citizens were "scarpering"'. At Frankfurt/Oder comments such as 'keep up the red-light treatment' were among the milder insults, paling before 'kiss my arse' and '*Scheißgesetz*'. Officials were at the 'end of their tether'. Young Cottbusers were also openly threatening to 'go on the streets' or 'via Hungary'.[65] In other words, Hirschman's 'voice' was threatening to spill over into some very public spaces.

For reasons of geography, Czechoslovakia had acted as a potential firewall for the GDR against Hungary. Yet, once East Germans started occupying the Federal embassy in Prague in late September, Czech police found themselves having to guard the compound fence against mass scalings. Soon, thousands of East Germans were camping out in the muddy embassy grounds, sharing inadequate toilet facilities, in what resembled a refugee camp. On 25 September the Czech leadership informed their GDR opposite numbers that they were no longer prepared to carry out this damaging role. In the background, the Soviets, in statements issued by foreign minister Shevardnadze, as well as the Kremlin's Germany specialist Falin, commiserated with the East Germans, but maintained a hands-off stance.[66] The Soviet response throughout had been to lend only

[59] SED-ZK (PO), 'Stellungnahmen von Bürgern der DDR zum Menschenhandel der BRD', 19 Sept. 1989, SAPMO-BArch, DY30/IV2/2.039/309, fos. 133–40.

[60] Maier, *Dissolution*, 126.

[61] Konrad Jarausch, *The Rush to German Unity* (New York: Oxford University Press, 1994), 16.

[62] Seidel to Hager, 6 Oct. 1989, SAPMO-BArch, DY30/IV2/2.039/309, fos. 144–6.

[63] 'Aktualisierte statistische Angaben . . .', 24 Oct. 1989, SAPMO-BArch, DY30/IV2/2.039/309, fos. 147–47a.

[64] MdI (PM), 'Information . . . (Monat August 1989)', BAB, DO-1/8/54472.

[65] MdI (PM), 'Information . . . (Monat September 1989)', BAB, DO-1/8/54472.

[66] Gedmin, *Hidden Hand*, 90–5.

moral support. Attempts by the GDR's foreign office to convene a meeting of Warsaw Pact foreign ministers failed. The SED's security section then proposed three options: (a) to demand that Bonn recognize GDR citizenship, but then to liberalize travel; (b) to close all borders temporarily with the prospect of reopening them before Christmas, while demanding FRG recognition; (c) the expansion of travel in and out of the GDR, but with no commitment to providing hard currency, and exceptions only for security personnel.[67] Wolfgang Herger, head of security, pleaded for the third variant, even at the cost of further losses, otherwise 'the situation in the interior could heat up to ungovernability', but Krenz, who forwarded the proposals to Honecker on 3 October, pressed for the second. On the same day the border to Czechoslovakia was closed, and the next day transit routes to Bulgaria and Rumania followed. The GDR was effectively sealed off from the rest of the eastern bloc. The immediate response among citizens at police stations was 'incomprehension and outrage', 'escalating sometimes to the point of hard confrontations which include insulting workers'. Individuals felt 'punished for wanting to stay in the GDR', or 'locked in and may have to take steps regarding actions to apply for permanent emigration'.[68] Blocking tactics led to 'massive queries' at visa offices. 'In hundreds of interviews and telephone calls they vented their outrage and bitterness at this measure, frequently escalating to insults against the Volkspolizei.'[69] Individuals threatened to stop work as well as to take part in the demonstrations (of which, more below). In some cases even Vopos petitioned the party leadership against this decision, feeling discriminated against![70] Subsequent interviews reinforce the view that the Czech border closure represented a tipping point in popular grievances.[71]

Despite the closure, however, a daily trickle of people managed to cross into Poland and Czechoslovakia. Further negotiations by Federal Foreign Minister Hans-Dietrich Genscher led to a compromise solution, that asylum seekers in Prague might be released to the West, but only if conveyed via sealed train through GDR territory, to preserve the fiction of formal deportation. Standing on the embassy balcony, Genscher, himself a *Republikflüchtiger* in the 1950s, announced the deal to an overjoyed audience.[72] Thus, on 30 September the first consignment of 6,300 left, but despite the border closures, thousands more GDR citizens managed to enter the FRG embassy to join other expellees on sealed trains in early October. By the fall of the Wall, 10,000 had followed the embassy route via Budapest, 17,000 via Prague, and nearly 5,000 through

---

[67] Krenz to Honecker, 3 Oct. 1989, SAPMO-BArch, DY30/IV2/2.039/309, fos. 141–3.

[68] Hertle, *Fall der Mauer*, 140.

[69] MdI (PM), 'Zuarbeit zur Lage im Zusammenhang mit der zeitweiligen Aussetzung des paß- und visafreien Reiseverkehrs mit der CSSR', 25 Oct. 1989, BAB, DO-1/8/41781.

[70] DVP-Kreisamt Sebnitz, Eingabe, 16 Oct. 1989, SAPMO-BArch, DY30/1094, fos. 79–80.

[71] Gareth Dale, *The East German Revolution of 1989* (Manchester: Manchester University Press, 2006), 14.

[72] Jarausch, *Rush*, 21.

Warsaw.[73] *Neues Deutschland*'s leader reflected Honecker's personal view that: 'Their behaviour is a kick in the teeth for moral values and they have excluded themselves from our society. No-one should shed any tears for them.'[74] Such callousness backfired, however. As one young female chemist wrote: 'I believe we should and will shed a river of tears. . . . Can you not imagine that as a young person I do not wish to be confined forever within concrete walls, barbed wire and state directives?'[75] Indeed, it was this aspect of soul-searching which prompted many of the civil rights protestors to ask why so many were leaving the land, overcoming some of their previous hostility to the emigrationists.[76]

Hirschman has already pointed out that the growing exodus played a pivotal role in raising the consciousness of those determined to stay put, and even of those previously indifferent. In an important revision of his original theory, this time applied directly to the experience of the GDR, he postulated that exit and voice could be mutually reinforcing, acting in tandem rather than diametrically.[77] Pollack, too, has pointed out that the numbers of demonstrators in Leipzig only rose significantly, from hundreds to thousands, after the full opening of the Hungarian border on 11 September.[78] Detailed exit-voice studies carried out since the events have plotted the correlation between regional losses and willingness to protest. Steven Pfaff has suggested that GDR society was particularly susceptible to exit, since its social structure of local niche networks was vulnerable to erosion. In other words, without social bonds at the intermediate level of a public sphere, it only took a few disappearing acts at grass-roots level to disrupt local milieux.[79] Even the Evangelical Church Federation found itself on 19 September playing the role of mediator, pointing out the debilitating consequences of the emigration:

Families and friendships are torn apart, old people feel themselves abandoned, the ill are losing their caretakers and doctors, workers' collectives are decimated. . . . Today we find ourselves facing the challenge of preserving what has proved its worth while we search for new ways to advance a society of greater justice and participation. . . . We need an open and public confrontation of our social problems, we need everybody for responsible cooperation in our society.[80]

Trade unionists also began to complain to their leadership at the conspiracy theories used to explain the losses. Others took the exodus as the symptom of a sick society, in need of reform, and were determined to use it to protest for change at home. The phrase 'We're staying here' was meant as a challenge to the

[73] Maier, *Dissolution*, 131.   [74] *Neues Deutschland*, 2 Oct. 1989.

[75] Heike Sch., Eingabe, 7 Oct. 1989, SAPMO-BArch, DY30/1096, fos. 47–9.

[76] Timmer, *Aufbruch*, 103–5.

[77] Albert O. Hirschman, 'Exit, Voice, and the Fate of the German Democratic Republic: An Essay in Conceptual History', *World Politics*, 45 (1993), 173–202.

[78] Detlef Pollack, *Politischer Protest: Politisch alternative Gruppen der DDR* (Opladen: Leske & Budrich, 2000), 210–11.

[79] Pfaff, *Exit-Voice Dynamics*, 150–1.   [80] Maier, *Dissolution*, 133.

regime, as well as to the emigrationists. Indeed, there could have been no autumn revolution inside the GDR without the exodus. As the pre-eminent expert on the fall of the Wall, Hans-Hermann Hertle, put it: 'Mass emigration became the precondition of the unfolding mass protest.'[81]

Leipzig became the focus for demonstrations for a number of reasons. The Leipzig Fair, held there every spring and autumn, provided an international audience of visitors and western media, which acted to restrain SED crackdowns. At the same time, East Germans could see the goods for export unavailable at home. As part of the GDR provinces there was also greater resentment at the lack of infrastructural renewal, at a time when money was being poured into East Berlin for its 750th anniversary celebrations in 1987. Leipzig itself was surrounded by a wasteland of worked-out lignite mines, scarring the Saxon landscape. At the Nikolaikirche, a baroque church in the very centre of the old town, its reformist deacon, Günter Johannsen, had held peace prayers on Monday evenings ever since 1982. Yet, in March 1989, congregationists began ancillary marches with posters calling for 'Travel Freedom not Officialdom', timed to coincide with the opening of the Leipzig Fair, leading to police intervention.[82] Demonstrators sought refuge in the church in the city centre, and the following Monday the numbers had swollen at what became regular peace vespers. The authorities then maintained a strong police presence at these gatherings, videoing participants and patrolling with dogs, while the western media circled. Individuals were arrested, but not without petitioning to know the law being used against them, in one case simply for photographing events.[83]

Tellingly, however, when the Leipzig Monday demonstrations resumed after the summer break on 4 September, the crowd divided between those demanding civil liberties, chanting 'We are staying!', and emigration seekers shouting 'We want out!'[84] Only two weeks later did the reformers win the upper hand, drowning out the emigrationists. The words 'We are staying here!' came to represent a struggle for public space within the GDR, not only against the massed ranks of the Volkspolizei, with their dogs and water cannon, but against the increasingly frustrated young emigrationists who were turning to stone-throwing and scuffles. This, too, partly explains the growing prevalence of the slogan 'No violence' among the more law-abiding protestors who felt that 'their' demonstration was being hijacked. On 9–10 September oppositionists formed 'New Forum', and on 19 September applied for recognition, the first of several civil rights groups such as Democracy Now and the more centre-right Democratic Awakening to emerge over the autumn, all prompted to go public

---

[81] Hertle, *Fall der Mauer*, 109.
[82] 13 Mar. 1989 in Mitter and Wolle (eds), *'Ich liebe euch'*, 28.
[83] Johannes B., 10 May 1989, SAPMO-BArch, DY30/1094, fos. 11–12.
[84] Maier, *Dissolution*, 136.

by the opening of the Hungarian border. The refugee wave thus acted as an important catalyst to formalization of the citizens' initiatives.[85] Yet, even then such groups seemed unaware of a potential leadership role, set for a long-term struggle rather than a knockout blow. Honecker, convalescing from his gall-bladder operation, ordered a hard line. On 21 September the new party applications were duly turned down with the argument that there was no 'social need' for such organizations.[86] The MfS ordered its unofficial collaborators to sow dissension.[87]

The first truly massed Leipzig demonstrations occurred, nevertheless, on 25 September, when gatherers spilled out of the Nikolaikirche and 5,000 people paraded around the city ring road, calling for the legalization of New Forum. In the first tentative steps, however, demonstrators observed traffic signals, waiting for green, before bringing the traffic to a standstill.[88] Pastor Wonneberger had told worshippers: 'In the words of Jesus: "Do not be afraid, unto me is given all power in heaven and earth." ... Against such power Stasi apparatus, dogs, and police phalanxes are but paper tigers. ... We can renounce violence.'[89] As events threatened to get out of hand in the ensuing days, local church leaders developed a language of non-violent protest. Others cited the words of Martin Luther King: 'We shall overcome.' A week later, on 2 October, more focused political demands were made for the legalization of New Forum. Demonstrators chanted 'We are staying here', 'Now or never', 'Freedom, equality, fraternity', 'Gorby, Gorby', as well as singing the 'Internationale'. A crowd of 6–8,000 then marched around the Leipzig Ring, shouting 'Stasi out' and 'Release the prisoners' before the MfS offices. Only baton charges by the police could break up the evening procession.[90]

Internal SED damage limitation analyses on the new movements reveal a self-destructive unwillingness to compromise. The reviving social democrats' call for a social market economy meant the restoration of capitalism and thus made it 'anti-constitutional'. The Democratic Initiative group was viewed as simply an 'underground movement' with internationalist connections, bent on civil disobedience. Democracy Now was seen as attacking the territorial integrity of the GDR and also anti-constitutional. 'Aufbruch 89—Neues Forum' was a catch-all movement, 'offering no new social conception'. Analysts believed that the movements could only gain a mass basis by dealing on SED terms. Simply banning them would achieve little. Fines would not be paid. Arrests were even more difficult because of the 'solidarity effects' they would cause, so the reporters argued. The only solution proffered was for the SED to publicize its 'socialist democracy', and to co-opt church circles and some of the 'alternative' groups

[85] Pollack, 'Zusammenbruch', 51. [86] Gedmin, *Hidden Hand*, 95.
[87] Süß, *Staatssicherheit*, 223 ff. [88] Pollack, 'Zusammenbruch', 52.
[89] Maier, *Dissolution*, 134.
[90] Krenz to Honecker, 3 Oct. 1989, SAPMO-BArch, DY30/IV2/2.039/317, fos. 1–2.

under the motto: 'Striving together for a *better, more beautiful socialist GDR.*'[91] This was much too little, much too late. Moreover, the party was beginning to witness the shearing away of the penumbra of mass organizations which had always lent it a veneer of respectability, leaving it isolated to face the growing tide of anger.

The first serious trial of strength came with the last act of the emigration movement, when former embassy occupiers were spirited out of Prague via Dresden and on to Bavaria aboard sealed trains. On 3 October thousands in Saxony waited at stations and bends in the track, hoping to hitch an unofficial ride. In Dresden alone about 3,000 people attempted to storm the station, with one person suffering serious injury underneath a train.[92] Violent clashes occurred the following night, as further deportees passed through. A crowd of up to 20,000, the largest since 1953, massed outside the main railway station, hoping to board the trains, and throwing stones, to which the security forces responded with tear gas and baton charges.[93] Meanwhile, army units were mobilized in support, armed with machine-pistols and live ammunition.[94] In the following days several thousand demonstrators were taken into custody by Volkspolizei and MfS. It was only a matter of months since Egon Krenz had publicly defended the Chinese use of force on Tiananmen Square and no-one was sure if there would not be a 'Beijing solution' in Germany too.

Berlin, the traditional functionary capital, had not experienced the same dissident activity as the provinces. Because of the GDR's fortieth anniversary celebrations, however, culminating on 7 October, it became a magnet for western media attention. In the run-up, as party activists tried to justify the achievements of four decades of socialism, audiences began to heckle with questions such as: 'Why are so many GDR citizens now emigrating?'[95] Visits by the SED *Prominenz* degenerated into disorderly scenes. When youth secretary Gerd Schulz toured one Hennigsdorf factory, workers refused to follow the birthday script and wanted to discuss the exodus.[96] The large anniversary rallies offered perfect cover for dissidents. On 7 and 8 October demonstrators began filling the city centre, chanting in the Alexanderplatz and marching on the Palace of the Republic, where Honecker was entertaining his illustrious guests, shouting 'Gorby help us' and 'No violence'. As darkness fell, the Volkspolizei cordoned off streets and made 1,047 arrests. The accompanying police brutality meted out on 7 and 8 October, often against passers-by, was clearly a shock for those on the receiving

---

[91] 'Zu den Aufrufen der "Bürgerbewegung—Demokratie Jetzt", "Demokratische Initiative", von "Aufbruch 89—Neues Forum" und der "Initiativgruppe Sozialdemokratische Partei" ', n.d., SAPMO-BArch, DY30/IV2/2.039/326, fos. 31–8.

[92] MdI, 'Information vom 04.10.1989', BAB, DO-1/8/41781.

[93] Dickel to BDVPs, 5 Oct. 1989, BAB, DO-1/8/41781.   [94] Hertle, *Fall der Mauer*, 113.

[95] SED-ZK (Propaganda), 'Information über einen Einsatz in der Bezirksparteiorganisation Berlin', 5 Oct. 1989, SAPMO-BArch, DY30/IV2/2.039/324, fos. 35–7.

[96] SED-ZK (Jugend), 'Information', n.d. (Sept. 1989), SAPMO-BArch, DY30/IV2/2.039/324, fos. 72–9.

end, and many sought redress, no longer afraid to speak out.[97] Petitions to the SED also attest that victims were no longer prepared to keep silent when loaded onto Volkspolizei lorries and taken to garages where they were forced to stand facing the wall, complaining that 'the arbitrariness and violence of the VP comrades was shocking'.[98] Subsequently, on 21 October 1,200 people formed a human chain around the Palace of the Republic, demanding the dropping of charges against those involved.[99]

The real showdown, however, occurred on 9 October in Leipzig. The MfS, now carrying side arms at all times,[100] reported 'a situation like shortly before the counter-revolutionary events of 17.6.1953'.[101] Police watched as thousands travelled in from surrounding Saxony by train and car. A total of 8,000 security personnel were on standby, as well as 5,000 functionaries. The regime was also rumoured to be preparing hospital beds and blood plasma, as well as the Leipzig exhibition centre for massed detentions. Demonstrators themselves felt that they were genuinely putting their lives on the line. The Nikolaikirche was full by lunchtime, surrounded by police, who could hear shouts of 'Gorby, Gorby', 'We are staying here', 'No violence', and 'We are the people' coming from the 6,000 inside.[102] SED plans to pack the meeting with loyalists backfired, however, when outsiders were spotted, hissed at and asked to leave. Behind the scenes, the local leadership had also been seeking direction from Berlin, with police making it clear that they would not act unless given direct orders, while the Interior Ministry in Berlin monitored proceedings on closed-circuit television. Three regional SED reform leaders, as well as Pastor Zimmermann of the Nikolaikirche, and Kurt Masur of the Leipzig Gewandhaus orchestra, signed a statement calling for dialogue, somewhat defusing the tension. At 6.15 p.m. 70–80,000 demonstrators then braved the show of force, at a point when the bluff of the GDR regime was effectively called, carrying candles and shouting 'We are the people', 'Legalize New Forum', 'Gorby, Gorby, Gorby' and '2, 3, 4, we are staying here, we are not hooligans', accompanied by rhythmic clapping. As the giant procession wheeled past the police and Stasi headquarters, there were whistles and boos, as well as playful shouts of 'join us'.[103] The crowd had lost its fear. At 6.35 p.m. the local police chief received the order from the Interior Ministry to go on the defensive.[104] By the time Krenz phoned through at 7.15 p.m., authorizing this course, the moment had already passed. Only ten people had been arrested.

[97] *Schnauze! Gedächtnisprotokolle 7. und 8. Oktober 1989: Berlin, Leipzig, Dresden* (Berlin: BVA Union, 1990), 20.

[98] Eveline G., 10 Oct. 1989, SAPMO-BArch, DY30/1094, fos. 61–3. See also Peter K., Eingabe, 12 Oct. 1989, SAPMO-BArch, DY30/1095, fos. 38–41.

[99] MdI, 'Information vom 22.10.1989', BAB, DO-1/8/41781.

[100] Süß, *Staatssicherheit*, 301–14.   [101] Mitter and Wolle, *'Wir lieben euch'*, 204 ff.

[102] Maier, *Dissolution*, 142.

[103] MdI, 'Information vom 10.10.1989', BAB, DO-1/8/41781.

[104] Hertle, *Fall der Mauer*, 116.

Meanwhile, in Dresden on the same evening approximately 22,000 church-goers gathered, and in Berlin 2,000 people congregated in the Gethsemane church, where rumours circulated that tanks had been deployed in Leipzig, and that security personnel were wearing gas-masks, until church leaders could reassure them that non-violence would prevail. Other smaller demonstrations in Jena, Magdeburg, Karl-Marx-Stadt, and Halle passed off peacefully.[105] Each home town was having its own revolution. In Wernigerode on 10 October, a group of young people attempted to place candles before the Rathaus, followed by others chanting, 'The Wall must go' and 'We don't want violence'.[106] Groups of a few hundred to several thousands continued to agitate. Initially, the security forces still broke up these events, but gradually local civic officials began to mediate with people's representatives. Churches continued to hold services for those arrested, as well as to marshal silent processions. In the Church of the Resurrection in Berlin-Friedrichshain, for instance, on 14 October a reading of forbidden texts was led by Stephan Hermlin, the author who had once defended 13 August 1961 against Günter Grass.[107] The following day in the Church of the Saviour a 'concert against violence' was held, including well-known bands such as Pankow, Silly, and City.[108] Leaflets were distributed. Occasionally there were calls for the organization of newspapers to go beyond the information sheets being distributed.[109] Banners called for 'Freedom of speech and the press', 'We are the people—we want reforms', or 'Freedom of opinion, travel and the press.' Students also started mobilizing for their own body. Amid the almost carnival atmosphere MfS officers were taunted with the words 'Stasi onto the production line'. By the Monday demonstration in Leipzig of 16 October, with 70–80,000 participants, slogans now included 'Legalize free media', 'Ecology not Economy', 'Free Elections', as well as continued calls for 'Where is our freedom to travel?', and for New Forum. Flyers warned not to be drawn into delaying dialogues, in which the church might become a 'brake': 'There is now no more time for nice fireside chats. If dialogue, then dialogue of equality, in other words, the conditions for dialogue cannot always come "from above", but must be co-set by us. That is why the actions and non-violent demonstrations cannot let up.' As well as demanding civil and political rights, including electoral reform and the right to strike, freedom to travel was included, although by now significantly last on the list.[110]

A delayed palace coup also took place. Although President Gorbachev had famously warned at the time of the anniversary celebrations that history punishes those who arrive too late, he had remained restrained. Soviet embassy

[105] MdI, 'Information vom 10.10.1989', BAB, DO-1/8/41781.
[106] MdI, 'Information vom 11.10.1989', BAB, DO-1/8/41781.
[107] MdI, 'Information vom 15.10.1989', BAB, DO-1/8/41781.
[108] MdI, 'Information vom 16.10.1989', BAB, DO-1/8/41781.
[109] MdI, 'Information vom 14.10.1989', BAB, DO-1/8/41781.
[110] MdI, 'Information vom 17.10.1989', BAB, DO-1/8/41781.

staff were under orders to offer no advice and the military were confined to barracks. On 6 October he attended an FDJ torchlit parade, but even Gorbachev noticed that all was not well with even the handpicked cream of the SED's youth movement. The Soviet leader then met Honecker and Stoph on the morning of 7 October, and sat in with the Politbüro, warning that 'if we lag behind, life will punish us immediately'.[111] Nobody at that stage was prepared to make a decisive bid for power, however, despite Honecker's genuine health problems. Any crucial decisions on the unfolding crisis were thus fatally postponed. On 8 October there were tentative efforts by Krenz and Schabowski for a Politbüro communiqué addressing the crisis, with a number of potential reformers being lined up. On 10 October the gathered leadership indeed admitted it was in trouble, and, backtracking from Honecker's 'no tears' speech, pronounced that 'we are not indifferent to the fact that people who worked and lived here have chosen to leave'.[112] Yet Honecker would not go voluntarily. Only at the Politbüro session of 17 October did Willi Stoph move for him to step-down, ignoring arguments that cadre changes would open the party up to 'blackmail'.[113] The next day Honecker complied, but departed from the script by recommending Krenz as his successor.

The popular movement outside the politbureaucracy was unimpressed by the partial reforms. Whereas in the week 16–22 October the MfS counted twenty-four demonstrations with 140,000 participants, the following week it was 145 demonstrations with 540,000.[114] On 23 October in Leipzig alone it was 300,000. 'The land needs new men', chanted demonstrators.[115] During an attempted party counter-demonstration against New Forum the same day in Schwerin, as the district SED leader began his speech, the majority of the bussed-in party faithful promptly joined in the opposition procession.[116] On the twenty-fourth, following Krenz's election as chairman of the Council of State, the first demonstration in Berlin following the anniversary debacle, swelling to 12,000, moved from the Alexanderplatz to the Palace of the Republic, as well as the Central Committee building, before converging on the Gethsemane church in Prenzlauer Berg. Banners included 'No Ego(n)ism' and 'Krenz cannot be left alone—Modrow [a reform communist] must be given a home'.[117] The Council of State even granted protestors an audience, only to hear: 'Only because we put pressure on you from the streets have you moved; only if we continue to apply pressure will you keep moving.' There were also calls for a separation of powers, complaints that petitioners were being 'fobbed off', and demands for

[111] Hertle, *Fall der Mauer*, 119.   [112] *Neues Deutschland*, 11 Oct. 1989.
[113] Hertle and Stephan (eds), *Ende der SED*, 53–4.   [114] Hertle, *Fall der Mauer*, 136.
[115] MdI, 'Information vom 23.10.1989', BAB, DO-1/8/41781.
[116] Grix, *Role of the Masses*, 115–16.
[117] MdI, 'Information vom 25.10.1989', BAB, DO-1/8/41781.

publication of the economic facts.[118] At the end of October the regime finally legalized demonstrations, but with the forlorn plea to turn to a more civilized form of dialogue. In response, on 30 October 200,000 people, the most so far, marched around Leipzig, now making militant demands 'which are long-term in their scope': slogans included 'we are posing the power-question', 'democracy instead of SED monopoly', 'free elections under UN supervision', 'without Wall for us all', and, as 4,000 people stood outside district Stasi headquarters, 'Mielke, your days are numbered'.[119]

As the dam broke, so did the tone of petitions. Whereas after Krenz's accession many had concerned supply and travel, since 1 November there had been more *want* calls for structural reform of the economy, with fewer subsidies, but also a 'true socialist democracy' with electoral reform with multiple parties, as well as critique and autocritique of the SED, including a block replacement of the Politbüro. Regarding travel, citizens wanted to know how the hard currency problem would be solved, as well as clarification of the situation for citizens wishing to re-enter the GDR. Accordingly, the term *Republikflucht* should be abandoned.[120] The petitions reaching the top in this phase were unlike anything previously encountered. One lady pensioner and non-comrade wrote on 13 October how she had arrived in the Soviet Zone in 1946, citing the experiences which had taught her to ' "keep my trap shut" in order not to completely flip out. On top of that the indescribable hypocrisy and the demonstration of the "power of the little men"—sickening!' But now, 'for the first time in years the red flag flew on my balcony. *I* was celebrating the 40th birthday of *my* Republic in *my* way.'[121] Meanwhile, previously loyal regime-carriers began to question their role, too. One Volkspolizei officer, an SED member since 1947, explained how sour the mood had been at the fortieth anniversary celebrations among his comrades in Gera. In his apartment block where normally thirty to thirty-five flags flew, there had been four or five. What followed was an indictment of the whole system of moral bribery.[122]

Despite the Party Information's best efforts, it could not conceal how quickly *military imposed* the veneer of ideological conformity had fallen away to expose a morass of material fears and resentments, and a feeling of betrayal by the top leadership.[123] The party mood was 'sensitive and sometimes tetchy'. According to the Party Information, criticisms of the Politbüro were spreading to regional and district

---

[118] 'Einige Fragen und Probleme, die Bürger der DDR in Diskussionen vor dem Staatsrat am 24. Oktober 1989 aufgeworfen haben', 25 Oct. 1989, SAPMO-BArch, DY30/IV2/2.039/317, fos. 30–7.

[119] SED-BL Leipzig to Krenz, 31 Oct. 1989, SAPMO-BArch, DY30/IV2/2.039/317, fos. 42–4.

[120] SED-PB (Eingabenbüro), '1. Information', 3 Nov. 1989, SAPMO-BArch, DY30/IV2/2.039/317, fos. 48–56.

[121] Anne A., 13 Oct. 1989, SAPMO-BArch, DY30/1094, fos. 2–4.

[122] Helmut S., Eingabe, 9 Oct. 1989, SAPMO-BArch, DY30/1096, fos. 2–5.

[123] SED-ZK (PO), 'Information über die aktuelle Lage in der DDR', 20 Oct. 1989, SAPMO-BArch, DY30/IV2/2.039/330, fos. 55–9.

leaderships: 'The breach of confidence at the grass roots is often glaringly obvious.'[124] Journalists complained that *Neues Deutschland* was making fools of factory cadres: 'Disappointment is turning to human resignation, and then bitterness and hatred.'[125] There was scepticism at Krenz's so-called 'turn' or *Wende*. Most regional and district parties felt 'left in the lurch by the party leadership', doubting 'the ability and readiness of leading comrades to complete the rethink, or to assess the situation realistically and to change it fundamentally'. A 'pogrom mood' was dominating rallies. As one party member reported: 'Yesterday a foreman from my former factory said to me: "Now you are standing with your backs to the wall, if you keep on like this for another two weeks you will be facing the wall".'[126] Yet things were only going to get worse with the revelations of the SED leaders' luxurious lifestyle at the Wandlitz compound. An article in the *Berliner Zeitung*, showing container-loads of luxury goods, including Dior perfume and Persil washing powder, caused particular offence. Each revelation created a 'wave of indignation' among comrades, who were increasingly turning to the opposition.[127]

On 4 November the GDR's largest ever rally of 500,000 took place in Berlin's Alexanderplatz, inspired by artists, including New Forum leaders, who welcomed 'colleagues and friends, like-thinkers and stayers-here'. The chief demands were for freedom of speech and association, as well as the renunciation of the SED's constitutional leading role. Overhung with witty banners—one depicting Krenz as a wolf in a nightdress above the motto 'Grandmother, what big teeth you have'—the event had a carnival atmosphere. Stilt-walkers warned Krenz not to 'trip up'. At the same time, rage was vented on the security services, with calls for 'Stasi onto the production line'. The former MfS counter-intelligence chief, Markus Wolf, accused the leadership of living in a 'fairytale world', but warned against the MfS being turned into whipping boys. Berlin party boss Günter Schabowski, drowned out at times, tried to make the SED's reform spirit plausible. Jens Reich for New Forum called for proper elections, but also for the return of those who had departed. Pastor Schorlemmer, too, enjoined listeners to: 'Stay here! Now we literally do need every man and woman' for a 'coalition of common sense'. Christa Wolf expressed her 'dream': 'Imagine there is socialism and no-one runs away!' Like many others, the writer Christoph Hein challenged the view that the Politbüro had inaugurated the *Wende*: 'It was the reason of the street, the demonstration of the people', inveighing against 'bureaucracy, demagogy, spying, corruption, paternalism and even criminality'.[128] The SED

---

[124] SED-ZK (PO), 'Information über die aktuelle Lage in der DDR', 2 Nov. 1989, SAPMO-BArch, DY30/IV2/2.039/330, fos. 65–9.

[125] Matthias L. to Krenz, 2 Nov. 1989, SAPMO-BArch, DY30/IV2/2.039/323, fos. 116–18.

[126] Karl-Heinz Z. to Herger, 1 Nov. 1989, SAPMO-BArch, DY30/1096, fos. 131–5.

[127] SED-ZK (PO), 'Information', 27 Nov. 1989, SAPMO-BArch, DY30/IV2/2.039/317, fos. 144–9.

[128] Annegret Hahn *et al.* (eds), *4. November '89* (Berlin: Propyläen, 1990), 195.

Central Committee's propaganda section praised the lack of violence, but SED speakers had 'great difficulty being heard'. Behind closed doors, the party could accept demands for non-violence, as well as free elections, although not 'bourgeois party pluralism'. The National Front, face of the single list, would have to remain. The SED could also join in calls for a restructuring of the MfS, but not its abolition. 'Demands for a removal of the leading role of the SED are unacceptable for us communists.' In order to regain control of the situation, analysts suggested the usual salami tactics of small-scale talks 'in order gradually to push back the barely controllable mass rallies', suggesting that little had changed.[129] The party's only consolation was that previous rumours of a mass border breakout at the rally had not materialized.[130]

THE OPENING OF THE WALL

The new SED leadership under Krenz had been seriously considering liberalizing travel almost as soon as he succeeded Honecker. As already noted, Krenz had much hands-on experience with the travel and emigration complex as former security secretary. Already on 10 October, his subordinate, Wolfgang Herger, had secured support from other ministries for a detailed travel law, which was mooted for December. There were already worries about the possible effects on the GDR's manpower, as well as the hard currency situation (each traveller currently was entitled to exchange 15 deutschmarks, not enough to reach even nearby rail destinations in the FRG, but sufficient to bankrupt the GDR if claimed en masse).[131] On 23 October the Politbüro then considered a draft travel law that would dispense with previous requirements about relatives and justification for travel, but would still have reserve blocking clauses in the interests of 'national security, public order, health and morals'.[132] Yet, internally, the GDR leadership was still concerned that opening the borders could expose the state's sovereignty, and was still seeking formal recognition from the FRG before such a move.

Yet at this stage the GDR was hardly in a position to bargain. The full horrific truth of the GDR's economic plight only became fully clear after Honecker's fall, when the Politbüro took stock on 31 October 1989. State Planning Commissioner Schürer revealed that, whereas most lending banks advised that debt should never exceed 25 per cent of export capacity, in the GDR it was currently running at 150 per cent. The repayable debt would reach 57 billion hard marks by the end of 1990. In order to stabilize this alone, 30 billion marks

---

[129] SED-ZK (Propaganda), 'Erste Einschätzung der Demonstration und Kundgebung am 4. November 1989 in Berlin', 6 Nov. 1989, SAPMO-BArch, DY30/IV2/2.039/317, fos. 62–87.
[130] SED-ZK (PO), 'Information über die aktuelle Lage in der DDR', 3 Nov. 1989, SAPMO-BArch, DY30/IV2/2.039/330, fos. 70–4.
[131] Hertle, *Fall der Mauer*, 140.   [132] Stephan (ed.), *'Vorwärts immer'*, 173–4.

would have to be deployed—the equivalent of three years' worth of planned economic growth, or 25–30 per cent of domestic consumption. In short, the GDR was facing financial ruin and a terminal balance of payments crisis. The only alternatives were a moratorium, in which case the International Monetary Fund would have a say in the GDR, or to turn to the FRG again. Although this solution was for the moment rejected, the notion of bargaining for a lifeline with the Wall was moot. Indeed, over the coming days Chancellor Kohl abandoned his previous non-interventionism to make considerable demands in return for economic aid, such as the recognition of new parties, the renunciation of the SED's leading role, and the timetabling of free elections. The SED was to shift on all three points, but the Wall was to be retained as a trump card.[133]

The border to Czechoslovakia had been reopened on 1 November. At the same time the occupation of the FRG's Prague embassy resumed, with Czech party leader Jake putting renewed pressure on the East Germans to permit their citizens to cross direct into the West, and indeed, on 3 November the Politbüro authorized the GDR embassy in Prague to stamp passports with exit visas and the promise of retained citizenship and non-punishment. Over the weekend of 4–6 November 23,000 East Germans left via this route. Effectively, the Czech iron curtain was now breached. Yet new regulations announced in the GDR press on 6 November did not go anywhere near as far as the population wanted. Travel abroad still had to receive official approval and could not exceed one month; foreign currency could not be taken in any quantity; the Berlin sector boundary remained closed. It seemed to be another case of offering too little, too late. The Czechoslovak leadership was still not happy. Meanwhile, events got ahead of the legislators. On the same day a 300,000-strong Leipzig demonstration demanded visa-free travel—*visafrei bis Hawaii*—and an end to the Wall, and even the SED.[134] Demonstrations across the GDR took up this call for unrestricted travel without SED strings attached. By 9 November the Party Information was labelling the situation as 'very tense with widespread fears for the continuation of socialism in the GDR'.[135]

The Foreign Ministry, along with the MfS and Interior Ministry then worked out revised regulations, proposing on 7 November a single crossing-point in the south-west, clearly aimed only at would-be émigrés, but not those wishing to come and go. To its credit, the slowly democratizing Volkskammer rejected this as inadequate, leading to the resignation of the Council of Ministers (the GDR's government) and a serious power vacuum as the Politbüro was also reshuffled. Then, on the morning of 9 November, in response to renewed calls to solve the Czech impasse, two Interior Ministry and two Stasi officials met to produce a credible draft travel law. They agreed that by liberalizing emigration

---

[133] Hertle, *Fall der Mauer*, 162.   [134] Maier, *Dissolution*, 159.
[135] SED-ZK (PO), 'Information über die aktuelle Lage in der DDR', 9 Nov. 1989, SAPMO-BArch, DY30/IV2/2.039/330, fos. 81–5.

while doing nothing serious about short-term travel would only exacerbate the situation. Those denied the right to come and go would simply join the queue to leave permanently.[136] The Politbüro's new security secretary, Wolfgang Herger, also hoped to use the absence of previous hardliners to get the revised version through. The troubleshooters produced a new draft that all passport holders were entitled to leave by any checkpoint, including Berlin. Since only about 4 million GDR citizens possessed a passport at this point, it was hoped that passport applications would buy some time to regulate the flow. The Soviets gave the green light from Gorbachev personally (although the ambassador later claimed to have understood only an opening of the Demarcation Line, not the Berlin sector boundary[137]), and during the afternoon Krenz read out the new draft to the SED Central Committee, which, besides permanent emigration, included 'private trips'. Whether the gathered delegates, or even Krenz for that matter, realized the implications is unclear, since there was no substantial discussion. It was approved with immediate effect, ignoring the original reporting ban until the following day.[138] Günter Schabowski, who had been absent from this part of proceedings, was then sent off to announce the decree that evening at a press conference. What amounted to the Wall's death certificate was then read out from a scribbled text in an atmosphere of improvisation and confusion. On live television Schabowski simply read what was in front of him, appearing slightly baffled himself about whether the measures were to take place with immediate effect.[139] Meanwhile the gathered journalists rushed to file their stories.

Within hours, bemused East Germans watching western news programmes heard that the Wall was to all intents and purposes already open, and by 9 p.m. a large group had congregated at the Bornholmer crossing-point between Prenzlauer Berg and Wedding, in a mixture of expectation and anger. The Trabis tailed back a kilometre. Local border guards had not been forewarned, but when they telephoned for confirmation from their superiors, clear instructions were not forthcoming. Eventually, the officers in charge requested to be allowed to filter out some of the crowd to relieve the pressure, although ID cards were secretly invalidated with a stamp over the photograph, effectively deporting leavers. Almost immediately, however, some wanted to return. For those thousands remaining, this was not the signal to give up, as they began chanting 'Open the gate, open the gate!' and, hoping to reassure the border guards, 'We are coming back!' By 11.30 p.m. the border units were no longer able to control the situation and informed their superiors that they were opening the swing barriers. Around 20,000 people flooded over the bridge at Bornholmer Straße. A more complex situation had been developing at Checkpoint Charlie and Invalidenstraße, where West Berliners were also demanding entry, requiring

---

[136] Hertle, *Fall der Mauer*, 217–18.   [137] Hertle, *Fall der Mauer*, 266–7.
[138] Hertle and Stephan (eds), *Ende der SED*, 304–5.
[139] Günter Schabowski, *Der Absturz* (Berlin: Rowohlt, 1991), 306–9.

the West Berlin police to restrain them. MfS and Interior Ministry officials were paralysed by the indecision of their superiors, however, but were evidently not prepared to initiate a bloodbath on their own initiative, although many saw their life's work evaporating before their eyes. Around midnight all the checkpoints were opened up amid scenes of tears and joyful hysteria, while border officials looked impassively on, occasionally letting slip a furtive smile. At the Brandenburg Gate, where the Wall was several metres thick, West Berliners began to climb up onto the edifice, defying the water jets aimed at them. Already, some were beginning to chisel away at the Wall. Soon after 1 a.m. East Berliners simply climbed over the fencing around Pariser Platz and milled around under the Gate itself, with some joining westerners on the Wall. During that night at least 70,000 East Germans explored the new freedom, to be greeted with flowers and sekt, or headed off to the Kurfürstendamm or the nearest hostelry.

The following morning the SED Central Committee was seemingly in denial about the importance of what had happened, indulging in personal recriminations over the economic disaster, until repeated telephone calls from the Soviet ambassador prompted Krenz to broach the subject. Indeed, Foreign Minister Sheverdnadze subsequently claimed that the Soviet military had been gearing up for a defence of the iron curtain, against the will of the politicians.[140] Krenz explained: 'The pressure which was directed until yesterday at the Czechoslovakian border, has been applied since last night against our frontier. . . . The pressure could not be contained, there could only have been a military solution, comrades.'[141] Rather pathetically, he tried to hitch the muddle of 9 November to the statesmanlike vision of Gorbachev:

You know, in a game of football when a free kick is awarded, a wall is formed in front of the goal. Free kicks are the result of fouls by the other team. Let us make sure together of fair play. . . . May this historical edifice, the witness of dramatic chapters of changing German history . . . be a symbol for cooperation, stability, peace and friendship in the heart of Europe. Indeed, a building block . . . for the formation of the new European house, which needs many entries and exits.[142]

In the course of the meeting, the Central Committee drew up an Action Programme, promising free elections, a planned economy 'orientated to market conditions', and the uncoupling of party and state. Yet the following weeks witnessed repeated revelations about the lifestyle of the politbureaucracy at its country retreat in Wandlitz. The SED rank and file grew increasingly alienated from the leadership, demanding an extraordinary party convention in December, at which most of the surviving old guard were voted out and the party renamed Party of Democratic Socialism. On 1 December the party had even voted in the Volkskammer for the removal of its own constitutionally guaranteed 'leading

[140] Loth, 'Sowjetunion', 136.   [141] Hertle, *Fall der Mauer*, 243–4.
[142] SAPMO-BArch, DY30/IV2/2.039/320, fos. 1–2.

role'. Although the perceived moderate Hans Modrow took over the caretaker government, it was widely accepted that once free elections had been set, the SED would be consigned to the wilderness.

The Wall was opened up in a desperate gamble to persuade East Germans to stay or to come back after they had satisfied their curiosity in the West. In the first ten days after its opening 11 million East Germans visited West Germany and West Berlin! The regime watched with trepidation. On 10 November reports were reaching the Central Committee that 'panic and chaos are spreading', as workers were leaving work to apply for visas at police stations.[143] Krenz set up an 'operative leadership group' on the morning of the same day to restore order at the border. The Interior Ministry reported that this move had 'defused the situation somewhat'. There was less frenzied curiosity about checking that the changes were real. There were also cases of citizens appearing at the Demarcation Line and demanding egress. At Nordhausen border troops relented when 400 people appeared, opening a gate in the fencing. Later that afternoon they were back, demanding re-admittance.[144] Moreover, in the days following the dramatic nocturnal opening, West Berliners began hacking away at the Wall, trying to create their own unofficial openings. South of the Brandenburg Gate one slab was dragged away on 11 November, only to be returned and welded back into place. Alongside West Berlin police, the border troops succeeded in clearing the reinforced wall at the Brandenburg Gate of revellers. Yet, in the ensuing days dozens of impromptu crossing-points had to be cut out of the Wall in response to the inundation of those wishing to travel.[145]

Yet it was not just the party which watched the fall of the Wall with anxiety. The citizens' groups and the *Hierbleiber* were by no means the unqualified champions of toppling it so quickly. For some conspiracy theorists, the SED had opened up the border in order to make the country ungovernable in a last suicidal fit of Machiavellianism. In a BBC interview soon after 9 November, New Forum had expressed concern that the new travel freedoms would reduce the pressure of protests against the SED's monopoly. Leaders such as Bärbel Bohley were ambivalent about the border opening, labelling it a misfortune, although she was persuaded not to go public with this view. Finally the New Forum leaders resolved on the following statement: 'We have waited almost thirty years for this day. Sick of the Wall, we rattled the bars of our cage. Youth grew up with the dream one day to be free and experience the world. This dream is now fulfillable. This is a festival day for all of us.' Yet, the reformists warned against being 'diverted from demanding a political reconstruction of society'. 'We will be poor for a long time, but we don't have to have a society in which profiteers

---

[143] Hertle, *Fall der Mauer*, 245.

[144] MdI (Operative Führungsgruppe), 'Information', 13 Nov. 1989, SAMPO-BA, DY30/IV2/268,2.029/317, fos. 91–7.

[145] Hertle, *Fall der Mauer*, 292.

and sharpies elbow ahead.'[146] Friedrich Schorlemmer, one of the spokesmen for Democratic Breakthrough, even pleaded that the remains of the Wall might 'exist a bit longer'.[147] The seeds were nevertheless sown for the marginalization of the civil rights groups, who soon showed that they did not have a finger on the more materialist popular pulse, representing instead narrower church reformism or green-alternative interests.[148]

Despite pleas to stay, the exodus of permanent leavers continued over the winter of 1989–90: 133,429 in November; 43,221 in December; 73,729 in January 1990; 63,893 in February; 46,241 in March, until the authorities stopped collecting the statistics in July.[149] Since the same qualified young people were leaving as had gone before the Wall, the economic impact of the hole left behind began to be felt in the spring of 1990. The loss of qualified workers was accelerating the free fall of the economy. By late January 1990 Modrow as caretaker leader was reporting serious economic problems, and a number of strikes spread across the GDR. The influx of new citizens also strengthened the FRG's resolve to become more interventionist with the GDR. Despite Kohl's initial claims that he was only interested in a ten-point plan and confederation, the continuing exodus provided the rationale for a more radical solution. Modrow had offered a 'contractual community' in November, but as the chaos spread, in January Bonn announced that it would only negotiate with an elected government. In February Kohl sounded out Gorbachev about his opposition to unity. The Kremlin leader realized that the GDR was by then a lost cause. The most he could argue for was that a united Germany should not be part of NATO.

At the same time the demonstrations took on a fundamentally different tone. Rather than democratically announcing that 'we are the people', the slogan became the more nationalist 'we are one people'. Over the winter, the Leipzig demonstrators became more proletarian and male, carrying flags rather than candles.[150] Behind the political rhetoric, Pfaff has also tried to prove statistically that, beyond a certain critical mass of exodus which had goaded the protestors of September–October into action, leavers will always fatally undermine voice: 'as more and more people have walked out of the game, the exodus erodes social capital among the residents of a country, thereby undermining the movement potential of the population'.[151] The reforming civil rights campaigners soon found

---

[146] Maier, *Dissolution*, 198.   [147] Maier, *Dissolution*, 199.

[148] See for instance the disarmingly frank letters to New Forum in Tina Krone (ed.), *"Sie haben so lange das Sagen, wie wir es dulden": Briefe an das Neue Forum September 1989-März 1990* (Berlin: Robert-Havemann-Gesellschaft, 1999).

[149] Schumann, 'Flucht und Ausreise', 2401.

[150] Peter Förster and Günter Roski, *DDR zwischen Wende und Wahl: Meinungsforscher analysieren den Umbruch* (Berlin: LinksDruck, 1990), 162; Dieter Voigt et al., 'Die innerdeutsche Wanderung und der Vereinigungsprozeß: Soziodemographische Struktur und Einstellungen von Flüchtlingen/Übersiedlern aus der DDR vor und nach der Grenzöffnung', *Deutschland Archiv*, 23 (1990), 732–46.

[151] Pfaff, *Exit-Voice*, 161.

themselves isolated, even once they had established themselves as interlocutors at the Round Tables instituted in December 1989. When Federal Chancellor Kohl visited Erfurt, the crowd was a sea of black, red, and gold, the colours of the West German flag, significantly devoid of the GDR emblem of the hammer and dividers. This was a disaster for those who saw themselves as the genuine reformers who had put their necks on the line in the hot autumn of eighty-nine. Dismissing the SED as a travesty of socialism, they had wanted to seize the chance to build a truly socialist state, with equality for men and women, as well as some social guarantees for the millions of workers now facing redundancy. Instead, they saw themselves being drawn irresistibly closer to West Germany's capitalist bigger brother. The chance of a third way for Germany now seemed a forlorn and utopian hope.

In the unfolding crisis, the new Volkskammer elections were brought forward from May to 18 March 1990. They ended by becoming a referendum on unity. Unlike the political parties emerging in other eastern bloc states, such as Civic Forum in Czechoslovakia, who had no outside option, politics in the terminal GDR became linked to western patronage. The CDU under Chancellor Kohl soon forged links with the former bloc party, the CDUD, and the Christian Socialists in Bavaria sponsored the emergent DSU. An 'Alliance for Germany' was founded, campaigning specifically on the promise of rapid reunification. Likewise, the initially semi-autonomous Social Democratic movement in the GDR, the SDP, soon came into line with its western sister party, which provided it with the wherewithal to campaign. Unlike the Alliance, the Social Democrats were more hesitant about unification, for which they paid in the elections. The former protest movements had coalesced into an Alliance '90 list, but many had from the outset been resistant to remodelling themselves from movements into formal parties, and scored surprisingly poorly at the polls. The surprise winners, in what had been an SPD heartland in the Weimar Republic, was the Alliance for Germany, which won 48.1 per cent (CDU 40.6 per cent). As Maier noted: 'Voting for Kohl represented the equivalent of going West the previous fall.'[152] The civil rights movement represented by New Forum received only 2.9 per cent. The final nail in the coffin of the GDR was the currency union of 1 July, which created a single economic space. On the same day the Federal Government stopped the policy of asylum for East Germans.

[152] Maier, *Dissolution*, 214.

9

Seeking Closure: Remembering the Wall

THE WALL IN THE HEAD

The Wall is now history, but it still casts an invisible shadow. In a now famous phrase, the West German author Peter Schneider claimed prophetically that: 'It will take longer to pull down the wall in the head than any demolition contractor needs for the visible Wall.'[1] Echoing this, Willy Brandt added: 'Walls in the head often stand for longer than those erected from concrete blocks.'[2] Despite all the euphoria of 9 November 1989, when *Wessis* greeted *Ossis* with bottles of bubbly, the following decade seemed to confirm the engrained differences between East and West. As the realities of reunification became apparent, a wave of disillusionment and so-called *Ostalgie*, or 'nostalgia for the East', swept eastern Germany. Even for West Berliners, who had themselves often mocked West Germans as *Wessis*—tourists who regarded Berlin as a Cold War theme park—there was a sense that the old, 'alternative' West Berlin would succumb to corporate interests.[3] Indeed, in the new, reunited capital Kreuzberg ceased to be the place to be for the fashionable urban guerrilla, who increasingly migrated to Prenzlauer Berg or Friedrichshain in the eastern boroughs of the city.

Here, too, there was a rapid sobering up after the elation of 1989. This feeling of eastern loss was perhaps best captured in Wolfgang Becker's film *Good Bye, Lenin!* (2003), a black comedy in which a symbolic East German mother figure temporarily falls into a coma on the eve of the Wall's fall. To preserve her from a rude and potentially fatal awakening in a post-Wall Germany, the film's comedic conceit is that her family must pretend that the Wall still stands. Her son then excavates the rubbish bins of the former GDR to find now long-gone, favourite brands of Mokkafix coffee or Spreewald gherkins. This was a tongue-in-cheek homage to what had become a retro cult in the 1990s for post-modernly cool,

---

[1] Peter Schneider, *Der Mauerspringer: Erzählung* (Darmstadt and Neuwied: Luchterhand, 1982), 102.

[2] *Westdeutsche Allgemeine Zeitung*, 21 Dec. 1990.

[3] Herbert Beckmann, *Atlantis Westberlin: Erinnerungsreise in eine versunkene Stadt* (Berlin: Links, 2000).

extinct GDR products. At a deeper level, however, the film played with the distortions of memory by the mother, a lone parent who had raised her children with the explanation that their absent father had committed *Republikflucht* for another woman. (In fact, he had wanted her to follow, so that it is partially her betrayal.) Yet, while living the lie of real existing socialism a second time around, the friends and neighbours roped into maintaining the pretence gradually discover that they actually like being back in their fake GDR. Obviously, Becker realized that this was not a realistic solution—the mother dies, just as East Germany did—but the hero Alex briefly constructs an idealized GDR from all of the positive fragments of his memories of the past.

Now, one might say that this was selective memory, but it was a reflection too of the cocktail of resentments which unification had brought. As Alex rummages in the bins, his elderly neighbour grumbles about being 'betrayed and sold down the river' by the Wessis. In the face of the condescension of 'Besserwessis' (a pun on *Besserwisser* or know-it-all) from the other Germany, former GDR citizens found themselves forced into defending aspects of their past which perhaps had not been so close to their hearts at the time. There were jokes circulating in 1990 that the Wall should be rebuilt, but this time twice as high and with the front and hinterland walls 200 kilometres apart (which would, of course, have placed most of the Federal Republic in no-man's land!). In a survey in May 1990 every fourth West Berliner and every fifth East Berliner was even prepared to admit to regretting the passing of the Wall.[4] Other satirists had taken Becker's idea one step further, imagining how a mirror-image reunification under GDR auspices might have looked, including the arrest of a corrupt Federal Chancellor Kohl, in a flight of fancy which permitted side-swipes at both East and West.[5]

For East Germans the act of remembering was doubly fraught, because of the negative experiences of unification which many had after the Wall's fall. The widespread perception that the GDR had been 'annexed' by the Federal Republic led to considerable resentment, as the eastern *Länder* succumbed to a prolonged period of high unemployment. As one East Berliner told me while staring morosely into his pint: while the Wall was up, everyone thought the grass was greener on the other side; now the grass closer to home seemed greener through rose-tinted spectacles. A number of personal as well as collective memoirs did appear in the nineties and noughties, in which 13 August 1961 and 9 November 1989 act as landmarks of recollection. These were dates which supposedly had the same salience as the Kennedy assassination had had for Americans; everybody seemed to be able to remember where they had been at the time. It was also mnemonic that such a troubled day had happened on a thirteenth. It was therefore an obvious reference point for oral historians to pitch their questions

---

[4] Feversham and Schmidt, *Berliner Mauer*, 125.
[5] Reinhold Andert, *Rote Wende: Wie die Ossis die Wessis besiegten* (Berlin: Elefanten Press, 1994).

around, especially in search of the state's impact on the individual's life course.[6] Yet many of the memories went against the grain of the expected. It was clear from some that events such as the building of the Wall had been so deeply woven into personal biography that the prospect of exhuming its meaning for a whole lifetime was too painful.[7] There was also a wave of 'everyday memoirs', aimed either at ignorant westerners or nostalgic easterners, which presented life in the GDR as an absurd obstacle course, negotiated with Schwejkian resourcefulness and good humour.[8]

Some retrospective films on the experience of national division drew out the theme of parallel, what-if biographies—what would have happened if there had been no Wall. The West German Margarethe von Trotta's rather sentimental movie, *The Promise* (1994), starts with the historical accident of a pair of undone shoelaces separating two lovers as they try to escape in 1961: Sophie starts a new existence in the West; Konrad remains behind, fatalistically coming to accept this altered destiny: 'Staying here was a challenge. It was an adventure. We wanted to build something completely new here.'[9] Although he never loves the system, he comes to value what he has made of his life behind the Wall and is not prepared to consign it to the dustbin of history. More recent filmic versions of the past have tended to revert to simple heroicization of the role of the West, for instance in the film for television *The Tunnel* (2001),[10] in which the West comes to the aid of the East; or the docudrama *The Wall: Berlin '61* (2005) which starts with a complex dilemma of loyalties for a 14-year-old boy stranded behind the Wall, who at one point seems to have lost his soul to the party, but which resorts to a more conventional escape narrative.[11]

Other cultural reckonings with the past, especially from former East Germans, have not taken such a tragic view. Black comedy bordering on farce characterized the approach of Thomas Brüssig in his novel *Heroes Like Us* (1996).[12] Brüssig extrapolated the sort of Stasi conspiracy theories which were simultaneously filling history bookshelves in the 1990s, inflating them to absurd proportions in the fantasy world of Klaus Uhltzscht. This Stasi anti-hero, with a mother syndrome and a penis complex, claims even to have caused the fall of the Wall on 9 November by inadvertently flashing the border guards at Bornholmerstraße with his private parts, which have assumed monumental proportions following a

---

[6] Erika M. Hoerning, 'Memories of the Berlin Wall: History and the Impact of Critical Life Events', *International Journal of Oral History*, 8 (1987), 95–111; Cornelia Heins (ed.), *The Wall Falls: An Oral History of the Reunification of the Two Germanies* (London: Grey Seal, 1994), 181–248.

[7] Manfred Butzmann in Carl-Christoph Schweitzer *et al.* (eds), *Lebensläufe—hüben und drüben* (Opladen: Leske & Budrich, 1993), 77.

[8] Reinhard Ulbrich, *Spur der Broiler: Wir und unser goldener Osten* (Berlin: Rowohlt, 1998); Bernd-Lutz Lange, *Mauer, Jeans und Prager Frühling* (Berlin: Kiepenheuer, 2003).

[9] *Das Versprechen* (von Trotta, 1994).   [10] *Der Tunnel* (Richter, 2001).

[11] *Die Mauer: Berlin '61* (Schoen, 2005).

[12] Thomas Brüssig, *Helden wie wir* (Berlin: Verlag Volk & Welt, 1996).

botched blood transfusion for the ailing Honecker. Using a brand of grotesque exaggeration already familiar from Günter Grass's confrontation with National Socialism, Brüssig deploys his satire to ridicule many of the 'heroes' of socialism, including the asexual mother–matriarch and a vicious, but hilarious, dissection of Christa Wolf and *Divided Heavens*.[13] Brüssig represented a thirty-something, post-communist GDR generation which had little time for means/ends justifications of socialist excesses. Uhltzsch's narration of the novel to an American reporter nevertheless undermines the veracity of a history which is simultaneously selling a story, sensitizing the reader to the distorting possibilities of the past. And he is highly critical of the GDR populace: 'Only the march of time, and further events in Germany, will make my version of the fall of the Wall altogether plausible: look at the East Germans, before and after the fall of the Wall. Passive before and passive after—how are they supposed to have toppled the Wall?'[14]

Brüssig's next venture, scriptwriting Leander Haußmann's 1999 film *Sonnenallee*, was less unforgiving, but again presented GDR history as farce, even though it was set in the direct shadow of the Wall in the Exclusion Zone. The beat subcultures encountered in Chapter 6 provide the setting and suggest a less drab version of East German history. The casting of Katharina Thalbach as yet another eastern mother, but this time harbouring dreams of escape disguised as a pensioner, lent the film an intertextual layer of irony, since she had herself left the GDR in more serious circumstances after the Biermann affair. The patrolling police constable is a busybody and a pedant. Yet, the protagonist, Michael, is also revealed falsifying his past, writing a forged diary of his resistance activities to impress a would-be girlfriend. The fall of the Wall becomes a choreographed musical fantasy, as crowds, shot in the commercialized style of a music video, shimmy towards the border as forerunners of the massed crowds of 1989. Indeed, some critics found *Sonnenallee* too anodyne and even prepared to make a joke of shootings at the Wall.[15] At the close of the film, however, there are still warnings of premature forgettings, as the hero intones: 'Once upon a time there was a land and I lived there. And if people ask me how it was, it was the best time of my life, because I was young and in love.' Yet this defiant injunction is simultaneously undermined by a reverse framing shot, as the camera pulls back through the border checkpoint, as if through a portal of memory, fading from colour to grey. The GDR has been returned to the stereotypical and, for western observers perhaps, safer world of black and white.

This 'popular culturalization' of the GDR has found further outlets in mass publishing. One popular sub-genre of GDR publications has been the playful

---

[13] His final chapter, 'Der geheilte Pimmel' (the healed willy), is even a pun on Wolf's *Der geteilte Himmel*. Ibid., 277 ff. See also Paul Cooke, *Representing East Germany since Unification: From Colonization to Nostalgia* (Oxford: Berg, 2005), 74–9.
[14] Brüssig, *Helden*, 319–20.   [15] Cooke, *Representing*, 111–19.

coffee-table guide to East–West differences.[16] How does one spot an *Ossi* or a *Wessi*? The defence of East German identity could revolve around the most mundane of symbols, such as the shape of the little green man on pedestrian crossings facing standardization by the new Federal authorities. There has been a great emphasis on the material culture of the former GDR. An almost endless array of books appeared on the everyday experience of the East, from the P2 high-rise block of flats to the advertising industry under socialism.[17] It was Proust, after all, who had recognized that the everyday object could effortlessly transport the individual back to the lost world of the past. Without wishing to undermine the importance of the everyday for historical understanding, at times one senses that post-Wall commercial interests have seized on the 'Spreewald gherkin' factor to present an image of the GDR cast purely in product placement terms, an inverted form of the materialism which characterizes the West. Thus, television shows have ridden the wave of *Ostalgie*, but, as Paul Cooke has recently suggested, this could be viewed as part of the 'colonization' of East German culture by the West. The shows were invariably produced there, even having to bus their studio audiences in from the East to laugh in the right places.[18] Former East German publishers such as Eulenspiegel, purveyors of satire to the party, have been equally guilty of jumping on the *Ostalgie* bandwagon, however, producing board- and card-games that require arcane knowledge of the authentic 'East' experience.

One can perhaps laugh about East Germany in ways that one cannot laugh about the Third Reich, partly because the system imploded in 1989, going out with a whimper rather than a bang. Behind the veneer of Prussian military efficiency there was often complacency and incompetence. Yet one should also remember that humour is often a facade for more aggressive intents. Nearly all of the tongue-in-cheek dealings with the past have been of the black variety, and should not be dismissed as mere entertainment. In some of my own interviews for this project, it became clear that, as well as those who could look back philosophically, the experience had deeply damaged others; the past still pursued them in ways which members of open societies might find difficult to understand.[19] Stasi victims would sometimes set up stall outside museums and memorial sites, ready to give lectures and laments, or very occasionally wander into the reading room of the Bundesarchiv, thumping their hands on the service desk in search of 'what the state had on them'.

Historical memory, on the other hand, is something slightly different from such personal, lived memory. It is that set of retrospective, second-hand images and

---

[16] Jürgen Roth and Michael Rudolf, *Spaltprodukte: Gebündelte Ost-West-Vorurteile* (Leipzig: Reclam, 1997).

[17] Simone Tippach-Schneider, *Messemännchen und Minol-Pirol: Werbung in der DDR* (Berlin: Schwarzkopf, 1999).

[18] Paul Cooke, *Representing East Germany since Unification: From Colonization to Nostalgia* (Oxford and New York: Berg, 2005), 141–75.

[19] Gerhard R. interview, 1 Sept. 1997.

narratives which inhabit the collective conscious, usually generated after the event and often to serve the interests of the present. Indeed, historical scholarship in the 1990s, influenced by post-modern relativism, became almost obsessed with acts of remembering. Pierre Nora and the 'sites of memory' school have suggested that the state has a greater interest than most in predisposing official commemorations of the past to legitimate itself. Yet the sites of memory need not be tangible places, but can be collections of images, in the media or in the history book (just like the one you are reading). To complicate things even further, in the German context, there was also a half-century-long tradition of *Vergangenheitsbewältigung* or 'coming to terms with the past', ever since the Second World War. The two German states had both produced highly selective versions of the common past to bolster their own post-national identities. For the remainder of this chapter, I will focus on monumental and historical attempts at dealing with this contested past, but also briefly touch on popular culture and the law. As will soon become evident, however, the closure being sought in all these areas was still marked by Cold War divisions, by the interests of the West in 'decommunizing' the former adversary, and by many East Germans attempting to put the past behind themselves and move on in a difficult and disorientating present.

THE WALL ON TRIAL

Attempts at *Vergangenheitsbewältigung* often begin with the obvious targets and in this case it was the border guards of the closed society. Any researcher on the Wall in the 1990s soon noticed that the interest was not simply academic. I recall sharing files with none other than Egon Krenz in the Party Archive, as he prepared his trial defence in 1996. Archivists of the SED's successor, the PDS, became wary of prosecution teams or investigative journalists looking for 'smoking guns' on those responsible for the Wall and the maintenance of its security regime. In what was otherwise a very open archive policy, Wall researchers could hardly fail to notice the withdrawal of sensitive documents which named names. Indeed, in the early 1990s the public prosecutor's office had the Archive Foundation of Parties and Mass Organizations of the former GDR sealed off in the search for incriminating material. Federal data protection forbids historians from identifying private individuals and the Stasi files are assiduously blacked out in this regard. (Ironically, of course, it was to be former Federal Chancellor Helmut Kohl who sought in vain to close down the Stasi files for inflicting too much 'collateral damage' on western politicians.)

Part of the post-Wall healing process was in seeing justice done for the violence committed at the border.[20] There was still intense anger among the relatives

[20] Herwig Roggemann, *Systemunrecht und Strafrecht: am Beispiel der Mauerschützen in der ehemaligen DDR* (Berlin: Berlin-Verlag, 1993); Henning Rosenau, *Tödliche Schüsse im staatlichen*

of those shot. Yet, there was also growing resentment as the trials unfolded that western justice was being applied to eastern perpetrators. The accusation was levelled of retrospective 'victors' justice', like that allegedly dispensed at Nuremberg. However much the presiding judges denied any parallels, the media drew direct comparisons with the post-fascist experience, when SS camp guards had been put in the dock for wartime atrocities. Reckoning with the past after the Third Reich has usually been viewed as a series of compromises and missed opportunities, buried in Cold War realpolitik. Yet these were not completely abstract comparisons—even as the border guard trials began, some of the last trials against Nazi war criminals were ending.[21] They also coincided with a massively revived interest in the role of the Wehrmacht as trigger-pullers in the racial war on the eastern front, in which the left-wing public became more sceptical of arguments that soldiers were 'only obeying orders', but where conservatives felt the need to rally to young men in uniform. Others have also drawn tendentious parallels between victims of Auschwitz and the 20 July 1944 and the 'victims of the recently ended dictatorship, above all those who lost their lives at the Wall in Berlin and at the inner German border'.[22] Sensitive to these failings, but also propelled by anticommunism, the Federal authorities were determined that those responsible for the shoot-to-kill policy at the Berlin Wall should be brought to justice. In fact, the normal thirty-year statute of limitations was suspended on the grounds that perpetrators had not been prosecutable at the time.

In the 1990s a number of 'Wall shooter' trials thus began, starting with the 'trigger-pullers' immediately responsible. In the first, in the autumn of 1991, four guards were accused of killing Chris Gueffroy and wounding Christian Gaudian in February 1989, the last shooting victims of the Wall.[23] The defence objected to the Berlin state judge's past connections with escape organizations in the 1960s, as well as the fact that two of the prosecution lawyers were being retained by national news magazines. There were a number of juridical problems, moreover, for instance of *nulla poena sine lege previa*, or no crime without a prior law. Defendants could claim that guards had only been obeying GDR law. As part of the political plea-bargaining, the accused were charged not with murder but manslaughter, but still based on the argument that conscience should have dictated that their actions were illegal, thus overruling GDR law. This was to become enshrined at later trials by the so-called Radbruch formula, that natural

Auftrag: Die strafrechtliche Verantwortung von Grenzsoldaten für den Schusswaffengebrauch an der deutsch-deutschen Grenze (2nd edn; Baden-Baden: Nomos, 1998); Toralf Rummler, *Die Gewalttaten an der deutsch-deutschen Grenze vor Gericht* (Berlin: Nomos, 2000).

[21] *Der Spiegel*, 23 Dec. 1991, 30.

[22] Wolfgang Georg Fischer and Fritz von der Schulenberg, *Die Mauer: Monument des Jahrhunderts* (Berlin: Ernst & Sohn, 1990), dedication. Both were relatives of victims of the Nazis.

[23] Antje C. Petersen, 'The First Berlin Border Guard Trial' (Indiana Center on Global Change and World Peace, occasional paper no. 15, Dec. 1992).

justice superseded positive law. The defence argued that this was retrospective justice, and that the guards had only been obeying orders from above. At the trial, Fritz Streletz, ex-Chief of Staff of the National People's Army, testified that there was never a conscious attempt to kill fleers. Citing the many cases where border violators had been taken alive—of 3,600 attempts in the final decade, 187 had involved shooting—he claimed 'that use of firearms was the exception and there was no direct order to kill border violators. There was never a so-called shoot-to-kill order.'[24] Part of the cross-examination dealt with the guards' socialization under GDR norms, although the court dismissed the notion that they could not have known that their actions were wrong, citing the high degree of secrecy surrounding shootings. One telling piece of evidence was that, despite the official decorations and promotions for shootings, peers informally awarded border guards who had never fired in anger a pair of white gloves, a symbol of clean hands. In January 1992 the main accused, Ingo H., was nevertheless sentenced to three-and-half years (later reduced and suspended); a second guard was given a two-year suspended sentence; and the remaining two acquitted. Public opinion was mixed: some wanted to see justice done; others wanted to forget the past. Many East Germans felt that they were being subjected to an arbitrary interpretation of West German law, and some even collected signatures to end the trial. Other border guard trials, of the 450 brought by 2002, used similar defences, and judges handed down similar verdicts, with all convictions but seven leading to suspended sentences, although there were a third acquittals too.[25] One might view these trials as symbolic acts of justice, in which the prosecuting authorities were keen to show restraint, but not to leave crimes completely unpunished.

One of the accusations against denazification in the late 1940s was that it had prosecuted the smallfry, while allowing those truly responsible to escape. To avoid a repetition, the judiciary was determined to pursue some of the 'desk-killers' higher up the command chain, including members of the National Defence Council. In November 1992 the first leadership trial took place against Honecker, Mielke, Stoph, Keßler, and two other National Defence Council members, although the first three were let off for health reasons. In September 1993 Keßler, Streletz, and Albrecht were sentenced to between five and seven-and-a-half years, with appeals against retrospective justice thrown out by the Bundesgerichtshof, which set these aside on the grounds that the GDR itself had not respected human rights. Here, the court explicitly rejected arguments that the German–German border was a special case as the dividing line between two military blocs, and hence was the political responsibility of the former Soviet Union and the Warsaw Pact. Commanders of the Border Troops were also

---

[24] Ritter and Lapp, *Grenze*, 97.
[25] Roman Grafe, *Deutsche Gerechtigkeit: Prozesse gegen DDR-Grenzschützen und ihre Befehlsgeber* (Berlin: Siedler, 2004), 309.

put in the dock in 1994. At the beginning of proceedings officers had issued a statement that the Border Zone was always marked as a military exclusion zone, but claimed that firearms were only used to detain not to kill escapers. The court discussed the semantics of the term 'annihilate' in the guards' order of the day, whether it was of rhetorical or literal intent, but was not prepared to give the benefit of the doubt. In September 1996 the head of Border Troops, General Klaus-Dieter Baumgarten and five of his subordinates were sentenced to three to six years for manslaughter on eleven counts, although Baumgarten was pardoned after serving half of his sentence. The accused again called this victors' justice, and there were ugly scenes in court from the defendants' supporters. Later, in 1999 four colonels in the Border Troops were also tried by the Berlin Landgericht.[26]

In March 1995 the state prosecutor had, in addition, switched his attention back to the top political leadership, charging seven Politbüro members—Krenz, Schabowski, Kleiber, Dohlus, Hager, Mückenberger, and Tisch (the last one died before proceedings, and all but the first three were eventually deemed unfit to stand trial)—with manslaughter of refugees.[27] This was to be the jewel in the crown for the prosecution. In September 1995 Gorbachev wrote a letter for Krenz to use in court, stating that 'the border between the GDR and the FRG was not only a border between two UN member states, but also between two hostile military–political alliances. This undoubtedly deeply influenced the border regime.' The attempt to make Krenz responsible was an attempt 'to settle political accounts', a 'relapse into the practices of the times of the "Cold War"'.[28] This was echoed by the former Soviet ambassador, Abrassimov, who reiterated that the GDR's state border had also been the western frontier of the Warsaw Pact, and that the NVA had been part of its command structure.[29] Indeed, cynics could argue that the Federal Republic had accepted the status quo when it signed the *Ostpolitik* treaties in the early 1970s, but was suddenly changing the rules. A first session of the Berlin Landgericht met in November 1995, in which the impartiality of one of the judges was questioned but not enough to delay proceedings. The long-awaited Politbüro trial duly commenced in January 1996, seeing three members sentenced in August 1997—Krenz, Schabowski, and Kleiber—although they claimed that the military border had been under Soviet jurisdiction. Yet, it was argued by the state prosecutor that since the death of Brezhnev, the GDR had enjoyed a certain room for manoeuvre, which included the GDR's unilateral dismantling of the SM-70 fragmentation

---

[26] Kurt Frotscher and Wolfgang Krug (eds), *Im Namen des Volkes: Grenzer vor Gericht* (Schkeuditz: GNN, 2000).

[27] Neue Justiz (ed.), *Der Politbüro-Prozeß: Eine Dokumentation* (Baden-Baden: Nomos, 2001). Three other Politbüro members, Herbert Häber, Siegfried Lorenz and Hans-Joachim Böhme were acquitted or found not guilty in a trial ending in July 2000, on the grounds that they had joined too late to influence policy.

[28] Gorbachev to Krenz, 22 Sept. 1995, in Dietmar Jochum, *Der Politbüro-Prozeß* (Kückenshagen: Scheunen-Verlag, 1996), 17–20.

[29] Abrassimov to Krenz, 17 Oct. 1995, in ibid., 20–3.

devices, and that the Politbüro had nevertheless failed to humanize the frontier. Only Schabowski expressed any regret, conceding his moral guilt, but viewing his criminal responsibility as a 'juristic construction'. Krenz was unrepentant, denying that 'I am making circumstances responsible for my actions by invoking phenomena such as the "Cold War" or "Systems Conflict" ': 'These proceedings are about elevating self-serving propaganda against the "GDR illegal state" [*Unrechtsstaat*] to historical fact. . . . I feel the wave of trials against the GDR and its politicians as a new German variant of McCarthyite persecution.'[30] Krenz received six-and-a-half years, the others three. This verdict went to appeal but the Bundesgerichtshof upheld the sentences in 1999, although in October 2000 the ruling mayor of Berlin, the Christian Democrat Eberhard Diepgen, pardoned both Schabowski and Kleiber. Meanwhile, Krenz did not turn himself into the authorities until 2001, having failed to convince the European Court of Human Rights of his case. Even then, his open prison conditions only required him to spend the night in prison.

As a gesture of even-handedness, one escape helper who caused the death of border guard Reinhold Huhn received a one-year suspended sentence in December 1998. At the time, after the shooting on 18 June 1962, the media on both sides of the Wall had given very conflicting views, with the West claiming that Huhn had been shot by his own side. An investigation by the West Berlin state attorney exonerated the individual concerned. After the fall of the Wall, however, M. admitted his deed.[31] It is probably true that most East Germans preferred to draw a veil over the legal coming to terms with the Wall, but there were lone voices who have argued that, in the interests of integrating middle-ranking GDR military leaders into the united German armed forces, legal corners were cut. Roman Grafe in particular has pleaded for greater consequentiality, comparing unfavourably the relatively short length of sentences with those for 'conventional' crimes: 'German justice? . . . While the privately motivated killing of an individual as a rule is shunned by society, the prosecution of state–political multiple murder has remained the exception.'[32] Such views are in danger of rocking the all-German boat and tend to cause academics to move uncomfortably in their seats. Nevertheless, the trials of the guardians of the Wall, which ended in 2004, now remain a closed chapter in its history.

A MONUMENT UNTO ITSELF?

What of the edifice itself? The Wall was an instrument of division, but became more than that, a symbol of national partition and of the entire Cold War bloc

[30] Neue Justiz (ed.), *Politbüro-Prozeß*, 277–85. [31] *Der Spiegel*, 28, 1991.
[32] Grafe, *Deutsche Gerechtigkeit*, 319.

confrontation, indeed of the twentieth century's total wars of ideology.[33] Berlin, largely a product of the nineteenth century, was of course already filled with memorials, both triumphalist monuments to Prussian victories as well as more sombre commemorations of the war dead of the First World War. The city is also scattered with monuments to the victims of National Socialism and the last war, including injunctions to remember the dead of the Holocaust. The German terms *Denkmal*, *Gedenkstätte* and *Mahnmal* denote slightly different things, however. *Denkmal* is more positively loaded, a testament to achievements past; a *Gedenkstätte* a place for remembrance and contemplation; whereas a *Mahnmal* is a warning to the future not to repeat the past. What is common to all is their uniting function, making a statement on behalf of the nation. Yet what distinguishes the Wall, and indeed most monuments to the Cold War in Germany, is the existence of two distinct constituencies within the united nation, the 'winners' in the West and the 'losers' in the East.[34] What might appear obvious to a West Berliner, might cause offence to an East Berliner.

different views

In 1961, of course, the 'losers' of 1989 thought they were the winners, and the 'Antifascist Defence Rampart' was celebrated during its lifetime. The 13 August 1961 certainly belonged to the GDR's official calendar of dates, so much so that postage stamps were even issued to commemorate it. The anniversary of 13 August was celebrated with the same pomp and circumstance as Britain's trooping the colour. Walking around the centre of East Berlin, it was possible to find plaques to the heroic activities of the factory militias. Whether 13 August was received by the population in the same vein is more doubtful. The Stasi always kept an especially close eye out for provocative actions on its anniversary. On the eastern side streets were renamed after dead border guards, for instance Egon-Schultz-Straße for Strelitzer Straße, and monuments erected, such as that in Jerusalemer Straße, almost directly opposite the Fechter memorial (see below), originally unveiled in 1963 to Reinhold Huhn, 'cowardly murdered by West German fascist bandits', but expanded in 1973 to commemorate seven other border comrades and inscribed 'Their Death is Our Obligation'. A rather ugly stonework structure, surrounded by pine fronds, this was an official stop for western tourists in guided tours of the East, as well as parties of East German schoolchildren.[35] In 1994, after the *Wende*, the border guard memorial was removed with the official explanation:

This is no censure against those who died. Their possibly unwitting involvement is acknowledged by the commission. However, after the fall of the Wall and the

[33] Fischer and Schulenberg, *Die Mauer: Monument des Jahrhunderts*.
[34] Brian Ladd, *The Ghosts of Berlin: Confronting German History in the Urban Landscape* (Chicago, IL: University of Chicago Press, 1997), 10. See also Leo Schmidt and Henriette von Preuschen, *On Both Sides of the Wall: Preserving Monuments and Sites of the Cold War Era* (Bad Münstereifel: Westkreuz, 2005).
[35] Gerhard R. interview, 1 Sept. 1997.

reunification of Germany there can no longer be any justification for regarding them as heroes and for honouring a service which was by no means honourable.[36]

The streets have thus returned to their original names while official sculptures have become museum pieces, leaving ghostly 'shadows' on the pavement.

The Wall was hardly days old before first acts of commemoration began to appear on the other side, in the West, as floral tributes and crosses were mounted at places where victims had died trying to cross, such as Bernauer Straße, sometimes symbolically entwined in barbed wire. These were then gathered in a row near the Reichstag for the benefit of tourists, while slabs in the pavement now commemorate the spots where people had met their deaths. At the point where Peter Fechter bled to death near Checkpoint Charlie a wooden cross was donated and tended by the conservative newspaper tycoon Axel Springer, and replaced in 1999 by a cylindrical steel memorial with the inscription ' . . . he only wanted freedom'. Before 1989 this was the main focus of anti-Wall sentiment. On 13 August every year the West Berlin assembly would lay wreaths here, joined by international representatives, while for the left, such ceremonies became rituals of the Cold War. The West Berlin authorities also erected viewing platforms at regular intervals, from which visitors could peer over the Wall. It became part of the itinerary of visiting schoolchildren and overseas tourists to ascend these scaffolds, including John F. Kennedy in 1963 and Ronald Reagan in 1987. Throughout its existence, the Wall was a ready-made piece of anticommunist propaganda.

One of the earliest museums to the Wall had also accompanied it almost from the start, the Haus am Checkpoint Charlie, set up in 1963 under Rainer Hildebrandt, a tireless campaigner against the GDR. Originally the Haus was to be situated at Bernauer Straße, the 'natural' location, given the dramatic events which had unfolded there, but found its home instead next to the American checkpoint. Its exhibits focused on escape attempts made under and over the Wall, displaying vehicles with false compartments and armour-plating, as well as the burners of a hot-air balloon and a micro-submarine used to haul escapees to safety. These now have the feeling of religious relics, some rather the worse for wear, but exude authenticity. Over the years, however, the exhibition took on a more universal tone, stressing global human rights and civil disobedience. Over the decades millions of tourists have tramped through its rather cramped rooms. Halfway up the stairs a peephole allowed a voyeuristic peek at the GDR checkpoint, only a hundred yards away. The Haus naturally became a target for the Stasi, who already knew Hildebrandt from his activities for the libertarian Fighters against Inhumanity, which would launch balloons with propaganda leaflets into the eastern sector. In the 1980s, in search of détente, the SPD-led West Berlin Senate became increasingly embarrassed by this Cold War memento

---

[36] Feversham and Schmidt, *Berliner Mauer*, 146.

and threatened to starve it of funding, which eventually occurred in 1995 under CDU budget cuts, when it lost its annual 130,000 deutschmarks. The expansion of the Haus to become a 'Mauermuseum', which includes trophies from the eastern side of Checkpoint Charlie, such as its swing barriers and the white line chiselled out of the road, could only occur with lottery funding and the increased sale of souvenirs from its gift shop, such as 'You are leaving the American Sector' mugs, keyfobs, and chocolate bars. In 1999 a replica of the original 1960's military police cabin was also reinstalled on the site of the one ceremonially hoisted away in 1991. Yet its somewhat eccentric jumble of exhibits still drew 500,000 visitors a year ten years after the fall of the Wall, the most frequented museum in Berlin.[37] The Haus's 'maverick' status was also underlined in October 2004, when it erected a thousand memorial crosses on a private piece of land before being ordered to remove them amid much press publicity.[38]

A more neglected site is the former reception camp for refugees at Marienfelde, housed in a still functioning centre for asylum seekers, mainly of eastern European origin. A small exhibition shows the various stations that *Republikflüchtige* had to go through upon arrival, as well as recreating a few rooms with bunk beds and luggage. Photographs of refugees also convey a sense of the scale of the exodus. The local association was short of funds in the 1990s, but more recently the exhibition there was expanded and made permanent.[39] Along the former intra-German border more than a dozen museums exist.[40] Some have been set up by aficionados of the Border Troops themselves, such as the Tetterborn museum. Vitrines are full of weapons and pennants of the former border troops. At Helmstedt is the Zonal Border Museum, which contains exhibits on the 'Face of the Frontier', with sections of fence and models of self-firing devices, as well as sections on 'Flight', the 'Border Opening' of 1989, and 'Frontier Art'. The last one has exhibits from eastern and western artists. The control-point at Marienborn has been preserved as a monument to 'German Division'. The drive-through areas for cars and lorries have been preserved. In the staff building an exhibition, tracing the changes from the wooden barracks of 1946 to the modern installation of the early 1970s, has been set up. Further south, in Mödlareuth, the divided village displays relics of the intra-German border, including a watchtower on a foreshortened pedestal, as well as bunkers and vehicles of the border troops. A three-mile 'historical walk' is also offered. Other rural reminders include the 'village republic of Rüterberg' at the Elbe, the hamlet of Zicherie, with a cross to a journalist shot at the border, the border monument

---

[37] Rainer Hildebrandt, *Es geschah an der Mauer* 18th edn (Berlin: Verlag Haus am Checkpoint Charlie, 1992).

[38] Maren Ullrich, *Geteilte Ansichten: Erinnerungslandschaft deutsch-deutsche Grenze* (Berlin: Aufbau, 2006), 213.

[39] Bettina Effner and Helge Heidemeyer, *Flucht im geteilten Deutschland: Erinnerungsstätte Notaufnahmelager Marienfelde* (Berlin: bebra, 2005).

[40] Ullrich, *Geteilte Ansichten*.

at Hötensleben, including a section of wall and an observation tower, as well as the Coburg Bundesgrenzschutz Museum, which includes GDR exhibits.[41]

The Wall was, of course, a great attraction in itself. From the late 1970s, its western face, especially the final-generation wall, had become an unofficial canvas for graffiti artists, a *tabula rasa* irresistible to paintbrush and spray-can.[42] Much of this was ephemeral verbal graffiti, often applied by tourists for their own photo-call at the Wall, or for the gratification of others (for example, 'Kate, Your name is now on the BERLIN WALL. From Jim'). In time-honoured fashion teenagers recorded their crushes on each other. More wittily, 'I like Beuys', the avant-garde artist, was crossed out to read 'I like boys'. Others treated the Wall like a church prayer board, registering hopes, or like a totem pole to ward off evil spirits. One could read pacifist slogans such as 'Make Love not Walls' or 'The Wall is only a symbol that every wall can be overcome' or 'Jesus' Love Will Conquer'.[43] When the Wall did fall, it vindicated a certain 'new ageist' belief that it had been felled by collective good karma or by biblical prophecy: 'And the people let out a loud shout and the wall fell down and the people entered the city. (Joshua 6: 20)'. One particular Californian self-help book cited everyone from Napoleon to Eisenhower, from Gandhi to Bob Dylan, in support of the graffito 'Love is thicker than concrete'.[44]

Some inscriptions were more overtly political, such as 'DDR = *Deutscher DReck*' (German scum) or the frequent 'DDR = KZ' (concentration camp). One cartoon spelled out a '3' with a pair of handcuffs, an SS-20 missile launcher as a '5', and 'Years' picked out in barbed wire, with two prison windows for 'D' and a truncheon-toting Vopo for the 'R': '35 Years of GDR'.[45] Another ascribed the blame more evenly between the superpowers, depicting the two halves of Berlin as faces attempting to embrace while pulled apart at gunpoint by two pairs of hands. Or a Humpty-Dumpty labelled 'détente' possibly toppling from, possibly leaping over, the Wall.[46] To the rhetorical question: 'Have you ever seen an antifascist defence wall?', another answered: 'All that I want to know is which side the fascists are on so that I can be on the other side.'[47] The fact that the downtown Wall was almost literally built on the ruins of Hitler's bunker seemed symbolic to some. Self-styled 'freedom fighters', such as John Runnings,

---

[41] Ritter and Lapp, *Grenze*, 147.

[42] For a selection see Helmut Schmitz, *Spray-Athen: Graffiti in Berlin* (Berlin: Rixdorfer, 1982); Harry Lorenz, *Mauerkunst: Ein Berliner Zeitdokument* (Berlin: Edition StadtBauKunst, 1991).

[43] Kurt Ausfelder, *Kunst oder Chaos? Graffiti an der Berliner Mauer* (Darmstadt: Das Beispiel, 1990), 9 and 37.

[44] Terry Tillmann, *The Writings on the Wall: Peace at the Berlin Wall* (Santa Monica, CA: 22/7, 1990), 31. The author was a leader of personal growth seminars, teaching pupils 'how to remove their personal walls', 13.

[45] Ausfelder, *Kunst oder Chaos?*, 69.

[46] Leland Rice, *Up Against It: Photographs of the Berlin Wall* (Albuquerque, NM: University of New Mexico Press, 1991), 11 and 16.

[47] Ibid., 8.

used the Wall as a Cold War political noticeboard, announcing the 'political declaration of war on military authority' and the end to 'kaputt diplomacy'. Others used it simply to publicize their own issues, such as the census boycott in 1986, pasting their blank census forms against the concrete. The anarchism symbol appeared frequently, beside the nuclear disarmament sign, a message from the 'autonomous' scene in Kreuzberg to more strait-laced tourists.

Other sprayings were more surreal: invitations to 'Go over the Top' or fake street signs showing 'Berlin City Limits: Next Town Berlin'. Or logos such as 'Made in Germany'. Others were visual *trompe l'oeil* jokes—painted-on ladders and doorways or extensions of the streetscape, including one elaborate continuation of a real church steeple on the other side. During the *Wende*, when makeshift openings appeared, emergency exit symbols were painted on the western side. In one case, a prankster decorated a section of the Wall with flowery wallpaper, besides which appeared the slogan: 'If they can't take a joke, fuck 'em.'[48] At this ephemeral level, layer upon layer of signs and symbols appeared, each amending what had gone before, so that the Wall was constantly in flux. Periodically, GDR border troops would appear in the night through secret doors and respray its western face off-white, although they were fighting a losing battle. Within weeks the graffiti would be back.

More accomplished street artists such as Thierry Noir and Christophe Bouchet became famous for their pop art, including lines of Easter Island-like cartoon heads or multiple Warholesque statues of liberty, preaching speed as the essence of their approach. Keith Haring's primitivist paintings drew on American street art. In 1986 he produced a 100-metre section by Checkpoint Charlie of intertwining aboriginal figures against a yellow background. Richard Hambleton's shadow figures were more brooding, as was his 1985 'Who Is Afraid of Black Red Gold?', covering 20 metres of Wall in black paint, with a thin red line at one end, a gold one at the other, thus mimicking the German flag, and a 20-centimetre gap in the middle. 'This place has symbolic meaning to me', commented Hambleton. 'It represents a shadow of Germany. One can look at it as a school blackboard. I hope people will write serious things on it.'[49] Another then painted a blackboard with the text 'German lesson', placing a real desk and chair as an installation against the Wall.[50] Nearby, in Zimmerstraße, in 1987 Peter Unsicker covered the Wall opposite his 'Wall Street Gallery' with plaster masks, peering through sheeting. The next year he attached shards of mirror, thus reflecting back a fragmented view of the West to viewers seeking the East.[51] On the eastern side of this anarchic and ever-changing *Gesamtkunstwerk*, of course, the Wall remained pristine, a chain of white rectangles framed in dark grey.

---

[48] *Up Against It*, Rice, 28.
[49] Heinz J. Kudas, *Berliner Mauer Kunst* (Berlin: Elefanten Press, 1998), 52–3.
[50] Ibid., 23.   [51] Ibid., 48.

This does raise the question of whether something as grisly as the Wall could be treated as art. According to one critical view, 'The kaleidoscopic Western side of the Wall became either a showcase of Western freedom or embarrassing evidence of Western decadence.'[52] In 1986 a group of former easterners objected to the Wall's aestheticization by painting through some of the graffiti at eye level with a white line, explaining: 'The Wall has to be seen as a wall again. It should not be a tourist attraction.'[53] Whereas in the 1960s the picture books on the Wall had shown stark black-and-white photographs of human misery, in the 1980s the Wall had become coffee-table literature, aimed at 'Wall tourists'. Were the graffiti artists helping to render it invisible as an imprisoning mechanism by turning it into an object of fun and spectacle? Some commentators have seen this as a positive attribute. The avant-garde artist Joseph Beuys wrote to the GDR Interior Ministry, teasingly suggesting that the Wall should be raised 5 centimetres for aesthetic reasons:

> Considering the Berlin Wall from a point of view which only takes account of the proportions of this edifice must be permissible. It immediately defuses the Wall. By laughter within. Annihilates the Wall. One is no longer caught on the physical wall. One is diverted to the spiritual wall, and overcoming this is the main point.[54]

According to Gareis, 'long before it physically vanished, art was able to erase the Wall from our mind thanks to the absurd and often chaotic works which anticipated future reality'.[55] To a certain extent, this was wish fulfilment that the Wall did not exist, and that westerners should not have to feel guilty.

Certainly this (understandable) interest in the image of the Wall did obscure its real purpose. The perspective of the photographer is often betrayed by how shots were framed (and whether East Berlin features in the background or not). For the purposes of my thesis here, it tended also to reflect a predominantly western view. Many of the literal 'writings on the Wall' were introspective and self-absorbed. The act of painting on the Wall released something dark and foreboding inside that was summoned up when confronting it. The only antidote was often humour. Although some of the motifs were self-related, addressing universal themes, these could be adapted to the Wall's message. Paintings of hearts divided down the middle above the motto 'torn apart' or an eye producing a large teardrop were perhaps the most effective statements. Parodies of cave art suggested the primitive nature of the object in view.[56] There could also be a postmodern self-awareness of the process, such as young people photographing themselves being photographed at the Wall, and pasting the results on its surface, or one injunction to 'look at yourself looking' at the 'Berlin ghetto'.[57] At a meta-level, there was also a poetic justice that a structure representing order was subjected to such disorder.

---

[52] Ladd, *Ghosts*, 27.   [53] Ibid., 58–9.   [54] Cited in Frech, *Berliner Mauer*, 25.
[55] Raimo Gareis, *Berliner Mauer: Die längste Leinwand der Welt* (Leichlingen: Krone, 1998), 96.
[56] Ausfelder, *Kunst oder Chaos?*, 21–3 and 40.   [57] Rice, *Up Against It*, 22.

From the night of 9 November 1989 the Wall's days were numbered. Mechanical equipment ripped improvised gateways out of what had appeared impenetrable. A strange limbo period followed over the winter of 1989–90, when temporary checkpoints were carved out of no-man's land. After the first free elections in March 1990 the new Minister of Disarmament and Defence, Pastor Eppelmann, ordered the dismantling of the Wall by the Border Troops themselves. After unification in October 1990, these, aided by Bundeswehr soldiers and British Army engineers, completed the task by the end of November, carting off stacks of L-shaped 'Border Wall 75' segments to depots in and around Berlin. Heaps of dismantled pieces gathered at 'Wall graveyards' in Pankow and Bernau, where they were ground down into aggregate. Elsewhere, former border troops worked on the recultivation of border land.

In the medium term, the removal of the Wall has transformed the cityscape of Berlin, above all in the area around Potsdamer Platz. What had once been the busy intersection of Wilhemine Berlin had become a wasteland. Tramlines literally disappeared into the Wall. Previous thoroughfares, such as the Leipziger Straße, became backwaters of East Berlin. The area on the western side, between the Brandenburg Gate and the Staatsbibliothek, had gone to seed, a zone almost beyond history where Wim Wenders had let the troubled angels of his 1987 film *Wings of Desire* roam in existential reverie. By the early 1990s, however, this area had become a massive building-site sitting on top of prime real estate. The Senate erected a giant red 'Infobox' on stilts, from which tourists could peer at the cavernous holes and towering steel building-shells. A diorama showed what the new Berlin would look like, as government buildings were projected for the still devastated Reichstagsufer. A new mental geography has opened up, as previously disused underground lines were taken back into use and connected up in different combinations. Although the trains and the passengers are often the same, the destinations have changed.

The East German government had soon realized, however, the marketability of the Wall, setting up VEB Limex-Bau in spring 1990, an import–export company. In August Eppelmann then ordered the sale of its remnants. Elements with prominent graffiti were auctioned off as works of art at Monte Carlo, reaching art-house prices of up to $300,000 apiece. Other pieces were donated to statesmen or institutions, including Ronald Reagan and George Bush; the Vatican; the Imperial War Museum in London; and CIA headquarters at Langley, Virginia. Private souvenir hunters, so-called 'wallpeckers'—including myself, I must confess—also joined the fray. This act of appropriation turned what had been a symbol of oppression into a symbol of freedom, however naively. Soon the Wall bore heavy scars, its reinforcing steel rods protruding rather forlornly in places, corroding in the rain. Stalls were set up at tourist traps selling pieces of Wall, mainly multi-coloured fragments from the western side. In some cases, bland pieces were sprayed up to make them appear even more 'authentic'. Postcards with perspex blisters containing fragments were sold, like holy relics. A large number of fakes also appeared on the market, so that genuine 'wallpeckers' accompanied their wares with photographs of themselves in action, hammer and chisel in hand.

With so much authorized and unauthorized destruction going on, there was a danger that nothing would remain. Some Wall artists painted up 'No hammering' symbols, to little avail. There were already German precedents for the removal of painful reminders of the past, such as some Nazi architecture. Again, some members of the new city government appeared to want to eradicate any vestige of the Wall in a form of cultural amnesia. Streets named after communist luminaries and martyrs were systematically renamed, including not only Egon-Schultz-Straße, named after the border guard killed in the Tunnel 57 incident, but Clara-Zetkin-Straße, named after the Weimar communist. In the 1990s it was ironically tourists who were most interested in rediscovering the Wall and the tourist guide industry catered for them with tours and special guidebooks, such as *Where was the Wall?*, which provided before-and-after shots of the Wall pre- and post-1989, or close readings in urban industrial archaeology.[58] There had already been some press voices calling for some sections to be kept.[59] Wolfgang Templin, a civil rights campaigner linked to the Haus am Checkpoint Charlie, also lent his voice: 'It may well be true that the Wall was torn down in a destructive rage. Everyone wanted to be rid of the imprisoning Wall, that stone document of freshly defeated oppression and separation. Yet what was at the time an act of emancipation will gradually become an act of historical suppression if the last pieces of the Wall are not preserved.'[60] The 'Arbeitsgemeinschaft 13. August' of the Haus am Checkpoint Charlie also pointed out that the Wall brought tourists to Berlin:

Berlin visitors ask if this wall will ever have the significance of the wall of Troy or the Great Wall of China. The material for history and literature, film and theatre is great and will certainly find employment. Even the Iliad only came to be centuries after the Trojan war. The task of contemporaries, however, is to save the salvageable.[61]

While politicians deliberated about a fitting monument, artists took an early lead. In the spring of 1990 an art competition was held at the Oberbaum Bridge, where a long section of hinterland wall nearly a mile long became the 'East Side Gallery'. A total of 118 artists from twenty-one countries painted on the then still pristine eastern face. A decade of weathering and graffiti took their toll, until in June 2000 the Gallery was listed and the artwork partially restored. The large amount of broken glass at its foot also indicated that the Wall still had a cathartic function. Many of the frescos reflected the ecological concerns

[58] Harry Hampel and Thomas Friedrich, *Wo die Mauer war* (Berlin: Nicolai, 1996); Axel Klausmeier and Leo Schmidt (eds), *Mauerreste—Mauerspuren* (Berlin: Westkreuz Verlag, 2004).
[59] *Berliner Morgenpost*, 14 June 1990, cited in Ladd, *Ghosts*, 32.
[60] Feversham and Schmidt, *Berliner Mauer*, 140.
[61] Arbeitsgemeinschaft 13. August, '119. Pressekonferenz', 11 Aug. 1998, 20.

of the time, or hip-hop pieces in primitivist style. Some humorously poked fun
at the recent past. Wenzel's 'Persistence of Ignorance' shows Honecker's head
superimposed on the body of Louis XVI, against a background of bricks and
smoking chimneys. Kinder's Trabi bursts through the Wall under the motto
'Test the Best' (a parody of a cigarette slogan). Only a few, such as Jost and
Steglich's 'Politics is the continuation of war by other means', showing a death-
bed corpse with a 100-mark note in its mouth (a reference to the 'welcome
money' given to East Germans arriving in the West), used the gallery for more
sardonic protest. More notable pieces such as Vrubel's 'Fraternal Kiss', showing
an embrace between Brezhnev and Honecker above the legend 'My God, help
me to survive this deadly love', has been reproduced elsewhere.[62]

The real controversies arose over how to mark the rapidly disappearing course of
the remaining Wall. Tensions developed between self-help initiatives and official
commemorations. In the early summer of 1990 former East German citizens
launched a scheme to sow the death strip with lupins. East Berlin landscape
architect Stefan Strauß suggested turning the former death strip into a green
belt, which would be visible from the air, but also 'like a scar which must heal,
and this greening would be a sign for Berlin'.[63] Late in 1990 Rosemarie Köhler
proposed a more permanent 'silver band' of aluminium to show the course of
the Wall, but the city-planning department demurred. The Kreuzberg municipal
works then came up with a more prosaic double row of cobblestones, with some
actually laid in Stresemann- and Wilhelmstraße and at the Schlesischer Busch
in 1991. Unfortunately, the effect blended all too easily into the surrounding
streetscape. In isolated places, such as the Sonnenallee checkpoint, a plaque has
been laid in the pavement, commemorating the opening of the Wall.[64]

Yet, *where* did the 'real' Wall run? Along the front Wall, visible to Wessis,
or along the hinterland Wall encountered by Ossis? As Feversham and Schmidt
rightly point out, nearly all sections deemed worthy of preservation are from
the front wall which faced west and thus represent a highly western view of
the edifice.[65] On the Wall's thirtieth anniversary Gerwin Zohlen, concerned to
avoid amnesia, proposed an endless copper strip with the inscription 'Berlin
Wall 1961–1989', but designed to run along the 'western' course of the Wall.[66]
Copper, the symbol of conductivity and communication would offset the banality
of the real Wall. A year later Angela Bohnen, by contrast, suggested two lines of
concrete intarsia inlays, red for the front wall, and blue for the hinterland wall,
as part of a *'Mauer-Markierung'*. For her it was more important to engage in 'a

[62] *Mauerkatalog: 'East Side Gallery'* (Berlin: Oberbaum, 1991).
[63] Feversham and Schmidt, *Berliner Mauer*, 151.
[64] Gabriele Camphausen *et al.*, *Eine Stadt wächst zusammen: 10 Jahre Deutsche Einheit: Was aus der Berliner Mauer wurde* (Berlin: Jaron, 1999), 61.
[65] Feversham and Schmidt, *Berliner Mauer*, 125.
[66] *Markierung des Mauerverlaufs: Hearing am 14. Juni 1995: Dokumentation* (Berlin: Senatsverwaltung für Bau- und Wohnungswesen, 1995), 58.

collective will to commemorate', rather than a ready-made monument. Concrete was a less monumental material for a 'memento muri'. The parallelism of the intarsia was also designed to create an interstitial space 'between ideologies', 'between state and individual'.[67] In October 1992 a test section was laid south of the Brandenburg Gate in the Ebertstraße, supported at the time by the Senator for Cultural Affairs and the borough planning offices of Mitte and Tiergarten, as well as the Berlin Bündnis 90/Green faction. A majority of the Berlin Landtag then voted to allow Bohnen and Zohlen to test their designs before the parliament building in the Niederkirchenerstraße. These were unveiled in November 1994, although later Mayor Eberhard Diepgen, mocking the protracted proceedings, suggested simply painting a red line along the former course of the wall, handing out tins of paint and pitching in himself, although this caused regular traffic accidents under the Brandenburg Gate as cars mistook the line for a traffic signal. A hearing was held in June 1995 at the Academy of Arts, filled with academics, experts, and journalists, prompting contradictory press comment. There were fears in some quarters of a 'Disneyfication' of the former Wall. One city-planner supported symbolic markings, but wanted to see authentic pieces of Wall too, so that 'visitors to Berlin have the chance to experience the symbol of the Cold War directly'. Elsewhere, there should be the possibility to remember without dividing again. Others preferred to contain memories of the Wall in museums and monuments, libraries, and film archives, rather than have constant reminders all around the city. Compromise suggestions were for markers to link the various surviving sites. Only reluctantly, however, did discussants concede that the artists' proposals represented a one-sidedly western view, an 'extension of the viewing platforms', as architect Wolfgang Kil put it; historian Andreas Graf was more forthright: 'Here an exclusively West German or West Berlin discourse is taking place.'[68]

In 1996 an artistic competition entitled *Übergänge* was held with projects to commemorate the former crossing-points, which had slightly less uniformly negative resonances than the Wall. The jury was clearly somewhat nonplussed by the results, but Karla Sachse's 'rabbit markings' concept was recommended, which envisaged a number of brass inlays of rabbit silhouettes to commemorate the creatures who had inhabited the no-man's land of the death strip, too light-footed for the trip-wires. According to the contestant, this was also a reference to a club she belonged to as a child in the GDR, which had the rabbit as the emblem on its flag—a subtle reference to the German phrase *das Hasenpanier ergreifen* or to 'do a runner'.[69] Other successful entries included Frank Thiel's giant portrait photographs of American and Russian soldiers, erected back-to-back on steel girders at Checkpoint Charlie, and lit from inside. These stared out neutrally. And at the Oberbaum Bridge between Kreuzberg and Friedrichshain

---

[67] *Markierung*, 7 and 56–7.   [68] *Markierung*, 53 and 67.
[69] Feversham and Schmidt, *Berliner Mauer*, 159.

two neon hands by Thorsten Goldberg have been built into the renovated bridge, which play an eternal game of paper–scissors–stone. Elsewhere markers were installed in the Berlin subway, reminding passengers that the border ran even underground.

At the outset, the GDR's Conservator General had tagged several sections of Wall for preservation. Hagen Koch was then entrusted with the job of listing selected sites for conservation, until it was discovered that his cartographic skills had been learnt in the Stasi.[70] One such section—although very dilapidated—runs down the Niederkirchnerstraße, along the back of the former Gestapo headquarters with its exhibition 'Topography of Terror'. The excavated Gestapo cellars, literally in the shadow of the Wall, now present a strange juxtaposition of Nazism and Communism. The viewer is invited to equate one with the other in a form of totalitarian systems comparison. A 'Wall Park' was opened in November 1994 at the boundary between Prenzlauer Berg and Wedding along Gleimstraße. At the border stands a row of swings, on which visitors can swing between 'East' and 'West'. A remaining watchtower in the Schlesischer Busch in Treptow housed an exhibition of border guard photographs of the death strip, as well as some western Wall art and 'forbidden eastern art'. Documentation also existed on the function of the border installation. Near the Invalidenfriedhof a watchtower has been left overlooking the canal, on the initiative of the Haus am Checkpoint Charlie, now looking rather out of place amid the pastel colours of the new housing complex surrounding it. A park nearby has a sculptured wall sinking into a pond by the French architect Christian Girot. In the former Steinstücken exclave, a tiny settlement inside the GDR but belonging to West Berlin, and supplied by US helicopters between 1961 and 1976, a pair of rotor-blades commemorate this miniature airlift.[71]

Elsewhere, the Wall has been rapidly disappearing. At Checkpoint Charlie, where the East German checkpoints were hoisted out to reveal a pleasant cobbled square, corporate interests took over. A large business complex has arisen, which for a time displayed larger than life photographs of famous confrontations from the empty offices, such as the tank stand-off of October 1961. The watchtower which stood across the way was also left in situ, if rather the worse for wear, with plans to cocoon it within the office space of the Central European Development Corporation. Beside the tower, sections of wall, fence and other border installations will be shown as part of an open-air museum, although at the time of writing they languished in storage. One of the last actions to preserve a section occurred at Potsdamer Platz in November 1998, when a group of artists painted the remaining segments of hinterland wall, some in reference to the East

---

[70] Since then Koch has set up his own Wall Archive at his apartment in Hohenschönhausen, and fights a running battle with the Berlin Senate over the ownership of the documents and artefacts he keeps, many of them rescued from the skip.

[71] Presse- und Landesamt des Landes Berlin (ed.), *Die Mauer und ihr Fall* (Berlin: Senat, 1994), 69–70.

Side Gallery, as well as covering two monoliths in gold foil as a 'Sun Gate'. The site was a stone's throw from the new glitzy skyscrapers emerging around the Sony Center at the 'world's biggest building-site', as the nearby 'Infobox' liked to tell visitors. In April 1999, however, the Senate had most remaining sections removed, to muted protest. A few pieces lingered in early 2001, with defiant injunctions to passers-by not to forget. There have also been legal disputes over the ownership of the land on which the Wall stood. Former owners of properties in Bernauer Straße have demanded back their land: 'We, who were driven out from here in contravention of human rights and international law, condemn this money-changing with stolen property as a scandal for our land.'[72]

More potentially abiding is a 212-metre section of Wall at Bernauer Straße, acquired by the German Historical Museum, which urged a full reconstruction of the border installation, using even elements in storage, to create an exhibition–museum–monument complex. In the chaos of demolition work in June 1990, however, various artefacts were removed, until what remained was mothballed inside a protective fence. The East Berlin Magistrat underwrote the project on 2 October 1990, one day before reunification, and the all-Berlin Senate confirmed the protected status in February 1992.[73] This scheme had optimistically envisaged a monument to be unveiled on 13 August 1991, the thirtieth anniversary of the building of the Wall. However, it provoked opposition from residents, victims, and politicians. The boroughs of Wedding and Mitte, but above all the Evangelical Sophien-Gemeinde and Lazarus clinic, an old people's home, complained that they had had to live long enough with the Wall. The Sophien-Gemeinde parish demanded the return of cemetery land on the other side of Bernauer Straße, expropriated under the GDR to consolidate the frontier, upon which the Wall remnants stood. On top of this came plans by Berlin transport to expand Bernauer Straße into a multi-lane freeway. In a compromise solution by a coordinating committee, all parties agreed to a 70-metre section of Wall and a 'Monument to Victims of the Second World War and to Victims of the Division of Germany' to be erected at the site.

This was enshrined in a competition launched in 1994 by the German Historical Museum on behalf of the Federal Government, with a budget of 1.5 million deutschmarks. A total of 259 entries were received, mainly from West Germany or abroad, rarely from Berlin, and never from the former GDR. With no overall winner, three were shortlisted. Bühren and Schulz from Allensbach wanted to leave the site largely intact, restoring a path to the cemetery under the motto: 'This place cannot be transformed into a monument. This place simply is.' The Berliners Winkler and Thiel would simply have ringed 110 metres of the border strip with 15-metre-high mesh, while Kohlhoff and Kohlhoff of Stuttgart

---

[72] Interessengemeinschaft Mauerstreifen Berlin e.V., hoarding at corner of Bernauer and Swinemünder Straßen, Feb. 2001.
[73] Verein "Berliner Mauer" (ed.), *Berliner Mauer*, 19.

envisaged 70 metres of the death strip, flanked by two polished steel walls. In July 1995 the Federal government chose the latter. Financial difficulties further delayed the project until the government granted 2.2 million deutschmark in April 1997, scheduling work to begin in May. At the eleventh hour, however, the municipality and the Sophien-Gemeinde unilaterally removed thirty-two Wall segments, purportedly to protect the mass graves suspected there. This unforeseen action seemed to galvanize previously apathetic public opinion, so much so that the Senate resolved to reconstruct the entire 212-metre section and to provide a Documentation Centre.

The monument itself was finally opened on 13 August 1998. At each side, reminiscent of the iron curtain, are two massive steel sections, higher than the real Wall, and deliberately rusted on the outside to symbolize the corrosion of the iron curtain, but polished on the inside and thus reflecting the scene trapped in between like infinitely receding mirrors. Accessible only from the rear on the eastern side, visitors can peer through what used to be the hinterland wall at the death strip, which has been denuded of most of the paraphernalia of surveillance. A vandalized signals box remains, and some rather unkempt sand. (The original control tower is to be seen at the Allies' Museum in Dahlem.) The whole installation has the tantalizing aspect of a peep show. A plan for a western viewing platform, as used by western tourists, was dropped for safety reasons. However, the glacis of the Wall, previously pockmarked by wallpeckers, has now been restored and is kept free of graffiti.[74] This was still not the end of the controversy, however. The original inscription upon the unveiling of the monument had read:

BERLIN WALL MEMORIAL
IN MEMORY OF THE DIVISION OF THE CITY
FROM 13 AUGUST 1961 TO 9 NOVEMBER 1989
AND IN REMEMBRANCE OF THE VICTIMS

This prompted protests from victim support groups, so that a plate had to be affixed over the old inscription, expanding it to 'VICTIMS OF COMMUNIST DESPOTISM', thus echoing the monuments to Nazi terror around the city and providing a more explicit totalitarian equation.[75] Contemporaries and lobby groups have continued to criticize the aestheticization of the Wall and the failure to reconstruct fully the death strip, which would not convey the true horror of the place, although this has occurred mainly at the insistence of local residents.

It is, however, a highly contested site. At the time of the Kosovo crisis, when Bundeswehr troops were controversially deployed, a graffito appeared on it that 'this Wall prevented us from going to war against other peoples'.[76] On another

[74] Verein 'Berliner Mauer' (ed.), *Berliner Mauer*, 20–21.
[75] Feversham and Schmidt, *Berliner Mauer*, 180. More recently the whole side panel was replaced.
[76] Interview with Marianne Nooke, 17 Aug. 2001.

occasion intruders climbed into the death strip and trod a swastika into the sand. During the fortieth anniversary commemorations Wall politics entered municipal Berlin politics. The recently deposed Christian Democrats, mired in financial scandal, mobilized the past against the acting Social Democratic mayor, Klaus Wowereit, protesting at the possibility of coalition with the communists' successor party, the PDS. The CDU therefore looked to the past, invoking the libertarian ideology of the Cold War. One poster advertising a commemorative Christian Democratic rally on 12 August 2001 showed the Brandenburg Gate in 1961 behind barbed wire, above the injunction 'Remembering means defending freedom'. At the rally CSU leader Edmund Stoiber accused the PDS of being 'the old socialist SED, repainted on the outside'. The then CDU leader and subsequently Federal Chancellor Angela Merkel, herself a former East German, asked what previous Social Democrats Ernst Reuter, Willy Brandt, and Kurt Schumacher would have made of the current situation. The communists 'had cut deep into the flesh of this city and divided it', and attempts to suppress the memory of the past 'is an injustice to freedom'.[77] (This account, of course, conveniently suppressed Adenauer's passive behaviour during the Wall crisis.)

Anticipating criticism, the PDS's Historical Commission and the Rosa Luxemburg Foundation had held a conference in May 2001 that debated whether the building of the Wall had been part of a 'consensual crisis', a 'silent agreement' between East and West.[78] Pressure was then put on the PDS by the SPD to apologize for the Wall. PDS mayoral candidate Gregor Gysi, himself only a boy at the time of the Wall's construction, denied any personal culpability: 'I stand for bridges, not walls.'[79] Nevertheless, the PDS leadership did issue a 'Wall declaration' in July, which conceded that the Wall had become the GDR's 'mark of Cain'. Yet the successor party revealed its dilemma: 'The constant demand that the PDS should apologize for the injustice committed by the SED is aiming at precisely this tactical goal: by apologizing, the PDS affirms its supposed continuity with the SED—by not doing so, all the more so.' The document emphasized the geopolitical constraints operating on the GDR at the time, but conceded that the Wall was 'the concrete proof of the inferiority of the GDR's Stalinist-style socialism compared with the real current capitalism in the Federal Republic'. By the current yardsticks of democracy and socialism, the unilateral incarceration of the population could not be justified. The PDS focused now on 'overcoming the wall in people's heads'.[80]

Bernauer Straße was also to provide the backdrop to national protests, when Federal Chancellor Gerhard Schröder was due to commemorate the fortieth

---

[77] 'Jahrestag des Mauerbaus: Streit um PDS', *Tagesspiegel*, 13 Aug. 2001, 1.
[78] Daniel Küchenmeister (ed.), *Der Mauerbau: Krisenverlauf—Weichenstellung—Resultate* (Berlin: Berliner Debatte, 2001), 4; in a similar vein, Werner Paulsen, *13. August 1961: Ereignisse und Zusammenhänge* (Schkeuditz: GNN, 2001), 147.
[79] PDS *Landtag* election leaflet, 2001.   [80] *Pressedienst PDS*, 27 (6 July 2001), 2–3.

anniversary of the Wall there. Flags were flown at half-mast. When Wowereit and Schröder laid wreaths at the memorial, in what must have been the fastest ceremony in history, conducted at a sprint, they were booed by young conservatives and members of victim support groups with cries of 'hypocrites'. For the first time the PDS had laid a wreath. Victim groups had warned that they would not lay theirs alongside. Protestors stood in front with signs around their necks labelled 'victim'. One PDS wreath was trampled, another thrown in a ditch, its remover arrested while the offending object was replaced. In the night it finally disappeared, as did the ribbons on the Chancellor's and leader of the Bundestag's wreaths. One former GDR prisoner claimed: 'Just as neo-Nazi wreaths have no place at the Plötzensee memorial [to victims of Hitler], so no PDS wreaths can lie here.'[81]

The Wall monument is part of a larger complex. At the nearby site of the demolished Church of the Reconciliation, which stood in no-man's land, but was dynamited by the East German authorities in 1985 to improve 'security, order, and cleanliness' at the border, a memorial chapel has been constructed. Its pastor, Manfred Fischer, had always been one of the keenest proponents of an effective memorial which made the past tangible, and had many times to physically intervene against bulldozers further down the Bernauer Straße. The old foundations were uncovered, and relics of the church, including the altar, steeple-point, and a statue of Christ, recovered. The salvaged bells have been brought back to the site, and a sculpture donated by the city of Coventry placed at the entrance. 'Windows' in the ground permit viewers to look at the foundations below, while an oval structure rises above, surrounded by a walkway of vertical wooden slats. The original name of the church has thus been appropriated, positively, for the needs of overcoming division.

As a third component to the site came the much-needed Berlin Wall Documentation Centre, housed in the former Reconciliation parish hall and opened on 9 November 1999, ten years after the fall of the Wall. It is staffed by both former East and West Germans. In a mixture of multi-media installations and conventional exhibits, including at one point a former western observation platform, visitors are encouraged to find their own way around. It also encourages consideration of the nexus between 'public–political' history and 'personal–private' experience, placing the local history of Bernauer Straße in its larger context.[82] According to the project leader the Wall is also a 'chance for rapprochement' between East and West, who can learn the differences between each other.[83] More recently a tower was erected at the eastern end of the Centre, consciously harking back to the old tourist viewing platforms, but because of its wire-mesh construction and nocturnal lighting, unconsciously reminiscent

[81] *Berliner Kurier*, 14 Aug. 2001, 2–3.
[82] Verein 'Berliner Mauer' (ed.), *Berliner Mauer*, 28.
[83] Interview with Marianne Nooke, 17 Aug. 2001.

of a guard tower.[84] For the fortieth anniversary of the building of the Wall, a special exhibition was mounted, combining film, audio listening stations, as well as displays of documents.

Most recently, following a Berlin Senate resolution of June 2006, it was agreed to bring together the disparate elements of the Bernauer Straße site into one national memorial. North of the existing buildings an open-air museum will encourage visitors to explore the virtual archaeology of an area under which tunnels used to run. Information pillars will be augmented by an information pavilion. A central feature of the open structure will also be 'windows of remembrance', which show the photographs and names of the victims of the Wall. All of this is scheduled to be ready by 2011, the fiftieth anniversary of the Wall, and will cost 11.6 million euros, including Federal funding, in order to make this the national Wall memorial. Of course, if it had not been for the private initiatives of various citizens' groups to preserve the various fragments, there would have been nothing for government to have coordinated in this way. And despite all the high-tech of the interactive exhibits, it is the original pieces of concrete and steel which lend Bernauer Straße its stark authenticity.[85]

THE WALL AS HISTORY

As with most Cold War histories, the history of the Wall has a pedigree almost as long as the Cold War itself.[86] Since it has been such a newsworthy topic, it has also attracted popular as well as academic histories, and it is sometimes difficult to disentangle the different genres. In the early days and years of the Wall's existence, the first accounts served as propaganda. In the West a number of picture books soon appeared, documenting the human misery caused by the Wall. In these the classic images of the crisis—barbed wire and border guards, tanks, sundered families, and last-minute escapes—were recorded with brief commentaries for an international as well as German audience. Arno Scholz, editor of West Berlin's *Telegraf*, thus brought out *Barbed Wire around Berlin* in 1961, which described the GDR as a 'concentration camp' without a safety-valve: 'The flag and the name of the tyrant have changed since 1945, but the methods are the same.'[87] An impression of upstanding East Germans, incarcerated but unbowed, was conveyed, but also the nervousness of West

---

[84] Dokumentationszentrum Berliner Mauer and Zerr Hapke Nieländer Architekten (eds), *turm* (Berlin: Aedes, 2004).

[85] http://www.competitionline.de/site/20012003133010/20012003133010.php?wettbewerb_id =8366 (1 Jan. 2008).

[86] For an overview of the first twenty years see Michael Haupt, *Die Berliner Mauer—Vorgeschichte, Bau, Folgen: Literaturbericht und Bibliographie zum 20. Jahrestag des 13. August 1961* (Munich: Bernhard & Graefe, 1981).

[87] Arno Scholz, *Stacheldraht um Berlin*, 2nd edn (Berlin: arani, 1961), 5 and 16.

Berliners cut off from the outside world. The term 'wall of shame' was duly coined. An eponymous paperback appeared in 1961, recording in impressionistic style one West Berliner's frustrations, in the slightly bathetic tone of the time, comparing the Wall to the Wailing Wall in Jerusalem, as well as Warsaw, but this time a 'ghetto for Germans, built by Germans'.[88] Another who invoked the past and criticized the Germans for their lack of civil courage in protesting was Wolfdietrich Schnurre, who had raised his voice alongside Günter Grass. He tried to keep alive contacts with East Berliners by playing up the personal fates involved. The Berlin Wall was a latter-day Warsaw ghetto: the failure to protest in the past was no excuse for remaining silent in the present.[89]

The official view remained somewhat more restrained. The Federal Ministry of All-German Affairs produced a pamphlet soon after the events, filled with emotive pictures, but arguing against the legality of the measures: 'A regime from which millions have fled and which finds no other solution than to erect a demarcation line with barbed wire, concrete walls and bayonets, has no legitimation as a partner in a peace treaty with Germany.'[90] The GDR was contravening the principles of the United Nations as well as occupation law. Liberal pictures of the protection forces, including a British armoured car accompanying a boy on his way to school, reinforced the message that the West would not abandon West Berlin. Another government pamphlet starkly recorded the dimensions of the border and the numbers of victims,[91] as well as a more critical collection of press comment, which repeated the accusation of moral bankruptcy on the part of the GDR. Voices included those of Vice President Johnson and the Congress for Cultural Freedom, condemning the communist action.[92]

The GDR engaged in offensive–defensive propaganda. Leaflets handed out to tourists entering the GDR explained how a 'reliable control was introduced, as is usual at the borders of any sovereign state' (revealing the old touchiness about lack of diplomatic recognition), 'with the support of the population'. (Tellingly, the 'rhetorical' hostile questions heading each section of this particular leaflet correspond almost exactly with the real questions posed in the Party Information's opinion reports.) The official view instead externalized the causes, blaming the economic exploitation to the tune of 3.5 billion marks per annum and nuclear armament in the FRG. It also projected guilt by association into the past, by making references to Hitler's march through the Brandenburg Gate on 30 January 1933. As for the appearance of armed troops on 13 August, 'far less

---

[88] Wolfgang Paul, *Mauer der Schande* (Munich: Bechtle, 1961), 18 and 23.

[89] Wolfdietrich Schnurre, *Berlin: Eine Stadt wird geteilt* (Olten: Walter-Verlag, 1962), 12.

[90] Bundesministerium für gesamtdeutsche Fragen (ed.), *Berlin, 13. August: Sperrmaßnahmen gegen Recht und Menschlichkeit* (Bonn, 1961).

[91] Bundesministerium für gesamtdeutsche Fragen (ed.), *Ulbrichts Mauer: Zahlen, Fakten, Daten* (Bonn, 1962).

[92] Bundesministerium für gesamtdeutsche Fragen (ed.), *Ein Schandmal im Urteil der Welt: Äußerungen ausländischer Politiker angesichts der Mauer* (Bonn, 1962).

occurred than at an average rock'n'roll concert at the West Berlin Sportpalast'.[93]
Another pamphlet, which interestingly called the Wall a wall, explained how
even 'we are not particularly fond' of walls. Citing western politicians, it painted a
picture of a revanchist West surrounding a peace-loving East. Yet the Wall would
permit peaceful co-existence of 'two fundamentally different social orders'.[94]
Another was at pains to show that deportees had received proper housing, as well
as drawing Wehrmacht/NATO parallels, and much visual material on spies and
black marketeers. Pictures of East Berlin depicted a thriving city with shopping
and theatres.[95] By 1967 the welcome literature was slightly less hectoring: 'You
have almost certainly read at home the usual horror stories about the Wall and
the order to shoot.' The brochure invited tourists to form their own opinion.
The same line of pre-emptive blaming of the Federal Republic occurred. In
answer to the question 'Can Germans shoot at Germans?', Kaiser Wilhelm's
civil war contingency measures were cited, as well as the murders of Luxemburg
and Liebknecht, before showing photographs of the dying Benno Ohnesorg and
victims in Vietnam. The 'victims of the Wall' were on the consciences of the
Federal president and chancellor, according to this diffusion of guilt.[96] Another
showed pictures of execution victims from 1919 before a wall, SS guarding a
ghetto wall, and Federal troops in a similar stance, practising detentions under
the new emergency legislation which was so annoying the West German New
Left.[97] There was a fundamental tension in these documents between such
histrionics and the call on the western reader to ponder soberly the causes of
the Wall.

In the West, the passage of the 1960s created slightly more distance from
events, although the Springer press continued to wage a campaign against the
Wall of Shame and the government's 'détente talk'.[98] A form of entertainment
propaganda was the 'escape book', usually written by journalists or freelance
writers. Journalists recognized the market potential for these real-life adventures,
including chapter headings picked out in chains,[99] or insider accounts by
tunnellers such as Harry Seidel, focusing on 'the heroism and the suffering', and
playing on readers' sense of suspense.[100] This genre has, of course, continued
even after the fall of the Wall.[101] In the Anglo-American context, this fixation
on the Wall was considerably reinforced by the espionage fiction of the likes

[93] Ausschuß für Deutsche Einheit (ed.), *Was geschah am 13. August?* (East Berlin, n.d. [1961]).
[94] Nationalrat der NF (ed.), *Warum Mauer? Wie lange Mauer?* (East Berlin, n.d. [1964]).
[95] Ausschuß für Deutsche Einheit (ed.), *Die Wahrheit über Berlin* (Berlin, n.d.).
[96] Nationalrat der NF (ed.), *Berlin und die Mauer: Fragen, Probleme, Antworten* (Berlin, 1967).
[97] Ausschuß für Deutsche Einheit (ed.), *Du und die Mauer* (Berlin, n.d.).
[98] Frech, *Berliner Mauer*, 22.
[99] William A. Heaps, *The Wall of Shame* (New York: Meredith, 1964). Heaps had worked as a
librarian for the UN.
[100] Pierre Galante with Jack Miller, *The Berlin Wall* (Garden City, NY: Doubleday, 1965), 63.
[101] Bodo Müller, *Faszination Freiheit: Die spektakulärsten Fluchtgeschichten* (Berlin: Links, 2000);
Christopher Hilton, *The Wall: The People's Story* (Thrupp: Sutton, 2001).

of John le Carré and Len Deighton. Nevertheless, these stories usually tell us more about the western self than the Cold War 'other'. It is a world where a few well-placed agents can wreak world-historical change, without the inconvenience of involving the masses.

Other journalists took the trouble to visit the border or the East. These sometimes became anthropologies or travelogues, as reporters explored the lost land behind the Wall. The goal of one was to prevent West Germans from losing touch with the East. A large part of this account dealt with border controls from the perspective of the westerner, but accepted that some East Germans were for the new situation. The daily lives of East Berliners, shopping and going to the park, were mixed with the indoctrination of a younger generation, and an everyday steeped in regulations and suspicion. Yet even Hildebrandt noticed how things in the West 'suddenly seem so far away, so alien'; the 'ideology of point of view asserts itself swiftly and brusquely'.[102] A number of readable journalistic accounts appeared in the 1960s, some reliant on stereotypes of the witty westerner abroad in a humourless (but normalizing) East, steeped in much non-communist history.[103] David Shears acknowledged that much of what had come before was propaganda of a kind, writing a part-history, part-reportage of the border, more in line with Brandt's *Ostpolitik*.[104] For Anthony Bailey, the journey along the iron curtain was something of a pilgrimage.[105] He, like other Anglo-American observers, went to great lengths to contextualize the border in a long history of Central European strife, from the Romans, through the Middle Ages to the National Socialist debacle. Division was somehow normal: 'the border seems so fixed that it is hard to realize that it was not always so'.[106] In addition, the focus on the landscape of the border—its rivers, forests, and mountains—presented it almost as a natural phenomenon, or at least as a man-made 'anti-wonder' of the world. The thriller writer Len Deighton perhaps best captured this view of the Wall-as-natural-disaster: 'bricked-up buildings and sections of breeze block that bisect the city, ending suddenly and unpredictably like the lava flow of a cold-water Pompeii'.[107]

Nevertheless, it was not long before academics began turning to the Wall. Soon after its building there were a series of political treatments of the second Berlin Crisis, dealing largely in high-level international history based on diplomatic correspondence.[108] As more documents became available, political commentary became political science.[109] Some treatments remained particularly

[102] Dieter Hildebrandt, *Die Mauer ist keine Grenze: Menschen in Ostberlin* (Düsseldorf and Cologne: Diederichs, 1964), 140.

[103] Newman, *Behind the Berlin Wall*.

[104] David Shears, *The Ugly Frontier* (New York: Knopf, 1970).

[105] Bailey, *Along the Edge*, 9.   [106] Ibid., 16.

[107] Len Deighton, *Funeral in Berlin* (London: Jonathan Cape, 1964), 22.

[108] Hans Speier, *Die Bedrohung Berlins: Eine Analyse der Berlin-Krise von 1958 bis heute* (Cologne: Kiepenheuer & Witsch, 1961).

[109] Robert M. Slusser, *The Berlin Crisis of 1961: Soviet-American Relations and the Struggle for Power in the Kremlin, June–November 1961* (Baltimore: Johns Hopkins University Press,

legalistic.[110] A particular sub-field of Berlin Wall studies has been the diplomatic history, which treats the 1958–62 crisis as an episode in crisis management at the very top.[111] One designed for school-teaching purposes focused exclusively on the high politics and nuclear brinkmanship.[112] From these diplomatic accounts it became axiomatic that the western powers had become more 'realistic' in the wake of the Wall. Adenauer's 'politics of strength' gave way to Bahr's 'change through rapprochement', the precursor to Brandt's *Ostpolitik*. The Wall forced the gradual de facto recognition of the GDR by the West. Willy Brandt, in his memoirs, talks of the stage of western diplomacy being laid bare.[113] As mayor of West Berlin at the time, the Wall forced a major rethink of how to deal with the East. The policy of 'small steps' in the mid-1960s would have been unthinkable without the Wall. Even after the fall of the Wall, however, this trend to treat the second Berlin crisis as purely an episode in superpower relations continued. The only modifications were more insights into the relations between patrons and junior allies, in line with the post-revisionist trends in Cold War historiography of the 1980s.[114]

East German historians did not tend to write about the Wall during its lifetime. A rare exception was Siegfried Prokop, one of the GDR's leading official historians, who embedded the account in the socioeconomic necessities of the 'transition to socialism'. On 13 August 1961, however, 'imperialism had been shown the limits of its power'.[115] After the fall of the Wall, Prokop did rapidly produce a new history, based on mainly published sources, it has to be said, and not the top-level materials which one might have expected from an insider. In the new account, Prokop conceded that 'Antifascist Defence Rampart' had not been an appropriate term, but still adhered to a version which stressed western anticommunism as a key aggravating factor.[116] Likewise, Hartmut Mehls, the blind GDR historian who with his wife had produced a popular illustrated history aimed at schoolchildren during the liftetime of the Wall,[117] quickly published a series of documents after its fall on popular opinion which conveyed

1973); Walther Stützle, *Kennedy und Adenauer in der Berlin-Krise 1961–1962* (Bonn: Verlag Neue Gesellschaft, 1973); Heribert Gerlach, *Die Berlinpolitik der Kennedy-Administration: Eine Fallstudie zum außenpolitischen Verhalten der Kennedyregierung in der Berlinkrise 1961* (Frankfurt: Haag & Herchen, 1977).

[110] Dieter Mahncke, *Berlin im geteilten Deutschland* (Munich: Oldenbourg, 1973); Udo Wetzlaugk, *Berlin und die deutsche Frage* (Köln: Verlag Wissenschaft & Politik, 1985).

[111] See the first reference at the start of Chapter 2 for an overview of this literature.

[112] Klaus Horn, *Die Berlin-Krise 1958/61: Zur Funktion der Krise in der internationalen Politik* (Frankfurt: Europäische Verlagsanstalt, 1970).

[113] Willy Brandt, *People and Politics* (London: Collins, 1978), 20.

[114] Joachim Arenth, *Der Westen tut nichts! Transatlantische Kooperation während der zweiten Berlin-Krise (1958–1962) im Spiegel neuer amerikanischer Quellen* (Frankfurt: Peter Lang, 1993).

[115] Siegfried Prokop, *Übergang zum Sozialismus in der DDR* (East Berlin: Dietz, 1986), 85.

[116] Siegfried Prokop, *Unternehmen 'Chinese Wall': Die DDR im Zwielicht der Mauer* (Frankfurt: Fischer, 1992), 168.

[117] Hartmut and Ellen Mehls, *13. August (illustrierte historische hefte* 17, 1979).

re-evaluation of GDR history (handwritten note in left margin)

a much more nuanced picture, although Mehls invited readers to draw their own conclusions rather than provide any commentary.[118] The Academy of Sciences also quickly altered course in the autumn of 1989, organizing conferences in December 1989 for a 're-evaluation of GDR history'.

There had, of course, been other East Germans who had written from outside the GDR. The dissident East German communist, Rolf Henrich, wrote an influential study of the 'guardian state', using Marxist terminology to critique the neo-feudal chaining of the citizenry to the state machine, denying the rational basis of liberty: the freedom to say no.[119] Henrich's basic diagnosis was that the failure of economistic mechanisms to stabilize the country had led to the imposition of political restraints which undermined even Marx's liberation project. Without freedom there could be no meaningful loyalty, thus questioning whether Hirschman's 'loyalty' is applicable to citizens without choice. But whereas Henrich meant loyalty to the state, ordinary East Germans had a whole range of sub-state loyalties: to their region, their family, their confession, and even to the idea of true socialism. After the *Wende* various young, non-party historians, previously denied an outlet, also began to write accounts which saw the building of the Wall as one of the stepping stones to the state's collapse, rather overstating the revolutionary will of the East German populace before 1961, in a teleological account which was implicitly written from the perspective of the Wall's collapse in 1989.[120]

Do any of these accounts have anything in common, beneath the Cold war rhetoric which was at times in danger of generating more heat than light? Leaving aside the foreign policy implications of the Wall, there has been considerable consensus on the significance of 13 August 1961 as a domestic caesura in East German history. The Communist authorities celebrated it. As none other than Erich Honecker, East German leader in the 1970s and 1980s, and original architect of the Wall, reflected: 'The 13 August 1961 is a milestone in the development of our socialist republic. In the truest sense of the word it was a moment when, intimately bound with the Soviet Union and the other Warsaw Pact states, we showed German and international monopoly capital the limits of its power.'[121] Among western historians there was also consensus on the momentous changes associated with the border, if they had reached the stage of considering East German history at all.[122] Hermann Weber wrote of 1961 as the 'incisive caesura of the GDR's development', signalling a shift from Stalinist

---

[118] Hartmut Mehls (ed.), *Im Schatten der Mauer. Dokumente. 12. August bis 29. Sept. 1961* (Berlin: Deutscher Verlag der Wissenschaften, 1990).

[119] Henrich, *Der vormundschaftliche Staat*, 153–77.

[120] Armin Mitter and Stefan Wolle, *Untergang auf Raten: Unbekannte Kapitel der DDR-Geschichte* (Munich: Bertelsmann, 1993).

[121] Honecker at Kampfgruppen rally, 29 Sept. 1973, in Mehls, *13. August*, 43.

[122] See for instance Martin Broszat (ed.), *Zäsuren nach 1945: Essays zur Periodisierung der deutschen Nachkriegsgeschichte* (Munich: Oldenbourg, 1990), which equates 'Germany' with the Federal Republic.

terror to 'neutralization and manipulation of the masses'.[123] The SED now entered a more pragmatic, 'conservative' phase, taking into consideration the practical needs of building a modern economy to provide for a basic consumer society. Dietrich Staritz was perhaps the most forthright, and most cited, claiming that the 13 August was the 'secret founding day of the GDR'.[124] This has been echoed by others, such as Charles Maier, talking of the 'second founding of the regime'.[125] Most recently, this version has received another lease of life from the GDR military historian Torsten Diedrich and the dissident-turned-historian Ilko-Sascha Kowalczuk, who, in an edited collection, have suggested that both the repression following 17 June 1953 and the building of the Wall should be viewed as 'stages' in the 'inner state-foundation' of the GDR.[126] (The concept of a 'second founding' was in fact borrowed from the historiography of Imperial Germany, when Bismarck had allegedly marginalized the liberals within the new Reich in the late 1870s, although its applicability seems misleading in the GDR case—from the very outset, in 1945, the Soviet occupation power had brought a heavy dose of 'state' with it.) This state foundation thesis also relies on the same teleological view of East German history which had been the source of criticism in Mitter and Wolle's work. Kowalczuk's qualified thesis that 'the path from the failed revolution of 1953 to the averted revolution of 1961' may not have been a causal one, but was still historically connected, is problematic in assuming a revolution in 1961 in the first place.[127] Yet if 'inner state-foundation' was a process which reached all the way from 1953 to 1961, it seems logical to argue that this continued after 1961 and was in fact part of a continuum of power consolidation. Caesura and process are not compatible concepts. Furthermore, methodologically the secret state foundation thesis still views the GDR's development largely through the state's eyes, from the point of view of the security apparatus.

Nevertheless, there has been some questioning of 13 August as a total caesura. The British historian Mark Allinson, in his local study of Erfurt, concluded on the Wall that 'patterns of conformity and non-conformity across the population were not particularly affected by its construction, and that after August 1961 life quickly settled back into the previously established contours'.[128] Moreover: 'In terms of political consolidation, then, the importance of the Berlin Wall as a watershed in the GDR's domestic history must be relativised.'[129] Corey Ross, too, has pointed out the 'important threads of continuity' before and after the

---

[123] Weber, *Geschichte der DDR*, 327.

[124] Dietrich Staritz, *Geschichte der DDR* (2nd edn; Frankfurt/M.: Surhkamp, 1996), 196.

[125] Maier, *Dissolution*, 24.

[126] Torsten Diedrich and Ilko-Sascha Kowalczuk (eds), *Staatsgründung auf Raten? Auswirkungen des Volksaufstandes 1953 und des Mauerbaus 1961 auf Staat, Militär und Gesellschaft der DDR* (Berlin: Links, 2005).

[127] Kowalczuk, 'Die innere Staatsgründung', in Diedrich and Kowalczuk (eds), *Staatsgründung*, 369.

[128] Allinson, *Politics*, 119.   [129] Ibid., 165.

Wall. Rather than solving the GDR's domestic problems, the border closure 'reconfigured' them.[130] Indeed, as more and more histories move from the early phase of the GDR to its later manifestations, it seems likely that this continuity thesis will gain more ground, although as I shall suggest, there were both breaks and continuities.

CONCLUSIONS

We require multiple timescales to understand the effects of 13 August: or at the risk of oversimplification, short, medium, and long. In the short-term, over the days and weeks following border closure, there was an undoubted shock to the system. The physical sealing off of a whole country literally overnight could not but force the populace to reconsider their position vis-à-vis communism. As Chapter 5 showed, the regime attempted to grasp some of the 'hot potatoes' such as work norms, collective farming, and military service, and the hard line persisted until the end of the year. Individuals certainly felt that the rules of the unwritten social compact had been broken and that the dictatorship would take off the gloves. Yet there were very mixed results on these various disciplinary fronts. Collective farmers were probably on the slippery slope to rationalization anyway and would not have been able to maintain smallholdings indefinitely. The building of the Wall therefore coincided with a long-term trend. The case of military service is slightly different, however. Although young men had little choice but to sign up for conscription, we have seen that even behind the Wall there was resistance to doing so on a purely voluntary basis; it required a law. This reflected the perceived transgression of the unwritten social compact which had existed in the 1950s, that there was a limited private sphere in the GDR, and the party would limit itself to voluntary campaigns. Indeed, while a large part of its peace propaganda liked to distinguish itself from the authoritarian West German state with its NATO rearmament, it would have been politically difficult for the party to introduce conscription. Yet, even when the geopolitical power parameters had supposedly shifted after August 1961, the party still could not rely on voluntarism. The populace demanded that it formalize the power relationship and abandon the fiction of a populist movement. Similarly, workers soon reverted to low productivity and work sciving. The 13 August ultimately failed where 17 June had failed, unable to solve the conundrum of labour productivity.

If we think in terms of years rather than months, however, in the medium term, we are forced to re-evaluate the impact of the Wall. Looking back to the 1950s, it soon became evident that many of the complaints and grouses of the populace had a prehistory from the early years of the regime. It was also

---

[130] Ross, 'East Germans', 41.

clear that there had been miniature border crises, such as 1952, which had fed significantly into the insurrectionary crisis of 1953. Whereas previously we tend to have thought of domestic upset on the eve of 1953 primarily in terms of rations and living standards, we should view the effective closure of the border as one of the major contributory factors of discontent. Moreover, one of the great pacifiers was a relaxation of the border, but this only illustrated the dilemma in which the party would find itself again in the 1970s and 1980s: the more one liberalized the real frontier, the more it could be exploited by the population as a means of negotiating their own grass-roots power struggles. There is a direct causal link, therefore, between 1953 and 1961, in that the abandonment of the post-1953 reforms in 1957 ushered in the second Berlin Crisis in 1958 by re-establishing the importance of the Berlin sector boundary. This was not a calculated ploy, but an accident of abandoned reform. Foreign policy experts may, however, wish to re-examine the causes of this major crisis of the European Cold War. There is no doubt that politicians such as Ulbricht manipulated it to address diplomatic problems (yet in fact solved very little), but the fundamental causes were domestic, related to the functioning of the East German economy and the popular disillusionment with the socialist experiment. Thus, although 'people power' may be more evident in 1989, it was still working as an aggregate of micro-challenges to the system in 1961.

There has been much discussion of the concept of 'niches' in East German society, whereby the population could duck out of the public ritual of communism into the privacy of the home and family. I would argue that in the 1950s one of the most important GDR niches was the city of West Berlin. As well as providing the permanent point of exit for millions of East Germans, it acted as the revolving door into and out of the West for millions more. In the short term, this provided a safety-valve function for the system. Yet, once access to this temporary relief was blocked, the West acted more and more as the forbidden fruit for East Germans, becoming more sought-after by its very inaccessibility. Yet before a physical barrier could be constructed, the GDR relied on moral arguments to construct an invisible border of transgression. Unfortunately, GDR officials, including Krenz at his trial, were to cling to a line of argumentation which was to become less and less convincing, drawn as it was from the Stalinist lexicon of the emotive 'other' which bore little relationship to the Social Democratic FRG of the 1970s. Helmut Kohl's Federal Republic continued this basic liberal approach, and it is illusory to think that even Adenauer's Germany had ever been as neo-fascist as SED propaganda claimed.

There were also continuities forward in time after 1961. The captive nature of the audience of East Germans after 1961 meant that the SED did have to learn to negotiate with its citizenry too. If anything, the Wall reinforced this quid pro quo attitude, since the population could no longer seek illicit compensation from outside the system, and now looked to the state to deliver. As citizens questioned by the local ideological commission in Anklam argued: 'Their relationship to the Workers' and Peasants' State is often dependent on the fulfilment of personal wishes which are nevertheless unfulfillable at our present stage of development (travel to West Germany, purchase of a car, etc.).'[131] Economically, in the medium term, the Wall did serve to stabilize the economy, by making the planning process more predictable, based on a finite labour pool. Yet the ambitious hopes to make the GDR autarkic from the economic miracle of the Federal Republic proved exaggerated. Perhaps not so much in raw materials, but in financial services, the East Germans became increasingly enmeshed with the West. On the negative side of the political balance sheet, the same sort of asymmetric civil war continued in the 1960s, as workers engaged in small-scale *nicht* strikes, or individuals withdrew into the private niche. Yet, just as there was an opening within in the shadow of the Wall, this was not a linear process. The party soon lost heart, and therefore we should not see the liberalization of 1963–65 as the norm. Nevertheless, as the short term moved to the long term, from the 1960s to the 1970s, the party increasingly turned a blind eye to non-conformity and confined itself to policing opposition. It was to become the prisoner of its own logic that, in an enclosed GDR, it would be able to build a more humane form of socialism, but also became the prisoner of its own unkept promises.

One of the ironies of the connections between the foreign and domestic was that although 13 August achieved the de facto international recognition from the outside world in the 1960s, and from the Federal Republic in the 1970s, this was to be at the cost of weakening its internal power position. Now, it might be easy with hindsight to criticize the West German government's *Ostpolitik* for stabilizing the East German state without prizing from it some of the liberal reforms which the authors of détente had hoped for. Yet it is difficult to see how the sorts of internal pressures brought to bear on the regime, which were attested in Chapter 6, could have occurred without some external handholds. Here again, we see the fatal meshing of domestic and international, economics and politics. Because of economic weakness, the party had sought external legitimation as a form of political stopgap, ever since the 1950s. When it came in the 1970s, because the social compact did not allow genuine economic reform, the regime became dependent on ever more western subsidies. Yet, while this may have stabilized the GDR in the medium term of the 1970s, in the long term it was making 'socialism in half a country' exceedingly vulnerable. Therefore, the GDR's foreign and domestic policies were pulling in different directions. In order to quell the sorts of hopes which had been raised by the state's human rights commitments, the SED had to resort to more and more police tactics in the 1980s. Moreover, the guarantee of a basic standard of living may have produced a more modest version of the post-material values which had encouraged the western New Left in the 1960s; by the 1980s an idealist opposition was beginning

---

[131] SED-KL Anklam (Ideol. Komm.), 'Analyse über die Lage in den Wohngebieten', 30 Sept. 1963, MLHA Schwerin, BPA SED Neubrandenburg, IVA2/8/1433.

to emerge, trying to save socialism from 'real existing socialism'. Yet, my focus on the everyday travellers hoping for compassionate leave demonstrates that freedom of travel was an aspiration which cut across all sections of the populace, even into the ranks of the party. The self-selecting nature of the family connections which enabled this did perhaps more than anything else to delegitimize the egalitarian claims of socialism. If there is one fundamental truth about state socialism, it is that while it may be a good idea in theory, in practice it ended in alienation. The issue of travel, but even access to the consumer delights of the West, created a two-tier society which became a travesty of socialism.

I hope, also, that the reader will come to see the merits of reconsidering the power of the individual, even within a dictatorial system. Paradoxically, this only becomes evident by viewing everyday actions through the eyes of the local party apparatchiks entrusted with governing them. Often, the individuals themselves, like Kafka's man from the country, may have felt powerless and alone. But East Germans were capable of voicing serious dissent. It has become fashionable recently to downplay the role of the citizens' movements in the great change of 1989. Yet, we should beware of conflating the reform movement with the general public at large. Of course, there were serious differences in aims between reform elites and the hundreds of thousands who eventually came out on the streets in 1989. It would be a mistake, nonetheless, to see ordinary East Germans as all 'free riders' on the coat-tails of the risk-takers. As well as complaining about the general standard of living, as Chapter 6 has shown, individuals with private agendas were capable of waging guerrilla campaigns which absorbed a great deal of state resources. 'Western' citizens probably expend only a fraction of the self-organization and stubbornness which *Ossis* were forced to expend in the defence of their political and human rights. It was these additional pressures which created the critical mass of change in 1989, as a combination of exit and voice. It was nevertheless to be an irony of history that the same will to exit the system which strengthened the hand of the reformers during a brief window of opportunity in September–October 1989, was also to spell the doom not only of the Wall, but of the GDR itself.

Bibliography

NATIONAL ARCHIVES

Bundesarchiv Berlin (BAB)
DA-5: Staatsrat der DDR
DO-1: Ministerium des Innern
  DO-1/8: Hauptabteilung Paß- und Meldewesen (PM)
  DO-1/11: Hauptverwaltung Deutsche Volkspolizei (HVDVP)
  DO-1/34: Hauptabteilung Innere Angelegenheiten (IA)

Stiftung Archiv der Parteien und Massenorganisationen der DDR im Bundesarchiv (SAPMO-BArch)
NY 4182: Nachlaß Walter Ulbricht
*DY 30: Sozialistische Einheitspartei Deutschlands (SED)—Zentralkomitee
  DY 30/J IV 2/2 J; J IV 2/201; J IV 2/202: Büro Walter Ulbricht
  DY 30: Büro Erich Honecker
  DY 30/IV 2/2.023: Büro Gerhard Grüneberg
  DY 30/IV 2/2.024: Büro Kurt Hager
  DY 30/IV 2/2.026: Büro Alfred Kurella
  DY 30/IV 2/2.029: Büro Dr. Erich Apel
  DY 30/IV 2/2.039: Büro Egon Krenz
  DY 30/IV 2/1: Tagungen des Zentralkomitees der SED
  DY 30/J IV 2/2: Protokolle der Sitzungen des Politbüros
  DY 30/J IV 2/3: Protokolle der Sitzungen des Sekretariats
  DY 30/IV 2/2.111: Jugendkommission beim Politbüro
  DY 30/IV 2/5: Abteilung Parteiorgane
  DY 30/IV 2/6.03: Abteilung Grundstoffindustrie
  DY 30/IV 2/6.04: Abteilung Maschinenbau und Metallurgie
  DY 30/IV 2/6.07: Abteilung Forschung & technische Entwicklung
  DY 30/IV 2/6.08: Abteilung Planung und Finanzen
  DY 30/IV 2/6.10: Abteilung Handel und Versorgung
  DY 30/IV 2/6.11: Abteilung Gewerkschaften und Sozialpolitik
  DY 30/IV 2/7: Abteilung Landwirtschaft
  DY 30/IV 2/9.02: Abteilung Agitation
  DY 30/IV 2/9.04: Abteilung Wissenschaften
  DY 30/IV 2/9.05: Abteilung Volksbildung
  DY 30/IV 2/9.06: Abteilung Kultur
  DY 30/IV 2/12: Abteilung Sicherheitsfragen
  DY 30/IV 2/13: Abteilung Staat und Recht
  DY 30/IV 2/16: Abteilung Jugend
  DY 30/IV 2/19: Abteilung Gesundheitswesen

*Freier Demokratischer Gewerkschaftsbund-Archiv
DY 34: FDGB-Bundesvorstand

*Freie Deutsche Jugend-Archiv
DY 24: FDJ-Zentralrat

Bundesarchiv Koblenz (BAK)
B 136: Bundeskanzleramt
B 150: Bundesministerium für Vertriebene, Flüchtlinge und Kriegsgeschädigte

Bundesarchiv—Militärisches Zwischenarchiv, Potsdam (BA-MZAP)
(since moved to the Bundesarchiv—Militärarchiv, Freiburg)

VA-01: Ministerium für Nationale Verteidigung, Stellvertreter des Ministers und Chef des Hauptstabes

Der Bundesbeauftragte für die Unterlagen des Staatssicherheitsdienstes der ehemaligen DDR, Zentralarchiv (BStU-ZA)
Sekretariat des Ministers [Erich Mielke] (SdM)
Zentrale Auswertungs- und Informationsgruppe (ZAIG) files

The National Archives/Public Record Office, Kew (TNA)
FO 371: Foreign Office—General Correspondence
FO 1050: Control Commission for Germany (British Element), Public Safety Branch
FO 1110: Information Research Department

National Archives and Records Administration, College Park, MD (NARA)
Record Group 306: United States Information Agency

REGIONAL ARCHIVES

Landesarchiv Berlin (LAB)
Bezirksparteiarchiv der SED Berlin
B Rep. 004: Senatsverwaltung für Inneres

Landesarchiv Berlin, Außenstelle Breite Straße (LAB-STA)
(since consolidated with the above at Berlin-Reinickendorf)

C Rep. 124: Magistrat von Berlin/Erster Stellvertreter des Oberbürgermeisters
C Rep. 303/26.1: Präsidium der Volkspolizei Berlin 1960–
STA Rep. 411: VEB Transformatorenwerk "Karl Liebknecht" (TRO)

Brandenburgisches Landeshauptarchiv, Potsdam (BLHA)
Bez. Ctb. Rep. 930: SED-Bezirksleitung Cottbus
Bez. Pdm. Rep. 401: Bezirkstag und Rat des Bezirkes Potsdam
Bez. Pdm. Rep. 530: SED-Bezirksleitung Potsdam

Mecklenburgisches Landeshauptarchiv, Schwerin (MLHA)
Bezirksparteiarchiv Schwerin: SED-Bezirksleitung Schwerin
Bezirksparteiarchiv Neubrandenburg: SED-Bezirksleitung Neubrandenburg

Sächsisches Hauptstaatsarchiv, Dresden (SächsHStA)
Bezirksparteiarchiv der SED Dresden

Sächsisches Staatsarchiv Chemnitz (StAC)
Bezirksparteiarchiv der SED Karl-Marx-Stadt

Sächsisches Staatsarchiv Leipzig (StAL)
Bezirksparteiarchiv der SED Leipzig
Bezirkstag und Rat des Bezirkes Leipzig (BT/RdB)
BDVP 24: Bezirksbehörde der Deutschen Volkspolizei Leipzig

Landesarchiv Merseburg (LAM)
Bezirksparteiarchiv der SED Halle

Thüringisches Hauptstaatsarchiv Weimar (ThHStAW)
SED Bezirksleitung Erfurt (1952–62)

SECONDARY LITERATURE

Ackermann, Volker, *Der 'echte' Flüchtling: Deutsche Vertriebene und Flüchtlinge aus der DDR 1945–1961* (Osnabrück: Universitätsverlag Rasch, 1995).
Agde, Günter (ed.), *Kahlschlag: Das 11. Plenum des ZK der SED 1965: Studien und Dokumente* (2nd edn; Berlin: Aufbau, 2000).
Ahonen, Pertti, *Death at the Berlin Wall* (Oxford: Oxford University Press, 2011).
Allan, Seán, 'Projections of History: East German Film-makers and the Berlin Wall' (unpublished paper at Liverpool conference, Sept. 2006).
Allgemeiner Deutscher Nachrichtendienst (ed.), *Tatsachen über Westberlin: Subversion, Wirtschaftskrieg, Revanchismus gegen die sozialistischen Staaten* (East Berlin: Kongreß, 1962).
Allinson, Mark, *Politics and Popular Opinion in East Germany 1945–68* (Manchester: Manchester University Press, 2000).
Andert, Reinhold, *Rote Wende: Wie die Ossis die Wessis besiegten* (Berlin: Elefanten Press, 1994).
Arenth, Joachim, *Der Westen tut nichts! Transatlantische Kooperation während der zweiten Berlin-Krise (1958–1962) im Spiegel neuer amerikanischer Quellen* (Frankfurt: Peter Lang, 1993).
Armstrong, Anne, *Berliners: Both Sides of the Wall* (New Brunswick: Rutgers University Press, 1973).
Ausfelder, Kurt, *Kunst oder Chaos? Graffiti an der Berliner Mauer* (Darmstadt: Das Beispiel, 1990).
Ausland, John C., *Kennedy, Khruschchev and the Berlin–Cuba Crisis, 1961–1964* (Oslo: Scandinavian University Press, 1996).
Ausschuß für Deutsche Einheit (ed.), *Was geschah am 13. August?* (East Berlin, n.d.).
Badstübner, Evemarie (ed.), *Befremdlich anders: Leben in der DDR* (Berlin: Dietz, 2000).
Bailey, Anthony, *Along the Edge of the Forest: An Iron Curtain Journey* (London: Faber, 1983).
Balfour, Alan, *Berlin: The Politics of Order 1737–1989* (New York: Rizzoli, 1990).
Barck, Simone *et al.* (eds), *Zwischen 'Mosaik' und 'Einheit': Zeitschriften in der DDR* (Berlin: Links, 1999).

Bauerkämper, Arnd, *Ländliche Gesellschaft in der kommunistischen Diktatur: Zwangsmodernisierung und Tradition in Brandenburg 1945–1963* (Cologne: Böhlau, 2002).

Beckmann, Herbert, *Atlantis Westberlin: Erinnerungsreise in eine versunkene Stadt* (Berlin: Links, 2000).

Beevor, Antony, *Berlin: The Downfall 1945* (London: Penguin, 2002).

Bender, Peter, *Neue Ostpolitik: Vom Mauerbau zum Moskauer Vertrag* (Munich: dtv, 1986).

Bennewitz, Inge and Rainer Potratz, *Zwangsaussiedlungen an der innerdeutschen Grenze: Analysen und Dokumente* (Berlin: Links, 1994).

Berdahl, Daphne, *Where the World Ended: Re-unification and Identity in the German Borderland* (Berkeley, CA: University of California Press, 1999).

Beschloss, Michael, *Kennedy versus Khrushchev: The Crisis Years 1960–63* (London: Faber, 1991).

Bessel, Richard and Ralph Jessen (eds), *Die Grenzen der Diktatur: Staat und Gesellschaft in der DDR* (Göttingen: Vandenhoeck & Ruprecht, 1996).

Bethlehem, Siegfried, *Heimatvertreibung, DDR-Flucht, Gastarbeiterzuwanderung: Wanderungsströme und Wanderungspolitik in der Bundesrepublik Deutschland* (Stuttgart: Klett-Cotta, 1982).

Bispinck, Henrik, ' "Republikflucht": Flucht und Ausreise als Problem für die DDR-Führung', in Dierk Hoffmann et al. (eds), *Vor dem Mauerbau: Politik und Gesellschaft in der DDR* (Munich: Oldenbourg, 2003), 285–309.

Boberach, Heinz (ed.), *Meldungen aus dem Reich: Die geheimen Lageberichte des Sicherheitsdienstes der SS 1938–1945*, 17 vols (Herrsching: Pawlak, 1984).

Bonwetsch, Bernd and Alexei Filitow, 'Chruschtschow und der Mauerbau: Die Gipfelkonferenz der Warschauer-Pakt-Staaten vom 3.–5. August 1961', *Vierteljahrshefte für Zeitgeschichte*, 48 (2000), 155–98.

Borneman, John, *Belonging in the Two Berlins: Kin, State, Nation* (Cambridge: Cambridge University Press, 1992).

Brandt, Willy, *People and Politics: The Years 1960–1975* (London: Collins, 1978).

Braun, Matthias, *Drama um eine Komödie: Das Ensemble von SED und Staatssicherheit, FDJ und Ministerium für Kultur gegen Heiner Müllers 'Die Umsiedlerin oder Das Leben auf dem Lande' im Oktober 1961* (Berlin: Links, 1995).

Broszat, Martin (ed.), *Zäsuren nach 1945: Essays zur Periodisierung der deutschen Nachkriegsgeschichte* (Munich: Oldenbourg, 1990).

Buckler, Alois, *Grenzgänger: Erlebnisse aus den Jahren 1947–1961 an der innerdeutschen Grenze* (Leipzig: Thomas, 1991).

Bundesministerium für gesamtdeutsche Fragen (ed.), *Jeder Fünfte* (Bonn, n.d.).

—— (ed.), *Berlin, 13. August: Sperrmaßnahmen gegen Recht und Menschlichkeit* (Bonn, 1961).

—— (ed.), *Ein Schandmal im Urteil der Welt: Äußerungen ausländischer Politiker angesichts der Mauer* (Bonn, 1962).

—— (ed.), *Ulbrichts Mauer: Zahlen, Fakten, Daten*, 2nd edn, (1962).

Bundesministerium für innerdeutsche Beziehungen (ed.), *Die Sperrmaßnahmen der DDR vom Mai 1952: Die Sperrmaßnahmen der Sowjetzonenregierung an der Zonengrenze und um Westberlin: Faksimilierter Nachdruck des Weißbuches von 1953* (Bonn: Bundesministerium für innerdeutsche Beziehungen, 1987).

Bundesministerium für innerdeutsche Beziehungen (ed.), *Der Bau der Mauer durch Berlin: Die Flucht aus der Sowjetzone und die Sperrmaßnahmen des kommunistischen Regimes vom 13. August 1961 in Berlin: Faksimilierter Nachdruck der Denkschrift von 1961* (Bonn: Bundesministerium für innerdeutsche Beziehungen, 1986).

Burgess, John P., *The East German Church and the End of Communism* (New York: Oxford University Press, 1997).

Burr, William and National Security Archive (eds), *The Berlin Crisis 1958–1962: Guide and Index* (2 vols; Washington, DC: National Security Archive and Chadwyck-Healey, 1992).

Catudal, Honoré M., *Kennedy and the Berlin Wall Crisis: A Case Study in US Decision Making* (West Berlin: Berlin-Verlag, 1980).

Chaussy, Ulrich, *Die drei Leben des Rudi Dutschke: Eine Biographie* (Berlin: Links, 1993).

Ciesla, Burghard *et al.* (eds), *Sterben für Berlin? Die Berliner Krisen 1948: 1958* (Berlin: Metropol, 2000).

—— '"Über alle Sektorengrenzen hinweg...": Die deutsche Reichsbahn und die Berlinkrisen (1945–1958)', in id. (ed.), *Sterben für Berlin? Die Berliner Krisen 1948: 1958* (Berlin: Metropol, 2000), 133–51.

—— and Patrice Poutrus, 'Food Supply in a Planned Economy: SED Nutrition Policy between Crisis Response and Popular Needs', in Konrad H. Jarausch (ed.), *Dictatorship as Experience: Towards a Socio-Cultural History of the GDR* (New York: Berghahn, 1999), 143–62.

Connelly, John, 'Zur "Republikflucht" von DDR-Wissenschaftlern in den fünfziger Jahren', *Zeitschrift für Geschichtswissenschaft*, 4 (1994), 331–52.

Cooke, Paul, *Representing East Germany since Unification: From Colonization to Nostalgia* (Oxford: Berg, 2005).

Creuzberger, Stefan, 'Abschirmungspolitik gegenüber dem westlichen Deutschland im Jahre 1952', in Gerhard Wettig (ed.), *Die sowjetische Deutschland-Politik in der Ära Adenauer* (Bonn: Bouvier, 1997), 12–36.

Dale, Gareth, *Popular Protest in East Germany, 1945–1989* (London and New York: Routledge, 2005).

—— *The East German Revolution of 1989* (Manchester: Manchester University Press, 2006).

Darnton, Robert, *Berlin Journal, 1989–1990* (New York: Norton, 1991).

Dasbach Mallinckrodt, Anita, *Propaganda hinter der Mauer: Die Propaganda der Sowjetunion und der DDR als Werkzeug der Außenpolitik im Jahre* (Stuttgart: Kohlhammer, 1971).

Davey, Thomas, *Generation Divided: German Children and the Berlin Wall* (Durham, NC: Duke University Press, 1994).

Davies, Sarah, *Popular Opinion in Stalin's Russia: Terror, Propaganda and Dissent, 1934–1941* (Cambridge: Cambridge University Press, 1997).

Davison, W. Phillips, *The Berlin Blockade: A Study in Cold War Politics* (Princeton, NJ: Princeton University Press, 1958).

Deighton, Len, *Funeral in Berlin* (London: Jonathan Cape, 1964).

Delius, Friedrich Christian and Peter Joachim Lapp, *Transit Westberlin: Erlebnisse im Zwischenraum* (Berlin: Links, 1999).

Detjen, Marion, *Ein Loch in der Mauer: Die Geschichte der Fluchthilfe im geteilten Deutschland* (Munich: Siedler, 2005).

Deutscher Bundestag (ed.), *Materialien der Enquete Kommission 'Aufarbeitung von Geschichte und Folgen der SED-Diktatur in Deutschland'*, 9 vols (Baden-Baden: Nomos/Suhrkamp, 1995).

Diedrich, Torsten and Ilko-Sascha Kowalczuk (eds), *Staatsgründung auf Raten? Zu den Auswirkungen des Volksaufstandes 1953 und des Mauerbaus 1961 auf Staat, Militär und Gesellschaft der DDR* (Berlin: Links, 2005).

Dittfurth, Udo, *August 1961: S-Bahn und Mauerbau: Die Berliner S-Bahn im Jahr 1961* (Berlin: GVE, 2006).

Dokumentationszentrum Berliner Mauer and Zerr Hapke Nieländer Architekten (eds), *turm* (Berlin: Aedes, 2004).

Dolphin, Ray, *The West Bank Wall: Unmaking Palestine* (London: Pluto, 2006).

Donnan, Hastings and Thomas M. Wilson, *Borders: Frontiers of Identity, Nation and State* (Oxford: Berg, 1999).

Dowty, Alan, *Closed Borders: The Contemporary Assault on Freedom of Movement* (New Haven and London: Yale University Press, 1987).

Effner, Bettina and Helge Heidemeyer, *Flucht im geteilten Deutschland: Erinnerungsstätte Notaufnahmelager Marienfelde* (Berlin: bebra, 2005).

Eisenfeld, Bernd, *Die Zentrale Koordinierungsgruppe: Bekämpfung von Flucht und Übersiedlung* (Berlin: BStU, 1995).

—— 'Flucht und Ausreise—Macht und Ohnmacht', in: Eberhard Kuhrt (ed.), *Opposition in der DDR von den 70er Jahren bis zum Zusammenbruch der SED-Herrschaft* (Opladen: Leske and Budrich, 1999), 381–424.

Eisman, April, 'Picturing the Berlin Wall in 1960s East Germany', paper at 'Berlin, Divided City' conference, Austin, Texas, 28–29 March 2008.

Ernst, Anna Sabine, *'Die beste Prophylaxe ist der Sozialismus': Ärzte und medizinische Hochschullehrer in der SBZ/DDR 1945–1961* (Münster: Waxmann, 1997).

Eulenspiegel (ed.), *Spötterfunken: Karikaturen aus zehn Jahren deutscher Entwicklung* (East Berlin: Eulenspiegel Verlag, 1959).

Evans, Jennifer V., 'Bahnhof Boys: Policing Male Prostitution in Post-Nazi Berlin', *Journal of the History of Sexuality*, 12 (2003), 605–36.

Feinstein, Joshua, *The Triumph of the Ordinary: Depictions of Daily Life in the East German Cinema, 1949–1989* (Chapel Hill, NC: University of North Carolina Press, 2002).

Fernandez-Armesto, Felipé, 'This Story Doth a Wall Present', *Index on Censorship (Writing on the Walls)*, 33/3 (2004), 38–45.

Feversham, Polly and Leo Schmidt, *Die Berliner Mauer heute: Denkmalwert und Umgang* (Berlin: Verlag Bauwesen, 1999).

Filmer, Werner and Heribert Schwan (eds), *Opfer der Mauer: Die geheimen Protokolle des Todes* (Munich: Bertelsmann, 1991).

Fischer, Wolfgang Georg and Fritz von der Schulenberg, *Die Mauer: Monument des Jahrhunderts* (Berlin: Ernst & Sohn, 1990).

Fitzpatrick, Sheila, *Everyday Stalinism: Ordinary Life in Extraordinary Times: Soviet Russia in the 1930s* (Oxford: Oxford University Press, 1999).

Förster, Peter and Günter Roski, *DDR zwischen Wende und Wahl: Meinungsforscher analysieren den Umbruch* (Berlin: LinksDruck, 1990).

Foreign Office (ed.), *Selected Documents on Germany and the Question of Berlin, 1944–1961* (London: HM Stationery Office, 1961).

Foucault, Michel, *Discipline and Punish: The Birth of the Prison* (Harmondsworth: Penguin, 1981).

Frech, Birgit, *Die Berliner Mauer in der Literatur: Eine Untersuchung ausgewählter Prosawerke seit 1961* (Pfungstadt: Edition Ergon, 1992).

Fricke, Karl Wilhelm, *Politik und Justiz in der DDR: Zur Geschichte der politischen Verfolgung 1945–1968: Bericht und Dokumentation,* 2nd edn (Cologne: Verlag Wissenschaft und Politik, 1990).

Frotscher, Kurt and Wolfgang Krug (eds), *Im Namen des Volkes: Grenzer vor Gericht* (Schkeuditz: GNN, 2000).

Fulbrook, Mary, *Anatomy of a Dictatorship: Inside the GDR 1949–1989* (Oxford: Oxford University Press, 1995).

—— *The People's State: East German Society from Hitler to Honecker* (New Haven and London: Yale University Press, 2005).

—— (ed.), *Power and Society in the GDR, 1961–1979: The 'Normalisation of Rule'?* (New York: Berghahn, 2009).

Fulcher, Kara S., 'Walling in and Walling Out: The Politics and Propaganda of the Second Berlin Crisis, 1958–1962' (PhD thesis, Princeton, 1997).

Funder, Anna, *Stasiland: Stories from behind the Berlin Wall* (London: Granta, 2003).

Fursenko, Aleksandr and Timothy Naftali, *Khrushchev's Cold War: The Inside Story of an American Adversary* (New York and London: Norton, 2006).

Gaddis, John Lewis, 'On Starting All Over Again: A Naïve Approach to the Study of the Cold War', in Odd Arne Westad (ed.), *Reviewing the Cold War: Approaches, Interpretations, Theory* (London: Cass, 2000), 27–42.

Galante, Pierre with Jack Miller, *The Berlin Wall* (Garden City, NY: Doubleday, 1965).

Galenza, Roland and Heinz Havemeister (eds), *Wir wollen immer artig sein. . .: Punk, New Wave, HipHop, Independent-Szene in der DDR 1980–1990* (Berlin: Schwarzkopf, 1999).

Gareis, Raimo, *Berliner Mauer: Die längste Leinwand der Welt* (Leichlingen: Krone, 1998).

Garton Ash, Timothy, *In Europe's Name: Germany and the Divided Continent* (London: Jonathan Cape, 1993).

Gaus, Günter, *Wo Deutschland liegt: Eine Ortsbestimmung* (Hamburg: Hoffmann and Campe, 1983).

Gearson, John P., 'British Policy and the Berlin Wall Crisis 1958–61', *Contemporary Record*, 6 (1992), 108–77.

—— *Harold Macmillan and the Berlin Wall Crisis, 1958–62: The Limits of Interest and Force* (Basingstoke: Macmillan, 1998).

—— and Kori Schake (eds), *The Berlin Wall Crisis: Perspectives on Cold War Alliances* (Basingstoke: Palgrave, 2002).

Gebert, Anke (ed.), *Im Schatten der Mauer: Erinnerungen, Geschichten und Bilder vom Mauerbau bis zum Mauerfall* (Berne: Scherz, 1999).

Gedmin, Jeffrey, *The Hidden Hand: Gorbachev and the Collapse of East Germany* (Washington, DC: AEI Press, 1992).

Geisel, Christof, *Auf der Suche nach einem dritten Weg: Das politische Selbstverständnis der DDR-Opposition in den 80er Jahren* (Berlin: Links, 2005).

Gellately, Robert, *Backing Hitler: Consent and Coercion in Nazi Germany* (Oxford: Oxford University Press, 2001).

Gentzen Udo and Karin Wulf, *'Niemand wußte, wohin wir gebracht werden. . . ': Zwangsumgesiedelte von 1952 und 1961 berichten über ihr Schicksal* (Hagenow: Boizenburg, 1993).

Geraghty, Tony, *Brixmis: The Untold Exploits of Britain's Most Daring Cold War Spy Mission* (London: HarperCollins, 1996).

Gerig, Uwe, *Morde an der Mauer* (Böblingen: Tykve, 1989).

Gerlach, Heribert, *Die Berlinpolitik der Kennedy-Administration: Eine Fallstudie zum außenpolitischen Verhalten der Kennedy-Regierung in der Berlinkrise 1961* (Frankfurt: Haag & Herchen, 1977).

Goeckel, Robert F., *The Lutheran Church and the East German State: Political Conflict and Change under Ulbricht and Honecker* (Ithaca and London: Cornell University Press, 1990).

Goldhagen, Daniel J., *Hitler's Willing Executioners: Ordinary Germans and the Holocaust* (London: Little, Brown & Co., 1996).

Grafe, Roman, *Deutsche Gerechtigkeit: Prozesse gegen DDR-Grenzschützen und ihre Befehlsgeber* (Berlin: Siedler, 2004).

Grashoff, Udo, *'In einem Anfall von Depression . . . ': Selbsttötungen in der DDR* (Berlin: Links, 2006).

Gray, William Glenn, *Germany's Cold War: The Global Campaign to Isolate East Germany, 1949–1969* (Chapel Hill, NC: North Carolina University Press, 2003).

Grieder, Peter, *The East German Leadership, 1946–1973: Conflict and Crisis* (Manchester: Manchester University Press, 1999).

Grix, Jonathan, *The Role of the Masses in the Collapse of the GDR* (Houndmills: Palgrave, 2000).

Grube Frank and Gerhard Richter, *Die Schwarzmarktzeit: Deutschland zwischen 1945 und 1948* (Hamburg: Hoffmann & Campe, 1979).

Grunenberg, Antonia, *Aufbruch der inneren Mauer: Politik und Kultur in der DDR 1971–1990* (Bremen: Temmen, 1990).

Härtel, Christian and Petra Kabus (eds), *Das Westpaket: Geschenksendung, keine Handelsware* (Berlin: Links, 2000).

Hager, Kurt, *Erinnerungen* (Leipzig: Faber, 1996).

Hahn, Annegret *et al.* (eds), *4. November '89* (Berlin: Propyläen, 1990).

Hampel, Harry and Thomas Friedrich, *Wo die Mauer war* (Berlin: Nicolai, 1996).

Harrison, Hope M., 'Ulbricht and the Concrete "Rose": New Archival Evidence on the Dynamics of Soviet-East German Relations and the Berlin Crisis, 1958–1961' (Working Paper No. 5 of the Woodrow Wilson Cold War International History Project, 1993).

—— 'The Berlin Crisis and the Khrushchev-Ulbricht Summits in Moscow, 9 and 18 June 1959', *Cold War International History Project Bulletin*, 11 (1998), 204–17.

—— *Driving the Soviets up the Wall: Soviet-East German Relations, 1953–1961* (Princeton, NJ and Oxford: Princeton University Press, 2003).

Hartmann, Andreas, *Grenzgeschichten: Berichte aus dem deutschen Niemandsland* (Frankfurt: S. Fischer, 1990).

Haupt, Michael, *Die Berliner Mauer—Vorgeschichte, Bau, Folgen: Literaturbericht und Bibliographie zum 20. Jahrestag des 13. August 1961* (Munich: Bernhard & Graefe, 1981).

Havel, Václav, *Living in Truth* (London: Faber, 1987).

Haydock, Michael D., *City under Siege: The Berlin Airlift, 1948–1949* (Washington, DC: Brassey's, 1999).

Heaps, William A., *The Wall of Shame* (New York: Meredith Press, 1964).

Heerma van Voss, Lex (ed.), *Petitions in Social History* (Cambridge: Cambridge University Press, 2001).

Heidemeyer, Helge, *Flucht und Zuwanderung aus der SBZ/DDR 1945/49–1961* (Düsseldorf: Droste Verlag, 1994).

Heins, Cornelia (ed.), *The Wall Falls: An Oral History of the Reunification of the Two Germanies* (London: Grey Seal, 1994).

Henrich, Rolf, *Der vormundschaftliche Staat: Vom Versagen des real existierenden Sozialismus* (Hamburg: Rowohlt, 1989).

Hertle, Hans-Hermann, *Der Fall der Mauer: Die unbeabsichtigte Selbstauflösung des SED-Staates* 2nd edn (Opladen and Wiesbaden: Westdeutscher Verlag, 1999).

—— *Die Berliner Mauer: Monument des Kalten Krieges* (Berlin: Links, 2008).

—— and Gerd-Rüdiger Stephan (eds), *Das Ende der SED: Die letzten Tage des Zentralkomitees* (Berlin: Links, 1997).

—— *et al.* (eds), *Mauerbau und Mauerfall: Ursachen–Verlauf–Auswirkungen* (Berlin: Links, 2002).

—— and Stefan Wolle, *Damals in der DDR: Der Alltag im Arbeiter- und Bauernstaat* (Munich: Bertelsmann, 2004).

—— and Gerhard Sälter, 'Die Todesopfer an Mauer und Grenze: Probleme einer Bilanz des DDR-Grenzregimes', *Deutschland Archiv*, 39 (2006), 667–76.

Hilbig, Wolfgang, *'Ich'* (Frankfurt: Fischer, 1993).

Hildebrandt, Alexandra, *Die Mauer: Zahlen, Daten* (Berlin: Verlag Haus am Checkpoint Charlie, 2001).

Hildebrandt, Dieter, *Die Mauer ist keine Grenze: Menschen in Ostberlin* (Düsseldorf: Diederichs, 1964).

Hildebrandt, Rainer, *Es geschah an der Mauer*, 18th edn (Berlin: Verlag Haus am Checkpoint Charlie, 1992).

Hilmer, Richard and Werner Hilse, 'Die Flucht- und Ausreiseproblematik als innenpolitischer Konfliktstoff in der DDR und innerhalb der DDR-Opposition', in Deutscher Bundestag (ed.), *Materialien der Enquete Kommission 'Aufarbeitung von Geschichte und Folgen der SED-Diktatur in Deutschland'*, vol. 7 (Baden-Baden: Nomos/Suhrkamp, 1995), 390–7.

Hilton, Christopher, *The Wall: The People's Story* (Thrupp: Sutton, 2001).

Hirschman, Albert O., *Exit, Voice and Loyalty: Responses to Decline in Firms, Organizations and States* (Cambridge, MA: University Press, 1970).

—— 'Exit, Voice, and the Fate of the German Democratic Republic: An Essay in Conceptual History', *World Politics*, 45 (1993), 173–202.

Höpfner, Jürgen, *Gleisverwerfung* (Halle: Mitteldeutscher Verlag, 1982).

Hoerning, Erika M., 'Memories of the Berlin Wall: History and the Impact of Critical Life Events', *International Journal of Oral History*, 8 (1987), 95–111.

—— *Zwischen den Fronten: Berliner Grenzgänger und Grenzhändler 1948–1961* (Cologne: Böhlau, 1992).

Hoffmann, Dierk *et al.* (eds), *Vor dem Mauerbau: Politik und Gesellschaft in der DDR der fünfziger Jahre* (Munich: Oldenbourg, 2003).

Hoffmann, Frank, *Junge Zuwanderer in Westdeutschland: Struktur, Aufnahme und Integration junger Flüchtlinge aus der SBZ und der DDR in Westdeutschland (1945–1961)* (Frankfurt: Peter Lang, 1999).

Hohmann, Joachim S., ' "Wenn Sie dies lesen, bin ich schon auf dem Weg in den Westen": "Republikflüchtige" DDR-Lehrer in den Jahren 1949–1961', *Zeitschrift für Geschichtswissenschaft*, 45 (1997), 311–30.

—— *Lehrerflucht aus SBZ und DDR 1945–1961: Dokumente zur Geschichte und Soziologie sozialistischer Bildung und Erziehung* (Frankfurt: Peter Lang, 2000).

Holm, Hans Axel, *The Other Germans: Report from an East German Town*, trans. Thomas Teal (New York: Random House, 1970).

Horn, Klaus, *Die Berlin-Krise 1958/61: Zur Funktion der Krise in der internationalen Politik* (Frankfurt: Europäische Verlagsanstalt, 1970).

Hornstein, Erika von, *Die deutsche Not* (Cologne and Berlin: Kiepenheuer & Witsch, 1960).

Hübner, Peter, *Konsens, Konflikt und Kompromiß: Soziale Arbeiterinteressen und Sozialpolitik in der SBZ/DDR 1945–1970* (Berlin: Akademie, 1995).

Huinink, Johannes *et al.*, *Kollektiv und Eigensinn: Lebensverläufe in der DDR und danach* (Berlin: Akademie, 1995).

Humm, Antonia Maria, *Auf dem Weg zum sozialistischen Dorf? Zum Wandel der dörflichen Lebenswelt in der DDR von 1952 bis 1969 mit vergleichenden Aspekten zur Bundesrepublik Deutschland* (Göttingen: Vandenhoeck & Ruprecht, 1999).

Infratest (ed.), *Empfangsmöglichkeit und Nutzung westdeutscher und westlicher Auslands-Sender in der SBZ: Ergebnisse einer Umfrage bei Ostzonenflüchtlingen* (Munich, September/October 1955).

Infratest (ed.), *Jugendliche Flüchtlinge aus der SBZ: Die menschlich-soziale, geistige und materiell-berufliche Eingliederung jugendlicher Sowjetzonen-Flüchtlinge* (Munich, May 1957).

Infratest (ed.), *Die Intelligenzschicht in der Sowjetzone Deutschlands*, 2 vols. (Munich, October 1959).

Infratest (ed.), *Fernsehempfang in der SBZ: Empfangsmöglichkeiten, Zuschauerverhalten, Beurteilung* (May 1961).

Inglés, José D., *Study of Discrimination in Respect of the Right of Everyone to Leave any Country, including his own, and to Return to his Country* (New York: United Nations, 1963).

Inkeles, Alex and Raymond Bauer, *The Soviet Citizen: Daily Life in a Totalitarian Society* (Cambridge, Mass.: Harvard University Press, 1961).

Jäger, Andrea, *Schriftsteller aus der DDR: Ausbürgerungen und Übersiedlungen von 1961 bis 1989* (Frankfurt: Lang, 1996).

Jaforte, Alessandra, *Die Mauer in der literarischen Prosa der DDR* (Frankfurt: Peter Lang, 1991).

Jakobsen, Ursula, *Berührungen: Deutsche Schriftsteller vor und nach der Mauer* (Rottenburg: Mauer Verlag, 2005).

Jarausch, Konrad, *The Rush to German Unity* (New York: Oxford University Press, 1994).

—— (ed.), *Dictatorship as Experience: Towards a Socio-Cultural History of the GDR* (New York: Berghahn, 1999).

—— 'Care and Coercion: The GDR as Welfare Dictatorship', in id. (ed.), *Dictatorship as Experience: Towards a Socio-Cultural History of the GDR* (New York: Berghahn, 1999), 47–69.

—— and Martin Sabrow (eds), *Weg in den Untergang: Der innere Zerfall der DDR* (Göttingen: Vandenhoeck & Ruprecht, 1999).

Jessen, Ralph, 'Mobility and Blockage during the 1970s', in Konrad Jarausch (ed.), *Dictatorship as Experience: Towards a Socio-Cultural History of the GDR* (New York: Berghahn, 1999), 341–60.

Jochum, Dietmar, *Der Politbüro-Prozeß* (Kückenshagen: Scheunen-Verlag, 1996).

—— *Die Beweisaufnahme im Politbüro-Prozeß: Eine Dokumentation* (Berlin: Magnus, n.d.).

Johnson, Uwe, *Zwei Ansichten* (1965; Frankfurt: Suhrkamp, 1992).

Jokiniemi, Miriam, 'From "Mauer-Blues" to "Der Tag, an dem die Mauer fiel": The Berlin Wall in Contemporary Songs and Ballads', in Ernst Schürer *et al.* (eds), *The Berlin Wall: Representations and Perspectives* (New York: Peter Lang, 1996), 228–49.

Joppke, Christian, *East German Dissidents and the Revolution of 1989: Social Movement in a Leninist Regime* (Houndmills: Palgrave, 1994).

Kaelble, Hartmut *et al.* (eds), *Sozialgeschichte der DDR* (Stuttgart: Klett-Cotta, 1994).

Kaiser, Monika, *Machtwechsel von Ulbricht zu Honecker: Funktionsmechanismen der SED-Diktatur in Konfliktsituationen 1962 bis 1972* (Berlin: Akademie, 1997).

Kaiser, Paul and Claudia Petzold, *Boheme und Diktatur in der DDR: Gruppen, Konflikte, Quartiere 1970–1989* (Berlin: Fannei & Walz, 1997).

Karau, Gisela, *Grenzerprotokolle: Gespräche mit ehemaligen DDR-Offizieren* (Frankfurt: dipa, 1992).

Karlsch, Rainer, *Allein bezahlt? Die Reparationsleistungen der SBZ/DDR 1945–1953* (Berlin: Links, 1993).

Keiderling, Gerhard, *'Rosinenbomber über Berlin': Währungsreform, Blockade, Luftbrücke, Teilung* (Berlin: Dietz, 1998).

—— and Percy Stulz, *Berlin 1945–1968. Zur Geschichte der Hauptstadt der DDR und der selbständigen politischen Einheit Westberlins* (East Berlin: Dietz, 1970).

Kemp, Anthony, *Escape from Berlin* (London: Boxtree, 1987).

Kershaw, Ian, *Popular Opinion and Political Dissent in the Third Reich: Bavaria 1933–1945* (Oxford: Clarendon, 1983).

Kershner, Isabel, *Barrier: The Seam of the Israeli-Palestinian Conflict* (Houndmills: Palgrave Macmillan, 2006).

Khrushchev, Nikita, *Khrushchev Remembers: The Last Testament*, ed. and trans. Strobe Talbott (Boston: Little, Brown, 1974).

Kirschey, Peter, *Der Tod des Gefreiten Reinhold Huhn* (Berlin: Spotless, 1999).

Klausmeier, Axel and Leo Schmidt (eds), *Mauerreste–Mauerspuren* (Berlin: Westkreuz Verlag, 2004).

Klein, Johannes Kurt, 'Ursachen und Motive der Abwanderung aus der Sowjetzone Deutschlands', *Aus Politik und Zeitgeschichte*, B 26/55 (15 June 1955), 361–83.

Kleindienst, Jürgen (ed.), *Mauer-Passagen: Grenzgänge, Fluchten und Reisen 1961–89* (Berlin: Zeitgut, 2004).

Klötzer, Sylvia, 'Über den Umgang mit heißen Eisen: *Eulenspiegel*(eien)', in Simone Barck *et al.* (eds), *Zwischen 'Mosaik' und 'Einheit': Zeitschriften in der DDR* (Berlin: Links, 1999), 105–15.

Knobloch, Heinz, *Geisterbahnhöfe: Westlinien unter Ostberlin* 3rd edn. (Berlin: Links, 1994).

Kocka, Jürgen, 'Eine durchherrschte Gesellschaft', in Hartmut Kaelble *et al.* (eds), *Sozialgeschichte der DDR* (Stuttgart: Klett-Cotta, 1994), 547–53.

Köhler, Günter, *Notaufnahme* (Berlin: Stapp, 1991).

Köhler, Tilo, 'Einmal Varna und zurück: Tramp nach Osten', in Michael Rauhut and Thomas Kochan (eds), *Bye Bye Lübben City: Bluesfreaks, Tramps und Hippies in der DDR* (Berlin: Schwarzkopf & Schwarzkopf, 2004), 296–304.

Koenigswald, Harald von, *Menschen von drüben* (Bonn: Bundesministerium für gesamtdeutsche Fragen, 1958).

—— *Sie suchen Zuflucht* (Esslingen: Bechtle, 1960).

—— *Bauern auf der Flucht* (Bonn: Bundesministerium für gesamtdeutsche Fragen, 1960).

Kopstein, Jeffrey, *The Politics of Economic Decline in East Germany, 1945–1989* (Chapel Hill, NC: University of North Carolina Press, 1997).

Koop, Volker, *'Den Gegner vernichten': Die Grenzsicherung der DDR* (Bonn: Bouvier, 1996).

Koop, Volker, *Kein Kampf um Berlin? Deutsche Politik zur Zeit der Berlin-Blockade 1948/1949* (Bonn: Bouvier, 1998).

Kowalczuk, Ilko-Sascha *et al.* (eds), *Der Tag X: 17. Juni 1953: Die 'Innere Staatsgründung' der DDR als Ergebnis der Krise 1952/54* (Berlin: Links, 1995).

—— *Geist im Dienste der Macht: Hochschulpolitik in der SBZ/DDR 1945 bis 1961* (Berlin: Links, 2003).

—— (ed.), *Freiheit und Öffentlichkeit: Politischer Samisdat in der DDR 1985 bis 1989* (Berlin: Robert Havemann Gesellschaft, 2002).

Krätzschmar, Sabine and Thomas Spanier, *Ankunft im gelobten Land: Das erste Mal im Westen* (Berlin: Links, 2004).

Krönig, Waldemar and Klaus-Dieter Müller, *Anpassung–Widerstand–Verfolgung: Hochschule und Studenten in der DDR 1945–1961* (Cologne: Verlag Wissenschaft und Politik, 1994).

Krone, Tina (ed.), *'Sie haben so lange das Sagen, wie wir es dulden': Briefe an das Neue Forum September 1989–März 1990* (Berlin: Robert-Havemann-Gesellschaft, 1999).

Kuczynski, Rita, *Mauerblume: Ein Leben auf der Grenze* (Munich: Claassen, 1999).

Küchenmeister, Daniel (ed.), *Honecker–Gorbatschow: Vieraugengespräche* (Berlin: Dietz, 1993).

—— (ed.), *Der Mauerbau: Krisenverlauf–Weichenstellung–Resultate* (Berlin: Berliner Debatte, 2001).

Küsters, Hanns Jürgen, 'Konrad Adenauer und Willy Brandt in der Berlin Krise 1958–1963', *Vierteljahrshefte für Zeitgeschichte*, 40 (1992), 483–542.

Kudas, Heinz J., *Berliner Mauer Kunst* (Berlin: Elefanten Press, 1998).

Kuhn, Anna, *Christa Wolf's Utopian Vision: From Marxism to Feminism* (Cambridge: Cambridge University Press, 1988).

Kuhrt, Eberhard (ed.), *Die SED-Herrschaft und ihr Zusammenbruch* (Opladen: Leske & Budrich, 1996).

Kunze, Gerhard, *Grenzerfahrungen: Kontakte und Verhandlungen zwischen dem Land Berlin und der DDR 1949–1989* (Berlin: Akademie, 1999).

Kwizinskij, Julij A., *Vor dem Sturm: Erinnerungen eines Diplomaten* (Berlin: Siedler, 1993).

Ladd, Brian, *The Ghosts of Berlin: Confronting German History in the Urban Landscape* (Chicago, IL: University of Chicago Press, 1997).

Land, Rainer, and Ralf Possekel, *Fremde Welten: Die gegensätzliche Deutung der DDR durch SED-Reformer und Bürgerbewegung in den 80er Jahren* (Berlin: Links, 1998).

Landsman, Mark, *Dictatorship and Demand: The Politics of Consumerism in East Germany* (Boston, MA: Harvard University Press, 2005).

Lange, Bernd-Lutz, *Mauer, Jeans und Prager Frühling* (Berlin: Kiepenheuer, 2003).

Lapp, Peter Joachim, *Gefechtsdienst im Frieden: Das Grenzregime der DDR* (Bonn: Bernhard & Graefe, 1999).

Lee, Sabine, 'Perception and Reality: Anglo-German Relations and the Berlin Crisis 1958–1959', *German History*, 13 (1995), 47–69.

Lemke, Michael, *Die Berlinkrise 1958 bis 1963: Interessen und Handlungsspielräume der SED im Ost-West-Konflikt* (Berlin: Akademie Verlag, 1995).

Lindenberger, Thomas, 'Alltagsgeschichte und ihr möglicher Beitrag zu einer Gesellschaftsgeschichte der DDR', in Richard Bessel and Ralph Jessen (eds), *Die Grenzen der Diktatur: Staat und Gesellschaft in der DDR* (Göttingen: Vandenhoeck & Ruprecht, 1996), 298–325.

Lindenberger, Thomas (ed.), *Herrschaft und Eigen-Sinn in der Diktatur: Studien zur Gesellschaftsgeschichte der DDR* (Cologne: Böhlau, 1999).

Litfin, Jürgen, *Tod durch fremde Hand: Das erste Maueropfer in Berlin und die Geschichte einer Familie* (Husum: Verlag der Nation, 2006).

Lochen, Hans-Hermann and Christian Meyer (eds), *Die geheimen Anweisungen zur Diskriminierung Ausreisewilliger: Dokumente der Stasi und des Ministeriums des Innern* (Cologne: Bundesanzeiger, 1992).

Lovell, Julia, *The Great Wall: China against the World, 1000 BC to 2000 AD* (London: Atlantic, 2006).

Lüdtke, Alf, *Eigen-Sinn: Fabrikalltag, Arbeitererfahrungen und Politik vom Kaiserreich bis in den Faschismus* (Hamburg: Ergebnisse, 1993).

—— (ed.), *The History of Everyday Life: Reconstructing Historical Experiences and Ways of Life* (Princeton, NJ: Princeton University Press, 1995).

—— and Peter Becker (eds), *Akten, Eingaben, Schaufenster: Die DDR und ihre Texte* (Berlin: Akademie, 1997).

—— ' " . . . den Menschen vergessen"? — oder: Das Maß der Sicherheit: Arbeiterverhalten der 1950er Jahre im Blick vom MfS, SED, FDGB und staatlichen Leitungen', in: id. and Peter Becker (eds), *Akten, Eingaben, Schaufenster: Die DDR und ihre Texte* (Berlin: Akademie, 1997), 189–91.

Lutz, Annabelle, *Dissidenten und Bürgerbewegung: Ein Vergleich zwischen DDR und Tschechoslowakei* (Frankfurt: Campus, 1999).

McAdams, A. James, *Germany Divided: From the Wall to Reunification* (Princeton, NJ: Princeton University Press, 1993).

McLellan, Josie, *Antifascism and Memory in East Germany: Remembering the International Brigades 1945–1989* (Oxford: Oxford University Press, 2004).

Maaz, Hans-Joachim, *Der Gefühlsstau: Ein Psychogramm der DDR* (Berlin: Argon, 1990).

Madarász, Jeannette Z., *Conflict and Compromise in East Germany, 1971–1989: A Precarious Stability* (Houndmills: Palgrave, 2003).

Maddrell, Paul, *Spying for Science: Western Intelligence in Divided Germany 1945–1961* (Oxford: Oxford University Press, 2006).

Mählert, Ulrich, 'Walter Ulbricht über die Aufgaben der FDJ im August 1961', *Deutschland Archiv*, 8 (1994), 890–93.

Mahan, Erin R., *Kennedy, de Gaulle and Western Europe* (Houndmills: Palgrave, 2002).

Maier, Charles S., *Dissolution: The Crisis of Communism and the End of East Germany* (Princeton, NJ: Princeton University Press, 1997).

Major, Patrick and Jonathan Osmond (eds), *The Workers' and Peasants' State: Communism and Society in East Germany under Ulbricht 1945–71* (Manchester: Manchester University Press, 2002).

—— 'Coming in from the Cold: The GDR in the British Spy Thriller', in Arnd Bauerkämper (ed.), *Britain and the GDR: Relations and Perceptions in a Divided World* (Philo: Vienna, 2002), 339–52.

Markierung des Mauerverlaufs: Hearing am 14. Juni 1995: Dokumentation (Berlin: Senatsverwaltung für Bau- und Wohnungswesen, 1995).

Mauer, Victor, 'Macmillan und die Berlin-Krise 1958/59', *Vierteljahrshefte für Zeitgeschichte*, 44 (1996), 229–56.

Mauerkatalog: 'East Side Gallery' (Berlin: Oberbaum, 1991).

Mayer, Wolfgang, *Flucht und Ausreise: Botschaftsbesetzungen als Form des Widerstands gegen die politische Verfolgung in der DDR* (Berlin: Tykve, 2002).

Mehls, Hartmut (ed.), *Im Schatten der Mauer. Dokumente. 12. August bis 29. Sept. 1961* (Berlin: Deutscher Verlag der Wissenschaften, 1990).

—— and Ellen Mehls, *13. August* (*illustrierte historische hefte* 17, 1979).

Melis, Damian van and Henrik Bispinck (eds), *'Republikflucht': Flucht und Abwanderung aus der SBZ/DDR 1945 bis 1961* (Munich: Oldenbourg, 2006).

Menzel, Rebecca, *Jeans in der DDR: Vom tieferen Sinn einer Freizeithose* (Berlin: Links, 2004).

Merritt, Richard L. and Anna J. Merritt (eds), *Living with the Wall: West Berlin, 1961–1985* (Durham, NC: Duke University Press, 1985).

Meuschel, Sigrid, *Legitimation und Parteiherrschaft: Zum Paradox von Stabilität und Revolution in der DDR 1945–1989* (Frankfurt: Suhrkamp, 1992).

Michael, Christel, *Ein Alptraum oder der Weg in die Freiheit*, 2nd edn (Frankfurt: R.G. Fischer Verlag, 1994).

Mitter, Armin, *Brennpunkt 13. August 1961: Von der inneren Krise zum Mauerbau* (Berlin: Presse- und Informationsamt des Landes Berlin, 2001).

Mitter, Armin and Stefan Wolle (eds), *'Ich liebe euch doch alle!': Befehle und Lageberichte des MfS Januar-November 1989* (Berlin: BasisDruck, 1990).

—— —— *Untergang auf Raten: Unbekannte Kapitel der DDR-Geschichte* (Munich: Bertelsmann, 1993).

Mühlberg, Felix, 'Eingaben als Instrument informeller Konfliktbewältigung', in Evemarie Badstübner (ed.), *Befremdlich anders: Leben in der DDR* (Berlin: Karl Dietz, 2000), 233–70.

—— *Bürger, Bitten und Behörden: Geschichte der Eingabe in der DDR* (Berlin: Dietz, 2004).

Müller, Bodo, *Faszination Freiheit: Die spektakulärsten Fluchtgeschichten* (Berlin: Links, 2000).

Müller, Torben, 'Vom Westen lernen, heißt improvisieren lernen: *Guter Rat*—eine sozialistische Verbraucherzeitschrift', in Simone Barck *et al.* (eds), *Zwischen 'Mosaik' und 'Einheit': Zeitschriften in der DDR* (Berlin: Links, 1999), 69–76.

Müller-Hegemann, Dietfried, *Die Berliner Mauer-Krankheit: Zur Soziogenese psychischer Störungen* (Herford: Nicolaische Verlagsbuchhandlung, 1973).

Mummert, Hartmut, 'Die Arbeiter-und-Bauern-Inspektion in der DDR zwischen Anspruch und Wirklichkeit: Zur Geschichte eines Volkskontrollorgans', *Hefte zur DDR-geschichte*, 58 (1999).

Murphy, David E. *et al.*, *Battleground Berlin: CIA vs. KGB in the Cold War* (New Haven: Yale University Press, 1997).

Neubert, Ehrhart, *Geschichte der Opposition in der DDR 1949–1989* (Berlin: Links, 1997).

Neue Justiz (ed.), *Der Politbüro-Prozeß: Eine Dokumentation* (Baden-Baden: Nomos, 2001).

Newman, Bernard, *Behind the Berlin Wall* (London: Hale, 1964).

Niemann, Heinz, *Meinungsforschung in der DDR: Die geheimen Berichte des Instituts für Meinungsforschung an das Politbüro der SED* (Cologne: Bund, 1993).

—— *Hinterm Zaun: Politische Kultur und Meinungsforschung in der DDR: die geheimen Berichte an das Politbüro der SED* (Berlin: edition ost, 1995).

Nieske, Christian, *Republikflucht und Wirtschaftswunder: Mecklenburger berichten über ihre Erlebnisse 1945 bis 1961* (Schwerin: Helms Thomas Verlag, 2002).

Niethammer, Lutz *et al.*, *Die volkseigene Erfahrung: Eine Archäologie des Lebens in der Industrieprovinz der DDR: 30 biographische Eröffnungen* (Berlin: Rowohlt, 1991).

Österreich, Tina, *Ich war RF: Ein Bericht* (Berlin: Verlag Haus am Checkpoint Charlie, 1988).

Ohse, Marc-Dietrich, *Jugend nach dem Mauerbau: Anpassung, Protest und Eigensinn* (Berlin: Links, 2003).

Otto, Wilfriede, '13. August 1961: Eine Zäsur in der europäischen Nachkriegsgeschichte', *Beiträge zur Geschichte der Arbeiterbewegung*, 39 (1997), 1: 40–74 & 2: 55–92.

Palmowski, Jan, *Inventing a Socialist Nation: Heimat and the Politics of Everyday Life in the GDR, 1945–90* (Cambridge: Cambridge University Press, 2009).

Parrish, Thomas, *Berlin in the Balance: The Blockade, the Airlift, the First Major Battle of the Cold War* (Reading, MA: Addison-Wesley, 1998).

Paul, Wolfgang, *Mauer der Schande* (Munich: Bechtle, 1961).

Paulsen, Werner, *13. August 1961: Ereignisse und Zusammenhänge* (Schkeuditz: GNN, 2001).

Pence, Katherine, 'Herr Schimpf und Frau Schande: Grenzgänger des Konsums im geteilten Berlin und die Politik des Kalten Krieges', in Burghard Ciesla *et al.* (eds), *Sterben für Berlin? Die Berliner Krisen 1948: 1958* (Berlin: Metropol, 2000), 185–202.

—— ' "A World in miniature": The Leipzig Trade Fairs in the 1950s and East German Consumer Citizenship', in David F. Crew (ed.), *Consuming Germany in the Cold War* (Berg: Oxford, 2003), 21–50.

Petersen, Antje C., 'The First Berlin Border Guard Trial' (Indiana Center on Global Change and World Peace, occasional paper no. 15, Dec. 1992).

Plato, *The Laws*, trans. Trevor J. Saunders (Harmondsworth: Penguin, 1970).

Plato, Alexander von and Wolfgang Meinicke, *Alte Heimat—neue Zeit: Flüchtlinge, Umgesiedelte, Vertriebene in der Sowjetischen Besatzungszone und in der DDR* (Berlin: Verlags-Anstalt Union, 1991).

Plowman, Andrew *et al.* (eds), *Divided, But Not Disconnected: German Experiences of the Cold War* (Oxford: Berghahn, forthcoming).

Plück, Kurt, 'Innerdeutsche Beziehungen auf kommunaler und Verwaltungsebene, in Wissenschaft, Kultur und Sport und ihre Rückwirkungen auf die Menschen im geteilten Deutschland', in Deutscher Bundestag (ed.), *Materialien der Enquete Kommission 'Aufarbeitung von Geschichte und Folgen der SED-Diktatur in Deutschland'*, vol. 3 (Baden-Baden: Nomos/Suhrkamp, 1995), 2015–64.

Poiger, Uta G., *Jazz, Rock and Rebels: Cold War Politics and American Culture in a Divided Germany* (Berkeley, CA: University of California Press, 2000).

Pollack, Detlef, 'Der Zusammenbruch der DDR als Verkettung getrennter Handlungslinien', in Konrad Jarausch and Martin Sabrow (eds), *Weg in den Untergang: Der innere Zerfall der DDR* (Göttingen: Vandenhoeck & Ruprecht, 1999), 43–74.

—— *Politischer Protest: Politisch alternative Gruppen der DDR* (Opladen: Leske & Budrich, 2000).

Port, Andrew I., *Conflict and Stability in the German Democratic Republic* (Cambridge: Cambridge University Press, 2007).

Potthoff, Heinrich, *Im Schatten der Mauer: Deutschlandpolitik 1961 bis 1990* (Berlin: Propyläen, 1999).

Power, Daniel and Naomi Standen (eds), *Frontiers in Question: Eurasian Borderlands 700–1700* (Houndmills: Palgrave, 1999).

Prescott, John, *Boundaries and Frontiers* (London: Croom Helm, 1978).

Pritchard, Gareth, *The Making of the GDR, 1945–53* (Manchester: Manchester University Press, 2000).

Prokop, Siegfried, *Übergang zum Sozialismus in der DDR: Entwicklungslinien und Probleme der Geschichte der DDR in der Endphase der Übergangsperiode vom Kapitalismus zum Sozialismus und beim umfassenden sozialistischen Aufbau (1958–1963)* (East Berlin: Dietz, 1986).

Prokop, Siegfried, *Unternehmen 'Chinese Wall': Die DDR im Zwielicht der Mauer* (Frankfurt: R. Fischer, 1992).

Prowe, Diethelm, 'Der Brief Kennedys an Brandt vom 18. August 1961: Eine zentrale Quelle zur Berliner Mauer und der Entstehung der Brandtschen Ostpolitik', *Vierteljahrshefte für Zeitgeschichte*, 33 (1985), 373–83.

—— ' "Ich bin ein Berliner": Kennedy, die Mauer und die "verteidigte Insel" West-Berlin im ausgehenden Kalten Krieg im Spiegel amerikanischer Akten', in Landesarchiv Berlin (ed.), *Berlin in Geschichte und Gegenwart: Jahrbuch des Landesarchivs Berlin 1989* (Berlin: Siedler, 1989), 143–67.

Przybylski, Peter, *Tatort Politbüro: Die Akte Honecker* (Berlin: Rowohlt, 1991).

Raschka, Johannes, 'Die Ausreisebewegung —eine Form von Widerstand gegen das SED-Regime?', in Ulrich Baumann and Helmut Kury (eds), *Politisch motivierte Verfolgung: Opfer von SED-Unrecht* (Freiburg: iuscrim, 1998), 257–74.

Rauhut, Michael, *Beat in der Grauzone: DDR-Rock 1964 bis 1972—Politik und Alltag* (Berlin: BasisDruck, 1993).

—— *Schalmei und Lederjacke: Udo Lindenberg, BAP, Underground: Rock und Politik in den achtziger Jahren* (Berlin: Schwarzkopf, 1996).

Read, Anthony and David Fisher, *The Fall of Berlin* (London: Hutchinson, 1992).

Rehlinger, Ludwig, *Freikauf: Die Geschäfte der DDR mit politisch Verfolgten 1963–1989* (Berlin: Ullstein, 1991).

Reimann, Brigitte, *Die Geschwister* (Berlin: Aufbau, 1963).

Reißig, Rolf, *Dialog durch die Mauer: Die umstrittene Annäherung von SED und SPD vor der Wende* (Frankfurt: Campus, 2002).

Renft, Klaus, *Zwischen Liebe und Zorn: Die Autobiografie* (Berlin: Schwarzkopf, 2001).

Rice, Leland, *Up Against It: Photographs of the Berlin Wall* (Albuquerque: University of New Mexico Press, 1991).

Richie, Alexandra, *Faust's Metropolis: A History of Berlin* (London: HarperCollins, 1998).

Richter, Hans Werner (ed.), *Die Mauer oder der 13. August* (Reinbek bei Hamburg: Rowohlt Taschenbuch, 1961).

Richter, James G., *Khrushchev's Double Bind: International Pressures and Domestic Coalition Politics* (Baltimore: Johns Hopkins University Press, 1994).

Ritter, Jürgen, and Peter Joachim Lapp, *Die Grenze: Ein deutsches Bauwerk* (Berlin: Links, 1997).

Röder, Werner, 'Die Emigration aus dem nationalsozialistischen Deutschland', in Klaus J. Bade (ed.), *Deutsche im Ausland–Fremde in Deutschland: Migration in Geschichte und Gegenwart* (Munich: Beck, 1993), 348–51.

Roesler, Jörg, 'Ende der Arbeitskräfteknappheit in der DDR? Erwartete und unerwartete Wirkungen der Grenzschließung auf wirtschaftlichem Gebiet' in Daniel Küchenmeister (ed.), *Der Mauerbau: Krisenverlauf–Weichenstellung–Resultate* (Berlin: Berliner Debatte, 2001).

—— 'Rübermachen': Politische Zwänge, ökonomisches Kalkül und verwandtschaftliche Bindungen als häufigste Motive der deutsch-deutschen Wanderungen zwischen 1953 und 1961, *hefte zur ddr-geschichte*, 85 (2004).

Roggemann, Herwig, *Systemunrecht und Strafrecht: am Beispiel der Mauerschützen in der ehemaligen DDR* (Berlin: Berlin-Verlag, 1993).

Rosenau, Henning, *Tödliche Schüsse im staatlichen Auftrag: Die strafrechtliche Verantwortung von Grenzsoldaten für den Schusswaffengebrauch an der deutsch-deutschen Grenze*, 2nd edn (Baden-Baden: Nomos, 1998).

Ross, Corey, *Constructing Socialism at the Grass-Roots: The Transformation of East Germany, 1945–65* (Houndmills: Macmillan, 2000).

—— 'Before the Wall: East Germans, Communist Authority, and the Mass Exodus to the West', *Historical Journal*, 45 (2002), 459–80.

—— *The East German Dictatorship: Problems and Perspectives in the Interpretation of the GDR* (London: Arnold, 2002).

—— 'East Germans and the Berlin Wall: Popular Opinion and Political Authority before and after the Border Closure of August 1961', *Journal of Contemporary History*, 39 (2004), 25–43.

Roth, Jürgen and Michael Rudolf, *Spaltprodukte: Gebündelte Ost-West-Vorurteile* (Leipzig: Reclam, 1997).

Rüddenklau, Wolfgang, *Störenfried: DDR-Opposition 1986–1989* (Berlin: BasisDruck, 1992).

Rühle, Jürgen and Günter Holzweißig, *13. August 1961. Die Mauer von Berlin*, 3rd edn (Cologne: Verlag Wissenschaft und Politik, 1988).

Rummler, Toralf, *Die Gewalttaten an der deutsch-deutschen Grenze vor Gericht* (Berlin: Nomos, 2000).

Sampson, Charles S. (ed.) *Foreign Relations of the United States, 1958–1960*, viii: *Berlin Crisis, 1958–1959*, (Washington, DC: USGPO, 1993).

Sampson, Charles S. (ed.) *Foreign Relations of the United States, 1961–1963*, xiv: *Berlin Crisis, 1961–1962* (Washington, DC: USGPO, 1993).

Sauer, Heiner and Hans-Otto Plumeyer (eds), *Der Salzgitter Report: Die Zentrale Erfassungsstelle berichtet über Verbrechen im SED-Staat*, 2nd edn (Frankfurt: Ullstein, 1993).

Schick, Jack M., *The Berlin Crisis, 1958–1962* (Philadelphia: University of Pennsylvania Press, 1971).

Schivelbusch, Wolfgang, *In a Cold Crater: Cultural and Intellectual Life in Berlin, 1945–1948*, trans. Kelly Barry (Berkeley, CA: University of California Press, 1998).

Schlechte, Helga and Klaus-Dieter (eds), *Witze bis zur Wende: 40 Jahre politischer Witze in der DDR* (Munich: Ehrenwirth, 1991).

Schlosser, Horst Dieter, *Die deutsche Sprache in der DDR zwischen Stalinismus und Demokratie* (Cologne: Verlag Wissenschaft und Politik, 1990).

Schmelz, Andrea, *Migration und Politik im geteilten Deutschland während des Kalten Krieges: Die West-Ost-Migration in die DDR in den 1950er und 1960er Jahren* (Opladen: Leske & Budrich, 2002).

Schmidt, Eberhard *et al.* (eds), *Gehen oder bleiben: Flucht und Übersiedlung von Pfarrern im geteilten Deutschland* (Leipzig: Evangelische Verlagsanstalt, 2002).

Schmidt, Leo and Henriette von Preuschen, *On Both Sides of the Wall: Preserving Monuments and Sites of the Cold War Era* (Bad Münstereifel: Westkreuz, 2005).

Schmidthammer, Jens, *Rechtsanwalt Wolfgang Vogel: Mittler zwischen Ost und West* (Hamburg: Hoffmann & Campe, 1987).

Schlechte, Helga and Klaus-Dieter (eds), *Witze bis zur Wende: 40 Jahre politischer Witze in der DDR* (Munich: Ehrenwirth, 1991).

Schneider, Peter, *Der Mauerspringer: Erzählung* (Darmstadt and Neuwied: Luchterhand, 1982).

Schnurre, Wolfdietrich, *Berlin: Eine Stadt wird geteilt* (Olten and Freiburg im Breisgau: Walter-Verlag, 1962).

Scholz, Arno, *Stacheldraht um Berlin*, 2nd edn (Berlin: Arani, 1961).

Scholze, Thomas and Falk Blask, *Halt! Grenzgebiet! Leben im Schatten der Mauer* (Berlin: BasisDruck, 1992).

Schreyer, Wolfgang, *Tempel des Satans* (East Berlin: Verlag des MfNV, 1960).

Schroeder, Klaus, *Der SED-Staat: Geschichte und Strukturen der DDR* (Munich: Landeszentrale für politische Bildungsarbeit, 1998).

Schröter, Gerhard, *Jugendliche Flüchtlinge aus der Sowjetzone* (Munich: infratest, 1958).

Schütrumpf, Jörn, 'Zu einigen Aspekten des Grenzgängerproblems im Berliner Raum von 1948/49 bis 1961', *Jahrbuch für Geschichte*, 31 (1984), 333–58.

Schwabe, Uwe and Rainer Eckert (eds), *Von Deutschland Ost nach Deutschland West: Oppositionelle oder Verräter?* (Leipzig: Forum, 2003).

Schwarz, J.C., *Das gespaltene Herz* (East Berlin: Tribüne, 1962).

Schweitzer, Carl-Christoph et al. (eds), *Lebensläufe - hüben und drüben* (Opladen: Leske & Budrich, 1993).

Scott, James C., *Domination and the Arts of Resistance: Hidden Transcripts* (New Haven and London: Yale University Press, 1990).

Selvage, Douglas, 'The End of the Berlin Crisis, 1961–62', *Cold War International History Project Bulletin*, 11 (1998), 218–29.

Sesta, Ellen, *Der Tunnel in die Freiheit: Berlin, Bernauer Straße* (Berlin: Ullstein, 2001).

Sevin, Dieter, *Textstrategien in DDR-Prosawerken zwischen Bau und Durchbruch der Berliner Mauer* (Heidelberg: Winter, 1994).

Shadrake, Alan, *The Yellow Pimpernels: Escape Stories of the Berlin Wall* (London: Hale, 1974).

Sharp, Tony, *The Wartime Alliance and the Zonal Division of Germany* (Oxford: Clarendon, 1975).

Shears, David, *The Ugly Frontier* (New York: Knopf, 1970).

Sheffer, Edith, 'On Edge: Building the Border in East and West Germany', *Central European History*, 40 (2007), 307–39.

Simmons, Michael, *The Unloved Country: A Portrait of East Germany Today* (London: Abacus, 1989).

Skyba, Peter, *Vom Hoffnungsträger zum Sicherheitsrisiko: Jugend in der DDR und Jugendpolitik der SED 1949–1961* (Cologne: Böhlau, 2000).

Slusser, Robert M., *The Berlin Crisis of 1961: Soviet-American Relations and the Struggle for Power in the Kremlin, June–November 1961* (Baltimore, MD: Johns Hopkins University Press, 1973).

Smith, Arthur L., *Kidnap City: Cold War Berlin* (Westport, CT: Greenwood, 2002).

Smith, Jean Edward, *The Defense of Berlin* (Baltimore, MD: Johns Hopkins University Press, 1963).

—— *Germany beyond the Wall: People, Politics . . . and Prosperity* (Boston and Toronto: Little, Brown & Co., 1969).

Solga, Heike, *Auf dem Weg in eine klassenlose Gesellschaft? Klassenlage und Mobilität zwischen Generationen in der DDR* (Berlin: Akademie, 1995).

Speier, Hans, *Die Bedrohung Berlins: Eine Analyse der Berlin-Krise von 1958 bis heute* (Cologne and Berlin: Kiepenheuer & Witsch, 1961).

Spilker, Dirk, *The East German Leadership and the Division of Germany: Patriotism and Propaganda 1945–53* (Oxford: Oxford University Press, 2006).

Staadt, Jochen, 'Eingaben: Die institutionalisierte Meckerkultur in der DDR; Goldbrokat, Kaffee-Mix, Büttenreden, Ausreiseanträge und andere Schwierigkeiten mit den Untertanen' (Berlin: Forschungsverbund SED-Staat paper, 1996).

Stafford, David, *Spies beneath Berlin* (London: Murray, 2002).

Staritz, Dietrich, *Geschichte der DDR*, 2nd edn (Frankfurt: Suhrkamp, 1996).

Staatliche Zentralverwaltung für Statistik (ed.), *Statistisches Jahrbuch der Deutschen Demokratischen Republik* (East Berlin: VEB Deutscher Zentralverlag, 1956 ff.).

Statistisches Jahrbuch für die Bundesrepublik Deutschland: 1962 (Stuttgart and Mainz: Kohlhammer, 1962).

Steege, Paul, *Black Market, Cold War: Everyday Life in Berlin, 1946–1949* (Cambridge: Cambridge University Press, 2007).

—— 'Totale Blockade, totale Luftbrücke? Die mythische Erfahrung der ersten Berlinkrise, Juni 1948 bis Mai 1949', in Burghard Ciesla *et al.* (eds), *Sterben für Berlin: Die Berliner Krisen 1948: 1958* (Berlin: Metropol, 2000), 59–77.

Steele, Jonathan, *Socialism with a German Face: The state that came in from the cold* (London: Jonathan Cape, 1977).

Steiner, André, 'Auf dem Weg zur Mauer? Ulbricht an Chruschtschow im November 1960', *Utopie kreativ*, 4/31–32 (1993), 94–111.

—— 'Zwischen Konsumversprechen und Innovationszwang: Zum wirtschaftlichen Niedergang der DDR', in Konrad Jarausch and Martin Sabrow (eds), *Weg in den Untergang: Der innere Zerfall der DDR* (Göttingen: Vandenhoeck & Ruprecht, 1999), 153–92.

—— 'Vom Überholen eingeholt: Zur Wirtschaftskrise 1960/61 in der DDR', in Burghard Ciesla *et al.* (eds), *Sterben für Berlin? Die Berliner Krisen 1948:1958* (Berlin: Metropol, 2000), 245–62.

—— *Von Plan zu Plan: Eine Wirtschaftsgeschichte der DDR* (Munich: DVA, 2004).

Steininger, Rolf, *Der Mauerbau: Die Westmächte und Adenauer in der Berlinkrise 1958–1963* (Munich: Olzog, 2001).

Steinmüller, Angela and Karlheinz, *Andymon: Eine Weltraum-Utopie* (Berlin: Shayol, 2004).

Stephan, Gerd-Rüdiger (ed.), *'Vorwärts immer, rückwärts nimmer!': Interne Dokumente zum Zerfall von SED und DDR 1988/89* (Berlin: Dietz, 1994).

Stiftung Archiv der Akademie der Künste (ed.), *Zwischen Diskussion und Disziplin: Dokumente zur Geschichte der Akademie der Künste (Ost)* (Berlin: Henschel, 1997).

Stiftung Gedenkstätte Berlin-Hohenschönhausen (ed.), *Die vergessenen Opfer der Mauer: Flucht und Inhaftierung in Deutschland 1961–1989* (Berlin: KOMAG, n.d.).

Stivers, William, 'The Incomplete Blockade: Soviet Zone Supply of West Berlin, 1948–49', *Diplomatic History*, 21 (1997), 569–602.

Stokes, Gale, *The Walls Came Tumbling Down: The Collapse of Communism in Eastern Europe* (New York and Oxford: Oxford University Press, 1993).

Stokes, Raymond G., *Constructing Socialism: Technology and Change in East Germany, 1945–1990* (Baltimore and London: Johns Hopkins University Press, 2000).

Storbeck, Dietrich, 'Flucht oder Wanderung?', *Soziale Welt*, 14 (1963), 153–71.

Stützle, Walther, *Kennedy und Adenauer in der Berlin-Krise 1961–1962* (Bonn-Bad Godesberg: Verlag Neue Gesellschaft, 1973).

Süß, Walter, 'Die Stimmungslage der Bevölkerung im Spiegel von MfS-Berichten', in Eberhard Kuhrt (ed.), *Die SED-Herrschaft und ihr Zusammenbruch* (Opladen: Leske & Budrich, 1996), 237–77.

—— *Staatssicherheit am Ende: Warum es den Mächtigen nicht gelang, 1989 eine Revolution zu verhindern* (Berlin: Links, 1999).

Tantzscher, Monika, 'Die verlängerte Mauer: Die Zusammenarbeit der Sicherheitsdienste bei der Verhinderung von "Republikflucht" über andere Ostblockstaaten', in: Heiner Timmermann (ed.), *Die DDR—Erinnerung an einen untergegangenen Staat* (Berlin: Duncker & Humblot, 1999), 91–122.

Taylor, Frederick, *The Berlin Wall: 13 August 1961 to 9 November 1989* (London: Bloomsbury, 2006).

Thacker, Toby, 'The fifth column: Dance music in the early German Democratic Republic', in Patrick Major and Jonathan Osmond (eds), *The Workers' and Peasants' State: Communism and Society in East Germany under Ulbricht, 1945–71* (Manchester: Manchester University Press, 2002), 227–43.

Thomaneck, J. K. A. and James Mellis (eds), *Politics, Society and Government in the German Democratic Republic: Basic Documents* (Oxford: Berg, 1989).

Thoß, Hendrik, *Gesichert in den Untergang: Die Geschichte der DDR-Westgrenze* (Berlin: Karl Dietz, 2004).

Thurston, Robert W., *Life and Terror in Stalin's Russia, 1934–1941* (New Haven and London: Yale University Press, 1996).

Tillmann, Terry, *The Writings on the Wall: Peace at the Berlin Wall* (Santa Monica, CA: 22/7, 1990).

Tippach-Schneider, Simone, *Messemännchen und Minol-Pirol: Werbung in der DDR* (Berlin: Schwarzkopf, 1999).

Torpey, John, *The Invention of the Passport: Surveillance, Citizenship and the State* (Cambridge: Cambridge University Press, 1999).

Trachtenberg, Marc, *A Constructed Peace: The Making of the European Settlement, 1945–1963* (Princeton, NJ: Princeton University Press, 1999).

Turner, Frederick Jackson, *The Frontier in American History* (New York: Henry Holt, 1920).

Tusa, Ann and John, *The Berlin Blockade* (London: Hodder & Stoughton, 1988).

Tusa, Ann, *The Last Division: Berlin and the Wall* (London: Hodder & Stoughton, 1996).

Uhl, Matthias and Vladimir I. Ivkin, ' "Operation Atom": The Soviet Union's Stationing of Nuclear Missiles in the German Democratic Republic, 1959', *Cold War International History Project Bulletin*, 12/13 (2001), 299–304.

—— and Armin Wagner (eds), *Ulbricht, Chruschtschow und die Mauer: Eine Dokumentation* (Munich: Oldenbourg, 2003).

—— ' "Westberlin stellt also ein großes Loch inmitten unserer Republik dar": Die militärischen und politischen Planungen Moskaus und Ost-Berlins zum Mauerbau', in Dierk Hoffmann *et al.* (eds), *Vor dem Mauerbau: Politik und Gesellschaft in der DDR der fünfziger Jahre* (Munich: Oldenbourg, 2003), 307–26.

Ulbrich, Reinhard, *Spur der Broiler: Wir und unser goldener Osten* (Berlin: Rowohlt, 1998).

Ulbricht, Walter, 'Der Kampf um den Frieden' (Dietz: East Berlin, 1958).

Ullrich, Maren, *Geteilte Ansichten: Erinnerungslandschaft deutsch-deutsche Grenze* (Berlin: Aufbau, 2006).

Veith, Ines, *Die Frau vom Checkpoint Charlie: Der verzweifelte Kampf einer Mutter um ihre Töchter* (Munich: Knaur, 2006).

Verein 'Berliner Mauer—Gedenkstätte und Dokumentationszentrum' (ed.), *Berliner Mauer: Gedenkstätte, Dokumentationszentrum und Versöhnungskapelle in der Bernauer Straße* (Berlin: Jaron, 1999).

—— (ed.), *Die Berliner Mauer* (Dresden: Michel Sandstein Verlag, n.d.).

Voigt, Dieter *et al.*, 'Die innerdeutsche Wanderung und der Vereinigungsprozeß: Soziodemographische Struktur und Einstellungen von Flüchtlingen/Übersiedlern aus der DDR vor und nach der Grenzöffnung', *Deutschland Archiv*, 23 (1990), 732–46.

Vollnhals, Clemens and Jürgen Weber (eds), *Der Schein der Normalität: Alltag und Herrschaft in der SED-Diktatur* (Munich: Olzog, 2002).

Waldron, Arthur, *The Great Wall of China: From History to Myth* (Cambridge: Cambridge University Press, 1990).

Wagenaar, Cor *et al.*, *Ideals in Concrete: Exploring Eastern and Central Europe* (Rotterdam: NAi publishers, 2004).

Wagner, Armin, *Walter Ulbricht und die geheime Sicherheitspolitik der SED: Der Nationale Verteidigungsrat der DDR und seine Vorgeschichte (1953 bis 1971)* (Berlin: Links, 2002).

316   *Behind the Berlin Wall*

Walckhoff, Dirk-Arne, *Der 13. August 1961 in der Traditionsarbeit der Grenztruppen der DDR* (Hamburg: Lit-Verlag, 1996).

Walter, Joachim, *Sicherungsbereich Literatur: Schriftsteller und Staatssicherheit in der Deutschen Demokratischen Republik* (Berlin: Propyläen, 2001).

Wanstrat, Renate, *Strukturanalyse der politisch nicht anerkannten Flüchtlinge in West-Berlin* (West Berlin: Verwaltungsdruckerei, 1953), 2 vols.

Weber, Hermann, *Geschichte der DDR* (Munich: dtv, 1985).

——*DDR: Grundriß der Geschichte 1945–1990*, 2nd edn (Hannover: Fackelträger, 1991).

Weber, Max, *Economy and Society: An Outline of Interpretive Sociology*, 3 vols. (New York: Bedminster, 1968).

Werkentin, Falco, *Politische Strafjustiz in der Ära Ulbricht* (Berlin: Links, 1995).

Westad, Odd Arne (ed.), *Reviewing the Cold War: Approaches, Interpretations, Theory* (London: Cass, 2000).

Wettig, Gerhard, *Chruschtschows Berlin-Krise 1958 bis 1963: Drohpolitik und Mauerbau* (Munich: Oldenbourg, 2006).

Wetzlaugk, Udo, *Berlin und die deutsche Frage* (Köln: Verlag Wissenschaft & Politik, 1985).

Whittaker, C. R., *Frontiers of the Roman Empire: A Social and Economic History* (Baltimore and London: Johns Hopkins University Press, 1994).

Wierling, Dorothee, 'Die Jugend als innerer Feind: Konflikte in der Erziehungsdiktatur der sechziger Jahre', in Hartmut Kaelble *et al.* (eds), *Sozialgeschichte der DDR* (Stuttgart: Klett Cotta, 1994), pp. 404–25.

——*Geboren im Jahr Eins: Der Jahrgang 1949 in der DDR: Versuch einer Kollektiv-biographie* (Berlin: Links, 2002).

Williams, Derek, *The Reach of Rome: A History of the Roman Imperial Frontier 1st–5th Centuries AD* (London: Constable, 1996).

Wolf, Christa, *Der geteilte Himmel* (Halle: Mitteldeutscher Verlag, 1963).

Wolf, Markus, *Spionagechef im geheimen Krieg: Erinnerungen* (Munich: List, 1997).

Wright, Patrick, *Iron Curtain: From Stage to Cold War* (Oxford: Oxford University Press, 2007).

Zatlin, Jonathan R., 'Ausgaben und Eingaben: Das Petitionsrecht und der Untergang der DDR', *Zeitschrift für Geschichtswissenschaft*, 45 (1997), 902–17.

Zilch, Dorle, *Millionen unter der blauen Fahne: Die FDJ: Zahlen–Fakten–Tendenzen* (Rostock: Verlag Jugend und Geschichte, 1994).

Zubok, Vladislav M., 'Khrushchev and the Berlin crisis (1958–1962)' (Working Paper No. 6 of the Woodrow Wilson Cold War International History Project, May 1993).

——and Constantine Pleshakov, *Inside the Kremlin's Cold War: From Stalin to Khrushchev* (Cambridge, MA: Harvard University Press, 1996).

Index